LITERATURE AND UNION

LITERATURE

AND

UNION

SCOTTISH TEXTS, BRITISH CONTEXTS

Edited by

GERARD CARRUTHERS

AND

COLIN KIDD

OXFORD

UNIVERSITY PRESS

OXFORD

UNIVERSITY PRESS

Great Clarendon Street, Oxford, OX2 6DP,
United Kingdom

Oxford University Press is a department of the University of Oxford.
It furthers the University's objective of excellence in research, scholarship,
and education by publishing worldwide. Oxford is a registered trade mark of
Oxford University Press in the UK and in certain other countries

© the several contributors 2018

The moral rights of the authors have been asserted

First Edition published in 2018

Impression: 1

Published in the United States of America by Oxford University Press
198 Madison Avenue, New York, NY 10016, United States of America

British Library Cataloguing in Publication Data
Data available

Library of Congress Control Number: 2017948008

ISBN 978–0–19–873623–3

Printed and bound by
CPI Group (UK) Ltd, Croydon, CR0 4YY

Contents

List of Illustrations

List of Contributors

Gerard Carruthers is Francis Hutcheson Professor of Literature at the University of Glasgow. He is General Editor of the Oxford University Press edition of the *Works of Robert Burns* (published from 2014), co-editor with Colin Kidd of *The International Companion to John Galt* (2017), with Don Martin of *Thomas Muir of Huntershill: Essays for the Twenty First Century* (2016), and with Liam McIlvanney of *The Cambridge Companion to Scottish Literature* (2012).

Robert Crawford's seventh collection of poems is *Testament* (2014); his prose volumes include the history of Scottish literature, *Scotland's Books* (2007) and biographies of Robert Burns and T. S. Eliot. He is Professor of Modern Scottish Literature and Bishop Wardlaw Professor of Poetry at the University of St Andrews.

David Goldie is senior lecturer in the School of Humanities at the University of Strathclyde. He has written extensively on Scottish literature and popular culture in the early twentieth century and is editor, with Gerard Carruthers and Alastair Renfrew, of *Beyond Scotland: New Contexts for Twentieth-Century Scottish Literature* (2004) and *Scotland in the Nineteenth-Century World* (2012) and, with Roderick Watson, of *From the Line: Scottish War Poetry 1914–1945* (2014).

Andrew R. Holmes is Lecturer in Modern Irish History at Queen's University, Belfast. His publications include *The Shaping of Ulster Presbyterian Belief and Practice, 1770–1840* (2006) and *Revising Robert Burns and Ulster* (co-ed., 2009). He is currently working on a monograph for Oxford University Press provisionally entitled *The Irish Presbyterian Mind: Conservative Theology, Religious Revival, and Modern Criticism, 1830–1930*.

Richard Holmes completed his Ph.D. at Bristol University in 2012 on 'The Literary Career of James Arbuckle 1717–37'; and edited *James Arbuckle: Selected Works* (2014). His latest article is on the Whiggism of Hugh Boulter, Archbishop of Armagh 1724–42 (*Eighteenth-Century Ireland*, 2017). His current research is on Whig cultures in Ireland and Scotland.

Thomas Keymer is Chancellor Jackman University Professor of English at the University of Toronto and General Editor of *The Review of English Studies*. His books include *Sterne, the Moderns, and the Novel* (2002), *Pamela in the Marketplace: Literary Controversy and Print Culture in Eighteenth-Century Britain and Ireland* (2005, with Peter Sabor), *The Oxford History of the Novel in English*, i. *Prose Fiction in English from the Origins of Print to 1750* (2017, as editor), and *Poetics of the Pillory: English Literature and Seditious Libel, 1660-1820* (forthcoming, in the Clarendon Lectures in English series).

Colin Kidd is Wardlaw Professor of Modern History at the University of St Andrews and a Fellow of All Souls College, Oxford. A frequent contributor to the *London Review of Books* and the *Guardian*, he is the author of five books, most recently *The World of Mr Casaubon* (2016).

Alison Lumsden is a Professor in English Literature at the University of Aberdeen. While she has published on many aspects of Scottish literature, she has particular interests in the nineteenth century. She was a General Editor for the Edinburgh Edition of the Waverley Novels and is now lead editor for the Edinburgh Edition of Walter Scott's Poetry. She is co-director of the Walter Scott Research Centre at the University of Aberdeen and Honorary Librarian at Abbotsford House.

Catriona M. M. Macdonald is Reader in Late Modern Scottish History at the University of Glasgow. A former editor of the *Scottish Historical Review*, she has written widely on the socio-economic and political history of modern Scotland and the contested culture of Unionism. Works relevant to this volume include her edited volume, *Unionist Scotland* (1998), her monograph *Whaur Extremes Meet: Scotland's Twentieth Century* (2009), and recent historiographical studies relating to Andrew Lang and John Buchan. She is currently working on a major project exploring the evolution of Scottish historiography since 1832.

Donald Mackenzie is retired Lecturer in English Literature and Affiliate of the School of Critical Studies, University of Glasgow. He has edited Kipling's *Puck of Pook's Hill and Rewards and Fairies* for Oxford World's Classics (1993) and co-edited with Andrew Hook Scott's *The Fair Maid of Perth* for The Edinburgh Edition of the Waverley Novels (1999). He is the author of *The Metaphysical Poets* (1991) and has published articles on various authors and topics including Fulke Greville, Bunyan, Stevenson, Lawrence, Ford Madox

Ford, 'Borderlands of Tragedy' in the *Bacchae* and *Othello*, 'The Psalms' in *The Oxford History of Literary Translation in English, Volume 2* (2010) and (with Stuart Gillespie) 'Lucretius and the Moderns' in *The Cambridge Companion to Lucretius* (2007).

Ralph McLean is Curator of Manuscripts for the Long Eighteenth Century at the National Library of Scotland. He previously worked as a research associate at the University of Glasgow on the AHRC-funded project 'Editing Robert Burns for the 21ˢᵗ Century'. His most recent publications focus on the 1755–6 *Edinburgh Review*, and the decline of Latin in the Scottish Universities. Along with Ronnie Young he is the editor of *The Scottish Enlightenment and Literary Culture* (2016), which investigates the impact of imaginative literature on Enlightenment culture.

Alasdair Raffe is a Chancellor's Fellow in History at the University of Edinburgh. He is the author of *The Culture of Controversy: Religious Arguments in Scotland* (2012) and *Scotland in Revolution, 1685–1690* (2018). He has published articles and essays on various topics in Scottish religious, political, and intellectual history of the seventeenth and eighteenth centuries, including the Restoration settlement, the Union of 1707, and philosophical change.

Valerie Wallace is a Lecturer in History in the School of History, Philosophy, Political Science and International Relations at Victoria University of Wellington in New Zealand. In 2011–12 she was the inaugural US–UK Fulbright Scottish Studies Scholar at the Center for History and Economics at Harvard University and in 2016 a Visiting Fellow at the Institute of Scottish Historical Research at the University of St Andrews. Her work has appeared in *Utilitas*, the *Journal of Imperial and Commonwealth History*, *Scottish Historical Review* and in edited collections published by Oxford University Press and Palgrave Macmillan.

Professor Christopher A. Whatley OBE, FRSE, began his academic career as an economic historian and published titles such as *The Scottish Salt Industry 1570 to 1850: An Economic and Social History* (1988), and *Scottish Society 1707–1830: Beyond Jacobitism, Towards Industrialisation* (2000). Even so, he has long had an interest in Scottish literature and in 1979 edited *John Galt, 1779–1979*. Recent publications include the award-winning *The Scots and the Union: Then and Now* (2014), and *Immortal Memory: Burns and the Scottish People* (2016).

Brian Young is University Lecturer and Charles Stuart Student and Tutor in History, Christ Church, Oxford, where he is currently Senior Censor. He is the author of *Religion and Enlightenment in Eighteenth-Century England* (1998), and *The Victorian Eighteenth Century* (2007). He has co-edited a number of books, most recently with Karen O'Brien, *The Cambridge Companion to Edward Gibbon*. He is completing a study of relations between Christians and unbelievers in eighteenth-century England.

I

Union and the Ironies of Displacement in Scottish Literature

Colin Kidd

The Union between Scotland and England bulks large on today's Scottish literary scene as a symbol of negativity and oppression. Writers view the Union—almost unanimously—as an impediment to full Scottish self-realization, cultural as well as political. The British state, so the literary consensus runs, is not only an obstacle to the uninhibited implementation in the political sphere of measures appropriate to Scotland and its needs, but also a threat to a distinctive Scottish voice, vision, and ethos in the arts. Writers have been in the vanguard of the campaign for Scottish independence.

In the aftermath of the 1979 referendum on Scottish devolution—when Scots voted narrowly for an assembly, but without meeting the required supermajority threshold (40 per cent of the total electorate, inclusive of non-voters)—Scottish writers, artists, and musicians took up the supposed cause of 'Scotland' as their own.[1] Scotland in the 1980s went through a literary renaissance, which was highly politicized. Writers moved easily between high literature and polemic. Alasdair Gray (b. 1934), for example, the author of the monumental dystopian novel *Lanark* (1981), also published

1. Michael Gardiner, *The Cultural Roots of British Devolution* (Edinburgh: Edinburgh University Press, 2004).

the pamphlet *Why Scots Should Rule Scotland* (1992). Language itself inscribed difference. The novelist James Kelman (b. 1946) and the poet Tom Leonard (b. 1944) were the most vivid and accomplished practitioners of a literature in demotic Scots that was defiantly in-your-face. In the world of the radical vernacular, the cause of the working class and the cause of the nation blurred together, prefiguring uncannily—but by decades—the SNP's capture of much of the working-class electorate from Labour in 2014–15.

The new writers identified with the idea of Scottish popular sovereignty; moreover, they promoted the idea that Scottish culture, both in its ethos and in its mode of expression, was utterly different from the supposed georgic aesthetics of the English literary tradition. The notion of a common British heritage—of Jane Austen and Walter Scott, say, read and appreciated on both sides of the border—gave way to neo-colonialist perspectives in the new Scottish cultural criticism.[2] Anglican churches, country houses, and the genteel ways of village life were not only socially distant and for toffs; they were also foreign. Of course, popular reading and viewing habits in Scotland give the lie to the pronouncements of the literary elite. Nevertheless, seeming contradictions of this sort—between an older generation that had lived through the common British deprivations of the Second World War and younger age groups that felt more confidently Scottish, between the fastidious guardians of high culture and the undiscriminating consumers of popular literary fare—were symptomatic of the asymmetrically divided society so evident in the referendum campaign in 2014. From the 1980s the nationalist-tinged renaissance was understandably more visible—and voluble—than the complacencies of the comfortably middle class and the middle-aged. By the time of the referendum campaign, the arts in Scotland were ranged decidedly, if just short of unanimously, on the side of an independent future.[3]

Within literary circles, the Union is widely perceived as purely instrumental and lacking in deep indigenous cultural roots. During the recent campaign for Scottish independence that preceded the Referendum of 2014, Scottish writers were outspoken in their commitment to a future outside

---

2. Influential, if controversial and unconvincing to most historians, was Michael Hechter, *Internal Colonialism: The Celtic Fringe in British National Development, 1536–1966* (London: Routledge and Kegan Paul, 1975).

3. Scott Hames (ed.), *Unstated: Writers on Scottish Independence* (Edinburgh: Word Power Books: 2012); Colin Kidd, 'Scottish Independence: Literature and Nationalism', *Guardian*, 19 July 2014 <http://www.theguardian.com/books/2014/jul/19/scottish-independence-literature-nationalism> (accessed 21 May 2015).

the Union.[4] Dissenting notes among poets, novelists, and playwrights were sufficiently rare that, however modestly or tentatively expressed, they carried a frisson of transgression or shock value. Such near-unanimity, in a sector of society where dissonance and debate are usually the norm, is puzzling. Of course, in every area of life we encounter peer pressure and the confining attitudes of group think; but writers, on the whole, tend to be different, to relish the countercultural pose and the cut-and-thrust of disagreement. Why were Scotland's outlandishly colourful literary circles so atypically monochrome when it came to expressing views on the independence Referendum? The phenomenon of literary anti-unionism invites further investigation.

Unanimity on this scale derives from ideas of literary essentialism; to put it crudely, the notion that there is a direct one-to-one correspondence between a nation and its literature, each understood as a singular entity. If a unitary Scottish culture is adulterated with draughts of Englishness or some other foreign tincture, then it is at best a diluted version of what it might be, or worse a poisonous brew dangerous for Scots to consume. Since the inter-war era, generations of Scottish literary intellectuals have, under the inspiration of the poet and critic Christopher Murray Grieve (1892–1978), better known by his pen name Hugh MacDiarmid, rejoiced in essentialism, a rigidly binary set of values and a zero-sum approach to questions of union, Anglicization, assimilation, cultural integrity, and Anglo-Scottish hybridity. Nationalist bias complemented a unitarist conception of literary wholeness. Consider MacDiarmid's attitude to Edwin Muir's *Scott and Scotland* (1936), a controversial work of cultural analysis that he detested, not least because of Muir's sombre pessimistic conclusion about the limited potential of Scots as a revived literary medium. In MacDiarmid's eyes, *Scott and Scotland* amounted to nothing more than 'a restatement of the literary case for Scottish unionism—that hireling caste employed by English Imperialism to perpetuate the provincial status of Scotland'.[5] Posthumously, the MacDiarmid thesis in Scottish criticism received additional reinforcement from the colonial world, notably from Frantz Fanon's ideas of inferiorism[6] and from

---

4. Most comprehensively in Robert Crawford, *Bannockburns: Scottish Independence and Literary Imagination 1314–2014* (Edinburgh: Edinburgh University Press, 2014).
5. Hugh MacDiarmid, *Lucky Poet*, ed. A. Riach (Manchester: Carcanet, 1994), 199.
6. Craig Beveridge and Ronald Turnbull, *The Eclipse of Scottish Culture* (Edinburgh: Polygon, 1989); Cairns Craig, *Out of History: Narrative Paradigms in Scottish and British Culture* (Edinburgh: Polygon, 1996).

postcolonial criticism.[7] Moreover, the periphery has begun to deconstruct the centre, with an emergent nationalist critique of the political 'constitution' of English Literature as the literature of an imperial British Establishment.[8] Such developments have further entrenched interwar ideas in today's culture that might otherwise find the values of the 1920s and 1930s embarrassing, outdated, or redundant. MacDiarmid is still the principal authority in Scottish criticism,[9] and his influence also persists in the political sphere.

The Scottish National Party, founded in 1934, and its immediate forebear the National Party of Scotland, launched in 1928, were by-products of the interwar Scots literary renaissance, and both provided political homes for poets, novelists, and critics. Grieve was, of course, a member, though expelled for his Communism. Neil Gunn (1891–1973), one of Scotland's leading novelists, was more reliable than Grieve, and participated effectively in the councils of the party. The comic novelist Compton Mackenzie (1883–1972) was another prominent interwar nationalist. Indeed, literature has been integral to the life of Scottish Nationalist politics to a degree unimaginable in any mainstream UK party. At the opening of the devolved Scottish Parliament in 1999 SNP MSPs sported white roses in their lapels, by way of allusion to a MacDiarmid lyric:

> The rose of all the world is not for me
> I want for my part
> Only the little white rose of Scotland
> That smells sharp and sweet—and breaks the heart.[10]

Alex Salmond, the long-serving and inspirational leader of the SNP from 1990 to 2000, and again between 2004 and 2014, prized Scotland's literature; though this did not preclude appropriating it for political purposes when the opportunity presented itself. Salmond's cautious vision of Scottish independence as a halfway house short of full separation from England centred on a currency union, a shared monarchy under the auspices of the Union

---

7. Leith Davis, *Acts of Union: Scotland and the Literary Negotiation of the British Nation 1707–1830* (Stanford: Stanford University Press, 1998); Michael Gardiner, Graeme Macdonald, and Niall O'Gallagher (eds), *Scottish Literature and Postcolonial Literature: Comparative Texts and Critical Perspectives* (Edinburgh: Edinburgh University Press, 2011).

8. Michael Gardiner, *The Constitution of English Literature: The State, the Nation and the Canon* (London: Bloomsbury, 2013).

9. For a trenchant assessment of the state of Scottish literary and cultural studies, not least its unthinking debts to MacDiarmid, see Gerard Carruthers, *Scottish Literature: A Critical Guide* (Edinburgh: Edinburgh University Press, 2009).

10. Hugh MacDiarmid, 'The Little White Rose', in Hugh MacDiarmid, *Complete Poems, Volume I*, ed. Michael Grieve and W. R. Aitken (Manchester: Carcanet, 1993), 461.

of the Crowns, and what he termed—tellingly—a continuing 'social union'.[11] The social union suggested to the anxious or faint-hearted that common British standards of welfare provision would continue after independence— reassurance bolstered here by the very familiarity of the term, which was taken from the second stanza of Robert Burns's most canonical lyric, 'To a Mouse':

> Wee, sleeket cowran tim'rous beastie,
> O what a panic's in thy breastie!
> Thou needna start awa sae hasty,
> Wi' bickering brattle
> I wad be laith to run an' chase thee,
> Wi' murdering pattle
>
> I'm truly sorry man's dominion
> Has broken nature's social union
> An' justifies that ill opinion,
> Which makes thee startle,
> At me, thy poor, earth-born companion,
> An' fellow-mortal.[12]

Salmond's commitment to free university tuition was also couched in the phraseology of Burns. Echoing the famous lines in the third stanza of Burns's song 'O my luve's like a red, red rose'—'Till a' the seas gang dry my dear, And the rocks melt wi' the sun'[13]—Salmond said at his party's spring conference in 2011 that the SNP would cling to its policy of free university education until the 'rocks melt wi' the sun',[14] a vow later inscribed in stone at Heriot-Watt University in 2014.[15]

Salmond not only used his keen ear for Scottish poetry to serve party political ends. He also perceived literature as a vivid demonstration of why the UK as he saw it was doomed as a failed state. The very differences between Scottish and English literatures provided evidence that the ethics and value systems of the two nations were deeply incompatible. Salmond contended that it was impossible to mistake the fundamental differences

---

11. *Scotland's Future* (Scottish Government, 2013), 215.
12. Burns, 'To a Mouse', in *Burns Poems and Songs*, ed. J. Kinsley (1969; paperback edn, Oxford: Oxford University Press, 1990), 101.
13. Burns, 'A red, red Rose', in *Burns Poems and Songs*, ed. Kinsley, 582.
14. See https://stv.tv/news/scotland/234728-alex-salmond-the-rocks-will-melt-with-the-sun-before-we-allow-tuition-fees/ (accessed 7 August 2017).
15. <https://www.timeshighereducation.com/news/salmond-unveils-free-tuition-monument-at-heriot-watt/2017046.article> (accessed July 2017).

between a Scottish and an English novelist.[16] Basic divergences of this kind, it seems, undermined notions of a common democratic discourse and, by extension, the very idea of British nationhood.

MacDiarmid-inspired assumptions also enjoy a much wider influence in Scottish life, beyond literary studies. Over the decades MacDiarmid's views about the threat the Union poses to Scottish culture have come to exercise considerable influence on Scotland's political class, and not only among outright nationalists. The devolutionist manifesto, the Claim of Right (1988) of the Constitutional Steering Group of the Campaign for a Scottish Assembly, proclaimed starkly:

> Scottish nationhood does not rest on constitutional history alone. It is supported by a culture reaching back over centuries and bearing European comparison in depth and quality…Since the Union, the strength of that culture has fluctuated but there is no ground for any claim that, overall or even at any particular time, it has benefited from the Union.

The verdict was stark: 'the Union has always been, and remains, a threat to the survival of a distinctive culture in Scotland.'[17]

Given such a decisively negative assessment of the Union and its devastating impact on Scottish culture, we might expect union to be the great white whale of Scottish literature, a monstrous topic obsessively pursued down the ages. Rather, the reverse is the case. Union, it transpires, is a marginal presence in the history of Scottish literature. To be sure, it provides the subject matter of a celebrated poem by Robert Burns, Scotland's national bard, as well as some pungent lyrics by the eighteenth-century poet Robert Fergusson and by MacDiarmid himself. In 'Such a Parcel o' Rogues in a Nation', Burns both lamented the effects of the Union and highlighted the notorious bribery that had accompanied the Union's passage through the Scots Parliament:

> Fareweel to a' our Scottish fame
> Fareweel our ancient glory;
>
>   .   .   .   .   .   .
>
> We're bought and sold for English gold,
> Such a parcel o' rogues in a nation![18]

16. David Torrance, *The Battle for Britain: Scotland and the Independence Referendum* (London: Biteback Publishing, 2013), 197.
17. 'A Claim of Right for Scotland', in Owen Dudley Edwards (ed.), *A Claim of Right for Scotland* (Edinburgh: Polygon, 1989), 2.2, p. 14.
18. Burns, 'Such a parcel of rogues in a nation', in *Burns Poems and Songs*, ed. Kinsley, 511–12.

The message that Scottish independence had been sold out by a corrupt elite resonates with today's popular left-wing nationalism. The case of Robert Burns is, however, a complex one. How representative of Burns's overall political position are his much-quoted lines about Scotland being 'bought and sold for English gold' at the Union?[19] To what extent was Burns's complaint—and those of other authors, including later Scott—simply that the Union of 1707 had been accomplished by *means* of corruption? In other words, were the means (criticized) distinguished from the ends (laudable) of union?[20] How far, moreover, is there any real overlap between Burns himself and his champions within the cult of Burns Suppers and other festivals that flourished throughout the nineteenth and for much of the twentieth century? Was the iconic Burns of the Burns Cult a more unionist Burns than the poet himself?[21]

Robert Fergusson (1750–74), in his poem 'The Ghaists' (1773), a conversation in an Edinburgh kirkyard between two long-dead ghosts, Heriot and Watson, furious that their legacy to an Edinburgh hospital is at risk because of a British mortmain bill, features the celebrated anti-unionist lines:

> Black be the day that e'er to England's ground
> Scotland was eikit by the Union's bond.[22]

Fergusson was a conservative poet of Tory–Jacobite sympathies, and these underpinned a traditionalist critique of the Union.

Hugh MacDiarmid used 'The Parrot Cry'—initially a free-standing poem, later incorporated as a section of *To Circumjack Cencrastus* (1930)—to denounce the pro-unionist parrot cries of the English and their Scots collaborators:

> Tell me the auld, auld story
> O' hoo the Union brocht
> Puir Scotland into being
> As a country worth a thocht.
> England, frae whom a' blessings flow

19. Christopher Whatley, 'Burns and the Union of 1707', in Kenneth Simpson (ed.), *Robert Burns a Bicentenary Celebration* (East Linton: Tuckwell Press, 1997).
20. Colin Kidd, 'Eighteenth-Century Scotland and the Three Unions', in T. C. Smout (ed.), *Anglo-Scottish Relations from 1603 to 1900: Proceedings of the British Academy*, 127 (2005), 171–87, at p. 186.
21. Richard Finlay, 'The Burns Cult and Scottish Identity in the Nineteenth and Twentieth Centuries', in Simpson (ed.), *Robert Burns a Bicentenary Celebration*; Christopher Whatley, *Immortal Memory: Burns and the Scottish People* (Edinburgh: Birlinn, 2016).
22. Fergusson, 'The Ghaists: A Kirk-Yard Eclogue', in *Robert Fergusson Selected Poems*, ed. James Robertson (Edinburgh: Polygon, 2000), 136.

What could we dae withoot ye?
Then dinna threip it doon oor throats
As gin we e'er could doot ye
My feelings lang wi' gratitude
Ha'e been sae sairly harrowed
That dod! I think it's time
The claith was owre the parrot![23]

MacDiarmid wanted to restore the possibility that Scotland could redis-
cover a self-confident voice, but only if unionist parrot cries were silenced:

It's possible that Scotland yet
May hear its ain voice speak
If only we can silence
This endless-yatterin' beak.[24]

MacDiarmid's subject matter was not the events surrounding the Union
itself, but the dominance of unionist thinking on the Scottish mindset.

Indeed, the Union itself has rarely surfaced directly in Scottish literature.
While the historical matter of 1707 scarcely features in the Scottish canon,
retrospective flyting over the pros and cons of union has nevertheless been
a prominent set piece in Scottish fiction since the mid-eighteenth century.
Tobias Smollett's *The Expedition of Humphry Clinker* (1771) provided a decisive
postscript to the literary battle of Britain that had raged throughout the
1760s. Politically, the decade saw Lord Bute become the first Scot to rise—
as King's favourite—to the rank of Prime Minister, the scotophobic radical
John Wilkes edit the controversial anti-Bute magazine the *North Briton*, and
a host of other English pamphleteers, poets, and cartoonists denigrate the
Scots in various media.[25] In literature, moreover, the appearance of James
Macpherson's versions of the supposed epics of Ossian, a third-century
Caledonian poet, exacerbated Anglo-Scottish tensions; for it inspired
damagingly subversive questions: had ancient Scotland produced a Celtic
bard to rival Homer? Or, more plausibly, was the modern Scotland that
celebrated Ossian addicted to falsehood and forgery?[26] *Humphry Clinker*

23. MacDiarmid, 'To Circumjack Cencrastus', in MacDiarmid, *Complete Poems, Volume I*, 192.
24. MacDiarmid, *Complete Poems, Volume I*, 194.
25. John Brewer, 'The Misfortunes of Lord Bute: A Case Study in Eighteenth-Century Political
    Argument and Public Opinion', *Historical Journal*, 16 (1973), 3–43; Adam Rounce, 'Stuarts with-
    out End: Wilkes, Churchill and Anti-Scottishness', *Eighteenth-Century Life*, 29 (2005), 20–43.
26. Richard Sher, '"Those Scotch Imposters and their Cabal": Ossian and the Scottish Enlightenment',
    Man and Nature/L'Homme et la nature, 1 (1982), 55–63; Sher, *Church and University in the Scottish
    Enlightenment: The Moderate Literati of Edinburgh* (Princeton: Princeton University Press;

(1771) is an ingenious attempt by a North British novelist and journalist to have the last word. In place of a single authorial voice, this is an epistolary novel that records a tour around Britain by a Welsh family, whose presumed objectivity regarding the differences they observe between England and Scotland allows the Anglo–Scottish Smollett to puncture various scotophobic prejudices found in England during the controversies of the 1760s.[27] However, false expectation, drama, and contestation precede unprejudiced enlightenment. En route, two of Smollett's leading characters, the Scottish patriot Lieutenant Lismahago and the tourist Welsh squire Matthew Bramble, debate the merits of union. Bramble claims 'that the appearance of the country was much mended; that the people lived better, had more trade, and a greater quantity of money circulating since the union than before'. Lismahago rejects the 'inference': 'Before the union, there was a remarkable spirit of trade among the Scots, as appeared in the case of their Darien company.' Moreover, he adds, the 'maritime towns in Fife' had a thriving trade with France, 'which failed in consequence of the union'. In general, Lismahago asserts, 'the Scots were losers by the union.—They lost the independency of their state, the greatest prop of national spirit; they lost their parliament, and their courts of justice were subjected to the revision and supremacy of an English tribunal.' Bramble in turn points to more practical advantages for individuals: 'that by the union the Scots were admitted to all the privileges and immunities of English subjects; by which means multitudes of them were provided for in the army and navy, and got fortunes in different parts of England and its dominions.' Yet again the anti-unionist know-it-all has a sharp retort: 'All these (said he) become English subjects to all intents and purposes.' Not only does Bramble concede that 'his patience began to fail', but Lismahago's complaints are unobtrusively undercut by comments on the improvement of Scotland from the unbiased Welsh letter-writers in Smollett's epistolary travelogue.[28]

This argument is reprised in Walter Scott's Jacobite novel of the 1715 rising *Rob Roy*, in a disputation between the anti-unionist Andrew Fairservice and the canny Glasgow merchant, Bailie Nicol Jarvie: 'When Andrew Fairservice (whom, by the way the Bailie could not abide) chose to impute

Edinburgh: Edinburgh University Press, 1985), 242–61; Fiona Stafford, *The Sublime Savage: James Macpherson and the Poems of Ossian* (Edinburgh: Edinburgh University Press, 1988).

27. E. Rothstein, 'Scotophilia and *Humphry Clinker*: The Politics of Beggary, Bugs and Buttocks', *University of Toronto Quarterly*, 52 (1982), 63–78.

28. Tobias Smollett, *The Expedition of Humphry Clinker* (1771; Harmondsworth: Penguin, 1967; repr. 1982), 315–16.

the accident of one of the horses casting his shoe to the deteriorating influence of the Union, he incurred a severe rebuke from Mr Jarvie.' Bailie Jarvie asks Fairservice to desist, complaining that 'it's ill-scraped tongues like yours, that make mischief atween neighbourhoods and nations'. Jarvie notes that the people of Glasgow had been as loud as any other Scots in their protests against the Union in 1706–7, but now Glasgow's commerce was flourishing: 'What was ever like to gar us flourish like the sugar and tobacco-trade? Will ony body tell me that, and grumble at the treaty that opened us a road west-awa' yonder.' But Jarvie's arguments merely provoke Fairservice, who launches another anti-union diatribe:

> That it was an unco change to hae Scotland's laws made in England; and that, for his share, he wadna for a' the herring-barrels in Glasgow, and a' the tobacco-casks to boot, hae gien up the riding o' the Scots Parliament, or sent awa' our crown, and our sword, and Mons Meg to be keepit by thae English pock-puddings in the Tower o' Lunnon.[29]

The result in both flytings—as Smollett and Scott present them—is a victory for unionist pragmatism, prudence, and common sense over emotive nationalist rhetoric.

Indeed, the nationalist blowhard is, perhaps surprisingly, something of a stock character in Scottish fiction. The lineage of Lismahago and Fairservice continues with Archie Brown, the ultra-nationalist poseur in *The Singing Sands*, a novel by Josephine Tey (1896–1952),[30] and MacTavish, the loud-mouth nationalist publican in *Beside the Ocean of Time* by the Orcadian novelist George Mackay Brown (1921–96). Archie Brown, who 'calls himself Gilleasbuig Mac-a'-Bruithainn', is a Lowlander who has 'elected himself the champion of Gaeldom'; a would-be poetic genius, he had dabbled in Scots but got nowhere, so, opportunistically, has learnt some Gaelic and, as 'the self-appointed saviour of Gaeldom', promptly embarked upon an epic poem in his new language. 'This perversion of patriotism' lectures some picknickers 'on the glory of Scotland; its mighty past and dazzling future'. He mistakes Alan Grant, a detective from London, for an Englishman, and recites 'England's iniquities' at length: 'Scotland had groaned under the foreign yoke, she had come staggering behind the conqueror's chariot, she had paid tribute and prostituted her talents to the tyrant's needs.' However, Mac-a'-Bruithainn

---

29. Walter Scott, *Rob Roy* (1817; London: Penguin, 1962 edn; repr. 1986), 246–7.
30. Josephine Tey was one of the pseudonyms of Elizabeth MacKintosh. For Tey's distance from the nationalism of the Scottish literary scene, see Jennifer M. Henderson, *Josephine Tey: A Life* (Dingwall: Sandstone Press, 2015), 158–9.

has confidence in the nationalist dream: 'the fiery cross was about to be sent out once more, and soon the heather would be alight. There was no cliché that Wee Archie spared them.' However, in a later scene, Grant offers an incisive interpretation of the Union of 1707, which is, by contrast, sparing and understated: 'Scotland stepped thankfully onto England's band-wagon, and fell heir to all the benefits. Colonies, Shakespeare, soap, solvency and so forth.'[31]

In Mackay Brown's novel, MacTavish is an incomer to Orkney from Edinburgh, and flaunts his nationalist opinions on his drinkers, whether they like it or not: 'Mr MacTavish spoke at great length—too long, most of the smithy-men thought—about the mighty nation Scotland had been before that disastrous union with England in 1707.' MacTavish complains that all Scotland's 'glory was shorn away in 1707, except that we had our own laws and our Presbyterian kirk. We were a rump of England, nothing more.' A local Orcadian interjects that Orkney 'had never been part of Scotland anyway till 1472, and then the Scots had fallen on the once powerful earldom of Orkney and battened on it like hoodie crows'. The innkeeper 'brushed that aside', and the torrent continues: 'If only Mr MacTavish had lived in those days—how gladly would he have followed the troops converging on the little torrent, the Bannock Burn, under Stirling Castle... The inn-keeper's voice went on and on.'[32]

The events of the Union also feature, as we shall see, in a few minor novels and plays. But otherwise the central fact of modern Scottish history is surprisingly peripheral to the canon, certainly by comparison with other historical and political subjects, such as the late -seventeenth-century plight of the persecuted Presbyterian Covenanters and the Jacobite rebellions that occurred during the first half of the eighteenth century. Indeed, Fergusson's 'The Ghaists'—already identified as one of the few canonical moments in Scottish literature when the Union is directly addressed—resounds not only to anti-unionist lament, but also—and just as obviously—to a Tory encomium on the arch-royalist persecutor of the Covenanters, the King's Advocate Sir George Mackenzie of Rosehaugh, the Bluidy Mackenzie of Covenanting lore:

> Yonder's the tomb of wise Mackenzie fam'd
> Whase laws rebellious bigotry reclaim'd,
> Freed the hail land frae covenanting fools.[33]

31. Josephine Tey, *The Singing Sands* (1952; London: Arrow Books, 2011), 33–4, 39, 138.
32. George Mackay Brown, *Beside the Ocean of Time* (1994; Edinburgh: Polygon, 2011), 22–3.
33. *Fergusson Selected Poems*, 138.

What was true of poetry and song[34] was still more applicable to the Scottish
novel. Long after the passing of the movements themselves, Jacobitism and
Covenanting Presbyterianism came to constitute and to shape the political
and historical matter of the Scottish novel. The well-known romantic heroism of the Jacobites, which, from Walter Scott's *Waverley* (1814) onwards,
delighted nineteenth-century audiences sentimentally addicted to the lost,
defeated cause of the Stuarts, was paralleled by a romantic celebration of the
sufferings of the Covenanters, a movement antithetical to Jacobitism with
respect both to politics and to religion. Scots Presbyterians had been in
general loyal Whigs, supporters of the Revolution of 1688–9 that brought
William of Orange and his wife Mary to the throne of Scotland. Literature
is not written only on behalf of the losers; sometimes we forget—even in
Scotland—that the winners too had a voice.

The Whig–Presbyterian novel emerged in good part in reaction to Walter
Scott's shafts of anti-Presbyterian satire in *Old Mortality* (1816), and became
the dominant trope in nineteenth-century Scottish fiction through to the
Kailyard novel and beyond. However, so prevalent was Whig–Presbyterian
unionism in Scottish culture—and so remote any Jacobite or nationalist
threat after 1746—that it was safe within the capacious bounds of this genre
to subvert Presbyterian themes—whether, as Scott did, the extremism of the
Covenanters themselves, or the ultra-Calvinist antinomianism of James
Hogg's Justified Sinner[35] or the self-delusion of the Revd Micah Balwhidder
in John Galt's *Annals of the Parish*[36]—without calling into question the
Union or the standing of the Kirk. The genre's exponents have included
writers as various as Galt,[37] Hogg,[38] and Robin Jenkins (1912–2005).[39] Scott
occupies an unusual liminal space both outside the genre as its foremost
critic, and inside it as the founder of the novel of Calvinist excess and its
mutations. It continues to flourish in the early twenty-first century in the
work of James Robertson (b. 1958), notably in *The Fanatic* (2000) and *The
Testament of Gideon Mack* (2006). We need to be alert to the dominance of

34. Cf. William Donaldson, *The Jacobite Song: Political Myth and National Identity* (Aberdeen:
    Aberdeen University Press, 1988); Murray Pittock, *The Invention of Scotland: The Stuart Myth and
    the Scottish Identity 1638 to the Present* (London: Routledge, 1991); Pittock, *Poetry and Jacobite
    Politics in Eighteenth-Century Britain and Ireland* (Cambridge: Cambridge University Press, 1994).
35. James Hogg, *The Private Memoirs and Confessions of a Justified Sinner* (1824; Harmondsworth:
    Penguin, 1983).
36. John Galt, *Annals of the Parish* (1821; Oxford: Oxford University Press, 1986).
37. See also John Galt, *Ringan Gilhaize* (1823; Edinburgh: Canongate, 1995).
38. See also James Hogg, *The Brownie of Bodsbeck* (1818; Edinburgh: Scottish Academic Press, 1976).
39. Robin Jenkins, *The Awakening of George Darroch* (1985; Edinburgh: B&W Publishing, 1995).

ecclesiastical rather than political divisions in the Scottish past. Nineteenth-century Scotland was not without a kind of nationalism, but a religious nationalism, which reached boiling point at the Disruption of 1843, when the Free Church split from the established Presbyterian Kirk, and which did not challenge the British state politically.[40] By the same token, Scott's romantic Jacobitism flourished within the confines of the unionist novel, albeit in his case a very latitudinarian unionism. In all of his Jacobite and Cavalier tales Scott achieves a unionist outcome—usually by way of a marriage of reconciliation between Whig and Jacobite and an acceptance of the status quo.

Scottish literature is as much a reflection of Scott-land[41] as it is of Scotland itself, so overwhelming was Walter Scott's legacy for the nineteenth century and beyond. The matter of union played a much less prominent role in Scott-land than either Jacobitism or Presbyterian covenanting. Scott's novels do serve a 'nationalist' function, though a very particular one.[42] Scott's 'nationalist' purpose is to reconcile the conflicting party allegiances of Whigs and Jacobites, of Presbyterians and Episcopalians, of the old feudal ways of clan-ship and the new world of commerce. On the other hand, the reconciliation of unionism and nationalism barely registers in Scott's concerns. Scott is pre-eminently a novelist of Scotland's warring parties and churches.

The party novel—broadly conceived—has dominated Scottish litera-ture, to the exclusion of a comprehensively 'national' sensibility. Indeed, even novels seemingly dominated by questions of Anglo-Scottish differ-ence, such as Smollett's *Humphry Clinker*, also turn out to have a 'party' dimension.[43] The English novel, by contrast, is much less partisan in its concerns, and—ironically—an altogether more 'national' genre. The 'con-dition of England' novel has played a central role in shaping the norms and forms of modern English literature, notwithstanding obvious imbalances within the genre such as the assumption that the south and the country, rather than the north and the city, embody the essentials of Englishness. However, the 'condition of Scotland' novel is a relative rarity in the Scottish canon, and certainly marginal to the 'party' novels of Whig–Presbyterians

40. Michael Fry, 'The Disruption and the Union', in S. J. Brown and M. Fry (eds), *Scotland in the Age of the Disruption* (Edinburgh: Edinburgh University Press, 1993), 31–43.
41. Cf. Stuart Kelly, *Scott-land: The Man who Invented a Nation* (Edinburgh: Polygon, 2010).
42. Cf. Eric Hobsbawm, *Nations and Nationalism* (Cambridge: Cambridge University Press, 1990), 90.
43. W. Franke, 'Smollett's *Humphry Clinker* as a Party-Novel', *Studies in Scottish Literature*, 9 (1971–2), 97–106.

and Jacobite–Episcopalians, and to the continuators, inverters, and parodists of these party-denominational genres.

The very resonance and significance of these two traditions, one associated with Covenanting, Whiggery, and Presbyterianism, the other with Jacobitism, in the decades either side of the Union of 1707 go some way towards explaining the relative invisibility of the Union within the canon; but only some part of the way, for the very proximity of a seemingly semi-invisible 1707 to this subject matter still begs the question of why the Union itself should be—at the very most—tangential to the Scottish canon.

★

What follows is an attempt to make sense of a series of puzzles about the relationship of Scottish literature and the Union, and about literature and unions more generally. This introductory chapter will provide an overview of the Union in Scottish literature, and will set out the central objective of the volume, which is to effect a rapprochement between a new British-orientated Scottish historiography and an essentialist–nationalist tradition of Scottish literary criticism. The terrain on which we shall be operating is pockmarked with ironies. Why is the Union more obviously an absence than a presence in Scottish literature? Why do Scottish critics ignore the rather obvious historical fact that the vast bulk of Scottish literature—whether after the Union of the Crowns in 1603, or after the parliamentary Union of 1707—was created *within* the context of union? The Scottish canon as we know it is very largely a product of union, and much of it was composed by writers who favoured some sort of political and economic connection with England, even if their unionism was not overt. The Unions with England provided the normal habitat of Scottish poets, playwrights, and novelists, in which a literature of stunning richness and distinctiveness flourished. Indeed, it is very hard to accept the assumption of the Claim of Right (1988) that the Union was inimical to creativity. Scottish literature has thrived, not of course without nationalist grievance or complaint, largely within the parameters of union. In what ways did the Union curb or constrain the genius of Burns or Scott or Stevenson? What would the corpus of Scottish literature look like if one excluded as abnormal and Anglo-contaminated the work produced between 1603 and the present? The corpus would, of course, be a fraction of its current scale. Scottish literature composed outside of the Union, such as the achievements of the late medieval makars, is the exception rather than the rule. Why, moreover, do scholars of Scottish literature pay so little heed to the role of Scottish writers in creating so many of the iconic texts of British—and, indeed, English—identity?

Beyond Scottish peculiarities, why is the study of literature in general more concerned with national essences than with loyalties to multinational union states? This situation takes its rise from a more general imbalance within literary studies as a whole. There has been a great deal of academic work—both in the Scottish context and more broadly—on the relationship between literature and nationhood, yet almost none on the relationship between literature and unions. There appears to be an assumption—at least among literary scholars—that identity is indivisible.

There are certain marked incongruities in Scottish academic life between the findings of literary and historical research. Scottish literature seen critically, in terms of what's worth celebrating, looks rather different from Scottish literature seen historically—that is, all of it, including elements that now jar with modern tastes. Perhaps disjunctions of this sort arise as a result of a fundamental mismatch between the attitude of the critic and that of the historian, between aesthetic and political criteria, between enduring literary quality and mere representativeness? Two obvious examples of this are what might be called the Kailyard Problem and the MacDiarmid–Cronin Problem. In the first case, today's Scottish critics recoil—appalled and embarrassed—from a strain of Scottish literature that dominated popular reading in Britain and the Empire during the late nineteenth and early twentieth centuries.[44] However, did Kailyard literature have no redeeming qualities whatsoever?[45] And, even if it was entirely lacking in literary value, should we dismiss out of hand an overwhelming success story—at least in terms of sales and the wider cultural influence of its impresario Sir William Robertson Nicoll (1851–1923)—that was so integral a part of the historical record?[46] In the second instance, the MacDiarmid–Cronin Problem, there is an awkward gulf between what literary critics emphasize as the main feature of interwar Scottish literature—namely, the achievement of MacDiarmid and the Scottish Renaissance—and what ordinary people in vast numbers were actually reading—for example, the popular novels of A. J. Cronin (1896–1981). While MacDiarmid's works appeared in 'little magazines' or in limited editions

---

44. Critical revulsion set in with George Blake, *Barrie and Kailyard School* (London: A. Barker, 1951).
45. Andrew Nash, *Kailyard and Scottish Literature* (Amsterdam: Rodopi, 2007).
46. Phillip Waller, *Writers, Readers and Reputations: Literary Life in Britain 1870–1918* (Oxford: Oxford University Press, 2006), 112–14, 131–2, 505, 977, 1010.

published by 'small presses' (or were, indeed, effectively self-published), Cronin, by contrast, sold over 40,000 copies of *The Citadel* (1937) in nine days, and 100,000 in ten weeks.[47] Should questions of literary value entirely obscure issues of wider social influence and representativeness? The historian notes that the high literature of Scottish Renaissance was a minority pursuit, which had minimal political impact, as the SNP would win its first seat in a wartime by-election only in 1945 and its first seat in a general election in 1970. Quite apart from these inherent differences of disciplinary perspective, there is also the possibility that literary critics have quite simply got things wrong, and have failed to contextualize Scottish writers with appropriate sensitivity and discrimination. In particular, it seems that modern assumptions about the importance of nationhood and the salience of the Union have been back-projected willy-nilly onto the past.

Historians try to attune themselves to the alien otherness of the past, and aim to recover the values of our ancestors on their own terms. To assume that Scots of the eighteenth or nineteenth centuries thought about the Union or nationhood like Scots of the late twentieth or early twenty-first centuries is to be imprisoned in the mental categories of the latter. National identity is not an ahistorical given, whose continuity can be casually inferred from one generation to the next. Rather, a central part of the historical enterprise is the study of how identities—even within the same nation—are gradually reconfigured over the centuries, sometimes more dramatically and abruptly, as we have seen in Scotland's recent past, in a matter of decades.

Few works have been more influential within history than Benedict Anderson's *Imagined Communities* (1983), in which he argues that all communities beyond face-to-face communities such as small tribes or villages have to be imagined; in other words—and, as Anderson insisted, in a non-pejorative sense—all forms of national consciousness are artificial constructs that depend upon processes of imagination.[48] However, few historians have contemplated the implications of Anderson's work for Scotland and Britain. Scottishness, so the logic of the Anderson thesis runs, is no more natural or authentic than Britishness; both—indeed *all* forms of nationhood—are imaginative confections.

---

47. Andrew Nash, 'Authors in the Literary Marketplace', in David Finkelstein and Alistair McCleery (eds), *The Edinburgh History of the Book in Scotland*, iv. *Professionalism and Diversity, 1880–2000* (Edinburgh: Edinburgh University Press, 2007), 388–408, at pp. 393, 396–8.
48. Benedict Anderson, *Imagined Communities: Reflections on the Origin and Spread of Nationalism* (London: Verso, 1983), 15.

Since the pioneering field-clearing work of John Pocock from the 1970s on our 'Atlantic archipelago',[49] the massive achievement of Hugh Kearney in the 1980s in mastering the historiography of the four nations of these islands,[50] and the publication in the 1990s of Linda Colley's seminal work *Britons: Forging the Nation 1707–1837* (1992),[51] the subject of Britishness has come to the forefront of historical concerns.[52] In particular, historians of political thought have drawn attention to the richness of early modern Scottish engagement with ideas of Britishness and union.[53] The Union of 1707, it transpires, was a much more sophisticated affair—arguably much more principled indeed, a matter of preserving the Revolution principles of 1688–9—than a simple transaction whereby its corrupt elite was bought and sold for English gold.[54] Early modernists have also been alert to the phenomenon of concentric loyalties; a British political allegiance did not diminish an emotional identification with Scotland.[55]

Quite apart from the historiographical phenomenon of 'the new British history', historians also appreciate that the nation state was not the norm in early modern Europe. Unions and 'composite states'[56]—miscellaneous

49. J. G. A. Pocock, 'British History: A Plea for a New Subject', *New Zealand Journal of History*, 8 (1974), 3–21, repr. in *Journal of Modern History*, 47 (1975), 601–24. See also Pocock, 'The Limits and Divisions of British History: In Search of the Unknown Subject', *American Historical Review*, 87 (1982), 311–36; Pocock, *The Discovery of Islands* (Cambridge: Cambridge University Press, 2005).

50. Hugh Kearney, *The British Isles: A History of Four Nations* (Cambridge: Cambridge University Press, 1989).

51. Linda Colley, *Britons: Forging the Nation 1707–1837* (New Haven and London: Yale University Press, 1992).

52. See, e.g., A. Grant and K. Stringer (eds), *Uniting the Kingdom? The Making of British History* (London: Routledge, 1995); S. Ellis and S. Barber (eds), *Conquest and Union: Fashioning a British State 1485–1725* (London: Longman, 1995); Brendan Bradshaw and John Morrill (eds), *The British Problem: State Formation in the Atlantic Archipelago 1534–1707* (Houndmills: Palgrave, 1996); Brendan Bradshaw and Peter Roberts (eds), *British Consciousness and Identity: The Making of Britain 1533–1707* (Cambridge: Cambridge University Press, 1998); G. Burgess (ed.), *The New British History: Founding a Modern State 1603–1715* (London: I. B. Tauris, 1999).

53. See R. A. Mason (ed.), *Scots and Britons: Scottish Political Thought and the Union of 1603* (Cambridge: Cambridge University Press, 1994); J. Robertson (ed.), *A Union for Empire: Political Thought and the British Union of 1707* (Cambridge: Cambridge University Press, 1995).

54. See, e.g., J. Robertson, 'Andrew Fletcher's Vision of Union', in R. A. Mason (ed.), *Scotland and England 1286–1815* (Edinburgh: John Donald, 1987), 203–25; Robertson (ed.), *Union for Empire*; Christopher Whatley, *The Scots and the Union* (Edinburgh: Edinburgh University Press, 2007); K. Bowie, *Scottish Public Opinion and the Anglo-Scottish Union, 1699–1707* (Woodbridge: Boydell Press, 2007).

55. T. C. Smout, 'Problems of Nationalism, Identity and Improvement in Later Eighteenth-Century Scotland', in T. M. Devine (ed.), *Improvement and Enlightenment* (Edinburgh: John Donald, 1989).

56. H. G. Koenigsberger, 'Dominum regale or dominium politicum et regale: Monarchies and Parliaments in Early Modern Europe', in Koenigsberger, *Politicians and Virtuosi: Essays in Early*

collections of geographically dispersed and ethnically heterogeneous territories that were ruled individually with little in the way of uniform governance, having been acquired, variously, by the royal dynasties that controlled them through the accidents of marriage, inheritance, and warfare—were the norm. Sweden, Denmark, and Norway formed the Kalmar Union between 1397 and 1523, and, long after the break-up of the union, Denmark—which we now think of as a simple nation state—evolved as an imperial agglomeration of territories in Scandinavia, northern Germany, the north Atlantic, the Caribbean, and even Tranquebar in India. The Union of Lublin 1569 consolidated the late medieval Polish–Lithuanian Union.[57] The Dutch territories that seceded from the Spanish Empire were united by the Union of Utrecht in 1579. Even polities that we now think of as nation states, such as Spain and France, were agglomerations of territories and provinces.[58] Entities such as these comprised the Europe in which the British Unions of 1603 and 1707 were less remarkable or incongruent than we might mistakenly imagine in retrospect. Indeed, things were more complicated still. Between 1697 and 1763 the formal Polish–Lithuanian Union comprised a composite state with Saxony, as the Wettin dynasty provided rulers for both its Saxon patrimony and the elective monarchy of Poland–Lithuania. Similarly, the Hanoverian state between 1714 and 1837 was a composite dynastic agglomeration, Britain–Hanover, with the Hanoverian portion succeeding through the male line, which is why it split from Britain at the accession of Queen Victoria.

Oddly, literary scholarship has preferred to study the expression of straightforward and simple essences to the exclusion of such tangled hybrids. Nevertheless, there are exceptions. Interestingly, there has been some attention within literary scholarship to the role of 'Anglo-Irish' literature within the culture of the British–Irish Union of 1800–1.[59] Yet Scottish literary scholars

Modern History (London: Hambledon, 1985), 1–25; J. H. Elliott, 'A Europe of Composite Monarchies', *Past and Present*, 137 (1992), 48–71.

57. See, esp., Robert I. Frost, *The Oxford History of Poland–Lithuania*, i. *The Making of the Polish–Lithuanian Union 1385–1569* (Oxford: Oxford University Press, 2015).

58. Cf. the implications, variously, of Peter Sahlins, *Boundaries: The Making of France and Spain in the Pyrenees* (Berkeley and Los Angeles: University of California Press, 1989); Eugen Weber, *Peasants into Frenchmen: The Modernization of Rural France 1870–1914* (Stanford: Stanford University Press, 1976); F. H. Hinsley, *Sovereignty* (2nd edn; Cambridge: Cambridge University Press, 1986); A. Mackillop and M. O. Siochru (eds), *Forging the State: European State Formation and the Anglo-Scottish Union of 1707* (Dundee: Dundee University Press, 2009).

59. See, e.g., Marilyn Butler, *Maria Edgeworth* (Oxford: Clarendon Press, 1972); J. C. Beckett, *The Anglo-Irish Tradition* (London: Faber and Faber, 1976); W. J. McCormack, *Ascendancy and Tradition in Anglo-Irish Literary History* (Oxford: Clarendon Press, 1985).

have done little to align what might be called 'Scottish–British literature' comparatively with the Anglo-Irish literary tradition. It is also a mistake to assume that multinational unions are incapable of fostering the sort of visceral loyalties associated with nationhood. Poland's national epic *Pan Tadeusz* by the country's bard, Adam Mickiewicz (1798–1855), opens with the immortal—and disconcerting—line, 'O Lithuania, my country'.[60] Modern Poland has appropriated as its national epic a work imbued with the pre-nationalist latitudinarian loyalties to the united Polish–Lithuanian commonwealth. Might pre-nationalist allegiances lurk undetected—or misinterpreted—in the Scottish literary tradition?

Punctuated cross-border (and, often significantly, cross-denominational) literary warfare—largely ignored by navel-gazing Scottish literary critics— formed a fundamental feature of the background to Anglo-Scottish politics between 1603 and the early years of George III's reign. The Union of the Crowns did not mark the end of Anglo-Scottish frictions, so much as a new beginning.[61] National-cum-confessional differences were a major factor behind the turbulence of the seventeenth-century Civil Wars,[62] and were still evident long after the parliamentary Union in the early 1760s when Lord Bute was Britain's first short-lived Scottish Prime Minister. However, within a few decades, James Boswell's *Life of Johnson* (1791) saw the scoto-phobic jibe safely domesticated: a sycophantic Scot taking delight in, and seemingly laughing at, the good-humoured recounting of anti-Scottish witticisms by the dominant figure in English letters.[63] Indeed, not only did Boswell take a relaxed and indulgent view of what he regarded as innocent foibles, but he tried to explain away Johnson's instinctive, groundless, and thence insubstantial 'antipathy to the Scotch', which had become almost second nature and a mere comic turn: 'Surely the most obstinate and sulky nationality, the most determined aversion to this great and good man, must be cured, when he is seen thus playing with one of his prejudices, of which

60. Adam Mickiewicz, *Pan Tadeusz*, trans. K. R. Mackenzie (New York: Hippocrene Books, 1992), 2.
61. See, e.g., Brian P. Levack, *The Formation of the British State: England, Scotland and the Union 1603–1707* (Oxford: Clarendon Press, 1987); K. Brown, *Kingdom or Province? Scotland and the Regal Union, 1603–1715* (Basingstoke: Palgrave, 1992); R. A. Mason, 'Debating Sovereignty in Seventeenth-Century Scotland: Multiple Monarchy and Scottish Sovereignty', *Journal of Scottish Historical Studies*, 35 (2015), 1–24.
62. Conrad Russell, *The Causes of the English Civil War* (Oxford: Oxford University Press, 1990); Russell, *The Fall of the British Monarchies 1637–1642* (Oxford: Clarendon Press, 1991).
63. James Boswell, *Life of Johnson* (1791; World's Classics; Oxford: Oxford University Press, 1980), see, e.g., 301–2, 406–8, 494, 578, 621, 627, 752–3, 774, 924, 1143.

he candidly admitted that he could not tell the reason.'[64] Boswell's biography marks a crucial milestone in Anglo-Scottish reconciliation. Thereafter, the nineteenth century witnessed what the eminent modern historian Keith Robbins has called the 'blending' of Britain.[65] The ordeals faced by Bute were now a thing of the past. Since the mid-nineteenth century, indeed, there have been almost as many Scots or obvious descendants of Scots in Downing Street as Englishmen: Aberdeen, Gladstone, Rosebery, Balfour, Campbell-Bannerman, Bonar Law, MacDonald, Macmillan, Douglas-Home, Blair, Brown, Cameron.

The three kingdoms turn in early modern historiography has been matched by a similar change of emphasis in modern historiography. The multinational character of the British state has come more clearly into focus, and historians and political scientists have traced with greater sensitivity the lineaments of its component political cultures.[66] Scottish unionist culture has emerged from the shadows as something more distinctive and indigenous than either a quisling phenomenon or a mere brand of sectarianism.[67] Long before devolution, it is recognized, Scotland enjoyed very high levels of autonomy within an otherwise unitary British state.[68] In recent decades the seemingly oxymoronic category of 'unionist–nationalism' has become one of the most influential categories in modern Scottish historical analysis,[69] and there have been intimations of a 'unionist turn' in the historiography.[70] Historians recognize that, while separatism and anglicizing assimilation stand at extremes of a nationalist–unionist spectrum, the bulk of modern Scottish political debate over the past few centuries has been conducted within

---

64. Boswell, *Life of Johnson*, 1197.
65. K. Robbins, *Nineteenth-Century Britain: Integration and Diversity* (Oxford: Oxford University Press, 1988).
66. See, e.g., R. Rose, *Understanding the United Kingdom: The Territorial Dimension in Government* (Harlow: Longman, 1982); L. Brockliss and D. Eastwood (eds), *A Union of Multiple Identities: The British Isles c. 1750–c. 1850* (Manchester: Manchester University Press, 1997); W. L. Miller (ed.), *Anglo-Scottish Relations from 1900 to Devolution*, Proceedings of the British Academy, 128 (Oxford: Oxford University Press, 2005).
67. R. Finlay, *A Partnership for Good? Scottish Politics and the Union since 1880* (Edinburgh: John Donald, 1997); C. Macdonald (ed.), *Unionist Scotland 1800–1997* (Edinburgh: John Donald, 1998).
68. See Lindsay Paterson, *The Autonomy of Modern Scotland* (Edinburgh: Edinburgh University Press, 1994), for the striking level of autonomy enjoyed by an undevolved Scotland within the incorporating union. Cf. James Mitchell, *Governing Scotland: The Invention of Administrative Devolution* (Houndmills: Palgrave Macmillan, 2003); Mitchell, *Devolution in the UK* (Manchester: Manchester University Press, 2009).
69. Graeme Morton, *Unionist Nationalism: Governing Urban Scotland 1830–60* (East Linton: Tuckwell Press, 1999).
70. A. Raffe, '1707, 2007 and the Unionist Turn in Scottish History', *Historical Journal*, 53 (2010), 1071–83.

a broadly unionist idiom, though one that is also inflected by nationalist tropes.[71] Furthermore, Scottish nationalism itself has been revealed as a surprisingly capacious phenomenon, which has embraced both looser versions of union and reinvigorated notions of British[72]—or more properly, Anglo-Scottish—Empire. Hybridity of this sort barely registers in Scottish literary studies. 'Romantic Unionism' sounds like an oxymoron, notwithstanding the obstinate fact that Scotland's leading 'romantic' writers were not so much 'bardic nationalists'[73] as romantic in their aesthetics—Gothic, historicist, intrigued by abnormal psychologies—while conforming to contemporary unionist norms in their political allegiances. There has been no serious attempt to introduce the insights of the new British history into Scottish literary scholarship.

Traditionally, literary historians have assumed that Scottish writers became nationalistic and defensive after the Union of 1707, which induced an eighteenth-century Scottish crisis of identity and the emergence of a vernacular renaissance in Scots championed by Allan Ramsay (1686–1758), Fergusson and, of course, Burns.[74] These assumptions are questionable. Party identities—Whig–Presbyterian and Jacobite–Episcopalian—were, if anything, stronger than national identity, and certainly more ubiquitous in Scottish literature until the twentieth century.[75] Whig loyalties were inseparable from pro-union allegiance; indeed, Whigs tended to commemorate 1688—the date of the Glorious Revolution in England—as the source of their liberties, regarding the Union of 1707 as a kind of sequel to the Revolution of 1688.

In this volume, we shall look at the way in which union influenced Scottish self-fashioning in the fields of poetry and the novel. The presence of union in Scottish culture was not simply a matter of collaboration or assimilationist reaction to the realities of post-1707 power politics. Such approaches are too reductive and miss not only the confident and creative

---

71. Colin Kidd, *Union and Unionisms: Political Thought in Scotland 1500–2000* (Cambridge: Cambridge University Press, 2008).
72. R. Finlay, 'For or Against? Scottish Nationalists and the British Empire, 1919–1939', *Scottish Historical Review*, 71 (1992), 184–206; Kidd, *Union and Unionisms*, ch. 7.
73. Cf. Katie Trumpener, *Bardic Nationalism: The Romantic Novel and the British Empire* (Princeton: Princeton University Press, 1997).
74. David Daiches, *The Paradox of Scottish Culture: The Eighteenth-Century Experience* (London: Oxford University Press, 1964); K. Simpson, *The Protean Scot: The Crisis of Identity in Eighteenth-Century Scottish Literature* (Aberdeen: Aberdeen University Press, 1988).
75. R. C. Gordon, *Under which King? A Study of the Scottish Waverley Novels* (Edinburgh and London: Oliver and Boyd, 1969); James Anderson, *Sir Walter Scott and History* (Edinburgh: Edina, 1981); Alexander Welsh, *The Hero of the Waverley Novels with New Essays on Scott* (Princeton: Princeton University Press, 1992).

underpinnings of Scottish–British literature, but also the ways in which—
contrary to the assumed run of literary analysis—Scottish writers reshaped
English culture and identity. In place of the dominant existing mode of
literary interpretation that assumes a close relationship between Scottish
literature and Scottish nationhood, this project will challenge received ideas
about the 'national' basis of the Scottish literary tradition. To what extent has
Anglo-Scottish Union—notwithstanding the acknowledged role of Scottish
nationhood—influenced the Scottish literary tradition? The primary focus
of Scottish literary scholarship has been on what might be called expressions
of literary nationalism. In general, Scottish critics have yet to see through
the mirage of literary nationalism, though there have been a couple of
glaring instances of this delusion. The decidedly non-nationalist socialism
of Lewis Grassic Gibbon, the pen name of James Leslie Mitchell (1901–35),
in *A Scots Quair* and John McGrath (1935–2002) in *The Cheviot, the Stag and
the Black, Black Oil* (1973) have been eagerly and all too easily aligned with
nationalist shibboleths by their audiences. Alas, the findings of historical
scholarship do not always manage to dispel received assumptions in literary
criticism. These days we are used to being presented with a familiar alternative:
nationhood or union? However, identity is not a zero-sum game. Multiple
identities, as we have seen, have been a common feature of early modern
and modern Scottish history. Unionism is in some ways as Scottish as
nationalism. Nor is nationalism the opposite of union; the idea of union
was first conceived by Scots as an alternative to English *imperial* dominance
of Great Britain.[76]

Union, indeed, started out as a Scottish idea—and not simply as a justification of political realities. Unionism was an invention of sixteenth- and
seventeenth-century Scots as an inspired visionary alternative to English
empire. Indeed, unionism was invented in the 1520s almost a century before
the Union of the Crowns, in the work of the internationally renowned
philosopher John Mair (1467–1550), from Haddington in East Lothian.[77]
Where, asked Mair, had the imperial claims and national counterclaims of
England and Scotland led during the later Middle Ages? For Bannockburn
had not put an end to Anglo-Scottish conflict. The dispute between an
independent Scotland and an over-mighty England had brought about two
centuries of intermittent but economically destructive warfare in the south

76. Kidd, *Union and Unionisms*.
77. Hence, R. Mason, 'Posing the East Lothian Question', *History Scotland*, 8 (January–February
    2008), 40–8.

of Scotland and north of England. Some Scots, such as Mair, began to realize that Scottish independence had not brought peace to Britain; perhaps union might. An Anglo-Scottish union, Mair thought, would achieve the same political benefits for Scotland as independence, as well as a range of social and economic goods that Scotland's embattled independence on a small island alongside an ambitious England had conspicuously not delivered. Mair's unionism was a means of allowing Scotland to be Scotland within a British framework of institutions.[78]

The Reformation added a religious gloss to the notion of shared Anglo-Scottish interests. Several Scottish Protestants argued for a Britain united on Reformation principles, indeed for a strikingly 'imperial' Protestant Britain.[79] In other words, the assumed grammar of union—that England was the subject, Scotland always the object—needs to be re-examined. After all, post-1707 the canon of iconic Englishness owed much to the Scottish literary tradition. John Bull was the creation of the Scottish doctor, wit, and pamphleteer John Arbuthnot (1667–1735).[80] The lyrics of 'Rule, Britannia' were the work of the Scots poet James Thomson (1700–48), who co-authored the masque *Alfred* (about the reign of the English king Alfred the Great) with a fellow-Scot, David Mallet, in 1740.[81] The most influential account of the ethnic-making of the English nation—the fusion of a defeated Saxon peasantry and ruling Norman aristocracy into a single English people—appeared in Walter Scott's *Ivanhoe* (1820).[82] Even the classic parody of conventional village Englishness turns out to be the work of a Scottish writer, A. G. Macdonell (1895–1941), author of *England, their England* (1933).[83]

Multiple identities and even an assumption of Englishness were long characteristic features of post-Union Scottishness. The Scots dialect literature of the Lowlands was not, as is sometimes believed, a form of nationalist reaction against the Union. Rather Scots was celebrated as a sister-language

78. John Mair, *A History of Greater Britain*, trans. A. Constable (Edinburgh: Scottish History Society, 1892); R. A. Mason, 'Kingship, Nobility and Anglo-Scottish Union: John Mair's *History of Greater Britain*', *Innes Review*, 41 (1990), 182–222.
79. A. Williamson, 'Scotland, Antichrist and the Invention of Great Britain', in J. Dwyer, R. Mason, and A. Murdoch (eds), *New Perspectives on the Politics and Culture of Early Modern Scotland* (Edinburgh: John Donald, 1982); R. A. Mason, 'The Scottish Reformation and the Origins of Anglo-British Imperialism', in Mason (ed.), *Scots and Britons*; Mason, 'Divided by a Common Faith? Protestantism and Union in Post-Reformation Britain', in J. McCallum (ed.), *Scotland's Long Reformation* (Leiden: Brill, 2016), 202–25.
80. See Alasdair Raffe, Chapter 2, this volume.
81. See Ralph Mclean, Chapter 4, this volume.
82. See Alison Lumsden, Chapter 7, this volume.
83. See Brian Young, Chapter 14, this volume.

of Old English. When Scots took pride in their medieval and Renaissance literary heritage in Scots, it was not simply out of a straightforward kind of Scots literary patriotism, but in having preserved the Old English of Chaucer and Shakespeare,[84] unlike the English themselves, who, it was reckoned by some Scots, spoke a corrupted language. Scots philologists and lexicographers, such as Sir John Sinclair (1754–1835), Alexander Geddes (1737–1802), and John Pinkerton (1758–1826), delighted in their native tongue, but from a British unionist position.[85] Indeed, the close sisterhood of medieval Scots and English literatures was a familiar trope of late-eighteenth- and early nineteenth-century Scots literary criticism. The ideological significance of Lallans in the late eighteenth and early nineteenth centuries was unionist, not nationalist.[86] The late medieval Makars, whom MacDiarmid would later elevate as totems of a national literary language, were viewed by late-eighteenth-century Scots literary critics, antiquarians, and philologists as exponents of a shared Anglo-Scottish literary culture.[87]

One of the central features of Scottish literature—'the national tale', which provided the basis and initial inspiration for Scott's Waverley Novels—was unionist in provenance, kindled by the Anglo-Irish novels of Maria Edgeworth (1768–1849).[88] Scott acknowledged his indebtedness to Edgeworth's novels and noted precisely their significance:

> Miss Edgeworth, whose Irish characters have gone so far to make the English familiar with the character of their gay and kind-hearted neighbours of Ireland, that she may truly be said to have done more toward completing the Union than perhaps all the legislative enactments by which it has been followed up.[89]

---

84. Cf. the claim of the diehard Scots patriot Lismahago in Smollett, *Humphry Clinker*, 235, that Scots was 'genuine old English'.

85. John Sinclair, *Observations on the Scottish Dialect* (London: n.p., 1782); Alexander Geddes, 'Three Scottish Poems, with a Previous Dissertation on the Scoto-Saxon Dialect', *Archaeologia Scotica*, 1 (1792), 402–68; John Pinkerton, 'An Essay on the Origin of Scotish [sic] Poetry', in Pinkerton, *Ancient Scotish Poems* (2 vols; London: C. Dilly, 1786).

86. Cf. Colin Kidd, 'Race, Theology and Revival: Scots Philology and its Contexts in the Age of Pinkerton and Jamieson', *Scottish Studies Review*, 3 (2002), 20–33.

87. P. O'Flaherty, 'John Pinkerton (1758–1826): Champion of the Makars', *Studies in Scottish Literature*, 13 (1978), 159–95; Colin Kidd, 'British Literature: The Career of a Concept', *Scottish Literary Review*, 8 (2016), 1–16.

88. Ina Ferris, *The Romantic National Tale and the Question of Ireland* (Cambridge: Cambridge University Press, 2002).

89. Walter Scott, 'General Preface to the Waverley Novels', repr. in D. Hewitt (ed.), *Scott on Himself: A Selection of the Autobiographical Writings of Sir Walter Scott* (Edinburgh: Scottish Academic Press, 1981), 249.

Scott 'felt that something might be done for my own country, along the lines that she [Edgeworth] had undertaken with her Irish novels', in particular 'something which might introduce her natives to those of the sister kingdom, in a more favourable light than they had been placed hitherto, and tend to procure sympathy for their virtues and indulgence for their foibles'.[90] Scott's project to 'complete the Union' through national tales that educated the English in the history, customs, and manners of the Scots was a phenomenal success.

To be fair, literary critics have not been wholly oblivious of a 'unionist' element in the Scottish literary tradition. The decentring and devolving of English literature have in turn led to a recasting of Scottish literature, which is much less essentialist and more alert to a British dimension.[91] In recent years, moreover, there has been a growing interest in literary negotiations of union, not least from North America.[92] However, the most sophisticated literary engagement with the new British history has come from the Cambridge scholar John Kerrigan, in *Archipelagic English: Literature, History and Politics 1603–1707* (2008). Kerrigan cogently challenges the tired anglocentric orthodoxies associated with an 'Anglo-English' canon and its interpretation, but is equally alert to the danger of reading 'literary texts along national or ethnic lines even when they have more universal, or pointedly local, socio-economic and ideological determinants', a 'distortion' that is all 'the more likely' when 'it serves the interests of modern nationalism'.[93] How much of the Scottish literary canon is 'overdetermined' in this way?

After all, the 'English' dimension of Scottish literature does tend to be viewed pejoratively; not necessarily in the way it was understood by creative practitioners who were less rigidly nationalist than their latter-day interpreters. In particular, there is a recognition that Scottish literature is conducted—regrettably, it seems—for the most part through the mixed medium of Scots

90. Scott, 'General Preface', 249.
91. Robert Crawford, *Devolving English Literature* (1992; 2nd edn, Edinburgh: Edinburgh University Press, 2000); Crawford (ed.), *The Scottish Invention of English Literature* (Cambridge: Cambridge University Press, 1998).
92. Davis, *Acts of Union*; Rivka Swenson, *Essential Scots and the Idea of Unionism in Anglo-Scottish Literature, 1603–1832* (Lewisburg, PA: Bucknell University Press, 2016).
93. John Kerrigan, *Archipelagic English: Literature, History, and Politics 1603–1707* (Oxford: Oxford University Press, 2008), 9–12, 27.

vernacular and standard English. MacDiarmid thought hybridity of this sort
a fit subject for complaint:

> Curse on my dooble life and dooble tongue,
> Guid Scots wi' English a' hamstrung.
> Speakin' o' Scotland in English words
> As it were Beethoven chirpt by birds[94]

Doubleness—including the tension between Scots patriotism and English
commitments—has become established as one of the central themes of Scottish
criticism.[95] Indeed, the idea of doubleness had preceded MacDiarmid's
interventions. In 1919 the literary critic G. Gregory Smith (1865–1932)
launched the influential notion of the 'Caledonian Antisyzygy', 'a zigzag of
contradictions' in Scottish literature.[96] MacDiarmid latched onto Smith's
concept, and wrote an essay on 'The Caledonian Antisyzygy and the Gaelic
Idea' (1931–2).[97] Twentieth-century Scottish criticism was long obsessed with
doubleness, though from the 1990s the poet and critic Robert Crawford led
a move towards a more pluralistic appreciation of multiple 'Scotlands'.

Notwithstanding the strong unionist currents in Scottish literature and
culture up until the 1970s, the Union itself has rarely been discussed. Indeed,
it is more obvious now that it is overtly challenged than when it was quietly
cherished, unostentatiously, perhaps almost unconsciously. Tim Barrow's
play *Union* (2014)[98]—which dramatized political events around 1707—was
premiered in Edinburgh in the immediate prelude to the independence
referendum.[99] Why does the Union have such a low visibility in Scottish
literature? Is it perhaps because the Union sits at the eye of the hurricane?
Is it because other issues swirl around this central issue of contention—one
so obviously significant that it does invite superfluous treatment? However,
this is to approach the question from the wrong direction. For here historical
and literary analyses diverge. While literary scholars stress the centrality
of an identity crisis in Scottish literature since 1707, historians point to the
uncontested dominance of the Union in Scottish politics, certainly between
1746 and the mid-1880s, if not longer, and the striking marginality of

94. Hugh MacDiarmid, 'To Circumjack Cencrastus', in MacDiarmid, *Complete Poems, Volume I*, 236.
95. Karl Miller, *Doubles* (1985; London: Faber and Faber, 2008).
96. G. Gregory Smith, *Scottish Literature: Character and Influence* (London: Macmillan, 1919).
97. Hugh MacDiarmid, 'The Caledonian Antisyzygy and the Gaelic Idea', in Duncan Glen (ed.),
    Selected Essays of Hugh MacDiarmid, ed. Duncan Glen (London: Jonathan Cape, 1969), 56–74.
98. Tim Barrow, *Union* (Portsmouth: Playdead Press, 2014).
99. <http://www.scotsman.com/lifestyle/culture/theatre/tim-barrow-s-new-play-on-1707-act-
    of-union-1-3342518> (accessed July 2017).

nationalist politics in Scotland until at least the 1970s. If we accept, as some historians do, that the Union was so taken for granted that it became an unnoticed part of the background to Scottish public life, then this might help to explain its invisibility. Something so normal, so uncontroversial, was unlikely to set pulses racing. This is what has come to be known as 'banal unionism', a union so well established as to need no defence or justification, with the result that unionism was mute and inarticulate, part of the 'wall-paper' of Scottish life.[100] 'Banal unionism' has yet to become a term of art in Scottish literature. But was 'banal unionism' a literary as well as a political phenomenon? Is the relative marginality of the Union in Scottish literature between the mid-eighteenth century and the mid-twentieth century a literary manifestation of 'banal unionism'?

The study of union and its curious displacement in Scottish literature brings us close to the invisible core of Scottish culture, mundane workaday quotidian Scottishness, of the sort that lacks exoticism or the romance of difference. Behind the overt trappings of an assumed Highland identity lies an invisible and rarely trumpeted Lowland consciousness; behind Celticism, a Teutonic identity, which was the dominant form of Scottish self-consciousness throughout the nineteenth century;[101] behind nationalist posturing, unionist realism; behind industrial working-class machismo, bourgeois norms little different from those in Middle England. Above all, behind national identities lie denominational identities, which were, arguably, the primary expressions of identity in Scotland[102]—and certainly in the Scottish novel—until our own secular times, the point at which nationalism has appeared to fill the vacuum.

To view Scottish literature—in terms derived from MacDiarmid—as a clash between Scottish and English identities is to lose sight of the internal

---

100. Kidd, *Union and Unionisms*, 23–4.
101. C. Kidd, 'Teutonist Ethnology and Scottish Nationalist Inhibition, 1780–1880', *Scottish Historical Review*, 74 (1995), 45–68; Kidd, 'Race, Empire and the Limits of Scottish Nationhood', *Historical Journal*, 46 (2003), 873–92; K. Fenyo, *Contempt, Sympathy and Romance: Lowland Perceptions of the Highlands and the Clearances during the Famine Years, 1845–1855* (East Linton: Tuckwell Press, 2000).
102. See, e.g., A. L. Drummond and J. Bulloch, *The Scottish Church 1688–1843* (Edinburgh: St Andrew Press, 1973); Drummond and Bulloch, *The Church in Victorian Scotland 1843–1874* (Edinburgh: St Andrew Press, 1975); Drummond and Bulloch, *The Church in Late Victorian Scotland 1874–1900* (Edinburgh: St Andrew Press, 1978); A. Herron, *Kirk by Divine Right: Church and State: Peaceful Coexistence* (Edinburgh: St Andrew Press, 1985); G. I. T. Machin, *Politics and the Churches in Great Britain 1869 to 1921* (Oxford: Clarendon Press, 1987); J. L. Macleod, *The Second Disruption: The Free Church in Victorian Scotland and the Origins of the Free Presbyterian Church* (East Linton: Tuckwell Press, 2000); Kidd, *Union and Unionisms*, ch. 6.

Scottish ecclesiastical divisions, which, far more than issues of nationhood
and union, were the major sources of conflict in Scottish culture for most
of the period of union, until at least the early twentieth century. Indeed,
Presbyterianism—Covenanting in particular—was the primary basis of
popular identity, for radicals especially.[103] Only when the religious disputes
that had led, among other outcomes, to the Secession, the Disruption, and
the Free Church case had been largely resolved in the Church of Scotland
Act 1921 and the subsequent Kirk reunion of 1929 with the United Free
Church[104] did the issue of national—rather than ecclesiastical—identity
became a more prominent feature of cultural life within the Union.
Nevertheless, some of the older less secular strains still persist in the contemporary rhetoric of an otherwise secular Scottish radicalism.[105] Moreover,
literary critics have paid vastly more attention to the 'English problem' in
Scottish literature than to the 'Irish problem'—the perceived alien menace
of Roman Catholic Irish migration into Presbyterian Scotland—which so
exercised nineteenth- and early twentieth-century Scots.[106] The presence of
Catholic Irishness in Scottish towns and cities provoked more anxiety than
the high status and pervasive influence of Englishness, at bottom, however
obvious the differences, another kind of Protestantism. The date of 1690—
the year of the Protestant victory in Ireland of William of Orange's army
over the forces of Stuart Catholicism at the Battle of the Boyne—has long
had greater resonance in Scottish popular political culture than 1707.[107]
Religion was, until the early twentieth century at least, the primary marker

103. Cf. T. Brotherstone (ed.), *Covenant, Charter and Party: Traditions of Revolt and Protest in Modern
     Scottish History* (Aberdeen: Aberdeen University Press, 1989).
104. D. M. Murray, *Rebuilding the Kirk: Presbyterian Reunion in Scotland 1909–1929* (Edinburgh: T &
     T Clark, 2000); G. I. T. Machin, 'Voluntaryism and Reunion 1874–1929', in N. Macdougall
     (ed.), *Church, Politics and Society: Scotland 1408–1929* (Edinburgh: John Donald, 1983), 221–38.
105. J. Hearn, *Claiming Scotland: National Identity and Liberal Culture* (Edinburgh: Polygon, 2000).
106. Scottish historians and social scientists have not ignored the Irish dimension of modern Scottish
     political culture and debate: see, e.g., Steve Bruce, *No Pope of Rome: Militant Protestantism in
     Modern Scotland* (Edinburgh: Mainstream, 1985); Tom Gallagher, *Glasgow the Uneasy Peace:
     Religious Tension in Modern Scotland* (Manchester: Manchester University Press, 1987); Elaine
     McFarland, *Protestants First: Orangeism in Nineteenth-Century Scotland* (Edinburgh: Edinburgh
     University Press, 1990); S. J. Brown, 'Outside the Covenant: The Scottish Presbyterian Churches
     and Irish Immigration, 1922–38', *Innes Review*, 42 (1991), 19–45; R. Finlay, 'Nationalism, Race,
     Religion and the Irish Question in Inter-War Scotland', *Innes Review*, 42 (1991), 46–67;
     T. Devine (ed.), *Irish Immigrants and Scottish Society in the Nineteenth and Twentieth Centuries*
     (Edinburgh: John Donald, 1991); Devine (ed.), *Scotland's Shame? Bigotry and Sectarianism in
     Modern Scotland* (Edinburgh: Mainstream, 2000); M. J. Mitchell, *The Irish in the West of Scotland*
     (Edinburgh: John Donald, 1998).
107. See William L. Miller, *The End of British Politics? Scots and English Political Behaviour in the
     Seventies* (Oxford: Clarendon Press, 1981), 1.

of identity, and, by the same token, the major source of Scottish discontents (not that a reader would ever gain that impression from the canon of modern Scottish literary criticism).[108]

For secularizing literary modernists the continuing hold on Scots of old-time Calvinist religion was a massive bugbear. Indeed, the writers of the Scottish Renaissance complained about Calvinism as much as they did about the Union. The legacy of John Knox and a philistine Reformation had been just as devastating to Scottish culture as the corrupting march of anglicization. Edwin Muir (1887–1959), in his controversial classic *Scott and Scotland* (1936), blamed the twin influences of the English language and Calvinism for the decline of Scottish culture since the supposed organic wholeness of the pre-Reformation era. Scotland before the Reformation enjoyed a harmonious social and cultural wholeness, 'a concord which was destroyed by the rigours of Calvinism'. The Union of the Crowns played its part, of course, but it was 'the Reformation [which] truly signalized the beginning of Scotland's decline as a civilized nation'. By the seventeenth century 'Scotsmen already felt in one language and thought in another'. Lacking a national literary language that served as a vehicle for both 'sensibility and thought', Scottish culture degenerated into 'a confusion of tongues ranging from orthodox English to the dialects of various Scottish districts'. However, the Scottish Reformation—which was 'adverse...to poetry itself'—seriously exacerbated matters, undermining cohesion and producing in its stead only 'that reciprocally destructive confrontation' of 'irresponsible feeling' and 'arid intellect', for which 'Gregory Smith found the name of "the Caledonian Antisyzygy"'. Literature, in particular, had withered under the 'strict surveillance of Calvinism'.[109] This loss of organic wholeness became the theme of Muir's poem on the sad course of Scottish culture, 'Scotland 1941':

> But Knox and Melville clapped their preaching palms
> And bundled all the harvesters away,
>
> .   .   .   .
>
> Out of that desolation we were born.[110]

---

108. On the other hand, however, R. Crawford, 'Presbyterianism and Imagination in Modern Scotland', in Devine (ed.), *Scotland's Shame*, 187–96, supplies a sensitive corrective to sectarianism as an overdetermined and overused category.

109. Edwin Muir, *Scott and Scotland: The Predicament of the Scottish Writer* (London: Routledge, 1936), 17, 23–5, 42, 61.

110. Edwin Muir, 'Scotland 1941', in *Edwin Muir: The Complete Poems*, ed. P. Butter (Aberdeen: Association for Scottish Literary Studies, 1991), 100.

Muir's outlook was representative of broader trends in Scottish cultural criticism. The literary historian J. H. Millar (1864–1929) blamed religious conditions in Scotland for the decline of Scottish drama; the Reformation in Scotland had been 'hostile to every form of art, and fatal to that which finds its home on the stage'. For about 'a hundred fifty years' thereafter 'the desolating influence of a gloomy and intolerant fanaticism brooded over the country'. Millar went on to blame 'the sad and sorrowful Union' for the 'complete disappearance of the Scottish dialect as a vehicle of serious prose', but from his tone it seems clear that he regarded the Calvinist Reformation as a greater bane.[111] Similarly, the nationalist MacDiarmid—no friend to the dour, anti-aesthetic world view of bourgeois Calvinism—complained that Scots 'ha'e suffered frae Knox on the heid sae lang'.[112] In an essay denouncing 'Balmorality', George Scott-Moncrieff drew attention to the deadening effect of a plain, puritanical Presbyterianism on Scottish culture: 'What has the Kirk given us? Ugly churches and services, identifying in the minds of churchgoers ugliness with God, have stifled the Scottish arts almost out of existence.' Of course, the Kirk had also succumbed, like other parts of Scottish society, to 'Anglo-imitative' attitudes; but a philistine Reformation loomed much larger in the interwar Renaissance than the Union. As Scott-Moncrieff saw it, Calvinism and an Anglo-deferential provincialism were poisonous ingredients in 'the deadening slime of Balmorality, a glutinous compound of hypocrisy, false sentiment, industrialism, ugliness, and clammy pseudo-Calvinism; a slime that has made [Scotland] forget that she is a country and regard herself as a suburb'.[113] The intellectuals' obsession with independence would come later, as Scotland secularized and prim Victorian values lost their sway in the cities.

★

The momentous events leading up to the Anglo-Scottish negotiations for union and the Treaty's passage through the Scots Parliament in 1706–7 have caused barely a ripple in Scotland's literary tradition. The only novel that deals in full with the politics of 1707 comes in a piece of genre fiction by the historical novelist Nigel Tranter (1909–2000), whose principal terrain is the medieval Scotland of Wallace, Bruce, and the Wars of Independence.

---

111. J. H. Millar, *A Literary History of Scotland* (London: T. F. Unwin, 1903), 110, 312, 314.
112. Hugh MacDiarmid, 'To Circumjack Cencrastus', in MacDiarmid, *Complete Poems Volume I*, 215.
113. George Scott-Moncrieff, 'Balmorality', in David Cleghorn Thomson (ed.), *Scotland in Quest of her Youth* (Edinburgh: Oliver and Boyd, 1932), 69–86, at pp. 71, 86.

In *The Patriot* (1982), Tranter turned his attention to the renowned anti-union orator in the last Scots Parliament before union, Andrew Fletcher of Saltoun. The novel is historically informed, provides a full and reasonably accurate account of the run-up to union, and, in a fair-minded way, does try to capture multiple points of view, pro- as well as anti-unionist. However, it is as a result stilted and full of speechifying. Energy is sacrificed to accuracy, and the work lacks literary élan. Moreover, in another kind of displacement, Tranter's normal terrain—the War of Independence—never seems far away; indeed, the medieval past continues to frame Tranter's attitude to the early eighteenth century. The Union of 1707 is 'the final betrayal of the land of Bruce and Wallace'.[114]

The Union of 1707 has rarely featured in Scottish novels or plays as the central focus of attention. More often it constitutes the backdrop to other forms of action—religious division, family feuds, and, most notoriously, legal chicanery in Sir Walter Scott's revised version of *The Bride of Lammermoor* (1819). In Scott's original version of the novel—set at an indeterminate point in the immediate pre-Union period—there is a crucial legal appeal from the Court of Session to the Parliament. Embarrassingly, however, Scott, as a trained lawyer and Sheriff-Depute of Selkirkshire, had overlooked the fact that there was no provision for appeals from the Court of Session to the pre-Union Scots Parliament. As a result, a shamefaced Scott revised the novel, and, by a minor sleight of hand, relocated its action to an equally indeterminate moment in the immediate post-Union era, when Scottish legal appeals were accepted by the British House of Lords.[115]

Scott did write a union novel, but only a short, minor tale, *The Black Dwarf*, and even here the Union is still viewed obliquely, for his central focus is the failed Jacobite rising of 1708. Resentment of the Union provides the backdrop to the story and its motivating dynamic: 'all Scotland was indignant at the terms on which their legislature had surrendered their national independence... The fermentation was universal.' Scott notes that the general discontent brought together unlikely bedfellows—Covenanting Cameronians and Jacobites, 'papists, prelatists and presbyterians'—in the aim of reversing the Union.[116] However, Scott's depiction of an all-consuming,

114. Nigel Tranter, *The Patriot* (1982; London: Coronet Books, 1984), 370.
115. J. Millgate, 'Text and Context: Dating the Events of *The Bride of Lammermoor*', *Bibliotheck*, 9 (1979), 200–13; P. D. Garside, 'Union and the Bride of Lammermoor', *Studies in Scottish Literature*, 19 (1984), 72–93.
116. Walter Scott, *The Black Dwarf*, ed. P. D. Garside (1816; Edinburgh: Edinburgh University Press, 1993), 15.

all-pervasive anti-unionism is put to unionist ends. At the heart of the novel, which takes place in Liddesdale in the Scottish borders, is a set piece meeting of the conspirators, a far-from-impressive bunch of ideologues, opportunists, smugglers, and cattle-rustlers, whose limited good sense is further clouded by the toasts they have been drinking to their lawful Jacobite sovereign, 'King James the Eighth, now landed in Lothian, and, as I trust and believe, in full possession of his ancient capital!' The chief plotter, Ellieslaw, a sinister character, launches into a denunciation of the recent Union, 'a treaty, by means of which, he affirmed, Scotland had been cheated of her independence, her commerce, and her honour, and laid as a fettered slave at the foot of a rival'. This anti-unionist tirade strikes a chord with the assembled company:

> 'Our commerce is destroyed,' hollowed old John Rewcastle, a Jedburgh smuggler, from the lower end of the table. 'Our agriculture is ruined,' said the Laird of Broken-girth-flow, a territory which, since the days of Adam, had borne nothing but ling and whortleberries. 'Our religion is cut up, root and branch,' said the pimple-nosed pastor of the Episcopal meeting-house at Kirkwhistle. 'We shall shortly neither dare shoot a deer or kiss a wench, without a certificate from the presbytery and kirk-treasurer,' said Marischal-Wells. 'Or make a brandy jeroboam on a frosty morning, without licence from a commissioner of excise,' said the smuggler. 'Or ride over the fell on a moonless night,' said Westburnflat, 'without asking leave of young Earnscliff, or some Englified justice of the peace; thae were gude days on the Border when there was neither peace nor justice heard of.'[117]

Scott's attitude to 1707 could not be clearer, though his real subject is in fact changes in customs and manners, the passing of old superstitions and lawless feuds, and the long, slow birth of law-bound, civil society. Both anti-unionism and Jacobitism are emblematic of the old ways. Indeed, in much of Scott's oeuvre national distinctions are decidedly less important than sociological differences of this sort. The Marxist critic Georg Lukács made several major howlers in his influential study of Scott—not least aligning *Rob Roy* with the Jacobite rebellion of 1745, rather than the earlier rebellion of 1715 around which it is set.[118] Nevertheless, the Marxist is for the most part right in his parsing of Scott, whose principal emphasis on changing social and economic structures was, notwithstanding its antiquarian wistfulness and high tory reverence for hierarchy, strikingly pre-Marxian.

---

117. Scott, *The Black Dwarf*, 88–9.
118. Georg Lukács, *The Historical Novel*, trans. H. and S. Mitchell (London: Merlin Press, 1962), 57–8.

One of the central episodes in the run-up to union, the Worcester affair, provided depressing anti-nationalist matter for Josephine Tey, who, under her other main pseudonym, Gordon Daviot, composed a one-act play about the controversy, entitled *Leith Sands*, which was performed on the BBC in 1942. The affair of Captain Green and the *Worcester* occurred in 1704–5, and was emblematic of the crisis in Anglo-Scottish relations that reached its resolution in the Treaty of Union. What happened to Captain Green and two members of his crew also constitutes a dark blot on Scotland's independent governance and law. In the late summer of 1704, the *Worcester*, an English merchant vessel, was seized in retaliation for the English seizure of a Scottish ship, the *Annandale*. Then charges of murder and piracy were brought—on the flimsiest of trumped-up evidence—against Captain Green and his crew, who were alleged to be responsible for the capture of a Scottish trading vessel in the Indian Ocean, which had indeed been captured by pirates, but not by the crew of the *Worcester*. The Scottish political and legal establishment knew that there was no justification for the charges against Green and his crew, but decided—out of cowardice and a prudent concern for civil order—that the Edinburgh mob was so inflamed that its anglophobia needed to be appeased. The sacrificial victims—Captain Green, his first mate John Madder, and the ship's gunner James Simpson—were executed in 1705, in a cruel mockery of justice.[119] Green's fate and the dangers of mob rule were the dominant themes in Daviot's *Leith Sands*, which is set on the day of hanging. The atmosphere around the hanging is fervently nationalistic— with shouts of 'Down with England! Down with Englishmen! Scotland for ever!', 'Ay, a good day for Scotland', and the suggestion that the anniversary of Green's hanging be perpetuated as a 'national holiday'. However, the central character, a young law student—and later a prominent Scots politician, who was in real life deeply scarred by these events—Duncan Forbes of Culloden (1685–1747), dissents from the prevailing mood: 'If I could burn the Scot out of me with hot iron I would do it today. It's a dreadful thing to be ashamed of the very blood in one's veins.' Indeed, he perceives the black ironies of Green's career and ultimate fate: '[Green] had traded well, and his cargo was rich. He had taken his ship half round the world and back like a good seaman; and he was a proud young man sailing into the Forth; home again and safe. No one had told him that Scotland was still inhabited by

---

119. William Ferguson, *Scotland's Relations with England: A Survey to 1707* (Edinburgh: John Donald, 1977), 224–6.

savages.' Forbes has no doubt about why Green was executed—sheer envy
of English success: 'Because Scotland wanted a blood sacrifice. Because
we had failed to make colonies like the English, and failed to keep ships on
the sea like the English, and we were sick with jealousy and drunk with
hate and shouting for blood. Well, we have had our blood. But my business
is law, not murder.' The short play concludes with an ironic twist in which
hard evidence at last opens nationalist eyes to the monstrous wrong that has
been committed.[120]

The shocking treatment of Green and the crew of the *Worcester* also
frames the action in Douglas Galbraith's brilliant historical novel *The Rising
Sun* (2000), where the main narrative concerns the Scottish colony to the
Darien isthmus in Panama (1698–1700), but is itself a flashback bookended
by opening and closing sections on an early eighteenth-century present,
where—with an allowable sleight of chronology of the sort Scott had fruit-
fully pioneered—the *Worcester* episode (actually 1704–5) occurs during the
debates over union (actually 1706–7). Darien provides the main matter
of the book, but the Union—though displaced from the apparent heart of
the story—looms over the whole. Indeed, Galbraith's narrator, Roderick
Mackenzie, opens his account of Darien with the telling words: 'Hear the
story of a Britishman'. In the beginning Mackenzie buys into the idea that
the Darien colony will be the basis of Scotland's future as a self-sustaining
independent state, and at this stage he has contempt for 'the fainthearts, the
easy men who raised their old song about union'. The Company of Scotland,
which launches the Darien venture, 'had become the whole hope and faith
of the nation'. But the force of circumstance dents Mackenzie's sunny
patriotic optimism. *The Rising Sun* reads in several places like a parable on
nationalist delusion. Galbraith describes the Darien mania that induced
otherwise canny Scots to invest in a speculative colonial project (whose
failure swallows much of Scotland's limited capital resources). Moreover, he
uses the Darien colony itself—Caledonia, which had its chief settlement at
New Edinburgh and a defensive enclosure at Fort St Andrew—as a dark
satirical microcosm of the Scotland the colonists had left behind. Soon
'Caledonia is divided'; given 'our tendency to faction', the colony becomes
a 'fractured society', each segment of which was preoccupied 'with its own
enemies'. In echoes of the anti-Presbyterian tradition in Scottish literature,
the colony's rigid Presbyterian chaplains strive to make Caledonia a dour

120. Gordon Daviot, *Leith Sands and Other Plays* (London, 1946), esp. 10–12, 14.

place of righteousness, but are frustrated in their plans. Mismanagement compounds faction-fighting and the hostility of Spaniards—and, tellingly, the English, who resent Scotland's cack-handed intrusion into the colonial sphere. At least English interference against the colony permitted Scots to experience 'the relief of knowing that even in the least of their misfortunes they are the victims of another's injustice'. The colony fails disastrously, with a huge loss of life and the evacuation of its surviving inhabitants. Mackenzie imagines what the abandoned colony must now seem like, 'voided of its humanity and of all its madness too, absurd, incomprehensible, the not very interesting remains of an ancient people whose purpose no sane man could guess at'. Significantly, however, it is the Green affair and the question of union that bracket the main action. Galbraith pays discreet homage to Scott's *Heart of Midlothian* in his description of the lynch mob baying for the innocent blood of Captain Green and his crew members. Mackenzie is disgusted by the Green affair, an empty gesture of pseudo-patriotic defiance provoked by the Darien disaster: 'I saw a nation fouled by its own failures.' The novel ends on the brink of union with the narrator disillusioned, the young man's 'blithe baseless certainty' having evaporated, along with Scotland's 'money and hopes', both 'conjured inexplicably into air'. Mackenzie's friend James Minto launches into an anti-Darien tirade: 'how everyone involved in the Company had been a fool, how its failure had been predictable to the very last detail, how the country had played the Prodigal Son and now, having thrown its money in the sea, was whining all the more for being welcomed back, for having all its losses restored by its kindly southern uncle.' Mackenzie remonstrates—with an anger that derives, ironically, from his lack of conviction—that a grasping England had frustrated Scotland's colonial ambitions. Minto 'laughed at this, called it poetry and asked me if I really believed it. Because I didn't, I shouted at him, "I've lost my country."' However, a Jewish financier, D'Azevedo, reassures Mackenzie that nationhood in general is a sham: '"It wasn't God who made countries. What are they for? I ask. No one could ever tell me...No one needs a country."'[121]

The most prominent account of union concerns the Union of the Crowns of 1603 rather than the Union of 1707. Indeed, Scott's most explicit discussions of Anglo-Scottish relations come in his celebrated novel of the

---

121. Douglas Galbraith, *The Rising Sun* (2000; New York: Grove Press, 2001), esp. 5–6, 114, 203, 328, 390, 412, 424, 447, 469, 525, 531.

Union of the Crowns, *The Fortunes of Nigel* (1822) and its intertextual sequel, *The Letters of Malachi Malagrowther* (1826). The plot of *The Fortunes of Nigel* turns on the first appearance of Scots in London after King James VI of Scotland's accession to the throne of England in 1603, and the various layers and degrees of scotophobic prejudice that provokes, from the vulgar xenophobia of the lower orders to the insidious backbiting of courtiers. The Union of the Crowns did not create a sense of common Britishness. As Scott notes: 'it required a long lapse of time, and the succession of more than one generation, ere the inveterate national prejudices which had so long existed betwixt the sister kingdoms were removed, and the subjects either side of the Tweed brought to regard those upon the opposite bank as friends and brethren.'[122] In other words, grand symbolic moments—1603 and 1707—mattered less than gradual processes of peaceful interaction in the centuries after 1603. Piecemeal social processes underpinned the ethical bonds of union; the political events of 1603 and 1707 merely provided a foundation for the growth of civility. Indeed, in the further introduction to the novel that Scott wrote in 1831, he stressed that his real subject was not Anglo-Scottish quarrels. These, while of course colourful and engaging, were in fact epiphenomenal to a deeper set of developments:

> the most picturesque period of history is that when the ancient rough and wild manners of a barbarous age are just becoming innovated upon, and contrasted, by the illumination of increased or revived learning, and the instructions of renewed or reformed religion. The strong contrast produced by the opposition of ancient manners to those which are gradually subduing them, affords the lights and shadows necessary to give effect to a fictitious narrative... The reign of James I of England possessed this advantage in a peculiar degree...[123]

Scott inherited from the Scottish Enlightenment a keen sociological insight, which reckoned nationhood part of the foaming froth of history, and looked instead beneath the waves of historical events to deeper currents and undertows. Not that the particularities of history were irrelevant; Scott—a magpie antiquarian collector of trivia—insisted upon their importance. However, both the particular and the general needed to be brought together in historical analysis. The irreducible individuality of character mattered, both in history and, of course, in the novel. In the *Fortunes of Nigel* no character

122. Walter Scott, *The Fortunes of Nigel* (1822; St Albans: Panther, 1973), 33.
123. Scott, *The Fortunes of Nigel*, Ibid., pp. 8–9.

is more pointed or idiosyncratic than the 'peevish' Sir Mungo Malagrowther of Girnigo Castle—an 'atrabilarious' Scots courtier of 'blighted fortunes', an uninhibited and girning cynic whose 'satire ran riot' and whose 'envy could not conceal itself'.[124] Scott resurrected the Malagrowther line in 1826 in his polemical letters in defence of the Scottish one pound banknote, which was threatened by British currency reforms.

In his *Letters*, originally published in the *Edinburgh Weekly Journal*, and later collected into pamphlet form, Sir Mungo's growling—purported—descendant Malachi Malagrowther became the mouthpiece of Scott's attempt to restate the Union and its principles for the 1820s. Malagrowther lamented that Scottish nationhood was sinking into a merely 'provincial' contempt and 'degradation'. Centralization and uniformity—meaning in practice, of course, anglicization—were increasingly prized over diversity; and the demands of political economy further exacerbated the threat to established national differences within the Union. Yet, there seemed little point in invoking the Treaty of Union, which had slipped out of the English public memory, a half-forgotten 'old parchment' of little more than antiquarian significance: 'remembrances which are cherished by the weaker party in a national treaty, are naturally forgotten by the stronger, and viewed, perhaps, as men look upon an old boundary stone, half-sunk in earth, half-overgrown with moss.' Malagrowther remained committed to the grand principles of 1707, but insisted that diversity was integral to the Treaty: 'For God's sake, sir, let us remain as nature made us, Englishmen, Irishmen, and Scotchmen...scrupulously regardful of each other's rights.'[125] The debate continued, in an intertextual vein. In response to Malagrowther's intervention, his Anglo-Scots cousin, Edward Bradwardine Waverley—the supposed product of the marriage of the fictional characters Edward Waverley and Rose Bradwardine in Scott's novel *Waverley*, but whose ventriloquist was the Irish-born Secretary to the Admiralty, John Wilson Croker (1780–1857)—published letters presenting an alternative vision of union based on principles of assimilation, common interests, and the eradication of anomalies. Alluding to the pro- and anti-union flyting in *Rob Roy*, Waverley wished Malagrowther's views 'had partaken more of the candid and liberal spirit of Baillie Nicol Jarvie, than the narrow prejudices of Andrew

---

124. Scott, *The Fortunes of Nigel*, 99–101, 214–15, 404.
125. [Walter Scott], *Letters of Malachi Malagrowther on the Currency* (1826; Edinburgh: R Cadell, 1844), 1–4, 8, 14, 16, 23, 25.

Fairservice'.[126] Notwithstanding Croker's robust defence of the currency reform, the particular measure to abolish the Scottish small denomination banknote was ultimately withdrawn.[127] Victory belonged to the 'peevish' descendant of a fictional character.

★

The *locus classicus* of Scottish literary displacement is James Hogg's *Private Memoirs and Confessions of a Justified Sinner*, a novel set around the Union of 1707, but with a plot centred on the antinomian consequences of ultra-Calvinist obsession, which pushes the Union itself offstage. Indeed, the Union is simply an incident in the background, less prominent indeed than stock partisan themes, the matter of Covenanting and Jacobitism. The story largely takes place between 1703—whose daringly provocative parliamentary session set Scotland on a road to a constitutional conflict with England, which the Union ultimately resolved—and 1712; furthermore, much of the action takes place in Edinburgh, where the old Scots parliament sat.[128] The Union is ratified off to the wings. Hogg alludes to the momentous parliamentary events taking place in the background to the main action, and the unconstrained partisanship between Whig–Presbyterians and Cavalier–Jacobites, which are central *both* to that backstory and to the family psychodrama of the complacently Episcopalian Colwans and the rigidly Presbyterian Wringhims. Doubleness operates as a leitmotif of the ostensible novel of Calvinist psychology and the antinomian excesses that—taken to logical extremes—it is liable to engender in the self-assured elect. What remains tantalizingly elusive is the wider applicability of doubleness to the Scottish situation.[129] Does Edinburgh in the years of the last Scots Parliament before 1707 simply provide a convenient setting for a story about something altogether different? Or is the Union part of a deeper unacknowledged symbolism about Scots doubleness? My own inclination is towards the former reading; a vivid example of the Union's historic unobtrusiveness. However, in a highly sophisticated novel of demanding theological complexity[130]—one where

126. [John Wilson Croker], *Two Letters on Scottish Affairs from Edward Bradwardine Waverley, Esq, to Malachi Malagrowther, Esq* (2nd edn; London: John Murray and Oliver and Boyd, 1826), 12.
127. B. Hilton, *Corn, Cash and Commerce: The Economic Policies of the Tory Governments 1815–1830* (Oxford: Clarendon Press, 1977), 221–3; Graham McMaster, *Scott and Society* (Cambridge: Cambridge University Press, 1981), 88–90; John Sutherland, *Life of Walter Scott* (Oxford: Blackwell, 1995), 305–6.
128. Hogg, *The Private Memoirs and Confessions*, 45, 59.   129. Cf. Miller, *Doubles*.
130. Cf. C. Gribben, 'James Hogg, Scottish Calvinism and Literary Theory', *Scottish Studies Review*, 5 (2004), 9–26, who is emphatic that the novel is not a satire on *conventional* Calvinism.

the presentation side-by-side of two distinct narratives of the same events exhibits a consciously contrived ambivalence—deliberateness and emblematic coding seem far from implausible.

Michael Russell MSP, a leading SNP politician, has asked where is 'the great Unionist novel'?[131] Of course—as we have seen—the great novel of union is a rarity. However, Hogg's *Confessions* has a good claim to the title; or at least to be the great novel of banal unionism. Hogg's novel is characteristic of the Scottish literary tradition in its obsessive pursuit of Calvinist themes, immediately behind which lie questions of religious commitments, partisanship, and—ultimately—dynastic adherence, with the momentous contemporary events that comprised the making of the Anglo-Scottish Union of 1707 lurking unobtrusively in the recessive backdrop of the novel, a matter of seeming indifference. The great novel of banal unionism is one where the Union itself is so taken for granted that it does not need to be mentioned.

131. M. Russell, 'A Writer in a Time of Change: Gunn, Walsh and the Process of Independence', in Alistair McCleery (ed.), *Nation and Nationalism* (Dunbeath: Whittles Publishing, 2013), 15.

2

John Bull, Sister Peg, and Anglo-Scottish Relations in the Eighteenth Century

Alasdair Raffe

I

John Arbuthnot's *The History of John Bull* (1712) is an allegorical satire on the War of the Spanish Succession. In the work, Arbuthnot depicted the war as a lawsuit brought by the merchants John Bull (personifying England) and Nic. Frog (the Netherlands) against Lewis Baboon (Louis Bourbon, otherwise King Louis XIV of France). Bull and Frog contend that Lewis has illegitimately sought the custom of Philip Baboon, the character representing Louis XIV's grandson Philip Bourbon, over whose inheritance of the Spanish throne the war was fought. *John Bull* was published as a series of five pamphlets, from March to July 1712. Each part was reprinted that year in several further editions, indicating that *John Bull* sold in large numbers and reached a wide audience. All five parts were reprinted in Edinburgh by the bookseller James Watson.[1] One reason for the success of the enterprise was that *John Bull* appeared at an important juncture in the war, as the Tory

---

1. John Arbuthnot, *The History of John Bull*, ed. Alan W. Bower and Robert A. Erickson (Oxford: Clarendon Press, 1976), p. xvii. See the English Short-Title Catalogue at: <http://estc.bl.uk/F/?func=file&file_name=login-bl-estc> (accessed July 2017).

ministry of Robert Harley, Earl of Oxford, negotiated peace terms with France. While most Tories longed to extract Britain from the decade-long conflict, Whigs and some moderate Tories were appalled at the prospect of a 'separate' peace: a treaty between Britain and France alone, which would leave Britain's Dutch and German allies in the war.[2] In this context, Arbuthnot's satire contributed to a Tory campaign for peace. More imaginative and less virulently partisan than such Tory pamphlets as Jonathan Swift's *Conduct of the Allies* (1711), *John Bull* echoed their criticisms of the cost of war and cynicism about the motives of Britain's continental partners.[3]

Arbuthnot's Tory attitudes had long roots.[4] He was the son of Alexander Arbuthnot, episcopalian minister of Arbuthnot, Kincardineshire, from 1665 to 1689. The episcopalian clergy of Restoration Scotland strongly supported the monarchy; their sermons helped to propagate ideas of indefeasible hereditary right and non-resistance to divinely appointed authority. Most episcopalian ministers became Jacobites after the Revolution of 1688–90.[5] Moreover, the lay people of the Mearns readily acquiesced in the policies of Charles II and James VII; many in the region remained sympathetic to the deposed James and his son. Unfortunately for Alexander Arbuthnot, however, the local landowner and patron of the parish church, Robert, Viscount Arbuthnot, was willing to accept the outcome of the Revolution. When the minister failed to read a proclamation of the convention of estates commanding allegiance to William and Mary as monarchs, and absented himself from church to avoid praying for them, the viscount complained to the privy council, which deprived Arbuthnot of his living.[6] At least two of Alexander

2. Geoffrey Holmes, *British Politics in the Age of Anne* (London: Macmillan, 1967), 77–9.

3. Jonathan Swift, *The Conduct of the Allies*, ed. C. B. Wheeler (Oxford: Clarendon Press, 1916). See Robert C. Steensma, *Dr John Arbuthnot* (Boston: Twayne, 1979), ch. 3.

4. The following biographical information derives from George A. Aitken, *The Life and Works of John Arbuthnot* (Oxford: Clarendon Press, 1892); Angus Ross, 'Arbuthnot, John (*bap.* 1667, *d.* 1735)', *Oxford Dictionary of National Biography*; David E. Shuttleton, '"A modest examination": John Arbuthnot and the Scottish Newtonians', *British Journal for Eighteenth-Century Studies*, 18 (1995), 47–62.

5. Clare Jackson, *Restoration Scotland, 1660–1690: Royalist Politics, Religion and Ideas* (Woodbridge and Rochester: Boydell Press, 2003), esp. chs 3–4; Tristram Clarke, '"Nurseries of Sedition"?: The Episcopal Congregations after the Revolution of 1689', in James Porter (ed.), *After Columba— After Calvin: Community and Identity in the Religious Traditions of North East Scotland* (Aberdeen: Elphinstone Institute, 1999), 61–9; Bruce Lenman, 'The Scottish Episcopalian Clergy and the Ideology of Jacobitism', in Eveline Cruickshanks (ed.), *Ideology and Conspiracy: Aspects of Jacobitism, 1689–1759* (Edinburgh: John Donald, 1982), 36–48.

6. Hew Scott, *Fasti Ecclesiae Scoticanae: The Succession of Ministers in the Church of Scotland from the Reformation*, rev. edn, 8 vols (Edinburgh: W. Paterson, 1915–50), v. 453; *Records of the Parliaments of Scotland to 1707*, ed. Keith M. Brown et al. (St Andrews, 2007–15) <http://www.rps.ac.uk/> (accessed July 2017), 1689/3/116; *The Register of the Privy Council of Scotland*, 3rd ser., ed. P. Hume Brown,

Arbuthnot's sons were involved in the Jacobite cause. Robert, born two years after John, is said to have fought with the Jacobites at the battle of Killiecrankie; he later became a banker in Rouen and provided financial assistance to the movement. Following the rising of 1715, John's much younger half-brother George also sought asylum in France.[7] Unlike his father and brothers, John Arbuthnot did not espouse the exiled royal family's struggle. But his episcopalian upbringing made it unsurprising that he came to support the Tories' agenda under Queen Anne.

After the Revolution, John Arbuthnot settled in England, soon appearing in print for the first time. *Of the Laws of Chance* (1692) was a short book outlining the innovative work on probability of the Dutch mathematician Christiaan Huygens.[8] Arbuthnot trained as a physician, briefly returning to Scotland in 1696 to graduate as a medical doctor from St Andrews University. In 1705, he became one of the royal physicians. A courtier with particular influence during the ministry of Harley, his personal friend, Arbuthnot was active in the London Royal College of Physicians and the Royal Society, and was also a keen musician. His literary peers included Jonathan Swift, Alexander Pope, John Gay, and Thomas Parnell, the famous 'Scriblerus Club' whose members collaborated to satirize pompous learning in the fictitious memoirs of Martin Scriblerus. Though it has long been agreed that Arbuthnot was responsible for *John Bull*, which appeared anonymously, his fellow Tory wits were a source of ideas and encouragement.[9]

John Bull is described as an 'honest, plain-dealing Fellow', and a lively, generous companion. He is also 'Cholerick, Bold, and of a very unconstant Temper', characteristics that make him amenable to persuasion.[10] The narrative describes how Bull is manoeuvred into commencing the lawsuit by his attorney, Humphrey Hocus, a hostile portrayal of John Churchill, duke of Marlborough. Swift's *Conduct of the Allies* attacked Marlborough for his avarice and connivance with the self-interested Dutch.[11] In his newspaper

Henry Paton, and E. Balfour-Melville, 16 vols (Edinburgh: HM General Register House, 1908–70), xiv. 327–30.

7. Aitken, *Life and Works of Arbuthnot*, 5; Scott, *Fasti*, v. 453; Pat Rogers, 'Dr Arbuthnot and his Family', *Notes and Queries*, 51 (2004), 387–9.

8. [John Arbuthnot], *Of the Laws of Chance, or, a Method of Calculation of the Hazards of Game* (London: Randall Taylor, 1692).

9. On the authorship of *John Bull*, see esp. Lester M. Beattie, *John Arbuthnot: Mathematician and Satirist* (Cambridge, MA: Harvard University Press, 1935), 36–57; Thomas F. Mayo, 'The Authorship of The History of John Bull', *Proceedings of the Modern Language Association*, 45 (1930), 274–82.

10. Arbuthnot, *John Bull*, 9.   11. Swift, *Conduct of the Allies*, esp. 47–8, 52.

the *Examiner*, Swift calculated that Marlborough amassed more than half a million pounds through his military service.[12] Arbuthnot provided further ballast to this reading of the general, who had in December 1711 been dismissed as commander-in-chief of the allied forces. Thus *Law is a Bottomless-Pit*, the first part of *John Bull*, describes how Hocus increases his influence by seducing Bull's first wife, who personifies the war-making government of Sidney, first Earl of Godolphin. Bull becomes distracted by the legal battle, neglecting his normal affairs and resolving to become a lawyer. Meanwhile, Bull's rival in business Nic. Frog gains a commercial advantage, and Hocus enriches himself at his client's expense.[13] If individual details had to be guessed at, the overall message was clear: the English people had suffered from the war and the self-interested actions of their leaders.

Like Swift, Arbuthnot pinned the blame for this situation on the Whigs. Indeed, Arbuthnot may have helped another Tory satirist, his fellow physician William Wagstaffe, write *The Story of the St Alb[a]ns Ghost*, an anti-Whig satire published the month before the first *John Bull* pamphlet. Shorter and less elaborate than *John Bull*, the *St Albans Ghost* adopted the same allegorical approach.[14] Reflecting the books' similarity, and perhaps also the closeness of the authors, enterprising booksellers published several editions of a *Complete Key* to the allegory of both works.[15] The main targets of the *St Albans Ghost* were Godolphin, his Whig allies in parliament, and especially Marlborough and his wife Sarah Churchill, whose birth in St Albans is fictionalized in the pamphlet. Echoing Swift's criticisms, Wagstaffe described the characters representing the duke and duchess as 'extreamly Wealthy', having 'gain'd the Art of getting Money out of every Body they had to do with, and by the most dishonourable Methods'. At the end of the story, justice is done, and the avaricious Whigs face punishment for their misrule.[16]

12. *The Examiner*, no. 17, 16–23 November 1710. See the discussion in Ashley Marshall, *Swift and History: Politics and the English Past* (Cambridge: Cambridge University Press, 2015), esp. 45, 89, 91, 141–2.
13. Arbuthnot, *John Bull*, 8–9, 11–13.
14. [William Wagstaffe,] *The Story of the St Alb[a]ns Ghost, or the Apparition of Mother Haggy* (London: n.p., 1712). Published in at least five editions in 1712, this pamphlet was included in the *Miscellaneous Works of Dr William Wagstaffe* (2nd edn; London: Jonah Bowyer, 1726), 54–75. See also Arbuthnot, *John Bull*, 168; J.A. Downie, *Robert Harley and the Press: Propaganda and Public Opinion in the Age of Swift and Defoe* (Cambridge: Cambridge University Press, 1979), 166–7.
15. The first appears to be *A Complete Key to the Three Parts of Law is a Bottomless-Pit, and The Story of the St Alban's Ghost* ([London: S. Bolton,] 1712), which was probably issued before the publication of the fourth and fifth *John Bull* pamphlets.
16. [Wagstaffe], *Story of the St Alb[a]ns Ghost*, 9–10 (quotations), 15–16.

Arbuthnot also looked forward to a change in the nation's fortunes, placing his hopes in the Harley administration. *John Bull* tells how Bull's wife is exposed in her affair with Hocus by the local parson, representing the Tory preacher Henry Sacheverell. Bull's wife attempts to eject the clergyman from his living, and defends her relationship with Hocus in a hilarious speech advocating 'the indispensable Duty of Cuckoldom'. This episode—in mockery of the Whigs' trial of Sacheverell before the House of Lords in 1710—prompts the death of Bull's wife, the fall of the Godolphin ministry.[17] Tory polemicists made much use of the Sacheverell trial and the Tory landslide in the election of October 1710, which seemed to prove that partisan Whigs had abused their power and lost the support of the electorate. In the *St Albans Ghost*, a Sacheverell-like figure 'open'd the Eyes of all the honest Tenants' of the landlady representing Queen Anne, leading her to dismiss her corrupt servants.[18] In *John Bull*, Bull soon replaces his first wife with a 'sober Country Gentlewoman', the Tory government. Bull employs Sir Roger Bold (Harley) as his new lawyer, and arranges a meeting at the Salutation Tavern (the congress of Utrecht) to resolve the long-running lawsuit.[19]

Arbuthnot's use of a lawsuit to represent the War of the Spanish Succession was effective, but scarcely original. Scholars have found in the period's Whig and Tory periodicals several parallels with Arbuthnot's scheme. In April 1710, for example, Daniel Defoe's *Review* characterized Britain as a 'Fine House, exquisitely Built' and 'admirably Scituated'. Under the conduct of 'a certain Lady, of the Ancient and Royal Blood of the BRITANNIA's' (Queen Anne), the house had been improved and extended, in spite of 'a Troublesome and Perplexing *Law-Suit*, with an Envious and Powerful Neighbour'.[20] Another parallel to Arbuthnot's allegory can be seen in the coded cant used by contemporary conspirators, notably Jacobites, to convey information secretly. Letters written in this fashion disguised news of national significance by giving political parties and countries the names of individuals (often supposed to be merchants) and referring to conflicts and controversies as lawsuits.[21]

17. Arbuthnot, *John Bull*, 13, 15, 25–7; quotation at p. 25.
18. [Wagstaffe,] *Story of the St Alb[a]ns Ghost*, 11.
19. Arbuthnot, *John Bull*, 15, 16 (quotation), 18–19, 71.
20. *A Review of the State of the British Nation*, vol.VII, no. 7, 11 April 1710.This and other examples are discussed in Beattie, *John Arbuthnot*, 75–82; Arbuthnot, *John Bull*, pp. xix–xxii.
21. See, e.g., James Macpherson, *Original Papers; Containing the Secret History of Great Britain, from the Restoration, to the Accession of the House of Hannover*, 2 vols (London:W. Strahan and T. Cadell, 1775), i. 444–5, 501–2; Daniel Szechi, *Britain's Lost Revolution? Jacobite Scotland and French Grand Strategy, 1701–1708* (Manchester: Manchester University Press, 2015), 76.

depictions of dissenters' goggling eyes. The nasal twang of Jack's voice was another stock trait of the fanatic preacher.[32]

Arbuthnot emphasized religious differences in his account of Anglo-Scottish relations prior to the Union. For her part, Peg is suspicious of entering an alliance with Bull, not least because of the influence of 'that auld Carline his Mother', the Church of England, who 'rails at *Jack*', and insists on 'Spells', '*Pater-nosters*, and silly auld warld Ceremonies'. When the agreement between the siblings is completed, one of the terms is that Peg 'might have the Freedom of *Jack*'s Conversation', provided that 'he did not come into the House at unseasonable Hours, and disturb the Rest of the Old Woman, *John*'s Mother'.[33] Here Arbuthnot referred to the Acts of the Scottish and English parliaments, passed with the Union, to guarantee security for the two national Churches.[34] Arbuthnot recognized that, though the proponents of union excluded religious matters from the negotiation of the Treaty, they were obliged to maintain the ecclesiastical status quo in both countries.[35]

As well as emphasizing the religious concessions required to pass the Treaty through the parliaments, Arbuthnot hinted at a confessional agenda lying behind the English drive for union. There was 'a malicious Story', he reported, that '*John*'s last Wife' (the Godolphin ministry) 'had fall'n in love with *Jack*', and 'that she perswaded *John* to take his Sister *Peg* into the House, the better to drive on her Intrigue with *Jack*'.[36] The alleged love affair represented the influence of English nonconformists in parliamentary politics. Since the Revolution, Tories and high churchmen such as Sacheverell alleged, dissenters had infiltrated political life, which was formally restricted to Anglicans. They did so chiefly by means of occasional conformity, the practice by which dissenters took communion in the Church of England just often enough to qualify for public offices under the Test Act (1673) and Corporation Act (1661), but otherwise worshipped in their own meeting

32. Arbuthnot, *John Bull*, 51 (quotation), 80; Alasdair Raffe, 'Episcopalian Polemic, the London Printing Press and Anglo-Scottish Divergence in the 1690s', *Journal of Scottish Historical Studies*, 26 (2006), 23–41, at 33–5.

33. Arbuthnot, *John Bull*, 55.

34. *Records of the Parliaments of Scotland*, ed. Brown et al., 1706/10/251; 5 Ann. c. 5, in *The Statutes at Large, from Magna Charta, to the End of the last Parliament, 1761*, ed. Owen Ruffhead, 8 vols (London: Mark Baskett, Henry Woodfall and William Strahan, 1763–4), iv. 222, 231–2.

35. For modern discussions, see Christopher A. Whatley with Derek J. Patrick, *The Scots and the Union* (Edinburgh: Edinburgh University Press, 2006), 293; Jeffrey Stephen, *Scottish Presbyterians and the Act of Union 1707* (Edinburgh: Edinburgh University Press, 2007), 63–73.

36. Arbuthnot, *John Bull*, 54.

houses. In 1702–4, Tory MPs three times attempted to pass a bill restricting occasional conformity; at this stage, their efforts were resisted by the Whigs.[37] These events deepened the partisan rivalry at the heart of parliamentary politics, exacerbating Tory anxieties about the Whigs' alleged misgovernment of the Church. (Hence *St Albans Ghost* and *John Bull* feature hostile portrayals of Gilbert Burnet, the Whiggish bishop of Salisbury, who was widely disliked by Tories and suspected of religious heterodoxy, not least because of his Scottish background.[38]) Reflecting the importance of Tory concerns about the Church, Arbuthnot devoted the fourth *John Bull* pamphlet to the successful passage of an act against occasional conformity in 1711, at which point the Whigs abandoned the dissenters and accepted the Tory measure.[39] Yet in 1706–7, according to the rumour alluded to by Arbuthnot, some Whigs thought that union would magnify the effect of occasional conformity by creating a stronger Calvinist counterpoint to the Church of England. Thus Bull's wife hoped that, after reaching an agreement with his sister, Bull 'would follow his Mistress *Peg*' and become more sympathetic towards Jack. And yet Arbuthnot was dismissive of the reports: 'All I can infer from this Story, is, that when one has got a bad Character in the World [as the Godolphin ministry had], People will report and believe any thing of them, true or false.'[40]

As we have noted, moreover, Arbuthnot thought that Bull, as a man, would influence his sister Peg, rather than the reverse. After Peg moves in with her brother, he certainly seems to have the upper hand. We learn that 'The Purchase-Money of *Peg's* Farm was ill paid', a reference to the delayed delivery of the Equivalent, the financial compensation to Scotland for future payments on the English national debt. Peg's servants endure numerous minor slights, reflecting the exclusion of Scots from trading advantages and public offices, and to the House of Lords' refusal to admit Scottish peers with British titles. Again Arbuthnot drew attention to the religious dimensions of Anglo-Scottish relations. Bull's servants order 'Plumb-porridge and Minc'd Pies for *Peg's* Dinner', an allusion to the statutes of 1712 tolerating the worship of Scottish episcopalians and restoring the rights of lay patrons in the Kirk. Some argue that this rich food should be forced on Peg. Rather than

37. John Flaningam, 'The Occasional Conformity Controversy: Ideology and Party Politics, 1697–1711', *Journal of British Studies*, 17/1 (Autumn 1977), 38–62; Holmes, *British Politics*, 99–104, 113.
38. [Wagstaffe], *Story of the St Alb[a]ns Ghost*, 12; Arbuthnot, *John Bull*, esp. 68–9.
39. Arbuthnot, *John Bull*, 77–89.   40. Arbuthnot, *John Bull*, 54.

allowing Scottish influence to bring England back to Calvinism, the advocates
of these reforms hoped to make Scotland safe for episcopalian worship.
Nevertheless, 'the Wiser sort bid let' Peg 'alone, and she might take to' the
food 'of her own Accord'.[41]

Arbuthnot was probably among the 'Wiser sort'. At least some of the
proponents of toleration and the restoration of patronage hoped that the
measures would undermine presbyterianism and the Whig interest in Scotland
more generally, thus serving a Jacobite agenda.[42] Arbuthnot, the loyal subject
of Queen Anne, sympathized with the Scottish episcopalians, but was wary
of attempts forcibly to improve their situation. And, unlike the Jacobites,
Arbuthnot was a supporter of union who, in 1706, had published a pamphlet
in its favour. This work, the *Sermon preach'd to the People, at the Mercat Cross of
Edinburgh*, predicted that great economic benefits would flow from union with
England, and argued that, without it, Scotland's independence was 'Precarious
Imaginary and Fantastical'.[43] Arbuthnot also claimed that the 'putting an end
to uncharitable and unreasonable Divisions about our triffling Differences
in Religion, is one of the great Benefites *Scotland* will reap by this Union'. He
condemned as an 'unchristian' objection to union the presbyterian clergy's
fear of losing the power to coerce dissenters and delinquents. Whereas Lord
Belhaven, in one of his celebrated speeches before parliament, conjured the
nightmare vision of a society overrun with sectaries, Arbuthnot hoped that
Scotland would welcome Jews, Independents, Quakers, and Baptists, and
receive the fruits of their commercial dynamism.[44] It was not the persecuting
uniformity of Restoration Scotland, nor the intolerant Anglicanism of Henry
Sacheverell, that Arbuthnot had in mind for his native country. Rather it
was the religious pluralism of Amsterdam, or the confessional coexistence of
England under the Toleration Act of 1689.

Arbuthnot's account of John Bull and Sister Peg is an insightful reading
of the passage of the Anglo-Scottish Union. But the section of *The History of
John Bull* describing Bull's alliance with Peg constitutes less than 10 per cent

---

41. Arbuthnot, *John Bull*, 56–7.
42. On the passage of the acts, see esp. D. Szechi, 'The Politics of "Persecution": Scots Episcopalian
    Toleration and the Harley Ministry, 1710–12', in W. J. Sheils (ed.), *Persecution and Toleration*,
    Studies in Church History, 21 (Ecclesiastical History Society; Oxford: Blackwell, 1984),
    275–87.
43. [John Arbuthnot], *A Sermon Preach'd to the People, at the Mercat Cross of Edinburgh; on the Subject
    of the Union* ([Edinburgh?,] 1706), quotation at p. 13.
44. [Arbuthnot], *A Sermon Preach'd to the People*, 18–19; cf. John Hamilton, Lord Belhaven, *The Lord
    Beilhaven's Speech in Parliament Saturday the Second of November, on the Subject-matter of an Union
    betwixt the Two Kingdoms of Scotland and England* ([Edinburgh: n.p.,] 1706), 3.

of the work. Described in the text as 'some trifling Things', the passage feels like a digression from the main narrative, though the same can be said of other episodes.[45] And after the allegory of the Union, Peg appears only once. During negotiations with Lewis Baboon prior to the cessation of the lawsuit, Peg asks that Lewis 'would let his Servants sing Psalms a Sundays', a reference to Scottish concerns about the treatment of French Protestants.[46] Apart from this demand, Peg has no role to play, either in the politics of Bull's household or in his relations with the neighbours. Peg has vanished, just as Scotland would in later works imitating Arbuthnot's masterpiece.

III

Thanks to Arbuthnot's satire, John Bull became a recognizable symbol of the English people. Later writers reanimated Arbuthnot's character in prose and verse, and developed the enduring visual imagery of John Bull. But Sister Peg rarely walked the pages of imaginative literature again. As we examine later manifestations of John Bull, then, we shall also trace the process of Peg's disappearance. Her absence in later political satires is testimony to the marginalization of Scotland in the decades following the Union.

After the success of Arbuthnot's work, satirists repeatedly appropriated his allegory to discuss contemporary politics. In the five years after John Bull's publication, there were nine further pamphlets featuring the character of John Bull or making use of a scenario similar to Arbuthnot's.[47] Unsurprisingly, several writers continued with his theme of European diplomacy. The first two imitations of John Bull, published after the conclusion of the War of the Spanish Succession in 1713, used the character to develop a Whiggish critique of the peace terms. John Bull's Last Will and Testament (1713) featured many names familiar from John Bull, but offered alternative interpretations of some of the events satirized by Arbuthnot. Thus the Whigs' trial of Sacheverell is 'a *Moderate* Revenge for' the '*High*' affront of his preaching, and Bull's sudden adoption of Tory principles—after the fall of the Godolphin ministry—could be attributed only to mental illness. Far from being the

---

45. Arbuthnot, *John Bull*, 47.   46. Arbuthnot, *John Bull*, 102.
47. Of the nine, *A Dialogue between the Staff, the Mitre, and the Purse. With a Conclusion by Lord John Bull* (London: J. Roberts, 1715), has the least to do with Arbuthnot's scheme and is not discussed here.

heroic saviour of the nation, Roger Bold (Harley) is 'a Knavish Steward'.[48]
The last will and testament he draws for Bull, which stands for the Treaty
of Utrecht, is a betrayal of Bull's interests, and a boost to the cause of
Lewis Baboon and Don L'Abjurado (the Stuart Pretender). Indeed, Bull's
treacherous servants help him to hang himself. In *A Review of the State of
John Bull's Family* (1713), a sequel to *John Bull's Last Will and Testament*,
Bold then enriches himself through his management of Bull's estate.[49]
Though there is much reference in these pamphlets to Bull's children,
there is no mention of Sister Peg. We read that Bull has three farms, but
otherwise the Scottish (and Irish) dimensions of European politics, and
even of Jacobitism, are ignored.

A more substantial appropriation of Arbuthnot's satire was the five-part
History of the Crown-Inn (1714). Perhaps for commercial reasons, the first
instalment was entitled *A Postscript to John Bull*. It was printed in seven
impressions, and the next three parts were also reprinted, albeit in declining
numbers of impressions.[50] If this suggests that the initially high level of interest in the *History of the Crown-Inn* dropped away, it also supports Walter
Scott's judgement of the work. It is, he wrote, 'so far inferior' to *John Bull*
'as to excite some question whether it be the composition of Arbuthnot'.[51]
In fact, the Whig politics of the *History of the Crown-Inn* are a stronger reason
for assigning the work to an unknown imitator of the Tory physician.

The *Crown-Inn* pamphlets were written after Queen Anne's death, and it
was possible to refer to her more directly than Arbuthnot had done. Probably
for this reason, Anne (in the character of a widow) displaces John Bull as
the main focus of the *History of the Crown-Inn*. Moreover, in the fourth
pamphlet Bull is depicted as a Tory, and his family history becomes that of
a party, rather than of the English people as a whole.[52] The *Crown-Inn's*

---

48. *John Bull's Last Will and Testament, as it was Drawn by a Welch Attorney* (London: S. Popping,
    1713), 10–11.
49. *John Bull's Last Will and Testament*, 12–13; *A Review of the State of John Bull's Family, ever since the
    Probat of his Last Will and Testament* (London: J. Moor, 1713), 4.
50. *A Postscript to John Bull, Containing the History of the Crown-Inn* (London: J. Moor, [1714]);
    A Continuation of the History of the Crown-Inn (London: J. Moor, [1714]); *A Farther Continuation
    of the History of the Crown-Inn* (London: J. Moor, [1714]); *The Fourth and Last Part of the History
    of the Crown-Inn* (London: J. Moor, [1714]). *An Appendix to the History of the Crown-Inn* (London:
    J. Moor, [1714]) continued the satire and supplied a key to the whole work.
51. *The Works of Jonathan Swift, D.D;*, ed. Walter Scott, 19 vols (Edinburgh: Archibald Constable
    and Company, 1814), vi. 236. Scott included *John Bull* itself in his collected works of Swift
    because it had been published with writings by the Irishman in the second volume of
    Miscellanies in Prose and Verse (1727).
52. *Fourth and Last Part*, 13–19; *Appendix*, 20.

author made no reference to Peg, and concentrated overwhelmingly on a partisan evaluation of English politics. There is a brief reference to the abortive Jacobite invasion of Scotland in 1708, a plot 'to give the *Young Gentleman* Possession of the *North* Farm, with design to burn and plunder it, if he could not hold it by Law'. But this detail serves more to blacken the reputation of James Hamilton, fourth duke of Hamilton (Jacob Booty), than to analyse Anglo-Scottish relations.[53] The *Crown-Inn* pamphlets manifest little of Arbuthnot's interest in national characteristics and the difficulties of incorporating Scotland into the United Kingdom.

The Present State of the Crown-Inn (1717), purportedly by the author of the other *Crown-Inn* pamphlets, contains a more detailed allegory of the Jacobite rising of 1715. In this satire, Lord Hump (John Erskine, sixth Earl of Mar, who probably had a hump on his back) 'silently withdrew himself to the *North-Farm*, where he rais'd a considerable Rabble, and openly proclaim'd' the right of Shute (the Pretender). Though it is remarked that 'many considerable Tenants who had been always attach'd to that Interest, join'd' Hump, the pamphlet offers no explanation for the popularity of Jacobitism in Scotland.[54] Again there is no attempt to characterize the Scottish people, and Peg has no role in the narrative. The same can be said of *The History of John Bull. Part III* (1744), which alludes briefly to the 1715 rising.[55] In these pamphlets, Scotland receded from view.

IV

The major, well-known, exception to the departure of Peg from eighteenth-century literature is *The History of the Proceedings in the Case of Margaret, commonly called Peg* (1761). Probably by the influential professor of moral philosophy at Edinburgh, Adam Ferguson, this work satirized Anglo-Scottish relations during the Seven Years War, a time when various politicians and intellectuals campaigned for the reintroduction in Scotland of a citizens' militia, following its revival in England. The work begins by correcting Arbuthnot's understanding of the 1707 Treaty. The agreement between Bull and Peg did not arrange for her 'to come to live in his house', as Arbuthnot had narrated,

---

53. *Postscript to John Bull*, 12–13, quotation at p. 13. See also *Fourth and Last Part*, 9.
54. *The Present State of the Crown-Inn, for the First Three Years under the New Landlord* (London: S. Baker, 1717), 13.
55. *The History of John Bull. Part III* (London: M. Cooper, 1744), 4.

since Peg remained resident at Thistledown farm. Rather, Peg had engaged 'merely to shut up her own compting-room, dismiss her overseers, and send clerks to John's house, to manage their affairs together with his accomptant, under the inspection of the great lawyer', the king.[56] After early disappointment, Peg became comfortable with the arrangement. If Jack (or the Kirk's Calvinism) had formerly made friction between the siblings, he had by this time 'sown his wild oats, and was grown an orderly conversable fellow'.[57] Rather than religious differences, the main source of tension now is lingering support for Squire Geoffrey (the Pretender), whose followers dwell in Peg's attic and once tried to invade Bull's farm.[58] When the panic resulting from the invasion subsided, however, John and Mrs Bull (parliament) began to neglect Peg, and her servants grew reluctant to stand up for her interests.[59]

For Ferguson, the relationship between John Bull and Sister Peg was an obvious framework within which to discuss the state of the Union at a time when Scottish intellectuals felt that their country was slighted. Adapting Ferguson's approach for more parochial purposes, the broadside *Speedily will be Published, the History of Rachel, commonly called Auld Reikie, eldest Daughter of Sister Peg* (1761) addressed the affairs of Edinburgh, personified as Peg's eldest daughter Rachel. The broadside, in the form of an advertisement for a forthcoming book, claims to be the work of 'the Author of the History of MARGARET' (that is, Ferguson). But, because the broadside intervened in a short-lived controversy over the election of Edinburgh's MP, there was probably no intention of publishing a fuller *History of Rachel*.[60] Nevertheless, Sister Peg evidently remained a recognizable figure, at least to Scottish readers.

When we turn to the polemical writing of the early 1760s, during the ascendancy of John Stuart, third Earl of Bute, the first Scottish prime minister, we repeatedly find John Bull, but rarely Sister Peg or the other

56. *Sister Peg: A Pamphlet Hitherto Unknown by David Hume*, ed. David R. Raynor (Cambridge: Cambridge University Press, 1982), 50. On the work's authorship, see the review of David Raynor's edition by Richard B. Sher, in *Philosophical Books*, 24 (1983), 85–91; John Robertson, *The Scottish Enlightenment and the Militia Issue* (Edinburgh: John Donald, 1985), 125. Walter Scott thought that the author was alive in 1814, which rules out Hume and most of his pro-militia contemporaries, and supports the attribution to Ferguson: *Works of Swift*, ed. Scott, vi. 236.
57. *Sister Peg*, 50, 77 (quotation).   58. *Sister Peg*, 50, 57–60.   59. *Sister Peg*, 72–3, 77–81.
60. *Speedily will be Published, the History of Rachel, commonly called Auld Reikie, eldest Daughter of Sister Peg* ([Edinburgh: n.p.,] [1761]). For the context, see Alexander J. Murdoch, 'The Importance of Being Edinburgh: Management and Opposition in Edinburgh Politics, 1746–1784', *Scottish Historical Review*, 62 (1983), 1–16, at 9.

elements of Arbuthnot's allegorical scheme. John Bull was mobilized against Scotland by the opponents of Bute, notably by the government's leading critic, John Wilkes, in his newspaper the *North Briton*. It carried the following mock obituary: 'Some time since died Mr John Bull, a very worthy, plain, honest, old gentleman, of Saxon descent; he was choaked by inadvertently swallowing a thistle, which he had placed by way of orna-ment on the top of his sallad.'[61] Tobias Smollett, whose *Briton* newspaper defended the government from Wilkes's attacks, drew an ironical comparison between John Bull and Wilkes himself.[62] Peg made a rare appearance in *Sister Peg's Memorial to one of her Clerks* (1763), which objected to the abuse of one of her 'principal domestics' (Bute) by a rabble-rousing '*Bullhall* champion' (Wilkes).[63]

Visual satire referring to or picturing John Bull was common at the time of the agitation against Bute. In criticizing the Scottish prime minister, these prints also drew on a new repertoire of symbols, notably the jackboot (to represent Bute) and the priapic staff of Gisbal, the Bute figure in the satirical pamphlet *Gisbal, an Hyperborean Tale* (1762).[64] Arbuthnot's allegorical world was not quite forgotten in the prints of 1762–3: as well as John Bull, we can find Lewis Baboon and the Salutation Tavern.[65] But, among the many visual satires commenting on Anglo-Scottish relations, only one in the British Museum's collection features Peg. 'A Poor Man Loaded with Mischief, or John Bull and his Sister Peg' (1762) (Figure 2.1) shows the unfortunate Bull carrying his tartan-clad sister on his back. A boot hangs above them. Though it suggested that Scotland was a burden on England, this image's criticism of Scots at Westminster was milder than that of other contemporary prints such as 'The Caledonians Arrival, in Money-Land' (1762).[66]

The text beneath the 'Poor Man' plays on stereotypes of Scotland and refers to Bute as 'Sawney Mackenzie'. Indeed, the hostile representation of Scots and Scotland as 'Sawney'—referring to the legendary cannibal Sawney

61. *North Briton*, no. 7, 17 July 1762.   62. *Briton*, no. 16, 11 September 1762, p. 93.
63. *Sister Peg's Memorial to one of her Clerks, on the Subject of Some Late and Present Grievances* (Edinburgh: n.p., 1763), 9, 11.
64. Frederic George Stephens and M. Dorothy George (eds.), *Catalogue of Prints and Drawings in the British Museum*, 11 vols (London: British Museum, 1870–1954), iv, esp. nos 3848–9, 3860; *Gisbal, an Hyperborean Tale: Translated from the Fragments of Ossian the Son of Fingal* (London: printed for the author, 1762).
65. Stephens and George (eds), *Catalogue of Prints and Drawings*, iv, nos 3917, 3953.
66. Stephens and George (eds), *Catalogue of Prints and Drawings*, iv, nos 3904, 3857. There are also two etchings based on the engraved 'Poor Man': nos 3905–6.

56   ALASDAIR RAFFE

Figure 2.1. 'A Poor Man Loaded with Mischief' (BM Satires 3904). © The Trustees of the British Museum. All rights reserved.

Figure 2.2. 'Sawney ganging back again' (BM Satires 6005). © The Trustees of the British Museum. All rights reserved.

Bean—was common in the period's prints.[67] What appears to be the only other reference to Peg in an eighteenth-century satirical print comes in the verse accompanying 'Sawney ganging back again' (1782) (Figure 2.2). This print shows a Scotsman, probably Bute, leaving an inn. Through its windows can be seen several figures—one is clearly Charles James Fox, appointed foreign secretary in March 1782—who are giving directions for the refurbishment of the premises. The print celebrated the fall of Lord North's ministry in 1782, suggested that Bute's political influence was finally extinguished, and implied that the new cabinet would restore effective government. The verse reinforced the message by telling how Sister Peg, having been taken into Bull's house, 'perverted JOHN's Wife' (parliament) and advanced Sawney, a greedy servant who let Bull's property decay. A group of Bull's friends then 'turn'd out his sister, divorc'd his bad wife' and 'kick'd SAWNEY out', thus salvaging his affairs.[68]

After the early 1760s, John Bull was rarely depicted for anti-Scottish purposes. Rather he was a symbol of the English people in their struggles with overseas foes and high-taxing governments.[69] In some images, such as James Gillray's 'French Invasion: or John Bull bombarding the Bum Boats' (1793), Bull clearly represents England. But in others he stands for the British people. An example is William Dent's 'The Free-Born Briton, or a Perspective of Taxation' (1786), which depicts John Bull as a 'Briton' weighed down by taxes. The representation of John Bull had evolved far beyond its original context, and Arbuthnot's subtle dissection of Anglo-Scottish differences had been left behind.[70]

V

The History of John Bull was a witty allegory of England's relations with its continental friends and foes. It also contained a convincing interpretation of the Union of 1707. Arbuthnot argued that English unionists were concerned primarily to secure the Hanoverian succession and preserve peace in Britain, while Scottish supporters of the Treaty looked especially to its promised

67. Gordon Pentland, ' "We speak for the ready": Images of Scots in Political Prints, 1707–1832', *Scottish Historical Review*, 90 (2011), 64–95, at 79–80, 81, 85.
68. Stephens and George (eds.), *Catalogue of Prints and Drawings*, v, no. 6005.
69. Miles Taylor, 'John Bull and the Iconography of Public Opinion in England, c.1712–1929', *Past and Present*, 134 (February 1992), 93–128.
70. Stephens and George (eds.), *Catalogue of Prints and Drawings*, vii, no. 8346, vi, no. 6914.

economic benefits. He hoped that union would bring about a more tolerant culture in Scotland, but he identified religious sticking points in both countries. Many Scots warned that the presbyterian settlement of 1690 was at risk; the reforms of 1712 proved their alarm justified. And in England, Anglo-Scottish reconciliation exacerbated Tory fears about the safety of the Church of England, already under threat from occasional conformity and the Whigs' mismanagement.

However, while Arbuthnot had the background and knowledge to comment on Anglo-Scottish relations, he placed greater emphasis on European diplomacy and Westminster politics. Many of his imitators neglected Scotland and omitted Sister Peg entirely from their allegorical writings. Unsurprisingly, the satires mentioning Peg were largely the work of Scots. The disappearance of Peg from eighteenth-century literature had two effects. First, the character of John Bull was only occasionally invoked in discussions of Scotland's place in the Union. Bull played this part during the Earl of Bute's premiership, but scarcely thereafter. Second, in the absence of his Scottish sister, Bull's specifically English characteristics became obscure. Indeed, recent art historians of John Bull—and some scholars of satire writing about Arbuthnot—have entirely elided the distinction between England and Britain.[71] If the evolution of Bull into a Briton was the logical outcome of his reconciliation with Peg, it nevertheless suppressed part of what is valuable in the History of John Bull. Arbuthnot, an episcopalian Scot in England, could observe national characters, religious commitments, and party prejudices with a degree of critical distance. This perspective allowed him to create John Bull and Sister Peg, and ensured that the History of John Bull would rarely be equalled in the satirical literature of Anglo-Scottish Union.

71. Tamara L. Hunt, *Defining John Bull: Political Caricature and National Identity in Late Georgian England* (Aldershot: Ashgate, 2003); Reva Wolf, 'John Bull, Liberty and Wit: How England Became Caricature', in Todd Porterfield (ed.), *The Efflorescence of Caricature, 1759–1838* (London: Ashgate, 2011), 49–60; Ashley Marshall, *The Practice of Satire in England, 1658–1770* (Baltimore: Johns Hopkins University Press, 2013), 177; Vincent Carretta, *George III and the Satirists from Hogarth to Byron* (Athens, GA: University of Georgia Press, 1990), 320.

3

Bagpipes no Musick
Allan Ramsay, James Arbuckle, and the Significance of the 'Scots' Poetic Revival

Richard Holmes

*B*agpipes *No Musick*, an attack on the 'Scots' poetry of Allan Ramsay, appeared shortly before his first major collection was published in London 1721.[1] The collection included a defence of Ramsay by a Glasgow student, James Arbuckle, and an 'Epistle' from Ramsay to Arbuckle, which lavished praise on Arbuckle's mock-heroic poem *Snuff*.[2] There is an apparent paradox in this mutual support. Ramsay's work helped initiate a 'Scots' poetic revival, often seen as a form of Jacobite, nationalist resistance to union, to Whiggish illusions of progress that threatened Scottish cultural authenticity.[3] Arbuckle was a firm Whig, whose poem *Glotta* (1721) celebrated union as a step towards enlightenment.[4] Why was Arbuckle defending him? Was the 'Scots' revival in fact a unionist project? Ramsay's collection was indeed sponsored at the highest level of the Whig and unionist establishment. Subscriptions for it, at the time of the *Bagpipes* attack, were being organized

1. *The Works of Allan Ramsay*, ed. Burns Martin, A. M. Kinghorn, and A. Law, 6 vols (Edinburgh: Scottish Text Society, 1951–74), iii. 32.
2. Ramsay, *Works*, i, pp. xxviii–xxx, 212–17; *James Arbuckle: Selected Works*, ed. Richard Holmes (Lewisburg, PA: Bucknell University Press, 2014), 3–25.
3. Murray Pittock, *Poetry and Jacobite Politics in Eighteenth-Century Britain and Ireland* (Cambridge: Cambridge University Press, 1994), 152–4.
4. Arbuckle, *Selected Works*, 25–39.

by Sir William Bennet, the Duke of Roxburghe's Scottish agent.[5] Roxburghe was Secretary of State for Scotland, leader of the Squadrone Whigs who had ensured the passage of the Articles of Union (Bennet was at that time also a Squadrone MP).[6] Roxburghe himself was a patron and admirer of Ramsay. The *Bagpipes* attack had come to Bennet's attention through Roxburghe's son, Lord Bowmont, an Eton schoolboy, and an enthusiast for 'Scots song'.[7] The Squadrone Whigs were also Arbuckle's principal patrons. *Snuff* (1719) was dedicated to Roxburghe. His celebration of Joseph Addison as a Whig hero, *An Epistle to Thomas, Sixth Earl of Haddington* (1719), was addressed to Roxburghe's friend and colleague (Haddington had also praised *Snuff*).[8] *Glotta* praised another Squadrone leader, the Duke of Montrose.[9] This chapter will examine Ramsay through a comparison with Arbuckle, for the light it can shed on Ramsay's early success in the period 1719–21, on the role of their patrons among the Scottish Whig politicians, and on the significance of the 'Scots' revival in a broader process of cultural change.

Arbuckle, born to a Scottish mercantile family in Belfast, attended Glasgow University in 1716–22, latterly as a student of Divinity. He was a near-contemporary of Francis Hutcheson ('Father of the Scottish Enlightenment'), who later collaborated with him in Dublin on the literary journal *Hibernicus's Letters*.[10] Ramsay, in 'To My Kind and Worthy Friends in Ireland' (1727), referred to Arbuckle, whose career thereafter was in Ireland. Apart from the verse epistles, there is no surviving correspondence between them.[11]

Arbuckle's 'To Mr Allan Ramsay' focused on a defence of Ramsay's use of 'Scots' as a poetic language, describing his critics as 'snarling curs' and 'fustian coxcombs'. He called on classical tradition in justification, comparing

---

5. Robert Wood to Bennet, National Records of Scotland, Papers of the Ogilvy family of Inverquharity (hereafter Bennet Letters), GD 205/35/5/8/12.

6. D. J. Patrick and C. A. Whatley, 'Persistence, Principle and Patriotism in the Making of the Union of 1707: The Revolution, Scottish Parliament and the *Squadrone volante*', *History*, 92/306 (April 2007), 162–86.

7. Roxburghe to Bennet, 9 November 1720, Bennet Letters, GD 205/31/25 [AR]; Robert Wood to Bennet, 1 December 1720, Bennet Letters, GD 205/35/5/8/10-2; Ramsay, *Works*, i. 236, iii. 161, vi. 52.

8. Arbuckle, *Selected Works*, 3.

9. Arbuckle, *Selected Works*, 25 (it was dedicated to the son of the Duke of Chandos, a visitor in Glasgow at Montrose's invitation; his father negotiated with Montrose a gift towards a new library).

10. T. D. Campbell, 'Hutcheson: "Father of the Scottish Enlightenment"', in R. H. Campbell, and A. S. Skinner (eds), *The Origins and Nature of the Scottish Enlightenment* (Edinburgh: John Donald, 1982). Hutcheson contributed six essays to *Hibernicus's Letters* (Dublin and London: Smith and Bruce, Grierson and others, 1729).

11. Ramsay, *Works*, ii. 203–4.

Ramsay's 'Scots' to Virgil's pastorals. He went on to draw a distinction between two kinds of originality, native genius and learned talent:

> Your muse, upon her native Stock
> Subsisting, raises thence a Name;
> While they are forc'd to pick the Lock
> Of other Bards, and pilfer Fame.[12]

The latter joke was at his own expense, as *Snuff*, like Ramsay's *The Morning Interview*, had played extensively with allusions to Pope's *Rape of the Lock*. Ramsay himself, on a number of occasions, preferred 'natural' to 'learned' poetry.[13]

The formal title of Ramsay's 'Epistle to Mr James Arbuckle of Belfast A.M.' suggests a defensive mockery of the learned by a poet who himself did not attend university. His poem began with an imitative tribute to *Snuff*, pretending that he needed an inspiring 'pinch' before he could write. He moved on to Arbuckle's rising reputation among 'men o' mettle' in Edinburgh, who may have included Bennet or his associates (the *Snuff* of 1719, dedicated to Roxburghe, was an extended version of the poem originally published in Glasgow in 1717). *Snuff* is a very unlikely poem for a student of Divinity, especially at Glasgow ('this most strictly Presbyterian of cities'), but it gives a good indication of what drew Ramsay to Arbuckle.[14] It is bawdy, irreverent, delighting in the pleasures of commercial society, full of allusions not only to Pope, but to Virgil, Dryden, Addison, and Gay, and above all a hymn to poetry, concluding with a statement of artistic vocation that is a studied challenge to religious piety (his Muse required him to 'Renounce thou therefore all the World for me'[15]). In a later essay Arbuckle discussed 'contempt of the world', the view, shared by the religious and by neo-Stoics, that virtue was incompatible with 'the innocent pleasures of life'. The advocates of virtue, he said, were too often 'Men of a saturnine and melancholy Humour'.[16] Ramsay's 'Epistle' similarly encouraged Arbuckle to resist the pious, whom he called:

---

12. Ramsay, 'To Mr Allan Ramsay on the Publication of his Poems', ll. 17–20, in *Works*, i, p. xxix.
13. Ramsay, 'The Preface', in *Works*, i, pp. xix, 27–38. Similar points were made by another friend of Ramsay, the English Whig MP Josiah Burchet (further discussed later in the chapter); see Burchet, 'To Mr Allan Ramsay', in Ramsay, *Works*, i, pp. xxi–xxiv.
14. M. A. Stewart, 'John Smith and the Molesworth Circle', *Eighteenth-Century Ireland*, 2 (1987), 89–102, at 92; Nicholas Phillipson, *Adam Smith: An Enlightened Life* (London: Allen Lane, 2010), 32.
15. Arbuckle, *Snuff*, l. 612, in *Selected Works*, 16.   16. Arbuckle, *Selected Works*, 85.

these Fellows Girning
Wha wear their Faces ay in Mourning

. . . . .

Terming ilk Turn that's witty vicious.[17]

The English poet Ambrose Philips (also addressed as one of Ramsay's 'Friends in Ireland' in 1727) sent encouragement in 1719 to the new Scottish poets 'Who in a rude and sullen country write'.[18] Ramsay and Arbuckle shared a commitment to Scotland's cultural improvement. Ramsay's 'Epistle' described Arbuckle as 'brushing up our sister Glasgow' and referred to conflict in Glasgow between modernizers and Calvinist orthodoxy.[19] This began with student protests over university governance, the protesters including Hutcheson and John Hamilton, son of the Earl of Haddington.[20] Ramsay's 'Epistle' refers to another friend of Arbuckle, John Smith, who was expelled over the protests. Smith published a pamphlet that described the Principal's 'Act to suppress Immorality', directed at Arbuckle and his friends who 'haunted' taverns, and the charge against Arbuckle in particular that he 'attended at a house of ill-fame at unseasonable hours'.[21] It may have been these protests that first brought Arbuckle and his friends to Ramsay's attention; their lawyer was his friend, Duncan Forbes.[22] Perhaps the greatest concern to Ramsay was the University's opposition to Arbuckle staging plays (they called the theatre 'wicked and ungodly').[23] Ramsay's own battles over the theatre in Edinburgh are well known; a later letter described his fear that 'antichristian priestcraft and gloomy enthusiasm' would prevail over 'politeness'.[24]

17. Ramsay, 'Epistle to James Arbuckle', ll. 39–40, in *Works*, i. 212–7.
18. *Lugubres Cantus* (Edinburgh: M'Euen, 1720).
19. Ramsay, 'Epistle to James Arbuckle', i.36 and in *Works*, iv. 15.
20. Stewart, 'John Smith and the Molesworth Circle'; John Hamilton matriculated in 1716, *The Memorials of the Earls of Haddington*, ed.W. Frazer, 2 vols (Edinburgh: privately printed, 1889), i. 261.
21. John Smith, *A Short Account of the Late Treatment of the Students of the University of G—w* (Dublin, 1722).
22. Smith, *Short Account*, 34; Ramsay, *Works*, vi. 212.
23. Joseph Mitchell, a contemporary student of Divinity at Edinburgh, believed that he had been driven out of Scotland because of his involvement in drama (*Poems on Several Occasions* (London: L. Gilliver, 1729), 19, 313). Ramsay's poem to Mitchell urged him (in terms similar to the 'Epistle' to Arbuckle) 'to thwart the gowks' (Ramsay, 'To Mr Joseph Mitchel', l. 18, in *Works*, i. 239.
24. Ramsay, *Works*, iv. 39. See Ramsay, *Some Few Hints in Defence of Dramatical Entertainment* (1728), and the criticism of Ramsay by Revd George Anderson, *The Use and Abuse of Diversions* (1733). One difference between Ramsay and a critic of Calvinist philistinism like Archibald Pitcairne was that Ramsay was a Presbyterian, not an Episcopalian: Ramsay, *Works*, iv. 25.

These conflicts, and the determined secularism of Arbuckle and Ramsay, should be understood in the context of a society in the process of change.[25] Increasing secular control of the Church and universities was an important part of this (for Hugh Trevor-Roper an essential condition for the Scottish Enlightenment was a kirk 'de-Calvinized').[26] Control was exercised by Whig grandees such as Arbuckle's and Ramsay's patrons in the Squadrone party, many of them with a family background in persecuted presbyterian orthodoxy.[27] The appointment of men such as Arbuckle's friends Hutcheson and William Wishart to important positions in Church and university helped foster 'polite Whiggism', 'a civil presbyterianism', and ultimately the conditions for Moderatism and Enlightenment.[28] Arbuckle, rejecting a career in the church for 'polite' literature, exemplified these changes. Ramsay has been described as striking 'the first note of rebellion against the tyranny of the kirk'.[29] These 'improvers' were distinguished from religious orthodoxy partly by their willingness to seek moral guidance in secular and literary, as opposed to theological, sources. Two literary models were of particular importance, Horace and Addison, and both had considerable influence on Ramsay and Arbuckle.

Arbuckle translated sixteen of Horace's Odes, Ramsay ten, and there is a Horatian influence in much of their other work (in Ramsay's longer poems 'Content' and 'Health', for example).[30] Arbuckle's translations were first

25. 'Scotland in 1720 stood at the threshold of a new age' (Richard Sher, *Church and University in the Scottish Enlightenment: The Moderate Literati of Edinburgh* (Princeton: Princeton University Press; Edinburgh: Edinburgh University Press, 1985), 23).

26. Hugh Trevor-Roper, *Religion, the Reformation and Social Change* (London: Macmillan, 1972), 204 (which understates the extent to which 'de-Calvinization' was the work of moderate Presbyterians; see, e.g., Colin Kidd, 'Religious Realignment between Restoration and Union', in John Robertson (ed.), *A Union for Empire: Political Thought and the British Union of 1707* (Cambridge: Cambridge University Press, 1995), 153–7).

27. Patrick and Whatley, 'Persistence, Principle and Patriotism', 162–86; Kidd refers to 'the hard headed erastianism common to the political elite', 'Religious Realignment between Restoration and Union', 153. For examples concerning Bennet, see *The Manuscripts of the Duke of Roxburghe*, Historical Manuscripts Commission 14th Report (London: HMSO, 1894), 54–5; and Sir John Clerk, *Memoirs of Sir John Clerk of Penicuik*, ed. John M. Gray (Edinburgh: T. and A. Constable, 1892), 247.

28. Sher, *Church and University*, 15; William Wishart to Viscount Molesworth, 7 November 1723, National Library of Ireland, Molesworth correspondence, microfilm no. 4082; Colin Kidd, *Subverting Scotland's Past: Scottish Whig Historians and the Creation of an Anglo-British Identity* (Cambridge: Cambridge University Press, 1993), 60.

29. W. J. Courthope, *A History of English Poetry*, 6 vols (London: Macmillan, 1910), vi. 54. See also Arbuckle's support for 'non-subscribing' Presbyterians in Glasgow: William McKnight to Robert Wodrow, 28 December 1722, National Library of Scotland, Wodrow Letters Quarto, fos 290–1.

30. Ramsay, 'Content', in *Works*, i. 90–105; 'Health', in *Works*, ii. 5–17.

published in James M'Euen's *Edinburgh Miscellany* of 1720 along with the first work of James Thomson.[31] In a later essay he discussed the difficulty of translating Horace and recommended a cooperative effort, such as the famous 'Wits' Horace' (substantial parts of Arbuckle's own versions were borrowed for the eighteenth century's best-known translation, by the Irish clergyman Philip Francis).[32] It may be that, in translating so many odes in a short time, Arbuckle and Ramsay were considering a Scottish Horatian miscellany. The obvious difference between Arbuckle's versions and Ramsay's is that the former were close translations in standard English, the latter loose imitations and, mostly, in Scots (Ramsay called them 'dressed in British').[33] Ramsay's freedom with Horace attracted a bitter attack that began 'Damned brazen face'.[34] Arbuckle's later essay justified such loose imitation in terms borrowed from Dryden, as his poem to Ramsay had expressly defended his use of Scots.[35]

These versions were part of a contemporary vogue for the modest epicureanism of the Horatian 'Happy Man' (in Ramsay's 'Content' 'Godlike is he whom no false fears annoy, | Who lives content, and grasps the present joy'[36]). The Horatianism of Sir John Clerk ('Scotland's Maecenas') has been particularly noted. The writers patronized by him included Ramsay and Samuel Boyse, a close friend of Arbuckle's at Glasgow.[37] Less remarked is the literary patronage of Bennet, now living on his Borders estate at Marlefield and closely associated with the Haddington as well as the Roxburghe families.[38] Bennet embodies the cultural shift among the modernizing Scottish Whigs, from the persecuted piety of the Covenanting period to moderation and civility.[39] As Roxburghe's Scottish representative, he advised on patronage, exchanging the latest literature with Roxburghe in London and supervising

31. Arbuckle, in *Edinburgh Miscellany* (Edinburgh: M'Euen, 1720) and 'Hibernicus's Letters', Arbuckle, *Selected Works*, 77–85, 159–60; Ramsay, *Works*, i. 90–106, 217–27 [6], ii. 5–18, iii. 340–3 [4].
32. Arbuckle, *Selected Works*, 72–3, and, for examples, *Selected Works*, 82–3; Philip Francis, *The Odes, Epodes, and Carmen Secularae of Horace in Latin and English*, 2 vols (Dublin: S. Powell, 1742).
33. Ramsay, 'Preface', to *Poems* (1712), in *Works*, i, p. xviii.
34. *A Satyr upon Allan Ramsay Occasion'd by a Report of his Translating Horace* (Edinburgh, 1720).
35. Arbuckle, *Selected Works*, 73.   36. Ramsay, 'Content', ll. 15–16.
37. Iain Gordon Brown, The Clerks of Penicuik, Portraits of Taste and Talent (Edinburgh: Penicuik House Preservation Trust, 1987), 15. Samuel Boyse, 'To the Honourable Sir John Clerk, Baronet', Translations and Poems (London, 1738), 180–2. On Boyse, son of one of Ireland's leading Presbyterians, see Arbuckle, *Selected Works*, p. xvi.
38. Countess of Roxburghe to Bennet, 27 July 1719, Bennet Letters, GD 205/31/1/45.
39. 'William Bennet', *The History of Parliament: The House of Commons 1690–1715*, ed. Eveline Cruickshanks, Stuart Handley, and D. W. Hayton, 5 vols (Cambridge: Cambridge University Press, 2002), iii. 175–9.

the construction of Floors Castle and its gardens (the project begun under William Adam in 1720). James Thomson stayed at Marlefield, and addressed three 'Happy Man' poems to Bennet.[40] Another protégé was John Ker, promoted at Aberdeen University through Roxburghe's patronage and a friend of Ramsay's. [41] In preparing his Latin poem on Aberdeen (a work with some echoes of Arbuckle's *Glotta*), Ker asked David Mallet to send him six copies of Arbuckle's poem.[42] Ramsay was a particular favourite at Marlefield. He and Bennet exchanged Horatian imitations, the best-known Ramsay's 'Epistle to Sir William Bennet', but including poems from Bennet himself, such as 'Upon Allan Ramsay parting from Marlefield 1721'.[43]

In *The Happy Man: Studies in the Metamorphosis of a Classical Ideal*, Maren Sophie Rostvig notes a change in the early eighteenth century in this Horatian genre that 'had been closely associated with a Royalist and Anglican bias'. The 'epicureanism and downright immorality' of the Restoration Horace was adapted by 'the pious sectarians': 'considerable interest was taken in more prudent versions emphasizing clean living and moderate pleasures tempered by piety.'[44] One example is Arbuckle's 'Ode III, 29', a favourite of carpe diem epicureanism, to which he adds a moralizing final line: 'My Vertue shall make all serene.'[45] Ramsay's 'Epistle to Bennet' is another. He contrasts those 'rack'd about on fortune's wheel' with Bennet's ease and serenity ('who can mean care despise'), his expression borrowing from Arbuckle.[46] This 'Happy Man' is not the libertine of Restoration Horatians, but a polite Augustan for whom moderation and knowledge

40. James Thomson, 'Upon Marle-field', in Thomson, *Liberty, The Castle of Indolence and Other Poems*, ed. James Sambrook (Oxford: Clarendon Press, 1986), 238–40.
41. John Ker to Sir William Bennet, 19 December 1717 and 29 April 1722, Bennet Letters, GD 205/37/7.20 and GD 205/37/7.4. For exchange of epistles with Ramsay, see Ramsay, *Works*, iv. 307–11, iii. 158–60. Ker is described in the *Oxford Dictionary of National Biography* as a Jacobite, but this is difficult to square with his verse ('Perfidious Tory, could'st thou once be brought | To quiet loyalty, and sober thought' ('To King George' (1723)), and his later work for Sir Robert Walpole, see Ker to Walpole, undated, Cambridge University Library, Cholmondeley (H) Corr. 2389 (which enclosed his *The Cause of Liberty, Addressed to the British Senate* (1734)).
42. Letters, David Mallet to John Ker, 10 September and 2 November 1722, *European Magazine* (May 1793 to February 1794), 24: 23, and 23: 415. Ker also introduced Mallet to Roxburghe when he moved to London: Mallet to Ker, 26 September 1723, *European Magazine*, 24: 24.
43. Ramsay, 'Epistle to Sir William Bennett' in *Works*, i.227–8; 'Upon Allan Ramsay parting from Marlefield 1721', in *Works*, i. 227–8; Bennet Letters, GD 205/38/8.
44. Maren Sophie Rostvig, *The Happy Man: Studies in the Metamorphosis of a Classical Ideal* (Trondheim: Norwegian Universities Press, 1971), 15.
45. Arbuckle, 'Ode III, 29', l. 95, in *Selected Works*, 79.
46. Ramsay, 'Epistle to Bennet', ll. 2, 7. Ramsay writes of Bennet's 'undaunted stalk and brow serene'. *Snuff* has 'stalk | With steady Courage', and Arbuckle's translation of 'Ode I, 22', 'Undaunted and serene he goes' (Arbuckle, *Selected Works*, 16; *Edinburgh Miscellany*, 60).

mean true happiness: Bennet possesses 'taste refin'd which does not easy cloy'.[47] Ramsay contrasts the 'purblind eyes' of the libertine ('gen'rous friendship's out of sight too fine, | They think it only means a glass of wine') with Bennet's wisdom ('he whose cheerful mind hath higher flown') and praises his learned and horticultural pursuits.[48]

Rostvig also suggests that Horace was one influence on 'Spectatorial' morality.[49] Addisonian 'politeness' was secular, replacing obedience to authority (divine or other) with cultivation of the skill to judge for oneself (in Ramsay's 'Content' 'wise and virtuous thought in constant course').[50] The shared admiration for Addison of Ramsay and Arbuckle is evident from the elegy each wrote on his death in 1719, Ramsay's 'Richy and Sandy' (representing Pope and Steele as 'Scots' shepherds), and Arbuckle's *Epistle to Haddington*.[51] Ramsay, as a member of Edinburgh's 'Easy Club', had appealed to Addison as an arbiter of taste.[52] *The Gentle Shepherd*, perhaps Ramsay's best work, is a 'Scots' pastoral informed by Addisonian politeness.[53] Arbuckle's task of 'Brushing up our sister Glasgow' was an Addisonian project of cultural improvement. Addison's influence on Arbuckle is clear not only in his *Epistle*, and in his poems on his Glasgow production of Addison's *Cato*, but in references and imitation throughout his career, particularly in his later essays as 'Hibernicus'.

The influence of Addison on eighteenth-century Scotland has usually been equated with Anglicization.[54] In fact, his promotion of 'natural' writing, his efforts to free British poets from classical influence, could encourage a distinctively Scottish culture: hence Arbuckle and Ramsay, in praising the 'natural' over the 'learned', defended 'Scots' poetry in Addisonian terms.[55]

---

47. Ramsay, 'Epistle to Bennet', l. 22.   48. Ramsay, 'Epistle to Bennet', ll. 39–40, 41.
49. Rostvig, *The Happy Man*, 16–18.
50. L. Klein, 'Joseph Addison's Whiggism', in David Womersley (ed.), *Cultures of Whiggism* (Newark: University of Delaware Press, 2005), 108–26. Addison, however, remained in some respects a churchman: L. Klein, 'Addisonian Afterlives: Joseph Addison in Eighteenth-Century Culture', *Journal for Eighteenth-Century Studies*, 35/1 (2012), 103.
51. Ramsay, 'Richy and Sandy', in *Works*, i. 106–12.   52. Ramsay, *Works*, v. 5.
53. Steve Newman, 'The Scots Songs of Allan Ramsay: "Lyrick" Transformation, Popular Culture, and the Boundaries of the Scottish Enlightenment', *Modern Language Quarterly*, 63 (2002), 277–314, at 291.
54. N. Phillipson, 'Politics, Politeness and the Anglicization of Early Eighteenth Century Scottish Culture', in R. A. Mason (ed.), *Scotland and England 1286–1815* (Edinburgh: John Donald, 1987), 226–47, at 233–5; Robert Crawford, *Devolving English Literature* (1992; 2nd edn, Edinburgh: Edinburgh University Press, 2000), 34.
55. See, e.g., 'A Letter from Italy, to the Right Honourable Charles Lord Hallifax', in Joseph Addison, *The Miscellaneous Works of Joseph Addison*, ed. A. C. Guthkelch, 2 vols (London: G. Bell & Sons Ltd, 1914), i. 49–62.

'Anglicization' also suggests an established English culture and might overlook the extent to which Addison's writing was closely involved in the politics of change (what sort of 'England' was 'Anglicization' imposing?). The liberation of British writing from literary 'fathers' was influenced by a broader Whig ideology of liberty.[56] Addison's 'politeness' set a politics of toleration for diversity and individual liberty against patriarchal Toryism, divine right, and rule based on a hereditary landed interest.[57] His tone of cultivated ease was a rhetorical strategy to claim cultural authority for the Whigs, who had been mocked in Tory propaganda as illiterate fanatics.[58] He was indeed not only a writer but a politician, closely allied (alongside Sir Richard Steele) with Scottish Whigs against Tory policies, especially those religious policies such as the Schism and Occasional Conformity Acts that were seen as threats to the Church of Scotland.[59]

This article has focused so far on the ways in which a shared commitment to secular culture is reflected in Ramsay's and Arbuckle's work. Their treatment of Addison suggests what may be a political difference. Arbuckle's *Epistle* emphasized the more radically Whig Addison, treating his 'Whig battle-hymn' *The Campaign*, and his play *Cato* as firmly Whig contributions to the partisan cultural wars of Queen Anne's reign.[60] He praised Addison for subverting an established tradition of Tory satire on Whigs: 'No longer Vice presumes to Ridicule | But wears itself the Habit of the Fool'.[61] This had a relevance to Scottish Whig efforts at cultural improvement. Scottish Tories like Archibald Pitcairne had mocked Scots Whig–Presbyterians as philistine bigots, like Lord Whigridden ('a Presbyterian peer, a rigid fool') in his play *The Assembly*.[62] But in a culturally improved Scotland Whigridden, following Addison's strategy, could be reinvented as a polite Augustan, a Horatian 'Happy Man', or even as Scotland's Maecenas. The radicalism of

---

56. David Womersley (ed.), *Augustan Critical Writing* (London: Penguin, 1997), p. xiv.
57. Klein, 'Joseph Addison's Whiggism'; Edward A. Bloom and Lilian D. Bloom, *Joseph Addison's Sociable Animal* (Providence, RI: Brown University Press, 1971), 55–6, 88–112.
58. Abigail Williams, *Poetry and the Creation of a Whig Literary Culture 1681–1714* (Oxford: Oxford University Press, 2005), 22–3.
59. G. M. Townend, 'Religious Radicalism and Conservatism in the Whig party under George I: The Repeal of the Occasional Conformity and Schism Acts', *Parliamentary History*, 7 (1988), 24–43; *A Guide to the Electors of Britain* (London: S. Popping, 1722), 13; Bloom and Bloom, *Joseph Addison's Sociable Animal*, 145. For Steele's relationship with the Squadrone MP George Baillie (closely linked to the Haddington family), see 'George Baillie', in 'William Bennet', *The History of Parliament: The House of Commons 1690–1715*, and *Notes and Queries*, 2nd ser. (12 June 1858), 472.
60. Womersley, *Augustan Critical Writing*, p. xxiii.   61. Arbuckle, *Epistle*, ll. 309–10.
62. Archibald Pitcairne, *The Assembly, A Comedy* (London, 1722).

the poem may also reflect the support of the Squadrone Whigs, at the time of its publication (1719), for Sunderland's controversial repeal of Tory religious legislation. The repeal was masterminded by Grey Neville and Shute Barrington, allies and friends of Bennet and Roxburghe, MPs for Berwick, a constituency within their sphere of influence.[63]

There is no trace in Ramsay's response to Addison, or in his work generally, of such radical Whiggism. This difference may be behind a note of criticism of 'Richy and Sandy' in Arbuckle's 'Epistle': 'Celestial Poets call for other strains | Than dying Shepherds on Arcadian Plains'.[64] Were Ramsay and Arbuckle despite their many affinities politically opposed? What were Ramsay's politics? Two contrasting poems written for the 'Easy Club' illustrate the difficulty of giving a simple answer. An elegy for the Jacobite Pitcairne, perhaps Ramsay's earliest work, gives voice to Pitcairne's bitter attack on the Union.[65] In 'The Gentleman's Qualifications', by contrast, Ramsay sounds like a polite Addisonian Whig, describing a debate on the principle of heredity that sets a radical Whig against a caricatured Tory (similar to Addison's 'Foxhunter' in 'an old redcoat and mangled face') before imposing, in the name of 'social friendship', a compromise, to 'end all controversy by a vote', which is more an endorsement of limited Hanoverian monarchy than of Jacobite invasion.[66] Both poems were very early. By the time of his 'Epistle to Arbuckle' (1719) Ramsay seemed keen to avoid politics altogether, describing himself as 'nowther Whig nor Tory. Believing truths and thinking free, | Wishing thrawn parties wad agree'[67] (which is not inconsistent with a 'polite' Whiggism). Nevertheless he has consistently been described as a nationalist Jacobite.[68] Murray Pittock puts the case at its

---

63. For both, see 'William Bennet', *The History of Parliament: The House of Commons 1690–1715*; and Grey Neville to Bennet, 11 July 1708, Bennet Letters, GD 205/36/19, and Roxburghe to Bennet, 23 December 1720, Bennet Letters, GD 205/31/1/27.

64. Arbuckle, *Epistle*, ll. 27–8. For the subversive quality of 'Richy and Sandy', see Murray Pittock, 'Allan Ramsay and the Decolonization of Genre', *Review of English Studies*, NS 58 (2007), 316–37, at 333. Note, however, the poem was published with a friendly exchange of poetic epistles between Ramsay and Josiah Burchet, and a 'translation' by Burchet, a Whig MP, who helped raise subscriptions for Ramsay's 1721 collection.

65. F. W. Freeman and Alexander Law, 'Allan Ramsay's First Published Poem: The Poem to the Memory of Dr Archibald Pitcairne', *Bibliotheck*, 9 (1979), 153–60.

66. Ramsay, 'The Gentleman's Qualification', ll. 52, 39, in *Works*, i. 199–20; Bloom and Bloom, *Joseph Addison's Sociable Animal*, 168–9.

67. Ramsay, 'Epistle to Arbuckle', ll. 108–9.

68. Alexander Tytler, 'Remarks on the Genius and Writings of Allan Ramsay', in *The Poems of Allan Ramsay*, ed. George Chalmers (London: T. Cadell and W. Davies, 1800), 49; David Daiches, *The Paradox of Scottish Culture: The Eighteenth-Century Experience* (London: Oxford University Press, 1964), 27; Pittock, *Poetry and Jacobite Politics*, 154.

strongest, uncovering Jacobite imagery and symbolism where a less skilled reader might overlook it. 'The Lamentation' (1715), for example, appears to be a polite critique of civil war, its attack on 'schismatic pride' arguably directed at Jacobite rebellion, but Pittock finds Jacobite sympathy in its 'ambivalence', in coded references to 'base blood' and 'new succession'.[69] It is difficult that many of the 'Jacobite' poems were not published or acknowledged by Ramsay: 'The Gentleman's Qualifications' was included in the 1721 collection, though the elegy for Pitcairne was not. However, was Ramsay's anxiety to avoid party identification a committed moderation, or, as has often been suggested, a discretion enforced by dependence on Whig patrons?[70] In the 1721 collection Pittock's case for the Jacobite, nationalist Ramsay relies principally on two poems, 'Tartana, or The Plaid' and 'Wealth, or the Woody', one of a series on the South Sea Bubble.[71] A detailed exam-ination will illuminate not only Ramsay's politics but also a close intertextual relationship with Arbuckle's work, especially *Glotta*.

'Tartana', a poem in praise of the traditional Scottish 'plaid', is in a sense a manifesto for Ramsay's promotion of 'Scots' poetry, similar in terms to his preface to *The Evergreen*.[72] It also shares the form of *Snuff*, a mock-heroic 'thing-poem', following and referring to a tradition, which included John Gay's *Wine* and *The Fan*, of cleverly using the paradox of small things mag-nified (he dares to 'Advance such Praises for a Thing despis'd').[73] Although *Snuff* is a more carefully worked, a more learned and allusive poem, there are many similarities in phrasing, style, and overall structure (probably deriv-ing from shared imitation of Pope).[74] The poem also aligns native culture with natural genius, humorously undercutting classical with Scots, as when

---

69. Pittock, *Poetry and Jacobite Politics*, 155–6.
70. Daiches, *The Paradox of Scottish Culture*, 27; see also Pittock, *Poetry and Jacobite Politics*, 160.
71. Pittock, *Poetry and Jacobite Politics*, 158; and 'Allan Ramsay and the Decolonization of Genre', 329; Ramsay, *Wealth or the Woody*, in *Works*, iv. 15.
72. Ramsay, 'Tartana, or the Plaid', in *Works*, i. 27–38; 'Preface', to *The Evergreen*, in *Works*, iv. 235–8.
73. Ramsay, 'Tartana, or the Plaid', l. 222. Barbara M. Benedict, 'Encounters with the Object: Advertisements, Time, and Literary Discourse in the Early Eighteenth-Century Thing-Poem', *Eighteenth Century Studies*, 40/2 (Winter 2007), 1.
74. They share an extended play on the idea that 'beauty masked' is enhanced ('The Fancy hightens ev'ry Charm that's vail'd' (Arbuckle, *Snuff*, l. 177); 'We by the Sample, tho no more be seen, | Imagine all that's fair within the Skreen' ('Tartana, or the Plaid', ll. 191–2)). There are repeated comparisons between female beauty and the sky or the sun ('At least the fairest Scene the Heavens display, | A Starry Confluence in a Milky-way' (*Snuff*, ll. 245–6); 'So through *Hamilla*'s op'ned Plaid, we may | Behold her heavenly Face, and heaving milky Way' ('Tartana, or the Plaid', ll. 243–4). Both refer to epic scenes in which Venus protects Aeneas in battle; in *Snuff* a shield becomes a snuffbox, and in 'Tartana', her cloud becomes a plaid (ll. 298–302).

Paris at the divine beauty contest: 'To *Jove's* high Queen, and the Celestial
Maids, | E're he wou'd pass his Sentence, cry'd, *No Plaids*'.[75] There clearly is
a Scottish patriotism in the poem's criticism of 'base foreign fashions', and,
for Pittock, this is Jacobite and anti-English because of the symbolic meaning of the plaid, the garment of 'the disaffected part of the nation'.[76]

Arbuckle's *Glotta*, a topographical poem describing the valley of the
Clyde, responds to *Tartana*, when it pauses at Glasgow Green to describe a
group of girls, beautiful as those of 'th' Arcadian Plain', but for one flaw:

> What envious Pow'r then first contriv'd, or made
> That Foe to Beauty, and to Love, a Plaid?
> Destruction seize the guilty Garb, that holds
> Conceal'd such Charms in its malicious Folds.
> Of this, O Thyrsis, could thy Strains unshrine,
> Thy Saccharissa, how the Fair would shine![77]

This is done with a friendly wit, not only recalling Ramsay's 'Paris', but
playfully reworking the rhyme in Ramsay's lines: 'Let bright *Tartana*s hence-
forth ever shine, | And *Caledonian* Goddesses enshrine'.[78] Ramsay's 'Scots'
may not be quite a 'Foe to beauty', but Arbuckle, by his references to the
'Thyrsis' of Virgil's *Eclogues*, and to Edmund Waller's 'Sacharissa', suggests
that Scottish culture should be capable of incorporating classical or English
culture. The form of his own poem supports this point, as does the next
passage, where he describes the very Scottish game of golf in a comical
reworking of Addison's Latin poem on bowling, 'Sphaeristerium'.[79] This
does not mean, however, that *Glotta* represents union as simply Anglicization.
His previous poems had very little to identify them as Scottish, but this is
explicitly a Scottish poem that unites classical, English, and Scottish references. Its starting point may be Ramsay's much slighter 'Clyde's Welcome
to his Prince', which similarly deploys the voice of the Clyde's river-god.[80]
Its structure is borrowed from Pope's topographical poem *Windsor Forest*.
The broad scheme is to turn Pope's celebration of Stuart English culture
into a poem about Scottish Whig culture, and its reconciliation with England
in the Union. A panegyric to the Union is given to George Buchanan, the
Scottish Latin poet associated with radical Presbyterian Whiggism, with a
supposed support for 'king-killing', a figure potentially embarrassing to the

75. Ramsay. 'Tartana or the Plaid', ll. 277–8.   76. Pittock, *Poetry and Jacobite Politics*, 158.
77. Arbuckle, *Glotta*, ll. 121–6.   78. Ramsay, 'Tartana or the Plaid', ll. 357–8.
79. *Poems on Several Occasions, with a Dissertation upon the Roman Poets* (London: [E.Curll], 1718).
80. Ramsay, 'Clyde's Welcome to his Prince', in *Works*, i. 233–6.

'polite' Scottish Whigs of Arbuckle's generation.[81] The *Epistle* on Addison's death had emphasized the more radical Whig in Addison, but *Glotta* seeks to incorporate Buchanan into Addisonian 'polite' Whiggism.[82] It is an instance of the poem's central theme, the reconciliation of diverse elements, the 'Concordia Discors' (the theme also of *Windsor Forest*).[83] Arbuckle also firmly rejects the 'bought and sold for English gold' tradition of the opponents of unionist Whiggism by turning the familiar rhyme against the rebellious Jacobites ('those that grown in impious Actions bold, | Boast all their Merit Kings and Countries sold?').[84] *Glotta* is indeed an early contribution to the Whig interpretation of history, celebrating progress, recalling conflict and neglect in Scotland's past, placing union in a narrative of improvement that will bring liberty and prosperity.

Pittock's *Poetry and Jacobite Politics* is premised on an opposition between a Jacobite or 'typological' and a Whig or 'incremental' view of history, with the revival of Scots on the Jacobite side: it 'defied the idea of Union as progress'.[85] Ramsay's 'ferocious attacks on the South Sea scandal' are inscribed in 'a period of feverish Jacobite political activity', and in an anti-union tradition.[86] *Wealth or The Woody* (1720) is the first of these poems, a prophetic attack on the South Sea company six months before its collapse. The morality of the poem is a Horatian caution about greed and speculation, and it includes an ironic sub-version of Horace's 'Happy Man' ('Happy that man wha has thrawn up a main | Which makes some hundred thousands a' his ain'[87]). He is a speculator, whose distorted values are marked by his taste in drink: 'Closs may he bend Champain frae e'en to morn, | And look on cells of Tippony with scorn'[88] ('tippony' is 'the Scots pint'); but whose fate is the one Horace knew waited for all: 'I canna guess how rich fowk cam to die'.[89] Horace's *Epode II* similarly praised the home product against foreign luxury: 'Let the luxurious, lolling at their ease, | Call plaise and turbit from the distant seas' (Arbuckle's translation).[90]

81. Kidd, *Subverting Scotland's Past*, 40, 59–60.
82. Richard Holmes, 'James Arbuckle's *Glotta* (1721) and the Poetry of Allusion', *Journal for Eighteenth-Century Studies*, 35/1 (March 2012), 85–100.
83. E. R. Wasserman, *The Subtler Language: Critical Readings of Neoclassic and Romantic Poems* (Baltimore: Johns Hopkins University Press, 1959), 107.
84. Arbuckle, *Glotta*, ll. 97–8. Pittock, 'Allan Ramsay and the Decolonization of Genre', 329.
85. Pittock, *Poetry and Jacobite Politics*, 2, 152.
86. Pittock, 'Allan Ramsay and the Decolonization of Genre', 329.
87. Ramsay, *Wealth or the Woody, Works*, i, 152–8, ll. 105–6.
88. Ramsay, *Wealth or the Woody*, ll. 111–12.
89. Ramsay, *Wealth or the Woody*, l. 126. 'To braw Tippony bid adieu', 'Elegy on Maggy Johnston', in Ramsay, *Works*, i. 10.
90. Arbuckle, *Epode II*, in *Selected Works*, 81.

Criticism of the South Sea Company was certainly not limited to Tories and Jacobites; the most ferocious came from the 'Real' Whigs Trenchard and Gordon, and the Squadrone were later aligned with the 'Real' Whigs in the opposition to Walpole.[91] It is also difficult to see Ramsay as intending an 'anti-union' poem in the light of the companion pieces *The Prospect of Plenty* and *The Rise and Fall of Stocks*.[92] In the latter, the ruin was inflicted not by the English on the hapless Scots but on a 'nation' defined in unionist terms: 'Since Poortith o'er ilk head does hover | Frae John a Groat's House, South to Dover';[93] 'Sae Britain brought on a' her troubles, | By running daftly after bubles'.[94] The poem subscribes to a narrative of progress, the Bubble a salutary lesson enabling an optimistic vision of future prosperity, when 'The honest man shall be regarded, | And villains as they ought rewarded'.[95] It is a unionist vision, in which 'Lombard-street shall be replenisht' and 'A glorious sun shall soon arise, | To brighten up Britannia's skies'.[96] These lines are indistinguishable in tone from the ardently unionist panegyric with which Arbuckle concludes *Glotta*.

The Prospect of Plenty (1720) celebrated a proposed company to exploit Scotland's sea fishery, and formed a pair to *Wealth*, deliberately contrasting disastrous South Sea speculation with improvement at home ('Thus, by fair trading, North-Sea stock shall thrive'[97]). It did not seem antagonistic to Roxburghe, who, on 9 November 1720, wrote to Bennet that 'Allan Ramsay upon the North Sea has diverted me very much tonight'.[98] Its language resembles an extended passage in *Glotta* on Scotland's marine resources, both no doubt influenced by poets such as Dryden and Gay, in the descriptions not only of the water-gods Nereus (Ramsay) and Glotta (Arbuckle) but in piscine vocabulary generally. A more substantial sharing is in the treatment of progress. Ramsay's poem begins with 'the Caledonians lang supine' who have neglected 'that store which heav'n | In sic abundance to their hands has given'.[99] He looks to a future, 'Where schools polite shall lib'ral arts

91. Marie McMahon, *The Radical Whigs, John Trenchard and Thomas Gordon* (Lanham: University Press of America, 1990). James Thomson was later an opposition poet; see Haddington's 'opposition' poem *The Faithful Few* (Edinburgh, 1734), which praises Scottish Whigs in their 'Real Whig' opposition to Walpole.
92. Ramsay, *Works*, i. 158–66, 176–82.   93. Ramsay, *The Rise and Fall of Stocks*, ll. 15–16.
94. Ramsay, *The Rise and Fall of Stocks*, ll. 31–2.
95. Ramsay, *The Rise and Fall of Stocks*, ll. 179–80.
96. Ramsay, *The Rise and Fall of Stocks*, ll. 183–4.   97. Ramsay, *The Prospect of Plenty*, l. 69.
98. Roxburghe to Bennet, 9 November 1720, Bennet Letters, GD 205/31/25.
99. Ramsay, *The Prospect of Plenty*, ll. 5–6.

display, | And make auld barb'rous darkness fly away'.[100] *Glotta* similarly sees
a Scottish past of barbarity.[101] Ramsay's poem also resembles *Glotta* in seeing
improvement as a unionist project: 'But dawns the day sets Britain on her
feet, | Lang look'd for's come at last, and welcome be't'.[102] There was in fact
contemporary controversy over the fishery scheme, with some in Scotland
objecting to an English initiative that, they feared, would mean English
exploitation.[103] An alternative Scottish company was to be formed by
the Convention of the Royal Burghs. Ramsay's poem was inscribed to the
Convention, but it criticized those in Scotland who had objected to the
English plan. The 'bonny prospect' that has inspired the poet is greeted by 'a
grumbletonian', a Scot who fears ruin by the English ('The Southerns will
with Pith your project bauk'[104]). Ramsay is dismissive: 'Thus do the dubious
ever countermine, | With party wrangle, ilka fair design'.[105] He approaches
the project with an optimistic unionism: 'Will Britain's King or Parliament
gainstand | The universal profit of the land?'[106] There is 'Nae sep'rate interest'
between the countries who 'never mind wha serves or wha commands | But
baith alike consult the common weal'.[107] This unionism again resembles *Glotta*:

> The Realm in Int'rest as in Name be One:
> Impartial Riches flow in ev'ry Stream,
> And Thames and *Glotta* mutual Friendship claim.[108]

The idea of a backward Scotland, failing to develop, a barbarous nation
awaiting the improvement of Anglicization, was commonplace. The unionist
Defoe's *Caledonia* opened with 'Northern heights, where nature seldom
smiles'.[109] The unionism of Arbuckle and Ramsay is very different. Arbuckle
insisted that 'Our Glotta yet with justice lays her claim | To share his [Thames']
beauty, tho not wealth or fame';[110] and turned Defoe's image of Scottish
barbarity: 'There Mountains cap'd with everlasting Snow, | Defend from
Storms the fruitful Vales below'.[111] Much of *Glotta* is devoted to demonstrating

---

100. Ramsay, *The Prospect of Plenty*, ll. 231–2.   101. Arbuckle, *Glotta*, ll. 265–76.

102. Ramsay, 'The Prospect of Plenty', ll. 52–3.

103. Bob Harris, 'Scotland's Herring Fisheries and the Prosperity of the Nation, *c*.1660–1760', *Scottish Historical Review*, 79/207, pt 1 (April 2000), 39–60.

104. Ramsay, *The Prospect of Plenty*, l. 82.   105. Ramsay, *The Prospect of Plenty*, ll. 84–5.

106. Ramsay, *The Prospect of Plenty*, ll.88–9.   107. Ramsay, *The Prospect of Plenty*, ll. 95–6.

108. Arbuckle, *Glotta* ll. 326–8.

109. Defoe, *Caledonia*, l. 1. Kidd, *Subverting Scotland's Past*, 48; Robert Crawford writes of 'suppression of native tradition in a process of cultural conversion that was thought of as a move from the barbarous Scottish to the polite British' (*Devolving English Literature*, 22).

110. Arbuckle, *Glotta*, ll. 21–2.   111. Arbuckle, *Glotta*, ll. 25–6.

the strength of Scotland's distinctive culture, from architecture (the Duke of
Hamilton's palace, Lord Belhaven's hanging garden at Barncleugh, Glasgow's
St Mungo's cathedral) to Scottish poets Buchanan, Maitland, and Douglas,
to scientific study in Scottish universities.[112] It is relevant that Arbuckle's Dublin
career began with a patriotic project (as 'Hibernicus') to challenge English
literary dominance.[113] But he did not see that as incompatible with Irish
dependence on Britain. Political discourse in contemporary Dublin was
dominated by this kind of patriotism, by campaigns such as that to promote
Irish linen.[114] This was in terms similar to 'Tartana's' defence of the plaid, and
Ramsay's preface to The Evergreen, where he criticized 'imported Trimming
upon our cloaths'.[115] A Scottish patriotism working within 'Britishness' was
widespread. William Hamilton's patriotic project of publishing Blind Hary's
Wallace depended on the support of the unionist Bennet.[116] Sir John Clerk
has been described as 'pro-Union and pro-Scotland'.[117] Such hybrid patriotism did not preclude occasional anti-English feeling on the part of Scottish
unionists. In the last years of Queen Anne, Scottish Whigs were so disquieted
by Tory policies (on religion and tax) that there were serious moves for the
Union's dissolution (this was the period of Ramsay's most anti-union poem,
the elegy on Pitcairne).[118] Colin Kidd says that unionism generally has been
about 'maintenance of semi-autonomy or nationhood within Union'.[119]

   Gerard Carruthers recognizes the diversity of Ramsay and his contemporaries, describing them as 'polyphonic... prone to try... the different options
of identity open to them'.[120] The analysis of 'Tartana' and the South Sea
poems shows him close to the Whiggish unionism of Arbuckle. For Pittock,
however, the Jacobite and anti-union notes represent the real Ramsay. David
Daiches finds him simply 'mixed and confused', and condemns him for a

---

112. Arbuckle, Selected Works, 29–30.   113. Arbuckle, Selected Works, 42.
114. Arbuckle, Selected Works, p. xxx.
115. See also Ramsay, 'On our Ladies being dressed in Scots Manufactory', in Works, iii. 78.
116. William Hamilton to Bennet, 31 May 1721, Bennet Letters, GD 205/37; Pittock, Poetry and
      Jacobite Politics, 152.
117. Crawford, Devolving English Literature, 50.
118. Daniel Szechi, 'The Politics of "Persecution": Scots Episcopalian Toleration and the Harley
      Ministry, 1710–12', in W. J. Sheils (ed.), Toleration and Persecution, Studies in Church History,
      21 (Ecclesiastical History Society; Oxford: Blackwell, 1984), 282–3.
119. Colin Kidd, Union and Unionisms: Political Thought in Scotland 1500–2000 (Cambridge:
      Cambridge University Press, 2008), 5–7.
120. Gerard Carruthers, 'James Thomson and Eighteenth-Century Scottish Literary Identity', in
      Richard Terry (ed.), James Thomson: Essays for the Tercentenary (Liverpool: Liverpool University
      Press, 2000), 173.

betrayal of 'Scots' authenticity.[121] The advantage of looking at Ramsay in relation to Arbuckle is not to place him decisively on the spectrum of political and national options, but to draw attention to aspects that a focus on his 'Scottishness' might overlook, to what brings Ramsay closer to Hutcheson as 'father of the Scottish Enlightenment' than to the Jacobite rebels of 1715. He and Arbuckle shared a support for the 'de-Calvinization' of the Scottish church in the movement towards Moderatism, an embrace of the world in place of Stoic and Christian asceticism. They found a model of a secular ethic in the moderate Epicureanism of the Horatian 'Happy Man'. Above all they shared the influence of Addisonian politeness, the essence of which was a mistrust of absolutes, a commitment to learning by exchange, or, as Shaftesbury put it, to 'polish one another, and rub off our Corners and rough Sides by a sort of amicable Collision'.[122] A long tradition of Scottish criticism, from Carlyle through Daiches to Pittock, is more concerned with opposition than 'amicable collision', setting 'Scots' poetry against Whiggism, Union, and Enlightenment, a resistance of national authenticity to Anglicizing artifice.[123] In Ramsay and Arbuckle, as in their patrons, these elements are not opposed but combined. Bennet in 1720 looked forward to a visit from Roxburghe and Bowmont, when he hoped that they would dance 'to the bagpipe'.[124] Bagpipes no music? On the contrary, their music was—at times—just what unionist Scotland wanted to hear.

---

121. Daiches, *The Paradox of Scottish Culture*, 27.
122. Earl of Shaftesbury, *Characteristics of Men, Manners, Opinions, Times*, ed. Lawrence Klein (Cambridge: Cambridge University Press, 1999), 31.
123. Thomas Carlyle, unsigned review of John Gibson Lockhart's *Life of Burns*, *Edinburgh Review* (December 1828), 288; Daiches, *The Paradox of Scottish Culture*. On Enlightenment interest in 'Scots', see F. W. Freeman, 'The Intellectual Background of the Vernacular Revival before Burns', *Studies in Scottish Literature*, 16/1 (1981), 160–87. For a view of Ramsay that unites 'Scots' and Enlightenment, see Newman, 'The Scots Songs of Allan Ramsay'.
124. Robert Wood to Bennet, 4 June 1720, Bennet Letters, GD 205/35/5/3.

4

James Thomson and 'Rule, Britannia'

Ralph McLean

While John Arbuthnot can reasonably be identified as the creator of the archetypically English figure of John Bull, the same cannot be said for the role of his fellow Scot James Thomson (1700–48) in establishing Britannia as an icon of Britishness. What can be said, however, is that the image of Britannia represented in Thomson's ode 'Rule, Britannia' became the dominant image of the expanding British Empire. Just as Bram Stoker's Dracula was not the first vampire, but was so vivid in its realization that it superseded all those that came before, so too did Thomson's reimagining of Britannia overshadow previous incarnations.[1] In effect this Britannia 2.0 endured in the nation's psyche, enjoying sustained exposure from its first appearance in 1740 right up to the present day, when its performance remains an enduring favourite on the last night of the proms. As a cornerstone of British pride and as a symbol of the country's naval supremacy in an expansive global empire, it is perhaps somewhat ironic that the creator of this icon should be a Scotsman, from a nation whose members found themselves caught uneasily during the eighteenth century between subaltern status at the Empire's English core and overseas as welcome co-equal partners in its management. However, an analysis of Thomson's motivations for utilizing

---

1. David Armitage identifies it as the 'most lasting expression of the conception of the Britain and the British Empire that emerged in the 1730s' (David Armitage, *The Ideological Origins of the British Empire* (Cambridge: Cambridge University Press, 2000), 173).

Britannia in his works reveals a man who was eager to further the cause of British integration in the aftermath of the Union of 1707, but who was also concerned that the Scottish contribution to the newly established British state be duly recognized. This chapter will therefore assess 'Rule, Britannia' in four main areas. First, I shall briefly look at the image of Britannia, and how she was used in British literature prior to Thomson's reimagining of her. Second, I shall investigate Britannia as she appears in a number of Thomson's works, as she was a muse to whom he returned throughout his poetic career. This point feeds into my third theme, which is to provide a sharper focus on the ode itself, in order to demonstrate how Thomson utilizes the image in *Alfred: A Masque* (1740), where it originally appeared. Finally, I shall look at the impact of the ode on eighteenth-century British culture with the aim of assessing the extent of its penetration into popular consciousness.[2]

The earliest extant image of Britannia is Roman in origin, but is to be found in south-west Turkey. Located on a rock relief, her first appearance is not one of triumph and patriotism, but rather one of defeat and subjugation. Britannia, clad as an amazon, is physically overpowered by the Emperor Claudius, who is in the process of forcing her to the ground as he readies himself to strike her.[3] Britannia's first appearance in a naval context can be traced to the Elizabethan polymath John Dee's *General and Rare Memorials Pertaining to the Perfect Art of Navigation* (1577), which in its frontispiece contains a small figure of Britannia kneeling by the shore, who urges Elizabeth I to protect her empire and strengthen her navy.[4] It is significant that at this point Britannia is still a passive figure: she is not the protector, she is the one in need of protection. However, the defeat of the Spanish Armada during the reign of Elizabeth seems to have accelerated the transformation of Britannia into the role of naval protectress.

Henry Peacham's book of emblems *Minerva Britanna* (1612) was the first to depict Britannia's metamorphosis. Peacham's woodcut has her repelling a naval invasion, and, while once she was 'As then their [the Romans] captive, and abandon'd quite', the tone has now changed to bombastic proclamation as 'Usurping Roome [*sic*], stands now in aw of thee'.[5] This version of Britannia

2. Herbert M. Atherton, *Political Prints in the Age of Hogarth* (Oxford: Clarendon Press, 1974), 91.
3. Kenan T. Erim, 'A New Relief Showing Claudius and Britannia from Aphrodisias', *Britannia*, 13 (1982), 279–81.
4. John Dee, *General and Rare Memorials Pertaining to the Perfect Art of Navigation* (London: John Daye, 1577).
5. Henry Peacham, *Minerva Britanna* (London: Wa: Dight, 1612), no pagination.

is also more truly pan-Britannic than previous representations, reflecting the desires of the ruling monarch James VI and I to bind Scotland and England together in closer union.[6] Indeed, Peacham dedicated the work to James's son Henry, the Prince of Wales, although, if this was an attempt to seek future patronage from the 18-year-old prince, it was ultimately in vain, as Henry died shortly after the publication of the book.[7] The premature death of the future king anticipated exactly the position that Thomson found himself in a century or so later when he dedicated *Alfred* to George II's son Frederick.

Britannia's position as guardian of the nation evolved throughout the seventeenth century. John Roettier created a series of medals commemorating naval battles and the Treaty of Breda signed in 1667; here Britannia is depicted sitting at the foot of a rock and overseeing her fleets at sea.[8] According to Samuel Pepys, Britannia's appearance was modelled on Frances Teresa Stuart, whom Charles II desired to have as his mistress.[9] Pepys noted in his diary that 'at my goldsmith's [I] did observe the King's new Medall, where in little there is Mrs Stewards face, as well done as ever I saw anything in my whole life I think—and a pretty thing it is that he should choose her face to represent Britannia by'.[10] The notion that Britannia was a guardian of the British fleet draws on the the the myth that Neptune surrendered his sovereignty of the sea to her, most obviously through the transferral of his symbol of power—the trident. Indeed, the political reformer John Cartwright later envisaged that just such a scene be carved in stone for his proposed temple dedicated to the successes of the British navy in 1802: 'On the new-born island is seen *Britannia*, receiving a sceptre from the hand of *Neptune*, terminating at top in the form of a rudder, on which is wrought the likeness of his own sceptre; a type as it should seem, of her future greatness of the ocean.'[11]

6. Keith M. Brown, 'The Vanishing Emperor: British Kingship and its Decline 1603–1707', in Roger A. Mason (ed.), *Scots and Britons: Scottish Political Thought and the Union of 1603* (Cambridge: Cambridge University Press, 1994), 80–1.
7. Peacham, *Minerva Britanna*, no pagination.
8. Jenny Uglow, *A Gambling Man: Charles II and the Restoration* (London: Faber and Faber, 2009), 402.
9. Stephen N. Zwicker, *Lines of Authority: Politics and English Literary Culture, 1649–1689* (Ithaca, NY: Cornell University Press, 1993), 118–19.
10. Samuel Pepys, *The Diary of Samuel Pepys*, ed. Robert Latham and William Matthews, 11 vols (London: Harper Collins, 2000), viii. 83.
11. John Cartwright, *The Trident: Or, the National Policy of Naval Celebration* (London: J. Johnson, J. White & T. Payne, 1802), 99–100; John W. Osborne, *John Cartwright* (Cambridge: Cambridge University Press, 1972), 68.

In 1672—during the reign of Charles II—Britannia made her first appearance on coinage since the time of the Roman occupation of Britain.[12] The newly formed Bank of England continued this trend at its foundation in 1694 by choosing the image of Britannia for its seal and placing her on their notes, which helped to consolidate her position as a figure of authority.[13] This financial link is important for understanding Thomson's view of Britannia, as the commercial interests of the nation were frequently folded into his conception of Britannia as an allegory for the nation. It should also be noted here that Britannia during the sixteenth and often during the seventeenth centuries had been a symbol of England exclusively, rather than associated with Britain as a whole. The coins issued in 1672 included Scottish iconography in Britannia's shield, which incorporated the crosses of St Andrew and St George.[14] As John Giuseppi noted, her appearance was not 'as a captive Barbarian maid, but as the tutelary goddess of a sovereign state'.[15] However, the first time that she appears on a Bank of England note, the shield carries only the cross of St George.[16] As we shall see, Thomson was to be instrumental in shifting the focus away from an English representation towards recasting Britannia as a symbol of inclusive Britishness. The emphasis henceforth was on naval supremacy and imperial expansion, though tempered with pride in liberty and a desire for peace, albeit a pax Britannica.

Two years after the masque of *Alfred*, an anonymous political pamphlet, *Britannia in Mourning* (1742), appeared in the form of a dialogue between two men, one of whom is a staunch patriot lamenting the current state of British affairs while imagining a Britannia from a bygone age: 'See the Riches of the World landed at her Feet: see *Liberty* supported by her on one Side, and the Gorgon *Tyranny* trampled upon on the other. See the *Great States of Europe* differently represented, courting her Smiles, and suing for her Alliance or Protection.'[17] Even during the latter part of the eighteenth

12. Virginia Hewitt, 'Britannia', in *The Oxford Dictionary of National Biography* <http://www.oxforddnb.com/view/article/68196?docPos=1> (accessed 9 January 2016).
13. Bank of England Archive, 'Britannia and the Bank 1694–1961', ADM 30/59, pp. 1–2.
14. Thomas Snelling, *A View of the Silver Coin and Coinage of England* (London: T. Snelling, 1762), 34, 36.
15. John Giuseppi, *The Bank of England* (London: Evan Brothers, 1966), 18.
16. Bank of England, 'Britannia and the Bank', p. 2. For a discussion on why Britannia was chosen as the Bank's symbol, see Valerie Hamilton and Martin Parker, *Daniel Defoe and the Bank of England: The Dark Arts of Projectors* (Alresford: Zero Books, 2016).
17. *Britannia in Mourning: Or, a Review of the Politicks and Conduct of the Court of Great Britain* (London: J. Huggonson, 1742), 5.

century, however, Britannia was not solely a figure of strength or victory. Often she was used to represent suffering or inequality in the nation, as on occasions where she appears to be beaten, abused, and, helpless against her enemies.[18] During the Seven Years War, for instance, she appeared with the other great patriotic figure of the age, John Bull, in the 1757 work *A View of the Assassination of the Lady of John Bull*, where John Bull watches on helplessly as Britannia is mutilated by French soldiers on the seashore.[19]

The perceived leniency of the Bute administration towards France and Spain during the negotiations that resulted in the 1763 Treaty of Paris provided an opportunity, not just to depict Britannia as a victim, but also to indulge in scotophobia—one of the most prominent strands in the political culture of the 1760s. Although the two countries were now joined in political union, Britannia herself could still be deployed as an exclusively English symbol.[20] In the print, Lord Bute—Britain's first Scottish Prime Minister—who is clad in Highland dress, threatens to stab Britannia in her heart unless she consents to the terms on offer. Britannia laments: 'What a situation I am in, sold by a Scot and purchased by France and Spain. O where's my Pitt.'[21]

Thomson's most famous invocation of Britannia was, of course, in 'Rule, Britannia'. However, he had employed her before this in *Britannia, A Poem*, first published in January 1729. In some versions of the poem the statement 'Written in the year 1719' is added. The suggested reasons for the appearance of this date range from Thomson's desire to make the poem less politically incendiary by distancing its creation from the then current animosity between Britain and Spain, which is the main thrust of the poem, to the suggestion that 1719 is merely a mis-transcription of the Roman numerals for 1729.[22] However, James Sambrook advances an interesting theory that Thomson may have chosen the date very deliberately, because 1719 witnessed

---

18. Madge Dresser, 'Britannia', in Harry Goldbourne (ed.), *Race and Ethnicity: Solidarities and Communities* (London: Routledge, 2001), 64–5. For a discussion on the treatment of the female body in the figure of Britannia, see Kathleen Wilson, *The Island Race: Englishness, Empire and Gender in the Eighteenth Century* (London: Routledge, 2003), 93–4.

19. M. John Cardwell, *Arts and Arms: Literature, Politics and Patriotism during the Seven Years War* (Manchester: Manchester University Press, 2004), 143.

20. John Richard Moores, *Representations of France in English Satirical Prints* (Basingstoke: Palgrave Macmillan, 2015), 187. For more on Britannia and her use in anti-Bute imagery, see Tamara L. Hunt, *Defining John Bull: Political Caricature and National Identity in Late Georgian England* (Aldershot: Ashgate, 2003), 122.

21. Moores, *Representation of France*, 187.

22. J. E. Wells, 'Thomson's *Britannia*; Issues, Attribution, Date, Variants', *Modern Philology*, 40 (1942), 46–9.

the only Spanish military invasion of Britain, when a small army supporting
a Jacobite rising was routed by the Hanoverians in north-west Scotland.[23]
The event itself resulted in a swelling of anti-Spanish feeling among the
Scottish Whigs when Thomson was an undergraduate at Edinburgh
University.[24]

The poem was in fact written at a time when public opinion in Britain
was calling for retaliation against Spanish interference in British trade in
the Spanish American colonies. British ships were being seized by Spanish
coastguards, and the two countries became embroiled in a war that neither
appeared to pursue with any vigour. In terms of engagements, a failed
British effort to blockade the port of Porto Bello was matched by the
Spanish failure to recapture Gibraltar. In Britain, the Whig opposition
attempted to stir British patriotic fervour in order to push for retaliation.
William Pulteney, a leader of the opposition, complained in 1729

> of the monstrous expence at which we have annually been of late neither to
> make war nor secure peace...the losses sustained by our merchants in the
> Indies, the insults offered there to them by the Spaniards, the cruelties exer-
> cised upon them and the injuries they sustained unrevenged; the loss of our
> fleet and so many brave seamen before Porto Bello under Admiral Hosier,
> who was sent thither with his hands tied up and was forced to suffer the galleons
> to pass under his nose unmolested.[25]

This response was typical of those who believed that Walpole's government
was operating an overly pacific foreign policy. James Sambrook believes that
the publication of *Britannia* in January of 1729 was therefore timed to coin-
cide with the opening of a new parliamentary session and was designed to
arouse public opinion.[26] Despite criticisms of his premiership and his handling of the war, Walpole emerged from the potential crisis with advanta-
geous terms for Britain in the Treaty of Seville, which was signed at the
close of the year.[27]

23. Jeremy Black, *Politics and Foreign Policy in the Age of George I, 1714–1727* (Farnham: Ashgate,
    2014), 118–19.
24. Bruce Lenman, *The Jacobite Risings in Britain, 1689–1746* (London: Eyre Metheun, 1980),
    189–95.
25. Lord Hervey, *Memoirs*, ed. Romney Sedgwick, 3 vols (London: Eyre Methuen, 1931), i. 107.
26. James Thomson, *Liberty, The Castle of Indolence, and Other Poems*, ed. James Sambrook (Oxford:
    Clarendon Press, 1986), 18.
27. W. A. Speck, *Stability and Strife: England, 1714–1760* (Cambridge, MA: Harvard University Press,
    1977), 232.

The poem itself is told from the perspective of Britannia, sitting by the shores and lamenting the inactivity of the British in the face of Spanish incursions:

> Deep in her anxious Heart, revolving sad
> Bare was her throbbing bosom to the gale,
> That hoarse, and hollow, from the bleak surge blew;
> Loose flow'd her tresses; rent her azure robe.[28]

Thomson describes her—though she is currently in a state of despondency—as the 'Queen of Nations',[29] who through his poem issues a rallying cry to all Britons, attempting to energize them with patriotic pride in national achievements, past military glories, and a sense of destiny. Britannia also plays upon the national love of liberty, which is currently threatened by Spanish aggression. Part of Thomson's sense of national pride is bound up with mercantile activity. Trade and commerce are powerful symbols of British national identity for him, and are inextricably bound together with a sense of maritime patriotism as personified in Britannia:

> And what, my thoughtless sons, should fire you more,
> Than when your well-earn'd empire of the deep
> The least beginning injury receives?
> What better cause can call your lightning forth?
> Your thunder wake? Your dearest life demand?
> What better cause, than when your country sees
> The sly destruction at her vitals aim'd?
> For oh it much imports you, 'tis your all,
> To keep your Trade intire, intire the force,
> And honour of your Fleets, o'er that to watch,
> Even with a hand severe, and jealous eye.
> In intercourse be gentle, generous, just,
> By wisdom polish'd, and of manners fair;
> But on the sea be terrible, untam'd,
> Unconquerable still.[30]

The desire to protect property and to maintain freedom of the Oceans forms a major part of Britannia's call to arms.

As with later works, when Thomson expresses a British identity he is careful to represent both Scottish and English involvement in a shared

---

28. Thomson, *Britannia, A Poem*, in Thomson, *Liberty, The Castle of Indolence, and Other Poems*, ed. Sambrook, 21–30, ll. 3–6.
29. Thomson, *Britannia, A Poem*, ll. 13–14.   30. Thomson, *Britannia, A Poem*, ll. 168–80.

enterprise. For example, the most obvious chest-thumping display of national pride in the face of Spanish military incursions is to raise the spectre of the defeat of the Spanish Armada. However, as this took place in 1588 and directly involved only the English, it would appear to be taking something of a liberty to project this as a genuinely British reference point. Nevertheless, Thomson includes a Scottish contribution first by referring to those who fought as Britons,[31] and then by alluding to the destruction wrought by the rugged coastline of Scotland's northern islands on the bedraggled remnants of the Armada:

> Round the glad isle, snatch'd by the vengeful blast,
> The scatter'd remnants drove; on the blind shelve,
> And pointed rock, that marks the indented shore,
> Relentless dash'd, where loud the Northern main
> Howls thro' the fractur'd *Caledonian* isles.[32]

This establishes a mythical element of divine intervention to the extent that Britannia herself sends winds and storms to destroy the Spanish fleet. Destiny is propelling 'Britain' forward to its status as the premier maritime nation.

Thomson also incorporates themes here that would reappear in *Alfred* over a decade later; most obviously praise for the potential of Frederick, Prince of Wales. By the time of *Alfred*, Thomson was committed to his camp and even dedicated his poem *Liberty* to him. In 1737 Thomson had been awarded an annual pension of £100 by Frederick.[33] However, in 1729 his praise is mixed with appreciation for the prevailing royal authority. In *Britannia*, Frederick is the '*Royal Youth*, | A freight of future glory',[34] who according to Thomson is interconnected with the British golden age of mercantile expansion. This also looks forward to a key theme in *Alfred*, where the future greatness of the monarch has yet to be realized, but, when this inevitably comes to pass, it will usher in a golden age for the country.

Unusually for Thomson, *Britannia* appeared anonymously, although part of the reason for this may have been the fact that Thomson had previously enjoyed the patronage of government politicians, and here he appeared to be backing the opposition. When his name was revealed as the author, Walpole's supporters latched on to what they saw as Thomson's ingratitude to those who had previously supported him. He had dedicated *Sophonisba*

31. Thomson, *Britannia, A Poem*, l. 75.   32. Thomson, *Britannia, A Poem*, ll. 85–9.
33. Alexander Scott, 'Arne's Alfred', *Music and Letters*, 55 (1974), 387.
34. Thomson, *Britannia, A Poem*, ll. 16–17.

to Queen Caroline,[35] and had been appointed as the travelling tutor to Charles Richard Talbot, who was the son of the Solicitor General.[36] *Britannia* continued to remain politically relevant for a number of years after its publication. When conflict with Spain was renewed in the War of Jenkins's Ear, Andrew Millar published an English translation of Milton's *Manifesto of the Lord Protector* (1738) 'Wherein is shewn the Reasonableness of the Cause of this Republic against the Depredations of the Spaniards'. The text included a quotation from *Britannia* on the title page, and a full reprinting of the work as an appendix.[37]

The menace of the Spanish military was still prevalent when *Alfred: A Masque* first appeared in 1740. Thomson was not the sole author of *Alfred*, it was in fact the product of a collaboration with his fellow Anglo-Scottish poet David Mallet (*c.*1705–65). It is still unclear how *Alfred* was constructed by the two men, as the earliest newspaper reports of the time attributed the words exclusively to Thomson, but the advertisement to the revised edition of the work of 1751 carried only Mallet's name. By the time that Mallet's collected works appeared in 1759 he appeared to have claimed 'Rule, Britannia' as his own.[38] In the advertisement to the masque Mallet notes that in revising it he was unable to 'retain, of my friend's part, more than three or four single speeches, and a part of one song'.[39] However, there does appear to have been early agreement that the ode was Thomson's creation. For example, the *Charmer* (1752) names him as the composer, along with other pieces by him that are accurate in their attribution.[40]

The association of Alfred with Frederick the Prince of Wales had already been established before the masque. In 1735 Frederick had erected a statue of Alfred by the sculptor John Michael Rysback in the garden of his London house, which bore an inscription championing him as the founder of the country's constitutional liberty.[41] This is echoed in the masque itself when Alfred swears, 'to build on an eternal base | On liberty and laws, the public weal'.[42] The position of Alfred in the masque is in fact similar to the position of Frederick, a figure whose power lies in the future. These allusions were

35. James Thomson, *The Tragedy of Sophonisba* (London: A. Millar, 1730), 3–4.
36. James Sambrook, *James Thomson: 1700–1748, A Life* (Oxford: Clarendon Press, 1991), 75.
37. John Milton, *A Manifesto of the Lord Protector* (London: A. Millar, 1738), 1, 31–9.
38. Mary Jane W. Scott, *James Thomson, Anglo-Scot* (Athens, GA: University of Georgia Press, 1988), 231.
39. David Mallet, *The Works of David Mallet*, 3 vols (London: A. Millar, 1759), iii, p. ii.
40. J.G., *The Charmer: A Choice Collection of Songs, Scots and English* (Edinburgh: J. Yair, 1752), 130.
41. Sambrook, *James Thomson*, 203.
42. James Thomson, *Alfred: A Masque* (London: A. Millar, 1740), 19.

certainly not lost on the prince's contemporaries. One anonymous writer, under the name of 'Philomathes', wrote in the *London Magazine* of August 1740 that the Prince of Wales's patronage of a masque celebrating the great king to whom we owed our spirit of liberty was a sort of pledge, 'that he will endeavour to build the publick Weal on *Liberty and Laws*'. For Philomathes, this '*Spirit of Liberty* . . . has for so many Ages animated the Breast of every *true Briton*'.[43]

As the performance was written as a short masque, it is very light on action. Alfred himself has just been defeated by the Danes and is currently in hiding, where he is being sheltered by the shepherd Corin and his wife Emma. In the course of the masque, Alfred meets a hermit who offers him a vision of national glories yet to be realized by the nation of England. This English view is reinforced by a train of spirits who appear prophesying success—Edward III, Queen Elizabeth, and William III. This list of monarchs of England is, however, brought into alignment with the idea of Britain. For example, in his vision of Edward III he specifically states that, 'Beneath his standard, Britain shall go forth'.[44] This is no accidental appearance though as the hermit goes on to say:

> In this Edward's time,
> Warm'd by his courage, by his honor rais'd,
> High flames the British spirit, like the sun,
> To shine o'er half the globe.[45]

The appearance of William is far more clear-cut in a British sense, as he arrives at a time when England and Scotland were on the brink of ruin. As Thomson viewed it, the Glorious Williamite Revolution laid the foundation for Britain to flourish in the post-Union period. While Alfred ponders these ghosts of Britain's future, the Earl of Devon arrives with news that he has won a decisive battle against the Danes. To celebrate this victory a bard appears and sings 'Rule, Britannia'; and the action concludes with the hermit predicting a glittering future of British maritime supremacy. In true Thomsonian style, trade and industry are vital to this British future, as the hermit announces: 'I see thy commerce, *Britain*, grasp the world.'[46] This echoes the ode itself, which envisages a future where 'Thy cities shall

43. *The London Magazine and Monthly Chronologer* (August 1740), 393.
44. Thomson, *Alfred: A Masque*, 30.   45. Thomson, *Alfred: A Masque*, 31.
46. Thomson, *Alfred: A Masque*, 43.

with commerce shine'.[47] The continual expansion of the British Empire is also forecast:

> See, where beyond the vast Atlantic surge,
> By boldest keels untouch'd, a dreadful space!
> Shores, yet unfound, arise! In youthful prime,
> With towering forests, mighty rivers crown'd!
> These stoop to Britain's thunder.[48]

Although it is the Danes who are ostensibly presented as the external enemies in *Alfred*, the current national enemy, the Spaniards, lurked behind the depiction of the 'Danes'. The appearance of Elizabeth is significant in this regard, because, as before, it provided an opportunity for a further direct reference to the defeat of the Spanish Armada. The hermit prophesizes that Queen Elizabeth

> shall rouse *Britannia's* naval soul,
> Shall greatly ravish from insulting *Spain*,
> The world-commanding scepter of the deep.[49]

'Rule, Britannia' would go on to enjoy a longevity that far outstripped the original masque. Thomas Arne (1710–78), the man who composed the rousing music to accompany Thomson's words, revived *Alfred* in 1745, with 'Rule, Britannia' as the grand finale.[50] Indeed, a large part of the enduring appeal of the ode is precisely because of Arne's musical contribution. Even to those on the European mainland, the music appeared to conjure a feeling that was quintessentially British. A century later Richard Wagner would recognize the first eight notes of 'Rule, Britannia' as an expression of Britain's national character, and he set himself the task of composing an overture with Arne's music as the motif.[51] As the popularity of 'Rule, Britannia' grew, it was sold in the streets in broadsides and was performed, as it is today, in concerts. It was sung in theatres by actors and audiences together, and, as Tim Fulford notes, served to unite the upper classes in their boxes with the common people watching from the gods.[52] It was also frequently employed

---

47. Thomson, *Alfred: A Masque*, 43.   48. Thomson, *Alfred: A Masque*, 43.
49. Thomson, *Alfred: A Masque*, 34.
50. James Thomson and David Mallet, *Alfred: An Opera. Altered from the Play Written by Mr Thomson and Mr Mallett* (London: A. Millar, 1745), 20–1.
51. W. H. Cummings, *Dr Arne and Rule, Britannia* (London: Novello and Co., 1912), 133.
52. Tim Fulford, 'Britannia's Heart of Oak: Thomson, Garrick and the Language of Eighteenth-Century Patriotism', in Richard Terry (ed.), *James Thomson: Essays for the Tercentenary* (Liverpool: Liverpool University Press, 2000), 197.

as the climax of dramatic entertainments that were designed to commemorate naval successes. In 1794, following the battle of the 'Glorious First of June', Admiral Howe's victory over Revolutionary France's navy was celebrated with a performance at Drury Lane. In the aftermath of the battle, the French also claimed a victory, for, despite their loss of ships to the British forces, their fleet held off the Royal Navy long enough for a vital grain shipment to reach France.[53] Nonetheless, the encounter was deemed to be such a success in Britain that the Drury Lane performance included a re-creation of the battle using model ships and a water tank. At the conclusion of the celebration there was a display of fireworks, including a set that spelled out the words Rule Britannia in capital letters while the song itself was sung by all the performers.[54]

As the popularity of 'Rule, Britannia' grew, the ode became a target for widespread imitation, emulation, and parody. While Britain was drawn further into a war with France in the 1790s, the philologist James Adams offered a counterpart to 'Rule, Britannia' entitled 'Gallia Rule the Waves'. In a prose introduction he set out the importance of Britain's separation from mainland Europe, a divine location that afforded the island many benefits. 'The Sea stops the progress of Invaders: the Sea alone, whilst *Britannia rules the waves*, has protected the island from modern Plunderers, from Rebels and Regicides, from impious and sacrilegious Wretches.'[55] Adopting an obvious mirror image of the heavenly sanctioned position of Britain, the song opens with 'When Discord late by Hell's command, | Arose in rebel Gaul's domain'.[56] The ultimate perversion of the song is to present an enslaved and conquered Europe should the French prevail in the war, with the chorus declaring: 'Rule Gallia; Gallia rule the waves, | And Europe ever shall be slaves'.[57]

While Adams believed that the sea had protected Britain from 'Rebels', the Jacobite challenge that had struck such fear into the heart of the establishment had brought a 'King from over the water' and drew almost exclusively on home-grown support. Despite the associations of 'Rule, Britannia' with the Hanoverian Whig establishment—albeit with the reversionary interest of Frederick, Prince of Wales—there was, perhaps surprisingly, an attempt by

---

53. *The Naval Chronicle*, i. *1793–1798*, ed. Nicholas Tracy (London: Chatham, 1998), 89.
54. *The Salopian Journal*, 9 July 1794.
55. James Adams, *Rule Britannia or the Flattery of Free Subjects, Paraphrased and Expounded* (London: n.p., 1798), 15. Adams also provided a Latin translation of 'Rule Britannia', which he believed to be the first of its kind.
56. Adams, *Rule Britannia*, 11.   57. Adams, *Rule Britannia*, 11.

the Jacobites to wrest the image of Britannia away from the Hanoverians and return it to the Stuarts.[58] The Jacobite version employed some of the imagery of the original transposed to support Charles Edward Stuart's claims to the throne:

> When royal Charles by Heaven's command
> Arrived in Scotland's noble Plain;
> Thus spoke the Warrior, the warrior of the Land,
> And Guardian Angels sung this strain;
> Go on Brave Youth, go combat & succeed,
> For Thou shall't conquer, 'tis decreed.[59]

The first thing to note between the two poems is that 'Heaven's command' has been retained in the Jacobite version. In this instance, however, it is used to reinforce the Jacobite belief in the divine right of kings through Charles's Stuart lineage. The patriotism in evidence here is also more overtly Scottish than British. However, there is also a juxtaposition of the image of the 'Warrior of the Land', who fills the role of the terrestrial Scottish military figure, in opposition to the oceanic British manifestation of the warrior protectress. The Guardian Angels line is identical to Thomson's version, probably because it effectively lends itself to Jacobite messianic prophecy, and therefore can remain unchanged. The final two lines, in place of the famous Rule Britannia refrain, are entirely altered from the original, almost to the extent that they are mirror images—one celebrating the unconquerable status of British people, the other championing the conquering spirit of the displaced Stuart monarch. In further adaptations of 'Rule, Britannia' by the Jacobites, an aggressive militarism is invoked in order to assert the authority of the deposed monarch: 'Rule, Britannia, Britannia rise and fight, | Restore your injured Monarch's right.'[60] However, not all pro-Jacobite interactions with Britannia were militaristic. A print that appeared in 1749, *The Agreeable Contrast*, had the Chevalier sitting in a library with Britannia beside him, looking at the Magna Carta while the works of John Locke are nearby. Underneath the image are the words 'Here hapless Britain tells her mournful

58. Murray Pittock believes that this reclamation of British iconography in the name of the Stuarts was reciprocated by the Whigs, who were in the process of seizing back 'God save the King' from the Jacobites: Murray Pittock, *Poetry and Jacobite Politics in Eighteenth-Century Britain and Ireland* (Cambridge: Cambridge University Press, 1994), 83–4.
59. *Jacobite Minstrelsy* (Glasgow: R. Griffin & Co., 1828), 350.
60. Cummings, *Dr Arne and Rule, Britannia*, 130.

Tales, | And may, again, till *One* prevails'.[61] Here laws and liberty are the dominant themes of Jacobite engagement with Britannia.

Despite this Jacobite effort to link liberty and Britannia with their cause, in his poem *Liberty* (1735–6) Thomson is at pains to disassociate himself from both the Jacobites and the wider Stuart line. In his panorama of British history, he denounces the Stuart era, but completely omits from his verse any mention of the dynasty's Scottish origins.[62] What he does do is make sure he mentions that it was the Scots, led by Alexander Leslie, who invaded England in 1640 in order to defend Scotland's Presbyterian regime against Stuart tyranny:

> When instant from the keen resentive *North*,
> By *long Oppression* by *Religion* rous'd,
> The *Guardian Army* came. Beneath its Wing,
> Tho' meant to furnish hostile Aid, was call'd
> The *more than Roman Senate*. There a Flame
> Broke out, that clear'd, consum'd, renew'd the Land.[63]

While Thomson was evasive about the nationality of the Stuarts, he was far more effusive about the role that Scotland had to play as a bastion of Britain's liberties. A key motif for Thomson in this poem is that liberty does not just emanate from a classical centre and radiate out to barbarous regions on the periphery of civilization, but instead has a distinctive northern trajectory. It was, after all, the north of Britain that repelled Roman imperial expansion. In this respect Thomson is most emphatic about the role that the ancient Scots played in maintaining liberty on the island when most of it had been brought to heel:

> The *North* remain'd untouch'd, where those who scorn'd
> To stoop reitr'd; and, to their keen Effort
> Yielding at last, recoil'd the *Roman* Power.
> In vain, unable to sustain the Shock,
> From Sea to Sea desponding Legions rais'd
> The Wall immense, and yet, on Summer's Eve,
> While sport his Lambkins round, the Shepherd's Gaze.
> Continual o'er it burst the *Northern Storm*...[64]

---

61. Atherton, *Political Prints in the Age of Hogarth*, 76–7.   62. Scott, *James Thomson*, 219–20.
63. James Thomson, *Liberty*, in James Thomson, *Liberty, The Castle of Indolence, and Other Poems*,
    143–7, IV.1016–21.
64. Thomson, *Liberty*, IV.647–54.

Viewed in this light, Scotland is a beacon of liberty that preserves its flame for subsequent generations, and, although it may flare violently on occasion, it also has the capacity to cleanse and regenerate. The 'Guardian Army' led by Alexander Leslie is therefore performing a Presbyterian corrective to the misrule of the Stuarts, in effect clearing the way for the extension of the liberties both of Scots and of English. What this demonstrates is that Thomson is comfortable in asserting a British identity, but in the aftermath of union it is an identity that is forged out of Scots as well as English values, and celebrates the contributions of both nations. As a result, Thomson's patriotism turns out to be more heterogeneous than it would first appear.

Indeed, so rich were its various associations that Britannia is seemingly the quintessential symbol of British nationhood. An anonymous piece, using Britannia as its inspiration, first appeared in the *Pennsylvania Gazette* in October 1774, entitled, 'An American Parody, On the old song of Rule Britannia'. The first verse is identical to Thomson's, indicating the shared origins—and Whiggish values—of the American colonists and their mother country. However, the chorus is altered at the end of the second verse to become, 'Rule, Britannia, rule the waves, But rule us justly—not like slaves'. The song then proceeds to chastise Britain for forgetting its commitment to freedom and opposition to tyranny. However, the song is conciliatory in the sense that it sees the two parties in the Anglo-American dispute as twin sides of the same coin, and urges Britain to view the colonists as equals. It ends with both a hope for the future and a warning about the failure to acknowledge the Americans' status:

> For thee we'll toil with cheerful heart,
> We'll labour, but we will be free—
> Our growth and strength to thee impart,
> And all our treasures bring to thee.
> Rule, Britannia, rule the waves;
> We're subjects, but we're not your slaves.[65]

'Rule, Britannia' was also adapted by conservatives in the 1790s to attack radicals and portray them as enemies of the nation. A broadside verse, 'Church and King', which was to be sung to the same tune as Arne's original, employed a raft of anti-Jacobin language, which fed off Thomson's original words. The verses play upon the fears of the establishment that the values of

---

65. Quoted in *Songs, Odes, and Other Poems, on National Subjects*, ed. William McCarthy (Philadelphia: Wm McCarthy, 1842), 291–2.

the French Revolution might spread to the British mainland. Significantly, in this instance it was used to shame false patriotism and to castigate disharmony among Britain's citizenry at a time of national crisis:

> The Gallic lilies droop and die
> > Profan'd by many a *patriot knave*;
> Her clubs command, her nobles fly,
> > Her Church a martyr—king a slave
> > CHORUS While Britons still united sing
> > > Old England's glory—Church and King.

This particular version was directed at Joseph Priestley (and others like him) for his support for the French Revolution complaining that:

> Yet Priestley, Faction's darling child,
> > Enjoys this sanguinary scene,
> And celebrates, with transports wild,
> > The *wrongs*, micall'd the *Rights of Men*.
> > CHORUS But Britons still united sing, &.[66]

The result of this particular unity was the mob chanting 'church and king' as they burnt his Birmingham house and laboratory to the ground in 1791.[67] Although Priestley moved to London in the aftermath of these riots, he eventually emigrated to the United States, away from the patriotic hordes.

Although 'Rule, Britannia' became an anthem of the patriotic, it was also used—somewhat ironically—to undermine such fervour when it threatened to rock the ship of state. The Scottish poet Thomas Blacklock (1721–91), for example, used the ode as a means to deflate Britain's hubristic notions of its naval supremacy. In the aftermath of one of its worst maritime defeats during the Anglo-Spanish naval conflict (1779–83)—an offshoot of the American War of Independence—which saw a British fleet of sixty-three ships almost entirely captured by the Spanish navy, Blacklock placed the swelling patriotism of Thomson's ode against the crushing humiliation of the events that took place in August 1780. Blacklock proclaims: 'Yield Britannia! yield the main | To faithless France & haughty Spain.'[68] The reference to 'haughty Spain' echoes Thomson's claim in verse four of 'Rule, Britannia'

---

66. *The Gentleman's Magazine* (1791), 760.
67. Harriet Guest, *Unbounded Attachment: Sentiment and Politics in the Age of the French Revolution* (Oxford: Oxford University Press, 2013), 47.
68. Thomas Blacklock, 'A Parody on the Ode, "Britannia rule the waves", written by Dr Blacklock on the Capture of the West & East India Fleet', National Library of Scotland MS.24593, fo. 7.

that 'Thee haughty Tyrants ne'er shall tame'.[69] In a note regarding verse five of Blacklock's parody, the original lines were as follows:

> To thee pertained the Sov'reign nod;
> The pose of Nations once was thine:
> Now debts at home & wars abroad
> To work thy fatal ruin join.[70]

In this version Blacklock places emphasis on the economic impact that the defeat would have had on British commerce. Indeed, such was the enormity of the loss that the Spanish victory, coupled with serious storm losses in the Caribbean, produced a financial crisis among marine insurance underwriters throughout Europe, with the result that war insurance rates were increased to extortionate levels.[71] Blacklock ultimately opted to alter the verse so that instead it read:

> To thee pertained the Sovereign nod;
> The poise of Nations once was thine:
> Till chear'd by thee, tho' curs'd of God,
> False Patriots Spring the fatal mine.

This time the spotlight is on those who supported the war with Spain, and who in Blacklock's eyes were prepared to destabilize the British state even though such actions attract divine censure. It is also clear that Blacklock believed that the appeal to patriotism had been twisted by the unscrupulous to make a trap for the credulous.

Although this is the darker obverse of Britannia as national icon, the fact that Arne's music and Thomson's lyrics were adapted to serve such a number of competing ideologies, and were parodied, copied, and repeated so continuously, is testament to the powerful image of Britannia that they created. Thomson's marriage of commercial–imperial expansion with a patriotic defence of the country's borders and its liberty influentially personified the British nation. That Thomson's Britannia was genuinely British in conception—and so much more than a figleaf for English imperial expansion—was owing in no small part to a Scot who passionately believed in the benefits of the Anglo-Scottish Union.

---

69. Thomson, *Alfred: A Masque*, 42, l. 19.   70. Blacklock, 'A Parody on the Ode', fo. 9.
71. James M. Volo, *Blue Water Patriots: The American Revolution Afloat* (London: Praeger Publishers, 2007), 78.

5

Fictions, Libels, and Unions in the Long Eighteenth Century

Thomas Keymer

To allegorize, in theory at least, is to bestow clarity on complexity. Distilled into a lucid, coherent set of figures in action accompanied by cues for interpretation, the mess and sprawl of morality, religion, politics, or history are transformed into singular meaning. It is no doubt for this reason that allegorical modes were so often enlisted to examine, promote, or contest union enactments, and to address the controversies that swirled around them, right back to the Jacobean Union of the Crowns, if not indeed to the Anglo-Welsh Union under Henry VIII. A conspicuous early modern example is Ben Jonson's court masque *Hymenaei* (1606), which uses the nuptials of two young nobles from politically rival dynasties, the puritan Essex family and the pro-Catholic Howards, to celebrate James VI and I's project of Anglo-Scottish union. In *Hymenaei* marriage becomes, as David Lindley puts it, 'an example of ordered passions on the personal level which both validate and are validated by analogy with the desirability of order on the political and cosmic levels'.[1] *King Lear*, performed at court the same year, is sometimes read as *Hymenaei*'s dystopian other, focused on the disastrous

---

1. David Lindley, *The Trials of Frances Howard: Fact and Fiction at the Court of King James* (London: Routledge, 1993), 31; see also Kevin Curran's reading of Jonson's masque as designed 'to link a personal union with the British national Union, and to see the cohesion at court in terms of the hoped-for domestic cohesion within the isle as a whole' (Kevin Curran, *Marriage, Performance, and Politics at the Jacobean Court* (Farnham: Ashgate, 2009), 46).

division of a British realm into three kingdoms roughly corresponding to England, Scotland, and Wales/Cornwall. 'The emptied, exhausted nation at the end of *King Lear* is at the farthest possible remove from the luminous globe that emblematises political union at the end of Jonson's *Hymenaei*, or the re-energised imperial Britain at the end of *Cymbeline*,' writes Leah S. Marcus.[2]

It is no surprise that literary methods continuous with Jonson's were adopted in response to the Acts of Union that frame the eighteenth century: the 1707 Union of Parliaments between England and Scotland (in some respects a fulfilment of James's vision) and, a century later again, the 1801 Union with Ireland. Yet the most memorable instances are animated by a hostility worlds away from Jonson's panglossian celebration of the Jacobean Union of the Crowns, and they are fiercely concentrated in form and style: first, Jonathan Swift's 'The Story of the Injured Lady', a terse prose narrative that was seemingly written just before the 1707 agreement, but that remained in manuscript until 1746, after Swift's death; second, 'The Painter Cut: A Vision', by another Irish writer, though one less equivocal about his Irishness than Swift, a journalist named Thomas Finn who wrote under the pseudonym 'Orellana' in Walter Cox's *Irish Magazine* for July 1810. For all the polemical energy behind these pieces, however, neither is quite as single-minded as it seems. Both encounter and to some extent articulate contradictions even as they seek to reduce their subject to the pure simplicity of allegory. Read in conjunction, Swift's fable and Finn's vision reveal tensions always inherent in the century's figurations of union, whether pro or con, even or at their most polemical. They suggest conclusions that can illuminate the far more complex and extended literary encounters with union produced in the intervening decades, notably in the aftermath of the Seven Years War (1756–63) and the ministry of the Earl of Bute (1762–3), which together forced questions of Anglo-Scottish relations and shared imperial destiny on writers as dissimilar (and mutually antagonistic) as James Macpherson, Charles Churchill, and Samuel Johnson. It was a crucial period for the construction of Britishness, for the development of concentric as opposed to competing national identities in a four-nations context, and for the notion of 'completing the union' in an overarching affective sense: a project in which 'literary' writers took a leading role. I concentrate below

---

2. Leah S. Marcus, 'Literature and the Court', in David Loewenstein and Janel Mueller (eds), *The Cambridge History of Early Modern Literature* (Cambridge: Cambridge University Press, 2002), 487–511, at 491.

on the riotously funny, yet also uniquely sophisticated, case of Tobias Smollett's
Humphry Clinker (1771), in Ian Duncan's words 'the early prototype of
Romantic national fiction', in which allegory is just one small, teasing, and
belated component of a technical arsenal trained throughout the novel on
national identity in all its mobility and multiplicity.[3]

True Pictures?

Swift's rancorous 'The Story of the Injured Lady' offers, in the wording of
its 1746 title page, 'a True Picture of Scotch Perfidy, Irish Poverty, and English
Partiality'. Here 'Scotch Perfidy' (pointedly reworking 'Perfidious Albion',
a phrase associated in eighteenth-century Ireland with the 1691 Treaty of
Limerick and its violated provisions)[4] is only the first of several unexpected
reversals, and as Swift's narrative proceeds it displays no trace of quasi-colonial
fellow-feeling, of common cause or bond between subordinate nations.
As a whole, indeed, 'The Story of the Injured Lady' is hard to square with
the progressive Swift who came to prominence in 1980s criticism, often
quite crudely retrofitted in modern colours: the committed speaker for the
subaltern, the voice of postcolonial protest *avant la lettre*. At one level, to be
sure, the narrative plays into the proto-nationalist aspect of Swift's complex
identity with its account of degradations experienced by the long-suffering
Lady (Ireland) at the hands of a callous 'Gentleman in the Neighbourhood'
(England): degradations that make her, Carole Fabricant wrote in 1982, 'a
victim of sexual violation, political despotism, and economic exploitation'.[5]
The gentleman, we learn, 'had two Mistresses, another and myself; and he
pretended honourable Love to us both. Our three Houses stood pretty near
one another; his was parted from mine by a River, and from my Rival's by
an old broken Wall.'[6] It would be hard to mark this down as deep encoding,
though by the early nineteenth century Walter Scott (whose great edition

3. Ian Duncan, *Scott's Shadow: The Novel in Romantic Edinburgh* (Princeton: Princeton University
   Press, 2007), 59.
4. Karl S. Bottingheimer, 'The Glorious Revolution and Ireland', in Lois G. Schwoerer (ed.), *The
   Revolution of 1688–89: Changing Perspectives* (Cambridge: Cambridge University Press, 2004),
   234–43, at 236. The subtitle, not present in two later 1746 editions, may be a bookseller's
   embellishment.
5. Carole Fabricant, *Swift's Landscape* (Baltimore: Johns Hopkins University Press, 1982), 49.
6. Jonathan Swift, 'The Story of the Injured Lady', in *The Basic Writings of Jonathan Swift*, ed. with
   introduction by Claude Rawson and notes by Ian Higgins (New York: Modern Library, 2002),
   293. Hereafter IL.

of Swift came out in 1814, the year of *Waverley*) felt it advisable to gloss every detail in his notes. The gentleman—a term that obviously denotes rank alone, not moral standing—is England; the mistresses are Scotland and Ireland; the river is the Irish Sea; the wall is 'the Picts Wall', a standard designation for Hadrian's Wall well into the nineteenth century.[7]

As the tale unfolds, Ireland is constant and loyal, though sorely tested by a long history of encroachment and exploitation, and undone, she laments, 'by the common Arts practised upon all easy credulous Virgins, half by Force, and half by Consent, after solemn Vows and Protestations of Marriage'.[8] Now these vows and protestations have come to nothing, for the gentleman has chosen, inexplicably to the narrating Injured Lady, a wife of quite a different kind. At this point Swift applies to his allegorized figure of Scotland an early instance of that virtuoso rhetoric of recoil and disgust that would characterize his later visions of the female body, as though already cranking himself expressively up for the Brobdingnagian nursemaid, the female Yahoo, and the Beautiful Young Nymph Going to Bed:

> As to her Person she is tall and lean, and very ill-shaped; she hath bad Features, and a worse Complexion; she hath a stinking Breath, and twenty ill Smells about her besides; which are yet more unsufferable by her natural Sluttishness: for she is always lousy, and never without the Itch.[9]

Here are the stomach-churning staples of scotophobic satire, among which, D. W. Hayton writes, 'the "Scotch itch", induced by rough clothing, or a prodigious infestation of lice, was proverbial'.[10] But there is more. Miss Scotland, it turns out, has moral and religious qualities to match (kleptomania, fanaticism), to the point that the gentleman now embarking on union with her can only be 'possessed' or 'bewitched'.[11] 'I have been always told', jilted Ireland sadly avows, 'that in Marriage there ought to be an Union of Minds as well as of Persons',[12] as though only she might offer England such a thing.

Let us fast-forward now to 1810, and to the journalist Thomas Finn of Carlow (1772–1842), later a Tory opponent of Daniel O'Connell, and a man remembered after his death as 'a well-known public writer and clever

7. Jonathan Swift, 'The Story of the Injured Lady', in *The Works of Jonathan Swift, D. D.*, ed. Walter Scott, 19 vols (Edinburgh, 1814), vii. 334 n.
8. IL 294.   9. IL 293.
10. D.W. Hayton, *The Anglo-Irish Experience, 1680–1730: Religion, Identity, and Patriotism* (Woodbridge: Boydell, 2012), 20.
11. IL 296.   12. IL 293.

man, not remarkable, however, for very strong political principles'.[13] Finn's mobility or pragmatism notwithstanding, during his time as an *Irish Magazine* contributor he was, or saw fit to pose as, a firebrand republican, certainly when writing under the incongruous pseudonym of Orellana.[14] A year later, he contributed trenchant material to the magazine deploring the slaughter of Carlow rebels during the 1798 rising, but 'The Painter Cut: A Vision' was easily his biggest splash. In it, the painter in question is not an artist or labourer but a painter in the nautical sense of 'a rope attached to the bow of a (usually small) boat for tying it to a ship, quay, etc.': in this case, a tie securing a small, subordinate vessel to a large, dominant mothership. Hence the metaphorical sense of 'to cut (also slip) the painter', first recorded in 1699, as 'to effect a separation, sever a connection; to free oneself of something; to break free': an idiom that obviously lends itself to political use, and indeed one *OED* illustration is a late Victorian passage about decolonization ('to "cut the painter", as the phrase then went, i.e., to throw off the sovereignty of the old country').[15] No prizes, then, for guessing the identity of the tethered vessels. Looking back after thirty-five years on 'the celebrated and very clever paper called "The Painter Cut"' as the finest hour of the *Irish Magazine*, the historian Thomas Mooney called Finn's vision 'ably, but mysteriously worded, in which Ireland was presented to the mind as a small boat attached, by cords, to a ship, (England,) which might be easily, and ought to be, cut away'.[16]

In truth there was little mystery about the basic allegory. Finn's vision begins with the narrator 'recapitulating the unparalleled sufferings that Ireland has borne for so many ages'; he later specifies 'a slavery already borne for six hundred years', which dates the suffering closely enough to the first Anglo-Norman incursions of the late twelfth century.[17] What follows is an allegory in which exploitative union with Britain is severed by means of French intervention, but this is an emphatically self-glossing allegory, and it ends

13. Maurice Lenihan, 'Portrait of Turlough O'Callaghan', *Notes and Queries*, 4th ser., 6 (15 October 1870), 324.

14. A man at the cutting edge of early modern genocide, Francisco de Orellana (1511–46), was a gold-hunting conquistador who fought his way through the Amazon basin and helped Pizarro conquer Peru: for a recent account, see Buddy Levy, *River of Darkness: Francisco Orellana's Legendary Voyage of Death and Discovery down the Amazon* (New York: Random House, 2011).

15. *OED Online*, s.v. Painter, 1.b, 2.

16. Thomas Mooney, *The History of Ireland, from its First Settlement to the Present Time* (Boston, 1845), 1114.

17. Thomas Finn, 'The Painter Cut: A Vision', in *The Irish Magazine, or Monthly Asylum for Neglected Biography* (July 1810), 293–5, at 293, 295. Hereafter PC.

with an unmistakable appeal to United Irishmen or their heirs: '*The Painter is Cut* and ✦✦✦✦✦✦✦ *is free*'.[18] At the close of this speech, it scarcely makes a difference that the word 'Ireland' is conventionally disguised by seven asterisks, exactly corresponding in number to the obliterated letters. Rather than shroud a meaning made inescapable in context, this token gesture of concealment merely calls attention to the structures of oppression (specifically, the threat of prosecution for seditious libel) that make subterfuge prudent. The typographical gesture validates the vision.

On the face of it, then, we have two direct, systematic allegories critiquing different Acts of Union. In the first, Ireland is excluded from the gross, unnatural Union of England with Scotland—a union that, by the time of the second allegory a century later, has swollen into a vast and sinister body to which Ireland is now tethered as a helpless appendage. Yet on inspection neither narrative, whatever we might conjecture about its author's intentions, is quite as straightforward in its message as first appears. In a pattern familiar throughout Swift's Irish writings, the narrating voice of his Injured Lady complicates, and in some respects destabilizes, the surface meaning. The 'true and plain Relation' she promises of her misfortunes with England, the 'very just impartial Character' she offers of her Scottish rival, and the 'Modesty and Truth' she attributes to her self-representation[19] are not quite in the territory of the Modest Proposer's jarring professions of sympathy and philanthropic concern. The alarm bells these blandishments trigger are not quite so shrill (and the Lady of 1707, unlike the Proposer of 1729, is not about to recommend a final solution). Even so, there is more than a hint at these points of protesting too much, while the adjectival overkill—true, plain, just, impartial—sorts oddly with the demonizing screed that follows: stridently partial, far from plain, and really no less lurid than Churchill or John Wilkes at their most xenophobic.[20] Are we in the territory, in fact, of ironic counter-suggestion or unreliable narration; are we being invited to mistrust the injured lady's account of her own treatment, much as the Modest Proposer's professions warn readers to keep up their interpretative guard?

Almost certainly not, according to Swift's agenda and that of Protestant Dublin at the time, anxious and resentful about the political and economic gains that Scotland seemed on the cusp of securing, with Ireland left out in the cold. But several further factors muddy the message. One constraint

18. PC 295.   19. PC 293.
20. For the larger pattern in Swift, see Christopher Fox, 'Swift's Scotophobia', *Bullan: An Irish Studies Journal*, 6/2 (2002), 43–66.

in Swift's sympathetic construction of the Injured Lady's voice is his own growing hostility to her first ambition: that of marriage with the neighbouring gentleman, in other words the integrationist union with England that had been unsuccessfully requested in 1703 by the Irish House of Commons, a goal Swift at first seems to have supported, but no longer.[21] Nearer the surface is his inability to exclude from his narrator's voice that visceral contempt for the native Irish, for Gaelic Ireland, that was to make *A Modest Proposal* so vividly imagined and rhetorically compelling. In one of the story's strangest turns, the Lady drifts seamlessly from complaint about her suitor's disparagement of her family to vigorous endorsement of his view: they were indeed 'none of the best, consisting of ignorant illiterate Creatures'.[22] At such points she speaks not for the nation as a whole (always a problematic concept in Swift, whose use of the term 'Whole People of Ireland' is a notorious scholarly crux) but merely for its anglicized, indeed originally settler, elite. She voices the distinctively Swiftian plague-on-two-houses position that Claude Rawson finds in the Irish tracts more broadly: 'no uncomplicated attack on the English oppressor, but an ambiguous and sometimes volatile blend of compassion and contempt for the Irish victims, in which their failure to help themselves was often deplored more than... their exploitation by the English.'[23]

Her attitude to the neighbouring gentleman is no less ambivalent. It may be a masterstroke of novelizing psychology, or a shrewd insight into colonial hegemony, that makes Swift's narrator so inconsistent in characterizing her lover, who oscillates in the allegory between desirable potential husband and callous libertine tyrant. That said, the effect of this inconsistency is to leave unclear how we should view the alternative constantly implied by her narrative, in which England chooses not sluttish, beggarly Scotland but virtuous, patient Ireland. Would such a union rectify the gentleman's abuses to date, or would it merely legitimize them? It only increases the uncertainty that Swift appends to the Lady's narrative the response of its imagined

---

21. As Evan R. Davis notes in his subtle account of the 'Story', 'It is one of the underappreciated twists of Swift's life that the writer who would later style himself the defender of Irish liberty was, like most of his Ascendancy peers, in 1703 an advocate for the union of England and Ireland' (Evan R. Davis, 'The Injured Lady, the Deluded Man, and the Injured Creature: Swift and the 1707 Act of Union', in David A. Valone and Jill Marie Bradbury (eds), *Anglo-Irish Identities, 1571–1745* (Lewisburg, PA: Bucknell University Press, 2008), 126–42, at 134).
22. IL 294.
23. Claude Rawson, *Swift's Angers* (Cambridge: Cambridge University Press, 2014), 47.

addressee, 'The Answer to the Injured Lady', rebuking her for having allowed herself to be outmanoeuvred by her manifestly less eligible Scottish rival.

As for 'The Painter Cut', the nationalist zeal of its surface notwithstanding, this work too is no less vexed by contradiction. Leaving aside Finn's grating pen name of Orellana, the allegory's largest incongruity is the identity of Ireland's saviour, an unmistakably Napoleonic figure whose imperialist character, far from being downplayed, is highlighted as he moves in on his 'ship of considerable magnitude' to cut the painter. 'I perceived on its deck a triumphant Marine Carr, in which was seated a benign looking personage wearing an *Imperial Diadem*, who held in his right hand a two edged sword, which had a map of Europe engraved thereon, as emblematic of the owners power':[24] this at the height of Napoleon's brutal campaign to subjugate the sovereign nations of Portugal and Spain. Perhaps sensing the problem, Finn makes no attempt to connect his painter-cutting scene with the vision of liberated Ireland that immediately follows, noting only that, 'as transitions in dreaming are very rapid, I found the scene suddenly changed and discovered myself to be on a large plain resembling the Curragh of Kildare'. There the dreamer meets 'an unaccountable multitude of every denomination *all Irish*', the attempt being to depict a ceremony of national union in which all competing factions participate with joy. But unaccountable is really the word at this point. The Curragh was certainly a traditional meeting-point that at one level suggests Irish unity, but in recent experience (following the massacre of rebel forces by the Dublin militia at Gibbet Rath in 1798) it more obviously called to mind civil war. Beyond this, the more Finn itemizes his denominations and interest groups—'there were Judges, Lawyers and Attorneys, Protestant and Catholic bishops with all their subordinate clergy, Protestants, Papists, Presbyterians, Quakers and Methodists, Orangemen and United Irishmen'[25]—the more he highlights the actual state of Ireland as profoundly divided: an effect further intensified by the publishing context of the *Irish Magazine*, filled as its pages are with violent Orangemen, vindictive judges (including the Fieldingesque figure of 'Judge Bladderchops'), and other endogenous sources or agents of conflict. To turn away from the diversity of four-nations Britain is not to retrieve some primary authentic coherence but instead to encounter yet more diversity and dissension within, as though in a process of infinite regress. Perhaps this is why Finn ends his vision not with the celebration of 'universal harmony' articulated

24. PC 293–4.   25. PC 295.

in his penultimate sentence, nor with his oddly evanescent imagery of con-cord, when 'grateful offerings ascended in volumes of smoak to the almighty dispenser of social love and *National Union*'. Instead he concludes with a further sentence recognizing the harmony and love of his dream to be sim-ply mirage, and wakes 'to the sad and ever to be regretted, certainty that the entire scene I had just witnessed was but a vision'.

First-person allegorical narrative, we might conclude, is an inherently untrustworthy medium for the communication of undivided meaning, and certainly political exhortation; there is always a lurking counter-meaning, a space for alternative interpretation, a dangling loose thread from which the larger fabric of argument threatens to unravel. Alternatively, for those reluctant to see contradiction as inevitably a property of discourse, we might point to evidence in the biographies of both Swift and Finn of unresolved mixed feelings, which, consciously or otherwise, find simultaneous expression at different levels of their writing, explicit or implicit. Whether traceable to unruly signification or authorial ambivalence, the effect is the same. These are allegories against political unions between nations (England and Scotland in 1707, Britain and Ireland in 1800) that incidentally destabilize the sense of pre-existing unity or integrity in which their critiques are first grounded. In Swift, the Lady's household is fragmented, morally and culturally, between her accomplished (elite) self and her uncouth (native) family; in Finn, the dream nation turns out to be fissured by political faction and confessional schism, no more natural or harmonious as a unit than the composite, four-nations Britain to which it has been joined.

A further and no less important point is that, even with the mildly pro-tective strategies of disguise or encoding at work in both these pieces, to write about union is always to court controversy, and perhaps retribution. Pre-publication censorship was no longer a factor following the fracturing of the king's printer's monopoly in 1680s Ireland and the 1695 lapse of the Licensing Act in England.[26] But it was still a recent memory when Swift wrote, and perhaps residually an internalized constraint on expression. Moreover, as Daniel Defoe argued with feeling during one of several official crackdowns on print after 1695, the retributive regime that succeeded the licensing system in England—retrospective prosecution under the common law of blasphemous, obscene or seditious libel—made dissident writing more

26. James Kelly, 'Regulating Print: The State and the Control of Print in Eighteenth-Century Ireland', *Eighteenth-Century Ireland*, 23 (2008), 142–74, at 142–3.

rather than less hazardous, because the borderlines of acceptable expression could no longer be known by authors and publishers until they were committed and exposed. If pre-publication licensing were restored,

> all Men will know when they Transgress, which at present, they do not; for as the Case now stands, 'tis in the Breast of the Courts of Justice to make any Book a Scandalous and Seditious Libel...and the Jury being accounted only Judges of Evidence, Judges of Fact, and not of the Nature of it, the Judges are thereby Unlimited.

Defoe goes on to compare good laws with buoys marking dangerous sands or rocks, 'and the Language of them is, *Come here at your peril*', whereas no such specificity applies to the new regime of press control by retrospective action. Uniquely, under the common law of seditious libel, 'the Crime of an Author is not known; and I think verily no Book can be wrote so warily, but that if the Author be brought on his Tryal, it shall be easy for a cunning Lawyer, ay for a Lawyer of no great Cunning, to put an *Innuendo* upon his Meaning, and make some Part of it Criminal'.[27]

Only the previous year, Defoe had suffered imprisonment, fines, and the pillory for writing *The Shortest-Way with the Dissenters* (1702). And, though to modern ears the most shocking thing about *The Shortest-Way* is its ironic advocacy of persecution, even perhaps genocide, on sectarian grounds (the aspect in which it anticipates *A Modest Proposal*), the legal record makes clear that at the time of publication the authorities were far more exercised by the pamphlet's hostile allusions to the delicate early stages of the union negotiations. Defoe was left to argue in vain that his fevered paragraphs decrying '*a union of Nations*, that *England* might unite their Church with the Kirk of *Scotland*, and their Presbyterian Members sit in our House of Commons, and their Assembly of *Scotch* canting Long-Cloaks in our Convocation' were mere ironic ventriloquism of Tory High-Church polemic. Prominent in his Old Bailey indictment was the charge that his pamphlet's motive was nothing less than 'to prevent the union of the said Kingdoms of England and Scotland'.[28]

Censorship in this alarming new sense is the constraint that pressed on Swift and Finn as they wrote, a constraint that both attempted but failed to circumvent by encoding their own reflections on national identities and

27. Daniel Defoe, *An Essay on the Regulation of the Press* (London, 1704), 14, 15.
28. Daniel Defoe, *The Shortest-Way with the Dissenters* (London, 1702), 11; City of London Record Office Sessions of the Peace SF 472, quoted by Paula R. Backscheider, 'No Defense: Defoe in 1703', *PMLA* 103/3 (1988), 274–84, at 277.

incorporations. Swift may have been joking two decades later when—alluding to the mutilations routinely inflicted in earlier generations on seditious or schismatic libellers—he suggested that *Gulliver's Travels* would remain unpublished until 'a printer shall be found brave enough to venture his Eares'.[29] But, as Ian Higgins demonstrates from a range of evidence, Swift's career may be interpreted as an extended cat-and-mouse game with the censoring authorities, one in which he personally never suffered arrest or prosecution, though his printers and other book-trade associates several times did on his account.[30] In the strictly policed print culture of the reign of Queen Anne, when Defoe's prosecution in London was mirrored by the official scrutiny bestowed in Edinburgh on scribally circulated pasquils against the Union Parliament, even the strategies of disguise to which Annabel Patterson has given the term 'functional ambiguity' could not make anti-union satire a risk-free endeavour.[31] In this context, 'The Story of the Injured Lady' was never a realistic publishing prospect, and Swift's tale remained in manuscript, though some degree of private circulation is not impossible.

'Why it should have surfaced in London in the year of his death is unclear', writes Jim McLaverty of the story's mysterious textual history, and again 'it is not clear why Mrs Cooper's name is used in the imprint here' (that is, in the earliest London printing, the first of three 1746 editions of differing provenance).[32] But posthumous publication of seditious libel is a familiar enough phenomenon, and in some cases an author's death could even license opportunistic publications by others, as when various anti-court satires appeared after 1678 with spurious attributions to Andrew Marvell.[33]

29. *The Correspondence of Jonathan Swift*, ed. Harold Williams, 5 vols (Oxford: Clarendon Press, 1963–5), iii. 103 (to Alexander Pope, 29 September 1725).
30. Ian Higgins, 'Censorship, Libel, and Self-Censorship', in Paddy Bullard and James McLaverty (eds), *Jonathan Swift and the Eighteenth-Century Book* (Cambridge: Cambridge University Press, 2013), 179–98.
31. Annabel Patterson, *Censorship and Interpretation: The Conditions of Writing and Reading in Early Modern England* (Madison: University of Wisconsin Press, 1984), 18. The anti-union ballads of 1702–7, some of them later published by nineteenth-century antiquarians, remain surprisingly under-researched. One 1703 example entitled 'Lynes upon the Nobility of Scotland' ('Our senat has had many fyrie a debate') survives in the State Papers for Scotland (TNA SP 54/1, fos 3–4), meticulously annotated with the name of the peer implicitly libelled in each verse. This item seems to have been first printed, from a different copy, in James Maidment (ed.), *A Third Book of Scotish Pasquils, &c.* (Edinburgh, 1828), 78–85.
32. Jim McLaverty, 'An Introduction to *The Story of an Injured Lady*', *Jonathan Swift Archive* <jonathanswiftarchive.org.uk/browse/year/intro_jsa_9_1_1.html> (accessed July 2017).
33. Nicholas von Maltzahn, 'Marvell's Ghost', in Warren Chernaik and Martin Dzelzainis (eds), *Marvell and Liberty* (Basingstoke: Macmillan, 1999), 50–74.

As McLaverty adds, Mary Cooper was a wholesaler or trade publisher, essentially just a distributor, a category of book-trade professional behind whom the real publisher could and frequently did conceal his agency. Perhaps in the hysteria of 1746, when establishment opinion typically failed to distinguish between Jacobite clansmen and their many categories of Scottish opponents, Swift's scotophobia may have seemed acceptable, and his specifically Irish grievances remote. The more urgent priority was a number of pro-Jacobite (or at least superficially sympathetic) pamphlets by Welsh and English authors and booksellers including Ralph Griffiths and Eliza Haywood, both of whom were arrested, though not convicted, in the later 1740s.[34]

As for 'The Painter Cut' in Dublin in 1810, this work attracted much closer scrutiny, and, though rarely noted in the rich scholarship on Romantic-era censorship that has been inspired over the past decade or two by John Barrell's work,[35] it set off proceedings no less significant in the history of press control than the well-known London prosecutions of Daniel Isaac Eaton. Finn stayed out of trouble, having reportedly struck a pre-emptive deal with Walter Cox, proprietor and editor of the *Irish Magazine*, 'either to give himself up as the writer of the prosecuted article, or to give Cox a sum of £300 in the event of the latter consenting to bear the brunt of a prosecution'.[36] Cox duly protected Finn's identity and was convicted of seditious libel, though not before an audacious defence in which Cox's barrister Leonard McNally exploited ambiguities inherent in the text, and manufactured others that were not, to turn the tables on the prosecution. In a version of the classic 'Gurney defence' that Barrell documents in Eaton's 1794 trial for the fable 'King Chaunticlere, or the Fate of Tyranny', McNally held that seditious meaning resided not inherently in 'The Painter Cut' but only in the interpretative gloss attached to it in the arraignment—which made Cox's prosecutors, not Cox himself, the only libellers in the room. On inspection, the text itself was innocent of political bias, or even loyalist in implication. The Napoleon reference was so contextualized as 'to stimulate

34. On Griffiths's *Ascanius: or, The Young Adventurer* (1746) and Haywood's so-called Goring pamphlet of 1749, see Kathryn R. King, *A Political Biography of Eliza Haywood* (London: Pickering & Chatto, 2012), 181–91.

35. See especially John Barrell, *Imagining the King's Death: Figurative Treason, Fantasies of Regicide, 1793–1796* (Oxford: Oxford University Press, 2000), including his discussion of Eaton's 1794 trial, pp. 108–18.

36. Richard R. Madden, *The United Irishmen, Their Lives and Times*, 2nd edn, 4 vols (Dublin: James Duffy, 1858), ii. 280.

every Irishman to destroy the French, wherever they met them invading their native land'; moreover, since dreams must be approached as imaginary counterfactuals, the only conclusion to be drawn about Cox was that 'he, in publishing the dream, has foretold not a separation between the countries, but a continuation of a strong, long, and natural Union'.[37] None of this carried much weight with a compliant jury, but the public pillorying to which Cox was sentenced was comprehensively subverted by his Dublin supporters, and this fiasco led fairly directly, with similar events in London when the law finally caught up with Eaton in 1812, to the abandonment of the pillory as a sanction against seditious libel. Far from being scapegoated and humiliated by the ritual of spectacular punishment, Cox was cheered and feted in the pillory by a sympathetic crowd, 'not less than twenty thousand persons', his magazine claimed.[38] In a turnaround familiar to connoisseurs of seditious libel and its management across the long eighteenth century, he later made sure not to repeat the experience by accepting a government pension to leave the country, and by launching, on his eventual return, a new periodical in vigorous defence of Dublin Castle.[39]

Spirit of Contradiction

In most respects the norms of acceptable or at least unpunishable discourse were more relaxed in the third quarter of the eighteenth century than in the reign of Queen Anne or in the revolutionary and Napoleonic period. During the Seven Years War—years of fraught and fascinating cultural politics in which the literary controversy launched by Macpherson's Ossian fabrications of 1760–3 became intertwined with virulent partisan dispute surrounding the Tory administration of the Earl of Bute, in effect the first Scottish prime minister of Great Britain[40]—the meticulous encoding of Walpole-era satire gives way to a more frank and strident style of polemic and lampoon. That said, by 1760 ministerial and other official exercises in

37. 'Second Trial of Walter Cox', *Irish Magazine* (April 1811), 149, 150.
38. 'Exhibition of Walter Cox', *Irish Magazine* (April 1811), 145.
39. Mooney, *History of Ireland*, 1111–15. Cox appears to have been on the government payroll before launching the *Irish Magazine*, and in his earlier venture the *Union Star* (1797–8), 'which supported the United Irishmen (without their approval) and advocated the assassination of named loyalists', he may have been acting as a paid agent provocateur (C. J. Woods, 'Cox, Walter', *Dictionary of Irish Biography*).
40. See Philip Connell, 'British Identities and the Politics of Ancient Poetry in Later Eighteenth-Century England', *Historical Journal*, 49/1 (2006), 161–92.

press control had reached their highest level since Walpole's fall in 1742 and the aftermath of the 1745 rebellion. One victim in 1760 was Smollett himself, when legal action launched privately by an admiral he had traduced in the *Critical Review* grew into criminal prosecution for 'certain misdemeanours in writing and publishing a scandalous libel', since the offending article also touched on naval policy and—in the usual convenient catch-all formulation—threatened to disturb the public peace.[41] On the upside, Smollett gained, his biographer writes, 'widespread publicity as a daring and dangerous libeler'.[42] But he also suffered enduring expressive constraint as well as immediate punishment on being fined £100, imprisoned for three months, and required to pay sureties, perhaps totalling a crushing £1,000, for future good behaviour. Similar constraint was recognized two years later by Smollett's chief antagonist during the Bute ministry, John Wilkes, who conducted his anti-ministerial periodical the *North Briton* (1762–3) with unflagging rhetorical vigilance. Before publication, each of Wilkes's leader columns would be put through two rounds of revision by other hands: Churchill would edit for style before consulting the seasoned bookseller William Johnston (or, later, an Inner Temple lawyer named Charles Sayer), 'who would advise whether the writing was libelous, "for fear," said Wilkes, "I have got too near the pillory"'.[43] Eventually, in the provocative 45th number of 23 April 1763, Wilkes did indeed get too near the pillory, and prudently absconded to France, leaving the printer of a later edition, John Williams, to be pilloried in his stead in 1765. In a pattern of crowd subversion that reaches from Defoe in 1703 to Cox and Eaton in 1811–12, Williams was cheered and toasted while his supporters draped the pillory with anti-Bute iconography (a jackboot, a scotch bonnet) straight out of Wilkes's scotophobic playbook; on Williams's release, the bonnet was put on the boot and beheaded with an axe.[44]

Despite this ongoing need for circumspection, by Smollett's account of the period's 'paper wars'—a term intensively used in 1756-63 to indicate a characteristic spillover of bellicosity into wartime writing[45]—discourse was

41. Alice Parker, 'Tobias Smollett and the Law', *Studies in Philology*, 39 (1942), 545–58, at 552, quoting TNA, Rule Book, 1757–62, KB 21/38, fo. 259.
42. Lewis M. Knapp, 'Rex versus Smollett: More Data on the Smollett-Knowles Libel Case', *Modern Philology*, 41/4 (1944), 221–7, at 221.
43. Arthur H. Cash, *John Wilkes: The Scandalous Father of Civil Liberty* (New Haven: Yale University Press, 2006), 72.
44. Cash, *John Wilkes*, 178–9.
45. For details, see Thomas Keymer, 'Paper Wars: Literature and/as Conflict during the Seven Years' War', in Frans De Bruyn and Shaun Regan (eds), *The Culture of the Seven Years' War:*

now too plain, too strident, too much untempered by judicious encoding, with corrosive or polarizing effects on the public realm. In particular, Smollett deplores, and in his one-nation journal *The Briton* (1762–3) he contests, the divisive rhetoric of Wilkes in the *North Briton*, which in its attacks on Bute opportunistically resurrected the 1707 Treaty of Union, and its more recent consequences, as a focus of specifically English grievance. The same line of attack was ferociously extended by Churchill in verse polemics like *The Prophecy of Famine: A Scots Pastoral* (1763), in which, wrote Smollett's *Critical Review*, 'every passage which history could furnish, that insinuated any thing, either true or false, to [Scotland's] prejudice, is artfully interwoven, every public prejudice against her heightened and inflamed'.[46] At the end of the war Smollett left Britain as a country on the brink, he feared, of fragmentation: a fragmentation he attributed, moreover, to the untrammelled agitations of factionalists in politics and print. 'I fled from my country', he writes, in tones still marked by the adjectival hyperbole of war-time journalism, 'as a scene of illiberal dispute, and incredible infatuation, where a few worthless incendiaries had, by dint of perfidious calumnies and atrocious abuse, kindled up a flame which threatened all the horrors of civil dissension'.[47] He was in Italy again, by this time seriously ill, when he composed *Humphry Clinker*, published in London shortly before his death in 1771. For all its startling effects of sensory immersion in the world it describes, it may be that the clarity with which *Humphry Clinker* represents post-Union Britain, both as diverse parts and as a meaningful whole, has something to do with the outsider perspective that Smollett finally achieved in self-imposed exile. Perhaps he was further stimulated to write about union, with his distinctive sense of national identity as energized by diverse identities within, by early theorizings of pan-Italian identity as able to embrace, without homogenizing, smaller constituent states: works such as Gianrinaldo Carli's pioneering essay 'Della patria degli Italiani' (1765).

We rarely think of novels, as opposed to satires or poems on affairs of state, as kinds of literature in need of protective encoding against censorship. But it was a *roman à clef* about the Jacobite rising that got Smollett's book-trade rival Ralph Griffiths arrested in 1747, and in 1754 another rival, the

---

Empire, Identity, and the Arts in the Eighteenth-Century Atlantic World (Toronto: University of Toronto Press, 2014), 119–46.

46. *Critical Review*, 15 (January 1763), 60.
47. Tobias Smollett, *Travels through France and Italy*, ed. Frank Felsenstein (Oxford: Oxford University Press, 1981), 2.

Jacobite journalist John Shebbeare, was arrested for casting aspersions upon parliament in his novel *The Marriage Act*. Four years later, Shebbeare was convicted of seditious libel for a pamphlet that dated the nation's woes to the expulsion of James II and alluded provocatively to the white horse of the House of Hanover in its title-page motto from Revelations: 'And I looked, and beheld a pale Horse: and his Name that sat on him was Death, and Hell followed with him.'[48] Unlike these largely forgotten works, *Humphry Clinker* was far too complex and multivocal to be reduced to a single thesis, and by dividing its narrative between five distinct epistolary voices the novel was able to articulate, without having to resolve, competing perspectives on the nation it represented. Nevertheless, several readers saw *Humphry Clinker* as directly continuous with the political journalism that Smollett had practised on Bute's behalf a decade beforehand, and as no less factional in spirit. It was, sneered Horace Walpole, 'a party novel, written by the profligate hireling Smollett, to vindicate the Scots and cry down juries' (the constitutional rights and threatened independence of which, especially in libel trials, were central to radical Wilkite argument in the 1760s).[49]

Potentially, 'party novels' had just as much need as short fictions like Swift's 'Injured Lady' or Finn's 'Painter Cut' of ambiguity, indirection, or more broadly the whole range of techniques developed in the period to build plausible deniability into literary texts. At the same time, novels could use techniques of this kind—the technique, for example, of figuring political union in gendered terms, from rape or seduction to equitable marriage—in order to enable literary explorations of greater amplitude than other genres could afford. As the Stuart licenser turned Jacobite libeller Roger L'Estrange put it in a classic statement about fable in 1692, political encoding and reliance on implication involved the twin advantage of authorial protection and expressive force: on the one hand, powerful, potentially vindictive authorities 'are not to be dealt withal, but by a Train of Mystery and Circumlocution'; on the other, 'there's Nothing makes a Deeper Impression upon the Minds of Men, or comes more Lively to their Understanding, then Those Instructive Notices that are Convey'd to them by Glances, Insinuations, and Surprize; and under the Cover of some *Allegory* or *Riddle*'.[50]

---

48. John Shebbeare, *A Sixth Letter to the People of England, on the Progress of National Ruin* (London: J. Morgan, 1757), title page (quoting Revelations 6:8).
49. Horace Walpole, *Memoirs of the Reign of King George III*, ed. G. F. Russell Barker, 4 vols (London: Lawrence and Bullen, 1894), iv. 218; on juries.
50. Roger L'Estrange, *Fables, of Aesop and Other Eminent Mythologists* (London: for R. Sare, 1692), sigs A2–A2ᵛ.

The second of these advantages could outlive the need for the first, and it applied as much to extended novels as to concentrated fables. There is a large secondary literature, especially on Irish national tales of the Romantic period, on just this expressive gain in the novel genre, where social and domestic relations could represent as realism, while figuring as allegory, the convergence of four-nations Britain in a shared identity (typically with an emphasis on harmonious intermingling, though sometimes disharmony and fracture).[51] It was exactly this capacity of the national tale, enhanced by the affective qualities of realist narrative, that Walter Scott famously detected when praising his Irish counterpart Maria Edgeworth in the 1829 preface to his Magnum Opus edition of the Waverley Novels: 'she may be truly said to have done more towards completing the Union, than perhaps all the legislative enactments by which it has been followed up.'[52]

To what extent might we view *Humphry Clinker* as attempting or per-forming a feat of this kind? Structurally, Smollett's work gives itself the equipment to do so by selecting as protagonists a group of Anglo-Welsh narrators who thus embody a union long antedating that of 1707, one that is ancient, stable, and broadly accepted—a 'completed... union', Hume called it in his *History*[53]—but one that has not erased heterogeneity within, as the characters bear obvious witness. Foremost among these protagonists is the splenetic valetudinarian Matthew Bramble, whose quest for a cure shapes the plot as a tour through Britain that begins in the spas of western England and reaches its farthest extent in Argyll, where Bramble seeks out 'the highland air, and the use of goat-milk whey'.[54] This is, among much else, the first novel ever written about medical tourism and consumerism; more strictly, it is as much travelogue as novel, though travelogue of a dis-tinctive and clever kind, using its multi-voiced narrative structure to give a kaleidoscopic representation of social reality that lays constant emphasis

51. See especially Ina Ferris, *The Romantic National Tale and the Question of Ireland* (Cambridge: Cambridge University Press, 2002), and, for a recent overview, Claire Connolly, 'The National Tale', in Peter Garside and Karen O'Brien (eds), *The Oxford History of the Novel in English*, ii. *English and British Fiction 1750–1820* (Oxford: Oxford University Press, 2015), 216–33.
52. Walter Scott, 'General Preface' (1829), in *Waverley; or, 'Tis Sixty Years Since*, ed. Claire Lamont (Oxford: Oxford University Press, 1981), 352. On the implications of this claim for the Romantic novel, see Mitzi Myers, '"Completing the Union": Critical *Ennui*, the Politics of Narrative, and the Reformation of Irish Cultural Identity', *Prose Studies*, 18/3 (1995), 41–77.
53. David Hume, *The History of England, from the Invasion of Julius Caesar to the Revolution in 1688*, intr. William B. Todd, 6 vols (Indianapolis: Liberty Fund, 1983), iii. 206.
54. Tobias Smollett, *Humphry Clinker*, ed. Lewis M. Knapp, rev. Paul-Gabriel Boucé (World's Classics; Oxford: Oxford University Press, 1984), 235. Hereafter *HC*.

on the relativity, and unreliability, of perceptions.[55] We visit a broad range of social environments—Bristol, Bath, London, Harrogate, Scarborough, Edinburgh, unspecified Highland settings, Glasgow, Manchester, then two rural English estates, one idealized, one satirized—with close attention to the vigorous diversity, geographical, material, social, human, of the new Britain: a diversity that turns out to be refracted and reflected in complex ways across internal national boundaries, constantly implying the value of hetero-geneous British identity as drawing out previously unsuspected affinities and providing a capacious, accommodating host for all. So, on crossing the Highland Line, one narrator finds the Highlanders 'a very distinct species' from their nominal compatriots in Lowland Scotland, against whom they 'indulge an ancient spirit of animosity';[56] yet these Highlanders at the same time profoundly resemble 'the mountaineers of Brecknock',[57] whose English neighbours in Herefordshire in turn resemble the farmers of Dunbartonshire, whose 'Scottish dialect' is in fact more English than anything now spoken in England: 'true, genuine old English'.[58] Another narrator puts it all more succinctly, with the wisdom of fools, when she reports that the Highlanders 'speak Velch, but the vords are different'.[59]

This pervasive idea finds its most telling microcosm in the playful cameo of himself that Smollett provides in the London section of *Humphry Clinker*. It is a gesture that anticipates the enigmatic late appearance of 'James Hogg' in *The Private Memoirs and Confessions of a Justified Sinner* (1824), and, like Hogg, Smollett says little but implies everything in the scene, which represents him as a kind Grub Street patron, presiding benignly in his Chelsea house over the swarming energy of a literary London drawn from all corners of four-nations Britain. It is a crazy but exuberant chorus. 'Not only their talents, but also their nations and dialects were so various, that our conversation resembled the confusion of tongues at Babel', writes one narrator with typically Smollettian relish for creative chaos: 'We had the Irish brogue, the Scotch accent, and foreign idiom, twanged off by the most discordant vociferation.' Yet the chaos is constantly celebratory in kind, and where it threatens anything else 'is effectually checked by the master of the feast,

55. The novel is in this respect, I argue elsewhere, Smollett's riposte to Defoe's *A Tour thro' the Whole Island of Great Britain* (London, 1724–6), implicitly critiquing the monological positiv-ism of Defoe's text and its Whiggish confidence in commercial progress ('improvement') as the ultimate social good (Thomas Keymer, 'Smollett's Scotlands: Culture, Politics and Nationhood in *Humphry Clinker* and Defoe's *Tour*, *History Workshop Journal*, 40/1 (1995), 118–32).
56. HC 253.   57. HC 239.   58. HC 199.   59. HC 261,

who exerted a sort of paternal authority over his irritable tribe'.[60] With this emphasis on Smollett's own authorial agency in channelling the energies of diverse nationhood into thriving community, the scene looks forward to the novel's conclusion, which pioneers the distinctive plot structure of the national tale, in which culminating mixed marriages—mixed in terms of social rank, regional or national origin, and sometimes both—are presented as metaphors, or more accurately metonyms, for the progress of national union.[61]

With characteristic self-consciousness and excess, Smollett brings about three such cases of 'matrimonial union'[62] at the close of *Humphry Clinker*, involving English, Scottish, and Welsh characters ranging in rank from servant to gentry. Nothing is without complication here, and Smollett avoids banality by giving the last words of the novel to a malapropian servant who, while attempting to celebrate health and concord, society and decency, inadvertently says that the characters will now live 'upon dissent terms of civility' (an ominous echo of 'civil dissension' in Smollett's *Travels through France and Italy*) and that their 'satiety is to suppurate'.[63] Nevertheless, the dominant trajectory of the novel is from sickness to health, and at the end of his tour Bramble is rejuvenated if not quite cured, like the wise old man he meets in the Highlands who 'had a slight fever the year before the union' but has flourished since 1707.[64] As Robert Folkenflik puts it in an influential account of the novel's comedic structure, the closing marriages bespeak a 'sense of unity in variety, of abundance and excess as the very stuff of life, a *discordia concors* in which distinct individuals, like the nations England, Scotland and Wales, come together in a union which gives health to all'.[65]

To some readers at the time, however, Smollett's handling of these enabling structures and themes was far from stabilizing. During the political turbulence of the Bute ministry, and responding to the toxic combination of radical populism and rank xenophobia that made Wilkes so dangerous, his response as a journalist had certainly been to embrace and promote an overarching British identity in harmony with his more specific identity as a Scot—the most obvious instances being his emphatically named periodicals

60. *HC* 127.
61. See Michael Murphy, 'Marriage as Metaphor for the Anglo-Scottish Parliamentary Union of 1707: The Case of *Humphry Clinker*', *Etudes Ecossaises*, 3 (1996), 61–5.
62. *HC* 140.   63. *HC* 352–3.   64. *HC* 251.
65. Robert Folkenflik, 'Self and Society: Comic Union in Humphry Clinker', *Philological Quarterly*, 53 (1974), 195–204, at 204.

of the early 1760s, *The Briton* and, before that, *The British Magazine*. Now, however, Smollett as novelist could look like the voice of disunion, and one reviewer worried out loud that *Humphry Clinker* would 'tend rather to widen than heal the breach that at present subsists betwixt the South and North Britons, whom every lover of his country would wish to see united without distinction or difference'.[66] A spoof newspaper advertisement, widely reprinted in the Wilkite press, represented Smollett as a kind of eighteenth-century Sean Connery, noisily proclaiming the superiority of Scotland, and implicitly deploring its union with England, from the vantage point of a distant, sun-drenched haven. His next publication would be

> A Dissertation tending to prove, that the cities of London and Bath are filthy, stinking, disagreeable, hateful places, filled with a *Mob of impudent Plebeians*...and that Edinburgh, and the whole kingdom of Scotland, is superior to every other part of the world for elegance, cleanliness, politeness of manners, learning, magnificence, good living, and universal plenty...By TOBIAS SMOLLETT.[67]

Why ever, this notice continued, did he not choose to live in Scotland himself?

These early responses, as cues for interpretation, should not be dismissed out of hand. When we look closely at Smollett's most explicit and extended writing about the Union of 1707, in his continuation of Hume's *History*, a picture emerges of quite complicated rhetorical cross-currents. Here Smollett places emphasis on Queen Anne's express hope that political union will in turn generate a deeper and fuller union of sympathetic identity, 'an union of minds and affections among her people'.[68] He endorses the Union as a long-term success in the face of anxiety and opposition both sides of the border: for 'we now see that it has been attended with none of the calamities that were prognosticated; that it quietly took effect, and fully answered all the purposes for which it was intended'.[69] Yet at the same time he devotes extensive space to anti-union sentiment at both high-political and street level; moreover, he represents this opposition as majority opinion on both sides of the border, and evokes it with more literary verve than he bestows on the settlement itself. He also hints at a personal preference

66. *Universal Magazine*, 49 (November 1771), repr. in Lionel Kelly (ed.), *Tobias Smollett: The Critical Heritage* (London: Routledge & Kegan Paul, 1987), 216–18, at 218.
67. *Middlesex Journal*, 18–20 July 1771.
68. Tobias Smollett, *The History of England, from the Revolution to the Death of George the Second*, new edn, 5 vols (London: T. Cadell; R. Baldwin, 1790), ii. 67. Hereafter *HE*.
69. *HE* ii. 103.

for confederal as opposed to incorporating union, so breaking with a family tradition established by his grandfather Sir James Smollett, MP for Dumbarton and a Union commissioner, who voted with the government throughout the proceedings without any absence or abstention.[70] He shows little sympathy for street opposition in Edinburgh, which he represents as an unholy alliance of Jacobites and Cameronians, and seems quietly amused by the learned civic humanist strictures of Andrew Fletcher of Saltoun, 'who professed republican principles, and seemed designed by nature as a member of some Grecian commonwealth'.[71] But he gives prominence to the critiques of other politicians on both sides of the border, and, though never endorsing them, he acknowledges their power. In Edinburgh 'the Lord Belhaven enumerated the mischiefs which would attend the Union, in a pathetick speech, that drew tears from the audience, and is at this day looked upon as a prophecy by great part of the Scottish nation',[72] while at Westminster the Tory 'Sir John Packington disapproved of this incorporating union, which he likened to a marriage with a woman against her consent'.[73] Horace Walpole was exaggerating as usual when he dismissed Smollett's continuation as 'compiled from the libels of the age and the most paltry materials...heightened by personal invective [and] strong Jacobitism'.[74] But the continuation was certainly more jagged and wayward than anything in Hume. This was the historiography of mixed feelings, in which explicit overall endorsement of the Union coexists with a discernible undertow of regret, expressed in particular through careful attention to the perspectives of opposition figures.

To move from here to *Humphry Clinker* is to detect something comparable at the fictional level. The most disruptive presence from this point of view is the half-pay Scots lieutenant Obadiah Lismahago, a crack-brained figure (literally scalped at Ticonderoga) whose face is 'half a yard in length, brown and shrivelled, with...a mouth from ear to ear, very ill furnished with teeth, and a high, narrow fore-head, well furrowed with wrinkles'.[75] He is the novel's most ludicrous comic butt: at one level a zealous puritan who bears

70. David Wilkinson, 'Smollett, Sir James (c.1648–1731), of Stainflett and Bonhill, Dumbarton', in David Hayton, Eveline Cruickshanks, and Stuart Handley (eds), *The House of Commons 1690–1715*, 5 vols (Cambridge: Cambridge University Press for the History of Parliament Trust), v. 515–17.

71. *HE* i. 494.   72. *HE* ii. 99.   73. *HE* ii. 106.

74. Horace Walpole, *Memoirs of the Reign of King George the Second*, quoted in Kelly (ed.), *Tobias Smollett: The Critical Heritage*, 171.

75. *HC* 188.

his Covenanter pedigree in his name[76] and contests all established maxims with obsessive 'spirit of contradiction' and 'polemical pride';[77] at another an abject fortune-hunter who courts Bramble's old-maid sister, and thus falls within Smollett's final comedic resolution by marrying an Anglo-Welsh gentlewoman, dressed for the occasion in 'his campaign wig that surpasses all description, and a languishing leer upon his countenance'.[78] Yet, alongside all this ridicule, and before the resolution, Lismahago is also the mouthpiece for two eloquent and extended denunciations of union and its consequences, the first largely implicit but the second fully explicit. In the first, Lismahago strikes an austere position against material progress and Whiggish 'improvement' on the grounds that commerce 'would, sooner or later, prove the ruin of every nation, where it flourishes to any extent',[79] and that the wealth generated by modern commerce has 'forced open all the sluices of luxury and overflowed the land with every species of profligacy and corruption; a total pravity of manners would ensue, and this must be attended with bankruptcy and ruin'.[80]

His second diatribe responds to Bramble's observation that 'the Scots were now in a fair way to wipe off the national reproach of poverty', an achievement Bramble attributes, very much in the style of Defoe's *Tour*, to the happy effects of the Union, so conspicuous in the improvement of their agriculture, commerce, manufactures, and manners'.[81] Lismahago replies with angry nostalgia for the virtuous austerity of pre-commercial Scotland:

> The Lacedaemonians were poorer than the Scots, when they took the lead among all the free states of Greece, and were esteemed above them all for their valour and their virtue. The most respectable heroes of ancient Rome, such as Fabricius, Cincinnatus, and Regulus, were poorer than the poorest freeholder in Scotland; and there are at this day individuals in North-Britain, one of whom can produce more gold and silver than the whole republic of Rome could raise at those times when her public virtue shone with unrivalled lustre; and poverty was so far from being a reproach, that it added fresh laurels to her fame, because it indicated a noble contempt of wealth, which was proof against all the arts of corruption—[82]

As for the Union, it was achieved only by parliamentary corruption ('no stone was left unturned, to cajole and bribe a few leading men, to cram the union down the throats of the Scottish nation'[83]) and as a result the Scots

76. The Lanarkshire town of Lesmahagow, though now the Scottish base of the International Society for Krishna Consciousness, was a hotbed of covenanting resistance under Charles II.
77. *HC* 203.   78. *HC* 347.   79. *HC* 204.   80. *HC* 205.   81. *HC* 275.
82. *HC* 275.   83. *HC* 278.

have lost 'the independency of their state, the greatest prop of national spirit'.[84] They have fallen instead into the moral and practical error of 'extravagant luxury', while allowing their substance to drain away south of the border: 'The Scots, not content with their own manufactures and produce, which would very well answer all necessary occasions, seem to vie with each other in purchasing superfluities from England'.[85]

If all this sounds familiar, it is not only because in constructing Lismahago's voice at such points Smollett was channelling an anti-luxury discourse of great antiquity in the classical republican tradition, one strongly reanimated in his own day to challenge the pervasive new discourse of progress or 'improvement'.[86] It is because he was drawing on the distinctively Scottish inflection given to this discourse during the union debates by Fletcher of Saltoun, whose reading of Machiavelli on Livy lent a theoretical rigour to the case against union that was otherwise far from the surface.[87] That is not to say that Smollett was quoting Fletcher verbatim, or had Fletcher open in front of him as he wrote. But he caught with some closeness the intonations of Fletcher's voice in *An Account of a Conversation Concerning a Right Regulation of Governments* (1704), his most important work, which gained renewed currency when reprinted in London (in *The Political Works of Andrew Fletcher* (1732; 2nd edn, 1737)) as a contribution to the Patriot campaign against Walpole. It is not simply that Lismahago echoes Fletcher's use of Sparta as a touchstone of republican virtue ('The Lacedaemonians continued eight hundred years free, and in great honour'), or his attribution of the Union to political corruption at the nation's expense ('For they bestow all offices and pensions; they bribe us, and are masters of us at our own cost').[88] He repeats Fletcher's economic arguments, and in the same tones, with only a change of tense. Even before union, in Fletcher, 'the perpetual issue of money to

84. HC 277.   85. HC 279.
86. See John Sekora, *Luxury: The Concept in Western Thought, Eden to Smollett* (Baltimore: Johns Hopkins University Press, 1977); Michael McKeon, 'Aestheticising the Critique of Luxury: Smollett's *Humphry Clinker*', in Maxine Berg and Elizabeth Eger (eds), *Luxury in the Eighteenth Century: Debates, Desires and Delectable Goods* (Basingstoke: Palgrave Macmillan, 2003), 57–70. For the broader context, see Berg and Eger's chapter on 'The Rise and Fall of the Luxury Debates', in their *Luxury in the Eighteenth Century*, 7–27; also Paul Slack, *The Invention of Improvement: Information and Material Progress in the Seventeenth Century* (Oxford: Oxford University Press, 2015), 170–214.
87. On Fletcher and political theory, see John Robertson, 'An Elusive Sovereignty: The Course of the Union Debate in Scotland, 1698–1707', in John Robertson (ed.), *A Union for Empire: Political Thought and the British Union of 1707* (Cambridge: Cambridge University Press, 1995), 198–227.
88. Andrew Fletcher, *Political Works*, ed. John Robertson (Cambridge: Cambridge University Press, 1997), 22, 133. Hereafter *PW*.

England... has reduced the country to extreme poverty';[89] after union, trade with England will achieve only 'a further exhausting of our people, and the utter ruin of all our merchants';[90] English luxuries will instill 'a horrid corruption of manners, and an expensive way of living, that we may for ever after be both poor and profligate'.[91] One interlocutor in Fletcher's *Account of a Conversation* is dire in his warnings about London as a sink of corruption that will contaminate virtue nationwide, and, in passing on these arguments to Lismahago, Smollett barely exaggerates them:

> that corruption of manners which reigns in this place, has infected the whole nation, and must at length bring both the city and nation to ruin. And if one may judge by the greatness of the corruption, this fatal period is not far off. For... no human prudence can preserve the manners of men living in great cities from extraordinary corruption; and... where great power, riches and numbers of men are brought together, they not only introduce an universal depravation of manners, but destroy all good government, and bring ruin and desolation upon a people.[92]

As a historian, Smollett only briefly summarized Fletcher's neo-Machiavellian case against union; as a novelist, we may now see that he gave it generous scope.

Yet how are we to explain this odd feature of *Humphry Clinker*? One option might be to invoke the hermeneutics of censorship and read the novel, albeit in the face of biographical evidence about Smollett, as repudiating the Union of Scotland with England by indirect, circumspect means. By assigning Fletcher's arguments to an obvious madman, Smollett finds a way to articulate but at the same time sanitize anti-union polemic, and to dissociate himself personally from it. He gives these arguments voice without endorsing them, but as he does so he also imbues them with vigour and conviction; he says here what he really thinks, but leaves room to disavow the effect as irony or satire. This was certainly a strategy practised by others in the period, as in Robert Southey's *Wat Tyler* (composed 1794, published 1817), which expresses Southey's youthful Jacobinism through a dramatic mouthpiece (the Lollard preacher John Ball) but could later be explained as dispassionate historical authenticity, not committed authorial opinion: Ball's speeches may indeed have been seditious, but 'for the book itself I deny that it is a seditious performance, for it places in the mouths of the personages who are introduced nothing more than a correct statement of their real principles'.[93] This is clearly how

89. *PW* 164.   90. *PW* 192.   91. *PW* 165.   92. *PW* 178–9.
93. 'A Letter to William Smith, Esq., M.P., from Robert Southey, Esq.', in *The Life and Correspondence of Robert Southey*, ed. Charles Cuthbert Southey, 6 vols (London: Longman's, 1849–50), iv. 372.

Horace Walpole read *Humphry Clinker*, for the passages he singles out for objection—notably Smollett's attack on partisan juries[94]—all come from Lismahago's mouth. In this view, what mattered was the argument itself, not the character who made it—or, if provenance mattered it all, it was not prickly Bramble or his witty nephew but ranting, Covenanting Lismahago who was the novel's most authentically Smollettian presence.

There is another way, however, of reading Lismahago's speeches: first, as cases of irony that is manifestly indicated within the speeches themselves; second, as articulations of a position that needed to be voiced in *Humphry Clinker* in order then to be refuted. As the novel constantly reminds its readers, Lismahago is a bundle of contradictions, perverse and 'paradoxical' by disposition,[95] and when one narrator calls him 'so addicted to wrangling, that he will cavil at the clearest truths, and, in the pride of argumentation, attempt to reconcile contradictions',[96] the indication to look for such contradictions in his speeches is plain enough. A modern reader might be tempted to find one such example of irony in the contamination of his civic–humanist rhetoric by casual anti-Semitism (contrasting Cincinnatus et al. with 'Jews and others in Amsterdam and London, enriched by usury, peculation, and different species of fraud and extortion'[97]), though early readers may have sensed nothing unusual here. A more telling example— characteristic, perhaps, of Fletcher too—is his unselfconscious ability to shift seamlessly from Scotland as Sparta—austere, uncorrupted, pre-commercial, self-sufficient—to enthusiastic recollection of the Darien venture, an attempt to launch a Scottish empire of trade, as indicating a national genius for commerce: 'Before the Union, there was a remarkable spirit of trade among the Scots, as appeared in the case of the Darien company, in which they had embarked no less than four hundred thousand pounds sterling'.[98] Beyond the obvious irony that the attempt at empire invoked by Lismahago was in human and financial terms a disastrous failure, Smollett also neatly pinpoints the incoherence of Fletcher's case against the Union as grounded in two equal, opposite, and entirely unreconciled visions of national destiny, one stressing virtuous, nostalgic isolationism, the other commercial modernity and imperial power.[99]

94. *HC* 205–6.   95. *HC* 275.   96. *HC* 190.   97. *HC* 275.   98. *HC* 276.
99. On Fletcher and Darien, see David Armitage, 'The Scottish Vision of Empire: Intellectual Origins of the Darien Venture', in Robertson (ed.), *Union for Empire*, 97–118; also, on Fletcher's difficulties in applying Machiavellian theory to the modern world of commerce, see Robertson's introduction to *PW*, pp. xviii–xxviii.

Again, it is important to recognize that neither of these visions was easy to dismiss for Smollett himself: both held strong imaginative appeal, and indeed one might read the whole novel as his own attempt to reconcile them in an overarching British context. For his lead narrator Matthew Bramble, who until Lismahago's appearance is the novel's most forthrightly anti-modern voice, the Scottish phase of his tour through Britain marks an ideological turning point, a moment in which he sees commercial modernity not as a threat to traditional hierarchies and values but as reconcilable with them. In the Highlands, he starts to argue, commerce will banish poverty and feudalism by giving clansmen 'a taste of property and independence' from patriarchal chiefs;[100] in the Lowlands, 'a noble spirit of enterprise' makes modern Glasgow 'one of the prettiest towns in Europe; and, without a doubt, one of the most flourishing in Great Britain'.[101] In this respect, if the novel was indeed written to 'vindicate the Scots', as Horace Walpole alleged, it does so by showing how emphatically Scots have now seized the opportunities of union in ways epitomized by the border town of Dumfries, whose inhabitants take Glasgow as their model 'not only in beautifying their town . . . but also in prosecuting their schemes of commerce and manufacture, by which they are grown rich and opulent'.[102] This is not the vision of republican Fletcher or blood-and-soil Belhaven, but it looks forward to the vision that would be more fully articulated in the novels of Scott, one of a union in which multiple identities coexist, collide, and are enabled to thrive together.

100. *HC* 255.   101. *HC* 246.   102. *HC* 272.

6

Jacobite Unionism

Gerard Carruthers

Arguably, amid the fierce ideological battles that raged in Scotland between the Revolution of 1689 and Reform in 1832, the Union of the nation's Parliament with its English counterpart in 1707 was almost incidental. Of more enduring concern, certainly after 1707, were religious and dynastic matters rather than any desire to restore Scotland's Parliament, whose reputation for either efficiency or democracy was not necessarily great.[1] The oft-repeated claim that Scotland remained more or less as culturally distinctive after 1707 cites the institutions of Church, Law, and Universities as the important capsules of Scottish identity. As regards the first of these, the ructions that recur throughout the eighteenth century and beyond are rooted specifically in the Church Patronage Act (Scotland) of 1711–12, which essentially allowed the landed classes to obtain control over ministerial appointments in the parishes, and superseded the previous rights—since 1690—of appointment by church congregations. Certainly, it should be mentioned that opponents of the Act repeatedly denounced it as contrary to the Union of 1707, since its passage had been accompanied by measures that guaranteed a separate sphere of Scottish church governance.[2]

1. Although see recent revisionist work here; e.g., K. Brown and A. J. Mann (eds), *The History of the Scottish Parliament II: Parliament and Politics in Scotland, 1567–1707* (Edinburgh: Edinburgh University Press, 2004).
2. See Andrew Herron, *Kirk by Divine Right: Church and State: Peaceful Coexistence* (Edinburgh: St Andrew Press, 1985), for a brilliantly clear summation of the very complex history surrounding eighteenth-century patronage disputes.

The Union also provided for a largely autonomous legal system in Scotland, at the core of which was the Faculty of Advocates in Edinburgh. A significant shift can be discerned in the change of Keeper (or principal librarian) at the Advocates from Thomas Ruddiman (1674–1757) to David Hume (1711–76) in 1752, a transition that exemplifies the diminution of Jacobite cultural power at the heart of the Scottish legal establishment, six years after the failure of the last Jacobite Rebellion of 1745–6.[3] Such changes in ideological complexion also enabled a smoother collaboration between the Faculty of Advocates and the Scottish universities in the broad project of the Scottish Enlightenment. These universities, thirled to civic and Kirk authorities, however, were the keepers of an educational legacy that was far from uncontested. Proponents of the Moderate Party (resigned to the fact of patronage and liberal in theology) and the Popular Party (decidedly anti-Patronage and more conservative in religion) vied for control of the universities, certainly at Edinburgh and Glasgow well into the nineteenth century.[4] Throughout the eighteenth century this internal fault line in the established church—a mainstay of Scottish culture—coexisted with other elements of disorder. Indeed, both Jacobitism and later Jacobinism were highly combustible. Moreover, the Covenanting zeal represented by the Popular Party in church and university and outside the establishment by varieties of Seceding churches and smaller Covenanting sects,[5] makes eighteenth-century Scotland look more like a nation on perpetual 'revolutionary' alert than in a state of settled enlightenment.

Issues of kingship and religion constituted the dominant themes in Scottish literature between 1689 and 1832. Both Jacobitism and the Whig–Presbyterian heritage provided the diet on which creative writers fed. Walter Scott's *Waverley* (1814) centred on the 1745 rebellion, while his *The Tale of Old Mortality* (1816) focused on the late-seventeenth-century Covenanters. These texts represent the twin pulses of the Scottish literary imagination for the best part of two centuries after 1688. Where was the novel about 1707 through the eighteenth and nineteenth centuries?

---

3. For an important account of Ruddiman's career, integral in the Scots literary 'revival' of the early eighteenth century, see Douglas Duncan, *Thomas Ruddiman: A Study in Scottish Scholarship of the Early Eighteenth Century* (Edinburgh: Oliver and Boyd, 1965).
4. Crucial to an understanding of the internal politics of the Scottish universities in the period is Roger L. Emerson, *Academic Patronage in the Scottish Enlightenment: Glasgow, Edinburgh and St Andrews Universities* (Edinburgh: Edinburgh University Press, 2008).
5. Colin Kidd, 'Conditional Britons: The Scots Covenanting Tradition and the Eighteenth-Century British State', *English Historical Review*, 117 (2002), 1147–76.

The answer might be that it did not occur to Scots that the surrender of their indigenous parliament impacted so particularly upon their identity as did wider—and deeper—confessional and dynastic issues or the partisan contexts in which they were mired. This came most sharply into focus with Scott's *Old Mortality*, which provoked strong reactions from his contemporaries James Hogg (1770–1835), who produced *The Brownie of Bodsbeck* in 1818, and John Galt (1779–1839), whose *Ringan Gilhaize* was published in 1823. Both Hogg and Galt created a whole series of fiction that reflected centrally on Scotland's Presbyterian identity. Hogg's *Private Memoirs and Confessions of a Justified Sinner* (1824)—a further contribution to the debate inaugurated by *Old Mortality*[6]—is now seen as a classic of the romantic period, with its deep psychological portrayal of fanaticism. Indeed, André Gide's revival of the tale in 1947 as a post-Holocaust novel demonstrates the portability of its concerns, a move that diverges from a marked line of culturally nationalist Scottish criticism that saw early nineteenth-century Scottish fiction's concern with religion as a (mass-psychological) displacement of what ought to have been authors' proper concerns with the 'secular' state after 1707.[7]

Like religion, the concern with dynasty in Scottish literature and song (these two things sharing an often symbiotic relationship) has been read by many critics as a rather anachronistic cultural formation. However, this was part of a long, interlinked and enduring ideological battle going back at least as far as the British Civil Wars of 1639–51, with loyalty to the Stuart cause most often a counterpoint to the Whig, Presbyterian, or Calvinist interest. Although frequently invoked by twentieth-century commentators as a reaction to 1707, the *Choice Collection of Comic and Serious Scots Poems* (1706, 1709, and 1711) edited by James Watson (d. 1722) was the work of a Catholic Jacobite whose pro-Stuart allegiance, rather than his anti-unionism per se, was here, in fact, writ large. The sensibility espoused in this series of anthologies published in the Scottish capital was in opposition to the puritanical city fathers of Edinburgh, seen as representatives too of a wider

6. Douglas Mack, 'The Rage of Fanaticism in Former Days: James Hogg's *Confessions* and the Controversy over *Old Mortality*', in Ian Campbell (ed.), *Nineteenth-Century Scottish Fiction* (Manchester: Carcanet, 1979), 37–50.
7. David Craig, for instance, sees the nineteenth-century Scottish novel of religion authorially engaged and of 'the people', yet his overarching secularism also sees it in the context of 'backward ideas of the past', not representing 'the whole life of the people' and even as 'pre-political' (David Craig, *Scottish Literature and the Scottish People 1680–1830* (London: Chatto and Windus, 1961), 197).

Calvinist Scotland and as existing within another, related 'uncultured' context, the rampant commercialism, as read by many Tories, symptomatic of the reign of Queen Anne. Early eighteenth-century Edinburgh saw men like Watson, Episcopalian Thomas Ruddiman, and the nominally Presbyterian Allan Ramsay (1684–1758) congregating around the intellectual leadership of Archibald Pitcairne (1652–1713).[8] Pitcairne satirized the hypocritical, covetous Calvinists of Scotland in his play *The Assembly* (1691), which mocked the General Assembly of Scotland and reprised the spirit of David Lindsay's satire on the medieval church in *Satire of the Three Estates* (c.1552) (itself usually read in literary history as a crucial sign of the changing winds that were bringing the Reformation). Indeed, here in Pitcairne's text, *The Assembly*, tellingly *before* the demise of Scottish parliament, was a negative tribute to the power of the Kirk Assembly as a guiding cultural force, more powerful perhaps in this respect than the secular gathering of MPs and Lords in the Scottish capital.

The rationalist, Tory–Jacobite mentality of Pitcairne and his circle encouraged the promotion of classical values in Scotland.[9] One product of this was Ruddiman's edition of Gavin Douglas's original 1513 translation of Virgil in the *Eneados* (1710). Importantly, the Scots glossary in this edition was an inspiration to Ramsay's attempted eighteenth-century revival of an older Scots poetry. Ramsay, like Pitcairne and Ruddiman, was a Jacobite who bought into the Stuart-loyal ideological position generally that Scotland needed a cultural revival in the face of the crass, enervating Whig domination of the country. This accounts for Ramsay's multitudinous activities as editor of poetry, in English as well as Scots, his promotion of music, theatre, and art.[10] It was Scots poetry that was to be Ramsay's enduring legacy through the eighteenth century and that represents an essential root in the Jacobitism of Robert Burns (1759–96). This was modal as well as thematically explicit, Ramsay's usage of the 'standard Habbie' stanza being

---

8. Crucial in the understanding of this relationship is F. W. Freeman and Alexander Law, 'Allan Ramsay's First Published Poem: The Poem to the Memory of Archibald Pitcairne', *Bibliotheck*, 9 (1979), 153–60; see also Murray Pittock, 'Were the Easy Club Jacobites?', *Scottish Literary Journal*, 17/1 (1990), 91–4.

9. Colin Kidd, 'The Ideological Significance of Scottish Jacobite Latinity', in Jeremy Black and Jeremy Gregory (eds), *Culture, Politics and Society in Britain 1660–1800* (Manchester: Manchester University Press, 1991), 110–30.

10. For modern accounts of Ramsay in his ideology and in his varied cultural activities, see Murray Pittock, 'Allan Ramsay and the Decolonization of Genre', *Review of English Studies*, NS 58 (2007), 316–37, and the same author's entry in the *Oxford Dictionary of National Biography* (Oxford, 2004).

taken from Watson's publication of 'The Life and Death of the Piper of Kilbarchan, Habbie Simpson'. Later, Burns's use of the stanza would find it rechristened the 'Burns stanza'. 'Habbie Simson' was dubiously attributed by James Watson to Robert Sempill of Beltrees (*c.*1505–76), staunch Catholic and supporter of Mary, Queen of Scots. Here is one stanza describing the kind of service that Habbie the bagpiper had provided:

> So kindly to his Neighbour neist,
> At Beltan and Saint Barchans Feast.
> He blew and then held up his Breast,
>   as he were weid,   [possessed
> But now we need not him arest?
> For Habbie's dead.[11]

We glimpse, then, the 'Catholic' calendar of festivity, with which Habbie assisted, rendered in a stanza-form (going back in origins probably to the troubadours of France) that in its jaunty arrangement of iambic tetrameter and trimeter conveyed the idea of joy that the Jacobite interest claimed was being lost in Calvinist Scotland (the lament for Habbie being metonymic of a nation's lament).

The other stanza form that Burns imbibed via Watson and Ramsay was the 'Christ's Kirk' stanza form from the medieval poem 'Christ's Kirk on the Green', attributed—again very dubiously—to not one but two Stuart kings, James I and James V. The important point of course was the idea of the Scottish-cradled Stuarts as men of culture, poets, and also—as 'Christ's Kirk on the Green' might be seen to exemplify—ready to involve themselves in a scene of integrated community celebration, involving the various strata of society. This myth of community, Tory–Jacobite in its outlook, including happy hoi polloi, represents one myth of 'the people' in Scotland in competition, broadly, with the 'democratic' kirk myth of the people. Does Burns, then, derive what were to become his populist themes (and indeed ultimate iconicity) from Jacobite or Presbyterian origins, or perhaps from a confection conflated from the cultural claims of both? It is interesting to note in the two main stanzas of the eighteenth-century Scots poetic renaissance, medieval and sixteenth-century revivalism, a backward-reflex reprojecting pre-Hanoverian and ultimately pre-Reformation times. Episcopalians and moderate Presbyterians such as Ramsay and Burns, as well as Catholics, could increasingly lament the puritanical form of Protestantism that had

---

11. *James Watson's Collection of Comic and Serious Scots Poems* (Glasgow: M. Ogle, 1869), 33.

emerged in sixteenth-century Scotland. Antiquarianism can be found elsewhere in the eighteenth-century Scots poetic project, including what might be its most famous text, 'Auld Lang Syne'. Allan Ramsay produces his own version of this old song in 1720, beginning, 'Should auld acquaintance be forgot, | Tho' they return with scars?'[12] In other words, part of the setting for Ramsay's version is returning comrades (presumably having fought together in the pro-Stuart cause). Burns loses such ideological resonance altogether in his version of 1788, producing instead a song appropriate to a new age of immigration and international travel. This is typical of the transitional creative effect that Burns often operates, so that today Scotland is largely oblivious of the song's ideological lineage (as well as of the Scots poetry revival of the eighteenth century, generally). Here, literary history shows us the elision of a particular ideology but also suggests an ongoing though transformed political significance (in which Burns—unconsciously—conspired). The result is that poetry in Scots, most especially in the twentieth century, comes to be associated with Scottish 'Nationalism', generally, and in a secularized, non-dynastic version that would be somewhat alien to Ramsay and Burns (notwithstanding the fact that, as we have seen, the latter helps effect this transition).

What, then, of Burns's explicit Jacobitism? Where does this come from, after the event, as it were, after 1745? One of the things we need to understand as background to the literary expression of Jacobitism and its longevity is the co-relative anti-Jacobite rhetoric of eighteenth-century Britain, persisting even as the threat of the Stuarts returning had receded. One example here is instructive. It is to be found in a poem by Charles Churchill (1732–64), 'The Prophecy of Famine', which very quickly went through large sales and four editions in London in 1763. At this time Great Britain had its first Scottish premier in John Stuart (1713–92), third Earl of Bute who is ironically attacked in Churchill's text:

> What mighty blessings doth not ENGLAND owe,
> What waggon-loads of courage, wit, and sense
> Doth each revolving day import from thence?
> To us she gives, disinterested friend,
> Faith without fraud and STUARTS without end.[13]

---

12. *The Works of Allan Ramsay*, i, ed. Burns Martin and John W. Oliver (Edinburgh: Scottish Text Society, 1944), 45.
13. Charles Churchill, *The Prophecy of Famine* (London, 1763), 6.

No matter that this Stuart was a stalwart favourite of George III and had
been hostile to Jacobitism, his name was used in cheap propaganda to imply
the ongoing disloyalty of the Scots, who are also, in general in Churchill's
text, intent on plundering their southern neighbour. Here we have the
prototype grumbling, seen much later in connection with Tony Blair and
then with Gordon Brown, that the Scots are unfairly taking the top political
posts in London. Perhaps even more revealing than Churchill's text is the
published frontispiece illustration. Here, a ragged (Jacobite) Highlander is
portrayed, the plaid barely covering his modesty, his want shown also in his
extreme skinniness, and his state of cleanliness indicated in the insects that
are attracted to him. Completing the scene are scant livestock, one unhealthy-
looking sheep sniffing another one's bottom. The Scottish land, clearly, has
nothing good to offer except, that there is a trace outline of some moun-
tains coming into view, not to be denied but not yet to be sharply drawn in
the detail of their sublime grandeur. The text and its illustration, of course,
were exactly contemporaneous with the Ossianic moment, when supposed
ancient Gaelic poetry translated into English by James Macpherson (1736–96)
represents a formative moment in the romantic re-evaluation of Scotland:
England has its green and pleasant land, but Scotland has other natural and
cultural resources that might at least be consumed aesthetically. In the illustration to 'The Prophecy of Famine' (Figure 6.1) we see a remarkable instance
of this emerging cultural debate.

   Churchill was a camp follower of John Wilkes (1725–97), who had
founded the *North Briton* a year earlier, the London newspaper that specialized in mocking the Scottish influence on government. Wilkes's paper was
a riposte to the periodical the *Briton*, edited by Tobias Smollett (1721–71),
and Smollett was to respond most extensively to what had become the
virulent anti-Scottish culture of 1760s Britain in his novel *The Expedition of
Humphry Clinker* (1771). The text repeatedly riffs on the supposed scarcity
of resource in Scotland, with Smollett pointing out, with great equanimity,
economic losses as well as gains in Scotland precipitated by the union of
Scotland and England in the eighteenth century. It proposes something that
looks like fish-farming for the Highlands and that the Highlanders might
well become excellent fighting units in the service of a united British army
(as they were already being marshalled by the time Smollett's text appeared
anyway).[14] Smollett also has one of his characters assured that, where there

---

14. See Tobias Smollett, *The Expedition of Humphry Clinker*, ed. Lewis M. Knapp; rev. Paul-Gabriel
    Boucé (World's Classics; Oxford : Oxford University Press, 1984), 256, 253–5.

Figure 6.1. Frontispiece from Charles Churchill, *The Prophecy of Famine. A Scots Pastoral* (1763). Courtesy of the National Library of Scotland.

are sheep's heads (the character Tabitha Bramble fears this will be her chief ration on reaching Scotland with her touring party), there are also sheep's bodies.[15] Smollett's novel is in a sense the great unionist text of Scottish literature, countering prejudice, embracing the term 'North Briton' as a positive identity, pointing out too the prodigiously enlightened parts of Scottish culture (famously coining the 'hotbed of genius' for what would later, in the twentieth century, become termed the Scottish Enlightenment) and also the attractions, especially the sophisticated aesthetic worth of the primitive Highland landscape, as well as its undeniable disadvantages. Scotland—and especially the post-45 Highlands—is not to be sneered at, but to be recuperated and reappraised.[16]

This positive cultural turn towards the Highlands, generally, seen in a unionist Scot partly explains why Burns might have been enabled to write positively about Jacobitism by the time he is writing in the 1780s. However, it does not fully comprehend a facet of the Lowland, Presbyterian poet that goes well beyond the rather trite label of 'sentimental Jacobitism'. Burns's first text where his Jacobite bite becomes apparent is scratched into a window in an inn at Stirling in August 1787:

> Here Stewarts once in triumph reign'd,
> And laws for Scotland's weal ordain'd;
> But now unroof'd their Palace stands,
> Their sceptre's fall'n to other hands;
> Fallen indeed, and to the earth,
> Whence grovelling reptiles take their birth.—
> The injur'd STEWART-line are gone,
> A Race outlandish fill their throne;
> An idiot race, to honor lost;
> Who know them best despise them most.[17]

These lines were written by Burns 'on seeing the Royal Palace [of Stirling] in ruins' during his travels through Stirlingshire following his first flush of fame as a poet. In that county, Burns was also, according to later legend, 'knighted', either humorously or more likely seriously, by an elderly Jacobite lady.[18] The lines on the window were seemingly answered by a Presbyterian

---

15. Smollett, *Humphry Clinker*, 220.
16. Smollett, *Humphry Clinker*, 233; see Robert Crawford, *Devolving English Literature* (1992; 2nd edn, Edinburgh: Edinburgh University Press, 2000), 55–75, for a highly illuminating reading of *Humphry Clinker* as a novel about prejudice.
17. *The Poems and Songs of Robert Burns*, ed. James Kinsley (Oxford: Clarendon Press, 1968), i. 348.
18. *The Mirror of Literature, Amusement and Instruction* (London: J. Limbird, 1832), 411.

clergyman, whose responding couplet on the same window called Burns an 'ass's heel', with Burns supposedly smashing the window two months later in an attempt to obliterate the controversy.[19] Shortly afterwards, however, in December 1787, Burns was writing yet again about the Stuarts, specifically about the Young Pretender, and if anything with even more passion than before, in a text occasioned by Charles Edward's birthday, 'A Birth-day Ode. December 31st 1787', in which our Lowland, west of Scotland poet cradled in Presbyterianism celebrates John Graham of Claverhouse (c.1649–89), or 'Bloody Clavers' in Covenanting folk memory. Indeed, in a reversal of a long-standing motif of the Covenanters being relentlessly hunted down, Burns transplants this idea to the Stuarts:

> Perdition, baleful child of Night,
> Ride and revenge the injur'd right
>   Of St—rts' Royal Race!
> Lead on th' unmuzzled hounds of Hell
> Till all the frighted Echoes tell
>   The blood-notes of the chace!
> Full on the quarry point their view,
> Full on the base, usurping crew.[20]

Burns had begun to tune into Stuart loyalism through reading the work of historian William Tytler of Woodhouselee (1711–92), author of *The Inquiry, Historical and Critical, into the Evidence against Mary Queen of Scots, and an Examination of the Histories of Dr Robertson and David Hume with respect to that Evidence* (Edinburgh and London 1760).[21] Several months before 'Here Stewarts once in triumph reign'd', Burns addressed a verse epistle to Tytler as 'revered defender of beauteous Stuart' [that is, Mary, Queen of Scots] and also alludes in several places in his text to his own family tradition that forebears had been out with the Jacobites in 1715. Burns writes:

> Tho' something like moisture conglobes in my eye,
>   Let no man misdeem me disloyal;
>
>   .   .   .   .
>
> Still in pray'rs for King George I most cordially join
>
>   .   .   .   .
>
> But Politics, truce! We're on dangerous ground;

19. *The Poems and Songs of Robert Burns*, i. 349.   20. *The Poems and Songs of Robert Burns*, i. 376.
21. Tytler had also published *The Poetical Remains of James I, King of Scotland* (Edinburgh: J. and E. Balfour, 1783) exemplifying the ongoing eighteenth-century loyalty to the Stuart cause as a highly cultured one.

Who knows how the fashions may alter:
The doctrines today that are loyalty sound,
Tomorrow may bring us a halter.[22]

Notwithstanding his later, antipathetic vehemence in the lines scratched on the window and in the birthday ode for Charles Edward, Burns here expresses loyalty to the Hanoverian monarch, though exercising a certain caution (and there is caution too, as mentioned, in the Stirling window episode). We might ask why: is this because he has an eye on future prospects (Burns was soon to have employment in the Crown Excise service)? Or, is he genuinely torn between past and present, a ubiquitous human condition not unique to Scotland? The poet, clearly, was not alone in what might possibly be described as an antiquarian patriotism with a Jacobite slant. As Nigel Leask has noted, Burns also formed a close friendship in his Dumfriesshire years of the early 1790s with Robert Riddell (1755–94), sharing 'sympathies for Jacobite as well as Jacobin politics, despite the fact that his [Riddell's] father Walter had been captured by the Jacobite army in 1745'.[23] There were plenty of people sympathetic to Jacobitism that the poet encountered during his lifetime. One of these, John Ramsay of Ochtertyre (1736–1814), was a Whig sympathetically interested in Jacobite history who listened to similar sentiments in Burns, concluding of his attitudes that these were 'abundantly motley, he being a Jacobite, an Arminian and a Socinian'.[24]

Ramsay's description of Burns's outlook is most often cited simply in evidence of the poet's inconsistency, or 'motley-ness', but perhaps there is here a description that points to a more congruent synthesis than is usually thought to be the case. 'Socinian' is a term of abuse thrown at Moderate Presbyterians in this period by Popular Party adherents. It was used especially against a friend of Burns, the Revd William McGill (173–1807), a clergyman in Ayr who published his *Practical Essay on the Death of Jesus Christ* (1786),

---

22. *The Poems and Songs of Robert Burns*, i. 332, 333.
23. Nigel Leask, *Robert Burns and Pastoral: Poetry and Improvement in Late Eighteenth-Century Scotland* (Oxford: Oxford University Press, 2010), 260.
24. *Scotland and Scotsmen in the Eighteenth Century from the MSS of John Ramsay of Ochtertyre*, ed. Alexander Allardyce (Edinburgh and London: W. Blackwood and Sons, 1888), 554. It might also be mentioned too though that a powerful influence on Burns was the Episcopalian poet and song writer John Skinner (1721–90), whose church was vandalized by the Duke of Cumberland's army following Culloden. Skinner, whom Burns met, with the two expressing mutual admiration, wrote about the Jacobites, about Bannockburn, and in Scots, English, and Latin (including Horatian odes) exemplifying the neoclassicism and Scots-language revivalism of the Jacobite mentality (see *John Skinner: Collected Poems*, ed. David M. Bertie (Peterhead: Buchan Field Club, 2005)).

which resulted in a long-running action against him for heresy by more
orthodox Calvinists. In seemingly downplaying the importance of the crucifixion, McGill was charged with being a 'Socinian', a term that had come
to stand as a crude but effective synonym for 'Unitarian'.[25] Burns was deeply
interested in this case from its beginnings through until 1789, when he wrote
his song 'The Kirk's Alarm', in which he defended McGill and castigated his
enemies in an act that Burns himself, picking up on the anticlericalism
then working to a pitch in France, described as 'priest-skelping'.[26] In the
same year, Burns's 'Holy Willie's Prayer' (written in 1785) was published
for the only time in the poet's lifetime in unauthorized chapbook form in
Ayrshire, with the highly probable connivance of its author.[27] The coincidence of the writing of 'The Kirk's Alarm' and the 'reappearance' of 'Holy
Willie's Prayer', indeed its publication in unofficial print-form run (where
previously it had circulated in the much rarer form again of manuscript and
in perhaps only a few copies), relates to the climax of the Popular Party
activity against McGill. Burns's most 'Arminian' text, in that, for instance,
it casts doubt on the doctrine of the elect and implicitly argues for the
agency of free will, 'Holy Willie's Prayer', was arguably the poem that made
his career. It had been written as a piece of poetic revenge in another
Popular Party versus Moderate dispute, where Burns's friend Gavin
Hamilton (1751–1805) had been subject to discipline via the kirk session of
Mauchline on charges of lax church attendance and maladministration of
the poor fund. Successfully defended by another friend of Burns, Robert
Aiken (1739–1807), Hamilton had the case against him kicked out by the
Presbytery of Ayr. 'Holy Willie's Prayer' lampooning the conservative theology
and supposed hypocrisy of Hamilton's arch-enemy in the proceedings,
William Auld (1709–91), was the triumph cry of the Moderate, Ayrshire
Enlightenment grouping around Hamilton. Following their delight at 'Holy
Willie's Prayer', Burns was rewarded by way of Hamilton and Aiken collecting many of the subscriptions for Burns's first appearance in print in his
book *Poems, Chiefly in the Scottish Dialect* (1786). Burns clearly thought it
prudent not to include his scurrilous poem in this collection, but it is likely
that he encouraged its appearance in chapbook form in 1789. It was his

---

25. See *A Memorial and Remonstrance Concerning the Proceedings of the Synod of Glasgow and Ayr and of the General Assembly in the Case of Dr William McGill* (Edinburgh: n.p., 1792), 79.
26. *The Poems and Songs of Robert Burns*, i. 474.
27. Patrick Scott, 'The First Publication of "Holy Willie's Prayer"', *Scottish Literary Review*, 7/1 (2015), 1–18.

signature anti-Popular Party text, written in the Habbie stanza, and its depiction of the character of Willie owed something to Pitcairne's hypocritical, canting worldly Calvinist, Timothy Turbulent in *The Assembly*. Here Burns, the 'Arminian', the 'Socinian' too in Ramsay of Ochertyre's loose usage of the term as standing for less than scrupulously observed Calvinist tenets, forcefully uses 'Jacobite' literary technology in the service of Moderate, enlightened Ayrshire. As a kind of footnote to this ideological-cum-cultural warfare, one of McGill's chief accusers, the Revd William Peebles (1753–1826), wrote a pamphlet attacking Burns in 1811, which included verse in English (as the appropriate mode for Presbyterian poetry as opposed to Burns's Jacobitical Scots) that depicted him as belonging in dangerously radical company: 'A Wilkes, a Pindar, Paine and Burns'.[28]

If the Jacobin threat had replaced the Jacobite one by the 1790s, Burns himself shows great imaginative dexterity in melding the two discourses together, and on more than one occasion. We see this in Burns's most famous patriotic song, 'Robert Bruce's March to Bannockburn' (1793), primed by his Stuart-loyalism (Robert the Bruce might be seen as progenitor of the Stuart dynasty), ostensibly about the Wars of Independence of course, but implicitly about 'freedom', 'tyrants', and 'liberty' in the present as well as in the past.[29] To advance this contemporary subtext, Burns allowed his text to be published in the reform-minded London *Morning Chronicle* for 8 May 1794, though, in his letter to an intermediary with the editor of the periodical, Burns requested, 'let them insert it as a thing they have met with by accident, and unknown to me'.[30] Yet again, we see Burns's periodic caution about political involvement, which was lifted to new codified heights in his song 'Is there for Honest Poverty' ('A Man's a Man') written in 1795. For a start, the refrain 'for a' that' was part of a tune that was Jacobite, 'Though Geordie Reigns in Jamie's Stead', which was collected in *Scotish* [*sic*] *Songs* (1794) edited by Joseph Ritson (1752–1803). Ritson was himself 'Jacobite turned Jacobin' and deeply involved in debates about national identity as well as interested in contemporary politics, where, like Burns, he

28. Donald Low (ed.), *Robert Burns: The Critical Heritage* (London and Boston: Routledge and Kegan Paul, 1974), 249.
29. *The Poems and Songs of Robert Burns*, ii. 708.
30. *The Letters of Robert Burns: Volume II, 1790–1796*, ed. J. De Lancey Ferguson; 2nd edn, ed. G. Ross Roy (Oxford: Clarendon Press, 1985); Robert Lomas, *Freemasonry and the Birth of Modern Science* (Gloucester, MA: Fair Winds Press, 2003), 288.

was one of the drivers in the age of discussions of Celticism.[31] The 'honest man' was also 'a leitmotif of Jacobite expression', while the trope of 'brotherhood' in the text could be ascribed to Burns's keen Freemasonry (though it might also be said that part of the attraction of the person of Charles Edward Stuart for Burns may well have been the Pretender's reputed status as 'Grand Master of the Masonic Royal Order of Scotland'). As a result of this position, a line of communication is alleged to have existed between the Pretender and another prominent Mason much admired by Burns, George Washington.[32] However much substance ought to be given to Charles Edward's Freemasonry, and however lurid the Freemasonic lore might be, these legends have persisted from Burns's own times down to the present day. What we see in the text of 'Is there for Honest Poverty' is at least two alibis should anyone question our Crown-sworn exciseman about the democratic overtones of his text. He could respond by claiming the centrality either of Jacobitism or of Masonry to the song rather than active, contemporary, reformist sensibilities.

Burns wrote, collected, and 'improved' a significant number of Jacobite or Jacobite-inflected songs, which would become staples of the Scottish folk canon down to the present day, for the series of anthologies *The Scots Musical Museum* edited by James Johnson (?1753–1811) from 1786 until 1803 (Burns material appearing posthumously in the later volumes). Here appeared 'Auld Lang Syne', 'Scots Wha Hae', 'Awa Whigs Awa' (1789), which Ritson reprinted in his *Scotish Songs*, 'The Battle of Sherramuir' (1790), 'Ye Jacobites by Name' (1792), 'Charlie he's My Darling' (1796), 'It was a' for our Rightfu' King' (1796), and 'The German Lairdie' (1796).[33] Burns and Johnson, a native of the Scottish Borders who was an engraver and sold music in Edinburgh, were generally inspired (as Ritson was too) by *Ancient and Modern Scottish Songs, Heroic Ballads* (1776) edited by David Herd (1732–1810); a text that also had a profound impact on Walter Scott when he edited his *Minstrelsy of the Scottish Border* (1802–3). What we see, clearly, is the progress of a song-collecting movement for Scotland, in which Jacobitism was undeniably a

31. Joseph Ritson (ed.), *Scotish Songs Volume II* (London: J. Johnson, 1794), 441–3. See Colin Kidd, *Subverting Scotland's Past: Scottish Whig Historians and the Creation of an Anglo-British Identity, 1689–c.1830* (Cambridge: Cambridge University Press, 1993), 253; see also pp. 253–7.
32. Murray Pittock, *Poetry and Jacobite Politics in Eighteenth-Century Britain and Ireland* (Cambridge: Cambridge University Press, 1994), 216; see also p. 274.
33. See Donald Low (ed.), *The Scots Musical Museum, 1787–1803* (Aldershot: Scolar Press, 1991); *The Scots Musical Museum* has been thoroughly re-edited by Murray Pittock for the *Oxford Press Edition of the Works of Robert Burns*, which will be published in 2017.

key theme, but that should be seen primarily as an important part of the growing historical and lyrical sentimental predisposition of the emergent romantic movement.

Carolina Oliphant (Lady Nairne) (1766–1845), the descendant of a Perthshire Jacobite family, was inspired by Burns's endeavours in the *Scots Musical Museum* to become a significant Jacobite songwriter herself from the 1780s, though many of her songs made their impact through a slow publication process well into the nineteenth century and long after her death. As for Burns, however, her oeuvre of Jacobite material has become an important component of the Scottish folk movement of the late twentieth and early twenty-first centuries.[34] However, the most cogent project in Jacobite song following the work of Burns is that of James Hogg, another Presbyterian, whose main motivation may simply have been the fee that he commanded when the Highland Society of London commissioned from him, *The Jacobite Relics of Scotland* (1819, 1821).[35] As William Donaldson notes, the prowess of Scottish and Highland units opposing Napoleon had effected a major change, unimaginable only a few years before: 'By the summer of 1815, real Highland Laddies [as opposed to those hymned in song] stood higher in public regard than at any time before, or possibly since.'[36] The Highland Society had been formed in 1778 and soon became a force to be reckoned with in British public life. It was the main agitator behind the repeal in 1782 of the Disarming Act, which had prohibited the wearing of the plaid after the final Jacobite rebellion. In 1786 it encouraged the organization that would lead to the British Fisheries Society as an important player in the economic administration of Scotland and other parts of the United Kingdom. The most visible result of this initiative was the setting-up of fishing villages in the north of Scotland, eventually mopping up some of the displaced people from the Clearances. Through the nineteenth and into the twentieth centuries it was often concerned with promoting Highland and Scottish units in the British army.[37] William Donaldson has noted

34. See Carol McGuirk, 'Jacobite History to National Song: Robert Burns and Carolina Oliphant', *Eighteenth Century*, 47/2–3, 'Ballads and Songs in the Eighteenth Century' (Summer/Fall 2006), 253–87.

35. James Hogg, *The Jacobite Relics of Scotland*, ed. Murray G. H. Pittock, 2 vols (facsimile edn; Edinburgh: Edinburgh University Press, 2002, 2003); see 'Introduction', i, p. xx.

36. William Donaldson, *The Jacobite Song: Political Myth and National Identity* (Aberdeen: Aberdeen University Press, 1988), 92; this book remains a crucial introduction to the topic of Jacobite Song.

37. See Katie Louise McCulloch, 'Building the Highland Empire: The Highland Society of London and the Formation of Charitable Networks in Great Britain and Canada, 1778–1857', unpublished Ph.D. thesis, University of Guelph, 2014.

various, broadly positive, components in Hogg's unionist-primed *Relics*, including the reversal of the idea of the Gàidhealtachd as a place of want; the oblique echoing of the loss of people and culture being engineered in the early stages of the Clearances; and—typical of Hogg's oeuvre more widely—scatological and sexual fun, notably in the mocking of the Elector of Hanover, a tradition that pre-dated Hogg's work in contemporary Jacobite expression.[38] Hogg, like Burns and Oliphant, is also in Donaldson's view 'a great songwriter', who helps propel creative Jacobite expression as a lively 'mythogenic force' through succeeding Scottish literature, song, and culture.[39] Hogg introduced his *Relics* with a large claim: 'It has always been admitted, that our Jacobite songs and tunes are the best that the country ever produced.'[40] This is why, he claims, there is a need for his anthology, effectively the first entirely Jacobite anthology to appear. He is, however, also quick to insert a Whiggish counter-narrative about these pieces:

> They actually form a delightful though rude epitome of the history of our country during a period highly eventful, when every internal movement was decisive towards the establishment of the rights and liberties that we have since enjoyed; and they likewise furnish us with a key to the annals of many ancient and noble families, who were either involved in ruin by the share they had in those commotions, or rose on that ruin in consequence of the support they afforded to the side that prevailed.[41]

Hogg's anthology was an important document 'in serving the contemporary purpose in the rehabilitation of Scotland as loyal'.[42] This was a cause that was embraced furth of Scotland—for instance, in the work of the composer Charles Dibdin (1745–1814), an arch-British patriot of the period of the Napoleonic Wars. He produced a song, 'There never was a Scot who was true to his clan', which in the most execrable Scots diction explicitly celebrates Ossian, who is granted an unproblematic historical location, then Robert the Bruce, and finally the Scottish troops in their successes against Bonaparte.[43] It might also be mentioned that Dibdin's patriotic naval song 'Tom Bowling', featured frequently over the years at the Last Night of the Proms, was based on a character from Smollett's novel *Roderick Random* (1748) and is therefore yet another aspect of the Scottish-engineered

---

38. Donaldson, *Jacobite Song*, 90–108.   39. Donaldson, *Jacobite Song*, 108–9.
40. Hogg, 'Introduction', in *Jacobite Relics* (1819), in Hogg, *Jacobite Relics* (2002), p. vii.
41. Hogg, 'Introduction', in *Jacobite Relics* (1819), Hogg, *Jacobite Relics* (2002), pp. vii–viii.
42. Pittock, 'Introduction', in Hogg, *Jacobite Relics* (2002), p. xvi.
43. *The Songs of Charles Dibdin*, i (London: E. Lloyd, 1847), 310.

British military patriotism of Britain's wars with France between the 1740s and 1815.

The fidelity of the Jacobite clans and their martial prowess—now repackaged as loyalty to the Hanoverians—allowed Whiggish Britons to become consumers of Jacobite culture. Something good could be strained from the failed rebellions, and this is how Walter Scott's *Waverley* (1814), a text that also played a large part in paving the way for Hogg's *Jacobite Relics* project, is often read. We see evidence for this effect in the testimony of one contemporary reader of *Waverley*, Maria Edgeworth (1768–1849), where Charles Edward Stuart is now safely to be enjoyed; in a letter to James Ballantyne (1772–1833), Scott's printer and literary agent, she writes:

> The Pre- [sic] the Chevalier is beautifully drawn—
>   'A prince: aye, every inch a prince!'
>   His polished manners, his exquisite address, politeness and generosity, interest the reader irresistibly, and he pleases the more from the contrast between him and those who surround him. I think he is my favorite character.[44]

Edgeworth's mock coyness, resisting the word 'Pretender' (a word somewhere between simply claimant, in its original definition, and by now carrying also the connotation of 'spurious'), would seem to be in deference to Ballantyne's nationality. Edgeworth is elaborately signalling that she does not wish to offend a Scot by referring to a failed compatriot claimant in negative terms. Edgeworth here, then, acknowledges Charles Edward's cultural efficacy in having now become an inclusive 'Scottish' character or symbol when in fact perhaps as many if not more Scots had stood *against* the Jacobites in 1745. The use of the word 'Chevalier' here is also a more neutral choice (popularly coined by Burns in his song 'Charlie is My Darling'), connoting knighthood and chivalry, generally, while leaving no precise sense of royalty. Charles Edward Stuart had become a pleasant delicacy for consumption more widely in the British Isles.

If Scott certainly helps rehabilitate Jacobitism for a wide British audience, does he deserve to have laid against him a wider set of charges: that he is responsible for the 'tartanization' and 'Highlandism' that supposedly ensue in the nineteenth century? Furthermore, Scott's Tory politics tend to be aligned with his purportedly phoney aesthetic offerings, and he is charged with tenderizing the Jacobites and other parts of Scottish history in order to make them easily palatable for English digestion within the Union.

---

44. John O. Hayden (ed), *Walter Scott: The Critical Heritage* (London: Routledge, 1970), 76.

Scott's reputation continues to suffer in today's nationalist and Left-leaning Scotland, even as outside Scotland the study of Scott is enjoying a renaissance, with an international array of scholars appreciating his work from a wide variety of critical approaches and acknowledging his crucial role in the development of western literature. Edwin Muir's *Scott and Scotland: The Predicament of the Scottish Writer* (1936), one of the most eloquent works of twentieth-century criticism, influentially diagnosed Scott as suffering from a 'curious emptiness behind... the wealth of his imagination', and as peddler of irresponsible romance disconnected from, indeed in denial of, the reality of modern Scotland.[45] Alternatively, in his *The Historical Novel* (1937)—published only a year later though without much English-language impact until its translation the 1960s—Georg Lukács (1885–1971) praised Scott for his realism and for his brilliant grasp of context, so that his work reflects:

> The organic character of English development [which] is a resultant made up of the components of ceaseless class struggles, and their bloody resolution in great or small, successful or abortive uprisings. The enormous political and social transformations awoke in England, too, the feeling for history, the awareness of historical development.[46]

For Lukács, then, Scott in his 'English'—or rather British—context is deeply authentic in demonstrating 'development' or the 'progress' of modern Britain, as exemplary in many ways of the modern European bourgeois state. Alongside Scott's apprehension of the modern, though, is an acknowledgement of the way in which parts of the people, classes and cultures, are marginalized or crushed, though often never with complete 'resolution' in the process (in spite of what 'organic' narratives might attest, most obviously the progressive Whig narrative of British history).

In keeping with the apprehensions of Lukács, we might suggest that *Waverley* features an uneasy dialogue between the hard-bitten facts of human history and romantic narrative, the latter generated by characters in the novel, we might say, rather than by Scott himself. Early on the narrator says: 'I beg pardon, once and for all, of those readers who take up novels merely for amusement, for plaguing them so long with old-fashioned politics, and Whig and Tory, and Hanoverians and Jacobites.'[47] Here, again, are the

---

45. Edwin Muir, *Scott and Scotland: The Predicament of the Scottish Writer* (Edinburgh: Polygon, 1982), 2.
46. Georg Lukács, *The Historical Novel*, trans. H. and S. Mitchell (Boston: Beacon Press, 1963), 32.
47. Walter Scott, *Waverley*, ed. P. D. Garside (EEWN; Edinburgh: Edinburgh University Press, 2007), 26.

Scots–British politics, cultural and constitutional, that Robert Burns and others earlier also had to pick their way through. These 'old-fashioned politics' are what have shaped Scotland and Britain more widely, but they are not to become site of a 'romantic' novel where the past, seemingly, is done and dusted. As Scott is well aware things are not so simple:

> This race [the Jacobites] has now almost entirely disappeared from the land, and with it, doubtless, much absurd political prejudice; but also, many living examples of singular and disinterested attachment to the principles of loyalty which they received from their fathers, and of old Scottish faith, hospitality, worth and honour.[48]

Waverley is precisely about reading the past properly. This past is *not* so easy to read, either because of our modern superiority or because of our equally lazy consumption of it, as something exotic, as 'othered'. If we are aware, history contains both noble and brutal human lessons, and, if unaware, potentially *misleading* romance that can seem all too deceptively cogent. This is why the fictional mode, rather than 'straight' history, is entirely apposite to Scott's intellectual and aesthetic purposes. The central character of the novel, Edward Waverley, is our mostly confused—wavering—avatar through the action. An officer in the Hanoverian army, he becomes a rebel, largely through the insidious plotting of the Jacobites. However, the son of a government loyalist, he is also nephew of Sir Everard, a Tory and a Jacobite and, as well as being part of an English family, as divided as much as any Scottish equivalent; Edward is, then, part of a problematic British nation. Scott's unionist purposes are seen again when his narrator says of Edward's upbringing: 'I know not whether the boy's nurse had been a Welch-woman or a Scotch-woman, or in what manner he associated a shield emblazoned with three ermines.'[49] Here, we have a reminder that Celtic sensibilities are potentially all around Edward, our British 'everyman', and not least since 1603, when the kingship of the British Isles (the three ermines of England, Ireland, and Scotland) was united. British history is suffused with complexities that are not easily disentangled into singular—rather than hyphenated— 'national' identities. Such hyphenation may be the result of programmatic action, 1603, 1707, and so on, but it is also the necessary consequence of the cultural consanguinity that preceded these constitutional moments. This, for Scott, is the British reality, more so than anything merely constitutional. For Scott too, it is not 'simply' progress towards British modernity that

48. Scott, *Waverley*, 363.   49. Scott, *Waverley*, 11.

preoccupies him in *Waverley*, but also the disruptions of the Union of 1603 and the intensified disputes of Kirk and kingdom that have in the early nineteenth century receded, though—as the heated response to *Old Mortality* demonstrated—not entirely. The disruption of British unity is noted yet again in Edward's formative years as is he is tutored by his uncle's chaplain, 'an Oxonian, who had lost his fellowship for declining to take the oath at the accession of George I'.[50] This tutor, Mr Pembroke, attempts to have his book published, *A Dissent from Dissenters, or the Comprehension Confuted; shewing the impossibility of any composition between the Church and Puritans, Presbyterians, or Sectaries of any description, illustrated from the Scriptures, the Fathers of the Church, and the soundest controversial Divines*.[51] To the early nineteenth-century readership these disputes over the religious word might seem arcane and antiquarian, bound up in a seventeenth-century mentality, but in one way or another they rumble on beyond Scott's time. Still to play out in the future were the Disruption of the Church of Scotland in 1843 and the Anglo-Catholic Oxford movement that emerged in England the year after Scott's death. These things illustrate, obviously enough, that the issue of religious authority, indeed, the settled constitution of British secular government, remained an issue of enduring importance beyond Scott's own time. *Waverley* is a novel about divided Britain as much as about divided Scotland, where underneath both states historical fault lines remained, and not far below the surface. It may have been 'sixty years since', but recent political perturbations such as Jacobin republicanism threatened the very existence of King and Kirk of any kind in Britain. Scott was not attempting to sugar coat the past or the present, or render magnificent a savage past, now having given way to rather boring, settled present. Katie Trumpener wisely sees Scott working in a context where he is aware of a largely unceasing, unsettled dialectic of 'political incorporation and disenfranchisement'.[52] Scott knows that there is no end of history, but rather repeated patterns of disunity, notwithstanding a striving for unity. That for him is the essential problem that he as a unionist confronted.

A crucial part of the cultural underfelt in *Waverley* is song generally, exemplifying how Scottish song, and Highland song particularly, had become such strong British mood music since the 1780s. Scott knows that,

50. Scott, *Waverley*, 13.   51. Scott, *Waverley*, 31.
52. Katie Trumpener, *Bardic Nationalism: The Romantic Novel and the British Empire* (Princeton: Princeton University Press, 1997), 19.

like other forms of romantic expansiveness, it can deceive. In the famous 'seduction' scene of *Waverley*, the Jacobite Flora Mac-Ivor sings:

> But the dark hours of night and of slumber are past,
> The morn on our mountains is dawning at last;
> Glenadale's peaks are illumin'd with the rays,
> And the streams of Glenfinnan leap bright in the blaze.
> O high-minded Moray!—the exiled—the dear!—
> In the blush of the dawning the Standard uprear!
> Wide, wide on the winds of the north let it fly,
> Like the sun's latest flash when the tempest is nigh![53]

Replete with Jacobite symbolism, of the rising sun, and hinting that the rising is already underway, or about to be, the passage demonstrates that hard facts are lost on Edward. A greyhound interrupts proceedings, much to Waverley's annoyance, enraptured as he is with Flora, her song, and its romantic words. Waverley is now in his 'tartan fever': dissociated from the actuality of events that are unfolding and oblivious of the fact that the canny Highlanders are playing him, withholding letters from his commanding officer summoning him to his garrison during his long sojourn in the Highlands, so that he believes he has been treated dishonorably by the army when eventually outlawed.[54] Of course, Scott is not dismissing romance altogether, understanding its attractions as he certainly did only too well. In the final chapter proper of the novel, Edward, now extricated from his entanglements, considers a portrait in the wild Highland landscape of the executed Jacobite warrior, Fergus Mac-Ivor, Flora's brother—and, in the novel, one of Charles Edward's right-hand men. Waverley himself also appears in the painting, and regards it, 'the ardent, fiery and impetuous character' of Fergus, 'finely contrasted with the contemplative, fanciful and enthusiastic expression' of himself.[55] The romance that was never really in Fergus, but in Edward, is now dissipated potentially for the consumption of the observer of the canvas, who, if wary, will see as Edward now does that it is only part of the story. Indeed, the romanticizing of events is attractive and even inevitable, but it is only one way of patterning and consuming history. Romance and reality (including human motivations that can be as noble or nefarious as romance) are confusing, potentially disunifying currencies that are each equally omnipresent in human culture. Like Burns, Scott is an artist of promiscuous sympathy, not least in *Waverley*, which, ending with the

53. Scott, *Waverley*, 115.   54. Scott, *Waverley*, 362.   55. Scott, *Waverley*, 361.

uncertainties of the painting just alluded to, is metonymic of this text itself.
It is also the Scottish text that more than any other says that the 'Jacobite'
problem, in its long historical complexities, is a British rather than only a
Scottish problem. Ironically enough, much like the career of Presbyterian
Jacobite Burns, Scott's *Waverley* is a great formative, indeed, unifying
moment in Scottish literature, but conjured out of the wider conditions of
British history. The historical novel, along with Jacobite song, is the invention of Scottish literature and dissatisfying as these things might be to
hopelessly, idealistic culturally nationalist versions of Scottish literature, real
Scottish and British literature they are, responsive to—rather than evasive
of—complex contexts.

Scott's *Waverley* is written at a time when rebellion or revolution on
British soil remained entirely imaginable, but for the many novelists who
have followed Scott over the succeeding 200 years this is perhaps much less
the case, and the charge of escapist romance might well stick. However, it is
interesting to observe Christian Isobel Johnstone (1781–1857), who finds a
historically well-observed and even gritty path, partly post-*Waverley*, in a
tale of Highland pride and chivalry. Her *Clan-Albin: A National Tale* (1815)
features a Highlander fighting in the British army in Ireland and Spain from
the 1780s onwards. All kinds of cultural dislocation and disunity are diagnosed, and its feminist author has a particularly good eye for strong female
characters at the centre of cultures and communities and also their scepticism about both war and the rapaciousness of commerce. The inheritor of
Scott's mantle as a historical novelist in Scotland, Robert Louis Stevenson
(1850–94), published *Kidnapped*, often seen as a 'children's book' (indeed it
was first published in the *Young Folks* magazine in 1886), but, featuring
child-murder and the enslavement of minors, it has rather more serious
undertones than is usually realized. Neil Munro (1863–1930) published
Doom Castle (1901), D. K. Broster (1877–1950) *The Flight of the Heron* (1925),
Georgette Heyer (1902–74) *The Masqueraders* (1928), John Prebble (1915–2001)
Glencoe (1966), Janet Paisley (b. 1948) *White Rose Rebel* (2007), all Jacobite
related and only a selection from a long line of post-Jacobite novels with
Scottish settings. The highly successful *Outlander* television series (2014
onwards) based on the novels of Diana J. Gabaldon (b. 1952) continues to
demonstrate the appeal of Highland Jacobite romance patented by Scott.
The genre exerts an attraction well beyond Scotland, given the American
popularity of *Outlander*. We should also note here the fact that Broster,
Heyer, and Prebble were all born in England and have enjoyed a large
international readership. In some sense all these texts play with the possibility

of honourable rebellion or disunity, a suppressed topic in the critical literature but one as central as nationhood or imagined communities.

Nor should we overlook the Scott-inspired unionist, cultural nationalism of William Edmondstoune Aytoun (1813–65), a pronounced Tory.
Aytoun became involved in the National Association for the Vindication
of Scottish Rights (established in 1853), an organization that partook of
Aytoun's mentality, whereby Scotland was emphatically a nation in its
own right, albeit in union with others in the British Isles.[56] Aytoun's collection *Lays of the Scottish Cavaliers* (1849) stitches together a national
cultural canon that includes Robert the Bruce, the Battle of Flodden, the
Duke of Montrose, Dundee (or Claverhouse), the Glencoe massacre, and
Charles Edward Stuart. Here we have a distinctive Scottish pantheon,
all congregated around 'Stuart' allegiance. *Lays of the Scottish Cavaliers* was
a hugely popular collection in Aytoun's lifetime, going through five editions and also appearing in *Blackwood's Edinburgh Magazine*. The use of
the term 'cavaliers' carried connotations of the British Civil War—a very
deliberate flying in the face of the overarching stereotype of Scotland
as 'Whiggish'—and was also somewhat Frenchified; Aytoun's characters
were in many ways read backwards through the lens of Charles Edward
Stuart. Montrose is introduced as 'among the devoted champions who,
during the wildest and most stormy period of our history, maintained the
cause of Church and king', even though Montrose's career was much
more chequered than that.[57] Here are romances lavishly annotated with
historical notes, and in their rather lachrymose tones they are not so different from what was happening to the treatment of iconic national figures,
elsewhere at this time in England, France, Germany, and other nations.
The point is aesthetic fashion, rather than (as over-read in some forms of
culturally nationalist criticism) vapidity of national consciousness unique
to Scotland. And what are we to make of a much later text that makes
use of the Jacobite symbol of the white rose by Christopher Murray
Grieve (Hugh MacDiarmid) (1892–1978) in his poem 'The Little White
Rose' (1934)?

> The rose of all the world is not for me.
> I want for my part

---

56. Graeme Morton, *Unionist Nationalism: Governing Urban Scotland 1830–60* (East Linton: Tuckwell
Press, 1999), 146.
57. *Poems of William Edmondstoune Aytoun* (London: H. Milford and Oxford University Press,
1921), 15; see also Catriona M. M. Macdonald, 'Montrose and Modern Memory: The Literary
Afterlife of the First Marquis of Montrose', *Scottish Literary Review*, 6/1 (2014), 1–18.

Only the little white rose of Scotland
That smells sharp and sweet—and breaks the heart.[58]

How should we interpret this Jacobite nationalist romance from the
hard-headed, republican communist MacDiarmid, who had, of course, very
little time for either the politics or the creativity of Walter Scott? The white
rose was worn by Scottish National party members at the opening of the
Scottish parliament and again at their biggest Westminster showing of
fifty-six MPs during the Queen's speech to parliament in 2015. By the same
token, and with a similar degree of irony, the rhetoric and symbols of
Whig–Presbyterian Scotland have been adopted for nationalist ends.[59] The
Whiggish language of 'covenant' has had an afterlife through the work of
John MacCormick (1904–61), founder in 1951 of the Scottish Covenant
Association for an independent Scottish parliament. It was invoked repeatedly and explicitly as the covenanted right of the Scottish people again in
the years immediately preceding the establishment of the devolved Scottish
Parliament at Holyrood (which came to pass in 1999). Since the 1800s
politicians and writers alike have put the partisan legacies of both Jacobitism
and Whiggery to incongruous uses, to versions indeed of what might be
called Jacobite unionism and Whig–Presbyterian nationalism. The curious
history of modern Scottish literature is in large measure the story of how
the defining century of religious and partisan strife between 1637 and 1746
was refurbished to meet later—and very different—ideological needs.

58. *Hugh MacDiarmid: Selected Poems*, ed. Alan Riach and Michael Grieve (Harmondsworth:
   Penguin, 1999), 198.
59. Jonathan Hearn, *Claiming Scotland: National Identity and Liberal Culture* (Edinburgh: Polygon,
   2000).

7

Inclusion and Exclusion
in the British State

Walter Scott's *Ivanhoe* and
The Fortunes of Nigel

Alison Lumsden

It is generally acknowledged that Walter Scott was a supporter of the British Union, if not one of its greatest advocates. While some critics such as Paul Scott and Peter Garside have suggested a movement away from this position after the financial crisis of 1825 and towards the end of his life, the dominant position persists that he was a supporter of union, and, until recently at least, most critics are in agreement that his work, on the whole, reflects this view.[1] Indeed the classic formulation of Scott's fiction is that offered by Lukács, which reads Scott as offering moments of conflict leading to resolution, often figured in terms of a movement towards union and stability.[2] In other words, Scott's novels are frequently figured in terms of *inclusivity*, seen as positing a process that allows disparate groups to come together in the formation of the modern nation state. Such readings are in turn bolstered by Scott's orchestration of George IV's visit in 1822, when,

1. See Paul Henderson Scott, *Walter Scott and Scotland* (Edinburgh: William Blackwood, 1981), where it is proposed that Scott's acceptance of the Union was always 'reluctant, grudging and conditional' (p. 73), and P. D. Garside, 'Union and *The Bride of Lammermoor*', *Studies in Scottish Literature*, 19 (1984), 72–93.
2. Georg Lukács, *The Historical Novel*, trans. H. and S. Mitchell (Lincoln, NE, and London: University of Nebraska Press, 1983).

as his biographer Lockhart describes, differences between Highland and Lowland Scotland were apparently elided in a new version of Scottish identity that conflated Highland and Lowland culture, thus informing a version of Scottishness within British union that has persisted (for some rather regrettably) ever since.[3]

However, recent revisionist views of Scott have recognized more complex dynamics within his work, suggesting that, while there may be a dominant movement towards reconciliation, there is frequently a counter-narrative at play within his fiction that pulls against any straightforward construction of the British nation. Julian D'Arcy goes as far as to suggest that Scott's work includes a covert nationalist agenda visible only to certain Scottish readers, while more cautious reassessments by those such as Penny Fielding, Ian Duncan, Susan Manning, and Caroline McCracken-Flesher have posited that the version of stability Scott's novels offer may be more complex than initially perceived.[4] Leith Davis, indeed, suggests that Scott engages with the fact that Britain is forged 'as a negotiation between the incommensurabili- ties of its internal populations', where some groups, like Highlanders, 'were forcibly silenced, while others were allowed to speak only in a particular fashion' so that they 'served as elements that could unsettle the illusion of consensus at any time'.[5] Within traditional readings of Scott, however, it is frequently the Author of Waverley who is seen as engaged in this very act of 'silencing', his work read as offering a colonial discourse that regrets the exclusion of certain groups while facilitating the emergence of a united Greater Britain. This chapter, however, will re-examine how that silencing or exclusion actually operates in Scott's work to suggest that, rather than *colluding* in this act, Scott may in fact be drawing our attention to it as a problem that is central to the modern nation state. It will do so not by looking at Scott's Scottish texts, but by considering his first English novel, *Ivanhoe* and his novel of the Union of the Crowns, *The Fortunes of Nigel*.

3. J. G. Lockhart, *Memoirs of the Life of Sir Walter Scott, Bart.*, 7 vols (Edinburgh: Robert Cadell, 1837–8), v. 206.
4. See Julian Meldon D'Arcy, *Subversive Scott: The Waverley Novels and Scottish Nationalism* (Reykjavic: University of Iceland Press, 2005), Penny Fielding, *Writing and Orality: Nationality, Culture, and Nineteenth-Century Scottish Fiction* (Oxford: Clarendon Press, 1996), Ian Duncan, *Modern Romance and the Transformations of the Novel: The Gothic, Scott, Dickens* (Cambridge: Cambridge University Press, 1992), Susan Manning, *Fragments of Union: Making Connections in Scottish and American Writing* (Basingstoke: Palgrave, 2002), and Caroline McCracken-Flesher, *Possible Scotlands: Walter Scott and the Story of Tomorrow* (Oxford: Oxford University Press, 2005).
5. Leith Davis, *Acts of Union: Scotland and the Literary Negotiation of the British Nation, 1707–1830* (Stanford: Stanford University Press, 1998), 5.

Published at the very end of 1819, *Ivanhoe* marks Scott's turn away from Scottish themes to the topic of 'merry England', a departure that was flagged up by an attempt to distance himself from his earlier work by having the phrase 'by the Author of Waverley' absent from the title page. Scott's publisher, Constable, however, was not about to see the Waverley brand disappear, and his authority prevailed; the phrase did indeed appear, aligning the novel with Scott's earlier productions.[6] Nevertheless, the attempt at change is evident in the introduction of a new narrating persona, Laurence Templeton, and in the shift in subject matter that *Ivanhoe* represents. Yet for many critics, while the novel may seem a radical departure in one sense, *Ivanhoe* may still be read as following the Lukácsian pattern, placing opposing sides—this time the Normans and Saxons—in a moment of conflict, only to have that conflict resolved in the marriage of the 'Normanized' Ivanhoe to the Saxon princess Rowena; as a consequence, such critics claim, the English state is thus imagined to move forward to form the foundation of the British nation finally consolidated in the eighteenth century. Indeed, some have gone as far as to argue that, in spite of its temporal and geographical shifts, *Ivanhoe* can be considered as simply a variation on the Scottish theme, with the rude Saxons acting as ersatz Highlanders and the Normans standing in for Lowland Scotland and its civilizing influence on the Scottish state. Ann Rigney, for example, suggests that the novel follows the familiar Scott pattern whereby we see the 'emergence of a modern nation from the conflict between two ethnic groups',[7] arguing that 'Scott was repeating in a new guise the story of *Waverley*', allowing readers 'to imagine and articulate the story of how one nation emerged from two'.[8] Similarly, Graham Tulloch suggests that, 'by creating a fictional Saxon claimant to the English throne, Scott was able to re-create in this new setting the equivalent of the Jacobite theme of *Waverley*'.[9]

There is, indeed, some evidence in the text to suggest that, in spite of its change of subject towards *English* nation-building, *Ivanhoe* operates as a vehicle to revisit the ostensible themes of the *Scottish* novels. In his 'Dedicatory Epistle', Scott, writing in the guise of his latest fictional persona Laurence Templeton, suggests that, when writing about England, one must

6. Graham Tulloch, 'Essay on the Text', in Walter Scott, *Ivanhoe*, ed. Graham Tulloch (Edinburgh Edition of the Waverley Novels (EEWN), 8; Edinburgh: Edinburgh University Press, 1998), 415.
7. Ann Rigney, *The Afterlives of Walter Scott: Memory on the Move* (Oxford: Oxford University Press, 2012), 83.
8. Rigney, *Afterlives*, 85.   9. Tulloch, 'Essay', 405.

delve deeper into the past in order to find the kind of conflict that is of interest to him as a writer. In Scotland, he suggests, 'all those minute circumstances belonging to private life and domestic character, all that gives verisimilitude to a narrative and individuality to the persons introduced, is still known and remembered... whereas in England, civilization has been so long complete, that our ideas of our ancestors are only to be gleaned from musty records and chronicles'.[10] This implies that Scott may be looking for a similar model of conflict and reconciliation, albeit in a more distant past.

However, Templeton also recognizes that delving 'amidst the dust of antiquity'[11] also necessitates a new kind of historical novel (a historical romance as the novel was later labelled, perhaps) and one that requires a greater imaginative engagement on the part of both the writer and the reader. This is a reminder to us that, while *Ivanhoe* may be similar to the earlier fictions of the Author of Waverley in one sense, it is also significantly different, prompting new kinds of aesthetic and intellectual responses in Scott. Indeed, *Ivanhoe* is potentially a far more disruptive text than those that have gone before it. If the Highlanders in Scott's work show the incommensurabilites within the British nation, something more complex and disturbing is at play in *Ivanhoe*. This is because *Ivanhoe* offers readers a far darker story of how two nations become one by embodying Scott's most overt counter-narrative to date about who can be included in the ideal state and, more significantly, who has to be excluded from it in order for it to reconstitute itself.

In fact, *Ivanhoe* is a novel that is deeply concerned with the subjects of belonging and exclusion. Following on from Templeton's epistle, the narrative opens with an account of the times as ones of 'national convulsion' brought about by the exile of Richard I from his kingdom. The tensions within the kingdom are then delineated, and the reader is reminded of the differences that persist at this time between Normans and Saxons, 'the wounds which the Conquest had inflicted', which 'maintain a line of separation betwixt the descendants of the victor Normans and the vanquished Saxons'.[12] Moreover, the first characters to appear in this landscape are none other than Wamba and Gurth, serf and jester, both clearly outlawed in their own ways; Gurth, the son of Beowulf, 'is [a] born thrall', thus without status in any state, while 'Wamba, the son of Witless' bears, like Gurth, a collar around his neck indicating that he too is in thrall to Cedric.[13]

10. Scott, *Ivanhoe*, 6–7.   11. Scott, *Ivanhoe*, 7.   12. Scott, *Ivanhoe*, 17.
13. Scott, *Ivanhoe*, 19.

This theme of exclusion continues once the characters have gathered at the home of Cedric the Saxon. Tensions between Norman and Saxon are immediately highlighted; and, while Prior Aymer and Brian de Bois-Guilbert are admitted entry, so that the 'hospitality of Rotherwood must not be impeached', they would have been 'more welcome' if they had 'ridden further on their way'.[14] Aymer and Bois-Guilbert are also accompanied by their guide, who wears a 'cloak or mantle of coarse black serge' that 'enveloped his whole body'.[15] This character 'withdrew to a settle placed beside and almost under one of the large chimnies, and seemed to employ himself in drying his garments, until the retreat of some one should make room at the board, or the hospitality of the steward should supply him with refreshments in the place he had chosen apart'.[16] This muffled person sitting apart is, of course, Ivanhoe, outlawed from his father's house and welcome there only in disguise. The final 'outlawed' character to join the group (and we could also note those other outlaws waiting outside in the forest with Robin Hood) is, of course, Isaac of York, the furthest outcast of all. Cedric's admittance of Isaac is, arguably, only to spite the Abbot and Templar, who are outraged at the presence of 'an unbelieving Jew', but it is on condition 'no man ... converse or ... feed with him' and that he has a 'board and morsel apart'.[17] Exclusion is, then, arguably a theme that is foregrounded from the very outset of the novel. And, while the whole text, read in terms of reconciliation and inclusion, could be seen as one of how those who, like Ivanhoe, have been 'disinherited' regain their place in the modern English state, it is, perhaps more compellingly, a narrative about those who *cannot* be reintegrated and who *cannot* belong. Nowhere is this more apparent than in the treatment of Rebecca and her father.[18] As has been recently noted, the character of Rebecca is disruptive in many ways; for example, the critique of chivalry she offers as the sickly Ivanhoe lies on a bed unable to participate in the battle cuts across repeated readings of the novel as an endorsement of chivalry, offering, rather, a feminist account of the limitations of it.[19] It is,

14. Scott, *Ivanhoe*, 38.   15. Scott, *Ivanhoe*, 40   16. Scott, *Ivanhoe*, 41.
17. Scott, *Ivanhoe*, 47.
18. Judith Wilt draws attention to the ways in which Rebecca operates as a dark and disruptive influence in this text ((Judith Wilt, *Secret Leaves: The Novels of Walter Scott* (Chicago: The University of Chicago Press, 1985), 45–48.), and Philip Cox notes that in George Sloane's dramatic adaptation *The Hebrew; A Drama* (1820) the treatment of Isaac 'acts as a pointed reminder of violent exclusions upon which images of national and cultural unity are established' (Philip Cox, *Reading Adaptation: Novels and Verse Narratives on the Stage, 1790–1840* (Manchester: Manchester University Press, 2000), 115).
19. See Alison Lumsden, 'Walter Scott', in Adrian Poole (ed.), *The Cambridge Companion to English Novelists* (Cambridge: Cambridge University Press, 2009), 116–31, Graham Tulloch, 'Introduction',

however, her ultimate exclusion from the novel that seems to have caused readers most disquiet and, as several critics have noted, that most effectively disrupts any straightforward account of national integration at the end of the text.

An awareness of the significance of Rebecca to the novel was quickly recognized. In a letter of January 1820, only days after the novel had been published, Scott's friend Lady Louisa Stuart wrote to him to comment:

> every body in this house has been reading...Ivanhoe...few things in prose or verse seize upon one's mind so strongly, are read with such breathless eagerness as the storming of the castle related by Rebecca...Few characters ever were so forcibly painted as hers...the hero and heroine are the people one cares least about.[20]

This effect of Rebecca on readers seems to have been replicated over and over again and, moreover, as Ann Rigney demonstrates, is apparent in the many adaptations of it; indeed as she compellingly demonstrates, of all of Scott's novels *Ivanhoe* has been most frequently adapted. There are multiple stage versions of it, several operas, children's versions, films, cartoons, and comic-book versions. More recently it has also been reinvented in the form of a science-fiction fantasy text.[21] But what many of these adaptations grapple with is the character of Rebecca and a seeming dissatisfaction with her exclusion at the end of the text. Many of them foreground her in ways that are not anticipated by Scott's novel. An early chapbook version of it bore the title *Ivanhoe, or the Knight Templar and the Jew's Daughter*, and illustrated Ivanhoe rescuing Rebecca.[22] The many dramatic adaptations that are based on *Ivanhoe* also grapple with the question of Rebecca's exclusion, and, as Rigney notes, usually end with Rowena off stage and with the focus on Rebecca's rescue: thus they sidestep the whole issue of Ivanhoe's marriage

---

in Walter Scott, *Ivanhoe* (London: Penguin, 2000), p. xxii, and Judith Wilt, *Secret Leaves: The Novels of Walter Scott* (Chicago: University of Chicago Press, 1981), 41.

20. *The Letters of Sir Walter Scott*, ed. H. G. C. Grierson et al., 12 vols (London: Constable, 1932–7), vi. 115–16.

21. I am indebted to Mary Nestor for drawing my attention to several of these adaptations. See Mary Catherine Nestor, 'Adapting the Great Unknown: The Evolving Perception of Walter Scott', unpublished Ph.D. thesis, University of Aberdeen, 2016. Nestor discusses the treatment of Rebecca in a range of adaptations and notes a 'consistent' quest to elevate Rebecca over Rowena (163).

22. *Ivanhoe; or, the Knight Templar, and the Jew's Daughter: An Ancient Tale of English Chivalry* (London, [1821]). This along with the comic book and other adaptations of the novel are held in the Bernard C. Lloyd Collection in the Sir Duncan Rice Library at the University of Aberdeen and can be viewed digitally at <http://digitool.abdn.ac.uk> (accessed July 2017).

to the Saxon princess, the potential for cultural inclusion that it may represent, and the exclusion of Rebecca from that unified state.[23]

Operatic versions also express this anxiety. As Jerome Mitchell notes, the operatic versions of *Ivanhoe* acknowledge a tension in Scott's treatment of Rebecca and the clear desire of readers to see her marriage to Ivanhoe. However, recognizing that to have Ivanhoe marry a Jewess would be out of step with the times, they frequently resolve the issue by having Rebecca revealed at the end of the text as an exiled (and recuperated) Saxon woman in disguise, thus facilitating the marriage. In Rossini's 1826 opera, for example, Rowena does not figure at all, and in its Covent Garden manifestation Rossini's version was reworked as 'The Maid of Judah'. Here, Leila, the character representing Rebecca, turns out to be Edith, a daughter of the Saxon nobleman Olric, which thus allows her to marry Ivanhoe.[24] Scott saw this version of the opera when he was in Paris and gives an account of it in his *Journal* for 31 October 1826: he is clearly taken with the costumes, which 'lookd very well', but notes: 'It was an opera and of course the story greatly mangled and the dialogue in a great part nonsense.'[25] 'Mangled' seems an appropriate choice of word (if one showing Scott's characteristic diplomacy), and other operatic adaptations follow a similar pattern. Only Arthur Sullivan's 1891 opera *Ivanhoe* follows the trajectory of Scott's novel and ends with the suggestion of the fact that Isaac and his daughter will leave England. Tellingly, it was to meet with little critical or popular acclaim.[26]

More recent adaptations also demonstrate a similar tension in response to the text. Again, Rebecca is frequently given a starring role. The 1952 MGM film follows the story fairly faithfully, but MGM's star of the day Elizabeth Taylor is given the role of Rebecca, thus ensuring her status as the most prominent character in the film. A Classic Comics version of *Ivanhoe* also places Rebecca prominently on the cover and, like the dramatic versions, ends with the rescue of Rebecca from Bois-Guilbert by Ivanhoe, thus once more sidestepping the question of Ivanhoe's marriage (which is briefly

---

23. See Rigney, *Afterlives*, 99; H. Philip Bolton, *Novels on Stage*, ii. *Scott Dramatized* (London: Mansell Publishing, 1992), 342–72.
24. Jerome Mitchell, *The Walter Scott Operas: An Analysis of Operas Based on the Works of Sir Walter Scott* (Alabama: University of Alabama Press, 1977), 146–56. See also Jerome Mitchell, *More Scott Operas: Further Analyses of Operas Based on the Works of Sir Walter Scott* (Lanham, MD, and New York: University Press of America, 1996). Some dramatic versions also offer this solution: see Rigney, *Afterlives*, 100.
25. *The Journal of Sir Walter Scott,* ed. W. E. K. Anderson (Oxford: Clarendon Press, 1972), 258.
26. Mitchell, *Scott Operas*, 197.

referred to in a closing lozenge) and Rebecca's expulsion.[27] The most bizarre rewriting of all, however, comes in Thackeray's 1850 novel *Rebecca and Rowena or, Romance upon Romance*. Again, the ending of Scott's novel is called to account, with Thackeray objecting to Ivanhoe's marriage to the 'icy, faultless prim Rowena'. It concludes with the now widowed Ivanhoe travelling across Europe and, by luck, encountering Rebecca, who has preserved her love for him. While the concluding chapter, 'The End of the Performance', can only be described as pastiche, once again exclusion is avoided, and Rebecca and Ivanhoe are united. It is worth quoting at some length:

> As for Rebecca, now her head is laid upon Ivanhoe's heart, I shall not ask to hear what she is whispering; or describe further that scene of meeting, though I declare I am quite affected when I think of it. Indeed I have thought of it any time these five-and-twenty years—ever since, as a boy at school, I commenced the noble study of novels—ever since the day when, lying on sunny slopes of half-holidays, the fair chivalrous figures and beautiful shapes of knights and ladies were visible to me—ever since I grew to love Rebecca, that sweetest creature of the poet's fancy, and longed to see her righted.
>
> That she and Ivanhoe were married follows of course; for Rowena's promise extorted from him was, that he would never wed a Jewess, and a better Christian than Rebecca now was never said her Catechism. Married I am sure they were, and adopted little Cedric; but I don't think they had any other children, or were subsequently very boisterously happy. Of some sort of happiness melancholy is a characteristic, and I think these were a solemn pair, and died rather early.[28]

Entertaining though such adaptations may be, this repeated need to rewrite Scott's novel in order to accommodate a distaste at Ivanhoe's marriage to Rowena and to avoid Rebecca's self-imposed expulsion is telling, illustrating that for generations of readers Rebecca's exclusion at the end of *Ivanhoe* is not satisfactory; so compelling is she as a character that an anxiety emerges when she is replaced by the more insipid Rowena. As Andrew Lincoln puts it: 'The presence of Rebecca complicates the pattern of reconciliation suggested by the union of Ivanhoe and Rowena... readers are led to feel the alternative possibility of a union between Ivanhoe and Rebecca as preferable.'[29] Marriage in Scott, of course, always operates tropically, as it

27. Walter Scott, *Ivanhoe* (Classic Comics 2; New York, Gilberton Company, 1946).
28. William Makepeace Thackeray, *Rebecca and Rowena, Or, Romance upon Romance*, first published *Fraser's Magazine* (August–September 1846); repr. in *Christmas Books: Rebecca and Rowena and Later Minor Papers, 1849–1861*, ed. George Saintsbury (The Oxford Thackeray; Oxford: Oxford University Press, 1908), 459–572, at 572.
29. Andrew Lincoln, *Walter Scott and Modernity* (Edinburgh: Edinburgh University Press, 2007), 77.

does in most nineteenth-century novels, and it signifies in most instances reconciliation and comic conclusion. However, if readers are *so* dissatisfied by the marriage at the close of *Ivanhoe*, then the trope of reconciliation is clearly compromised. Scott's depiction of Rebecca is, arguably, so powerful in this text that she refuses to be silenced, which pulls at the seams of the novel's movement towards national unity.

Ann Rigney suggests that Rebecca acts in the novel as an outsider and as such consolidates national identity by her outcast position,[30] which allows Scott both to posit difference and to sublimate it by way of her exclusion, her 'symbolic deportation' thus 'upholding the fiction of a unified national culture'.[31] However, she also recognizes that the many rewritings and re-mediations of *Ivanhoe* testify to the fact that Rebecca is in some ways the moral centre of the novel, cutting across national unity in the minds of its many readers to show 'the artificial limits of the national frame'.[32] She is, of course, correct, but like many readers she assumes that what Scott was *trying* to depict was a peaceful move towards a unified culture, and that somehow Rebecca's disruptive influence is pulling against his unionist agenda.

However, Scott was well aware of the desire of his readers to have *Ivanhoe* marry Rebecca and responded to it in his Magnum introduction to the text:

> The character of the fair Jewess found so much favour in the eyes of some fair readers, that the writer was censured, because, when arranging the fates of the characters of the drama, he had not assigned the hand of Wilfred to Rebecca, rather than the less interesting Rowena. But, not to mention that the prejudices of the age rendered such an union almost impossible, the author may, in passing, observe, that he thinks a character of a highly virtuous and lofty stamp, is degraded rather than exalted by an attempt to reward virtue with temporal prosperity.[33]

The prejudices of the age give some authority to his decision to exclude Rebecca then, but there is a something more complex at work here; Rebecca, Scott realizes, is in some ways the most appealing and virtuous character in this novel, and he refuses to have her incorporated into the new English state. Her exclusion, Scott suggests, is both fitting and necessary, for to include her within the fold of the emerging British nation would be both

30. Rigney, *Afterlives*, 86.   31. Rigney, *Afterlives*, 91.   32. Rigney, *Afterlives*, 91.
33. Walter Scott, 'Introduction to *Ivanhoe*', in *Introduction and Notes from the Magnum Opus*, ed. J. H. Alexander with P. D. Garside and Claire Lamont (EEWN 25B; Edinburgh; Edinburgh University Press, 2012), 17–18.

trite and demeaning. As so often in Scott, reconciliation at the conclusion of a novel must in some ways be contrived and, though expected by his readers, ultimately dissatisfying. There is, he seems to suggest, no room for Rebecca within this charade, not because she must be excluded in order for the charade to work but, rather, because the unity such closure symbolizes can never be wholly satisfactory. Rebecca, as Lincoln acknowledges, 'exposes the gap between the official agenda of the romance plot—the triumphant foundation of a unified nation anticipating future glories—and the actualities that complicate or are excluded by that version of history'.[34]

Reading *Ivanhoe* in this way suggests that the problem of exclusion is not an *accidental* question in his narrative of 'national unity' but, rather, the fundamental basis of it. Once issues of national identity and unity have been raised, this novel seems to suggest, questions of who must be excluded, silenced, or exiled are, perhaps, inevitable. It is hardly surprising, therefore, that similar issues arise in Scott's novel, *The Fortunes of Nigel*, which concerns the other Anglo-Scottish Union, the Union of 1603.

The Fortunes of Nigel was published in 1822 and is set around 1623 or 1624, twenty years after the Union of the Crowns.[35] National differences are almost by definition foregrounded in the text, and frequent reference is made to the fact that the English are dissatisfied with the many Scotsmen who are descending on the capital. On first encountering Nigel's servant Richie Moniplies, for example, the London apprentice Frank Tunstall complains: "'A raw Scotsman...just come up, I suppose, to help the rest of his countrymen to gnaw old England's bones; a palmer-worm, I reckon, to devour what the locust has spared'".[36] While it is just about possible to squeeze this novel into the paradigm of conflict, resolution, and reconciliation, its relative neglect by critics who wish to read Scott in this way suggests that it is in some ways a problematic piece in the Scott canon. Recently, Caroline McCracken-Flesher has advanced a revisionist interpretation that acknowledges the novel's disruptive tendencies. She suggests that its concerns with money and money-lending offer a metaphor for the ongoing circulation of ideas of Scottishness that inevitably disturb any sense of a settled or unified British nation state. Moreover, she also indicates that the novel appears to bring into focus the 'relationship between novel and author and nation and

34. Lincoln, *Scott*, 77.
35. See Frank Jordan, 'Essay on the Text', in Walter Scott, *The Fortunes of Nigel*, ed. Frank Jordan (EEWN 13; Edinburgh: Edinburgh University Press, 2004), 519.
36. Scott, *The Fortunes of Nigel*, 27.

narration'.[37] Elsewhere I have drawn attention to the fact that this novel is among the most linguistically challenging of all Scott's texts, including as it does passages in Latin, Greek, London street speech, and the thieves' cant spoken within the criminal world of Alsatia. Perhaps most surprisingly, however, is the density of Scots in this novel; while it is set in London and contains few lower-class Scottish characters, James and his courtiers speak largely in Scots. Such linguistic diversity is in itself a challenge to national unity, but is also suggests more overtly the difficulties of transition involved in combining two nations.[38]

The most marked features of exclusion in *The Fortunes of Nigel*, however, circle around its approach to space, the ways in which it can be controlled and prohibited, and the extent to which it can be used as a marker of both inclusivity and exclusivity. George A. Drake draws attention to the significance of space in this text, suggesting that 'it is not so much Nigel's moral failure that drives the plot as his spatial incompetence', for 'Scott's urban spaces are defined by his characters' trajectories and by the hidden connection and impediments that govern their movement through space'.[39] Drake argues that the treatment of urban space in *Nigel* is related to Scott's ongoing concern with borders and boundaries and suggests that it is used to articulate the uneven social development that London encapsulates as it moves towards capitalism and modernity in the early modern period. As in *Ivanhoe*, the novel's concern with space is first highlighted in the novel's 'Introductory Epistle', in which Captain Clutterbuck addresses the Rev. Dr Dryasdust. Clutterbuck reports that, since the Author of Waverley employed him as the conduit to bring *The Monastery* before the public, doors have opened for him that represent 'comforts reserved to such as are freemen of the corporation of letters'.[40] However, incorporation into this body requires exclusion from another: 'it is with no ordinary feelings of regret, that, in my annual visits to the metropolis, I now miss the social and warm-hearted welcome of the quick-witted and kindly friend who first introduced me to the public'.[41] With inclusion, this suggests, come a corresponding exclusion. Emboldened by his newfound status, however, Clutterbuck ventures into the interior of Scott's publishing house, until, having crossed a 'labyrinth of small dark rooms',

37. McCracken-Flesher, *Possible Scotlands*, 66.
38. Alison Lumsden, *Walter Scott and the Limits of Language* (Edinburgh: Edinburgh University Press, 2010), 141.
39. See George A. Drake, ' "The ordinary rules of the pave": Urban Spaces in Scott's *The Fortunes of Nigel*', *Studies in the Novel*, 33/4 (Winter 2001), 416–29, at 417, 423.
40. Scott, *The Fortunes of Nigel*, 3.   41. Scott, *The Fortunes of Nigel*, 4.

he encounters the representative of the Author of Waverley in 'a vaulted room, dedicated to secrecy and silence'.[42] Having reached this inner sanctum, Clutterbuck reports that his conversation with the Great Unknown results in a fear that his 'poor family' (the fictional conduits for his novels) 'shall fall into contempt and oblivion'.[43] The Author of Waverley responds that this is the fate of most literature, and Clutterbuck is eventually excluded when Mr C. (Constable one presumes) rebukes Mr F 'for suffering any one to penetrate so far into the *penetralia* of their temple'.[44]

The 'Introductory Epistle' has frequently been read in terms of its self-reflexive nature and as a commentary on Scott's attitudes to his own fame at the height of his popularity.[45] However, while the epistle clearly lends itself to being read in these ways, it is also a commentary on space and who can inhabit it, and it is notable that the word 'labyrinth' that occurs in the epistle recurs another seven times in the text, highlighting its concern with the complexities of space and how it may be negotiated. Clutterbuck's role has earned him the right to inclusion—incorporated as he is into the world of letters and given access to the body of the Author of Waverley—but the threat of exclusion, or oblivion, clearly stands as a constant threat to this privileged position. To read the epistle in this way is pertinent, for the story that follows hinges upon access to specific spaces and who can, and more significantly who cannot, approach the body of the king in the new emerging British state.

The Fortunes of Nigel tells the story of Nigel Olifaunt, who travels to London to try to redeem the mortgage that hangs over his ancient Scottish estate by asking the king to return a large sum of money lent to him by his father. In order to do so it is crucial that he gains direct access to the king. However, unlike his female counterpart, Jeanie Deans, who relatively easily wins an audience with the queen if not the king, Nigel is thwarted at every turn. Nigel cannot go to the king himself because 'he had no dress suitable for appearing at court'[46] and an attempt to deliver his petition via his servant results in Moniplies receiving a proclamation that apparently banishes all Scotsmen from James's London court. Moniplies asks his master what is in

42. Scott, *The Fortunes of Nigel*, 4.   43. Scott, *The Fortunes of Nigel*, 15.
44. Scott, *The Fortunes of Nigel*, 17.
45. McCracken-Flesher also reads this in terms of an expression of the economic relations that circulate in this text. See McCracken-Flesher, *Possible Scotlands*, 65.
46. Scott, *The Fortunes of Nigel*, 52.

the paper, and Nigel poignantly replies that 'it proclaims the shame of our country, and the ingratitude of our Prince':

> in this paper the Lords of the Council set forth, that, 'in consideration of the resort of idle persons of low condition forth from his Majesty's kingdom of Scotland to his English Court—filling the same with their suits and supplications, and dishonouring the royal presence with their base, poor, and beggarly persons, to the disgrace of their country in the estimation of the English; these are to prohibit the skippers, masters of vessels, and others, in every part of Scotland, from bringing such miserable creatures up to Court, under pain of fine and imprisonment'.[47]

It is clear that such a proclamation is indeed a shame or blight on the newly formed British state, since it acts to exclude Scots from what is now their own capital and the body of their own king, and, moreover, states that they are to be 'punished for their audacity with stripes, stocking, or incarceration'.[48]

Following the trajectory of comic reconciliation, one would expect Nigel's exclusion to be resolved along with his other predicaments, and in a sense this is what happens in the novel but only via a series of encounters that accentuate the parameters of particular spaces and who can rightly inhabit them. *Nigel* was never adapted to the same extent as *Ivanhoe*—it is notable that it gets virtually no mention in Rigney's study—but a review of a production of the novel at Drury Lane in 1868 concentrates on the depiction of London on the stage, recognizing that place and space are intrinsic to any remediation of this text.[49] Yi-Fu Tuan argues that 'space is an abstract term for a complex set of ideas' and that, while different cultures may conceptualize space in different ways, 'Man, out of his intimate experience with his body and with other people, organizes space so that it conforms with and caters to his biological needs and social relations'.[50] Nigel's journey towards resolution is, in fact, punctuated by an engagement with such concepts

47. Scott, *The Fortunes of Nigel*, 49.   48. Scott, *The Fortunes of Nigel*, 49.
49. 'The Fortunes of Nigel at Drury Lane', *Spectator*, 3 October 1868, pp. 1153–4 <http://archive.spectator.co.uk/> (accessed July 2017). Bolton states that 'The Fortunes of Nigel has been but a minor phenomenon in the context of the dramatization of Scott's novels' (*Novels on Stage*, ii. 426) and adds that 'Views of London were particularly appealing to London audiences in the early days of *The Fortunes of Nigel* on stage . . . The bills boast of scenery, which they mention especially when it has been newly painted . . . Sometimes the scenes were copied from highly regarded prints and drawings' (*Novels on Stage*, ii. 427).
50. Yi-Fu Tuan, *Space and Place: The Perspective of Experience* (University of Minnesota Press: Minneapolis and London, 1977), 34.

of space revolving around a series of encounters with the physical body of the king, and the social conventions that render him excluded from it.

After his first failed attempt to deliver his petition via Moniplies Nigel is aided by George Heriot, the king's Scottish goldsmith and banker, who informs him that, unlike more unfortunate Scots, he 'has direct access to the interior of the palace'[51] and will be able to place the petition 'in the King's hand',[52] a familiarity that is later elaborated upon:

> The Goldsmith to the Royal Household... was a person of too much importance to receive the slightest interruption from centinel or porter; and leaving his mule and two of his followers in the outer court, he gently knocked at a postern-gate of the building, and was presently admitted, while the most trusty of his attendants followed him closely with the piece of plate under his arm. This man also he left behind him in an anti-room, where three or four pages in the royal livery, but untrussed, unbuttoned, and dressed more carelessly than their place and nearness to a King's person seemed to admit, were playing at dice and draughts, or stretched upon benches, and slumbering with half-shut eyes. A corresponding gallery, which opened from the anti-room, was occupied by two gentlemen-ushers of the chamber, who gave each a smile of recognition as the wealthy goldsmith entered. No word was spoken on either side, but one of the ushers looked first to Heriot, and then to a little door half-covered by the tapestry, which seemed to say as plain as a look could—'Lies your business that way?' The citizen nodded, and the court-attendant, moving on tiptoe and with as much precaution as if the floor had been paved with eggs, advanced to the door, opened it gently, and spoke a few words in a low tone. The broad Scottish accent of King Jamie was heard in reply—'Admit him instanter, Maxwell—have ye hairboured sae lang at the court, and not learned that gold and silver is ever welcome?'
> The usher signed to Heriot to advance, and the honest citizen was presently introduced into the cabinet of the Sovereign.[53]

Shortly afterwards, Heriot takes Nigel to court, offering to conduct him as far as 'the presence-chamber', where he 'can point out the proper manner and time of approaching the King'.[54] However, while Heriot has access to the king on his own behalf, he cannot introduce Nigel to the king, and Nigel must face a further hurdle before he actually gets to speak to him. The Master Deputy-Chamberlain impedes his entrance on the grounds that, while 'Master Heriot's name will pass current for much gold and silver', it will not guarantee 'birth and rank'.[55]

51. Scott, The Fortunes of Nigel, 56.   52. Scott, The Fortunes of Nigel, 58.
53. Scott, The Fortunes of Nigel, 65–6.   54. Scott, The Fortunes of Nigel, 87.
55. Scott, The Fortunes of Nigel, 108.

It is not until towards the end of the first volume that Nigel finally gets to speak to the king, and a reader might imagine that this will be the end of his misfortunes. However, Nigel's path is not yet smooth, but is beset by a number of obstacles all involving space and who can inhabit it. At court Nigel meets the young Lord Dalgarno (who Heriot describes as the 'new fashion' of Scottish nobility[56]) and is enticed by him into an 'ordinary' or private gaming house, where his reputation is brought into disrepute.[57] As a consequence of inhabiting this prohibited space, he later is compelled to challenge Dalgarno within the precincts of the court in St James's Park. The events that lead up to this are telling. Yi-Fu Tuan observes that the built environment inscribes a 'hierarchy of values'[58] and that most societies have evolved a complex grammar of '"inside" and an "outside", of intimacy and exposure, of private life and public sphere'.[59] Following Levebvre, Drake suggests that Nigel must learn to 'negotiate the city according to conflicting representation of its high and low spaces and its insides and outsides'.[60] St James's Park is clearly one such public space, but its use and its rules are clearly delineated, and, when Dalgarno approaches in the company of Prince Charles and the Duke of Buckingham, the crowds draw off from the path. However, when the prince suggests that Nigel leaves the park, Nigel proclaims that 'he will quit this public walk for pleasure for no man'[61] and that he will stay to challenge Dalgarno as a false friend. In spite of being warned that 'the royal Park is no place to quarrel in', Nigel draws his sword.[62] The consequences are swift. Nigel is warned that 'this is a Star-Chamber business…and may cost [him his] right hand', and told to 'get into Whitefriars or somewhere, for sanctuary and concealment, till [he] can make friends or quit the city'.[63]

Nigel's misunderstanding of the ambiguities of private and public spheres that surround James's London court then lead him further into the labyrinthian complexities of space that this novel embodies. Banished from court and public life once again, Nigel is compelled to make his way via 'steep and

56. Scott, *The Fortunes of Nigel*, 129.
57. Andrew Lincoln suggests that '*The Fortunes of Nigel* shows how the introduction of the 'Ordinary' in Jacobean London provides a social space for those with 'good clothes and good assurance', in contrast to the unrefined pleasures of the tavern' (*Scott*, 11).
58. Tuan, *Space and Place*, 38.   59. Tuan, *Space and Place*, 107.
60. Drake reads the treatment of 'insides; and 'outsides' in *Nigel* in terms of Henri Lefebvre's concept of the three dimensions that cities possess: the symbolic, the paradigmatical, and the syntagmatic. See Drake, 'Ordinary rules', 416.
61. Scott, *The Fortunes of Nigel*, 176.   62. Scott, *The Fortunes of Nigel*, 179.
63. Scott, *The Fortunes of Nigel*, 180.

broken stairs'[64] into the outlawed underworld of Alsatia. When he does eventually escape, it is only to encounter the king in yet another prohibited space governed by strict rules, this time at Greenwich, where he is hunting, and Nigel is erroneously accused of attacking James. 'Can that unhappy man so soon have engaged in a new trespass', asks the prince,[65] and now Nigel is threatened with banishment or worse: 'I have had enough of him, and so has the country,' states James, and Nigel is sent to the most sinister expression of exclusion in the British state, the Tower of London.[66] It seems hard to see how Nigel will be extricated from this series of unfortunate engagements with space, but, perhaps ironically, his freedom is obtained by the king himself venturing into a forbidden or outlawed space. Keen to get to the bottom of Nigel's situation, James spies on him in the Tower. As James recounts to Prince Charles, he has built himself 'a lurking–place called the king's *lugg*, or *ear,* where he could sit undescried, and hear the converse of his prisoners'.[67] The prince is disgusted with this behaviour and the king admits that 'hearkeners hear ill tales of themselves';[68] and so he will have it built up. Yet it is by this further encounter with space that Nigel's innocence is proved and his misfortunes eventually resolved.

It is then via these strange negotiations with spaces and who can inhabit them that the novel reaches its comic conclusion. But, while Nigel does eventually both win back his estate and marry a suitable bride, the ending of the novel continues to engage with questions of expulsion and exile. While Nigel may regain his patrimony, we are left to presume rather than witness his return to it; there is no evidence in the novel that Nigel returns to Scotland. More significantly, James tells Lord Dalgarno, who is now exposed as a villain, that it is he who is banished 'frae our court and our countenance'.[69] In fact Dalgarno, in a last attempt to outwit Nigel, sets out for Scotland; but he is in turn outwitted by his own schemes and killed in a kind of no man's land just beyond London at Enfield Chase—'a wild woodland prospect' that 'led the eye at various points through broad and seemingly interminable alleys'.[70] While Dalgarno is never a particularly likeable character, Heriot has described him as the representative of the new Scotland, and his death in this way is clearly disruptive to any stable version of the British union and Scotland's position in it. Perhaps more significantly,

64. Scott, *The Fortunes of Nigel*, 182.
66. Scott, *The Fortunes of Nigel*, 306.
68. Scott, *The Fortunes of Nigel*, 370.
70. Scott, *The Fortunes of Nigel*, 391.

65. Scott, *The Fortunes of Nigel*, 307–8.
67. Scott, *The Fortunes of Nigel*, 368.
69. Scott, *The Fortunes of Nigel*, 363.

the character Jin Vin (the true Londoner of the tale) has no option but to leave the country as a result of the novel's comic conclusion. As in the 'Introductory Epistle', inclusion (Nigel's comic resolution) is accompanied by a concomitant exclusion from the space that is the new British state.

Through their treatment of character, generic conventions, and space *Ivanhoe* and *The Fortunes of Nigel* offer overt examples of a dynamic by which the idea of nationhood is constructed in part upon what it cannot contain, and it is in this, perhaps, rather than in unproblematic reconciliation of conflict towards unity, that they follow the paradigm of their Scottish predecessors. It is, after all, not only Rebecca and her father who are excluded from the unity at the end of *Ivanhoe*; there is no way forward, or back, for the Saxon Ulrika, who, having attempted to steer a path between her own heritage and a Norman one, is both reviled and outcast, and can only be redeemed by her own death. So, too, Rebecca's situation could be compared to others in Scott's 1820s English texts—Fenella in *Peveril of the Peak*, for example. *Nigel*, too, suggests a host of people who do not sit comfortably within the new British state; the criminals in Alsatia, Dalgarno, Lady Hermione, and perhaps even Nigel himself. If we look back at the Scottish novels in the light of this concern with a connection between exclusion and the emerging nation, we can see that Scott is drawing our attention to the fact that the modern nation state is as deeply entangled in questions of exclusion as in its obvious concerns with issues of belonging and national cohesion. Exclusion and inclusion are inextricably linked.

Throughout 2014, as Scotland both celebrated the bi-centenary of the publication of Scott's first novel *Waverley* and pondered how the boundaries of both the Scottish and the British state potentially might be renegotiated, the question of who may or may not be included within our definitions of national identity were present—and yet constantly evaded. While we would all wish that any new Scotland or reconstituted UK will be a pluralist, multicultural, and liberal state, there may lurk a darker question about who belongs in it, who can and who cannot be included within the ideal model of nationhood. These questions have, unfortunately, become all the more acute as the Scottish independence referendum was followed two years later by the referendum on the European Union. Larger issues of migration, national boundaries, and who can be said to belong have come to haunt Europe and a UK about to renegotiate its relationship with it following the British referendum decision of June 2016 to leave the EU. Ann Rigney argues that *Ivanhoe*, along with all of Scott's fiction, becomes forgotten (as the Author of Waverley may indeed have predicted of all literature) because at some point in the twentieth century the questions raised by it cease to be 'portable' and as a consequence cease to be relevant, which is why, she suggests, they also cease to be read and be adapted.[71] Yet the narratives of inclusion and exclusion that circle around *Ivanhoe*, *The Fortunes of Nigel*, and much of the rest of Scott's oeuvre—once we begin to read it in this way—continue to reverberate, and are, sadly, perhaps all too relevant.

71. Rigney, *Afterlives*, 222.

8

Union and Presbyterian Ulster Scots

William McComb, James McKnight, and *The Repealer Repulsed*

Andrew R. Holmes

This chapter explores the relationship between literature and union in nineteenth-century Ulster among Presbyterian writers who proudly traced their origins to the arrival of Scottish settlers in the seventeenth century. Literary scholars have largely focused on how links between Ulster and Scotland were expressed through the vernacular poetry associated with the so-called Rhyming Weavers in the late eighteenth and early nineteenth centuries. Often dismissed as mere imitators of Robert Burns, these writers have been rehabilitated as significant poets in their own right who utilized a shared literary culture in unique and significant ways.[1] Though some of these Presbyterian writers were associated with theological liberalism and the 1798 rebellion against British rule, others were theologically and politically conservative. These poets are undoubtedly part of the story of Ulster–Scottish literary connections, but this chapter will extend the narrative into the

---

1. For example, Carol Baranuik, *James Orr, Poet and Irish Radical* (London: Pickering and Chatto, 2014); Frank Ferguson and A. R. Holmes (eds), *Revising Robert Burns and Ulster: Literature, Religion and Politics, c. 1770–1920* (Dublin: Four Courts Press, 2009); Liam McIlvanney, *Burns the Radical: Poetry and Politics in Late Eighteenth-Century Scotland* (East Linton: Tuckwell Press, 2002), 220–40.

nineteenth century and beyond the focus on vernacular poetry. It will
demonstrate that Presbyterian writers saw Burns as only one part of a broader
literary culture they shared with Britain and that was usually expressed in
standard English, included prose as well as poetry, and employed a number
of literary genres. It emphasizes the variety of the connections that were
used by Presbyterian writers to reinforce and articulate political union in
the form of the United Kingdom, including a shared Gaelic heritage. In
particular, it draws attention to the common religious inheritance of early-
modern Presbyterianism and anti-Catholicism. As was the case after 1707,
Protestant religion in the nineteenth century continued to be instrumental
in providing the basis of a unifying British identity, not least amongst
Presbyterians in Ireland, where Catholics made up three-quarters of the
population.[2] Yet differences among British and Irish Protestants—Presbyterian
Scots and Ulster-Scots versus the episcopalian United Church of England
and Ireland—continued to cause friction after 1800, and, in many respects,
'Protestant religion was the grit in the Union, not its glue'.[3]

These themes are explored through a consideration of the literary output
of William McComb (1793–1873) and James McKnight (1801–76), who
were responsible for the publication in 1841 of *The Repealer Repulsed*. This
remarkable collection of reportage and literary fancy was written in response
to Daniel O'Connell's campaign to repeal the 1800 Act of Union between
Great Britain and Ireland. It has been described as 'one of the masterpieces
of Ulster Presbyterian polemical literature' and is considered 'a foundation
text of Ulster Unionism'.[4] Though the work was published by McComb,
and he is usually identified as the principal author, it is clear from the evidence presented here that it was mostly written by McKnight.[5] *The Repealer
Repulsed* and the other publications of both writers demonstrate how unionist
literary identity was a multilayered phenomenon and how it could change
over time. Frank Ferguson, the pre-eminent scholar of Ulster-Scots literature,
has observed how the physical location of such writers makes them sensitive

2. Linda Colley, *Britons: Forging the Nation 1707–1837* (New Haven and London: Yale University
Press, 1992); David Hempton, *Religion and Political Culture in Great Britain and Ireland from the
Glorious Revolution to the Decline of Empire* (Cambridge: Cambridge University Press, 1996).

3. Colin Kidd, *Union and Unionisms: Political Thought in Scotland 1500–2000* (Cambridge: Cambridge
University Press, 2008), 211.

4. Peter Brooke, *Ulster Presbyterianism: The Historical Perspective, 1610–1970* (2nd edn; Belfast: Athol
Books, 1994), 153; Patrick Maume (ed.), *The Repealer Repulsed by William McComb* (Dublin:
UCD Press, 2003), p. xvii.

5. This challenges the view of Patrick Maume, whose 2003 edition of the *Repealer Repulsed* states
that McComb was the principal author.

to the messiness of literary identity politics. 'To be Ulster-Scots...is to be aware of the constant traversal of national boundaries and sensitive to negotiating Irish and Scottish modes of being.' As demonstrated here, this sense of occupying a liminal space allowed Ulster Presbyterian writers to employ a variety of literary modes and subjects to suit their unionist purposes. For instance, 'When an Ulster-Scots writer is being serious, she/he exhibits a plain-spoken directness that cuts to the heart of the argument. When in satirical or sportive mode, these writers can play deftly between standard and vernacular registers with great inventiveness.' Ferguson is especially sensitive to the fact that polemical works in this tradition such as *The Repealer Repulsed* 'are much more unionist in design and execution: they employ a dense Scots idiom to remind Ulster readers of their Scottish antecedents and cultural similarities; they are purportedly written by plain-speaking Everyman characters who puncture the pretensions of their intended targets with homespun philosophy and "stage Ulster-Scots" mannerisms'.[6]

The chapter begins with an exploration of the careers of McComb and McKnight before 1841, particularly their shared commitment to evangelical Protestantism and desire to free Ireland from the influence of popery. It examines the influence of Thomas Moore, James Montgomery, and Irish patriotism on the poetry of McComb, before considering McKnight's attempt to vindicate early modern Presbyterians from the misrepresentations of, among others, Sir Walter Scott, as well as his promotion of the Irish language. The following section discusses the principal themes of *The Repealer Repulsed*, especially the fear that repeal would herald 'Rome Rule', and the various literary forms employed to underscore the commitment of Ulster Protestants to the Union. The chapter concludes with the increased attention of both writers to their Scottish Presbyterian heritage after 1841. It considers how this was used to express opposition to the imposition of English Protestant forms and principles, and to highlight the importance and distinctiveness of Presbyterian Scots and Ulster-Scots within the United Kingdom.

I

The failure and brutal suppression of the 1798 rebellion left Presbyterian Ulster bruised and fretful. Many erstwhile rebels were imprisoned, forced

6. Frank Ferguson (ed.), *Ulster-Scots Writing: An Anthology* (Dublin: Four Courts Press, 2008), 4, 6, 20.

into exile, or executed, while many others melted back into daily routine hoping that their past would not catch up with them.[7] The turmoil of the 1790s prompted significant changes within mainstream Presbyterianism, as evangelicalism reanimated the religious life of the bulk of Presbyterians, who had remained religiously conservative.[8] Clergy and laity began to interest themselves in a variety of voluntary societies formed to improve and redeem Irish society. Evangelical resurgence was certainly stimulated by the 1790s and led to Henry Cooke's campaign in the Synod of Ulster against the influence of Arianism, which paved the way for the formation in 1840 of the General Assembly of the Presbyterian Church in Ireland. Though Cooke was a political conservative, most of his ministerial colleagues were able to combine their conservative evangelicalism with reform politics.[9] In that regard, the early nineteenth century was a transitional period, and both William McComb and James McKnight were part of a new generation that reflected the complex relationships between religion, politics, literature, and identity. McKnight is often characterized as 'a Liberal of Liberals', yet he was editor of the conservative *Belfast News-Letter* in the 1830s and 1840s, and McComb, often portrayed as defender of Cooke's conservative politics, was a critic of British government policy in the 1840s and beyond.[10]

William McComb was born in Coleraine on the north coast of Ireland on 17 August 1793.[11] He was apprenticed to Thomas O'Neill, a wholesale draper in Belfast, and quickly became involved in popular education. McComb was a committee member of the Belfast Sunday School Society from its formation in 1811 and was given charge of the day school in 1820. In addition, he was founder and treasurer of the Ulster Institution for the Education of the Deaf and Dumb and the Blind (1831).[12] One of McComb's earliest collections of poems developed out of these experiences. *The School of the Sabbath* (1822) was a meditation on the role of Sunday school education

---

7. I. R. McBride, *Scripture Politics: Ulster Presbyterians and Irish Radicalism in the Late Eighteenth Century* (Oxford: Oxford University Press, 1998), chs 8, 9.

8. A. R. Holmes, *The Shaping of Ulster Presbyterian Belief and Practice, 1770–1840* (Oxford: Oxford University Press, 2006).

9. A. R. Holmes, 'Covenanter Politics: Evangelicalism, Political Liberalism, and Ulster Presbyterians, 1798–1914', *English Historical Review*, 125 (2010), 340–69.

10. 'Funeral of the Late Dr McKnight, Editor of the Derry Standard', *Londonderry Journal*, 14 June 1876.

11. Patrick Maume, 'McComb, William', *Dictionary of Irish Biography*.

12. Aiken McClelland, 'The Early History of Brown Street Primary School', *Ulster Folklife*, 17 (1971), 55; *Historical Sketch of the Ulster Institution for the Deaf and Dumb, and Blind* (Belfast: Belfast News-Letter, 1933), 1–7.

in inculcating religious and moral principles as an antidote to the infidelity and rebellion of the 1790s.[13] The collection included individual poems that McComb had published from the mid-1810s, most of which were eventually collected together in the *Poetical Works of William McComb* (1864). The form of his verse owed much to Thomas Campbell, Isaac Watts, James Montgomery, William Cowper, and Thomas Moore.[14] Whereas Robert Burns had little tangible influence on his poetry and he hardly ever employed dialect, McComb 'admired Byron as the first of all Britain's poets'.[15] McComb was also an admirer of James Montgomery, a Moravian poet with roots in County Antrim, whose poetry and hymns helped shape British evangelical culture.[16] McComb composed a poem in Montgomery's honour when he visited Belfast in October 1841 and recalled fondly his boyhood memories of reading the work of 'The Christian Bard'.[17] McComb preferred the evangelical respectability of Montgomery to the rougher and bawdier Ayrshire bard. When Burns's son visited Belfast in September 1844, McComb's poem for the occasion was indebted to Thomas Moore and presented Burns senior as 'a flawed individual'.[18]

Norman Vance has noted that McComb was 'often specifically, even aggressively, Protestant and Unionist in his outlook'. This was obvious in his concern with the fulfilment of biblical prophecy and the actions of the papal anti-Christ, themes discussed in *The Voice of a Year; or, Recollections of 1848* (1849). Nevertheless, McComb 'is at least fleetingly aware of the whole range of his country's imaginative heritage, English, Scottish, and European as well as Irish. He is able to draw on Anglo-Irish, Scots-Irish and Celtic traditions and on aspects of Ireland's general popular culture.' Vance observes that the results of this cultural fusion 'are sometimes bizarre'.[19] McComb's first collection, *The Dirge of O'Neill* (1817), was published in response to the death of the harper Arthur O'Neill, who is described as an Ossianic figure, 'simultaneously Scottish and Irish'. Patrick Maume notes that the use of

13. William McComb, *The School of the Sabbath: A Poem* (Belfast: T. Mairs, 1822).
14. Patrick Maume, 'From Scotland's Storied Land: William McComb and Scots–Irish Presbyterian Identity', in James McConnel and Frank Ferguson (eds), *Across the Water: Ireland and Scotland in the Nineteenth Century* (Dublin: Four Court Press, 2009), 78–9.
15. 'Reminiscences of the Late William M'Comb', *Ballymena Observer*, 27 September 1873.
16. G. Tolley, 'Montgomery, James (1771–1854)', *Oxford Dictionary of National Biography* (Oxford, 2004).
17. *Belfast Commercial Chronicle*, 26 October 1842.
18. Frank Ferguson, John Erskine, and Roger Dixon, 'Commemorating and Collecting Burns in the North of Ireland, 1844 to 1902', in Ferguson and Holmes, *Revising Robert Burns*, 132.
19. Norman Vance, *Irish Literature: A Social History. Tradition, Identity, and Difference* (Oxford: Basil Blackwell, 1990), 134.

Ossian and the celebration of Brian Boru allowed McComb 'to assert
his Irish patriotism without denying his Unionism'.[20] The importance
of Anglo-Irish Union was expressed in 'Waterloo—Wellington—Erin go
bragh' (1815), a celebration of the Irish field marshal, the 'Saviour of Europe
from war and commotion'.

> Oh! then shall the heroes of Waterloo slumber,
> And shall they forgotten remain in the grave?
>   Ah, no! whilst a string in my harp wakes a number,
> A strain patriotic their memory shall save;
>   Fame shall awaken a dirge to their glory,
> Bards yet unborn in their praise shall grow hoary,
> Europe with Erin will echo the story—
> 'Waterloo, Wellington, Erin-go-bragh!'[21]

McComb's Irish patriotism was clear in 'O Erin my country!', written in
1815 for St Patrick's Day and sung to the tune Kitty Tyrrel. McComb took
the opportunity to assert the superiority of his native land over the other
three kingdoms.

> Britannia may vaunt of her lion and armour,
> And glory when she her old wooden walls views;
> Caledonia may boast of her pibroch and claymore,
> And pride in her philabeg, kilt, and her hose:
> But where is the nation to rival old Erin?
> Or where is the country such heroes can boast?
> In battle they're brave as the tiger or lion,
> And bold as the eagle that flies round our coast!
>
> The breezes oft shake both the rose and the thistle,
> While Erin's green shamrock lies hushed in the dale;
> In safety it rests, while the stormy winds whistle,
> And grows undisturbed, 'midst the moss of the vale:
> The shamrock is emblem of Erin's fair daughters,
> In rustic retreat dwells her boast and her pride,
> And the old branching oak, clad with ivy, oft shelters
> The cottage where love, truth, and beauty reside.[22]

Owing to quarrels with some Sunday school teachers in Brown Street,
William resigned his schoolmaster's post in 1827 and the following year

20. Maume, 'From Scotland's Storied Land', 77–8.
21. William McComb, *Poetical Works of William McComb* (London: Hamilton, Adams & Co., 1864),
    166–7.
22. McComb, *Poetical Works*, 165.

entered business as a bookseller in Belfast.[23] He became publisher for the evangelical party within the Synod of Ulster, responsible for publishing a range of pamphlets and larger works throughout the 1830s and 1840s. He developed close friendships with Henry Cooke and other ministers, including the historian James Seaton Reid, the temperance advocate John Edgar, and the missionary enthusiast James Morgan. Around the same time, McComb made the acquaintance of Thomas Chalmers and James Emerson Tennent, the Conservative MP for Belfast.[24] In 1829 the first issue of the *Orthodox Presbyterian* was published by McComb in the wake of the Arian Controversy. Under the editorial direction of Reid, Cooke, and Morgan, who became the principal manager, the periodical was published monthly until 1840 and 'rendered efficient service to the orthodox cause'.[25]

The second of our authors, James McKnight, was born in February 1801 and until the 1840s spelt his surname as M'Neight. He was born and raised near Rathfriland in County Down, the 'son of an Irish-speaking Presbyterian smallholder'.[26] Writing later in life, McKnight was aware of the perceived incongruity between his Presbyterian religion and this cultural inheritance. He noted that he was

> passionately fond of the old Irish melodies, and have long been picking them up wherever I could find them. Indeed I was familiar with most of the airs in Moore, before his melodies were heard of. My father had an enormous store of scraps of this kind, and when a child he used to sing them to me in Irish. You would hardly expect this from an old black-mouthed Presbyterian.[27]

Alongside his immersion in Irish-language culture, the young McKnight sharpened his theological and philosophical skills by mastering Jonathan Edwards's *An Inquiry into the Modern Prevailing Notions of the Freedom of the Will which is Supposed to be Essential to Moral Agency, Virtue and Vice, Reward and Punishment, Praise and Blame* (1754), a defence of the Calvinist understanding of human sinfulness and the need of salvation by divine grace.[28]

---

23. McClelland, 'Brown Street Primary School', 55–6.
24. 'Reminiscences of the Late William M'Comb', *Ballymena Observer*, 27 September 1873.
25. *McComb's Presbyterian Almanac* (1874), 11. A. A. Campbell, *Irish Presbyterian Magazines, Past and Present: A Bibliography* (Belfast: Greer, 1919), 3–4.
26. Desmond McCabe, 'MacKnight (McKnight), James', *Dictionary of Irish Biography* (Cambridge: Cambridge University Press, 2009).
27. C. G. Duffy, *Young Ireland: A Fragment of Irish History, 1840–45. Final Revision* (London: T. Fisher Unwin, 1896), ii. 64–5 n.
28. W. T. Latimer, 'James M'Knight, LL.D.', in *Ulster Biographies, Relating Chiefly to the Rebellion of 1798* (Belfast: J. Cleeland, 1897), 94; George Marsden, *Jonathan Edwards: A Life* (New Haven: Yale University Press, 2003), 436–46.

He attended a classical school in Newry before entering Belfast Academical Institution in 1825 with the intention of becoming a Presbyterian clergyman. During his time as a student in Belfast, he excelled at languages and metaphysics, but was not a gifted speaker; he did not pursue his clerical calling and became instead librarian at the Linen Hall Library.

Before coming to Belfast, McKnight was already a published author and demonstrated his loyalty to the theology and example of seventeenth-century Ulster-Scots Presbyterians. In 1824 subscribers paid for the publication of his review of James Hogg's *The Brownie of Bodsbeck* (1818), in which McKnight praised the accuracy of Hogg's description of the character of late-seventeenth-century Presbyterians in comparison to the misrepresentations of Sir Walter Scott. According to McKnight, Scott's principal position was 'that our persecuted ancestors, to whose active, unremitting exertions we owe the possession both of Religion and Liberty, were the wild, extravagant, nonsensical madmen that "rave round the tenements" of Old Mortality'. Hogg, by contrast, offered a satisfactory account of their character, 'and lays the blame where it alone should rest—on the agents of arbitrary power'. Included with the review was an essay composed by McKnight on defensive war, originally published in the *Dublin Christian Instructor* in October 1823. He claimed that it was a relevant companion piece, 'for, had the sufferers passively sacrificed Religion and Liberty at the shrine of Despotism, the abhorred demon of Persecution had never scattered desolation through the south and west of Scotland'.[29] With regard to Hogg, McKnight noted that the 'satire is strongly pointed; and the Scottish dialect, rendered in some degree classical by the daring genius of BURNS, gives the whole description an additional charm, and to the lover of rustic simplicity, will furnish a fund of considerable amusement'. In addition to Hogg, his readers were directed to standard works on the later Covenanters such as Sir James Steuart's *Naphtali, or, The Wrestlings of the Church of Scotland for the Kingdom of Christ* (1667) and Robert Wodrow's *The History of the Sufferings of the Church of Scotland from the Restoration to the Revolution* (1721–2). McKnight returned in 1830 to early modern themes when he edited for publication the seventeenth-century manuscripts of the Montgomery family,

29. James M'Neight, *A review of the Brownie of Bodsbeck, with animadversions on Sir W. Scott's character of the Scottish nonconformists in his tale of 'Old Mortality', &c; an appendix, containing an essay on the lawfulness of defensive war, in answer to an article in that subject in the 'Dublin Christian Instructor'* (Newry: Printed by Alexander Peacock, 1824), pp. v, vi, 18, 36–7.

later viscount Ards, significant Scottish landowners and promoters of early Presbyterianism in Ulster.[30]

By early 1827, McKnight had become editor of the *Belfast News-Letter*. He would retain this position until he resigned in 1846, at which point he became, at various times, the editor of the *Londonderry Standard* (1847–8, 1854–76) and the *Banner of Ulster* (1849–54). During the 1830s, McKnight supported in general the religious policies and reforms advocated by Henry Cooke in the Synod of Ulster. He contributed to the orthodox cause by opposing the curriculum of John Ferrie, the professor of moral philosophy in the Belfast Institution, whose empirical, sensationalist, and utilitarian approach was at odds with the Scottish Common Sense philosophy upheld by Presbyterian evangelicals.[31] As editor, McKnight wrote on the course of the debate and contributed anonymously to the case against Ferrie through letters signed John Knox Junior on 'The Mode of Teaching Moral Philosophy' and 'A Presbyterian' on sceptical philosophy.[32]

Bringing together the language enthusiasm of his youth and his Protestant instincts, McKnight was a prominent member of the Ulster Gaelic Society and supported the efforts of evangelical Protestants to convert Catholic Ireland through the Irish language.[33] In editorials in the *Belfast News-Letter*, he commended the cultivation and extension of the Irish language, and he did so within the context of the shared Gaelic language community of Scotland and Ireland. One of his earliest editorials reviewed *Historical Sketches of the Ancient Native Irish* (1828) by Christopher Anderson, the Scottish Baptist evangelical. McKnight urged 'the propriety of improving the intellectual and moral condition of the Irish through the medium of their own language' and cordially recommended Anderson's plans to promote 'an exclusively Irish literature'.[34] McKnight drew his readers' attention to the considerable efforts of Scottish scholars to discover and list works in Gaelic, not least John Reid's

---

30. *The Montgomery manuscripts: containing accounts of the colonization of the Ardes, in the county of Down, in the reigns of Elizabeth and James. Memoirs of the first, second, and third Viscounts Montgomery, and Captain George Montgomery: also, a description of the barony of Ards, with various local and historical facts connected with the colonization of Ulster* (Belfast: News-Letter Office, 1830).

31. A. R. Holmes, 'From Francis Hutcheson to James McCosh: Irish Presbyterians and the Scottish Philosophy in the Nineteenth Century', *History of European Ideas*, 40 (2014), 622–43.

32. McKnight advertised his authorship of these letters on the title page of *The Ulster tenants' claim of right: or, landownership a state trust; the Ulster tenant-right an original grant from the British crown, and the necessity of extending its general principle to the other provinces of Ireland, demonstrated; in a letter to the Right Honourable the Lord John Russell* (Dublin: James McGlashan, 1848).

33. Roger Blaney, *Presbyterians and the Irish language* (Belfast: Ulster Historical Foundation, 1996), 143–51.

34. 'Historical Sketches of the Ancient Native Irish', *Belfast News-Letter*, 8 August 1828.

Bibliotheca Scoto-Celtica (1832). The lesson was obvious: 'if the energy and the zeal which are too frequently expended in teaching Irishmen how to hate each other most effectually, were employed in doing for our native language—and for the millions who understand no other, what Scotsmen have done for *their* country, how different in a little time would be our national condition!' He reviewed Reid's work 'for the purpose of holding up to our countrymen the example of Scotland, in regard to the cultivation of the Gaelic language, and the happy effects which have, in consequence, been produced'. McKnight was aware that the Irish language was identified with Catholicism and that Protestants were not interested in its promotion. Yet the success of Gaelic missions in Scotland provided proof of the strategy he supported.

> Here, then, lies the great secret of Ireland's conversion from Popery—let the vernacular language be studied—let the doctrines of Protestantism be propounded to the people through its fascinating medium—let it be no longer identified with Popery, and the happy results which a similar system has produced in the Highlands of Scotland, will, in due time, be produced in Ireland.[35]

In 1835 the Synod of Ulster decided to employ the Revd Dr Norman McLeod of Campsie, the noted Gaelic scholar and Church of Scotland minister, to translate the metrical psalms into Irish. In a letter to the Revd George Bellis, secretary of the Home Mission of the Synod of Ulster, McLeod outlined the similarities between the inhabitants of the Highlands and Islands of Scotland and much of Ireland—their 'tender and generous' minds, 'the same fond attachment for their own beloved language', and their 'love for story and for song'. If the Irish received the same treatment and opportunities as provided to Gaelic Scotland, 'I have no doubt they will soon exhibit the same delightful picture of simplicity, affectionate fidelity, social order, ardent devotional piety, which, I praise God, is this day to be seen in the lovely islands which gird the coast of Scotland, and in the lovely solitudes of our mountain land.'[36] When McLeod's version was eventually published in 1836, McKnight was rich in his praise of 'this truly admirable work'.[37]

In terms of politics, McKnight was on the reformist end of the conservative political spectrum and recognized the subordination of Presbyterians to the

35. Review of John Reid, *Bibliotheca Scoto-Celtica*, *Belfast News-Letter*, 23 October 1832.
36. 'Dr M'Leod and the Irish Psalms', *Belfast News-Letter*, 21 August 1835.
37. *Belfast News-Letter*, 15 October 1836.

Church of Ireland and to landlords belonging to that church. He shared the Peelite conservatism of James Emerson Tennent, who supported Catholic Emancipation and parliamentary reform as well as opposing popular Orangeism and Protestant ascendancy. By doing so, the *Belfast News-Letter* was roundly criticized by the ultra-Protestant *Ulster Times*.[38] During a period of popular opposition in southern counties to the Church of Ireland in 1832, he wrote to a friend that the 'chief subject of public anxiety now is the Church, and I should like right well to see the "old harlots daughter" spoiled of the possessions of which she stript her *mother* at the Reformation. The *old hag* may have no claim on them, but that is no reason why the *young* one should retain them.'[39] McKnight's critique of the Church of Ireland extended from its social and political dominance to its structure, liturgy, and theology. In 1840 he vindicated the principles of John Knox against the views of the Revd John Cuming, a popular evangelical preacher in London and minister of the Church of Scotland congregation in the city. Cuming had claimed that Knox's *Book of Common Order* (1562, 1564) was a liturgy, a claim strenuously denied by McKnight in the local press and in two pamphlets, the first of which was published by McComb.[40] Cuming's aim was to promote unity between episcopalians and Presbyterians in response to the resurgence of Catholicism in Britain and Ireland and the growing indifference of the state to Protestantism as represented by its allegedly shameful treatment of the Church of Ireland. McKnight fully agreed 'that union amongst Protestants of all classes is most desirable; but union as well as peace may be too dearly purchased, especially if a sacrifice of principle is to be the consideration yielded'.[41]

McKnight's opposition to the Church of Ireland, to landlords, and to their rejection of Irish national education put him at odds with Cooke and politically conservative Presbyterians who wanted closer political co-belligerence with their fellow protestants. Though a Calvinist and an evangelical, McKnight opposed the more hard-line approach of Cooke and some of his supporters.

---

38. John Bew, *The Glory of Being Britons: Civic Unionism in Nineteenth-Century Belfast* (Dublin: Irish Academic Press, 2009), 141, 148–50; Peter Brooke, 'Controversies in Ulster Presbyterianism, 1790–1836', Ph.D. thesis, University of Cambridge, 1980, pp. 186–9.
39. James McKnight to Ms Barber, 1 January 1833, in *Extracts from Original Letters of James McKnight, LL.D. Ninth Annual Report of the Presbyterian Historical Society of Ireland, 1915–16* (Belfast: Presbyterian Historical Society of Ireland, 1916), 8.
40. *John Knox and the Rev. Thomas Drew; Or, the Book of Common Order No Liturgy* (Belfast: William McComb, 1840).
41. *John Knox's Book of Common Order No Liturgy. To the Rev. John Cuming, Minister of the Scottish Church, London, from James M'Neight, Editor of the Belfast News-Letter* (Belfast: n.p., 1840), 14.

In particular, he opposed the reimposition of full subscription to the Westminster Confession of Faith by the Synod of Ulster in 1836 and especially the undertaking to support the teaching of Chapter Twenty-Three of the Confession, which, he argued, allowed for the persecution of those holding non-Presbyterian principles.[42] By insisting on full subscription, McKnight claimed that Cooke and others were no better than benighted Catholics who persecuted against the rights of personal conscience.

Cooke took part in public meetings throughout the United Kingdom during the summer and autumn of 1835 to protest at the weakening of the protestant character of the state. These meetings also protested against the persecuting principles of Roman Catholicism that were allegedly circulated at Maynooth College in a textbook written by the eighteenth-century Catholic theologian Peter Dens.[43] Writing as 'A Member of the Synod of Ulster', McKnight expressed his opposition to this campaign in two anonymous pamphlets, both published in 1836—*A letter to those Ministers and Members of the Church of Scotland, who have Lent themselves to the Dens' Theology Humbug* and *Persecution Sanctioned by the Westminster Confession*. In their mixture of close reasoning, biblical and theological learning, and righteous indignation, these publications are exemplars of Presbyterian controversial literature. The first demonstrated that the protestant Reformers, John Knox, the Westminster standards, and the modern-day Church of Scotland sanctioned the same intolerant principles as Catholic theologians who were assailed by Cooke and his supporters. The preface was addressed 'to my Roman Catholic Countrymen' and observed that all churches were guilty of intolerance and persecution. Though, 'in matters of mere religion, I believe you to be seriously wrong', 'I will never be a party to any scheme for doing you CIVIL OR POLITICAL INJUSTICE, either individually or as a body'. The main body of the text criticized the public pronouncements at Protestant meetings, and McKnight was especially critical of the views of Murtagh (later Mortimer) O'Sullivan, a prominent Church of Ireland anti-Catholic polemicist, and Robert Stewart, Cooke's right-hand man in the Synod.[44] McKnight's second

42. For an overview of this episode, see Brooke, 'Controversies', 243–53.
43. John Wolffe, *The Protestant Crusade in Great Britain 1829–1860* (Oxford: Clarendon Press, 1991), 88–92, 123–8.
44. A Member of the Synod of Ulster [James McKnight], *A letter to those ministers and members of the Church of Scotland, who have lent themselves to the Dens' theology humbug: showing from the Westminster Confession of Faith, the Larger Catechism, and other authorized documents, that John Knox, and our Protestant reformers, together with Assemblies of the Kirk, and even the National Kirk of Scotland itself, have all sanctioned the intolerant principles ascribed to Peter Dens* (Edinburgh: W. Tait, 1836), pp. v, 10, 18–19, 30, 33.

pamphlet addressed the persecuting principles in Chapter Twenty-Three of the Westminster Confession. While virtually every other denomination was 'trying to disengage itself from the trammels of a bigoted antiquity', his 'beloved' Synod was 'apparently made to leap back two centuries' at 'the bidding of a politico-religious dictator' to 'principles which that dictator himself lately denounced with all the fury of zealotism, when party objects were to be attained by their exclusive ascription to the poor Papists of this country'.[45]

Unsurprisingly, McKnight's pamphlets were well received by theological and political liberals but strongly criticized by conservative elements within Irish Presbyterianism.[46] The most interesting response to McKnight came in a pamphlet written in broad Scots dialect. *The McIlwham Papers* have been described as 'one of the most intriguing and linguistically complex polemics to be written in Scots in nineteenth-century Ulster' and whose 'fiery fusion of Scots vernacular, belligerent polemic and calculated personal insult make them worthy if uncouth additions to the corpus of Ulster-Scots writing'.[47] They purported to be a collection of letters edited by a student at Glasgow named John Morrison. The letters were written to McKnight by a childhood friend named Thomas McIlwham, who was now a weaver living in Scotland. They were originally sent to the *Ulster Times* and were published in Belfast by William McComb. The two letters criticized McKnight's alleged change of principles between his 1824 review of Hogg and his 1836 pamphlets. McIlwham recalled his fondness for the early review but could hardly reconcile this with the claims that his childhood friend was the author of the recent pamphlets. 'Is it him write Peter Dens! Is it him leebel the character an' principles o' he's ain great-great grandfather.' A friend of M'Ilwham's in Ulster said McKnight had 'writ twa pamphlets to prove that its what they ca' a mere *humbug* to accuse the Kirk o' Rome o' *persecution*, because the Kirk o' Scotlan', as your freen M'Neight is said to say, was as bad a *persecutor herself*". M'Ilwham was proud of his friend's achievements, but was cautious about the potential adverse effects of his intellectual attainments. 'Schulership

---

45. A Member of the Synod of Ulster [James McKnight], *Persecution sanctioned by the Westminster Confession: a letter, addressed to the clergy, eldership, and laity, of the Synod of Ulster, shewing, from the history and proceedings of the Westminster divines, and the public records of the Church of Scotland, the doctrines of intolerance to which the late vote of unqualified subscription has committed the general Synod of Ulster: with an humble dedication to the Rev. Dr. Cooke* (Belfast: J. Tate, 1836), 70–1.

46. For positive reviews, see *Northern Whig*, 24 March 1836; *Bible Christian*, NS 1 (December 1836), 381–4; for a negative review, see *Covenanter*, NS 4 (1837), 41–3.

47. Ferguson (ed.), *Anthology*, 257–8.

an' pheelosofy, o' which ye hae doubtless a hantle, are like fire an' water, gude in their ain places; capita servants, but awfu maisters.'[48] He also referred to McKnight's recent review in the *Belfast News-Letter* of James Meikle's *Our Scottish Forefathers* (1837), a rather unsuccessful novel about the earliest Scottish ministers in east Ulster. McKnight claimed that the narrative was 'utterly barren of incident and invention', while 'a tissue of historical anachronisms pervades the whole'.[49] M'Ilwham was at a loss to explain the review: 'Why naething but the speerit o' an elf or water kelpie cud hae dictated sic illeeberal, uncandid, an' unfounded observations.'[50]

II

After the 1832 general election, Daniel O'Connell led a group of thirty-nine Irish MPs who were pledged to bring about the repeal of the Act of Union.[51] Though that objective remained, for most of the following decade he attempted to work with Whig administrations to address specific Irish grievances. By the late 1830s, O'Connell was increasingly frustrated at the lack of progress and aware that the populist energies he had harnessed during the campaign for emancipation were ebbing away. As a consequence, he decided to renew agitation for repeal by touring Ireland and addressing large political meetings. In late 1840, plans were made to bring the campaign to Ulster. The prospect of repeal greatly alarmed Protestant opinion throughout Ireland, and in the province of Ulster it united Protestants from various political, social, theological, and denominational backgrounds. The figurehead of that united Protestant response was Henry Cooke, who publically challenged O'Connell to debate the merits of union in Belfast. After much obfuscation and mutual recriminations, O'Connell did visit the town in January 1841, though the obvious and deeply felt opposition to repeal among Ulster Protestants meant that his public engagements were few, and he quietly slipped away after a few days. Not wishing to waste the opportunity,

---

48. *The McIlwham Papers: In Two Letters from Thomas Mcilwham, Weaver, to his Friend, James Mcneight, Editor of the Belfast Newsletter. Edited, and Illustrated with Notes and a Glossary, by John Morrison, a Student, Glasgow* (Belfast: William McComb, 1838), 9, 18.
49. *Belfast News-Letter*, 24 November 1837. James Meikle, *Our Scottish Forefathers, a Tale of Ulster Presbyterians* (Belfast: H. Clark and Co., 1837).
50. *McIlwham Papers*, 19.
51. Patrick Geoghegan, *Liberator: The Life and Death of Daniel O'Connell, 1830–1847* (Dublin: Gill Books, 2010).

Cooke and his supporters held a series of public meetings at which he became the champion of the Union. Cooke's articulation of a world view that combined evangelicalism, anti-Catholicism, social conservatism, and unionism meant that he became the 'archetypal Ulster Protestant political parson'.[52] Unsurprisingly, the events and speeches received extensive coverage in the local and national press, but they also received permanent form in a pamphlet published by William McComb and entitled *The repealer repulsed! A correct narrative of the rise and progress of the repeal invasion of Ulster: Dr Cooke's challenge and Mr O'Connell's declinature, tactics, and flight. With appropriate poetical and pictorial illustrations. Also, an authentic report of the great Conservative demonstrations, in Belfast, on the 21 and 23 of January 1841.* A note written and signed by McKnight on the title page of a copy of the work held in the Gamble Library of the Union Theological College in Belfast reveals the authorship and division of responsibilities: 'The "Narrative" portion of this pamphlet was written by me; the squibs &c were contributed by the Publisher, and by other parties.'[53]

McKnight's introductory narrative ran to nearly forty pages and expressed many of the themes he had been developing over the previous fifteen years. He began by drawing historical parallels between O'Connell's campaign in Ulster with 'other Anti-British movements', including the United Irishmen. McKnight developed a comparison between O'Connell and Wolfe Tone, both of whom, he claimed, 'were salaried missionaries of Irish Roman Catholicism' who 'affected devotion to objects strictly constitutional' but whose careers told a more sinister story. For McKnight, repeal of the Union would bring about Rome Rule in Ireland: 'That Repeal is essentially a Roman Catholic interest, no one can doubt—its object and intended effect are to give Irish Roman Catholics an ascendant preponderance in the councils of the state; and, of course, to depress Protestants in a civil point of view, to the level of their numbers, as compared with the bulk of the general population.' Reflecting the tolerant tone of his 1836 pamphlets, he conceded that 'too much has sometimes been made of the intolerant character of the Romish system', yet when any sect achieved ascendancy in Ireland it would rule in favour of its own members. Moreover, the policy of Rome was marked by 'deep subtlety' and 'flexible adaptation', and its plan was 'no less than that of endeavouring to proselytize Ulster to Roman Catholicism'.

52. R. F. G. Holmes, *Henry Cooke* (Belfast: Christian Journals, 1981), 208. Cooke's response to O'Connell is well summarized on pp. 145–9.
53. This autograph note was reproduced in McKnight, *Extracts from Original Letters*, 9.

The recent assaults by priests on Protestantism in Belfast were calculated to prepare the ground for repeal.

> The plan was, first, to insult us and our religion, without distinction of sect or party; secondly, to attempt the putting of our necks under the feet of the Roman Catholics, even when the latter are in a local minority; and, lastly, to call upon us, in no very humble tone, to join them in the promotion of a scheme for exalting them to the dignity of a permanent national ascendancy! If *they* exhibited, and the *Church* patronized, such a spirit as this, when, in regard to Belfast at least, Roman Catholics constitute an insignificant, uninfluential minority, what would they not do, supposing them to have in their own hands the uncontrolled direction of the national councils?[54]

Though O'Connell had first been invited to Belfast by local repealers on 17 October, a definitive acceptance by him appeared in the *Vindicator* only on 2 January 1841, while on 6 January a formal challenge from Cooke was issued in the *Belfast Commercial Chronicle*. According to McKnight, Cooke's challenge disconcerted the repealers while also uniting 'the friends of British connexion', both liberals and conservatives. O'Connell responded on 9 January and referred to Cooke's challenge being taken up by a 'Hercules-Street Artizan', while a satire on a dialogue between two Belfast supporters of O'Connell appeared in the *Belfast News-Letter* on 12 January. The situation developed quickly over the next few days—O'Connell referred to 'my friend Bully Cooke, the cock of the North', while Cooke asserted that Presbyterian Ulster, despite minor political differences, was united against repeal. McKnight took delight in recording how O'Connell travelled north incognito and how a public meeting in the Victoria Theatre was not filled to capacity, despite the presence of a significant number of priests.[55]

The next hundred pages provided a full account of two Grand Conservative Demonstrations. The first was held on 21 January and had been called to support Lord Stanley's controversial voter registration bill and to oppose repeal.[56] The meeting 'formed a striking contrast, both in numbers and respectability, to the ragged pauperism' that characterized O'Connell's supporters. Friendly overtures were made towards politically liberal Protestants,

---

54. *The repealer repulsed! A correct narrative of the rise and progress of the repeal invasion of Ulster: Dr Cooke's challenge and Mr O'Connell's declinature, tactics, and flight. With appropriate poetical and pictorial illustrations. Also, an authentic report of the great Conservative demonstrations, in Belfast, on the 21 and 23 of January 1841* (Belfast: William McComb, 1841), 3, 4, 5, 7.
55. *Repealer Repulsed*, 13, 24, 31.
56. K. T. Hoppen, *Elections, Politics, and Society in Ireland 1832–1885* (Oxford: Oxford University Press, 1984), 15.

and the right of clergy to pronounce on political matters was defended. Cooke took to the stage and addressed the crowd as 'a Conservative, a Protestant, a Christian'. His speech covered the persecution of Protestants by Catholics in the sixteenth and seventeenth centuries, and he also discussed Presbyterian involvement in 1798. In particular, the massacre of Protestants by Catholic insurgents in Wexford had an invaluable impact on the political outlook of Presbyterians.

> Yes, yes; there was a time when the people of Ulster were nearly lured between the Scylla and Charybdis of disaffection and rebellion, and the genius of Popery was the syren that sung them amidst the breakers, the whirlpools, and the rocks. (Hear, hear, and cheers.) But the time will never come when the Presbyterians of Ulster will be found at the tail of O'Connell. (Cheers.) I tell you, Mr. O'Connell, the unhappy men and women who fell victims at Scullabogue barn and Wexford Bridge have been the political saviours of their country. (Loud cheering.) Though they perished, they live. They live in our remembrance—their deaths opened the political eyes of the many thousands of Ulster; and the names of Wexford and Scullabogue form an answer to all your arguments for Repeal.

In conclusion, Cooke offered a powerful economic argument for maintenance of the Union, the remarkable growth of Belfast, which had been nurtured by civil and religious liberty, benevolent episcopal landlords, and Protestant graft. 'In one word more I have done with my argument—Look at Belfast, and be a Repealer—if you can.' At a grand dinner held the next evening, Cooke returned to these themes and especially the dangers of religious ascendancy, calling on his audience to remember Catholic persecution in the past as a warning for the future. In such circumstances 'union' was used in a full range of meaning— the Act of Union, Protestant political union, and union with Christ.

> But, the cross represents union, while it seals the reconciliation between God and man. We'll stand, like Luther, so long as this Protestant kingdom stands, upholding that doctrine which he declared to be the sign of a standing or a falling Church—the doctrine of justification by faith, with humble hearts and uplifted hands. 'By the Cross of Christ crucified to the world,' and by the spirit of God 'rendered meet' for a better inheritance, an enduring kingdom. And if the enemy should ever repeat his invasion, the Protestants of Ulster will stand united, as the parts of that sad, yet glorious emblem of our religion to which I have referred; and we shall meet him again, as our rock-bound shores meet the waves of the Atlantic; and though again he may come in with lies, again must he go out in blasphemy.[57]

57. *Repealer Repulsed*, 46, 95, 103–4, 111, 131–2.

The narrative provided by McKnight ran to 140 pages, over 85 per cent of the total length of the pamphlet. In addition, the work contained six pictorial representations of the events of January 1841.[58] The final seventeen pages were entitled 'The Northern Lights; or Sketches and Songs All About Repeal'. The humorous introduction to this section signalled a change in authorial voice. It observed that the events covered in the previous narratives were 'equal in interest to the days of the French Revolution' and the author was 'now equal to Herodotus or Hume, Robertson or Rapin, Gillies or Gibbon, Schlegel or Smollet'. Now the writer could 'relax from our philosophical severity, and … condescend to regale thee with the Romance of the History of that ever-to-be-remembered epoch'. Such was the importance of these events, that a new period of literary endeavour in Protestant Ulster had been inaugurated.

> The talent of the North was roused; a new impulse was given to the mind; vast and gigantic conceptions struggled to obtain vent; poets who erst were unconscious of their powers, appeared in a multitude; lyrics and elegies were flung forth; nay, an epic was meditated, whose subject was Repeal—whose hero was Dan—whose episodes were soirees—whose moral was loyalty—and whose catastrophe was defeat.

The various literary efforts were collected from the *Belfast News-Letter*, the *Belfast Commercial Chronicle*, and the *Londonderry Standard*.[59]

The content of this section demonstrated a variety of literary influences and forms from Ireland, Britain, and North America. The first section was mainly composed of poems and songs, including 'O'Connell's Warning', a parody of 'Lochiel's Warning' (1802) by Thomas Campbell and probably composed by McComb. The following song was a rough satire of the supporters of O'Connell entitled 'The Blissin's of Repale'. It was claimed that it had been sung to the tune 'The Groves of Blarney' in 'a remote shebeen' by a Torlogh Mullan 'with all the euphoniousness of the Munster brogue'.[60] There then followed songs and poems on O'Connell's progress through Banbridge, the repeal dinner in Belfast, and his hasty departure from the town. There also was included 'A New Scene from Macbeth' that had 'never before exhibited on any northern stage'. It was based on the famous scene of the three witches around the caldron, the location of which was now

---

58. Patrick Maume, 'Repealing the Repealer: William McComb's Caricatures of Daniel O'Connell', *History Ireland*, 13/2 (March–April 2005), 43–7.
59. *Repealer Repulsed*, 144.   60. *Repealer Repulsed*, 147.

the office of the *Vindicator* in Belfast. The final two items were pieces of prose. The first was an imitation of the letters of Sam Slick, a creation of the English-born Nova Scotian writer Thomas Chandler Haliburton, who used the figure of Slick to poke fun at the manners and opinions of Canadians and Americans.[61] The conservative-inclined Slick had sympathy for Cooke's position.

> They want to break up a Union that has brought them most of the prosperity and true happiness that ever they have had. They want, like the cursedest fools ever I heard tell of, to cut away their sheet-anchor, at the very time that the storm may be ready to blart in their very teeth, and throw them upon all dangers of a lee shore.

The Repealer Repulsed concluded with two letters written in the style of the *McIlwham Papers*, purportedly composed by James Anderson of Ballintrae, who had sent them to John Hill, a bookseller in Belfast. In one of these, there was reference to a supporter of repeal from the predominantly Protestant town of Newtownards named M'Kitterty, though he was known to Hill and Anderson as Kitterty, perhaps a reference to his attempt to seem more Irish for his O'Connellite audience.

> I coulda leuk on the body without thinkin' on an auld hoose, whar the maist licht cams in through the cracks o' the roof. But losh man, had you seen him! how he rair'd an itampit, an' whappit, an' slappit his loof again his tides, an' shot out his nose like the heft o' a peggin' awl; an' sae raved about blood an' thunner, and peats, that sic nonsense ne'er was begatten, since or afore.[62]

McKnight observed at the conclusion of his narrative that Cooke's challenge to O'Connell had rendered invaluable service, 'not alone to the Protestants of Ireland, but to those of the British empire at large' (*Repealer Repulsed*, 143). This was certainly reflected in the many newspaper reviews that appeared after publication of *The Repealer Repulsed* in early March. The *Belfast Commercial Chronicle* described it as 'a very desirable book', 'exceedingly well got up', and 'well worth the low price'.[63] The *Belfast News-Letter* focused on the quality of the production and illustrations, which were 'in a high degree creditable to the taste and spirit of the publisher, as well as to the artistical talent of Belfast'. The reviewer (probably McKnight) recommended the work to all classes of political society, not least as 'it does justice to the manly,

61. Maume (ed.), *Repealer Repulsed*, 298; Fred Cogswell, 'Haliburton, Thomas Chandler', in *Dictionary of Canadian Biography*.
62. *Repealer Repulsed*, 157, 160.   63. *Belfast Commercial Chronicle*, 13 March 1841.

determined stand made by the Liberal Protestants of Belfast against the sectarian exclusiveness attempted to be established by the advocates of Repeal'.[64] The Protestant press in the rest of Ireland was equally enthusiastic about the publication. The *Wexford Conservative* stated that it deserved 'to be preserved as a faithful record of one of the most ridiculous and extraordinary occurrences, which the people of Ireland have ever witnessed'. 'Like the siege of Derry, the attack on Belfast, though a bloodless one, will be held long in the remembrance; and the event will be handed down to posterity, to remind them of what an united people can do, when lawless demagogues dare to infringe on their liberties, and to dragoon them into licentiousness.'[65] The *Dundee Warder* claimed that the reader would become acquainted in the publication with 'the most sarcastic of prose orations, and the most sky-rocketty of squib poetry'. In their opinion, 'certainly a more spirited publication has seldom been placed in our hands. It smacks of Ireland and Ulster from end to end.' The highlight for them, as well as *Cumberland Pacquet*, was Cooke's own contributions, which combined, to devastating effect, 'truth and reason, raillery and sarcasm' to overturn 'the nefarious projects of Repeal and Popish Ascendancy'.[66]

III

McComb's and McKnight's unionism remained with them for the rest of their lives, but they did not succumb to an unthinking form of Protestant politics. If anything, they became more vocal in their positive articulation of a distinctive Ulster–Scottish Presbyterian political identity. They did so because the principles and social position of Presbyterians seemed to be challenged on all sides during the 1840s.[67] The mother Church of Scotland suffered the catastrophe of the Disruption of 1843 that saw over 40 per cent of its membership secede to form the Free Church of Scotland over the

64. *Belfast News-Letter*, 26 March 1841.
65. *Wexford Conservative*, 31 March 1841. For similar opinions, see *Downpatrick Recorder*, 20 March 1841; *Dublin Evening Packet and Correspondent*, 18 March 1841; *Warder and Dublin Weekly Mail*, 27 March 1841.
66. *Dundee Warder*, 27 April 1841. *Cumberland Pacquet and Ware's Whitehaven Advertiser*, 30 March 1841
67. The following is based on: Holmes, *Henry Cooke*, 151–60; S. J. Brown, *Providence and Empire: Religion, Politics and Society in the United Kingdom, 1815–1914* (Harlow: Pearson Longman, 2008), 111–17; David Paton, *The Clergy and the Clearances: The Church and the Highland Crisis 1790–1850* (Edinburgh: John Donald, 2006).

failure of the state to recognize the spiritual independence of the church. In Ireland, many Presbyterian marriages were called into question on the basis of the High Church claim that only ceremonies performed by bishop-ordained clergy were valid. In both Scotland and Ireland, Free Church and Irish Presbyterian ministers became the spokesmen for crofters and tenant farmers who found themselves increasingly squeezed by Episcopalian and Church of Scotland landlords. Given all these pressures, Presbyterians asserted their privileges and turned to their shared histories in an effort to ensure that Scots and Ulster-Scots were not marginalized within the United Kingdom.

McKnight's response to developments after 1841 was through editorials written for the *Londonderry Standard* and the *Banner of Ulster* and works on political economy. In July 1847, he founded with William Sharman Crawford the Ulster Tenant Right Association to advocate the legalization of 'the Ulster Custom', the right of departing tenants to be recompensed for improvements they made to their holdings.[68] The significance of McKnight, according to Frank Wright, was that he shared the Protestant principles of northern farmers and based his understanding of tenant right on the early seventeenth-century articles of plantation yet encouraged his co-religionists to make common cause with Catholic farmers in the south whose economic position was more precarious than their own.[69] McKnight's most extensive discussion of the land question was *The Ulster Tenants' Claim of Right* (1848), in which he argued that landlords did not have an absolute right of ownership as the land was vested in trust to them at the Plantation. As a consequence of the growth of modern notions of equality, both Catholic and Protestant tenant farmers could now enjoy the profits accrued by their improvements.[70] His views on tenant right were extended further when he became editor of the *Banner of Ulster* in September 1849. McKnight's first editorial outlined the intrinsic relationship between Presbyterian principle, political non-partisanship, and the legalization of tenant right. McKnight and the people he spoke for wanted reform of 'an antiquated feudalism' because they were political reformers, free traders, and anti-revolutionists. More importantly, 'as Bible Presbyterians, we believe that, if the Mosaic

---

68. 'Definitive Formation of the "Ulster Tenant Right Association"', *Banner of Ulster*, 6 July 1847.
69. Frank Wright, *Two Lands on One Soil: Ulster Politics before Home Rule* (Dublin: Gill and Macmillan, 1996), 171.
70. For analyses of the *Ulster Tenants' Claim of Right*, see Wright, *Two Lands*, 171–6, and D.W. Miller, *Queen's Rebels; Ulster Loyalism in Historical Perspective* (Dublin: Gill and Macmillan, 1978), 76–8.

dispensation is calculated to teach any one doctrine to Christian communities, it is this, that, "fixity" of popular "tenure" is the universal law, specially sanctioned by the Deity himself in the arrangements of his own model commonwealth'.[71] His attempt to unite northern Protestant and southern Catholic farmers was initially successful, but the Tenant League fell apart over repeal and the fallout from the Papal Aggression in 1850–1.[72]

McComb combined these complex themes in his poetry during the mid-Victorian period. The prominent Ulster poet and critic John Hewitt too easily dismissed him as 'that sanctimonious bookseller' and *The School of the Sabbath* as 'weighty not to say flatulent, with piety'.[73] Yet McComb's didactic and respectable verse is not always subservient and reveals the interplay between Presbyterian principle and evangelical ecumenism. Maume has observed that through his publications 'he sought to disseminate to an Ulster Presbyterian audience a sense that they were part of a worldwide Evangelical culture at its purest in the tradition deriving from the Scottish Reformation and destined to find definitive expression in a world dominated by a united Presbyterian Church'.[74] An important means of doing so was *McComb's Presbyterian Almanac*. From the outset, the *Almanac* stressed the connection between the Scottish and Irish churches and offered wholehearted support for evangelicals in the Church of Scotland in their struggles with the Moderate Party and Peel's Erastian government. McComb urged his Presbyterian readers in 1841 to tell their local MPs 'that they should advocate your cause and that of Scotland's before the British Senate, or else, you will look out for those who will'. Presbyterian voters were to tell their landlords 'that conscience requires you... to act independently as freeholders, and that you will support no candidate who will not support your principles and struggle for the Church of your forefathers'.[75] Presbyterian pride was articulated by McComb in June 1843 at the bicentenary of the formation of the first presbytery on Irish soil by chaplains of the Scottish forces sent to quell the 1641 rising. McComb's poem for the occasion, 'Two hundred years ago', is perhaps his most well-known piece and, according to a fellow Presbyterian, 'stirs the spirit like the Marsellaise Hymn'.[76] It reflected pride

71. *Banner of Ulster*, 4 September 1849.   72. Wright, *Two Lands*, 192–207.
73. John Hewitt, *Rhyming Weavers and Other Poets of Antrim and Down*, new edn. (Belfast: Blackstaff Press, 2004), 103; John Hewitt, 'Ulster Poets', MA thesis, Queen's University Belfast, 1951, p. 67.
74. Maume, 'From Scotland's Storied Land', 76.
75. *McComb's Presbyterian Almanac and Christian Remembrancer* (1841), 62.
76. 'The Late William McComb', *Evangelical Witness and Presbyterian Review* (1873), 273.

in the Presbyterian past and the remarkable prosperity of Ulster in contrast with the rest of Ireland still gripped by the age-old enemy of popery.

> Two hundred years ago, there came from Scotland's storied land,
> To Carrick's old and fortress town, a Presbyterian band;
> They planted on the Castle-wall the Banner of the Blue,
> And worshipped God in simple form, as Presbyterians do.
> Oh! hallowed be their memory, who in our land did sow
> The goodly seed of Gospel Truth, two hundred years ago!
>
> Two hundred years ago, the hand of massacre was nigh;
> And far and wide o'er Erin's land was heard the midnight cry;
> Now Presbyterian Ulster rests, in happiness and peace,
> While crimes in distant provinces from year to year increase;
> O Lord! their bondage quickly turn, as streams in south that flow,
> For Popery is the same it was two hundred years ago.[77]

In the wake of the Disruption, McComb penned a poem in praise of the new Free Church of Scotland and its determined stand for Presbyterian and biblical principles. The last two stanzas expressed these themes and the identity of Presbyterianism and Scottishness.

> Soldiers of Christ! well done!
>   The struggle now is o'er;
> Wave, wave your banner blue on high.
>   As did your sires of yore:
> On every hill of Scotland plant
> The standard of the Covenant.
>   What though the martyrs' blood
>   Has stained its heavenly hue—
> Oh! ne'er forget that it was given
>   A sacred pledge to you;
> And may it still to Scotland be
> The flag of Scotland's liberty![78]

McComb obviously was appealing to a common Ulster–Scottish Presbyterian culture that was informed by a powerful historical myth about the purity and principle of early modern Presbyterianism. This was expressed by the flourishing of Presbyterian historiography in both countries and was commemorated in a spate of bi- and tri-centenaries, including the beginning of

---

77. McComb, *Poetical Works*, 210–12. The original appeared in the *McComb's Presbyterian Almanac* (1843), 62.
78. McComb, *Poetical Works*, 212–14. The original was published as 'The Free Presbyterian Church of Scotland', *McComb's Presbyterian Almanac* (1844), 65.

the Reformation in Scotland in 1560 under the leadership of John Knox.[79] It was the stand of Knox and his Presbyterian successors against the evils of popery that underpinned a shared identity. Some have claimed that McComb's 'virulent Anti-Catholicism' limited his national appeal, but that ignores the substantial support for that cause throughout the United Kingdom, most obviously seen in the reaction to the so-called Papal Aggression of 1850–1.[80] Furthermore, most nineteenth-century Protestants, including McComb, were hopeful that popery would wither in the face of the global expansion of evangelicalism, though they acknowledged that there would be a formidable conflict before the Second Coming.[81] Writing at the tercentenary of the Scottish Reformation in 1860, McComb noted: 'The days of ecclesiastical despotism are numbered, but Presbyterianism, which secures liberty without licentiousness, and unity without sameness, is the system which must eventually prevail over all Christendom.'[82] McComb's poem 'Three Hundred Years Ago' (1860) celebrated the 'race of brave and stalwart men' who freed Scotland from 'Popish thrall' and unleashed true religion, liberty, and missionary spirit; it also identified the connection between the Reformation in Scotland and the birth of Ulster Presbyterianism.

> Two Hundred Years Ago, there came to Ulster's fertile shore
> A goodly race of faithful men, our birthright to restore;
> We hailed them from the fatherland of mountain and of flood—
> The sons of sires who fought the fight, resisting unto blood.
> Hence Ireland's Presbyterian Church sends greetings on the day
> When Scotland's Presbyterian Church holds Tri-Centenary.
> The bulwark of our liberty to Scotland's sons we owe.
> And to our martyred ancestors. Three Hundred Years ago.[83]

79. James J. Coleman, *Remembering the Past in Nineteenth-Century Scotland: Commemoration, Nationality and Memory* (Edinburgh: Edinburgh University Press, 2014), 88–129; Coleman, 'The Scottish Covenanters', in Gareth Atkins (ed.), *Making and Remaking Saints in Nineteenth-Century Britain* (Manchester: Manchester University Press, 2016), 177–92; A. R. Holmes, 'Irish Presbyterian Commemorations of their Scottish Past, c.1830 to 1914', in McConnel and Ferguson (eds), *Across the Water*, 48–61; Holmes, 'The Scottish Reformations and the Origin of Religious and Civil Liberty in Britain and Ireland: Presbyterian Interpretations, c.1800–1860', *Bulletin of the John Rylands University Library*, 90 (2014), 135–54.

80. Thomas Hamilton, 'McComb, William (1793–1873)', rev. Katherine Mullin, *Oxford Dictionary of National Biography* (Oxford, 2004). For the Papal Aggression, see Wolffe, *Protestant Crusade*, 243–5, 247–9.

81. A. R. Holmes, 'The Uses and Interpretation of Prophecy in Irish Presbyterianism, 1850–1930', in Crawford Gribben and A. R. Holmes (eds), *Protestant Millennialism, Evangelicalism, and Irish Society, 1790–2005* (Basingstoke: Palgrave Macmillan, 2006), 144–73.

82. 'The Tri-Centenary of the Scottish Reformation', *McComb's Presbyterian Almanac* (1861), 62.

83. McComb, *Poetical Works*, 353–5.

McComb's progressive vision extended to politics, and his comments in 1841 show that he was sympathetic to political reform and critical of landlords. This was also seen in his positive description of the heroism of Protestant United Irishmen who fought against the Crown at the battle of Ballynahinch in 1798 and the rebel heroine Betsy Gray. The rebellion was 'a melancholy exhibition of folly and recklessness' and exhibited the infidel principles of Paine, yet it proved a providential 'turning point in the history of Ireland' as it brought about institutions for the spread of biblical Christianity as well as new modes of farming and communications. Intelligent Irish people in the mid-nineteenth century looked askance at the folly of attempting to separate from Britain, 'and every year, in the growing prosperity of the Emerald Isle, they are presented with fresh proofs of the benefits of the Union'. In addition to political reforms, 'English and Scottish capital has vastly contributed to Ireland's amelioration, and every sane person may now see that a separation from the sister country would be the harbinger of our national degradation'.[84]

McComb retired from business in 1864 and in the same year his collected poems were published. Most of the reviews remarked on his Irish patriotism as defined by Protestant liberty and religion. The *Weekly Review* noted that *The Dirge of O'Neill* was 'a patriotic elegy' that 'breathes the breath both of a true patriot and a lover of liberty of conscience—Protestant liberty'.[85] While Scottish reviewers observed that McComb was not well known in their country, the Presbyterian press in Ulster was very enthusiastic.[86] The *Derry Standard* hoped that 'the volume will inevitably give to the author an immeasurably higher place, both in the poetical and literary world, than that which he has hitherto occupied, in consequence of the scattered condition of his numerous writings'. As with British reviewers, it noticed that the early poems approached 'very closely to the genius and style of Thomas Moore'.[87] The *Banner of Ulster* emphasized his long-held position as 'Poet Laureate of Northern Presbyterianism'. His verse on the 'the early struggles of the Scottish Church in Ulster recalls reminiscences, which, like the music of their fathers' hills, ring on the ear of the descendants of the first settlers with all the thrilling effect of national harmony'.[88] The *Evangelical Witness and*

---

84. *McComb's Guide to Belfast, the Giant's Causeway, and the Adjoining Districts of the Counties of Antrim and Down* (Belfast: William McComb, 1861), 121–43, 143.
85. *Poetical Works of William McComb. Notices of the Press* (London, 1864).
86. For Scottish reviews, see *Notices of the Press*, 7–9.
87. *Notices of the Press*, 12.   88. *Notices of the Press*, 15.

Presbyterian Review declared that McComb was 'the poet of Ulster, and pre-eminently of Presbyterian Ulster', 'a true Irishman, in lively sympathy with the people of his land.' More significantly, 'he is all the more patriotic because he is a true Protestant and Christian'.[89] A memorial poem written by Francis Davis was published in *McComb's Presbyterian Almanac*. Though Davis was at this point a Protestant nationalist, he admired McComb's Ulster identity and religious seriousness.

> No more—no more!—ah, nevermore
>   Shall em'rald Ulster, midst her toil,
> With his loved voice essay to soar
>   In song that sanctified her soil.
> Yet, bless'd be heaven, doth Ulster know
>   That he who feels his God is love,
> And singeth but for Christ below,
>   Shall more His minstrel be above.[90]

The literary output of McComb and McKnight surveyed in this chapter shows the variety, complexity, and sophistication of Presbyterian Ulster-Scots writing. The identity they expressed was part of a Presbyterian culture they shared with Scotland, but it also reflected the multinational character of the United Kingdom. They were shaped by their Irish identity through, for instance, McComb's patriotic verse that followed the forms of Thomas Moore and McKnight's active support for the revival of the Irish language. In each case, these themes were refracted through a Protestant lens, and they both hoped that Presbyterian evangelicalism would transform Catholic Ireland and thus strengthen the United Kingdom. They shared this vision with most British Protestants and particularly with Scottish Presbyterians. Yet the problem was that the Protestant United Kingdom was not united, and from the late 1830s tensions between Ulster–Scottish Presbyterians and English and Irish episcopalians caused a political crisis that led to the Disruption of 1843. Both writers found that Presbyterian principle clashed with the dominant Anglican state churches, and they used a shared Ulster–Scottish Presbyterian discourse to condemn the inequalities of union. At the same time, this discourse also reinforced their opposition to O'Connell's campaign to repeal the Union and would provide the most potent symbol of Ulster Protestant opposition to Home Rule when the Ulster Covenant

89. *Notices of the Press*, 20, 21.   90. *McComb's Presbyterian Almanac* (1875), 10–11.

was signed in September 1912.[91] By that stage, of course, many Scottish Presbyterians were supporters of Irish Home Rule, yet that should not detract from the interpretation offered in this chapter. Ulster-Scottish Presbyterians in the mid-Victorian period shared a religiously-infused literary world view that asserted the superiority of the Presbyterian form of Protestantism and identified the threat from the age-old enemy of popery. For them, union was a Protestant, specifically Presbyterian, project.

91. A. R. Holmes, 'Presbyterian Religion, Historiography and Ulster Scots Identity, c.1800 to 1914', *Historical Journal*, 52 (2009), 615–40, especially 634–40.

9

Between Nationhood and Nonconformity

The Scottish Whig–Presbyterian Novel and the Denominational Press

Valerie Wallace and Colin Kidd

Scotland's literary past is an unacknowledged foreign country. What stands between the Scotland of a century ago and the very different country of today is a decisive process of secularization. According to the most recent census results in 2011, the largest grouping in Scotland comprised the thirty-seven per cent who declared themselves non-religious, reinforced by the nominal and indifferent Presbyterianism of the 1.7 million (thirty-two per cent) who self-identified as Church of Scotland, for the Kirk's actual membership is only 400,000.[1] While the literary scholars of today's secular, or, more precisely, post-Presbyterian Scotland obsess, understandably enough, over questions of independence and nationhood, the literati of the nineteenth and early twentieth centuries perceived identity primarily in denominational terms. The clash of Presbyterian and Episcopalian and interdenominational competition among rival strains of Presbyterianism were more obviously in evidence than grievances about how the English treated the Scots. For most Scots, certainly from the mid-eighteenth-century

1. Scottish Government, Religious Group Demographics, 2001 and 2011 <http://www.gov.scot/Topics/People/Equality/Equalities/DataGrid/Religion/RelPopMig> (accessed July 2017).

Secessions, by way of the Disruption of 1843, to the reunion of the Church of Scotland with the United Free Church in 1929, denominational allegiances, largely within Presbyterianism itself, were the principal vehicles of self-realization. However, one could go further. Religion rather than nationhood was the dominant feature of Scottish literature after 1707. In particular, the history of Scottish literature between the Napoleonic era and the First World War is in substance, or should be—if properly parsed—a matter of church history, inseparable from a saga of denominational divisions and alignments.

Literary critics are certainly aware of religious idioms and inflections in Scottish culture. The classic study is Susan Manning's *The Puritan–Provincial Vision* (1990), which traced a distinctive Calvinist ethos in the literatures of nineteenth-century Scotland and New England.[2] Nevertheless, it requires a further leap of the historical imagination to understand that religious identities were once more important than national identities. Historians recognize that Britishness and unionism were long inextricably linked with Protestantism, in particular with the twin Reformations of England and Scotland, with the pan-British vision of the Presbyterian Solemn League and Covenant of 1643, and with the anti-Catholic Revolution of 1688–9. The 'Glorious Revolution', in its turn, paved the way for the re-establishment in Scotland of Presbyterianism in 1690, and for the Union of 1707, which safeguarded both the Presbyterian Kirk establishment and the Revolution.

Presbyterianism was, of course, also long integral to Scotland's self-image. Scotland was in large part a Presbyterian nation, conclusively so from the religious settlement of 1690. Presbyterianism and Scottish nationhood were on occasions treated as synonymous, not least when the country was faced from the second quarter of the nineteenth century with substantial immigration from Ireland, a majority of it Roman Catholic. Sectarian divisions between a nativist Presbyterianism and Irish immigrants loomed large in Scottish culture for well over a century. Indeed, as a canonical date 1690—the year that the Battle of the Boyne in Ireland confirmed the anti-Catholic Revolution of 1688–9—remains even now a more resonant date in Scottish demotic parlance and graffiti than 1707. Indeed, hostility towards Irish Catholicism underpinned the pronounced nativism of the interwar era, nationalist as well as sectarian. During the 1920s and 1930s—the era when Scottish

2. Susan Manning, *The Puritan–Provincial Vision: Scottish and American Literature in the Nineteenth Century* (Cambridge: Cambridge University Press, 1990).

nationalism was first institutionalized in the *Scots Independent* (a monthly newspaper established in 1926), the National Party of Scotland (founded 1928), and the Scottish National Party (formed in 1934 from the merger of the left-of-centre NPS with the right-of-centre Scottish Party)—Irish Catholics were still seen as an alien presence in Scottish life: demonized by influential sections of the Church of Scotland, by leading journalists, and even by notable figures in the SNP, such as Andrew Dewar Gibb (1888–1974).[3] The very pronounced religious differences between Scots Presbyterianism and Irish Catholicism meant that for much of the nineteenth and early twentieth centuries the Scottish–Irish relationship was much more fraught than the relatively modest intra-Protestant frictions that disturbed Presbyterian Scotland's connection with its Anglican neighbour. The Union of 1800, which extended the Union of 1707 to incorporate Ireland, also introduced an outlandish third party into the Anglo-Scottish relationship. The assertion and projection of Scots Presbyterian nationhood belonged as much to a triangular relationship, including Ireland, as to a bilateral relationship with England.

Nevertheless, this alignment of Kirk and nation constituted a single thread in the complex tapestry of Scottish identity. For Scotland had also been for the previous two centuries a land of schism and secession; the land of Kirkmen and Seceders, of Free Churchmen and Free Presbyterians, of Reformed Presbyterians and the Relief Church, of New Licht Burghers and New Licht Anti-Burghers, of Auld Licht Burghers and Auld Licht Anti-Burghers.[4] Arguably, the denominational rivalry among the various branches of Presbyterianism was for much of the late eighteenth and nineteenth centuries the most prominent theme in Scottish literary culture, though not one that has left its mark on literary scholarship.

What has attracted more attention from literary critics is the long-standing contention between Presbyterians and Episcopalians, not least as these map onto well-established topics in Scottish literature—namely, the matter of the Covenanters, which has been a stock subject for Presbyterians, and

3. Andrew Dewar Gibb, *Scotland in Eclipse* (London: H. Toulmin, 1930); Catriona M. M. Macdonald, 'Andrew Dewar Gibb', in James Mitchell and Gerry Hassan (eds), *Scottish National Party Leaders* (London: Biteback, 2016), 105–25.
4. This is an area where the most comprehensive works date back to a bygone era when ecclesiastical history was the dominant area of Scottish historiography, in itself, of course, a telling phenomenon: John McKerrow, *History of the Secession Church* (Glasgow: A. Fullarton, 1841); Gavin Struthers, *The History of the Rise, Progress, and Principles of the Relief Church* (Glasgow: A. Fullarton, 1843); Matthew Hutchison, *The Reformed Presbyterian Church in Scotland: Its Origin and History 1680–1876* (Paisley: J and R. Parlane, 1893).

the matter of the Jacobites, which has been a staple of Episcopalian–Tory romanticizing. For each confessional tradition, the other represented tyranny— the grim authoritarianism of the Covenanters or the persecuting Cavaliers of the Restoration era—but also rebellion, in the form of the risings of the later Covenanters or of the Jacobite Pretenders. The Presbyterian Kirk established in 1690 also faced an enduring literary challenge from Episcopalians who questioned its legitimacy, and Episcopalians also resorted to satire in their critique of what they regarded as a vulgar, philistine creed devoid of cultural standards, refinement, or higher learning. This 'party-colouring'[5] in Scottish literature inherited from seventeenth-century polemic persisted well into the mid-nineteenth century, an era that witnessed ongoing skirmishes between Episcopalian and Presbyterian literati over controverted moments, personalities, and themes of Scotland's contested seventeenth-century past.

Some of the elements in the Episcopalian critique of Presbyterianism found their way during the eighteenth century into intra-Presbyterian disputes, especially as matter for liberal New Licht Presbyters who questioned the heavy-handed dominance of a stifling Auld Licht Calvinism in Scottish life, and the hypocrisies that it nourished. However, the division of Auld Lichts and New Lichts was only one of the many axes of division that fragmented Scots Presbyterianism during the eighteenth and nineteenth centuries: voluntaryism, the lines of demarcation between Kirk and State, the obligations of the Covenants, and patronage—all of these pitted Scots Presbyterians against fellow co-religionists who shared the same basic doctrines and worship. Gerry Carruthers, one of today's leading literary scholars, has recently argued that 1711–12—the date of the Patronage Act— was for much of modern Scottish history a more significant date than 1707.[6] Between the mid-eighteenth century and the 1920s huge amounts of mental effort and ink were expended in fighting the corners—often the very small corners—of Scotland's multiplicity of denominations. Scotland—as we shall see—had a rich periodical press during the nineteenth century, but one splintered along denominational lines. Every denomination had its own magazine, and Scottish reviewing bore marked denominational inflections.

---

5. David Reid (ed.), *The Party-Coloured Mind: Selected Prose Relating to the Conflict between Church and State in Seventeenth-Century Scotland* (Edinburgh: Scottish Academic Press, 1982).
6. Gerard Carruthers, 'Presbyterianism and the Legacy of Thomas Muir', unpublished paper presented at 'Presbyterianism and Scottish Literature' colloquium, University of St Andrews, 7 October 2016.

The divisions between Seceders and Kirkmen, Free Churchmen and Reformed Presbyterians, as well as between Presbyterians and Episcopalians, were as keenly felt, much more so in fact, than those between Scotland and England.

Party and denominational literature predominated in nineteenth-century Scotland, and novelists tended to relate Scotland's story not so much in terms of national grievance or nationalist assertion, but according to distinctive denominational perspectives. Confessional allegiances—rather than nationhood per se—framed the national story. However, matters were more complicated still, for there was also, of course, a moderate, latitudinarian readership in Scotland, sceptical of sectarian exclusiveness, which welcomed reconciliation and a degree of ecumenical good feeling, whether within Presbyterianism or within Scottish Protestantism more broadly. Scott, indeed, catered to this latter market and endeavoured to promote bipartisanship between Presbyterians and Episcopalians. Nevertheless, Scott's admiration for moderates on both sides of Protestant Scotland's religious divide did not preclude a marked asperity—sometimes serious, sometimes satirical— towards confessional extremists. This is why the author of *Old Mortality* was—as we shall see—misunderstood as a harsh, cyclopean partisan; which he was not.

Moreover, denominational partisanship was also tempered with an acknowledgement of deeper bonds—of doctrine and worship—which united the various rival elements in Scots Presbyterianism. Indeed, modest efforts towards intra-Presbyterian reconciliation constituted one of the hallmarks of nineteenth-century Scots churchmanship, notwithstanding the devastating drama of the Free Church split of 1843, which—naturally enough—tends to monopolize the attention of historians. Nevertheless, long-standing processes of fragmentation largely went into reverse, and the rival branches of the Scots Presbyterian tradition were gradually reconsolidated into larger denominations. Both branches of the New Licht Secession merged in 1820 as the United Secession, which joined with the Relief Church as the United Presbyterians in 1847; and this body later combined with the Free Church to become the United Free Church in 1900. Coincidentally—and on balance, it is perhaps, largely, coincidence—the United Free Church amalgamated with the Church of Scotland in a new broad-based national Kirk in 1929, at the very moment when nationalist parties first appeared on the Scottish scene. How far was the emergence of nationalism, one wonders, dependent on a prior settlement of the long-standing Scottish church question?

There are further complications in Scottish church history that prick our casual assumptions about past identities and allegiances. During the period when denominations were busy staking out their positions with respect to rival Presbyterian denominations, issues of union and independence faded into the background of debate. There were concerns in various denominations about the British state, but not about the Union as such. Rather there were concerns that the British state was Erastian, subordinating the supposed spiritual autonomy of the Scottish Church establishment to the sovereign claims of the British Parliament. However, political nationalism was in short supply. An article in the *Edinburgh Theological Magazine*, founded in 1826 as the mouthpiece of the United Secession Church, was attentive to the 'British problem'. Critical of moves to repeal the Irish union, it pointed to the success of 1707.[7] Denominational magazines like the *Edinburgh Theological Magazine* stridently defended Scotland's ecclesiastical distinctiveness without questioning the validity of the post-Union British state. Denominations were too busy sniping at the ecclesiological errors of their deviant co-religionists to bother with broader questions of nationhood. Although the ecclesiastical provisions that accompanied the Union of 1707 were open to interpretation and debate, the Union itself was taken for granted as an unquestioned fact of life.

Much of the incessant competition between Scotland's various Presbyterian denominations concerned the legacy of the seventeenth-century Covenanters, who had provoked the Civil Wars of the 1640s by rebelling against Episcopalian innovations in the late 1630s. Thereafter the later Covenanters of the 1670s had led the resistance to the Stuart regime, which eventually issued in the Revolution of 1688–9. Every Presbyterian denomination saw itself—at least in some measure—as the true heir of the heroic Covenanters, and jostled with its rivals to appropriate the mantle of historic Presbyterian righteousness. The ideals of the Covenanters were enshrined in two great documents, the National Covenant of 1638, which set out Scotland's grievances, and the Solemn League and Covenant of 1643, an alliance between the Covenanters and the English Parliamentarian cause, which exalted the ideal of an Anglo-Scottish union, on Presbyterian terms. In this way, a form of unionism was enshrined in the Covenanting tradition, which was in other respects a proxy for authentic Scots Presbyterian nationhood.

7. 'Union of Ireland and Britain', *Edinburgh Theological Magazine* (December 1829).

Indeed, one of the major themes in nineteenth-century Scottish literature, and a topic still not exhausted by the end of the twentieth century, was the vexed question of the Covenanters, their values and their psychology. The issue was provoked by the Episcopalian novelist and sentimental Jacobite Walter Scott, whose novel *Old Mortality* (1816) appeared to demonize the later Covenanters as dangerous fanatics and obsessives—not least by way of the novel's deluded preachers the Revds Habakkuk Mucklewrath and Ephraim Macbriar. The furore over *Old Mortality* generated a massive theological and literary debate over the next decade about the ethos of the Covenanters in particular, and Scots Calvinists in general. However, almost two centuries later the issues raised by Scott's *Old Mortality* were still a live issue for Scotland's finest contemporary novelist James Robertson (b. 1958), whose *The Fanatic* (2000) and *The Testament of Gideon Mack* (2006) continued to scratch the national itch left by the protagonists of the 1820s in the initial round of debate.

Of all the condemnations of *Old Mortality*, the review in the *Edinburgh Christian Instructor* of January, February, and March 1817 by the Revd Thomas McCrie (1772–1835), an Auld Licht Antiburgher, was the most powerful.[8] McCrie, like many evangelicals, regarded novel-reading as a time-killing activity for 'vacant minds', but he was still willing to read *Old Mortality* in order to criticize it.[9] Evangelical reviewers cared more about the function than the aesthetics of fiction. The departmentalization of religious periodicals, says Candy Gunther Brown, in which texts were organised according to their function rather than their literary genre, signalled to readers how texts should be used.[10] Poetry was sometimes included in magazines if it had a moralizing purpose,[11] but novels, especially historical novels, were more suspicious because they could express profanity and infidelity and misrepresent the past. Novelists had a duty, wrote one contributor in the *Edinburgh Theological Magazine*, to respect the sanctity of history.[12] Walter Scott, whose

8. Douglas M. Murray, 'Martyrs or Madmen? The Covenanters, Sir Walter Scott and Dr Thomas McCrie', *Innes Review*, 43 (1992), 166–75.

9. *Miscellaneous Writings, Chiefly Historical of the Late Thomas McCrie, DD*, ed. Thomas McCrie Jr (Edinburgh: Johnstone, 1841), 259.

10. Candy G. Brown, *The Word in the World: Evangelical Writing, Publishing, and Reading in America, 1789–1880* (Chapel Hill, NC, and London: University of North Carolina Press, 2004); Erin A. Smith, 'Religion and Popular Print Culture', in Christine Bolt (ed.), *The Oxford History of Popular Print Culture 1860–1920* (Oxford: Oxford University Press, 2012), 280.

11. The *Christian Magazine* announced when it launched in 1797 that religious poems would be admitted occasionally. 'Address to the Public', *Christian Magazine; or Evangelical Repository* (1797).

12. 'On Novel-Reading', *Edinburgh Theological Magazine* (December 1833).

novel, its critics declared, depicted the Restoration Covenanters as fanatical madmen, had failed in this regard. Scott had already been criticized in the *Edinburgh Christian Instructor* for praising Viscount Claverhouse too warmly in the *Lady of the Lake* (1810).[13] Claverhouse was the real-life figure who in the seventeenth century led the force directed to neutralize the Covenanting rebellion. Now, in *Old Mortality*, which featured Claverhouse as a somewhat noble character, Scott, the *Edinburgh Theological Magazine* declared, had vilified the 'defenders of our liberties'.[14]

In later years, McCrie's son, Thomas McCrie junior (1797–1875), explained that the elder McCrie had been indignant at Scott's attempt 'under the insidious form of fiction' to pour scorn on the Covenanters. Historical novelists 'must conform to historic truth'.[15] 'When [Scott] speaks', said the elder McCrie,

> of those men who were engaged in the great struggle for national and individual rights, civil and religious, which took place in this country previous to the Revolution, and of all the cruelties of the oppression, and all the sufferings of the oppressed, he is not to be tolerated in giving a false and distorted view of men and measures.[16]

According to McCrie's son, it was unsurprising that Scott, as a Jacobite sympathizer and Episcopalian, should represent the Covenanters in such a way. His depiction of the Covenanters struck deep, said McCrie junior, at his father's 'profession as a Seceder'.[17] In January, Scott defended his book in the *Quarterly Review*—a periodical with a predominantly Anglican readership—in which he accused his critics of allowing their 'religious or political creed' to be the 'sole gauge for estimating the good or bad qualities of the characters of past ages'.[18]

In the *Quarterly* in 1818, Scott expanded on his initial critique of McCrie in a positive review of *The Secret and True History of the Church of Scotland* (1817), another work that underlined the fanaticism of the Covenanters,

13. 'To the Editor of the Edinburgh Christian Instructor', *Edinburgh Christian Instructor* (October 1810).
14. 'On Novel-Reading', *Edinburgh Theological Magazine* (December 1833).
15. McCrie, *Miscellaneous Writings*, ed. McCrie Jr, 247, 268.
16. Thomas McCrie, 'Review of "Tales of My Landlord"', in *The Works of Thomas McCrie, DD: A New Edition*, ed. Thomas McCrie Jr (Edinburgh: William Blackwood, 1857), 12.
17. McCrie, *Miscellaneous Writings*, ed. McCrie Jr, 257.
18. 'Tales of My Landlord', *Quarterly Review* (January 1817). On the *Quarterly*, see Boyd Hilton, '"Sardonic Grins" and "Paranoid Politics"': Religion, Economics, and Public Policy in the *Quarterly Review*', in Jonathan Cutmore (ed.), *Conservatism and the Quarterly Review: A Critical Analysis* (London: Pickering and Chatto, 2007), 41–60.

edited by Charles Kirkpatrick Sharpe, a friend of Scott's and a fellow Episcopalian.[19] McCrie's indignation increased. The *Quarterly*, he thought, was ignorant on Scottish affairs. In a fragment commenting on this piece, McCrie accused Scott of lacking patriotism:

> We have writers of poetry and of romance, called National, who, amidst all the fine sentiments which they have uttered, have not uttered one sentiment truly Scottish, who have not yet been able to form a conception of the real Scottish character, who never were in the heart of Scotland, and are at home only when they are among marauding borderers, or demi-savage, pilfering, poignarding mountaineers.[20]

In McCrie's eyes, Scott's Jacobite Episcopalian sympathies rendered him un-Scottish. He equated Presbyterian denominationalism with Scottish patriotism. In a similar vein McCrie attacked the *British Review* and *British Critic* for their inaccurate endorsements of Scott. It was unsurprising, wrote McCrie, that the High Church Anglican *Critic* should write a positive review. Elsewhere in a letter to the Revd Andrew Thomson, editor of the *Edinburgh Christian Instructor*, McCrie jokingly remarked that the magazine was a good weapon to continue the Covenanting onslaught on the Anglican south: 'we should not be long in having a Solemn League and Covenant, and we would enter England at the head of 20,000 good, hearty, invincible (not soldiers armed with guns and swords, like General Leslie's, but) *Christian Instructors*, and we would easily put to flight the whole host of Christian Observers, British Critics, and Anti-Jacobin Reviewers.'[21] On account of their denominational proclivities, English periodicals—and Scottish writers of the wrong religious stripe—could not be trusted to give accurate accounts of Scotland's history.

The other leading novelists of Scott's day also participated in the debate over *Old Mortality*, contributing their own fictional interpretations of the Covenanting past and Presbyterian history more broadly.[22] James Hogg's *The Brownie of Bodsbeck* (1818) amounted to a straightforward rejection of the seeming anti-Covenanting message of *Old Mortality*. Instead, Hogg depicted a more conventionally heroic account of the beleaguered and

19. Sharon Ragaz, 'Walter Scott and the *Quarterly Review*', in Cutmore (ed.), *Conservatism and the Quarterly Review*, 107–32.
20. McCrie, *Miscellaneous Writings*, ed. McCrie Jr, 252.
21. Thomas McCrie Jr, *Life of Thomas McCrie, DD* (Edinburgh, 1840), 218.
22. Douglas Mack, 'The Rage of Fanaticism in Former Days: James Hogg's *Confessions* and the Controversy over *Old Mortality*', in Ian Campbell (ed.), *Nineteenth-Century Scottish Fiction* (Manchester: Carcanet, 1979), 37–50.

persecuted Covenanters after their defeat at the Battle of Bothwell Brig (1679). Hogg focuses on the simple virtues of the rural Lowlanders, and their modest desire to practise their religion unmolested.[23] John Galt's epic family saga *Ringan Gilhaize* (1823), which runs from the era of the Scottish Reformation through to the Revolution of 1689, seems for much of its course to be in the same modestly heroic tone as Hogg's *Brownie of Bodsbeck*.[24] However, by the end of the novel it is unclear whether Gilhaize remains a virtuous champion of the Covenanting cause or has been driven demented, either by the travails of his family or by imbibing religious zealotry to excess. By the novel's conclusion the reader is unsure about the grandiloquence of the Covenanting hero who is about to kill the Cavalier general Claverhouse at the Battle of Killiecrankie and thus deliver Scotland from the evils of religious persecution and Stuart tyranny. Has the hero succumbed to fanaticism? Is the slaying of Claverhouse tantamount rather to a godly execution or indeed to an assassination?[25] Galt, with masterly reticence, leaves the ending ambiguous, with enough of a seeming fanfare to satisfy the pro-Covenanting partisans among his readers, yet also with a sly instability of register that tantalizes the quizzical reader.[26] Galt's ambivalence seems understated by comparison with Hogg's second contribution to the debate the following year in his *Private Memoirs and Confessions of a Justified Sinner* (1824).[27] Hogg's celebrated novel picks up the theme of justified killing in *Ringan Gilhaize* and deliberately presents the reader with two parallel but incompatible accounts of an extreme Calvinist in the decades following the Revolution of 1689, who exercises righteous judgement—that is, murder— on individuals he deems backsliders and sinners. The two narratives Hogg sets out are the memoir of the deluded antinomian narrator and its interpretation in his critical apparatus by that document's editor, a rationalist product of the Scottish Enlightenment. The reader becomes all too obviously aware of the impasse between the two versions of the story, and is left with the chilling possibility, that a supernatural evil of the sort beyond the

23. James Hogg, *The Brownie of Bodsbeck* (1818; Edinburgh: Scottish Academic Press, 1976).
24. John Galt, *Ringan Gilhaize* (1823; Edinburgh: Canongate, 1995).
25. Colin Kidd, 'Assassination Principles in Scottish Political Culture from Buchanan to Hogg', in Roger Mason and Caroline Erskine (eds), *George Buchanan* (Farnham: Ashgate, 2012), 269–88.
26. P. Wilson, 'Ringan Gilhaize: A Neglected Masterpiece?' in Christopher Whatley (ed.), *John Galt 1779–1979* (Edinburgh: Ramsay Head Press, 1979), 120–50, esp. 138–9; Douglas Gifford, 'Myth, Parody and Dissociation: Scottish Fiction 1814–1914', in Gifford (ed.), *History of Scottish Literature Vol. III* (Aberdeen: Aberdeen University Press, 1987), 225.
27. James Hogg, *The Private Memoirs and Confessions of a Justified Sinner* (1824; Harmondsworth: Penguin, 1983).

comprehension of the enlightened editor, might in fact exist. We have come a long way from the particular circumstances and actions of the Covenanters. Nevertheless, as Douglas Mack has shown, Hogg's *Confessions* offers a sophisticated variation on the party novel. Instead of presenting a bipartisan conflict between groups of Covenanting Presbyterians and Episcopalian Cavaliers, Mack argues, Hogg grouped his protagonists into three camps: virtuous Presbyterian moderates, hyper-Calvinist extremists, and morally lax, if otherwise humane, Tory–Episcopalians.[28] Hogg is not anti-Presbyterian— or, arguably, anti-Calvinist as such[29]—but rather a critic of fanatical excess. He flirts with bipartisanship and roundly condemns a flagrant deformation of Calvinism that leads to an antinomian rejection of moral standards. Hogg's riposte to Scott's *Old Mortality* and Galt's *Ringan Gilhaize*, both of which he appears to have misunderstood, at least in part, was a precisely targeted condemnation of Presbyterian fanaticism: exactly what Scott and Galt were, in their different ways, trying to achieve—with, it seems, limited success among their contemporary readers.

Scott himself backtracked in his novel *The Heart of Midlothian* (1818), which—notwithstanding any continuity in personnel—was conceived as a thematic sequel to *Old Mortality*. Here Scott celebrated a strain of post-Covenanting heroism, in the person of Jeanie Deans, daughter of a Covenanting farmer, who travels to London to plead for the life of her sister Effie, tried and found guilty of the crime of presumptive infanticide. Mercy is at the core of the story, which pointedly contrasts the severity of Old Testament legalism and the more compassionate dispensation that follows, and suggests that in Scotland too the uncompromising rigour and inflexibility of the Covenanting cause was gradually modulating with the passing of generations into a culture of robust rectitude, fortitude, and uprightness, but devoid of the militant intensity that emerged in reaction to the years of Cavalier persecution. The novel concludes with a marriage between Jeanie and Reuben Butler, a Church of Scotland minister and the son of an English Cromwellian Independent who had settled in Scotland. Butler stands for second-generation moderation, and for 'common sense', which, he notes, 'accords with philosophy and religion more frequently than pedants or zealots are apt to admit'.[30] Behind the stories of Jeanie and Effie Deans,

28. Mack, 'Rage of Fanaticism'.
29. Crawford Gribben, 'James Hogg, Scottish Calvinism and Literary Theory', *Scottish Studies Review*, 5 (2004), 9–26.
30. Walter Scott, *The Heart of Midlothian* (1818; New York: Holt, Rinehart and Winston, 1963), 540.

which comprise the immediate foreground of the novel, lies a pointed backstory, the exhaustion of the volcanic religious enthusiasm of the seventeenth century and the changing manners of the eighteenth, which encompassed a greater emphasis on interdenominational civility and a growing tolerance for confessional difference.

★

Notwithstanding such shifts in manners, interdenominational rivalries long remained a feature of Scottish life and letters, most especially in the realm of periodicals and magazines. With the exception of one or two titles, the Scottish periodical press has been an understudied, almost 'invisible', aspect of the history of the book trade in Britain.[31] The denominational magazine, a subgenre of the periodical press, has been particularly neglected. While historians and literary critics have paid some attention to the famous literary reviews of the early nineteenth century—the *Edinburgh Review* and *Blackwood's Edinburgh Magazine*—the Wellesley Index includes only a few entries for religious magazines, regarded by the Index's compilers as too low brow to be worthy of serious critical study.[32] To fill this gap, Josef Atholz produced in 1989 a broad survey of the religious periodical press in Britain. His catalogue of titles, however, is far from comprehensive. It includes only brief sections on Scotland. According to Atholz, Scotland was an 'ecclesiastical world of its own' and thus, he implies, deserves a separate study.[33] Despite this acknowledgement, Joanne Shattock's analysis of the editorial practices of the *North British Review* remains the only focused consideration of the production of a Scottish religious periodical.[34] Yet the religious press was arguably the most popular branch of the book trade. As evangelicalism began to flourish, so too did the religious press; its output increased fourfold between 1790 and 1825.[35] One of the first Scottish evangelical magazines

31. Bill Bell, 'The Age of the Periodical', in Bill Bell (ed.), *The Edinburgh History of the Book in Scotland*, iii. *Ambition and Industry 1800–1880* (Edinburgh: Edinburgh University Press, 2007), 340.
32. Jane Platt, *Subscribing to Faith? The Anglican Parish Magazine 1859–1929* (Houndmills: Palgrave Macmillan, 2015), 6.
33. Jose L. Altholz, *The Religious Press in Britain, 1760–1900* (Westport, CT: Greenwood, 1989), 5. Terry Barringer has produced a catalogue of missionary periodicals drawing on the Missionary Periodicals Database hosted by Yale University. Some Scottish titles are included in this list; see Terry Barringer, 'What Mrs Jellyby Might Have Read: Missionary Periodicals: A Neglected Source', *Victorian Periodicals Review*, 37/4 (2004), 46–74, at 53–73.
34. Joanne Shattock, 'Problems of Parentage: The *North British Review* and the Free Church of Scotland', in Joanne Shattock and Michael Wolff (eds), *The Victorian Periodical Press: Samplings and Soundings* (Leicester and Toronto: Leicester University Press, 1982), 145–66.
35. Altholz, *Religious Press*, 10; Louise Billington, 'The Religious Periodical and Newspaper Press, 1770–1870', in Michael Harris and Alan Lee (eds), *The Press in English Society from the Seventeenth to Nineteenth Centuries* (London and Toronto: Associated University Presses, 1986), 113–32;

was established in 1797, five years before the *Edinburgh Review* kick-started what was, according to Bill Bell, the 'Golden Age' of the Scottish magazine.[36] As organs of improvement and conversion, religious magazines had a didactic purpose and were regularly sent to missionaries.[37] Reading had, of course, always been central to Protestantism, but nineteenth-century evangelicals, who believed that bible circulation and the diffusion of knowledge would facilitate conversion, reinforced its importance. According to the *United Secession Magazine*, the periodical press had acquired an 'ascendancy over the public mind'; it had the power to 'renovate' or to 'ruin'.[38]

As Candy Gunther Brown has argued, the denominational periodical press of the early nineteenth century constituted a distinctive branch of the book trade. Between 1789 and 1880, says Brown, whose study focuses on the United States, 'evangelical print culture' involved a distinctive set of writing, reading, and publishing practices.[39] The producers of religious magazines, for example, maintained working relationships with jobbing printers, who used hand presses, long after mainstream publishers had begun to machine-print in house. Some publishers were known for their religious brands,[40] while distribution networks were different from those of the secular press. As Jonathan Topham has argued, the *Wesleyan-Methodist Magazine,* distributed through particular Methodist networks in England, became 'institutionalized' within the authority structures of the church.[41] An informal English Nonconformist network, meanwhile, facilitated the distribution of the *Patriot* newspaper.[42] Owing to their relative cheapness, regular appearance, and geographical distribution, English and American religious periodicals helped to forge communities and functioned to maintain 'faith communities

Jonathan R. Topham, '*The Wesleyan–Methodist Magazine* and Religious Monthlies in Early Nineteenth-Century Britain', in Geoffrey Cantor, Gowan Dawson, Graeme Gooday, Richard Noakes, Sally Shuttleworth, and Jonathan R. Topham (eds), *Science in the Nineteenth-Century Periodical: Reading the Magazine of Nature* (Cambridge: Cambridge University Press, 2004), 67–90. See also the contributions by Peter Garside, David Finkelstein, and Padmini Ray Murray in Bell (ed.), *Edinburgh History of the Book*.

36. Bell, 'Periodical', 341.
37. Sujit Sivasundaram, 'The Periodical as Barometer: Spiritual Measurement and the *Evangelical Magazine*', in Louise Henson, Geoffrey Cantor, Geoffrey Dawson, Richard Noakes, Sally Shuttleworth, and Jonathan R. Topham (eds), *Culture and Science in the Nineteenth-Century Media* (Aldershot: Ashgate, 2004), 43–55.
38. 'Introductory Address', *United Secession Magazine*, Jan 1833.
39. Brown, *Word in the World*, 1.
40. Patrick Scott, 'The Business of Belief: The Emergence of "Religious" Publishing', in D. Baker (ed.), *Sanctity and Secularity: The Church and the World* (Oxford: Blackwell, 1973), 213–23.
41. Topham, '*Wesleyan–Methodist Magazine*', 73.
42. J. Nicoll Cooper, 'Dissenters & National Journalism: "The Patriot" in the 1830s', *Victorian Periodicals Review*, 14/2 (1981), 58–66, at 60.

over time'. Magazine producers were engaged in creating distinct, sectarian reading publics as opposed to *national* faith communities.[43] Religious monthlies, argues Topham with respect to the English press, 'typified the partisanship' of early nineteenth-century literature and addressed 'self-consciously distinct audiences'.[44] In the United States, before 1800, only two out of thirty-nine periodicals openly associated with a particular denomination. By 1830, however, 68 per cent of religious magazines were overtly affiliated with a church or religious group. To subscribe to a particular magazine was an act, says Brown, of declaring one's denominational loyalty.[45]

As with the American and English evangelical press, Scottish denominational periodicals appealed to distinctive sectarian reading communities. The *Christian Magazine* of 1797, conducted by both branches of the Scottish Secession Church—Burgher and Antiburgher—adopted, like the *Evangelical Magazine*—an earlier English publication on which it was modelled—an ecumenical tone.[46] Religious magazines, reported the Revd Gavin Struthers, minister of the Relief Church in Glasgow, 'started upon a broad basis of common support from churchmen and Dissenters'.[47] As competition sprang up between the churches in the first decades of the nineteenth century, however, there was less collaboration across denominations. In Britain in the aftermath of the Reform Acts of 1832, which enfranchised many dissenters for the first time, religion turned into a marketable commodity;[48] the established churches felt threatened, while dissenters felt more powerful. As Struthers commented in 1843, the 'rising spirit of civil and religious liberty [was] attended with rivalry and jealousy among different religious parties. The emulation was, who should take the lead among the people, whose favour now began to be courted because their power now began to be felt.'[49] Scotland's Protestant community was divided into an array of denominations. Anyone attempting, says Atholz, to draw up a 'scorecard of religious periodicals, must first draw up for Scotland a scorecard of denominations, seceding and merging'.[50] The Church of Scotland was itself divided internally between Moderates and Evangelicals. Evangelicals resented the law of patronage, which gave the right of electing ministers to lay patrons instead of congregations. They believed in the role of an established church but

43. Smith, 'Religion and Popular Print Culture', 280.
44. Topham, 'Wesleyan–Methodist Magazine', 70.   45. Brown, *Word in the World*, 145.
46. 'Address to the Public', *Christian Magazine; or Evangelical Repository* (1797); on the *Evangelical Magazine*, see Billington, 'The Religious Periodical', 113–32.
47. Struthers, *Relief Church*, 428.   48. Platt, *Subscribing to Faith*, 21.
49. Struthers, *Relief Church*, 432.   50. Altholz, *Religious Press*, 89.

thought it should manage its own affairs. Many Evangelicals would leave the Kirk to join the Free Church in 1843. Outside the Kirk, the Secession Church, which had evolved from a schism over patronage in the 1730s, was subdivided into Old Licht Burghers and New Licht Burghers, Old Licht Antiburghers and New Licht Antiburghers. The New Lichts—who came to support the disestablishment of national churches—reunited in 1820 to become the United Secession Church. This church would join in 1847 with the Relief Church, another sect with eighteenth-century origins and which shared many of the Secession's values. In 1827 the Old Licht Antiburghers united with the Synod of Protestors—a group of Seceders who had refused to join the United Secession—to become the Original Seceders. The Original Seceders had much in common with another fringe group: the Reformed Presbyterians. This sect evolved from the old Cameronians and still subscribed to the tenets outlined in the national Covenants of the seventeenth century. Original Seceders and Reformed Presbyterians opposed the emancipation of Catholics and hoped for a purified church establishment that would protect their version of truth. Outside the Presbyterian community, the Scottish Episcopalians—the sister church to the Church of England—constituted a minority dissenting sect.

Each sect—even the smallest—began to produce a magazine reflective of its distinctive views. The *Christian Magazine* folded as Burgher and Antiburgher Seceders went their separate ways and brought out their own titles: the Burghers had the *Christian Repository* (est. 1816) and the Antiburghers continued with their own *Christian Magazine*. When the new lights united, they launched the *Christian Monitor* in 1821 and the *Edinburgh Theological Magazine* in 1826, later replaced by the *United Secession Magazine* in 1833. The Church of Scotland's interests were represented by the *Edinburgh Christian Instructor* (est. 1810); the *Presbyterian Review* (est. 1831); the *Presbyterian Magazine* (est. 1832), and the *Church of Scotland Magazine* (est. 1834). In later years the Free Church had the *Home and Foreign Missionary Record for the Free Church* (est. 1843) as well as the incredibly successful newspaper the *Witness* (est. 1840). Meanwhile the Relief Church launched the *Christian Journal; or Relief Magazine* (est. 1833), which would merge with the *United Secession Magazine* when the churches united in 1847. The Reformed Presbyterians brought out the *Reformed Presbyterian Monitor* (est. 1826), the *Scottish Advocate* (est. 1832?), the *Scottish Presbyterian* (est. 1835), and, later, the *Reformed Presbyterian Magazine* (est. 1855). This list is by no means exhaustive. These magazines were sometimes supplemented by less frequent missionary records and single-issue periodicals like the Kirk-affiliated *Church Patronage Reporter* (est. 1831) or the Secession-affiliated *Edinburgh Voluntary Churchman* (est. 1835).[51]

Religious magazines affirmed the identity of denominations against assaults from other sects. They advocated the rights of the religious denominations they represented. Dissenters, says Michael Ledger-Lomas, relied on publishers to promote their case for disestablishment. This was an era, noted the *Edinburgh Theological Magazine* in 1831, in which ancient privileges were giving way and in which public opinion could be properly shaped in the cause of religious freedom.[52] Periodicals were more powerful than books at spreading the word; regular publications provided the news and 'phraseology' required for readers to participate in their chosen denominational community.[53] Newspapers were more regular and more powerful than magazines but much more expensive to run. Only in 1847, indeed, did the United Presbyterian Church launch a newspaper.[54] Denominational periodicals, says Altholz, stimulated readers' 'denominational consciousness'. Religious magazines, he adds, also promoted 'the religious self-identification' of readers as adherents of particular movements *within* denominations.[55] By subscribing to the *Presbyterian Review*, for example, readers signalled their adherence to the evangelical, non-intrusionist movement within the Kirk.

The little evidence we have on the editorial and production practices of Scottish denominational magazines suggests that most magazines acted as unofficial organs of denominations; they were edited by members of the churches whose views they tried faithfully to represent. According to Joanne Shattock, the Free Church weighed heavily on the editors of the *North British Review* and inhibited their creative freedom. The editors of the *United Secession Magazine* made it clear that they were members of the denomination; while their magazine was not officially sanctioned, it promoted the views of the church.[56] Even when the church did not fund the magazine explicitly, it still, to a certain extent, 'owned' the publication. The *Scottish Advocate* launched after members of the Reformed Presbyterian Church petitioned

---

51. The Scottish Episcopalians' publishing ventures were largely unsuccessful. According to Altholz, they had only one notable periodical, the *Scottish Magazine* (1849–54), before the appearance of the *Scottish Standard Bearer* in 1890. Altholz, *Religious Press*, 42.
52. 'To Correspondents', *Edinburgh Theological Magazine* (December 1831).
53. Michael Ledger-Lomas, 'Mass Markets: Religion', in David McKitterick (ed.), *The Cambridge History of the Book in Britain*, vi. *1830–1914* (Cambridge: Cambridge University Press, 2016), 341.
54. 'The Scottish Press Newspaper', *United Presbyterian Magazine* (September 1847).
55. Altholz, *Religious Press*, 141–2.
56. 'To the Readers of the Theological Magazine', *Edinburgh Theological Magazine* (December 1832).

for a periodical and requested that the editor be selected from among church members. The Revd Peter Macindoe took on the role.[57] An elder of the Reformed Presbyterian Church, Andrew Young, a printer in Trongate, Glasgow, specialized, it seems, in printing the works of Reformed Presbyterian ministers; his son, who took over the family business, was also responsible for printing issues of the church's second periodical, the *Scottish Presbyterian*.[58] Relationships with jobbing printers did indeed remain important in this particular subsection of the Scottish book trade.

As Francis Mineka has pointed out, early Victorian religious magazines, unattractive in design, octavo in size with two columns per page, were generally divided into five sections: theological discussion; moral essays; defences of the denomination's principles; poetry; and religious intelligence.[59] The Scottish magazines broadly followed this model. Most issues would contain items of biblical exegesis; reviews of theological works; original poems; letters from missionaries; denominational notices; and, oftentimes, general intelligence on public affairs. For its news the *Christian Monitor* relied on presbytery clerks who sent in regular reports.[60] Contributors were mostly other members of the church, often ministers. The *United Secession Magazine* printed a list of its contributors to encourage church members to get involved.[61] The *United Secession Magazine* also deliberately restricted its reviews department to publications of the United Secession Church alone.[62] The *Christian Journal* reported that its section on the history of the Relief Church was one of the most popular with readers.[63] Readers' denominational biases were thus continually reinforced in what were, in a sense, enclosed media echo chambers.

While women were avid readers of local Anglican parish magazines, which were distributed from the late 1850s and included didactic fiction and advice on home management,[64] the content of early nineteenth-century Scottish denominational magazines suggests that they were directed at male, middle-class office-bearers in the church and male heads of households. 'Early Victorian journals', writes Altholz, 'liked to characterise themselves as

57. 'Prospectus', *Scottish Advocate* (May 1832).
58. Andrew Aird, *Reminiscences of Editors, Reporters, and Printers during the Last 60 Years* (Glasgow: Aird and Coghill, 1890), 58.
59. Francis E. Mineka, *The Dissidence of Dissent: The Monthly Repository 1806–1838* (Chapel Hill, NC: University of North Carolina Press, 1944), 49–50, 89.
60. 'To Correspondents', *Christian Monitor* (January 1821).
61. 'United Secession Magazine', *United Secession Magazine* (1833).
62. 'United Secession Magazine', *United Secession Magazine* (1833).
63. *Christian Journal* (January 1838).   64. Platt, *Subscribing to Faith*.

manly; late Victorian periodicals appealed to families'.[65] McCrie, editor of
the *Christian Magazine*, though a strong advocate for congregational suffrage,
believed that women should have no role in the public life of the church
despite the fact, or because of the fact, that women formed a majority of
many dissenting congregations.[66] Denominational magazines did include
some didactic material on domestic affairs, but mostly their contents centred
on scriptural exegesis, controversy, and church business—considered to be
the domain of men alone.

At mid-century the *North British Review* tried to play down its Free
Church allegiance in order to broaden its appeal, but elsewhere the *United
Secession Magazine* and the *Christian Journal* underlined the importance of
denominational distinctiveness and the obligation to engage in controversy.[67]
Only by engaging in controversy between churches, the editors of the
United Secession Magazine declared, could the magazine propagate truth.[68]
The *United Secession Magazine* had formerly been known as the *Edinburgh
Theological Magazine* but had deliberately changed its name to highlight its
denominational link: 'The readers of the *Edinburgh Theological Magazine*', the
editors noted, 'will observe that it has latterly become less general and more
distinctive.' The conductors of the restyled *United Secession Magazine* had
'judged it best to avow at once their connection with the largest dissenting
body in Scotland and their intention to exert themselves in particular manner for advancement of its interests'. This exertion involved the vigorous
promotion of voluntaryism, disestablishment, and the social elevation of
dissenters. They hoped to encourage the church's members to 'rival the zeal'
of smaller denominations that already had their own magazines.[69] Elsewhere
the printer of the *Christian Journal; or Relief Magazine* changed type to
emphasize the word 'Relief' on the title page.[70] At a meeting of the magazine's supporters it was declared that the magazine had vindicated the
Relief's principles: voluntaryism as sanctioned by the 'scriptural constitution
of Christ's church'.[71] Even during the negotiations for union between the
Relief and the United Secession it was important, the magazine's producers

65. Altholz, *Religious Press*, 143.
66. Thomas McCrie, 'On the Right of Females to Vote in the Elections of Ministers and Elders',
    in McCrie, *Miscellaneous Writings*, ed. McCrie Jr, 669–74.
67. 'To the Readers of the Theological Magazine', *Edinburgh Theological Magazine* (December 1832).
68. 'Introductory Address', *United Secession Magazine* (January 1833).
69. 'United Secession Magazine', *United Secession Magazine* (1833).
70. 'Prefatory Notes', *Christian Journal; or Relief Magazine* (January 1845).
71. 'Edinburgh.—College-Street Church', *Christian Journal; or Relief Magazine* (March 1845).

argued, to maintain in the magazine the Relief's distinctive voice in order to highlight the principles of the respective parties. When the churches did finally unite to form the United Presbyterian Church in 1847, the editors of the *Relief Magazine* and *United Secession Magazine* joined forces and brought out a new magazine—the *United Secession and Relief Magazine*, which soon changed its name to the *United Presbyterian Magazine*.[72]

Meanwhile the *Edinburgh Christian Instructor*, which became the mouth-piece of the evangelical wing of the Kirk, praised the *Presbyterian Magazine* when it launched, describing the title as its auxiliary in propagating the 'old constitutional principles' of the Church of Scotland.[73] Both sought to reform the law of patronage in the Kirk and defend its spiritual independence. The *Church of Scotland Magazine*, meanwhile, was a combative opponent of the *United Secession Magazine* and Relief publications, championing the role of church establishments. The Reformed Presbyterian Church regarded its periodicals as useful weapons in their never-ending fight to establish a Covenanted Reformation. The magazines were designed to champion expli-citly their uncompromising agenda. A periodical, it was declared, was an essential weapon in the battle against Roman Catholics, who had launched their own magazine. The approaching struggle against Catholicism—the 'last conflict of great principle'—would be decided by discussion, the *Scottish Advocate* insisted, not force.[74] The *Scottish Presbyterian* aimed to coun-ter the 'infidel press' and 'disseminate in cheap form' the principles of Presbyterians who had 'Foil'd a tyrant's, and a bigot's bloody laws'.[75] In 1843 the editor observed that the 'Watchword of covenanting fathers' was 'less frequently heard'; the *Scottish Presbyterian*, however, would continue to be a 'vigilant and faithful sentinel' in 'eventful times'.[76]

As a result of their commitment to denominational principles, the circu-lation of these magazines was never anything but modest. The *Reformed Presbyterian Monitor* had little appeal outside of Reformed Presbyterian circles. One 'ill-natured student' was reported scornfully to have 'dissected' the first issue in a Glasgow shop. As a result the magazine denounced the city of Glasgow as 'illiberal and unmanly'.[77] Nevertheless, a subscription from a bookseller requested fifty copies of the magazine every quarter.

72. 'To our Readers', *United Presbyterian Magazine* (January 1847).
73. 'The Presbyterian Magazine', *Edinburgh Christian Instructor* (May 1832).
74. 'Prospectus', *Scottish Advocate* (May 1832).
75. 'To the Reader', *Scottish Presbyterian* (January 1835).
76. 'State and Prospects of the Scottish Presbyterian', *Scottish Presbyterian* (November 1843).
77. 'To correspondents', *Reformed Presbyterian Monitor* (April 1826).

Some subscribers at least hoped that the magazine would appear more regularly.[78] The magazine cost 6d., cheap when compared with the price of the more fashionable monthlies,[79] but the circulation of one of its successors, the *Scottish Presbyterian*, was low when compared with the same magazines. The *Scottish Presbyterian* had a circulation of around 1,200 in the 1840s, while about ten years earlier *Blackwood's* had 8,000 and the *Edinburgh* had about 12,000. The *Scottish Presbyterian* aimed to become a more compact and cheaper monthly and expressed concern that it was currently too expensive. In the event, the magazine doubled in size in 1843. The magazine's conductors urged ministers to use their pulpits to generate subscriptions, while elders were told to recommend the magazine during official visits.[80]

In 1870 the *United Presbyterian Magazine* declared that its circulation had been good considering that 'more showy and attractive periodicals [were] now in the field and moving in a sphere from which a Denominational Magazine is necessarily excluded'. The various branches of the United Presbyterian Church had managed to maintain denominational magazines—designed to defend the denomination's principles from attacks by 'assailants'—for seventy-four years.[81] In the late 1830s the Relief's *Christian Journal* sold less than 1,000, but it was believed that a circulation of 10,000 could be achieved with a little effort. The *Christian Journal* cost 7d., but its conductors insisted it would lower the price to 6d. if 300 more subscribers could be secured. Its long-term aim was to reduce the price to 4d., but this would be possible, it was thought, only with a much expanded readership. The Relief considered setting up a committee to promote the circulation of its magazine. The committee would print slips advertising the magazine to give to missionary societies, libraries, and Sabbath schools—an example of the institutionalized distribution networks outlined by Topham in his study of Methodist publishing.[82] A meeting of the Edinburgh College Street congregation suggested that members form four-person 1d. a month reading

78. 'A Request', *Reformed Presbyterian Monitor* (July 1826).
79. In 1834 the *Edinburgh Review* and *Quarterly Review* cost 6s. while *Blackwood's* and *Tait's Edinburgh Magazine* were 2s. 6d. The Scottish denominational magazines cost about the same as did, at the beginning of the century, the subsidized religious periodicals in England—the *Evangelical Magazine* and *Gospel Magazine*. Richard D. Altick, *The English Common Reader: A Social History of the Mass Reading Public 1800–1900* (Chicago and London: University of Chicago Press, 1957), 319.
80. 'State and Prospects of the Scottish Presbyterian', *Scottish Presbyterian* (November 1843); 'To our Readers', *Scottish Presbyterian* (January 1845).
81. 'Preface', *United Presbyterian Magazine* (1870).
82. 'To the Editor', *Christian Journal; or Relief Magazine* (February 1845); 'Extended Circulation of the Journal', *Christian Journal; or Relief Magazine* (March 1845).

clubs of people too poor to buy their own copies.[83] The magazine was so expensive, its editors declared, because it was impossible to send out issues from a publisher's warehouse at a rate proportional, say, to *Chamber's Journal*, since the magazine's content appealed only to members of the Relief: 'by seeking…to serve the Relief churches, we necessarily cut ourselves off from the support of the general religious public, and so limit within the bounds of some hundred congregations, the circulation of our work'. Despite its circulation problems, the *Christian Journal* insisted it was still important to have a denominational magazine, since the principle of 'equality of Christian brotherhood' was not yet enough acted upon.[84]

In order to legitimize their various positions on the church establishment question, each denomination claimed to be the legitimate heirs of the Covenanting tradition whose version of Presbyterianism was the most scripturally pure.[85] Magazines were littered with articles on the history of the Restoration Covenanters—their persecution by the authorities and their sacrifice for the cause of civil and religious liberty.[86] Contributors continually squabbled over how best to represent the Covenanters and honour their memory. The *Edinburgh Christian Instructor* angrily criticized the *Edinburgh Theological Magazine* for its review of *The Character and Claims of the Scottish Martyrs* (1831) by William Symington, a minister of the Reformed Presbyterian Church. The *Edinburgh Theological Magazine*'s reviewer, while agreeing with Symington that the Covenanters had secured to Scotland their civil and religious liberties, insisted that the Covenanters had ignored the precepts of the New Testament: that church and state should be separate.[87] The *Edinburgh Christian Instructor* passionately defended Symington's representation of the Covenanters, who, as a result of their belief in a national establishment, it was argued, had made provision for the poorest in Scotland.[88] The *Presbyterian Review* agreed. Symington, it was declared, had the 'true spirit' of the Covenanters, unlike the Seceders, who had been 'spoiled' by their disestablishment views.[89]

★

83. 'Edinburgh.—College-Street Church', *Christian Journal; or Relief Magazine* (March 1845).
84. 'Prefatory Notes', *Christian Journal, or Relief Magazine* (January 1845).
85. 'Who are the Successors of the Scottish Martyrs?', *Scottish Presbyterian* (January 1846).
86. Review of the 'Reformers of Scotland', *Edinburgh Theological Magazine* (January 1827).
87. Review of 'The Character and Claims of the Scottish Martyrs', *Edinburgh Theological Magazine* (April 1832).
88. 'Defence of Scottish Covenanters', *Edinburgh Christian Instructor* (August 1832).
89. 'Critical Notices', *Presbyterian Review* (September 1831).

The later nineteenth century added a further layer of complication and ambivalence to Scots Presbyterian literature. Publishers and editors recognized an identity of interest, taste, and discrimination between the Presbyterian readers of Scotland and a wider Nonconformist readership in other parts of Britain and the Empire. The presiding genius in this area was William Robertson Nicoll (1851–1923), a former Free Church minister turned literary impresario—critic, editor, publisher's reader—indeed the great dictator of literary reputations in the late nineteenth and early twentieth centuries.[90] Nicoll left Scotland for London in the mid-1880s, where he set up and edited a Nonconformist paper, the *British Weekly*.[91] 'Interdenominational'[92] in its intended catchment and subtitled 'A Journal of Social and Christian Progress',[93] the *British Weekly* published short stories and serialized fiction alongside homilies and sermons. Nicoll was also involved in a range of other activities, including a literary monthly the *Bookman*, which he established in 1891, and was an adviser to the publishers Hodder and Stoughton and editor of another monthly, the *Expositor*. Indeed, Nicoll—under a range of pseudonyms—reviewed in various outlets, and became the dominant arbiter of popular taste in the early twentieth century.[94] Arthur Conan Doyle was aghast to discover that, of six anonymous reviews that denounced as immoral his comic fiction *A Duet* (1899), all—three anonymous in the *Daily Chronicle*, the *American Bookman*, and the *London Bookman*; three pseudonymous (Claudius Clear and A Man of Kent, both in the *British Weekly*, and O.O. in *The Sketch*)—were authored by Nicoll.[95]

Nicoll promoted Scots and work strongly inflected by Scots Presbyterian themes, but his primary identity was as a supporter of British Nonconformity, whose cause he hoped to advance through the medium of fiction.[96] He championed the 'Free Churches' *south* as well as north of the border that stood outside the state connection, and supported the National Free Church Council.[97] He was also a staunch Liberal, a close ally first of Rosebery and

90. Philip Waller, *Writers, Readers and Reputations: Literary Life in Britain 1870–1918* (Oxford: Oxford University Press, 2006), 977; Stephen Koss, *Nonconformity in Modern British Politics* (London: Batsford, 1975), 41.
91. Waller, *Writers, Readers and Reputations*, 1010.   92. Koss, *Nonconformity*, 40.
93. Stephen Koss, *The Rise and Fall of the Political Press in Britain* (Chapel Hill, NC, and London: University of North Carolina Press, 1984), ii. 101.
94. Waller, *Writers, Readers and Reputations*, 131–2.
95. Andrew Nash, 'William Robertson Nicoll, the Kailyard Novel and the Question of Popular Culture', *Scottish Studies Review*, 5 (2004), 57–73, at 63.
96. Waller, *Writers, Readers and Reputations*, 1010.
97. T. H. Darlow, *William Robertson Nicoll: Life and Letters* (London: Hodder and Stoughton, 1925), 178, 190, 230, 237, 240.

Liberal Imperialism and later of Lloyd George, and he was knighted in 1909 for his services to literature. Nicoll favoured a broad measure of theological latitude in the Presbyterian writers he promoted, preferring a 'moderate' emphasis on bearing, conduct, character, and all-round goodness to any hint of doctrinal scruple or sectarian narrowness.[98] Nicoll introduced a series of Scottish writers to his Nonconformist readership, and effectively created what has come to be known as the Kailyard school.[99] Its members included the young J. M. Barrie (1860–1937); the Revd John Watson (1850–1907), who had been a Free Church minister in Edinburgh, Perthshire, and Glasgow, and was now the minister of a Presbyterian church in Liverpool, who, under the pseudonym of 'Ian Maclaren', wrote the bestselling *Beside the Bonnie Briar Bush* (1893); S. R. Crockett (1859–1914), a Free Church minister in Penicuik, who abandoned the ministry for writing, including *The Stickit Minister* (1893) and *The Lilac Sun-Bonnet* (1895). The most prolific of the writers promoted by Nicoll was Annie S. Swan (1859–1943), who authored around 200 novels, novelettes, and stories in her career, as well as running her own magazine. Swan had been brought up in the Evangelical Union, and later turned to the Church of Scotland.[100] The Kailyard school constituted a Liberal variant of Whig–Presbyterian fiction; though, interestingly, both Maclaren and Nicoll had sentimental Jacobite affinities (a not uncommon feature of Whig–Presbyterian culture).[101]

The virtuous wholesomeness on display in Kailyard fiction also provided a firm defensive buttress for British Nonconformity, the target of various literary assailants. Within the English critical tradition, Nonconformity had been associated, since the work of Matthew Arnold, with philistinism. Moreover, a succession of nineteenth-century English novelists had alighted on a stock character, the crafty, dissembling, and hypocritical evangelical, encapsulated in a Bulstrode, a Pecksniff, or an Obadiah Slope.[102] Although such despicable characters tended to be Low Church Anglican rather than overtly Nonconformist, the mud thrown splattered on the wider culture of evangelicalism, Nonconformity included. On the other hand, the inoffensive subject matter and tone of the Kailyard writers won over a Nonconformist readership that had a deep distrust of any non-sacred literature. The obvious

---

98. Waller, *Writers, Readers and Reputations*, 113.
99. Andrew Nash, *Kailyard and Scottish Literature* (Amsterdam: Rodopi, 2007).
100. Nash, *Kailyard*, 505.
101. W. Robertson Nicoll, *'Ian Maclaren': Life of the Rev. John Watson, DD* (London: Hodder and Stoughton, 1908), 1–3; Darlow, *Nicoll*, 2.
102. Waller, *Writers, Readers and Reputations*, 108, 1002–3.

virtues and mawkish sentiment of the Kailyard school answered English—as well as Scottish—taste and demands. As such, Kailyard fiction expressed a Nonconformist as much as any overtly ethnic or national allegiance, notwithstanding its couthy Scots language and settings. Moreover, the Kailyard also enjoyed a remarkable success in the Empire. Nevertheless, it would be wrong to push a straightforwardly unionist interpretation of this Anglo-Scottish literary phenomenon. Despite having spent much of her career in London, Swan, widowed and back in Scotland during the 1930s, became a staunch founding supporter of the Scottish National Party, which she served as Vice-President. Yet there is a further wrinkle still, for Swan (or Mrs Burnett Smith as she was known in public life) had been a Liberal all her life, 'since the days when Gladstone first stirred all my girlish imagination'.[103] She had been committed throughout her life to advanced Liberal causes and stood as an unsuccessful Liberal candidate at Glasgow Maryhill in the 1922 general election.[104] In the early twentieth century Scottish Home Rule was yet another radical Liberal issue, and sometimes needs to be parsed as such rather than pigeonholed simply as 'nationalism'. In her autobiography, published in the same year that the SNP was formed, she referred pointedly to 'these days of rabid nationalism', and confessed that she had once been rebuked by Rosebery for 'the unforgivable sin of putting the objectionable letters N.B. [an abbreviation for North Britain, which was used in preference to Scotland] on my notepaper'.[105] Indeed, Liberalism, it has been argued, functioned as a surrogate for much of the nineteenth and early twentieth centuries for a Scots Presbyterian conception of nationhood, a form of unionist–nationalism that was decidedly non-Anglican yet not anti-unionist as such. The Kailyard movement was a tame expression of this distinctive, largely forgotten, ethos.

However, the Kailyard movement has been a matter not of national pride but rather of acute embarrassment for most Scots, something that still makes literary critics squirm. Indeed, right from its heyday the Kailyard provoked a fierce backlash in Scottish literature, among both novelists and critics, which continues into the present. In particular, the Kailyard was understood as a saccharine substitute for life itself, and as such the antithesis of realism. In reaction, Scottish writers turned to grimness, anomie, despair, and dysfunction as a purported antidote to the unrealistic idylls of communal trust

---

103. Annie S. Swan, *My Life: An Autobiography* (London: Ivor Nicholson and Watson, 1934), 248.
104. Swan, *My Life*, 249–52.   105. Swan, *My Life*, 253–4.

and cohesion in rural and small-town Scottish life. Indeed, it was but a small step from virtuous parish life and the benevolent surveillance of its authority figures, the minister, schoolmaster, and elders, to the phenomenon of suffocating parochialism and stifled individualism. The classic of the genre was George Douglas Brown's studiedly anti-Kailyard depiction of his home village in Ayrshire, Ochiltree, which becomes the catty, unneighbourly, and claustrophobic Barbie of his novel *The House with Green Shutters* (1901). MacDiarmid led the critical charge against the Kailyard, and his sniping found corroboration in George Blake's celebrated monograph *Barrie and the Kailyard School* (1951).[106] A century on from *The House with the Green Shutters*, the anti-Kailyard turn remains inexhaustible. The Glasgow 'mean streets' genre, later the druggy grime of Irvine Welsh-land and the gritty Scottish crime novels of William McIlvanney (1936–2015) and his successors, all have their provenance—at some conscious level—in the anti-Kailyard. Of course, there is also a desire to be photographic, to capture in documentary form the undeniable squalor associated with industrial and then post-industrial Scotland. Nevertheless, the anti-Kailyard segues all too easily into a dark, urban version of Kailyard. For the principal flaw of Kailyard lurks in synecdoche, and the caricature of a portion of the Scottish experience stands representative of the whole. Just as the Kailyard writers turned their backs on the social problems of the urban and industrial central belt, so the dominant anti-Kailyard—or proletarian Kailyard—tradition in twentieth-century Scottish fiction tended to turn its back on neat lawns, privet hedges, bourgeois decorum, garden centres, trim suburbs, the service sector, the sprawling middle class—and, of course, the small-town parochialism and complacency of whose positive aspects the Kailyarders had once sung. Arguably, much of twentieth-century Scottish literature—as far removed as so much of it is from ostensibly religious matter—evolved in reaction to the arcadian Presbyterian whimsy of the late nineteenth and early twentieth centuries.

On the other hand, the vivid characterization, claustrophobic Calvinism, and ingenious plotting of the early nineteenth-century Whig–Presbyterian novel have continued in no small measure—in works by Robin Jenkins (1912–2005) and, more recently, James Robertson—to provide a narrative template for secularized, postmodern Scottish literature. In *The Awakening of George Darroch* (1985), Jenkins explored the confused conscience of a

106. George Blake, *Barrie and the Kailyard School* (London: Arthur Barker, 1951).

minister at the time of the Disruption, morally upright and committed to the non–intrusionist cause, but consumed with randy thoughts about his wife. The novel is rich in character development and context, but is also fully alert to the mid-nineteenth-century arguments about church polity that paved the way to the Free Church split from the established Kirk.[107] Robertson's oeuvre pays direct homage to the early nineteenth-century masters of the Whig–Presbyterian novel, not only Galt and Hogg, but its critical exponent, Walter Scott. *The Fanatic* (2000) alternates between the Covenanting Scotland of the 1670s and modern Edinburgh, where its disturbed central character Andrew Carlin—in thrall to an alter ego that speaks to him through his mirror—is obsessed with the milieu and personalities of the late-seventeenth-century Covenanting movement, especially James Mitchell, one of the murderers in 1679 of Archbishop James Sharp of St Andrews. Whereas *The Fanatic* acknowledges a general debt to the Whig–Presbyterian novel of the 1810s and 1820s, in *The Testament of Gideon Mack* (2006) Robertson specifically reworks the theological motifs, mechanics, and twists of Hogg's *Confessions of a Justified Sinner* (1824) in a highly plausible contemporary setting. Here, instead of an antinomian seductively inspired to murder by a diabolic counterpart, Robertson creates an unbelieving son of the manse who, for want of any other ambition, ends up a successful Presbyterian minister, with an enviable capacity to sublimate his unbelief into an enthusiastic and highly successful charitable commitment to the material welfare of his parishioners and the wider community in *this* life. However, things become more tortuous still when the successfully unbelieving minister makes the acquaintance—or so it seems—of the Devil, to whom he takes something of a shine. Again, as with Hogg's *Justified Sinner*, the reader succumbs to the compelling narrative of real-life diabolism, but still continues to harbour well-founded suspicions about the reliability of the narrator.

Robertson operates in a cultural mileu far removed from that of the 1820s. As he himself has explained—with great authority, subtlety, and conviction in *As the Land Lay Still* (2010)—contemporary Scotland has slipped the moorings of union, and seems set to launch itself on a journey to national independence.[108] Moreover, the loosening of Presbyterian restraints and a drift towards secularism are vital elements in this story. Nevertheless,

---

107. Robin Jenkins, *The Awakening of George Darroch* (1985; Edinburgh: B & W Publishing, 1995).
108. James Robertson, *And the Land Lay Still* (London: Hamish Hamilton, 2010).

The Testament of Gideon Mack was published to well-deserved acclaim, and reminds us that—notwithstanding the disorientation and dwindling relevance of what were once sharply distinctive denominational stances within Scots Presbyterianism, a more general loss of Christian faith, and even the decline of lukewarm, doctrinally empty Gideon Mack-like church attendance—the themes of the Presbyterian novel of the 1820s live on and continue to resonate as a major determinant of modern Scottish fiction.

10

Contested Commemoration
Robert Burns, Urban Scotland and Scottish Nationality in the Nineteenth Century

Christopher A. Whatley

Even a cursory glance backwards to the history of the national movements that swept Europe in the nineteenth century demonstrates the importance of literature and its creators—including peasant poets—in the formation of a collective sense of nationality.[1] As a means of communal memory-making, literature, Ann Rigney has observed, provides 'an imaginative template for articulating values and defining identities'.[2] Scottish writers in the twentieth and twenty-first centuries have performed just this role and by so doing have done much along with others in the creative arts to promote Scottish nationalist sentiment.[3] As far as the creation of cultural memory in nineteenth-century Scotland was concerned, the dominant figures were the nation's two literary giants, Sir Walter Scott and Robert Burns, alongside a canon of historic heroes—William Wallace, Robert the Bruce, John Knox, and the Covenanters. James Coleman's recent work has, along with that of Graeme Morton, Michael Penman, and others, established how significant

1. Cf. the Catalan peasant poet Jacint Verdaguer; see M. Eaude, *Catalonia: A Cultural History* (Oxford: Signal Books, 2007), 61–71.
2. Ann Rigney, *The Afterlives of Walter Scott: Memory on the Move* (Oxford: Oxford University Press, 2012), 6.
3. Alistair McCleery, 'Introduction', in A. McCleery (ed.), *Nation and Nationalism* (Dunbeath: Whittles Publishing, 2013), 1–4; Murray Pittock, *The Road to Independence? Scotland in the Balance* (London: Reaktion Books, 2013), 140–5.

the commemoration of Wallace, Bruce, and Knox was in forging a usable
sense of collective memory for the Scottish people in the nineteenth
century.[4] Scott's enormous influence too has been investigated, not only
in Scotland, where his impact for several decades was pervasive, but also in
Europe, and the English-speaking world.[5] Even so, in his native land, by
the time of the centenary of his birth in 1871, enthusiasm to celebrate the
occasion was 'muted'.[6]

The same could not be said of Burns. Of the two writers, Burns's cultural
'afterlife' was longer lasting. Indicative measures are the permanent memorials: more large-scale statues of Burns have been erected than for any other
Scot. Of those that are life-sized or larger, there are around fifty worldwide.
Most are in Scotland, Canada, and the United States. We should also note
the massive participation levels at Burns festivals held on key anniversary
dates in the nineteenth century, above all in 1859, the centenary of his birth,
which provoked an unprecedented crush of celebrations in Scotland, the
rest of the UK, and North America. The unofficial chronicler of the commemorations, James Ballantyne, managed to document an impressive 872,
which is almost certainly lower than the number that actually took place.[7]
There were those who were convinced that, as the century wore on, Burns
became even more important to his countrymen—his 'fame' and 'portent-
ous' influence grew rather than diminished, a process that was given formal
encouragement with the establishment, in 1885, of the Burns Federation.[8]

The focus of this chapter, however, is not the transient Burns festivals, the
first of which was in 1844, near Ayr, at Alloway, nor commemorative practices
like the Burns supper, now documented and comprehensively examined by

4. James J. Coleman, *Remembering the Past in Nineteenth-Century Scotland: Commemoration, Nationality
   and Memory* (Edinburgh: Edinburgh University Press, 2014); Graeme Morton, *William Wallace:
   A National Tale* (Edinburgh: Edinburgh University Press, 2014); M. A. Penman, 'Robert Bruce's
   Bones: Reputations, Politics and Identities in Nineteenth-Century Scotland', *International Review
   of Scottish Studies*, 34 (2009), 7–73.
5. Murray Pittock (ed.), *The Reception of Walter Scott in Europe* (London: Continuum, 2007); Stuart
   Kelly, *Scott-Land: The Man who Invented a Nation* (Edinburgh: Polygon, 2010).
6. Rigney, *Afterlives*, 178.
7. James Ballantyne, *Chronicle of the Hundredth Birthday of Robert Burns* (Edinburgh and London:
   Fullarton & Co, 1859); J. McVie, *The Burns Federation: A Bicentenary Review* (Kilmarnock:
   Kilmarnock Standard, 1959), 45; Murray Pittock, '"A Long Farewell to All My Greatness": The
   History of the Reputation of Robert Burns', in Murray Pittock (ed.), *Robert Burns in Global
   Culture* (Lewisburg, PA: Bucknell University Press, 2011), 32.
8. F. Ferguson, *Should Christians Commemorate the Birthday of Robert Burns?* (Edinburgh: A. Elliot,
   1869); McVie, *The Burns Federation*; Michael Lynch, *Scotland: A New History* (London: Century,
   1991), 357.

Clark McGinn.[9] Pauline Mackay and others have investigated the phenomenon of Burnsian memorabilia, much of which was highly commercialized and took the form of a wide range of domestic ware as well as personal items such as snuffboxes, pipes, and other ephemera.[10] What this chapter is concerned with is the more public aspects of Burns commemoration—that is, the permanent memorials of Burns that were erected in the nineteenth and early twentieth centuries. There were two waves of monument construction; that after 1859 has already been noted, but there was an earlier building round, which saw major memorials being erected in Dumfries, Ayr, and Edinburgh.

Despite Burns's importance in Scottish commemorative history, relatively little attention has been paid to statues of the poet.[11] They have not been ignored, however, and in recent decades some fine work on Burns memorials has begun to appear in print.[12] However, it is more than a century since the publication in 1911 of Edward Goodwillie's *World's Memorials of Robert Burns*; Goodwillie's observation—that, in terms of learning about Burns memorials, the 'well of information' was 'rather dry'—is still relevant.[13] There is still much to discover, interpret, and understand. What this chapter seeks to do is use the evidence of the campaigns for Burns statues, the proceedings that surrounded their unveiling, their reception, and the iconography of monuments erected to commemorate Scotland's best-known public figure in the nineteenth century as a means of better understanding the nature of Scottish nationality. Nationality at this time, it has been argued, signified 'the collective character of the nation', defined what made it great,

9. A. Tyrell, 'Paternalism, Public Memory and National Identity in Early Victorian Scotland: The Robert Burns Festival at Ayr in 1844', *History*, 90/1 (2005), 42–61; Clark McGinn, '"Every Honour Except Canonisation": The Global Development of the Burns Supper, 1801 to 2009', unpublished Ph.D. thesis, University of Glasgow, 2013.
10. Pauline A. Mackay, 'Objects of Desire: Robert Burns the "Man's Man" and Material Culture', *Anglistik*, 23/2 (2012), 27–39; see too James A. Mackay, *Burnsiana* (Alloway: Alloway Publishing, 1988).
11. Coleman, *Remembering the Past*, 17.
12. See Thomas Keith, 'Burns Statues of North America, a Survey', in G. Ross Roy (ed.), *Robert Burns & America* (Columbia, SC: Thomas Cooper Library and Akros Publications, 2001), 23–33; Johnny Rodger, 'The Burnsian Constructs', in J. Rodger and Gerard Carruthers (eds), *Fickle Man: Robert Burns in the 21st Century* (Dingwall: Sandstone Press, 2009), 50–79; Christopher Whatley, 'Robert Burns, Memorialisation, and the "Heart-Beatings" of Victorian Scotland', in Pittock (ed.), *Robert Burns in Global Culture*, 204–28; M. E. Vance, 'Burns in the Park: A Tale of Three Monuments', in Sharon Alker, Leith Davis, and Holly F. Nelson (eds), *Robert Burns and Transatlantic Culture* (Farnham and Burlington: Ashgate, 2012), 209–32.
13. Edward Goodwillie, *The World's Memorials of Robert Burns* (Detroit: Waverley Publishing, 1911).

and gave to the nation 'the right...to address itself as such'.[14] In this sense memorials to Burns become what in the French context Pierre Nora has termed memory sites (*lieux de mémoire*), which may reflect collective, even national, memory and identity.[15]

We should, of course, be wary of exaggerating the Scottish significance of the practice of large-scale permanent commemoration. Across Europe from the later eighteenth century there emerged a desire at what was a time of rapid modernization to construct national identities by celebrating key anniversary dates from the past, whether notable battles or the birthdays of nationally important figures.[16] New, and one of the most public and certainly the most permanent way of remembering these heroes, was the erection of memorials—mainly statues—in their honour. 'Statuemania' is the term used to describe the period when Britain—from the time of the death of Sir Robert Peel to that of Queen Victoria—went 'statue mad'.[17] Indeed urban statue-building was a Europe-wide practice that also crossed the Atlantic to the United States and Canada. There is nothing unusual either in the erection of statues of Burns, a poet (and other Scottish poets too—such as Thomas Campbell and Robert Tannahill). Universally there was a shift over the course of the century from statues of monarchs and military figures, to men of peace: poets, philosophers, and philanthropists.[18]

However, as Colin Kidd and James Coleman have recently observed, the national memory-building process—far from being static—was remarkably flexible over time.[19] What memory studies elsewhere have demonstrated are not only the fluidity of 'national' memory but also the extent to which it was contested, pluralist, and fractured by factors such as class, religion, gender, and ethnicity—and, at times, even contradictory.[20] Furthermore, behind the 'smooth surface of the finished memorial', its apparent permanency, and

14. Coleman, *Remembering the Past*, 5, 7–9.
15. B. Majerus, '*Lieux de memoire*—A European Transfer Story', in S. Berger and B. Niven (eds), *Writing the History of Memory* (London and New York: Bloomsbury Academic, 2014), 157–71.
16. R. Quinault, 'The Cult of the Centenary, *c*.1784–1914', *Historical Research*, 71 (1998), 303–23.
17. C. MacLeod, *Heroes of Invention: Technology, Liberalism and British Identity 1750–1914* (Cambridge: Cambridge University Press, 2007), 24.
18. P. Murphy, *Nineteenth-Century Irish Sculpture: Native Genius Reaffirmed* (New Haven and London: Yale University Press, 2010), 29.
19. Colin Kidd and James Coleman, 'Mythical Scotland', in T. M. Devine and Jenny Wormald (eds), *The Oxford Handbook to Scottish History* (Oxford: Oxford University Press, 2012), 62–3.
20. S. Berger and B. Niven, 'Writing the History of National Memory', in Berger and Niven (eds), *Writing the History of Memory*, 140–6; see too Eric Hobsbawm, 'Introduction: The Invention of Tradition', in E. Hobsbawm and Terence Ranger (eds), *The Invention of Tradition* (Cambridge: Cambridge University Press, 2010), 1–14.

the appearance of a well-planned project, were often bouts of political and perhaps aesthetic wrangling, and disputes over location, which in few places were as intense as in Ireland, where 'a war on statues' that represented British authority was fought.[21] Additionally, and as important as the monument or the purpose and intended meaning of the statue's makers (as commissioning agencies or artists) is the reception of the artefact, which implies the existence of a dialogue between producer and viewer.[22]

If in Scotland Burns statues were safe from attack, it is nevertheless clear that they were of immense importance to those individuals and small committees campaigning for them. What is striking is how rapidly funds were raised—certainly during the late-century wave of Burns statue-building in Scotland—that is between 1877 and 1896. Typically, the time taken from conception to completion was between three and five years, much faster than any of the memorials erected previously, and a lot more than the fifteen years or so it took to get the Scott monument in Edinburgh finished, although admittedly this was a more ambitious—and expensive—project. However, the fact that several of the statues were funded by public subscriptions indicates a high level of interest in and enthusiasm to commemorate Burns. In some places (Glasgow, Kilmarnock, and Paisley are good examples) the working classes were specifically targeted.[23] Indeed, Glasgow's Burns statue was largely paid for by individual payments that were limited to what was called the 'democratic shilling', some 40,000 of which were collected. Where a single sponsor was behind a statue, the time taken could be even shorter, as in Stirling—where the provost David Bayne first made enquiries about the cost of a Burns statue in the late summer of 1912 and saw it unveiled in September 1914.[24]

The same degree of enthusiasm for Burns seems to have encouraged many thousands of people to turn out at unveiling ceremonies. Processions and large crowds were a feature of nineteenth-century civic life. Members of crowds participated in and watched a host of highly orchestrated rituals, from the opening of public buildings, through funerals of national and local

21. Murphy, *Nineteenth-Century Irish Sculpture*, 3, 29, 238.
22. R. Crownshaw, 'History and Memorialization', in Berger and Niven (eds), *Writing the History of Memory*, 222–6.
23. *Glasgow Weekly Citizen*, 3 May 1873; *Aberdeen Weekly Journal*, 31 January 1877; *Paisley Daily Express*, 28 September 1896.
24. Stirling Council Archives (SCA), Stirling Burgh Records (SBR), SB1/15/6, correspondence relating to the Burns statue, 1912–14, J. W. Buchan to D. Morris, 24 September 1912; *Stirling Observer*, 29 September 1914, p. 3.

worthies, to commemorative festivals.[25] Yet the level of public interest in ceremonies held to unveil Burns monuments is impressive; from the time of his funeral in Dumfries in 1796 until the centenary in 1896 of his death, Burns-related events attracted crowds that in many towns were among the largest ever seen in their respective bounds.[26] Exceptions were rare, as in Paisley, where rain, but more importantly a 6d. charge—designed to reduce numbers and therefore damage to the gardens in which the statue was sited— deterred potential attendees from a ceremony that was afterwards described as 'boring'.[27] In Stirling the outbreak of war meant that the unveiling cere- mony in September 1914 had to be scaled down and muted, other than the unplanned contribution to the proceedings of a party of Royal Scots Fusiliers, who gave impromptu renderings of 'The Star o' Robbie Burns' and 'Ye banks and braes'—concluding though with 'It's a long, long way to Tipperary'.[28] In general, however, such was the intensity and extent of Burns-love that a number of evangelical Presbyterian clergymen were moved to speak out against 'Burnomania', the term coined by one of the Burns cult's first critics as early as 1811.[29] In the wake of the well-attended and widely reported Ayr Burns festival of 1844, Hugh Miller, founder and editor of what after 1843 became the mouthpiece of the Free Church, the *Witness*, pointed to the incongruity of Scotland's renown as 'pre-eminently a moral and religious land', and the 'universally known fact' that Burns was 'an immoral and religious man'.[30] These failings led more than one divine to ask whether it was right for Christians to honour a man who had pros- tituted his genius, whose principles were 'baneful' and sentiments 'polluted'.[31] Albeit the numbers of dissenting Presbyterian critics of Burns declined over time—with Dundee's Revd George Gilfillan (1813–78) of the United Presbyterian Church, for example, becoming one of Burns's best-known editors and biographers, while even Hugh Miller later conceded there was

25. S. Gunn, *The Public Culture of the Victorian Middle Classes: Ritual and Authority in the English Industrial City 1840–1914* (Manchester: Manchester University Press, 2000), 163–86; Rigney, *Afterlives*, 176.
26. W. McDowall, *History of Dumfries* (Edinburgh: Adam & Charles Black, 1867), 728–30; Dundee City Library, Lamb Collection, 228 (33), 'Inauguration of the Burns Statue, 1880'.
27. *Paisley Daily Express*, 28 September 1896; *Paisley and Renfrewshire Gazette*, 3 October 1896.
28. *Stirling Observer*, 29 September 1914.
29. William Peebles, *Burnomania: The Celebration of Robert Burns Considered: In a Discourse Addressed to All Real Christians of Every Denomination* (Edinburgh: J. Ogle, 1811).
30. *Witness*, 7 August 1844.
31. *Burns' Centenary: Are Such Honours due to the Ayrshire Bard?* (Glasgow: printed privately, 1959), 3–4; Ferguson, *Should Christians Commemorate*, 6–27.

merit in some of Burns's work[32]—there was a body of Scots in the Victorian era for whom Burns was no national hero, but instead a figure with conspicuous character flaws.

Acknowledging the enormous effort that went into Burns statue promotion is one thing; identifying the factors that motivated such behaviour is slightly more difficult. Yet in few places were more than a handful of determined individuals involved, who can be fairly readily identified. For instance, the Alloway monument owed much to the single-mindedness of Alexander Boswell of Auchinleck; the raising of the Kilmarnock Burns monument and statue was said to be owing to the 'indefatigable exertions' of James M'Kie and James Rose; and in Aberdeen the 'real originator' of the idea for a statue was Dr William Alexander.[33] Generally speaking the men—and Burns commemoration was mainly, though not exclusively, a male preserve—who led and took an active part in the campaigns for Burns statues were members of the new urban elites in Scotland, drawn from the emergent and increasingly wealthy manufacturing, commercial, and professional classes. Glasgow was typical in that the Burns statue committee members were generally substantial employers and civic leaders, men for whom Burns represented a role model as a hard-working man of independent thought and independent means.[34] They included Dr James Hedderwick, a freemason, a Conservative, and a stockbroker who was also the proprietor of the *Glasgow Weekly Citizen*; William Wilson, an umbrella manufacturer but also a Baillie of the town council and a Burns Club member who had had experience of fund-raising with the Wallace monument project, a few years earlier; and Charles Tennant of St Rollox, the world's largest chemical works. Indeed, even though it was from among the aristocracy and the landed classes that much of the funding for the Dumfries, Alloway, and Edinburgh memorials of the early nineteenth century derived, the chief initiator of the Dumfries mausoleum project and 'zealous' secretary of the committee formed to implement it was William Grierson, a merchant and respectable citizen of the burgh.[35]

32. A. Black, *Gilfillan of Dundee, 1813–1878: Interpreting Religion and Culture in Mid-Victorian Scotland* (Dundee: Dundee University Press, 2006), 192; (Hugh Miller), *Trinity College Church versus the Burns Monument* (Edinburgh: Shepherd & Elliot, 1856), 12–13.

33. A. M'Kay, *History of Kilmarnock* (Kilmarnock: Kilmarnock Standard, 1909), 195; Goodwillie, *World's Memorials*, 30, 85.

34. Richard J. Finlay, 'Heroes, Myths and Anniversaries in Modern Scotland', *Scottish Affairs*, 18 (Winter 1997), 111.

35. McDowall, *History*, 732.

The process of urban modernization can be dated to the end of the eighteenth century.[36] By the middle of the nineteenth century, however, in Scotland as elsewhere, it was self-made men of the sort just described who led the improvement and embellishment of the towns in which they held positions of influence. Under their leadership, the face of Scotland's industrial cities and townswas transformed, through projects that involved new civic buildings, open thoroughfares, parks, and squares. If civic leaders were to dominate urban culture, buildings had to be accompanied by works of public art that had the potential through their coded messages to lead to the material and social advancement of the working class.[37] The didactic potential of sculpture—and statues of 'great men'—situated in highly visible locations had long been recognized.[38] The 'educational value of works of art', declared a commentator on the Burns statue movement in Paisley, 'is enhanced when they are seen and admired, day after day, by countless thousands, and therefore statues of great men and women are . . . usually placed in the crowded streets and squares both of Continental and British cities'.[39] It was no accident, therefore, that the Glasgow Burns statue committee recruited John Carrick, the city architect who had been instrumental in designating George Square as a municipal centrepiece for the display of public art. He was also a necessary ally if Burns was to be allocated an appropriate location among the city's pantheon of heroes.

Guided by a revived sense of paternalism, urban elites sought to soften class antagonisms, where possible exploiting common bonds.[40] By involving especially urban artisans in the funding of, and ceremonials associated with, public artefacts, a sense of shared ownership of public space might be generated to become a moralizing place, and class confrontation and disorder and crime reduced.[41] Such considerations were very much in the forefront of the minds of the promoters of Glasgow's Burns: a 'statue erected on this principle', it was claimed, would be 'The People's own Monument to

36. Bob Harris and Charles McKean, *The Scottish Town in the Age of Enlightenment 1740–1820* (Edinburgh: Edinburgh University Press, 2014), 171–2.
37. D. S. Macleod, *Art and the Victorian Middle Classes: Money and the Making of Cultural Identity* (Cambridge: Cambridge University Press, 1996), 88–9, 103.
38. Murphy, *Nineteenth-Century Irish Sculpture*, I, 225, 243.
39. *Paisley Daily Express*, 5 May 1896.
40. R. Price, *British Society, 1680–1880* (Cambridge: Cambridge University Press, 1999), 307–11.
41. See Gunn, *Public Culture*, 65, but also J. Schmeichen, 'Glasgow of the Imagination: Architecture, Townscape and Society', in W. H. Fraser and I. Mavor (eds), *Glasgow*, ii. *1830 to 1912* (Manchester: Manchester University Press, 1996), 490–9.

BURNS'.[42] Comments by the editor of the *Glasgow Herald* on the Burns statue for George Square confirm this. The editor was pleased—and relieved—that George Ewing, the sculptor, had created 'a people's statue... as his peasant admirers would idealize him'.[43] Happily, however, he had '*resisted* the temptation of sacrificing *true artistic feelings* to the ideal of the mob'—that is, presumably, Burns as a political radical. Ewing, a founder member and one-time president of the Waverley Burns Club that had provided several of the members of the Burns monument committee, had modelled a 'safe' Burns. The poet's head was based primarily on the well-known portrait by Alexander Nasmyth, and the body is dressed in the period clothes of a small farmer, with a Kilmarnock bonnet under his right arm. Reinforcing the notion of craft pride rather than class distinction, Burns is portrayed as a contented but self-assured ploughman, and poet, of nature, symbolized by the daisy in his left hand—a flower that had 'led him in a train of glorious thought' manifested in one of his best-known poems, 'To a Mountain Daisy'. The unspoken message as conveyed through the semiotics of the statue was endorsed by the main speaker at the unveiling ceremony on 26 January 1877, the Liberal peer and acquaintance of Gladstone, Lord Houghton, formerly Richard Monckton Miles. Although for the public proceedings Houghton had played to the gallery, in the evening, at a private dinner where he addressed 250 or so of Glasgow's leading men, his message was rather different. Houghton praised Burns for those poems that had directed the 'popular imagination in good and wholesome lines'. Unchecked, imagination was a 'terrible power' in men and nations. Under the influence of Burns's poetry, he concluded, Scotland would not experience 'the violent socialistic extravagances and impossible forms of society... which have ended in the burning of Paris', a reference to the bloody, republican-inspired Paris Commune of 1871, only six years previously.[44]

Another explanation for the enthusiasm for Burns memorials on the part of Scotland's town and city fathers was the promotion of place. Attracting and impressing visitors was a major factor. In an early appeal for support for the mausoleum in St Michael's churchyard in Dumfries, the Revd Henry Duncan acknowledged that, whilst Burns's political principles might make it difficult for some people to contribute, the more important consideration was that a 'Mausoleum over the ashes of Burns' would be 'an ornament' to

42. *Glasgow Weekly Citizen*, 3 May 1873; *Glasgow Herald*, 11 April 1874.
43. *Glasgow Herald*, 10 September 1875.
44. *The British Architect and Northern Engineer*, 2 February 1877, pp. 75–7.

Dumfries, and might well 'conduce to the prosperity of the inhabitants by bringing strangers amongst us in their travels thro' Scotland'.[45] Literary tourism was becoming big business: in south-west Scotland, Burns Country was in the making.[46]

Towns vied with one another to have a Burns statue. Indeed, to be without one was a matter of civic shame, with the editor of the *Paisley Daily Express* in 1896, for example, conceding that Paisley 'had been somewhat slow, by the manner common throughout our country... to honour Scotland's peerless poet', with the argument being advanced (not wholly convincingly) that the delay had been due to the town waiting for an opportunity to erect a 'unique' monument.[47] Inter-town competition had begun early. It was news of the inauguration of the campaign for the mausoleum in Dumfries in 1813 that sparked an almost immediate response in Ayr, with the small group of men convened by Alexander Boswell noting that it was 'no less an interesting object to us, to raise a Monument to the memory of the Ayrshire Bard, where he first drew breath', and in the county 'where his genius was fostered and matured'.[48] The 'want' of a statue of Burns among the growing number of memorials in Glasgow's George Square—a failing, it was asserted, that was 'often noticed by strangers'—was one reason for the emergence of a campaign for a Glasgow Burns.[49] That Edinburgh's monument to Burns on Calton Hill had its critics provided another spur.[50] Within twenty-four hours of the unveiling of the Burns statue in Glasgow, Kilmarnock had launched a campaign, followed only a few weeks later by Dundee, even though here, as in Kilmarnock, the idea of such a monument had been mooted some time beforehand.[51] And, just before Dundee's Burns was unveiled, the news broke that Amelia Hill had won the commission for a marble Burns for Dumfries.[52]

Local pride insisted on having the best Burns, or at least a better one than those that were already in existence. This was a lesson learned the hard way

45. Quoted in Whatley, 'Robert Burns', 211.
46. Nicola J. Watson, *The Literary Tourist: Readers and Places in Romantic & Victorian Britain* (Houndmills: Palgrave Macmillan, 2006), 68–79.
47. *Paisley Daily Express*, 28 September 1896.
48. National Trust for Scotland Burns Birthplace Museum, Minutes, Monument to Robert Burns, 1814–41.
49. *Glasgow Weekly Citizen*, 29 June 1872.
50. Raymond McKenzie, *Public Sculpture of Glasgow* (Liverpool: Liverpool University Press, 2002), 141.
51. *Scotsman*, 16 September 1878; *Weekly News*, 23 October 1880; *Kilmarnock Standard*, 27 January, 7 September 1877.
52. *Glasgow Herald*, 13 September 1880.

by the promoters of Kilmarnock's Burns statue, who, to save on the expense of holding a competition for a sculptor, hoped to secure a replica of Glasgow's Burns. James M'Kie's request was politely but firmly rebuffed, with the advice that, to 'have any attraction or value, your movement, however inexpensive, should be original'.[53] The same message was conveyed to those concerned to find a sculptor for a Burns statue for Stirling. One possible candidate, W. Birnie Rhind RSA, had completed two or three Burns statues, but, it was reported, 'Mr Caw [a respected art critic and Director of the Scottish National Galleries] does not regard this as a recommendation...as you do not want a copy of another work'.[54] Consequently, a different artist created each Burns statue in Scotland; only overseas—in Australia, Canada, and the United States—were replicas or near replicas of statues already in place in Scotland acceptable, and in some cases even desirable.[55]

But from the time of his death it was apparent that Burns was a potent force—and a *Scottish* national icon—in the consciousness of tens of thousands of his countrymen both at home and overseas. Nevertheless, Burns was a poet with many voices, some of which seemed—and were—contradictory.[56] There was, therefore, a contest between competing interest groups who because of their different ideological standpoints wished to shape the memory of Burns in ways that reflected their vision of Scottish society.

A distinction can be drawn between the memorials to Burns raised during the early nineteenth century, and the statues that followed after 1859. The monuments completed in 1818, 1820, and the late 1830s respectively were, by and large, sponsored by Scotland's Tories, funded by Tories in both Scotland and England (as well as by monies from Scots abroad), and commemorated a Tory incarnation of Burns. Partly too they assuaged Tory guilt at having allowed Burns to die in comparative poverty, a stain on the country's landed classes they struggled to remove. With so many of the donations coming from the higher echelons of British society—the Prince Regent, for instance, and Lord Sidmouth, the Home Secretary, and also raised at London dinners hosted by Scottish aristocrats—the first memorials were very much British

53. *The Kilmarnock Burns Monument and Statue* (1882), 3–4.
54. SCA, SBR, SB1/15/6, J.W. Buchan to D. Morris, 24 September 1912.
55. Goodwillie, *World's Memorials*, 112, 115, 119, 123, 125–6, 129, 134; P.J. M. McEwan, *The Dictionary of Scottish Art and Architecture* (Ballater: Glengarden Press, 1988), 539.
56. Kenneth G. Simpson, *The Protean Scot: The Crisis of Identity in Eighteenth Century Scottish Literature* (Aberdeen: Aberdeen University Press, 1988), 184–218; Gerard Carruthers, 'Introduction', in Gerard Carruthers (ed.), *The Edinburgh Companion to Robert Burns* (Edinburgh: Edinburgh University Press, 2009), 3–5.

projects, even though Burns was commemorated as 'Scotia's bard', a national hero with roots set deeply in the Ayrshire countryside.[57] For his sponsors Burns was the 'heaven-taught' ploughman poet who had written 'The Cottar's Saturday Night', a patriotic hymn of praise that was widely interpreted by its many promoters as a paean to the virtues of the pious patriarchal family and the stoicism of the poor—as well as being a tribute to 'the benefits of a Presbyterian polity'.[58] Admittedly there were lines within the poem that could be read as dangerously subversive ('Princes and lords are but the breath of kings', 'What is a lordling's pomp? A cumbrous load, | Disguising oft the wretch of human kind'), but this is precisely why Scottish conservatives had taken it upon themselves to manage Burns's memory and to play down his social and political radicalism.[59] Significantly, too, the designer of both the Ayr and the Edinburgh monuments was Thomas Hamilton, who was also one of the organizers of the Ayr Burns festival, a spectacular, well-attended event that was much criticized for pandering to west central Scotland's social elites, and for patronizing the lower orders.[60] Although both of Hamilton's structures acknowledge the importance of geometry and mathematics in Scotland's Enlightenment, as with the Dumfries mausoleum (designed by the London architect Thomas Hunt), classical influences are clearly evident. They are there too in the sculptures for the Dumfries and Edinburgh memorials, both the work of London-based artists, Peter Turnerelli and John Flaxman respectively. The former, who had been appointed sculptor in ordinary to the royal family, portrayed Burns as a ploughman poet anointed by Coila, the goddess of Kyle, and Burns's muse in 'The Vision', while Flaxman wrapped a stolid marble Burns in a toga-like shawl, with a daisy in his right hand.[61]

Statues of Burns and figures from Burns's work were produced after the completion of the Edinburgh monument and prior to the late-century bout of memorialization. Indeed, instead of erecting copies of 'mutilated fragments of Athenian buildings', one correspondent to the *Scotsman* asked rhetorically, was there no 'native architect who will...give us something

57. Whatley, 'Robert Burns', 212–13.
58. Cairns Craig, *Intending Scotland: Explorations in Scottish Culture since the Enlightenment* (Edinburgh: Edinburgh University Press, 2009), 139.
59. Christopher A. Whatley, '"It is said that Burns was a Radical: Contest, Concession, and the Political Legacy of Robert Burns, *c*.1796–1859', *Journal of British Studies*, 50/3 (July 2011), 650.
60. Whatley, '"It is said that Burns was a Radical"', 650–2.
61. Rodger, 'Burnsian Constructs', 60–3.

original, something Scottish, something that will tell its meaning'?[62] Although
running against the grain of the Greek revival fostered by Scotland's gentle-
manly elite—inheritors of Enlightenment taste—there were, he believed, men
who fitted the bill. One was the self-taught sculptor James Thom (1802–50),
whose grey stone statues of characters from Tam O'Shanter to be housed in
the Alloway monument had very recently caught the public's attention—
and been praised for their attention to detail, and realism, an antidote perhaps to the classicism of the monument itself. Thom and others like him
would not only do better; Thom in particular, who carved from blocks of
sandstone directly, would do so at a lower cost. The existence of a powerful
pulse of pride in Burns as a Scot—across the classes—and as a counter-
weight to the 'drift towards Anglo-Britishness' identified by Colin Kidd and
others is reinforced by the remark made by a visitor from London to the
1844 festival. Even if provisions for the well-off, such as the banquet, had
not been made, he reflected, the event had been a 'manifestation' of the
ardour of 'the people to their poet'; what he had witnessed were the 'heart
beatings' of Scotland. Emblems of Scottishness like an 8-foot-high model
of a thistle, and the lion rampant, were carried in the procession at Ayr.
Not only were such devices prominent but they also induced positive, even
passionate, responses.

In terms of major statuary, however, a turning point does seem to have
been reached in 1859, the centenary of Burns's birth. While it is true that in
some places—Kilmarnock, for instance—unprecedented enthusiasm was
followed by the temporary demise of the town's Burns club,[63] elsewhere the
centennial celebrations spawned new clubs whose members were explicitly
committed to securing the memory of Burns in perpetuity. For many this
meant the erection of large-sized portrait statues, as opposed to the memorials
of the earlier part of the century, where in a sense Burns took second place
to the structures, and perhaps even to those who had built them. As with
other public statuary of the period, the new statues were placed lower, and
more easily seen, on impressive but relatively simple pedestals, rather on the
tall columns upon which statues of the nation's heroes had been set earlier
in the century.[64] Those in the forefront of his later commemoration were
inclined to emphasize Burns as the poet of the people. The editor of the

62. *Scotsman*, 20 August 1831.
63. Kilmarnock Burns Monument Centre, Ayrshire Archives, AA/DC/89, Kilmarnock Burns
    Club Minute Book, 1855–71.
64. Murphy, *Nineteenth-Century Irish Sculpture*, 29.

Illustrated London News who had ventured north in January 1859 to find out just what lay behind the choreographed national—and international—display of enthusiasm for Burns, explained this well: Burns, it seemed to him, had become 'the representative of one great democratic idea and formula... "A MAN'S A MAN FOR A' THAT".'This sentiment, he went on, was the one that above all Burns taught, and that 'has found its way into the hearts and souls of the foremost people in the world'.[65]

The campaign for a statue of Burns to be located in the city's George Square, which was rapidly filling up with generals, politicians, and royalty, was directly linked with the 1859 celebrations. Within a year the Waverley Burns Club had been founded. The club provided the impetus for the statue and also key members of the Burns statue committee referred to earlier, which was established in 1872. In addition to the knowledge that Edinburgh had long had a Burns statue (that begun by Flaxman, which, after his death in 1826, had been completed by his brother-in-law), but not—as reported already—a very good one, spurring them on was the sight in 1866 of an equestrian statue of the late Prince Albert being set in place in George Square to sit alongside Queen Victoria.[66] Burns, it was argued, was a glaring omission. Standing 2.7 metres high on a great 3.6-metre pedestal of Aberdeen granite, the statue was unveiled, in January 1877, five years after the campaign was launched, inaugurating a wave of Burns statue construction.

The Glasgow promoters' attempts, already described, to corral Burns or rather to blunt the edge of Burns's political radicalism—which had been an attraction for certain sections of the working classes, the Chartists, for example—was not unusual. Similar messages were conveyed both by the statue of Burns and by the platform speakers at the unveiling of the Kilmarnock Burns, two years later, in 1879. Colonel Charles Alexander MP acknowledged that the foundation of Burns's influence was the 'majesty' he accorded to the honest man—the 'noblest work of God'—but he warned against taking this idea too far. Because Burns deprecated the 'incense offered to rank', Alexander asserted, this should not be seen as implying 'any special merit in the absence of it'. If it was right, the MP went on, 'to avoid undue laudation of the upper, it is equally important to guard against the unwholesome and extravagant adulation of the lower classes of society... no class has any monopoly of virtue'.[67]

65. *The Illustrated London News*, 34/857 (29 January 1859), 97–8.
66. McKenzie, *Public Sculpture*, 141.   67. *Scotsman*, 11 August 1879.

The statue of Burns at Kilmarnock, by W. G. Stevenson of Edinburgh, was, like Ewing's in Glasgow, a representation of Burns the poet rather than Burns the democrat. Burns here is thoughtful, with his left hand holding a book and in his right, a pencil; a poet in slow motion. The same was true of the next Burns statue to be unveiled, Sir John Steell's in New York on 2 October 1880, followed by a replica in Dundee two weeks later.[68] This portrays a seated Burns, again in contemplative mode, looking upwards at the evening star as he wrote 'To Mary in Heaven', a poem written about Mary, or Margaret, Campbell, with whom Burns had had a fleeting but intense relationship, a love story the veracity of which caused dissention among Burns admirers, but not so much as to inhibit the rapid flow of funds for a statue to 'Highland Mary' that was unveiled in Dunoon by Lady Kelvin in August 1896.[69] The Dundee statue's semiotics did little to remind observers of Burns's social radicalism, and indeed soon after the statue had been unveiled comments were heard that, set low and with the poet's body seemingly twisted awkwardly, it lacked dignity.[70] It was left to the main speaker at the inauguration ceremony, Frank Henderson, one of the town's two Liberal MPs, to rouse the 25,000 people who had crowded into Albert Square by declaring that the 'Scottish working man became transformed' through two of Burns's ideas: 'the essential dignity of his labour and the possible nobility of his life'; thereby, the 'coward slave' struck off his chains, and 'stood erect in the dignity of his manhood'.[71]

However, it was not just the radical edge of Burns that those who commissioned Burns statues seem to have been keen to blunt. There is no sign in any of the major Burns statues of Burns's sociability, of his enjoyment, let alone his celebration, of drink and carnality. His satires on religion too were ignored. The former was represented only in the vernacular sculpture of men like James Thom, whose works were popular but evidently felt to be unsuitable as lasting memorials to be located in prestigious places. The more lascivious elements of Burns's poetry were confined to the panels that adorned some of the pedestals upon which the statues stood—which sometimes featured scenes from 'The Jolly Beggars' or 'Tam o'Shanter'.

68. Christopher A. Whatley, 'Contesting Memory and Public Spaces: Albert Square and Dundee's Pantheon of Heroes', in C. A. Whatley, B. Harris, and L. Miskell (eds), *Victorian Dundee: Image and Realities* (Dundee: Dundee University Press, 2000), 193.
69. Goodwillie, *World's Memorials*, 146–8.   70. Whatley, 'Contesting Memory', 195.
71. *Weekly News*, 23 October 1880.

Burns the celebrant of drink and sexual abandon was for private consumption, or the relatively closed circles of the Burns clubs.[72]

Although little direct evidence of the terms of reference for artists bidding for Burns statues appears to have survived, the monuments suggest that a key requirement was that Burns should be commemorated as a Scot. Recognition that Burns was Scotland's national poet was a primary reason why leading Scottish sculptors seem to have been especially keen to secure a commission for a Burns statue. This was certainly true for John Steell, who had been appointed as her Majesty's Sculptor for Scotland as early as 1838, and in 1846 had completed the marble statue of Sir Walter Scott for the Princes Street monument; the finished product (Burns statues in New York, Dundee, London, and Dunedin) he considered to be his best work.[73] Similarly, the Scottish nationalist sculptor and poet James Pittendrigh McGillivray, who competed unsuccessfully for the Ayr Burns statue but afterwards used the same model for that erected in nearby Irvine in 1896, reflected later that from early in his career he had 'longed to create a statue of Burns'.[74] In Glasgow, Birmingham-born George Ewing's awareness of the immensity of the task he had taken on—to produce 'the most complete [statue] of Burns in existence' and the first major public memorial of Burns for almost half a century—evidently caused him considerable anguish and certainly caused delay in presenting an acceptable memorial for public inspection.[75]

In most of the portrait statues, Burns is dressed in period clothes associated with men of his station in Lowland Scotland. In most of the groups there were symbols of Scottish-ness, such as an elm stump, thistles, and a Kilmarnock bonnet. In the speeches that were made at the various inauguration ceremonies, much pride was evinced from the fact that, not only was Burns Scots-born, but that his work was rooted in Scottish life and through his song Burns had 'preserved the simple- and soul-stirring music of his country'.[76] This was a recurrent theme for Archibald Primrose, Lord Rosebery, the Liberal MP described by some as 'Scotland's uncrowned

72. Murray Pittock and Christopher Whatley, 'Poems and Festivals, Art and Artefact and the Commemoration of Robert Burns, c.1844–c.1896', *Scottish Historical Review*, 93/1 (April 2014), 56–79.

73. R. Lieuallan, 'A Sculptor for Scotland: The Life and Work of Sir John Robert Steell, RSA (1804–1891)', unpublished Ph.D. thesis, 2 vols, University of Edinburgh, 2003, ii. 9; Whatley, 'Contesting Memory', 195.

74. NLS, Accession 3501/28, Scrapbook by J. Pittendrigh MacGillivray, notes (paper on Burns), c.1923.

75. McKenzie, *Public Sculpture*, 142.

76. *Scotsman*, 11 August 1879; *Dundee Courier & Argus*, 18 October 1880.

King', who was a popular, frequent, and eloquent speaker at Burns events in the 1880s and 1890s.[77] For Rosebery, it was Burns—above Wallace, Bruce, and all other Scottish heroes of the past—who had kept Scotland's 'enthusiasm' alive. Enthusiasm alone could not sustain a nation, he conceded, speaking in Paisley in 1896, but everywhere it was vital for national success, from the Revolution in France to the unification of Italy. It was the 'divine force' with which even the impossible might be achieved.[78] Later, in Ayr in 1906, Rosebery was even more specific about Burns's significance for the Scots. With the Union of 1707 Scotland had lost its parliament and the 'paraphernalia which distinguishes an independent kingdom'. But the songs of the common people of Scotland, responded Rosebery, had been revived, hallowed, and 'transmuted into gold, by the sublime alchemy of a great magician'; with these, he declared, there would be no end (of Scotland), 'as long as the world lasts, thanks to Robert Burns'. Rosebery's demand, however, was not for independence, but for Home Rule for a Scotland that was firmly embedded within the British Empire. This position was given eloquent expression by Edinburgh University's Professor David Masson (1822–1907) at the unveiling of Aberdeen's Burns statue in September 1892. In response to what he called some 'sneering' critics of the words of 'Scots Wha Hae', which had been written off as obsolete, Masson countered that the words of the song were exactly in accord with what he called the sentiment of Scottish nationality. This, he declared, 'exists indestructibly...among the powers and forces of the British body politic, and is capable of services in the affairs of that body politic that may be of incalculable utility even yet', not least in inspiring Scottish soldiers on the battlefield.[79] Both Masson and Rosebery were convinced of the significance of Scotland's cultural achievement, and were active in its preservation and promotion.[80]

The hypothesized 'amnesia' of some nineteenth-century Scots about their national past was not a universal condition.[81] The positive and occasionally rapturous reception given to speakers at the major Burns events who proclaimed Burns's association with and importance for Scotland is indicative of a vigorous sense of nationality at the popular level. Even so, there is little to suggest serious unease with the Union, or challenges to the essence of

77. Whatley, 'Robert Burns', 209–10.
78. *Burns Chronicle and Club Directory*, 6 (January 1897), 121.
79. *Glasgow Herald*, 16 September 1892.   80. Craig, *Intending Scotland*, 84–5.
81. C. Kidd, *Union and Unionisms: Political Thought in Scotland 1500–2000* (Cambridge: Cambridge University Press, 2008), 29–30.

the concepts either of unionist–nationalism or 'banal unionism', this last described as the 'background noise' in Scottish politics for the best part of two centuries after 1750.[82] Thus, at the laying of the foundation stone of the unmistakably Scottish, neo-baronial Burns monument in Kilmarnock in 1878, Mr Cochran-Patrick, the depute provincial Grand Master of Ayrshire's freemasons, hailed Burns as 'the bard of Scotland and the Scots', who had captured in his poetry the essence of Scottish nationality. Yet this had followed a rendition of the 'Old Hundreth' psalm played by the music bands in attendance, after which those present were treated to renditions of the 'Masons' Anthem' and 'Rule Britannia'.[83] For the unveiling of Dundee's Burns statue in October 1880, the town's buildings were decked in a variety of banners and flags, but the Union Jack was probably the most numerous. The statue too was covered in a large Union flag.[84]

The statues, too, were an antidote to national memory loss, and, far from being 'meaningless' images of Scotland's past (as they were described by the late Marinell Ash),[85] they became the focus of heated public argument by those concerned to harness Burns for the Scottish present and future. Until the later 1880s, praise for the portrait statues of Burns was usually effusive, not least from the proprietors and editors of local presses, who were strong on description, but who seem to be have been overawed by artistic endeavour and disconnected from cutting-edge aesthetic debates.[86] Scotland's Burns statues were of the traditional school. However, in 1889 what had been lone voices of disquiet multiplied to become a torrent of criticism, first articulated—trenchantly—by the *Glasgow Herald*, which considered all the Burns statues to date as 'painfully suggestive of incapacity'.[87] The *Scotsman* followed along similar lines, while an 'Art Student' writing for the *Burns Chronicle*, the mouthpiece of the Burns Federation, condemned most of Scotland's Burns statuary (except for the statues in Kilmarnock and Ayr), while those in in North America and Australia, he concluded, 'had better never been erected'.[88]

82. Graeme Morton, *Unionist Nationalism: Governing Urban Scotland, 1830–1860* (East Linton: Tuckwell Press, 1999); Colin Kidd, *Union and Unionisms: Political Thought in Scotland, 1500–2000* (Cambridge: Cambridge University Press, 2008).
83. *Scotsman*, 16 September 1878.   84. *Dundee Courier & Argus*, 18 October 1880.
85. Marianell Ash, *The Strange Death of Scottish History* (Edinburgh: Ramsay Head Press, 1980), 11.
86. In this sense Scotland and Ireland seem to have been similar; see Murphy, *Nineteenth-Century Irish Sculpture*, 5.
87. *Glasgow Herald*, 28 September 1889.
88. J. D. Ross (ed.), *Burnsiana: A Collection of Literary Odds and Ends* (2 vols; Paisley and London: A. Gradner, 1892), i. 102; Ross, 'Statues of Burns', *Burns Chronicle and Club Directory*, 4 (January 1895), 121–9.

There were several strands to the critics' complaint. The first was applicable to all or most of Scotland's public sculpture. In short, whereas the best in Greece was the 'rendering of the Ideal', in Scotland, it was alleged, the best sculpture 'is the rendering of the Real'. In part the blame was laid at the door of the committees of 'irresponsible men who usually know as little about sculpture as they do about the courses of the stars'. Accordingly, in relation to Burns, second-rate statues had been commissioned. Ewing's in Glasgow was 'not a highly imaginative work', Stevenson's in Kilmarnock lacked 'meaning' and in representing Burns musing was hardly original. It was, in the opinion of the *Scotsman*, 'nearly as much of a disappointment as that which graces Dundee', which was considered to be 'fictitious and frivolous'. There was nothing about this monument that embodied the 'manly, independent, great-hearted and liberty-loving Burns'. It was hoped that the statues that were in preparation in the early 1890s would provide for Scotland a Burns statue worthy of the poet, 'harmonizing in artistic merit with his position in Scottish literature', and capture Burns's 'worth, dignity, power and greatness'.

Commissioning bodies were not unresponsive to such comment. The Burns statue committee in Paisley, for example, appointed the French-inspired London sculptor F. W. Pomeroy, who was a prominent figure in the New Sculpture movement, for the Burns statue there. This, however, was a step too far for W. Craib Angus, who, writing in the *Glasgow Herald*, declared that Pomeroy's proposed statue 'was not Burns at all'. Rather the figure, modelled 'in the style of the modern French sculptors', was 'a Cockney masher' who 'never knew the toil of the fields'.[89] Other than the Kilmarnock bonnet, which, uniquely, Pomeroy has Burns wearing rather than carrying, there was—Craibe alleged—little else that identified this Burns with Scotland, a criticism underlined in the weeks immediately prior to the statue's unveiling when a panel for the pedestal in which Tam O' Shanter was dressed in a kilt had to be hastily redesigned with Tam attired in the more authentic (for a Lowland Scot) knee breeches.[90] It was seeing Pomeroy's Burns— a 'Sussex peasant leaning on his plough'—but also Flaxman's and Ewing's Burns that caused James Pittendrigh MacGillivray, the Inverurie-born (in 1856, d. 1924) sculptor, poet, and nationalist activist, to conclude that 'Burns by an Englishman is impossible'.[91] MacGillivray, however, had little respect

89. *Glasgow Herald*, 2 July 1894.   90. *Paisley and Renfrewshire Gazette*, 11, 25 July 1896.
91. National Library of Scotland, Dep. 349, Misc. correspondence and notes, J. Pittendrigh MacGillivray, n.d.

for Scottish sculptors either, although he was acutely conscious of the challenge of embodying 'so many stirring and superficially conflicting characteristics in one symbolic statue', of the man who personified the 'soul' of Scotland. By the mid-1920s, just prior to the formation of the National Party of Scotland (1927), MacGillvray was promoting Burns as 'social revolution incarnate', a 'potential Mussolini, with, in the browbeaten Scotland of his day, little stuff out of which to make black shirts'.[92] His statue of Burns, unveiled in 1896, was the first to break with the tradition whereby Burns's head was modelled on Nasmyth's well-known portrait; critical acclaim soon followed.[93]

The year 1896, however, marked the end of the period of greatest interest in Burns memorialization, although not in the United States, where several more statues were erected before the end of the 1920s.[94] In Scotland, however, funds were harder to raise. It had taken twelve years to bring the Paisley Burns statue project to completion.[95] In Montrose, a movement was begun in 1882, but it was not until 1912, thirty years later, that the statue was unveiled.[96] MacGillivray's commission for Irvine came from a single wealthy individual with a fondness for the burgh, as did the statue of Burns in Stirling. It is hard to be precise about just why the tide slowed, but the extension of the franchise in 1884 and the enhancement of the legal status of working men's rights were almost certainly factors; in these arenas Burns was now less important as an inspiration. Burns's role as tribune for the universal brotherhood of man lost much of its potency with the approach of the First World War, to the extent that even Andrew Carnegie, who at the launch of the Montrose Burns statue in 1912 had proclaimed Burns's influence as a peacemaker, chose to return to the United States rather than unveil the Burns statue in Stirling, his heart broken at the prospect of 'the impending destruction of the greatest number of civilized beings ever sacrificed in the history of the world'.[97]

Burns had never been entirely appropriated by any single interest group. As this chapter has shown, Burns was identified both with Scotland and with a wider set of causes (each, of course, with its Scots inflections) within

---

92. *Scotsman*, 24 January 1925.
93. McEwan, *Dictionary of Scottish Art and Architecture*, 336–7; Goodwillie, *World's Memorials*, 93–4.
94. *Burns Day in Detroit, Being a History of the Movement for a Burns Statue in Detroit* (Detroit: Detroit Burns Club, 1921), 91–3.
95. *Paisley and Renfrewshire Gazette*, 26 September 1896.
96. Angus Archives, Restenneth, Forfar, MS 628, Burns Statue papers.
97. SCA, SB1/15/6, A. Carnegie to D. Morris, 21 August 1914.

union and empire. Scottishness and broader British allegiances did not cancel one another out; nineteenth-century Scottish identity—unlike, perhaps, some of its later iterations—did not belong in a zero-sum game. Moreover, if anything, another lower layer of identity—that of localism and civic pride—was the prime focus of nineteenth-century Scottish commemorations of Burns. Competitiveness between Scottish towns in their attempts to commemorate the poet exceeded indeed the efforts of Tories and Liberals of various stripes to claim Burns as their own. The process would intensify in the twentieth century as the different political parties sought to make him their own.[98] However, Burns the familiar nationalist icon of the twenty-first century has a richly chequered, patriotically 'unionist' history that diverges decidedly from the seemingly inevitable monopoly conditions that prevail in today's cultural politics.

98. See William Power, as quoted in A. Noble, 'Burns and Scottish Nationalism', in K. Simpson (ed.), *Burns Now* (Edinburgh: Canongate, 1994), 176–7; R. J. Finlay, 'The Burns Cult and Scottish Identity', in K. Simpson (ed.), *Love & Liberty: Robert Burns, A Bicentenary Celebration* (East Linton: Tuckwell Press, 1997), 74–5.

II

Rogue Element

Charles Rogers and the Scotching of British History

Catriona M. M. Macdonald

The organic unity of Britain, dictated by geography and reinforced by the environment, is to the fore in this excerpt from Scott's accessible historical survey, *Tales of a Grandfather*. For Scott, Scotland exists only in terms of its people and its past: not a nation with a claim on the future, but an awkward if heroic episode on the journey to the Union of 1707, when nature and constitution at last coincided. The incorporating Union of 1707, according to Scott, was 'a healing measure', healing the past as much as the more recent wounds of the seventeenth century. Yet, after Scott's death in 1832, it was clear that historical traditions within the British Isles were still in need of 'healing': the emergent English historical profession would prove itself at times intolerant of contrasting historiographical traditions across the four nations and, as we shall see, apt to forget the Scottish influences that had shaped the early years of the British historical profession's own institutions.

I

In the absence of academic chairs in Scottish history until the twentieth century, and given the regular appointment of English academics to history posts in Scotland's universities in the final decades of the nineteenth century, such intolerance is understandable though not excusable. Apart from the work of Robert Anderson on history in the Scottish universities, little has been done in recent years to trace the development of Scottish historiography in the century after Scott.[1] Yet that does not quite explain the thrust of John Kenyon's reference to Sir Richard Lodge and George Prothero 'impos[ing] early English constitutional history, complete with Stubbs, on the *hapless* Scots at Glasgow and Edinburgh'.[2] Nor does it explain Doris Goldstein's silence on Scotland in her studies of the professionalization and organizational development of history in Britain.[3] Despite the emergence of 'Four Nations' perspectives on the British past over the last twenty years, conventional interpretations of the emergence of the British historical profession have—almost without exception—tended to stress a selective lineage of Oxbridge academics, the pre-eminence of English institutions, and a rather quixote interpretation of the scientific quality of historical scholarship as a litmus test for seriousness.[4] As a consequence, English historical practice has— whether by intention or by default—become the benchmark against which

1. See R. Anderson, 'University Teaching, National Identity and Unionism in Scotland, 1862–1914', *Scottish Historical Review* 91 (2012), 1–41; Anderson, 'The Development of History Teaching in the Scottish Universities, 1894–1939', *Journal of Scottish Historical Studies* 32 (2012), 50–73; Anderson, 'University History Teaching and the Humboldtian Model in Scotland, 1858–1914', *History of Universities*, 25 (2010), 138–84.
2. John Kenyon, *The History Men: The Historical Profession in England since the Renaissance* (London: Weidenfeld and Nicolson, 1983), 199 (emphasis added).
3. Doris S. Goldstein, 'The Organizational Development of the British Historical Profession, 1884–1921', *Bulletin of the Institute of Historical Research*, 55 (1982), 180–93; Goldstein, 'The Professionalization of History in Britain in the Late Nineteenth and Early Twentieth Centuries', *Storia della Storiografia*, 3 (1983), 3–27.
4. See A. T. Milne, 'History in the Universities: Then and Now', *History*, 59 (1974), 33–46. One exception would be Christopher Harvie, 'Nineteenth-Century Scotland: Political Unionism and Cultural Nationalism, 1843–1906', in R. G. Asch (ed.), *Three Nations—a Common History? England, Scotland, Ireland and British History c. 1600–1920* (Bochum: Universitatsverlag Dr N. Brockmeyer), 191–228.

Scottish histories and historians in the Victorian period have come to be judged, and typically been found lacking.[5] It is something of a long-standing convention: in 1887, Paul Frédéricq of the University of Ghent noted the 'almost utter poverty' in the science of history in the Scottish universities.[6]

This focus on university history, however, has resulted in what at best is but a partial appreciation of the evolution of British historical practice. The presumption that universities are the natural cradles of the most worthy historiographical traditions is flawed and is underpinned by an unhealthy and somewhat self-serving presentism. It is well to remember that in the middle decades of the nineteenth century most published historians did not boast the cushion of a university appointment.[7] In Scotland's case, this is of the utmost significance. As Ernst Bruckmüller, Neil Evans, and Lluís Roura y Aulinas have noted: 'Scottish history was advanced outside the universities.'[8] If we foreground this appreciation of Scotland's contribution to a maturing British cultural community, a very different history of British history emerges.

II

In what follows, a revisionist critique of the career of the Scotsman Charles Rogers (1825–90) and his role in the foundation of the Royal Historical Society (RHS) will serve to highlight how British historical practice was both formed and undone at the confluence of national traditions: how a strong associational dynamic perpetuated discrete national historiographies and professional and patronage networks, and how commerce, as much as university patronage, informed the professionalization of the discipline.

---

5. In 1900 Prothero wrote a nine-page letter to Dr William Wallace laying out the problems, as he saw it, with the Scottish universities: University College London (UCL), Royal Historical Society Archive (RHS), Prothero MS, Prothero to Wallace, 1900.
6. Paul Frédéricq, 'The Study of History in England and Scotland', *Johns Hopkins University Studies in Historical and Political Science* (October 1887), 50. A century later, David Cannadine would suggest simply that the origins of modern professional history date back to the 'first serious incumbents of the regius chairs at Oxbridge, the founding of the *English Historical Review* and the reform of the Royal Historical Society, and the establishment of history courses at the new, provincial, redbrick universities' (David Cannadine, 'British History: Past, Present—and Future?', *Past and Present*, 116 (1987), 169–91, at 170).
7. Philippa Levine, *The Amateur and the Professional: Antiquarians, Historians and Archaeologists in Victorian England, 1838–1886* (Cambridge: Cambridge University Press, 1986).
8. E. Bruckmüller et al., 'Striving for Visibility: Nationalists in Multinational Empires and States', in I. Porciani and J. Tollebeek (eds), *Setting the Standards: Institutions, Networks and Communities of National Historiography* (Basingstoke: Palgrave, 2012), 372–93, at 379.

More broadly, it points to the limitations of the unionist nationalism paradigm in a transnational context.[9]

It would appear from extant published works that the early years of the RHS resemble a false start in the pre-history of modern British historical studies. In 1909, George Prothero, president of the society between 1901 and 1905, ignored Charles Rogers altogether, attributing the foundation of the society to five others (including an earl, two lords, the Dean of Westminster, and the Vice Chancellor of the University of London).[10] J. W. Burrow refers to the society's 'decidedly murky history of the first decade' after 1868, and there has emerged something of a consensus that it was only after the resignation of the society's founder and historiographer, Charles Rogers, in 1881 that the life of this esteemed institution truly begins: Goldstein refers to the society's *Transactions* under Rogers as 'undistinguished and certainly not works of historical scholarship'.[11] After 1881 Burrow points to an improvement in management and respectability, and Levine refers to improved fortunes after Rogers's exit.[12]

Regardless of such posthumous disregard, Rogers was widely recognized as the founder of the RHS by contemporaries in the 1860s and 1870s, and in the early days his contribution to its growth was widely acknowledged and he himself was remunerated (his salary increasing steadily) for his efforts.[13] The development of the Society's *Transactions*, of which Rogers was the first editor, also seemed to galvanize interest, the membership growing to 270 within the first six years, encouraging supporters to back an initiative that led to Rogers acquiring a new London residence, Grampian Lodge.[14] The optimism of these early years was not to last, however, and Rogers's contested place in the society's history can be largely explained with reference to the events surrounding his departure. Despite a rising membership, the society incurred debts during Rogers's custodianship, with suspicions about financial irregularities aroused for the first time in 1879.[15] During

9. Graeme Morton, *Unionist Nationalism: Governing Urban Scotland, 1830–1860* (East Linton:Tuckwell Press, 1999).

10. G. W. Prothero, 'Historical Societies in Great Britain', *Annual Report of the American Historical Association for the Year 1909* (Washington, 1911), 229–42, at 232.

11. J. W. Burrow, 'Victorian Historians and the Royal Historical Society', *Transactions of the Royal Historical Society*, 39 (1989), 125–40, at 126; Goldstein, 'Organizational Development', 184.

12. Burrow, 'Victorian Historians', 126; Levine, *The Amateur and the Professional*,.55.

13. UCL, RHS, Minute Books (Mins), vol. 1, 12 April 1872, 24 November 1873, 10 February 1876, 9 November 1876.

14. UCL, RHS, Mins, vol. 1, 26 November 1872, 20 May 1875.

15. UCL, RHS, Mins, vol. 2, 21 May 1879, 10 July 1879, 3 November 1879.

Rogers's secretaryship, the RHS also amalgamated with or was attached to other societies in which he had an interest (Provincial Record Association, English Reprint Society, British Genealogical Institute, Grampian Club), and concerns were raised that Rogers was creatively financing the endeavours of some of these bodies with RHS funds. Soon, warring cliques formed in the society that would ultimately lead to Rogers's undoing, although not before he had publicized such rifts and defended himself vociferously in the press, in pamphlets, and even in the courts.[16] Despite the fact that Hubert Hall (the first director of the RHS from 1891) considered Rogers far less 'dangerous' to the society than Patrick Edward Dove, a joint secretary who embezzled money from the RHS and the Selden Society and committed suicide in 1894, still Charles Rogers seems to get the most attention.[17]

Taken at face value these are perhaps convincing reasons why it may be best to gloss over the early years of the RHS: indeed, scholarship on Rogers's earlier career certainly reinforces a certain scepticism. Before Rogers's arrival in London, he had courted controversy in Scotland as a divisive presence on committees connected with the raising of the Wallace monument in Stirling and the cultivation of Scottish literature.[18] As both a minister of the Church of Scotland, latterly chaplain to the garrison at Stirling Castle, and a son of the manse, he had also raised eyebrows as the founder of a number of short-lived publications and initiatives (for example, *The Workman's Friend*), mostly financed by subscriptions, which—despite often claiming an altruistic objective—appeared to some as simple money-making enterprises. By the time he left Scotland in 1863 he had also appeared as the accused in a military court for dereliction of duty and as a litigant in several civil court cases relating to libel and damages.[19] Ultimately, he headed south a bankrupt, only

16. *Athenæum*, 7 December, 14 December, 28 December 1878; 4 January 1879; 28 May, 4 June 1881; C. Rogers, *The Serpent's Track: A Narrative of Twenty-Two Years Persecution* (London, 1880), 51; *Royal Historical Society* (22 December 1880); *Royal Historical Society* (5 May 1881); *Parting Words to the Members of the Royal Historical Society in a Letter to the President, Rt Hon. Lord Aberdare* (London, 1881).

17. UCL, RHS, Tout Papers, Hubert Hall to Thomas Frederick Tout, 2 February 1926.

18. See James Coleman, 'Unionist–Nationalism in Stone? The National Wallace Monument and the Hazards of Commemoration in Victorian Scotland', in E. J. Cowan (ed.), *The Wallace Book* (Edinburgh: John Donald, 2007), 137–50; Coleman, 'The Double Life of the Scottish Past: Discourses of Commemoration in Nineteenth-Century Scotland', Ph.D. thesis, University of Glasgow, 2005.

19. *Scotsman*, 9 November 1861, 21 July 1863; *Caledonian Mercury*, 9 June 1862, 20 February, 21 July 1863; *Dundee Courier*, 18 December 1862.

to embark on schemes similar to those that had got him into trouble in the north, before embarking upon the RHS.[20]

The weight of the evidence against him might suggest that an attempt to rehabilitate Rogers is at best naive or precocious: this may be true, although errors in the membership billing and consultancy charges relating to his most cherished allies, such as David Laing and the Christie family, strongly point to incompetence as much as anything more serious.[21] This chapter, however, does not seek to condone, legitimate, or disprove Rogers's conduct; rather, what is proposed is that, in the case of Rogers, personality has been allowed to mask important processes through which British history was being formed during his lifetime—processes that his career exemplifies. The presence or otherwise in Rogers of a 'persecution complex', his 'puffing self justification', and his 'creative accounting' are of little consequence, although to date they have led to a misinterpretation of his contribution to Scottish historical studies and the relationship between Scottish cultural practices and unionism.[22]

III

Charles Rogers visited London in 1855, and in correspondence with the literary historian and librarian of the Advocate's Library, David Irving, noted that he had met with 'a number of literary characters'. 'Altogether I greatly enjoyed my visit to the metropolis,' he reflected.[23] The literary life of the imperial capital was apparently in stark contrast to life in Edinburgh at that time. The novelist James Grant wrote to Rogers eight months after his southern sojourn, claiming that

> the day has *gone past* for making Edinburgh a centre for anything, it must be content to consider itself, a little provincial town in literature, as in everything else. The spirit of flunkeyism is too strong in the modern Athens for anything

---

20. *Caledonian Mercury*, 9 October 1863; C. Rogers, *Leaves from my Autobiography* (London: Longmans, Green & Co., 1876), 234.
21. Edinburgh, Edinburgh University Special Collections (EUSC), La.iv.17, Charles Rogers (CR) to David Laing (DL), 22 January, 26 January 1875; Edinburgh, National Library of Scotland (NLS), MS Christie, CR to Captain J. E. Christie (Christie), 1 June 1877. Rogers had clearly not kept impeccable accounts: on his departure from the RHS many members were approached for unpaid subscriptions only for the treasurer to be told that they had already paid Rogers: UCL, RHS H3/1/No. 1, Treasurer's correspondence, 1879–81.
22. Coleman, 'Unionist–Nationalism in Stone?', 257, 274.
23. Glasgow, Mitchell Library (ML), DI, vol. 2, CR to David Irving (DI), 21 September 1855.

to compete with it; besides, except a few penniless advocates, who scribble in the papers, we have few or no literary men among us.[24]

The associational life of Edinburgh in the mid-nineteenth century seemed a pale reflection of what it had been at the height of the Scottish Enlightenment, or indeed in Scott's time, and yet its influence lingered in patronage networks and a societal tradition that would be the inspiration for Rogers's initiation of the Historical Society in London some years later.

Rogers' first literary publication in 1844 was an edited collection of the poems of Sir Robert Aytoun (1570–1638).[25] Rogers learned early that it was necessary, as an 'unknown', to cultivate the intellectual elite to support this venture, writing to Irving the year before for permission to dedicate the work to him, and thereafter seeking support from others, such as David Laing, the librarian to the Society of Writers to the Signet; William Spalding, Professor of Logic, Rhetoric, and Metaphysics at St Andrews; Daniel Wilson, the anthropologist; and the publisher Robert Chambers, as his interests matured and diversified.[26] He also learned much from the Edinburgh publisher Thomas Murray about subscription rates, sales, marketing, and optimizing the return on each printed volume, which would stand him in good stead as his literary career sought paths around fraught personal situations, many of his own making.[27] The subscription list to the Aytoun volume reveals a network of subscribers centred on Rogers's home county of Fife, but also reaching into the Scottish capital and the pockets of the 'penniless advocates' that Grant would deride some ten years later.

In the absence of formal historical research institutes in the late nineteenth century, Goldstein has emphasized the importance of cross-institutional 'invisible colleges', sustained by associations and journals, in nurturing the scholarship of university historians.[28] The fact that in Scotland (as well as elsewhere) such 'colleges' pre-date by some time the foundation of chairs in history in the universities suggests that associational culture was foundational to, rather than simply the outcome or by-product of, the institutionalization of the historical profession, and is testament to a vibrant (and necessary) historical fraternity beyond the university cloisters. Rogers's career is illustrative

24. NLS, MS 14303, James Grant to CR, 24 May 1856.
25. *The Poems of Sir Robert Aytoun*, ed. C. Rogers (Edinburgh: Adam and Charles Black, 1843).
26. ML, DI, vol. 2, CR to DI, 30 September 1843; EUSC, La.iv.17, CR to DL, 10 October 1843; NLS, MS 14303, CR to William Spalding.
27. NLS, MS 14303, Thomas Murray to CR, 14 September 1843.
28. Goldstein, 'Organizational Development', 192.

in this regard: while an alumnus of St Andrews, and with a boasted higher degree from Columbia University (the circumstances are hazy), his application for the Professorship of Ecclesiastical History at the University of St Andrews in 1857 got nowhere.[29] However, Rogers was a correspondent, as we have seen, of David Laing, who was the secretary of the Bannatyne Club, founded by Scott in 1823. Rogers himself was a Fellow of the Antiquaries of Scotland from December 1850, and by the time he arrived in London had become adept at exploiting patronage networks, which—though they did not deliver financial security—unlocked status, influence, advice, and, in practical terms (at least when it came to Irving, for example) book loans from Scotland's pre-eminent libraries.[30] Being regularly outwith professional clubs and without the resources to sustain his scholarship from independent means, it could be argued that Rogers's solution was simply to create his own 'invisible colleges'. It is in this light that we ought to read Rogers's attempt in 1855 to create a Scottish Literary Institution and, in turn, the RHS.

In 1855, the idea of a literary institution in Scotland attracted the interest of Lord Landsdowne, Professor Blackie (Edinburgh), Principal Tulloch (St Andrews), William Pyper (Professor of Humanity, St Andrews), the journalist Peter Bayne, the writer Robert Carruthers, and others.[31] Yet many were reluctant to take on executive or honorary positions, and—beyond some campaigning on university reform, Blackie's passionate interest—the scheme was largely unsuccessful. The Earl of Elgin in 1856 correctly suspected that 'the public have not yet shown such interest in the establishment of an Institution of this nature as to justify the hope that it w^d. be adequately supported'.[32] Far from there being a dearth of societies in Scotland at this time, however, the Rector of Dollar Academy bemoaned the 'multiplicity of organisations springing up for all sort of work' as his reason for not joining.[33] Ultimately, Rogers, having failed to set up a second rival body to the Institute, as his control of it slipped from his fingers, resigned.[34] The institution itself

29. C. Rogers, *A Few Testimonials in Favour of the Rev. Charles Rogers, LL.D.* (Edinburgh: Grant Bros., 1857).
30. The Advocate's Library refused to lend to Rogers after Irving was no longer in post, as he was not a member of the faculty: NLS, MS 14303, Samuel Halkett to CR, 7 April 1859.
31. NLS, MS 14303, Landsdowne to CR, 19 November 1857; Tulloch to CR, 18 July 1875; Pyper to CR, 16 July 1855; Bayne to CR, 26 May 1856; Carruthers to CR, 24 November 1856.
32. NLS, MS 14303, Elgin to CR, 26 November 1856.
33. NLS, MS 14303, Dr James Clyde to CR, 5 February 1857.
34. He had tried a similar strategy in relation to fundraising for the Wallace monument, instituting a Supplemental Committee. See Coleman, 'The Double Life of the Scottish Past'.

stumbled along for a short time before disappearing altogether then reappearing in London (with little success), sponsored by William Burns, Honorary Secretary of the London Burns Club (est. 1868), and Robert Crawford, a former director of the Grampian Club who had clashed with Rogers.[35]

Undaunted, Rogers by the 1850s knew that his patronage networks would reach as far as London: a Mr Dodds was working on behalf of Rogers, fund-raising in connection with the Wallace Monument, long before his own arrival in the metropolis.[36] Dodds noted in 1857 that 'the Wallace Monument is bringing me into contact with many of our leal-hearted Scotchmen here', and even offered to approach Thomas Carlyle in relation to the Literary Institution before dropping the notion altogether, as Rogers too cooled about the venture the following year.[37] William Jerdan, a Scottish journalist who had retired from the *Literary Gazette* in 1850, also prepared the ground for Rogers in London, noting in 1857 in connection with the monument fund-raising, 'I took a prominent part in the Burns' and Ettrick Shepherd's festivals. I am strongly of opinion that a Dinner at the London Tavern (say under Lord Elphinstone) would be a very productive measure...I think I could raise some hundreds of pounds (sterling not Scotch!)...'. He concluded that 'revival of the national feeling in the British Capital', every now and then' was a very excellent object, sustaining 'Scottish brotherhood, good feelings and charities'.[38]

Rogers, thus, had learned valuable lessons, and on his arrival in the south—after a short spell leading a religious tract initiative (something he had tried before)—founded the Grampian Club, which became the model he would use for the Historical Society in 1868. According to his autobiography, Rogers 'had contemplated the formation of a society or club, which might occupy the place of the Bannatyne Club at Edinburgh, the Maitland Club at Glasgow, and the Spalding Club at Aberdeen'.[39] Rogers followed a by now familiar strategy, approaching the Scottish elite before launching his scheme: the Duke of Argyll was the Grampian Club's first president. It was

---

35. This London society boasted a short-lived journal, the *London and Scottish Review* (1875). See also Rogers, *Leaves*, 311–18, 324–5; *Scotsman*, 10 May 1876.
36. Dodds would later become a member of both the Grampian Club and the Historical Society. A loyal friend, and not averse to scheming it appears, he cautioned Rogers in 1872 'not to bring me out in anyway until I am a member, when I shall always be ready to do duty, or take any little part you may wish' (NLS, MS 14303, Dodds to CR, 15 June 1872).
37. NLS, MS 14303, Dodds to CR, 22 January 1857; 13 March 1858.
38. NLS, MS 14303, William Jerdan to CR, 15 September 1856.   39. Rogers, *Leaves*, 331.

ostensibly a club founded for convivial purposes and to support the publication of works of Scottish interest; its first publication would be Rogers's own work *Scotland, Social and Domestic* (1869) and soon it would publish his *Monuments and Monumental Inscriptions in Scotland* (1871). The research for this latter work had commenced in 1861 as part of a scheme mimicking the approach of Sir John Sinclair's *Statistical Accounts,* involving the ministers of the Church of Scotland in recording the monumental inscriptions in their churchyards, while requesting that they pay 5s. to subscribe to the final published work.[40]

The Historical Society itself was established in London on 23 November 1868 in the offices of a Scottish insurance business on the Strand, and spent some time in 1871, during its rather peripatetic early years, in the Scottish Corporation Hall on Fleet Street. Of its earliest supporters a good many were Scots or had strong Scottish connections, among them the Earl of Mar, the Earl of Rosebery, the Marquis of Lorne, Henry Bruce (MP for Renfrewshire), William Euing (the Glasgow insurance broker and bibliophile), Kington Oliphant of Gask (also connected with the Grampian Club), the engineer, Sir William Fairbairn, and L. C. Alexander, the society's first secretary, whose offices hosted the first meeting. The Scottish vintage of the Historical Society is incontestable: the constitution of the society was almost identical to that of the Grampian Club, and among the first pieces featured in the society's *Transactions* were three papers by Rogers on Sir Robert Aytoun, the Roger family, and Sir John Scot of Scotarvit. [41] Indeed (compared to its later published works), a disproportionate number of the society's early papers and publications relate to Scottish history.

Should personality be our guide, we might simply interpret this Scottish influence as the consequence of the self-serving aims of Charles Rogers: as we have seen, many have done so and dismissed his years as an aberration. There are certainly grounds for this: in 1872 the society minutes record a payment of £1 11s. 6d. to a Mr James Paterson, 'searcher of Records, Edinburgh'—obviously Rogers's alternative source of research material following the passing of Irving and his own move to London.[42] After a

---

40. NLS, LC Folio 74, 26 August 1861. Rogers's father, Revd James Roger (Rogers added the 's' to his name in early adulthood), had written the *Old Statistical Account* entry for the parish of Monifieth, and the *New Statistical Accuont* entry for Dunino. See <http://edina.ac.uk/stat-acc-scot/> (accessed 13 March 2016).

41. UCL, RHS, Mins, vol. 1, 24 January 1871.   42. UCL, RHS, Mins, vol. 1, 12 April 1872.

promising start—he published his first Aytoun volume when just 19 years
of age—Rogers's career had been thwarted on a number of occasions in
Scotland. For example, it seems clear that he would have secured the post of
minister of the parish of Ballingry in 1851 had not patronage intervened
against him. The living—in the hands of Lady Scott of Lochore (daughter-
in-law of the late Sir Walter)—had been promised to a friend of the son of
William Lockhart, MP for Lanarkshire and half-brother of John Gibson
Lockhart (Sir Walter Scott's son–in law and biographer).[43] Instead, Rogers—
having been left little by his father, whose own literary tastes had exceeded
his income as minister of Dunino—eventually accepted a salary of £74 as
chaplain to the Stirling garrison, which he felt obliged to supplement, as we
have seen, by various schemes.[44] In this regard, Rogers's own financial straits
resemble the fragile foundations of the cultural community at large in Scotland
at this time. Indeed, it is telling that, in his preface to the first volume of the
History Society's *Transactions*, he noted the society's intentions of supporting
'individuals who, however earnest in prosecuting their inquiries, did not
possess facilities such as to render their researches available'.[45] And it is to
his credit that, more broadly, in supporting efforts to secure pensions for
Scottish writers and their families who had fallen on hard times, he recognized his own difficulties in the lives of others. Rogers, for example,
campaigned for a state pension for Thomas Dick, the Dundee-born scientist
and philosopher.[46]

The Scottish emphasis in Rogers's general approach, however, goes
beyond tactics borne of necessity, however one wishes to style it—national
or personal. It is testament to his attempted creation of a British historical
approach that drew as much on Scottish as English traditions, and—more
prosaically—the opportunities and challenges wrought by a new publication environment in the second half of the nineteenth century. This is most
notable in Rogers's genealogical publications and his creation of the British
Genealogical Institute.

It is interesting that the same authors who commend the amalgamation
of the Camden Society—'one of the most important of English publishing
societies', although one that collapsed through 'boredom'—and the RHS in

43. NLS, MS 14303, William Lockhart to 'Forbes', 25 May 1851.
44. C. Rogers, *The Issues of Religious Rivalry: A Narrative of Five Year's Persecution* (London: Alfred Boot, 1866), 9.
45. C. Rogers, 'Preface', *Transactions of the Historical Society*, 1 (1872).
46. NLS, MS 14303, Thomas Dick to CR, 18 August 1854. Further examples abound in Rogers, *Leaves*, 267, 278, 308

1897 tend to question if not deride Rogers's intentions of absorbing into the
RHS, on much the same terms, the British Genealogical Institute—a society
he, of course, had founded.[47] Rogers's own interests in genealogy are self-
evident: whether under the imprint of the Grampian Club or as independent
titles, Rogers published many genealogical studies of Scottish families,
variously styled 'memorials' and 'memoirs'.[48] In this regard, again, we might
suspect that Rogers was simply using the RHS to support his own private
interests, and that is clearly the case up to a point. Yet it is possibly more
than that. It was, after all, the monies from Sir William Fraser's various
genealogical studies of Scottish aristocratic houses that founded the first
chair in Scottish History at the University of Edinburgh in 1901. In many
ways, Rogers adopted Fraser's methods in his approach to publishing family
histories, although his client base would not generate the same profits. Indeed,
when it came to his Christie family volume, Rogers would complain that
sales of this 'labour of love' would not adequately recompense him for his
own effort and investment.[49]

It seems clear that the all-too-easy attribution of self-interest in Rogers's
relationship with the RHS has obscured cultural strategies and intellectual
shoots that have their roots north of the border. In volume eight of the
Transactions of the Royal Historical Society, Rogers laid out his approach to history as both a science and an art.[50] He sketched a trail of errors perpetuated
by Hume, Robertson, Macaulay, Carlyle, Alison, Tytler, and Hill Burton
that modern scholarship would seek to correct; the emphasis is resolutely
Scottish. This is understandable perhaps, but is worthy of comment in the
history of the RHS as it points to an alternative context within which these
early publications should be appreciated—not simply as the poor-quality
attempts of a group of amateurs, but as an indication that the institution
itself was an expression of a very Scottish unionist vision, transplanted to
London in the hope of grounding a genuinely British approach to history.

47. R. A. Humphreys, *The Royal Historical Society* (London: Royal Historical Society, 1969), 11, 14,
    26. It is interesting to note that John Bruce, a London antiquary educated at Aberdeen
    Grammar School, was one of the founders of the Camden Society, and that the Scot, William
    B.D.D. Turnbull—later a calendarer for the record commission—was both the founder of the
    Abbotsford Club in 1833 and the Camden Club's Scottish Secretary from 1838, following his
    move to London.
48. These continued even after Rogers's return to Scotland in the 1880s; e.g., C. Rogers, *Memorials
    of the Scottish Family of Glen* (Edinburgh: privately printed, 1888), and *Memorials of the Scottish
    House of Gourlay* (Edinburgh: privately printed, 1888).
49. NLS, MS Christie, CR to Christie, 18 January 1878.
50. C. Rogers, 'Notes on the Study of History', *Transactions of the Royal Historical Society*, 8 (1880),
    1–11.

In this context, it is worth mentioning that the Alexander Prize (awarded since 1898) is named after the society's first (Scottish) secretary,[51] and, even after Rogers's departure, the Scottish influence was evident in the presidency of Sir Mountstuart Grant Duff (1891–99).

Still, there was something revealing in Rogers's last contribution to the *Athenaeum* in relation to his debacle in the RHS: he noted: 'Virulence among men of letters is unseemly; it is Thracian, *not British*.'[52] Rogers's attempt to create in the RHS a vehicle for a new British history was thwarted by himself, by his pre-history in relation to the associational culture he hoped to grow beyond the bounds of provincial interests, by Scots themselves, and by the emergence of a professional nexus across the English universities that sought distance from an antiquarian past and protection from the increasingly commercially driven publishing industry.[53]

Curiously, given the strong Scottish influence in the executive positions of the society, by the end of the RHS's first decade it was clear that Scots made up a very small percentage of the society's fellows. An opportunity presented itself to rectify this in 1876, when the society instituted a network of local secretaries, but, despite most English provincial towns and even Belfast and Dublin acquiring secretaries, Scotland was awarded none.[54] The RHS minute books are silent on the rationale behind this, but the imbalance continued. The year before Rogers's departure, there were only eight fellows listed in Scotland (plus Hill Burton as an honorary member) out of a total membership of 670, and in 1886 the society boasted only ten fellows with Scottish addresses (there were fifteen American members).[55]

It is hard to say if Rogers might have reassured fellows of his own 'reach' into Scotland, thus making a Scottish secretary surplus to requirements, though equally it may have suited Rogers not to attract too much interest in the north. Only a partial explanation can be pieced together from miscellaneous correspondence in the RHS Archives. In 1881, Alexander, the society's secretary, revealed that he had relinquished his position as

---

51. The Berry Prize came to the RHS by default after an initial approach to the Society of Antiquaries of Scotland. The prize was originally intended for a work on the life and times of James Hepburn, Earl of Bothwell: UCL, RHS, Minute book, Anderson-Berry Prize, Extract from RHS Council Mins, 19 September 1929.
52. *Athenæum*, 4 June 1881 (emphasis added).
53. See Leslie Howsam, *Past into Print: The Publishing of History in Britain, 1850–1950* (London: British Library, 2009).
54. UCL, RHS, Mins, vol. 1, 9 November 1876.
55. *Transactions of the Royal Historical Society*, 8 (1880); *Transactions of the Royal Historical Society*, 2nd ser., 3 (1886).

a consequence of Rogers's 'unscrupulousness', the pressures of his other business ventures, and—more interestingly, perhaps—because 'I did not at all like to furnish further material for the merry-making of Scotch newspapers on the subject—in which, of necessity my name was brought into conjunction with that of Dr Rogers'.[56]

Charles Rogers was haunted by the reputation his various schemes and court actions had earned him in Scotland, and it was to have a material impact on his career in London. While divisions within the RHS were developing long before 1880, it was a letter in the *Athenaeum* on 17 January from a Scot, R. M. Spence of the 'Manse of Arbuthnott, 'N.B.', that ignited the controversy that would lead to Rogers's departure. A fellow of the society, Spence called on members dissatisfied with Rogers's conduct to send him their addresses.[57] It was just the opportunity many of Rogers's adversaries needed, particularly Cornelius Walford, a writer on insurance, and Hyde Clarke, a philologist who had already caused difficulties in the London Anthropological Society in the late 1860s. By the end of the year Spence had retracted the views he had expressed in the *Athenaeum*, apparently after legal action from Rogers. But, in March 1881 he would write directly to the RHS treasurer, William Herbage, that, before meeting Rogers, he had 'heard plenty about him in connexion with Wallace Monuments, Tract Societies etc.', and urged the Council to 'institute an inquiry into the financial management of a man whose financial career has been a peculiar one'.[58] These were Scottish battles being played out on English soil, not the wrangles of would-be professional historians impeded by the antiquarianism of the society, or necessarily the malign influence of Rogers.

In the middle of the *Athenaeum* controversy, in February 1880, Rogers wrote to William Herbage, the RHS treasurer, confirming that his recent problems had their origins in the north: 'The entire conspiracy is laid open—it has originated with two Scotsmen, Colin Rae Brown, whom I am now prosecuting for libel, and a Robert Crawford, whom I prosecuted for libel in 1876 and who then offered an apology when proceedings were abandoned. We now have the enemy in our hands, God be thanked.'[59] As the Chairman of the RHS, George Zerffi, despaired that 'nothing is going on

56. UCL, RHS, H3/No2., L. Alexander to unknown recipient (RHS), 18 May 1881.
57. UCL, RHS, Mins, vol. 3, 26 January 1880.
58. UCL, RHS H3/1/No. 1, Treasurer's correspondence, R. M. Spence to William Herbage (WH), 14 March 1881.
59. UCL, RHS H3/1/No. 1, Treasurer's correspondence, CR to WH, 23 February 1880.

but eternal squabbles or mere *personal* matters',[60] from an English perspective, the whole thing looked faintly ridiculous. Certainly, that was how it appeared to Chief Justice Coleridge in 1880, who sat in judgment on the case Rogers brought against Colin Rae Brown, the newspaper proprietor and a founder member of the London Burns Club, relating to allegedly libellous comments in the *Scotsman* concerning his past involvement in the Wallace Monument:

LORD COLERIDGE: I can scarcely understand why the Chief-Justice of the Common Pleas and a special jury of the county of Middlesex should try an action between a minister of the Scottish Church and another Scotchman about a purely Scotch question.

MR INDERWICK: There is no doubt that the Wallace Monument was erected in Scotland, but both parties to the action reside in England; the libels were published in England—

LORD COLERIDGE: The [*sic*] were published in the *Scotsman*.

MR INDERWICK: And the Scotsman is published in Fleet Street, London.

LORD COLERIDGE: But the *Scotsman*, if it is the same *Scotsman* that I have the honour of knowing, is a Scotch paper.

MR INDERWICK: No doubt it is the same paper, my Lord; but it has a considerable circulation in London.

LORD COLERIDGE: So has the *Manchester Guardian*; but the *Manchester Guardian* does not thereby become a London paper. I do not think that our time ought to be taken up with purely Scotch quarrels. We have plenty else to do. Englishmen will quarrel quite enough. (Laughter.)

MR INDERWICK: ...it seems rather hard that gentlemen living in London should be driven to Scotland to have their differences settled.

LORD COLERIDGE: In Scotland I can quite understand that this would be a useful inquiry, but why it should be gone into at Westminster Hall is a thing which I fail to appreciate.

Rogers emerged from this court case a laughing stock; Rae Brown's counsel pulled Rogers's case apart to the evident enjoyment of the court room, and the foreman of the jury interrupted the proceedings before Rogers's counsel could address them, stating that the jury felt the plaintiff had no case.[61] The *Scotsman*— while it bristled with indignation about Lord Coleridge's 'unjudicial impatience'

60. UCL, RHS H3/1/No. 1, Treasurer's correspondence, George Zerffi to WH, 24 March 1881.
61. *Scotsman*, 17 November 1880.

and 'superficiality' in his preliminary statements on jurisductions, clearly revelled in Rogers's defeat, declaring: 'It was not wise of him to invite an English jury to look into the Wallace Monument Transactions.'[62]

The court case, however, is more than simply the dénouement of Rogers's career: it reveals, in Coleridge's banal Anglo-Unionism, the impossible conditions in which Rogers had sought to grow British history from a Scottish root, and to foster an associational culture, previously cultivated at the civic level, on a properly British basis. The English origins of the majority of RHS members—a factor that protected Rogers in the short term—jeopardized his vision in the long term. The membership demographic goes a long way to explaining why Rogers's approach was unpicked so quickly and comprehensively: he had employed the structures of associationalism but had failed to take the members with him. It left the way open for a new breed of historian to take the reins of the society, and create a far more exclusive body. Between 1884 and 1886 'Acton, Maitland, Lecky, Seeley and Cunningham' were elected, notes Humphreys: 'The age of the dilettanti had ended.'[63] Within a few weeks of Rogers's departure, the genealogical section had been disbanded, the membership medals he had devised were treated as something of a youthful aberration, and, just a few years later, the RHS marked the 800th anniversary of the Domesday book, with scarce a thought as to what it meant for Britain as a whole.

Rogers's posthumous reputation has been shaped by a Whiggish and overtly English historiography that, to identify 'progress' in the evolution of the RHS, has simply accepted a particular vision of professionalization—one that invariably has at its apex the university history chairs of Oxford and Cambridge, supported by networks of professional historians producing works that meet the requirements of post-Rankean scholarship. It is a historiography that has used definitions of 'professional' and 'amateur' more in keeping with the twentieth century than with the nineteenth, which have in turn hidden the alternative routes that scholarship might just have taken. As it is, the Rogers era certainly stands as a missed opportunity, not necessarily because it delayed the professionalization of the RHS, but because a chance was lost to cultivate an approach to British history more in tune with the contrasting traditions of at least two of the four nations.

---

62. *Scotsman*, 18 November 1880.   63. Humphreys, *Royal Historical Society*, 16, 26.

12

Unspeakable Scots
Dialogues and Dialectics in Scottish–British Literary Culture before the First World War

David Goldie

I n a major recent work, *Acts of Union,* Leith Davis examines a series of dialogues between English and Scottish literary cultures for the century and a half from the making of the Union to the era of Thomas Carlyle and Matthew Arnold. Her argument describes a number of dialogues in which mutual recognitions of difference bring to the fore the contradictions that inhere in Britishness. As Davis puts it, in selecting 'historical moments when cultural difference was foregrounded', she intends to initiate a reading in which 'we can begin to understand the contradictions at the heart of Britain'.[1]

This dialogical model seems apt for the early stages of a union, in which each partner is feeling the other out—each coming from a relatively distinct and well-defined place and encountering the established views of a largely alien culture. But it is a model that has limitations when we come to a more developed union—the Union of the late nineteenth and early twentieth centuries that has been refined by two centuries of complex interaction. By the beginning of the twentieth century a combination of political and economic integration, labour migration, and a developed communications

---

1. Leith Davis, *Acts of Union: Scotland and the Literary Negotiation of the British Nation, 1707–1830* (Stanford: Stanford University Press, 1998), 17.

technology, along with the spread of cross-border academic, publishing, entertainment, and media networks, makes a simple dialogical idea of cultural encounter problematic.

Such changes make it difficult, too, to see the work of union as the operation of distinct and unaltering cultural identities. Davis talks of the 'intrinsically unstable' notion of British identity that demands 'constant renegotiation', but pays less attention to the instabilities that might exist in the negotiators themselves.[2] The Scots and the English (not to mention the Irish and Welsh) are not as they were in 1707 (or 1542, or 1801), and one of the factors that alters each is the engagement with the other. The relation-ships between them are no longer those of mutual definition by difference but of the blurring caused by repeated association, in which the edges of identity no longer butt hard up against each other but rather blend and merge. The incentives, not least those commercial ones created by industry and empire, are such that any contradictions that might generate friction are smoothed over and made productive. There may still be differences of tradition, character, and opinion, but within the larger operation of union such differences figure less as troubling contradictions than as paradoxes: inconsistencies that are not so much impediments to a common purpose as the means through which a more complex and multifaceted relationship might evolve.

The use of a dialogical model—a model that insists, at bottom, on the exchanges between self-consistent entities—to read the cultural relation-ships within union has proved an attractive and productive one to many Scottish critics, among them those attempting a Bakhtinian interpretation of Scottish literary culture.[3] But it perhaps needs to be augmented with a model that recognizes that the bases of difference are themselves subject to change, a model that places emphasis less on dialogue and more on dialectic.

Such a dialectic should not be thought of as the somewhat crude, Fichtean one of thesis–antithesis–synthesis, which might lend itself to a rather simpli-fying model according to which English and Scottish literatures become synthesized into something like a homogenous British literature. There are many very persuasive accounts of the ways in which a self-conscious British political and cultural identity came into being, not least those made by

2. Davis, *Acts of Union*, 168.
3. See, e.g., Alastair Renfrew, 'Brief Encounters, Long Farewells: Bakhtin and Scottish Literature', *International Journal of Scottish Literature*, 1 (Autumn 2006).

Linda Colley and Howard Weinbrot.[4] But, while these make ample scope for a unifying Britishness that remains heterogeneous in construction, their emphases are arguably uni-directional: investigating, so to speak, what the Scots did for union rather than what union did for Scottishness. An approach more along the lines of Hegelian dialectic, and particularly its notion of sublation, might give more room for a recognition of the persistence, and indeed the preservation in altered form, of the elements that comprise the synthesis of union. In so far as it is possible to translate Hegel's idealism into a pragmatic way of interpreting cultural formation, sublation offers a way of reading a synthetic culture as something that both supersedes the original terms of its formation and incorporates them. As Hegel puts it in his *Science of Logic*:

> The German 'aufheben' ('to sublate' in English) has a twofold meaning in the language: it equally means 'to keep', 'to "preserve"', and 'to cause to cease', 'to put an end to'. Even 'to preserve' already includes a negative note, namely that something, in order to be retained, is removed from its immediacy and hence from an existence which is open to external influences.—That which is sublated is thus something at the same time preserved, something that has lost its immediacy but has not come to nothing for that.[5]

It might just be that this is a long-winded, philosopher's way of explaining how it is possible to have one's cake and eat it (something many Scots proved adept at throughout the course of the Union). But it also allows for a means of conceptualizing the ways in which it was, and continues to be possible, to be both synthetically British and antithetically Scottish. It offers, too, a way of thinking about literary culture as a dynamic system: not a dialogue between two relatively well-defined subject positions, giving and taking from each other while retaining a sense of their distinctness and integrity, but a dialectic in which the subject positions themselves are dissolved, reformed, made discontinuous by their encountering of each other and their products; a model that insists that all subject positions and notions of identity are contingent and contextual rather than fixed and essential.

It is to suggest, too, that Scottish culture, or indeed any other culture, forms itself into a tradition not through a model of steady accretion or linear development, but dialectically as a set of practices that are continually

4. Linda Colley, *Britons: Forging the Nation, 1707–1837* (New Haven and London: Yale University Press, 1992); Howard Weinbrot, *Britannia's Issue: The Rise of British Literature from Dryden to Ossian* (Cambridge: Cambridge University Press, 1995).
5. Georg Wilhelm Friedrich Hegel, *The Science of Logic*, trans. and ed. George Di Giovanni (Cambridge: Cambridge University Press, 2010), 81–2.

being challenged, cancelled, and remade in their encounters with others, but that even in their remaking preserve and maintain in sublated form the markers of a recognizable identity. A culture is by this definition made up at any moment of iterations each of which is a product not only of the linear history of that culture but also of the lateral relations that that culture has had and continues to have with others; its coordinates are never simply temporal within that culture but are always also spatial in relation to others.

Unspeakable Scots

What prompts this latter emphasis on sublated identity at the turn of the nineteenth and twentieth centuries—the sense of a Scottishness that is both wholly integrated in British culture and yet strangely unfamiliar and dissonant—is a reading of T. W. H. Crosland's 1902 book *The Unspeakable Scot*. Crosland's book is a polemic against the infiltration of London literary culture and media by the Scots. At times humorously hyperbolic, at others humourlessly shrill, it offers a somewhat hard-nosed and confrontational version of the insinuations that were appearing in contemporary magazines, such as *Punch*, against the apparently unstoppable force of the proverbial Scotsman on the make in the metropolis.

> Your proper child of Caledonia believes in his bones that he is the salt of the earth. Prompted by a glozing pride, not to say by a black and consuming avarice, he has proclaimed his saltiness from the housetops in and out of season, unblushingly, assiduously, and with results which have no doubt been most satisfactory from his own point of view. There is nothing creditable to the race of men, from filial piety to a pretty taste in claret, which he has not sedulously advertised as a virtue peculiar to himself. This arrogation has served him passing well. It has brought him into unrivalled esteem. He is the one species of human animal that is taken by all the world to be fifty per cent cleverer and pluckier and honester than the facts warrant. He is the daw with a peacock's tail of his own painting. He is the ass who has been at pains to cultivate the convincing roar of a lion. He is the fine gentleman whose father toils with a muck-fork. And, to have done with parable, he is the clumsy lout from Tullietudlescleugh, who, after a childhood of intimacy with the crudest sort of poverty, and twelve months at 'the college' on moneys wrung from the diet of his family drops his threadbare kilt and comes South in a slop suit to instruct the English in the arts of civilisation and in the English language.[6]

6. T. W. H. Crosland, *The Unspeakable Scot* (London: Grant Richards, 1902), 4–5.

What seems particularly to irk Crosland, apart from the apparent ubiquity of successful Scotsmen across English literary and newspaper culture, is their seeming assumption of belonging to a unity but reluctance to integrate—the sense they have of forming English culture while being themselves resistant to it and refusing to subsume themselves in it. They want to assert their right to full membership of the common cultural projects enabled by union, but to maintain a distinctive sense of themselves outside it. To Crosland's frustration they appear to enjoy an elective, rather than an interpellated, relationship with the dominant culture. The project of a common British literary culture is compromised, Crosland implies, by the number of Scotsmen who carry about within them a set of reference points inaccessible, and to some extent incomprehensible, to their English peers, from Bannockburn to Burns, to which they refer on an annoyingly regular basis in order to assert not only their difference but, as he suspects, their assumptions of superiority.

Alex M. Thompson, who had co-founded the *Clarion* with Robert Blatchford in 1891, betrayed a similar anxiety in *The Haunts of Old Cockaigne*, even if his tone was more mischievously amicable than Crosland's. An episode in the book features a fantastic encounter between a fictionalized Thompson and a somewhat self-satisfied Roderick, the six-inch high, self-proclaimed 'Speerit o' Scottish Literature'. This tiny, pompous imp perhaps epitomizes the tiresome braggadocio of the Scottish literary man-on-the-make, as he buttonholes Thompson with his opinion that 'ye canna' alter the fact that a' great men are Scots' and informs him solemnly, in a sophisticated argument that is blissfully ignorant of the known facts, that Shakespeare was in fact a Scotsman, and not just any Scot, but William Drummond of Hawthornden no less.[7]

The idea that Scots were maintaining a disproportionate, and perhaps self-serving, influence on British literature and culture dated back to at least the late eighteenth century, from the time in which the work of the Scottish Enlightenment writers began to exert a dominant influence on popular reading and on the formation of a literary culture of politeness and self-improvement.[8] This had both positive and negative effects, leading to a widespread respect for Scottish writers in England but also a resentment

7. Alex M. Thompson, 'Was Shakespeare a Scotsman?', in Thompson, *The Haunts of Old Cockaigne* (London: Clarion, 1898), 87–115, at 98–9.
8. David Allan, *Making British Culture: English Readers and the Scottish Enlightenment, 1740–1830* (New York and London: Routledge, 2008), 237.

when that influence seemed to become overweening. David Hume and Lord Kames had been esteemed regulators of taste, but their commercial successors, Francis Jeffrey, Henry Brougham, John Wilson, and John Gibson Lockhart among them, provoked not only similar kinds of admiration but also the ire of some, and particularly those who felt slighted by their assumptions of superiority. Lord Byron—half-Scottish himself—famously led the charge in his *English Bards and Scotch Reviewers* (1809), where he not only noted resentfully that 'Scottish taste decides on English wit', but that Scottish literary critics were in practice little more than 'Northern Wolves': a 'coward brood, which mangle as they prey, | By brutal instinct, all that cross their way'.[9]

The particular Scotch reviewer who raised the hackles of Crosland a century later was—in his view at least—a particularly odious type of northern wolf in sheep's clothing, William Robertson Nicoll, the founding editor of the *British Weekly* and *Bookman*. Nicoll was a pious Presbyterian entrepreneur of impressive energy and enormous ambition: a man with an unerring instinct for connecting Scottish writers with the British popular mainstream. To some he seemed a monster of sanctimonious sentimentality, but to others he was 'an inexhaustible fount of sound commercial ideas' and 'the cleverest, shrewdest Scot of his generation'.[10] At first a literary adviser to Hodder and Stoughton, he created in the *British Weekly* (launched in 1886) a paper that thrived by marrying evangelical nonconformism with literary criticism. This paved the way for the massive British and international success of the Kailyard school of fiction, which Nicoll—who fostered J. M. Barrie, S. R. Crockett, and Ian Maclaren—effectively founded.[11] His work as editor and critic made him probably the most influential figure in popular, and what would later come to be called middlebrow British literature in the last years of the nineteenth century and early years of the twentieth.

He was equally influential in his editorship of the *Bookman*, where he showed (as at *British Weekly*) an unerring instinct for the commercial potential of books. According to his contemporary Dixon Scott, he

addresses an audience far more numerous, far more responsive, far more eagerly in earnest, than that controlled by any other literary critic. He praises

---

9. *Lord Byron: The Complete Poetical Works*, ed. Jerome McGann (Oxford: Clarendon Press 1980–93), i. 244, 242, ll. 503, 429–31.
10. George Blake, *Barrie and the Kailyard School* (London: Arthur Barker, 1951), 25. Donald Carswell, *Brother Scots* (London: Constable & Co., 1927), 237.
11. See T. H. Darlow, *William Robertson Nicoll: Life and Letters* (London: Hodder & Stoughton, 1925); Andrew Nash, *Kailyard and Scottish Literature* (Amsterdam: Rodopi, 2007).

a book—and instantly it is popular. He dismisses one, gently—and it dies. He controls the contents of the bookshelves of a thousand homes—they change beneath his fingers like bright keyboards—and every alteration means the modification of a mind. What Claudius Clear [Nicoll's pseudonymous critical persona] reads on Wednesday, half Scotland and much of England will be reading before the end of the week.[12]

Nicoll was only the most prominent of many Scots who had relocated to England and established themselves as the controllers and arbiters of popular literary taste. One was James Milne, who founded *Book Monthly* in 1903 and was from 1904 to 1918 the influential literary editor of the *Daily Chronicle*. Another was J. M. Robertson, the Liberal politician, polymath, Shakespeare scholar, and author in 1908 of a series of articles in *T. P.'s Weekly* on 'The Best Hundred Books of Today'.[13] Together, these Scots were largely responsible not only for regulating literary taste as Hume and Kames had done over a century before, but also for commercializing it through the introduction of modern phenomena such as the creation of bestseller lists.[14]

Scots could also be found not only dispensing advice but offering 'models of the self' in the causeries and correspondence columns that transformed the British sixpenny magazine market in the 1890s. The two stars of this new form were the Scots Andrew Lang in *Longman's Magazine* and Annie S. Swan in another Nicoll venture, *Woman at Home*.[15] Lang was already an established maker and breaker of reputations—his professed preference for 'more claymores and less psychology' pleased many general readers, but exasperated writers like Henry James, who blasted Lang's 'beautiful thin facility to write everything down to the lowest level of Philistine twaddle'.[16] Swan, who had emerged as a writer by winning a Christmas short-story competition in the Dundee *People's Friend*, had, by the First World War, become a public figure and a confidante not only of Nicoll and the wartime director of British propaganda, John Buchan, but also powerful magnates

12. Dixon Scott, *Men of Letters* (1916; London: Hodder & Stoughton, 1923), 205.
13. Philip Waller, *Writers, Readers, and Reputations: Literary Life in Britain 1870–1918* (Oxford: Oxford University Press, 2006), 104–6.
14. Peter Keating, *The Haunted Study: A Social History of the English Novel 1875–1914* (London: Secker & Warburg, 1989), 439.
15. Margaret Beetham, 'The Agony Aunt, the Romancing Uncle and the Family of Empire: Defining the Sixpenny Reading Public in the 1890s', in Laurel Brake, Bill Bell, and David Finkelstein (eds), *Nineteenth-Century Media and the Construction of Identities* (Houndmills: Palgrave, 2000), 253–70, at 255.
16. Roger Lancelyn Green, *Andrew Lang: A Critical Biography* (Leicester: Edmund Ward, 1946), 167, 57.

like Sir George Riddell, majority shareholder of the *News of the World* and the Pearson and Newnes publishing groups.[17]

In some respects, Nicoll offered a successful example of Scottish integration into a synthetic Britishness, an idea reinforced by the titling of his magazine as the *British Weekly* and his successful collaboration with its English nonconformist publishers, Hodder & Stoughton. Nonconformism, indeed, offered many from Scotland and England a fertile ground for a common British identity in which their various cultural and commercial projects could flourish.[18]

In this, Nicoll was only the first in a long line of Scots who had found themselves influencing the composite cultures of Britishness, both highbrow and popular, in the nineteenth century. And not only influencing, but infiltrating: Swan, Lang, Barrie, and McLaren all relocated south of the border to be nearer the metropolitan centres of culture. The extent of such influence and of such increasing proximity is well known by now, moving from the Scottish academics who, following Adam Smith and Hugh Blair, effectively invented the academic discipline of English Literature; through popular writers like J. M. Barrie and Kenneth Grahame, who in *Peter Pan* and *The Wind in the Willows* did so much to define British Edwardian children's literature; to the peddlers of popular culture who helped shape what British people consumed on the page and on the stage (and later, via the influence of John Reith (1889–1971)—the long-serving and influential Director General of the BBC—heard on the airwaves and saw on the screen).[19]

Such figures ranged from academics such as David Masson, author of *British Novelists and their Styles: Being a Critical Sketch of the History of British Prose Fiction* (1859), and George Lillie Craik, whose *A Manual of English Literature* (1862) was still in print in the Everyman's Library fifty years after its publication. It included the great Scottish publishers, John Murray, Macmillan, and Smith Elder & Co, who had become established in London early in the century, as well as those who set up offices in London later, such as A & C Black, William Blackwood & Sons, Nelson & Sons, W. & R. Chambers, Blackie & Sons, Collins & Co. of Glasgow, who were, by the

---

17. Mildred Robertson Nicoll (ed.), *The Letters of Annie S. Swan* (London: Hodder & Stoughton, 1945), 5. Annie S. Swan, *My Life: An Autobiography* (London: Ivor Nicholson and Watson, 1934).
18. For an illustration, see Keith A. Ives, *Voice of Nonconformity: William Robertson Nicoll and the British Weekly* (Cambridge: Lutterworth Press, 2011).
19. See Robert Crawford, *Devolving English Literature* (1992; 2nd edn, Edinburgh: Edinburgh University Press, 2000), 16–44; Robert Crawford (ed.), *The Scottish Invention of English Literature* (Cambridge: Cambridge University Press, 1998).

turn of the century, running London offices while also maintaining a strong presence across the Empire. Many of these publishers were also responsible for the journals that dominated literary culture in the nineteenth century and that survived well into the twentieth: Archibald Constable had been responsible for the *Edinburgh Review* (1802–1929); John Murray for the *Quarterly Review* (1809–1967); David Masson had, like many literary academics of the mid-century, offered a bridge between the academy and commercial publishing as the founding editor of *Macmillan's Magazine* (1859–1907), which joined other influential journals named for their Scottish publishers, among them *Blackwood's Magazine* (1817–1980) and *Chambers's Journal* (1832–1956). When a commentator in *Book Monthly* in 1917 asked, 'Has the English bookman ever reflected on the debt of service he owes to publishers of Scottish family and name', the question was plainly rhetorical. For, as he quickly went on to say, 'the Murrays, the Macmillans, the Blackwoods, the Blacks, the Nelsons, and other names famous on the imprints of books' have all ensured the presence of a distinctive 'Scottish note in publishing'.[20]

A 'Scottish note' was also audible in the newspaper press through the presence of people such as Robert Donald, editor of the *Daily Chronicle*, and James Nicol Dunn, editor of the *Morning Post*, as well as all the hordes of hacks and self-important subeditors who, according to Crosland at least, ensured that '"Hoo are ye the noo?" is the conventional greeting in most newspaper offices'.[21] It was present, too, in the commercial arm of literature, which saw the rise of the phenomenon of the literary agent. Easily the most significant of these new figures on the literary scene was the Glaswegian A. P. Watt, who not only represented most significant authors—from Marie Corelli and Arthur Conan Doyle, to Arnold Bennett, Rudyard Kipling, and W. B. Yeats—but who also acted as a crucial middleman for the publication of the great majority of the serialized and syndicated fiction in the British magazine market.[22]

Theatre, both high and low, was also strongly inflected with the Scottish accent. William Archer was probably the most influential theatre critic of the day, in his ground-breaking *English Dramatists of Today* (1882) and his

20. 'Personal and Particular: Small Talk of Letters at a Time of Great Affairs', *Book Monthly* (1917), 301–16, at p. 316.
21. Crosland, *The Unspeakable Scot*, 58–9.
22. Mary Ann Gillies, *The Professional Literary Agent in Britain, 1880–1920* (Toronto: University of Toronto Press), 27–39.

championing of realism and his promotion of Ibsen. And it was Archer who was responsible, in collaboration with the Englishman Harley Granville Barker, for making the first serious attempt to establish the idea of a British National Theatre, as expressed in their *Scheme & Estimates for a National Theatre* (1904). The two great theatre-owning companies of the late nineteenth and early twentieth centuries, which not only offered space for performance but also effectively controlled much of the touring repertoire of theatre and variety throughout Britain, were also substantially Scottish. Howard and Wyndham, a dominant theatre-owning, production, and management company, famed for its lavish pantomimes, was established in Glasgow in 1895, by the Irishman John Howard and the Scotsman Frederick Wyndham, and ran the major theatres in Edinburgh and Glasgow, but also in London, Newcastle, Liverpool, and Nottingham. Moss Empires, the company that transformed British variety and made it a respectable activity for the middle classes, eventually controlling thirty-nine theatres, had grown out of the experiences of its founder Edward Moss in his father's music hall in Greenock and his first lease at the Gaiety Music Hall in Edinburgh in 1877.[23]

'England' for the English, and 'Britain' for the Scots?

For probably as long as the Union itself, and certainly in the decades since the advent of the National Association for the Vindication of Scottish Rights in the 1850s, there was an anxiety among Scots that the national distinctiveness of their contributions was not being adequately recognized. While the huge majority of Scots were, for the most part, content with union, some occasionally voiced a frustration that England was taking credit too readily for them. This manifested itself most notably in what J. H. Grainger has called 'The English Presumption': the use of the adjective 'English' to describe things that are, more accurately, British, and the associated prejudice that files all Scots' successes under 'British' but their failures in the category 'Scottish'.[24]

23. Paul Maloney, *Scotland and the Music Hall, 1850–1914* (Manchester and New York: Manchester University Press, 2003), 64–9
24. J. H. Grainger, *Patriotisms: Britain 1900–1939* (London: Routledge & Kegan Paul, 1986), 48–64. See also, e.g., Brian Viner, 'Why Murray is a Brit when he wins and a Scot when he loses', *Independent*, 1 July 2010 <http://www.independent.co.uk/voices/columnists/brian-viner/brian-viner-why-murray-is-a-brit-when-he-wins-and-a-scot-when-he-loses-2016381.html> (accessed 12 August 2016).

In this context it is perhaps interesting to note some examples from the early twentieth century that suggest analogous counter-resentments among the English. A contribution to the *Publishers' Circular* of 1916 was one such. Tellingly titled 'If it's Scotch it's Scotch; if it's English—it's British', its arguments followed Crosland in suggesting that, if there was bias in the British press, it was in fact systematically exercised in favour of the Scots—a consequence perhaps of the fact that 'English journalism is crowded with Scotsmen who plaster their papers with Scotch matter'.[25] The Anglo-Scottish writer Ian Hay picked up on this, albeit in a somewhat tongue-in-cheek way, in his book *The Oppressed English* (1917), in which he professed sympathy with the English for lacking the kinds of aggressive nationalism found in other parts of the United Kingdom and thus gaining none of the plaudits for British successes but many of the brickbats for the nation's failures: 'why should the credit for the good deeds of the British Empire be ascribed to those respectively responsible—except the English—while the odium for the so-called bad deeds is lumped on to England alone?'[26]

Whatever the truth of these claims, what they disclose is an unresolved tension arising from the presence of so many self-identifying Scots at or near the centre of British culture. This might be a low-level anxiety, raised mainly in a bantering, humorous context, but it suggests a continuing resistance among Scots to the idea of a wholly assimilative, synthetic Britishness. Masson had signalled such a resistance in his *British Novelists and their Styles* in 1859, even as he celebrated British integration and the opportunities it offered Scottish cultural workers:

> Scotticism is not one invariable thing, fixed and intransmutable. It does not consist merely in vaunting and proclaiming itself, in working in Scottish facts, Scottish traditions, Scottish reminiscences—all of which has perhaps been done enough; it may be driven inwards; it may exist internally as a mode of thought; and there may be efficient Scotticism where not one word is said of the Thistle, and where the language and the activity are catholic and cosmopolitan. And, seeing that it is so, need we suppose that we have yet seen the last of the Scotchmen, the last of the men of Edinburgh? No! The drain may still be southwards; Scotland now subserves, politically at least, the higher unity of Great Britain, just as that unity in its turn subserves a larger unity still, not so obviously carved out in the body of the surrounding world.

25. Henry R. Brabrook, 'If it's Scotch it's Scotch; if it's English it's British', *Publishers' Circular*, 29 July 1916, p. 89.
26. Ian Hay, *The Oppressed English* (London: J. M. Dent & Sons, 1917), 6.

Welcoming the opportunities for Scots to assimilate, Masson nonetheless insists on a Scottish exceptionalism that allows them, even as they adopt the practices and language of the English, to maintain a distinctive 'internal Scotticism':

> at the time when Scotland was united to her great neighbour, she was made partaker of an intellectual accumulation and an inheritance of institutions, far richer, measured by the mode of extension, than she had to offer to that neighbour in return; and since that period, while much of the effort of Scotland has been in continuation of her own separate development, much has necessarily and justly been ruled by the law of her fortunate partnership. And so for the future, it may be the internal Scotticism working on British, or on still more general objects, and not the Scotticism that works only on Scottish objects of thought, that may be in demand in literature as well as in other walks. But while Scotland is true to herself, and while nature in her and her social conditions co-operate to impart to her sons such an education as heretofore, there needs be no end to her race of characteristic men, nor even to her home-grown and home-supported literature.[27]

This was, presumably, a compelling argument for many Scots. Not least because it aligns quite closely with the arguments of the National Association for the Vindication of Scottish Rights (NAVSR), which staunchly supported union while recognizing the desirability of maintaining distinct national identities. The NAVSR's *Address to the People of Scotland* of 1853 stated clearly such support for union alongside a belief that 'Scotland will never be improved by being transformed into an inferior imitation of England, but by being made a better and a truer Scotland'.[28] Masson and the Vindicationalists acknowledge the desirability of a hybrid British culture, but what both refuse to do is to entertain the idea that what Masson describes as an innate 'Scotticism' might itself be a hybridized form subject to alteration through its encounter with a persisting 'Anglicism'. As such, the 'better and truer Scotland' conjured by Vindicationists is implicitly an essential quality, a spirit not blended in combination with Englishness but distilled in isolation from it. For all its subtleties and careful equivocations, Masson's idea of cultural, as distinct from political, union is essentially of a unidirectional flow in which an axiomatically homogenous 'Scotticism' contributes to a hybrid Britishness without itself suffering alteration.

27. David Masson, *British Novelists and their Styles: Being a Critical Sketch of the History of British Prose Fiction* (Cambridge: Macmillan, 1859), 205–7.
28. National Association for the Vindication of Scottish Rights, *Address to the People of Scotland, and Statement of Grievances* (Edinburgh: Johnstone & Hunter, 1853), 3.

Unspoken Englishmen

The story so far is a recognizable one—the familiar legend of the many Scots who made their distinctive and disproportionate contributions to the British imperial project and its culture. But there is another story to be told about the other side of this relationship: of the significant part played by England in Scottish culture, whether that was through the active presence of the English in Scotland or their influence on the country at a distance.

This is not simply a discourse of hegemony or cultural imperialism—the rise of a dominant Englishness suppressing Scottish domestic politics and education, and excising Scots dialect along the way; or of having to live under the English sentimental gaze, the indulgence of which leads to Balmorality, the Kailyard, and the tartan shortbread tin. Rather it is the progress of Englishmen doing in Scotland the same kind of cultural work that many Scots were doing more visibly in England: teaching English, editing newspapers, running theatres, writing for an eager readership—bringing elements of their particular culture with them and engaging them in a Scottish context.

The Scots—Masson among them—may lay a claim to having invented English literature, but many Englishmen returned the compliment and came north of the border to help educate Scots in their own invention. Masson was succeeded in the Regius Chair at Edinburgh by probably its most celebrated incumbent, the Englishman George Saintsbury, while the chair in English at Glasgow University was held successively by two distinguished English scholars, A. C. Bradley and Walter Raleigh. Another Englishman who ventured north of the border was W. E. Henley, who, in 1889–92, ran the *Scots Observer* (from late 1890 the *National Observer*) from Edinburgh, and who did much to bring the work of Robert Louis Stevenson, W. B. Yeats, George Bernard Shaw, Thomas Hardy, J. M. Barrie, Rudyard Kipling, Kenneth Grahame, Alice Meynell, and H. G. Wells to a British reading public.

The Scottish theatre, that most apparently localized phenomenon, was similarly hybridized. A number of pioneers of Scottish music-hall management in the nineteenth century had been English, including James and Christina Baylis, who ran Glasgow's Scotia Music Hall and dominated the city's entertainment scene for many years. A. E. Pickard, the enterprising owner of Glasgow's Panopticon music hall and American museum and

waxworks, was an Englishman.[29] And, while the theatre-owner Edward
Moss might be regarded as a Scot, he was born in Ashton-under-Lyne and
was educated in Manchester; his partner Oswald Stoll was raised in Liverpool.

Scottish newspaper culture, too, was strongly influenced not just by professional and technical influences from south of the border but also by the
presence of English journalists and proprietors. An example is offered by
Scotland's most widely read weekly newspaper at the turn of the century,
the *People's Journal*. The paper, and its stablemates, including the *People's
Friend* and the *Dundee Advertiser*, was owned and run by John Leng & Co.,
which would amalgamate with its Dundee rival W. & D. C. Thomson & Co.
in 1905.

In 1891 Leng was advertising the *People's Journal* as the 'mouthpiece' of
'Scottish Radicalism' and was claiming for it a weekly readership of one
million.[30] The *Journal* offers an important piece of evidence for William
Donaldson, who argues the case that this 'organ of the Scottish democracy'
played a vital part in maintaining a vibrant vernacular culture in north-
eastern Scotland in the later Victorian period—effectively an autochthonous culture that had grown directly from indigenous folk traditions.[31] The
paper's significance in maintaining the vernacular culture, particularly before
the 1880s, is manifest, and has been reinforced by Kirstie Blair's recent
research into the poetry published in the paper.[32] But it is also the case that,
as the *People's Journal* grew beyond its regional base, the more deracinated
and the less vernacular it became. It had begun in 1858 as a paper strongly
committed to a local vernacular, and it had become by the turn of the century Scotland's most popular paper: but it was not both of these things at the
same time. The *Journal* of the 1890s and 1900s was, in fact, an outstanding
success of the New Journalism of the 1880s and 1890s, having broadened its
reading community beyond Scotland, to Ulster and northern England
through its industry-leading experiments in editionizing—creating bespoke
versions of the paper to cover regional preferences in politics, sport, and
local interest.

29. Paul Maloney, *The Britannia Panopticon Music Hall and Cosmopolitan Entertainment Culture*,
    Palgrave Studies in Theatre and Performance History (London: Palgrave Macmillan, 2016), 163–210.
30. *How a Newspaper Is Printed: Being a Complete Description of the Offices and Equipments of the
    Dundee Advertiser, People's Journal, Evening Telegraph, and People's Friend* (Dundee: John Leng &
    Co, n.d. [1891]), 18–19.
31. William Donaldson, *Popular Literature in Victorian Scotland: Language, Fiction and the Press*
    (Aberdeen: Aberdeen University Press, 1986), 1–34.
32. Kirstie Blair (ed.), *The Poets of the People's Journal: Newspaper Poetry in Victorian Scotland*
    (Glasgow: Association for Scottish Literary Studies, 2016).

If the *People's Journal* was, as Leng advertised, a mouthpiece of 'Scottish Radicalism' or an organ of what Masson called an 'internal Scotticism', it seemed by the turn of the century more than happy to speak to its diverse audiences in a variety of voices: its coverage of news, comment, and sport in standard English journalese, with odd Kailyard corners of Scots in its humour pieces and the occasional poem. In case it should be thought that this represented a falling-away from an autochthonous purity, as Donaldson suggests, it is worth noting that the paper from its earliest days had been ready, indeed designed, to operate in a wider British, as well as narrowly Scottish, marketplace. Leng had exploited from early on the commercial possibilities of syndication, in which A. P. Watt would later corner the market. From its very beginning, the stories that appeared in the *People's Journal* were being syndicated for publication in other Scottish and northern English papers. This had been the case, for example, with David Pae's *Lucy the Factory Girl; or, The Secrets of the Tontine Close* (1860).[33] An anticipation of the requirements of national British syndication might explain why this Glasgow novel keeps Scots dialect to a minimum: the only vernacular speaker is the salt-of-the-earth Hugh the knife-grinder, who finds himself assailed and assaulted by various apparently cockney-speaking criminals and embedded in a relentlessly polite and sentimental standard-English romance narrative.[34]

A similar process of adapting Scottish localism for the British market can be seen at work in the *People's Friend*—the paper started in 1869 as a sister paper to the *Journal* with the express intention of publishing serial stories and competitions written by and for local audiences (again, in an early anticipation of some of the techniques and participative emphases of New Journalism). The *Friend* had been founded with the aim that it 'should be the exponent and conserver of Scottish literature, and should contain Scotch stories, poetry, and other articles written by Scotchmen'.[35] But it had quickly spread its net more widely (partly under David Pae's guidance as editor), printing fiction by, among others, Anthony Trollope, Dora Russell, and Mrs Braddon, and even discovering and bringing to the fore English popular writers, like Adeline Sergeant, through its competitions.

33. Bob Harris, 'The Press, Newspaper Fiction and Literary Journalism, 1707–1918', in Susan Manning (ed.), *The Edinburgh History of Scottish Literature*, ii. *Enlightenment, Britain and Empire (1707–1918)* (Edinburgh: Edinburgh University Press, 2007), 308–16, at 314.
34. See, e.g., David Pae, *Lucy, the Factory Girl: Or the Secrets of the Tontine Close* (Edinburgh, Thomas Grant, 1860), 120–4, for a flavour of this linguistic hybridity.
35. *How a Newspaper Is Printed*, 53.

The Leng papers were not only open to the influences of the wider British market; they were in fact directly a product of it—not least owing to the fact that their founder and proprietor, Sir John Leng, was in fact an Englishman. Leng had, in the early 1850s, done exactly what Crosland would complain of Scots men-on-the-make doing some fifty years later: having crossed the border in search of commercial opportunities in the media. This was much more than carpet-bagging: there can be little doubt of Leng's commitment to Dundee's politics and culture, and of his seriousness in taking on the role of 'conserver of Scottish literature'—he became one of the city's Eminent Men and represented the city as a Liberal MP. But it is likely that Leng's commitment to Dundee arose from a paradox: that his and his company's advocacy of 'Scottish Radicalism' and 'Scotch stories' arose less from a rooted sense of national identity than from the deep beliefs in subsidiarity and civil society inculcated by the British Liberalism in which he grew up (as well as from a canny understanding of how to create and captivate a self-identifying public for his product—a businessman's realization that local identity might be manipulated as a form of brand identity).[36] His status as one of the defenders of Scottish popular culture—of a sublated 'Scottishness'—was, in other words, the product of the synthetic British Liberalism from which he had emerged.

And Leng was not the only Englishman at the helm of a Scottish newspaper institution. A contemporary of his from Hull Grammar School (and indeed co-editor with him of the school newspaper and then fellow reporter on the *Hull Advertiser*) was Charles Cooper, who would go on to become one of the *Scotsman*'s legendary editors. Cooper edited the *Scotsman* from 1876 to 1905, during which time it moved from being a staunchly Liberal, pro-devolutionary, paper to a solidly Unionist one—although Cooper had initially been an ally of Lord Rosebery and Gladstone throughout the Midlothian campaigns and had used the paper to campaign for Scottish Home Rule and the creation of a Scottish Secretary in Westminster in 1885. He also did his own bit for Scottish literature by being the first president of the Sir Walter Scott Club.[37]

Leng and Cooper were, in fact, fairly typical products of a British-wide provincial newspaper network that allowed for frequent cross-border traffic

36. And he was, of course, only one of many eminent English Liberals who represented Scottish parliamentary constituencies, from Gladstone and Asquith to Arthur Ponsonby and Winston Churchill.
37. *The Glorious Privilege: The History of 'The Scotsman'* (London: Nelson, 1967), 69–78.

between newsrooms. The great editor of the *Manchester Guardian*, C. P. Scott, for example, had trained on the *Scotsman*, and from 1909 to 1917 the *Glasgow Herald* was edited by a *Times*-trained Englishman, F. Harcourt Kitchin, who by all accounts had rather limited sympathies with Scotland.[38] Sir Linton Andrews (another former pupil of Hull Grammar School) was news editor of the *People's Journal* and *Dundee Advertiser* and would go on after the First World War to edit the *Leeds Mercury* and *Yorkshire Post*.[39]

English newspaper groups, too, had a strong purchase on Scotland from the 1890s. The daily paper with the largest circulation in Scotland before the First World War, the *Daily Record and Mail*, was owned by the Anglo-Irish Harmsworth brothers, Lords Northcliffe and Rothermere. Likewise, Sabbatarian Scotland lacked indigenous Sunday papers before the war, which meant the English-owned *News of the World* had a wide circulation, until the establishment during the First World War of Scottish Sunday papers including the *Sunday Post*.[40]

By the outbreak of the war there was little, apart from the details of their coverage of local topics, to distinguish the Scottish-owned regional and national newspapers from southern equivalents such as the *Birmingham Daily Post*, *Western Mail*, or *Yorkshire Post*. A reader of the *Aberdeen Free Press* in 1914 could find out the latest goings-on in the city council while also keeping up to speed with the English county cricket scores through the scorecards printed in full in its back pages: a person browsing the *Glasgow Herald* might see, side-by-side, reviews of the latest book by Ian Hay and a play currently causing a splash in London's West End; the *Daily Record and Mail* might feature a story from the Glasgow courts on one page and a feature on the latest London fashions on the next.

Scottish culture, as it was constructed in the pages of these papers, and as it was expressed in the literature and theatre that was consumed by the majority of Scots in the years before the war, was evidently not so much a single entity as a complex and dynamic system. The Scottish cultural identity to which these newspapers spoke was more than simply the nested grouping of 'concentric identities' described by Christopher Smout, but comprised rather a myriad of intersecting and overlapping identifications

---

38. See A. McL. Ewing, *A History of the Glasgow Herald 1783–1948* (Glasgow: Printed for Private Circulation, [c. 1948]), 64; Alastair Phillips, *Glasgow's Herald: 1783–1983* (Glasgow: Richard Drew, 1983), 110.

39. Linton Andrews, *The Autobiography of a Journalist* (London: Ernest Benn, 1964).

40. See Cyril Bainbridge and Roy Stockdill, *The News of the World Story: 150 Years of the World's Bestselling Newspaper* (London: HarperCollins, 1993), 60–1.

with the local, the national, and the international.[41] The sum of such referents might, at times, usefully amount to a quality that might be described as Scottishness, but it might equally be the formula for one of a range of other intranational or supranational subject positions.

Sublated Scots

What this complex cross-border cultural activity shows is how problematic it is to constitute the cultural and political relations between England and Scotland in the early twentieth century as a dialogue between two distinct traditions. The presence of influential Scottish people in England, and powerful English people in Scotland, created not only a hybrid or synthetic Britishness, but also an alteration in the nature of both England and Scotland themselves. John Leng helped establish Dundee as a powerhouse of Scottish and British journalism and Charles Cooper would play a part in reshaping Scottish and British politics, just as Macmillan, Smith Elder, and Blackwoods created, and William Robertson Nicoll and A. P. Watt refined, the British and English markets in publishing.

Cultural exchange, though, and especially literary exchange, needs little actual proximity. Given a common language and the functioning of an efficient means of book, magazine, and newspaper distribution, culture can operate at a distance. Benedict Anderson recognized this when he noted the importance of print culture in the formation of the imagined communities of emergent nations.[42] But what Anderson says is equally true of nations that are born through union as nations that come into being through separation. The imagination that John Leng wanted to inculcate in his readers was distinctly local and Scottish, relying as it did on the reporting of local news stories, municipal politics, and local sports teams. But it was also recognizably national and British, with detailed coverage of Westminster politics, metropolitan and international news, and national literary culture and sport. One of his early innovations, much vaunted in his papers, was to establish in 1870 a Fleet Street office with a direct telegraphic

---

41. T. C. Smout, 'Perspectives on the Scottish Identity', *Scottish Affairs*, 6 (Winter 1994), 101–13.
42. Benedict Anderson, *Imagined Communities: Reflections on the Origin and Spread of Nationalism*, rev. edn (London: Verso, 2002), 37–46.

link back to Dundee.[43] D. C. Thomson, similarly, established an office in Manchester in 1913. The implication was that an important part of being Scottish was being British: that localism was not to be confused with parochialism, and that its interests were best served by entering into a working relationship with the wider world. As such, the local became a locus—its newspaper not a kind of parish pump around which a culture might talk to itself but a place in which the diverse issues of a larger world might be focused and find expression within that culture.

Crosland was concerned that the metropolitan and imperial public spheres were, at the beginning of the new century, being distorted by hordes of semi-alien, unspeakable Scots—and he was not alone in both his amusement and bemusement at that fact. But the dichotomy he raised was a false one, for the Scots that he pilloried were not aliens at all but the products of that public sphere. The very distinctiveness they claimed, for all their references to Bannockburn and 'that heaven-sent date, A. D. 1314', was itself a direct product of, and manifestation of their reaction to, their union with the English.[44] The Scottishness they bruited forth was a token not so much of independence as of interdependence, not a quality that had been given once and for all at some originating moment in history, but a varying and relational means of self-identification that, like any complex identity, was constantly being remade in its continuing encounter with a familiar, antithetical Englishness.

43. This distinctive building remained a Scottish outpost in the capital into the twenty-first century. As a *Sunday Post* office latterly, it housed the last working journalists in Fleet Street, closing only in August 2016. See Michael Holden, 'Stop Press: Last Two Journalists Leave London's Fleet Street' <http://www.reuters.com/article/us-britain-fleetstreet-idUSKCN10G1LZ> (accessed 11 August 2016).
44. Crosland, *The Unspeakable Scot*, 24.

So Scott draws to a close his introduction to *The Minstrelsy of the Scottish Border*. The *Minstrelsy* is, in multiple ways, matrix and seedpod for the Waverley novels; and nowhere more so than in this passage as it modulates from the fieldwork of the Romantic folklorist through the enterprise of the antiquarian-as-nationalist to the tribute of the Romantic elegist for a vanishing nation. (Scott speaks—significantly?—not of a nation but of 'my native country' and of 'a kingdom, once proud and independent', with England segueing into position as 'her sister and ally').

The continuing presence of the folklorist in Scott's oeuvre will find a climax in *Redgauntlet* with 'Wandering Willie's Tale', that classic of Scottish *diablerie* that feeds into both the novel's deployment of Gothic and its sieving of history. The antiquarian-as-nationalist will fork one way to the debating of Scottish historical identity in *The Antiquary*; another to the projected four-volume *Tales of My Landlord* covering four Scottish regions, with their epigraph from Burns's poem to Captain Grose; and a third to the Abbotsford massing of historical relics so mordantly catalogued by Edwin Muir in *Scottish Journey*.[2] *The Lay of the Last Minstrel* incorporates the elegiac in its titular figure and framing; *The Lady of the Lake* in the Spenserian proem and epilogue that invoke the 'Harp of the North'. And the elegiac provides a key strategy for the mediation of history and defeat both in *Waverley*, which opens the sequence of Scott's Jacobite novels, and in *Redgauntlet*, which advances from, and answers to, it at the close of that sequence.

The elegiac ranks as one of the canonical modes through which the human imagination refigures and configures the world of human experience. Within literature its central genre is the elegy as such, but it crosses, or infuses, other genres, from epic to pastoral ('Et in Arcadia Ego') to the novel. Across and beyond the borders of literature the elegiac can occupy varied sites of memory: epitaphs, funeral games, monuments, relics, acts of commemoration, political or other, down to the affectionate comedy, with its mock-heroic roll call of history as provincial memory, of the Apparitor in *Pan Tadeusz* reading the Court Calendar of cases in which he has been involved:

> To common men the Calendar seems a mere list of names, but to the Apparitor
> it was a succession of magnificent pictures. So he read and mused: Oginski and

poems, culminating in *The Bronze Horseman*, trans. Oliver Elton. I am much indebted to Laurence Davies for conversation on things Polish.

2. For the original *Tales of My Landlord*, see Walter Scott, *The Black Dwarf*, ed. P. D. Garside (Edinburgh: Edinburgh University Press, 1993), 125. Edwin Muir, *Scottish Journey* (Edinburgh: Mainstream Publishing, 1979), 57–61.

Wizgird, the Dominicans and Rymsza, Rymsza and Wysogierd, Radziwill and Wereszczaka, Giedrojc and Rodultowski, Obuchowicz and the Jewish commune, Juraha and Piotrowski, Maleski and Mickiewicz, and finally Count Horeszko and Soplica; and, as he read, he called forth from these names the memory of mighty cases, and all the events of the trial; and before his eyes stand the court, plaintiff, defendant and witnesses; and he beholds himself, how in a white smock and dark blue kontusz he stands before the tribunal, with one hand on his sabre and the other on the table, summoning the two parties. 'Silence!' he calls. Thus dreaming and finishing his evening prayer, gradually the last court apparitor in Lithuania fell asleep.[3]

Elegy as genre, and the elegiac as mode, alike mark themselves off sharply from nostalgia as mood or stance. Nostalgia aches for an unrealizable return:

> Into my heart an air that kills
>   From yon far country blows:
> What are those blue remembered hills,
>   What spires, what farms are those?
>
> That is the land of lost content,
>   I see it shining plain,
> The happy highways where I went
>   And cannot come again.[4]

Elegy and the elegiac, by contrast, articulate defining and irreversible loss; and their contemplation of that loss has the quality C. S. Lewis found in his first schoolboy reading of Arnold's elegiac epic vignette *Sohrab and Rustum*: 'a passionate, silent, gazing at things a long way off'.[5] Elegy works through its specific generic conventions to orchestrate presence and absence, absence *as* presence.

It is the kind of poem where our need of the world and the frustration of that need, and the troubled relation of words and things, are taken to the highest degree of intensity and clarity: where the world as focused in a loved person is sought, and lost, and also reappears as an image, as 'Lycidas' or 'Adonais'.[6]

The elegiac, when it occupies sites of specifically political memory, evokes past loss in an act of commemoration that creates a celebratory community of the present. And, through celebration, it invokes that past to orientate the present community towards its inherited future, as in those polar

---

3. Adam Mickiewicz, *Pan Tadeusz*, trans. G. R. Noyes (London: J. M. Dent, 1930), 29–30.
4. A. E. Housman, *A Shropshire Lad* (Ludlow: Palmers, 1987), XL.
5. C. S. Lewis, *Surprised by Joy* (London: Geoffrey Bles, 1955), ch. III, p. 56.
6. Michael Edwards, *Poetry and Possibility* (London: Macmillan, 1988), 120.

classics of political commemoration, Pericles' Funeral Oration and the Gettysburg Address.

What we may call the political elegiac provides a natural vehicle for nineteenth-century romantic nationalisms of a once and future kingdom, whether it be a primal kingdom of the *Volk* or the lost kingdom of a vanished state. The first half of this chapter considers such lost kingdoms in texts from Scott and one of his major European heirs, Mickiewicz. In Scott, the loss is brought about by a political union; in Mickiewicz, by union's cannibal antithesis, partition. Over against these, the second half of the chapter considers a myth of English history as an organic growth into unity. And both halves touch on the myth of a counter- kingdom, whether the primeval Lithuanian forests in Mickiewicz, a Jewish diaspora world in Kipling, Buchan's morphing of the Robin Hood Greenwood, or the ocean world of Byron's Corsair and Verne's Captain Nemo.[7]

As a mode, the elegiac can presence itself in tragedy and romance alike; it can also mediate between them. It can be incorporated into tragedy as an inset (Gertrude in *Hamlet* on the drowning of Ophelia); or, as in the final book of Malory, it can retrospectively suffuse and synthesize different kinds of tragedy. In romance it can both align itself with, and counter, the latter's deep gravitational movement towards an Ecclesiastes-style tolling of vanity, the dissolving of illusion in a final bareness that is desolate (Prospero's Epilogue) if not deadly (*La belle dame sans merci*). Its mediation between tragedy and romance can be tracked at the European foundations of both in the movement from the *Iliad* to the *Odyssey*. The *Aeneid*, which telescopes Homeric epic as tragedy and as romance into the Virgilian epic of history—a history, from start to finish, of once and future kingdoms—has the elegiac as one of its dominant modes. And Virgilian tags orchestrate the penultimate movement (chapters 63–9) of *Waverley*.

Those chapters incorporate four confrontations with the Jacobite defeat as tragedy: the frontal shock of Tully-Veolan sacked (chapter 63); the Baron's threnody (chapter 65); Waverley's last interview with Flora (chapter 68); and the final conversation between Waverley and Fergus in chapter 69. The second confrontation counters and modulates the first. It centres on the Baron's 'To be sure we may say with Virgilius Maro, *Fuimus Troes*—and there's the end of an auld sang. But houses and families and men have a' stood lang enough when they have stood lang enough to fall wi' honour—'.[8] This is the consummate instance of the novel's polyphony of voices that can become an orchestration of cultures: the blade-edged plangency of the Virgilian phrase, lodged in that untranslatable *Fuimus*, is locked with a distinctively northern heroic idiom of ballad or saga. The incised serenity their conjunction achieves is challenged by the conversation with Flora where the end-stopped tragedy of personal loss and political defeat is internalized in a flicker of Websterian horror: 'there is, Mr Waverley, there is a busy devil at my heart, that whispers—but it were madness to listen to it—that the strength of mind on which Flora prided herself has—murdered her brother!'[9] And that, in its turn, is met by the commanding interplay of Fergus's farewell to Waverley, which modulates from a Johnsonian firmness ('Nature has her tortures as well as art'), to a mordant variation, for the law of high treason, on a technique of Enlightenment conjectural history:

> I suppose one day or other—when there are no longer any wild Highlanders to benefit by its tender mercies—they will blot it from their records, as levelling them with a nation of cannibals and out into the mingling of satire, self-satire and pathos in the mummery, too, of exposing the senseless head—they have not the wit to grace mine with a paper coronet; there would be some satire in that, Edward. I hope they will set it on the Scotch gate though, that I may look, even after death, on the blue hills of my own country, that I love so well. This would risk sentimentality were it not caught up into the wry amusement of: The Baron would have added Moritur, et moriens dulces reminiscitur Argos.[10]

And we are played out of the whole sequence through the novel's last Virgilian tag, *Fungarque inani munere*, quoted by Waverley to himself as he gives money to the attendant priest with the reflection, 'Yet why not class these acts of remembrance with the other honours, with which affection in all sects, pursues the memory of the dead'.[11]

The fading sequence of the elegiac is crossed by an upward movement of romance integration. The ending of chapter 61, where Waverley 'felt himself entitled to say firmly, though perhaps with a sigh, that the romance of his life was ended and that its real history had now commenced', has been

---

8. Walter Scott, *Waverley*, ed. P. D. Garside (EEWN; Edinburgh: Edinburgh University Press, 2007), 323.
9. Scott, *Waverley*, 344.
10. Scott, *Waverley*, 348–9. For 'paper coronet', EEWN compares *3 Henry VI*, 1.4.93–5, and *Richard III*, 1.3.175.
11. Scott, *Waverley*, 351.

frown), and the metaphysical (his uncle's rejection of individual freedom in society or history). Protean flexibility radiates into both the name-shifting and the fluidity of history as memory that are among the controlling motifs of the novel. And all manifestations of the protean counterpoint not only the single-mindedness of Redgauntlet's devotion to his cause but also the motif of doom and the fated, central to the dialectic in which history and the Gothic interrogate each other.

That dialectic can manifest itself equally in the folk memory of Wandering Willie's Tale and in the key chapters (V–VIII) that probe the relations of law, history, and freedom. At the centre of those chapters stands the interrogation before Justice Foxley. This begins as a Fieldingesque comedy of the incompetent country magistrate and his crafty subordinate; it modulates into the comedy of self-enclosed monologue as Justice Foxley addresses Darsie; and that, in turn, swirls into a Dostoevskeyean comedy of polyphony[19] with the entry of Peter Peebles at the end of chapter VII. His recognition of Redgauntlet releases a potent elegiac imaging of the latter as the Miltonic Satan, that master archetype, together with the biblical Cain, for the Byronic Hero:

> However little Peter Peebles might resemble the angel Ithuriel, the appearance of Herries, his high and scornful demeanour, vexed at what seemed detection, yet fearless of the consequences, and regarding the whispering magistrate and his clerk with looks in which contempt predominated over anger or anxiety, bore, in my opinion, no slight resemblance to
>
> > –'the regal port
> > And faded splendor wan'–
>
> with which the poet has invested the discovered King of the powers of the air.[20]

This exemplifies Ian Duncan's pregnant formulation 'Scott resorts to comedy for the elegiac key of failure, renouncing the Ossianic sublime and emptying history of its metaphysical charge'.[21] But here, and still more in the novel's final sequence, I would argue that the elegiac remains in polyphonic play of resistance against, and acute-angled interaction with, the comic—not to mention with and against the saga-laconicism of Nanty's

---

19. I am, of course, thinking of Bakhtin's classic exploration in *Problems of Dostoevsky's Poetics*, ed. and trans. Caryl Emerson (Minneapolis, University of Minnesota Press, 1984), specifically chs 1, 5.
20. Scott, *Redgauntlet*, 181.
21. Ian Duncan, 'Walter Scott, James Hogg and Scottish Gothic', in David Punter (ed.), *A Companion to the Gothic* (Oxford: Blackwell, 2000), 78.

death-word.[22] And polyphony refuses finality—including the finality of escape from history.

In the final scene General Campbell's 'this will be remembered against no one'[23] dissolves that threefold cording of memory as historical, political, and legal that has controlled the novel. It is met by Redgauntlet's bursting cry 'the cause is lost forever', and the sealing of that cry in his final gesture (with its echo of Prospero in that most elegiac of romances, *The Tempest*) of sinking Darsie's father's sword 'forty fathom deep in the wide ocean'.[24] Darsie himself passes out of the Gothic doom of his house in the freedom of the unpredictable for which he has argued with his uncle.

The editors of the authoritative Edinburgh Edition of the Waverley Novels end their Historical Note on this last of Scott's Jacobite novels with

> *Redgauntlet* is not a historical novel; it is, rather, a novel about denying history, about abnegating the forces of historical determinism. Darsie's memorable debate with his uncle is about historical determinism, and his eloquence is more than a rationalization of the whig tradition in which he has been reared. It is about being free of the past.

That is eloquently put. But one may still register that almost the novel's last word is the motto of the (contested) relic found on the dead Prior Hugh, who had been Redgauntlet, with its gerundive command: *Haud obliviscendum*.

II

Greater Lithuania—the old Grand Duchy that would partner the Polish Kingdom in the Polish–Lithuanian union—'is now altogether a thing of the past; its history offers a happy field for poetry from the fact that a poet who sings of its ancient annals must occupy himself only with his subject, with historical study of events and artistic reproduction of them, without calling to his aid the interests, passions, or fashions of his readers'.[25] Set alongside the end of Scott's introduction to the *Minstrelsey*, Mickiewicz's preface to *Konrad Wallenrod* transposes a native history—Mickiewicz writes as a poet of the Commonwealth that issues from the 1569 Union of Lublin

---

22. Scott, Red Gauntlet, 361.   23. Scott. Red Gauntlet, 373.
24. Scott, Red Gauntlet, 376.
25. Adam Mickiewicz, Konrad Wallenrod and Other Writings of Adam Mickiewicz, trans. G.R. Noyes at al. (Berkeley and Los Angeles: University of California Press, 1925), p.8.

between Poland and Lithuania, 'a posthumous child of the old *Respublica*'[26]—
into a transhistorical region of the aesthetic—albeit with a transposing
possible only through absolute loss: 'What is to have eternal life in song
must perish in actual life.' In fact, Mickiewicz's Byronic tale of a medieval
Lithuanian warrior who infiltrates the order of the Teutonic Knights and
becomes its Grand Master in order to lead it to military disaster against his
homeland is firmly attuned to the condition of Poland, which, after the
Third Partition of 1795, is, in brute historical fact, a once and future kingdom for the next 123 years. Published in St Petersburg in 1828, during
Mickiewicz's banishment (1824–9) to Russia for involvement in the illegal
Wilno University Society of Philomaths, it passed the Censor, but Senator
Novosiltsov, the Tsar's plenipotentiary in Poland, read it and, as Milosz drily
observes, 'sent in an alarm report containing an analysis that could have
been envied by any literary critic'.[27]

   Konrad Wallenrod, like *Redgauntlet*, is a Byronic hero text that mobilizes the
Gothic (in the secret tribunal, and the inset ballad of Moorish victory-in-
defeat through infecting the Christian victors with plague). Its gloomy and
mysterious leader has a secluded love (like Medora in *The Corsair*). He is a
renegade, like Alp, the jilted Venetian in *The Siege of Corinth*: but Konrad is a
married man who has sacrificed his marriage to pursue his mission. The
moral ambivalence of that mission is signalled by the poem's epigraph from
Machiavelli. And Konrad's position as double agent between two kingdoms
makes him, self-destructively, a *homo duplex*. If national identity, in any
extended history, is constituted as a theatre of conflicting traditions—and
this is certainly what is dramatized in *Waverley* or *Old Mortality*—then the
figure of the *homo duplex* is likely to be recurrent, if not mainstream.[28] In
a national history such as that of partitioned Poland, the figure can readily
become fraught, if not tragic. This can be traced in subsequent critical Polish
reaction, beginning with Mickiewicz's own, to the moral ambiguity of
Konrad Wallenrod.[29] It is flamboyantly advanced by Mickiewicz's self-
appointed rival among the Polish romantic poets Slowacki, in *Kordian*

26. Czesław Miłosz, *The History of Polish Literature* (Berkeley and Los Angeles: University of
    California Press, 1983), 232.
27. Miłosz, *The History of Polish Literature*, 220.
28. For national identity and conflicting traditions, cf. the trenchant critique in Cairns Craig, *The
    Modern Scottish Novel: Narrative and the National Imagination* (Edinburgh: Edinburgh University
    Press, 1999), 9–36, of accounts, from Edwin Muir to Alasdair MacIntyre, of the loss of Scottish
    identity.
29. See Miroslawa Modrzewska, 'Pilgrimage or Revolt?: The Dilemmas of Polish Byronism', in
    Richard A. Cardwell (ed.), *The Reception of Byron in Europe*, 2 vols (London: Thoemmes
    Continuum, 2004), ii. 310–14.

(1834), his systematically anti-Mickiewicz drama of a failed assassination of the Tsar. It can find an echo in Moniuszko's *Haunted Manor House* (1865), which handles the renunciation of marriage for patriotic calling in comic-opera terms but not without Romantic nationalist undercurrents.[30] (One can add that Verne at one point conceived that extreme avatar of the Byronic Hero as liberation fighter, Captain Nemo, as a Pole.[31]) And it is no accident that the founding and overarching classics of the spy story, as a serious modern genre, with its burden of dual agency, betrayal, revolutionary violence, and the interacting politics of bureaucracy and the underworld, are Conrad's *Secret Agent* (1907) and *Under Western Eyes* (1911).

Konrad Wallenrod morphs the Byronic tale into a national tale for a nation that has ceased to exist. Central to this morphing is its figuring of the poet in Konrad, the self-lacerating Byronic Hero as lutenist,[32] who ends as an avenging, self-destroying Samson; and in the counter-figure of his father-counsellor, the monk and poet Halban, who will outlive him to inspire the Lithuanian people with his story. It

> is...a narrative about two poets, or, rather, about just one symbolically bifur-
> cated. If Halban is a Tyrtean poet, whose songs are an inspirational call to arms,
> the eponymous hero is depicted as an elegiac poet, 'Chasing after his youth in
> the depths of the past [...] in the land of his memories'.[33]

Both figures of the poet are transfigured in Konrad, the revolutionary protagonist of *Forefather's Eve, Part III*. Written at Dresden in the wake of the crushing of the Polish Insurrection of 1830–1 (in which Mickiewicz had failed to participate), that extraordinary work is a Romantic cosmological drama, akin to *Prometheus Unbound* in its graphing of contemporary politics as apocalyptic myth, akin to Goethe's *Faust* in its soaring protagonist and its stylistic range, from the prophetic self-rapture of Konrad's improvisation in scene ii, or the radiant rococo lyricism of Ewa's vision in scene iv, to the

30. For the nationalist dimension of Moniuszko's work at large, see the entry on him in *The New Grove Dictionary of Music and Musicians*, ed. Stanley Sadie (2nd edn, London: Macmillan, 2001), xvi. For *The Haunted Manor*, see the review by Roderic Dunnett of a 2001 production (accessed at http://www.mv.daily.com/articles/2001/04/dwor1.htm (accessed July 2017). I am indebted to Laurence Davies for directing me to this work.

31. See Verne, *Twenty Thousand Leagues under the Sea*, pp. xvii, 436–7. For Nemo as bankrolling liberation movements, see pt II, chs 6, 8; of Nemo as hyperbolic and morally ambivalent avenger, see ch. 21.

32. Adam Mickiewicz, *Konrad Wallenrod*, in *Konrad Wallenrod and Other Writings of Adam Mickieiwcz*, trans. G. R. Noyes et al. (Berkeley and Los Angeles: University of California Press, 1925), i. 136–62.

33. Ramon Kompeckyj, 'Adam Mickiewicz and the Shape of Polish Romanticism', in Michael Ferber (ed.), *A Companion to European Romanticism* (London: Blackwell, 2005), 334.

mordantly or grotesquely satiric in scenes vi–viii. But *Part III* is also, and axially, a medieval mystery play whose Passion is the crucifixion, resurrection, and ascension of the Polish nation martyred at the hands of Europe.

> The cross has arms that shadow all of Europe,
> Made of three withered peoples, like dead trees.
> Now is my nation on the martyr's throne.[34]

This is Father Peter's vision in scene v. It responds, redemptively, to Konrad's Promethean–Christian challenge to God in the self-creation of scene ii, which as it mounts to its climax becomes an act of vatic—and blasphemous?—unification with, and of, his tormented country:

> Now is my soul incarnate in my country
> And in my body dwells her soul;
> My fatherland and I are one great whole.[35]

In its final scene *Part III* curves back to the Romantic ballad-opera dramatizing of *Part II* nine years before. But the closing focus is on the kibitkas, the travelling carriages of the Tsarist gendarmes that are carrying Konrad and his fellows into their exile. From here *Part III* looks to the suite of five poems, titled 'Digression', which stands as an epilogue to the drama, and to *The Books of the Polish Nation and of the Polish Pilgrimage* (1832), a pamphlet 'aiming…at nothing less than becoming a sort of fifth Gospel for Polish émigrés'.[36]

'The Digression' becomes a conversation partner for Pushkin in *The Bronze Horseman* (1834), that master-meditation on the achievements of Tsarist autocracy and their cost.[37] In it Mickiewicz recurrently images Russia as an anti-kingdom, unified only through the exercise of autocratic will, whether by the creation of St Petersburg, in the swamplands of the Neva, or by the imposing of a purely mechanical–military order in the settlements of the Russian waste:

> Like cartridge boxes their small windows shine,
> Such houses here march in a double line;
> There form a circle, there a hollow square.

34. Adam Mickiewicz, *Forefather's Eve, Part III*, in *Polish Romantic Drama*, ed. Harold B. Segal (Amsterdam: Harwood Academic Publishers, 1997), 97–8.
35. Mickiewicz, *Forefather's Eve, Part III*, 80.
36. Wiktor Weintraub, *The Poetry of Adam Mickiewicz* ('S-Gravenhage: Mouton & Co, 1954), 195
37. See Waclaw Lednicki, *Pushkin's Bronze Horseman: The Story of a Masterpiece* (Westport, CT: Greenwood Press, 1978), 7–9, 21–2, 25–42.

> This regiment of houses, squat and brown,
> Is called with conscious pride a district town.[38]

The context for such an ordering is Russia as a geographical blank, ambivalently open to an apocalyptic history:

> Will God's finger write on it, and using good people as letters, inscribe the truth of the holy faith that love rules the human race, that sacrifices are the trophies of the world? Or will the old God's foe come and carve there with his sword that the human race must be kept in fetters, that knouts are the trophies of mankind?[39]

(In *Under Western Eyes* Conrad will secularize and reverse that image in the night-walk vision that converts Razumov into betraying Haldin, the idealistic revolutionary assassin who has taken refuge with him, and so trapping himself into the *duplex homo* life of a Tsarist double agent).

The Books of the Polish Nation and Polish Pilgrimage mount the national history as Passion-myth onto an ontological myth of universal history graphed as idolatry and Fall. In them the union of Poland and Lithuania becomes a messianic icon: 'A great nation, Lithuania, united itself with Poland, as husband with wife, two souls in one body. And there was never before this such a union of nations. But hereafter there shall be.'[40] That signals how this mythicizing of Polish history might feed into the Mazzinian nationalism of what F. R. Leavis characterized, à propos of the old Garibaldino in Conrad's *Nostromo*, as 'the heroic age of the liberal faith—of *Songs before Sunrise* and the religion of humanity'.[41] And it separates decisively Mickiewicz's Passion-myth from the Passion-myth of Irish history that, some eighty years later, at the other end of Europe, Padraig Pearse forges in the pamphlets he wrote in preparation for the Easter Rising.

In Janus-headed conjunction with *The Books*, Mickiewicz writes in his Parisian exile his last major poem, *Pan Tadeusz*. This is both a Waverley novel in verse and an elegiac epic of the gentry life in the old Lithuania of the lost Commonwealth. Its first, elegiac invocation is of 'Lithuania, my country, thou art like health; how much thou should'st be prized only he can learn

---

38. 'The Road to Russia', in Lednicki, *Pushkin's Bronze Horseman*, 110

39. Translation in Weintraub, *The Poetry of Adam Mickiewicz*, 188.

40. Mickiewicz, *Konrad Wallenrod and Other Writings*, 141.

41. F. R. Leavis, *The Great Tradition* (London: Chatto & Windus, 1948), 194. For a summary of European reception of the *Books*, see, e.g., Roman Koropeckyj, *Adam Mickiewicz: The Life of a Romantic* (Ithaca, NY: Cornell University Press, 2008), 200–1; for Mickiewicz and Mazzini, see pp. 399–401.

who has lost thee'; its second is of that icon of a Catholic myth of Polish history the 'Holy Virgin, who protectest bright Czenstochowa'.[42] But, if epic, it is also idyllic. The idyllic as a mode is rooted in a vision of human life harmoniously integrated with the non-human in a shared world of spontaneous fertility.[43] In *Pan Tadeusz* such integration is carried, partly, by the dolphin play of metaphor that continually morphs human action into and out of the natural world. The farthest reach of this comes in book IV's celebration of the Lithuanian forests, which creates not an anti- but a counter-kingdom, a beast-fable mirroring of human society that is not satirical but paradisal:

> It is said that there in the capital the beasts lead a well-ordered life, for they govern themselves; not yet corrupted by human civilization, they know no rights of property which embroil our world; they know neither duels nor the art of war. As their fathers lived in paradise, so their descendants live today, wild and tame alike, in love and harmony... Even if a man should enter there, though unarmed, he would pass in peace through the midst of the beasts; they would gaze on him with the same look of amazement with which on that last sixth day of creation their first fathers, who dwelt in the Garden of Eden, gazed upon Adam, before they quarreled with him.[44]

Idyllic morphing has its counterpart in a shot-silk play of the mock-heroic—a *Rape-of-the-Lock* mock-heroic, enchanted by and enchanting the mundane.[45] But idyll is also continually embossed with history, from the ekphrastic vignettes of the opening to its full-stretch penetration by an apocalyptically tinged history in the opening of book XI, whose title 'The Year 1812' is for the reader of 1834 fraught with an elegiac foreknowledge. And, in a final twist of the kaleidoscope, some epilogue verses, unpublished in Mickiewicz's lifetime, bring together, wonderfully, elegy and nostalgia in the work of poetry as the constructing of a site of memory, liberation, return:

> How many memories, what long sorrow,
> There where a man shall cleave to his master

42. For the historical source of the Virgin of Czenstochowa cult, see, e.g., Norman Davies, *God's Playground: A History of Poland*, 2 vols (Oxford: Clarendon Press, 1981), i. 450–4; for a concise overview of it and other myths of Polish history, see Norman Davies, 'Polish National Mythologies', in Geoffrey Hosking and George Schöpflen (eds), *Myths and Nationhood* (London: Hurst & Company, 1997), 141–57.
43. I have sketched an account of the idyllic in Donald Mackenzie, 'Edwardian Idyll, Edwardian Mapping', in Laura Colombino and Max Saunders (eds), *The Edwardian Ford Madox Ford* (Amsterdam: Rodolpi, 2013), 105–24.
44. Mickiewicz, *Pan Tadeusz*, trans. Noyes, 107. Simon Schama, *Landscape and Memory* (London: Harper Collins, 1995), 37–74, provides a long-range Polish cultural context for Mickiewicz here.
45. Weintraub, *Poetry of Adam Mickiewicz*, 59, notes the popularity of Pope, 'known mostly through the intermediary of French translations' in 'Classical Poland'.

As here no wife cleaves to her man:
There where a man grieves for loss of his weapons
Longer than here for him who sired him;
And his tears fall more sincerely and faster
There for a hound than this people's for heroes.

My friends of those days made my speech come easy,
Each good for some singable idiom. Spring
Brought in the fable cranes of the wild island flying
Over the spellbound castle and the spellbound
Boy lamenting, who was loosed
By each pitying bird as it flew, one feather:
He flew out on those wings to his own people.[46]

III

See you our stilly woods of oak,
  And the dread ditch beside?
O that was where the Saxons broke,
  On the day that Harold died.

        .   .   .   .   .   .

And see you marks that show and fade,
  Like shadows on the Downs?
O they are the lines the Flint Men made,
  To guard their wondrous towns.

Trackway and Camp and City Lost,
  Salt Marsh where now is corn;
Old Wars, old Peace, old Arts that cease,
  And so was England born!

She is not any common Earth,
  Water or Wood or Air,
But Merlin's Isle of Gramarye,
  Where you and I will fare.[47]

Kipling's lines from 'Puck's Song' in *Puck of Pook's Hill* (1906) give expression—
dream-lucid and incantatory—to an organicist myth of English history.
As a myth it has an extended history of its own. It reaches back into the
seventeenth-century arguments of lawyers and antiquarians on the ancient

---

46. Donald Davie, *The Forests of Lithuania* (1959; repr. in Davie, *Slavic Excursions*).
47. Rudyard Kipling, *Puck of Pook's Hill and Rewards and Fairies*, ed. D. Mackenzie (World's Classics; Oxford: Oxford University Press, 1993).

constitution.[48] It can interact, variously, with the myth of the Norman Yoke.[49]
It is potently mobilized by Burke,[50] and is still sounding in the neo-Burkean
celebration of English history and the English political tradition offered by
Butterfield's 1944 lectures on *The Englishman and his History*—nowhere
more so than on the Revolution of 1688, where

> what might have been levered into a trenchant breach of the continuity of our
> history, was closed up—was made ready for the healing processes of time—by
> stitchings, blood transfusions, and countless little solicitudes. The result was
> like the grafting of an appropriate sprig on to a growing tree. It maintained
> the continuity of organic life—a unity more close and rich than the calcu-
> lated dove-tailing and the neat geometry of the carpenter could ever have
> produced.[51]

Butterfield's insistent metaphors for the continuity of English history include
metaphors of craft (weaving or, as here, medicine); but grafting, at the climax
of this passage, subordinates human skill to non-human organic process (and
shrinks, in passing, the Glorious Revolution of Whig foundation myth to 'an
appropriate sprig'). That separates it from an older organic metaphor of the
body politic. The organic here is diachronic, not synchronic; aligned with
history as growth by slow process from within and by assimilation of what
comes from without. As historiographical concept it downplays individual
human agency, denies rupture or tragic loss, and subsumes conflict. It is a
metaphor of unification, not union; but—unlike the unification of Petrine
Russia—a unification sanctified by a teleology of the natural.

The Norman Conquest—the last successful invasion of England—is pivotal
for the myth of organic assimilation.[52] Scott opens *Ivanhoe* (1819) with an
England schematized in terms of the Norman Yoke: 'Four generations had

48. See J. G. A. Pocock, *The Ancient Constitution and the Feudal Law*, rev. edn (Cambridge:
    Cambridge University Press, 1987).
49. The classic survey is Christopher Hill's essay in *Puritanism and Revolution* (London: Penguin
    Books, 1986), 58–125.
50. See, e.g., Edmund Burke, *Reflections on the Revolution in France*, ed. J. G. A. Pocock (Indianapolis:
    Hackett Publishing Company, 1987), 27–31; J. G. A., Pocock, 'Burke and the Ancient
    Constitution', in *Politics, Language and Time* (London: Methuen & Co, 1971), 202–32.
51. Herbert Butterfield, *The Englishman and his History* (Cambridge: Cambridge University Press,
    1944), 91. For 'neo-Burkean', cf. Pocock, *Ancient Constitution*, p. viii.
52. See the survey of nineteenth century historiography of the Norman Conquest in Marjorie
    Chibnall, *The Debate on the Norman Conquest* (Manchester: Manchester University Press, 1999),
    53–68; also John Burrow, *A Liberal Descent* (Cambridge: Cambridge University Press, 1981), esp.
    ch. 8 ('Conquest, continuity and restoration'), pp. 193–228; G. A. Bremner and Jonathan Conlin
    (eds), *Making History: Edward Augustus Freeman and Victorian Cultural Politics* (Oxford: Oxford
    University Press, 2015); Colin Kidd, *The Forging of Races: Race and Scripture in the Protestant
    Atlantic World, 1600–2000* (Cambridge: Cambridge University Press, 2006), 192–200.

not sufficed to blend the hostile blood of the Normans and Anglo-Saxons, or to unite by a common language and mutual interests, two hostile races, one of which still felt the elation of triumph, while the other groaned under all the consequences of defeat'.[53]

In chapter 27 Wamba rejects an offer of Norman service with a proverbial rhyming:

> Norman saw on English oak,
> On English neck a Norman Yoke;
> Norman spoon in English dish,
> And England ruled as Normans wish;
> Blithe world in England ne'er will be more
> Till England's rid of all the four.[54]

This exchange comes at the turning point of a chapter that opens with the conversation between Cedric and Ulfrida, the long-cast-off Saxon mistress of Torquilstone castle's Norman tyrants, now wrought into a figure of the subterranean Gothic vengeance she will consummate in firing the besieged castle. The siege itself is carried through by the Saxon outlaw band, led by the as-yet-undisclosed Coeur de Lion and the as-yet-undisclosed Robin Hood ('I am', said the forester, 'a nameless man; but I am the friend of my country, and of my country's friends'[55]). And the narrative moves to a romance closure of marriage, uniting Ivanhoe, originally disinherited by his father for becoming a Norman knight, and his father's ward, the Saxon heiress, Rowena in a ceremony 'that marked the marriage of two individuals as a type of the future peace and harmony betwixt two races, which, since that period, have been so completely mingled that, the distinction has become utterly invisible'.[56]

The conflicted England of *Ivanhoe*'s organicist myth is flanked by the green-wood kingdom of Robin Hood, and counterpoised by the future kingdom of Bois-Guilbert's oriental fantasy (chapter 39) and the lost kingdom of the Jews that Rebecca opposes to it. The first of these can be brought to bear on Buchan's post-First World War novels of failed rebellion, *Midwinter* (1923) and *The Blanket of the Dark* (1931), both the latter on the climactic story in *Puck of Pook's Hill*, 'The Treasure and the Law'. (In each case I am citing analogues not claiming sources.)

53. Scott, *Ivanhoe*, 16.   54. Scott, *Ivanhoe*, 225.   55. Scott, *Ivanhoe*, 169.
56. Scott, *Ivanhoe*, 398.

Bulwer Lytton's *Harold: The Last of the Saxon Kings* (1848) and Charles Kingsley's *Hereward the Wake: The Last of The English* (1866) offer a contrast with, and a bridge between, versions of the organicist myth in Scott and in Kipling. Both tap into an elegiac myth of the last of the race.[57] Both finally vaporize that myth in a triumphalist vision of English continuity expanding into a moralized world history. Bulwer uses the story of Harold buried by the sea to create a counter-Ossianic site of historical memory: 'the tombless shade of the kingly freeman still guards the coasts...and wherever, with fairer fates, Freedom opposes Force, and Justice, redeeming the old defeat, smites down the armed Frauds that would consecrate the wrong, smile, O soul of our Saxon Harold, smile appeased on the Saxon's land!'[58] Kingsley ends *Hereward* by an invocation whose rhetoric wambles on the edge of an imperialist Resurrection myth. The defeated English

> knew not that The Wake was alive for evermore...that above them, and around them, and in them, destined to raise them out of that bitter bondage, and mould them into a great nation, and the parents of still greater nations in lands as yet unknown, brooded the immortal spirit of The Wake...even the spirit of Freedom which can never die.[59]

And he follows this with an epilogue chapter where the draining of the Fens illustrates 'the true laws of God's universe, peace and order, usefulness and life' reasserting themselves, and whose woefully stuck-on quality can point up Kipling's much subtler rendering of an English history of assimilation that conjoins 'Old Wars, old Peace, old Arts that cease'.

Kipling, like T. S. Eliot, Namier, and (to some extent) Buchan, is an alien-assimilated-as-Tory, and *Puck of Pook's Hill* cross-hatches the organicist myth through the alien perspectives of 'The Runes on Weland's Sword' at the centre of the book, and the Jewish narrator of its final story. In the Norman Conquest stories, 'Young Men at the Manor' enacts the myth at the subaltern level of comradeship between Hugh and Richard in the creating of a local order; 'Old Men at Pevensey' enacts it at the level of high politics through its presiding figure, the wise baron De Aquila, who declares:

57. See Fiona Stafford, *The Last of the Race: The Growth of a Myth from Milton to Darwin* (Oxford: Clarendon Press, 1994), 1–11, for an overview of the myth, and pp. 261–88 on the myth in Bulwer Lytton.
58. Bulwer Lytton, *Harold: The Last of the Saxon Kings* (London: George Routledge and Sons, 1887), 490.
59. Charles Kingsley, *Hereward the Wake: The Last of The English* (London: Collins, 1954), 408.

'I think for England, for whom neither King nor Baron thinks. I am not Norman, Sir Richard, nor Saxon, Sir Hugh. English am I'.[60] But with a characteristic art of implication Kipling brings into play the polemical division between Anglo-Saxon and Nordic ancestries within a Victorian genealogy for the English history of freedom. That polemic is at its most trenchant in Samuel Laing's Preliminary Dissertation to his translation (1844) of *Heimskringla*:

> the introduction of social arrangements, establishments, ideas of polity and government, cast in one mould for all countries of Christendom by the Romish church, had during those five centuries [5th–10th] altered, exhausted and rendered almost effete, the original spirit and character of Anglo-Saxon social institutions.[61]

In Kingsley's Prelude to *Hereward*, 'The men of Wessex, priest-ridden, and enslaved by their own aristocracy, quailed before the free Norsemen, among whom there was not a single serf' in the Danish invasions; and it is the men of the Danelagh ('not knowing, like true Englishmen, when they were beaten') who 'kept alive in their hearts that proud spirit of personal independence, which they brought with them from the moors of Denmark and the dales of Norway; and they kept alive, too, though in abeyance for a while, those free institutions which were without a doubt the germs of our British liberty'.[62]

In *Puck of Pook's Hill* Weland, the smith-god of its opening story, belongs to a common Germanic stock before the Nordic branch has separated itself off. He forges his sword for the Saxon novice and future warrior Hugh as a gift that 'shall do him good the wide world over and Old England after him'. It does so through the treasure brought back from Hugh and Richard's voyage to Africa with the Viking trader–pirate Witta, which, in the final story of the book, will secure the bringing of the Law in Magna Charta. Kipling homes in here on two key foci of northern (as opposed to classical Mediterranean) story and myth: the named, talismanic weapon (Mjolnar, Gram), and gold, whether ring-wrought or dragon-hoarded. Both come together in the riddling incantation of 'The Runes on Weland's Sword',

---

60. Kipling, *Puck of Pook's Hill and Rewards and Fairies*, 70–1.
61. *The Heimskringla or, Chronicle of the Kings of Norway, Translated from the Icelandic of Snorro Sturleson*, 3 vols (London: Longman, Brown, Green, and Longmans, 1844), i. 4.
62. *Hereward the Wake*, 21–2; see further the comments on *Harold* and *Hereward* in Andrew Wawn, *The Vikings and the Victorians* (Cambridge: D. S. Brewer, 2000), 315–20.

where the Norse law-assembly becomes metonymic for an English history centred in freedom under Law:

> A Smith makes me
> To betray my Man
> In my first fight.
>
> To gather Gold
> At the world's end
> I am sent.
>
> The Gold I gather
> Comes into England
> Out of deep Water.
>
> Like a shining Fish
> Then it descends
> Into deep Water.
>
> It is not given
> For goods or gear,
> But for the Thing.

This is matched by the off-hand incantation of the final story. 'Well,' said Puck calmly, 'what did you think of it? Weland gave the Sword! The Sword gave the Treasure, and the Treasure gave the Law. It's as natural as an oak growing.' Except that, in the sequence of the Norman Conquest stories that leads to this climax, and within 'The Treasure and the Law' itself, it rather isn't. The politics of Magna Charta are indeed decided by treasure; but treasure now caught up into the mythic-cum-fairy-tale image of the geo-political underground river that Jews control: 'There can be no war without gold, and we Jews know how the earth's gold moves with the seasons, and the crops, and the winds; circling and looping and rising and sinking away like a river—a wonderful underground river. How should the foolish Kings know *that* while they fight and steal and kill'.[63] In a conventional children's historical adventure story the treasure would have fortified the barons against King John. Instead it secures the signing of Magna Carta by not being used. Located in the wall well of Pevensey castle by the charismatic, mocking Jewish money-lender (and deflected messianic figure) Kadmiel, it is taken out—through the refuse gate, we note—to be sunk ('A King's ransom—no, the Ransom of a People!') in the sea.

In this climactic fable English triumphalism is ironically relocated to the Jewish narrator, whose alienation effects control the story from his birth

---

63. Kipling, *Puck of Pook's Hill*, 166.

prophecy that 'I should be a Lawgiver to a People of a strange speech and a hard language'[64] to the climax where 'Kadmiel halted, all black against the pale green sky beyond the wood—a huge robed figure, like a Moses in the picture Bible'.[65] And it is the alienation of one living in the abiding absence between a once and a future kingdom that breaks out unforgettably in his cry over the meeting of the Jewish moneylenders with the barons against John: 'We did not seek to be paid *all* in money. We sought Power—Power—Power! That is *our* god in our captivity. Power to use!'[66]

A School History of England (1911), on which Kipling collaborated with the pugnaciously Tory–Protestant Oxford historian C. R. L. Fletcher, can provide a coda on the organicist myth and its unifications. For the debate on the Conquest, Fletcher proclaims with a schoolmasterly swashbuckling that the Normans 'brought England back by the scruff of the neck into the family of European nations' and 'it cost William about six years of utterly ruthless warfare to become master of all England. England resisted him bit by bit; its leaders had a dozen different plans; he had but one plan, and he drove it through. He was going to make an England that would resist the next invader *as one people*.'[67]

This is capped by Kipling's poem:

> England's on the anvil—hear the hammers ring—
>   Clanging from the Severn to the Tyne!
> Never was a blacksmith like our Norman King-
>   England's being hammered, hammered, hammered into line!
>
> England's on the anvil! Heavy are the blows!
>   (But the work will be a marvel when it's done)
> Little bits of Kingdoms cannot stand against their foes.
>   England's being hammered, hammered, hammered into one.
>
> There shall be one people—it shall serve one Lord—
>   (Neither Priest nor Baron shall escape!)
> It shall have one speech and law, soul and strength and sword.
>   England's being hammered, hammered, hammered into shape!

The image here is technological, not organic (though it chimes with a key motif in Kipling's 1910 sequel to *Puck of Pook's Hill*, *Rewards and Fairies*). And the poem invests unification driven through by a single masterful

---

64. Kipling, *Puck of Pook's Hill*, 165.   65. Kipling, *Puck of Pook's Hill*, 170.
66. Kipling, *Puck of Pook's Hill*, 168.
67. C. R. L. Fletcher and Rudyard Kipling, *A School History of England* (Oxford: Clarendon Press, 1911), 44.

leader with echoes ('There shall be one people—it shall serve one Lord', 'It shall have one speech and law, soul and strength and sword') from the Deuteronomic summons (Deuteronomy 6:4–5) to Israel. But Fletcher's succeeding narrative shifts to a joint emphasis on Law and on the incorporation of ruler and people.[68] And, preceding both, through the chapters (I–III) up to and including the Norman Conquest and settlement, is a motif of the land captivating its invaders. This Kipling had already sounded through the Norman stories in *Puck of Pook's Hill*. In a letter to Fletcher, discussing their prospective collaboration, he writes: 'I take it you are going to insist on the spirit of the land—the queer unchangeable force that persists at the back of everything and, indirectly, by means of many compromises, pushes things more or less into some order and coherence.'[69] Compounding a deep Tory pragmatic agnosticism about historical process with a sense of mythic hinterland, that gives the organicist myth a voicing at once persuasive and haunting.

IV

In chapter 32 of *Ivanhoe*, Locksley, taking his seat on a throne of turf (at 'the centre of a sylvan amphitheatre, within half a mile of the demolished castle of Torquilstone'), apologizes to the Black Knight and Cedric for placing them on his right hand and left 'but in these glades I am monarch—they are my kingdom; and these my wild subjects would reck but little of my power, were I, within my own dominions, to yield place to mortal man'.[70] This draws on, and draws the sting of, Ritson's radical challenge: 'what better title king Richard could pretend to the territory and people of England than Robin Hood had to the dominion of Barnsdale or Sherwood is a question humbly submitted to the consideration of the political philosopher.'[71] In later Robin Hood texts the Greenwood can become a locus of nostalgia, a nostalgia laced with comedy in Keats's octosyllabic 'Robin Hood', deliquescent in Alfred Noyes's 'Sherwood'.[72] In the two Buchan romances the Greenwood

68. See Fletcher and Kipling, *A School History of England*, 64 (Henry II), 88 (Edward I), 128 (Elizabeth), 221–3 (Queen Victoria and her immediate successors).
69. *The Letters of Rudyard Kipling*, ed. Thomas Pinney, 6 vols (London: Macmillan, 1990–2004), iii. 430.
70. Scott, *Ivanhoe*, 272.
71. Joseph Ritson, *Robin Hood: A Collection of all the Ancient Poems, Songs and Ballads, now extant, Relative to that Celebrated English Outlaw*, 2 vols (London: Routledge/Thoemmes Press, 1997; repr. of 1887 edn), i, p. v.
72. Both poems included in *Rymes of Robin Hood*, ed. R. B. Dobson and J. Taylor (London: Heinemann, 1976).

morphs into the myth of an Old England as a counter-kingdom whose seamless continuity plucks at the edges of history. In the first chapter of *Midwinter* ('In Which a Highland Gentleman Misses his Way') the eponymous oracular protagonist tells the Jacobite soldier and undercover agent, Alastair Maclean:

> There is an Old England which has outlived Roman and Saxon and Dane and Norman and will outlast the Hanoverian. It has seen priest turn to presbyter and presbyter to parson and has only smiled. It is the land of the edge of moorlands and the rims of forests and the twilight before dawn, and strange knowledge still dwells in it. Lords and Parliament-men bustle about, but the dust of their coaches stops at the roadside hedges, and they do not see the quiet eyes watching them at the fords. Those eyes are their masters, young sir.[73]

That risks an Edwardian gypsy fantasy of escape from history. In the cardinal chapter IX, however, Old England takes on a quality of fairyland, twined and twined with a lost pagan world of wild nature. But now it carries the challenge and danger of a true fairyland: 'It makes a man look into his heart, and he may find that in it which destroys him. Also it is ambition's mortal foe.'[74] In chapter XI, General Oglethorpe brushes off insinuations of Jacobitism ('I am a Tory, sir, I serve the ancient constitution of this realm')[75] and challenges Alastair with the rise of the Methodists: 'With them is the key of the new England, for they bring healing to the souls of the people ...What can your fairy Prince say to the poor and the hungry?'[76] At the end of that chapter both versions of England lock to exclude, in their unifying vision, the Jacobite dream, as Alastair 'mused on this strange thing, England, which was like a spell on sober minds'.

> Midwinter had told of Old England like a lover of his mistress, and here was this battered traveller, this Oglethorpe, thrilling to the same fervour. That was something he had not met before. He had been trained to love his family and clan and the hills of his home, and a Prince who summed up centuries of wandering loyalty. But his devotion had been for the little, intimate things, and not for matters large and impersonal like a country or a people. He felt himself suddenly and in very truth a stranger and alone. The Prince, the chiefs, the army—they were all of them strangers here. How could they ask for loyalty from what they so little understood?[77]

---

73. John Buchan, *Midwinter* (2nd edn, London: Thomas Nelson and Sons, Ltd., 1925), 36; subsequent page references are to this edition.
74. Buchan, *Midwinter*, 170.   75. Buchan, Midwinter, 213.
76. Buchan, *Midwinter*, 212.   77. Buchan, *Midwinter*, 217–18.

And in the penultimate chapter ('In Which Three Gentlemen Confess their Nakedness') Midwinter's Old England returns as offered escape for Alastair and Samuel Johnson, the idealists defeated by history. But it is now not escapist because of the purgation that is its prerequisite. And it is an escape that both refuse.

In *The Blanket of the Dark* Old England is at once more aligned with the Robin Hood Greenwood and more realistically conceived. It is an underworld of gypsies, of professional beggars and thieves with their own social groupings, but also of those dispossessed by the wool-trade economy, which is itself part of the new Tudor historical world of the 1530s. In a suggestive image, their 'life passes like a shuttle through England'.[78] They live under the blanket of the dark, an image that can encompass both a pagan nature and a land under tyranny.[79] Against the new order the Catholic aristocracy mount their betrayed (and self-interested) rising. Peter Pentecost, son of an executed Duke of Buckingham, who is deployed as its figurehead leader, goes down willingly at the end into the underworld of Old England. But not before he has grappled, in an encounter at once personal and apocalyptic (chapter XIV, 'How Peter Strove with Powers and Principalities'), with the new historical world as embodied by Henry VIII, a figure of autocratic (and daemonic) power bent on a ruthless unification of his realm, but a unification under Law: 'I have sworn', he tells Peter in their night-time dialogue in the ruined minster, isolated by flood waters, 'that I too shall be imperial, and England an empire... There will be one rule within these isles, not of Henry or Henry's son, but of English law'.[80] And this romance leaves that claim in tension with both the underworld outside of history and Peter's visionary glimpses of a transcendence that can knit together the paganism of a wild nature and a Platonic Christianity, the virgin Artemis and the Virgin Mother of God.

V

In terms of history as that which we make, is there a necessary dialectic... between remembering and forgetting? Strangely, Arthurian legend offers to such a dialectic a coherent and suggestive context. It certainly encourages remembering; but since Arthur is a once and future king it invites one into history both as the memory of the past and as a present activity with

---

78. John Buchan, *The Blanket of the Dark* (2nd edn, London: Thomas Nelson and Sons Ltd, 1933), 116.
79. Buchan, *The Blanket of the Dark*, 366-7, 120, 361.   80. Buchan, *The Blanket of the Dark,* 330,

a view to the future...the historian and the storyteller meet in their function as makers of images. History opens to the heuristic power of the imagination; even fabulous poetry may open to the real, as when Spenser claims, in the proem to Book II of *The Faerie Queene*, that his Arthurian domain is 'matter of just memory' (l. 5).[81]

This chapter and the texts it considers—or, rather, the topics it has elicited from those texts—step back or aside from unions as such, whether federal, dynastic, or incorporating. The topics elicited include the cost of union and the experience of defeat; partition as the cannibal antithesis of union; unifications that can stand in oblique or antithetical relation to unions. Partition, union, and unification can each call out, call into play, the imagining of a counter-kingdom. They can marshal the iconic figures of the Byronic Hero and the last of the race, or mobilize the troping of a national history as Passion myth or myth of organic growth.

All these topics generate the experience of the present as an absence, that experience to which elegy and the elegiac are, by definition, attuned, and that the figure of the homo duplex may embody with a particular intensity of oxymoron. Within politics and history such absence can be answered by the imagining (in the sense of a fictive re-creation that incorporates history and vision) of a once and future kingdom. The shift of that phrase from the epitaph for Arthur (*quondam rex et rex futurus*) acknowledges a replacement of mythic hero by polity worked upon by, or (in the extreme Mickiewicz cases) wrought into, myth. But it also acknowledges the paradigmatic resources of Arthur's story for such an imagining, as Michael Edwards demonstrates. His elegant construing hovers between literary theory and metaphysics. It should be balanced by one that calls up the immediate human and historical involvement a once and future kingdom can demand. Poland, in the texts discussed by this chapter, is the most acute case of such a kingdom. And, since Conrad has been at least an attendant presence throughout this piece, he may have the last word. In a letter of 1903 to his compatriot Kazimierz Waliszewki, he wrote: 'Both at sea and on land my point of view is English, from which the conclusion should not be drawn that I have become an Englishman. That is not the case. Homo duplex has in my case more than one meaning.'[82]

---

81. Michael Edwards, *Of Making Many Books* (London: Macmillan, 1990), 132–3.
82. Conrad, letter to Kazimierz Waliszewki, 5 December 1903, in *The Collected Letters of Joseph Conrad*, ed. Frederick R. Karl, Laurence Davies, et al., 9 vols (Cambridge: Cambridge University Press, 1988–2007), iii. 89.

14

A. G. MacDonell's *England, their England*

Brian Young

A. G. Macdonell's *England, their England*, published in 1933, is a largely forgotten bestseller, remembered, if at all, more for its title than for its content.[1] Whenever it is referred to, it is under the deeply chilling category of a 'classic of light humour'. Testimonies to its influence are, however, not difficult to find; in his recently published (and bestselling) memoir *The Unexpected Professor*, John Carey, a lifelong champion and connoisseur of all things middlebrow, instanced the book as one occasionally read from to him and his classmates by his English master at Richmond and Sheen Grammar School, in the early 1940s.[2] It is noteworthy that *England, their England* is a book that Carey, who was born in 1934, chose to isolate in this way; it is a surprisingly bookish book, and one can readily see its appeal to a bookish child from a not-so-bookish household, and also why Macdonell's making fun of modern art and literature originally appealed to Carey, the author of *The Intellectuals and the Masses*; it was a habit of mind that Carey

1. I am indebted to the late Rory Allan and Christopher Pelling, the latter particularly for his insights on cricket and the Classics; and we will simply have to forgive a character in a Macdonell detective novel for ignorantly referring to 'Christchurch College, Oxford': *The Shakespeare Murders* (London: Arthur Baker, 1933), 153.
2. John Carey, *The Unexpected Professor: An Oxford life in Books* (London: Faber and Faber, 2013), 53–4, and, for his likemindedness with Macdonell, see Carey, *The Intellectuals and the Masses: Pride and Prejudice among the Literary Intelligentsia, 1880–1939* (London: Faber and Faber, 1992).

would return to, more than once, in later years. Indeed, MacDonell and Carey have a deep literary connection: both are intellectual anti-intellectuals, both target much the same literature, and among their primary victims is Aldous Huxley, that elderly *enfant terrible* of the 1920s and 1930s. Huxley was someone Macdonell quietly despised: owing to his poor eyesight, Huxley had been a non-combatant in the First World War, the shattering event that marked out Macdonell's future as a survivor who reacted to this experience with a humour that often verged on the flippant and even more frequently that escaped into something like a rural twilight, experienced and rhapsodized both in England and in Scotland. Huxley's sharply urban satires, in which rural idylls are conspicuously not experienced by urban sophisticates who occasionally constitute desultory country-house enclaves, were not to MacDonell's nostalgic taste; and Huxley, unlike many of his literary contemporaries, had not only a distinctive style but also a distinctive intelligence, and neither appealed to the hack writers of the intellectually inert interwar years. In *Parody Party*—to which Macdonell contributed 'Eden week-end', an acute if affectionate sketch of Arnold Bennett and J. B. Priestley as disguised toffs—Huxley was patronizingly singled out by the editor, Leonard Russell, as the clever young man, 'perhaps the most gifted of post-war writers', who demanded to be parodied, the result being Cyril Connolly's wincingly 'clever' 'Told in Gath'.[3]

Parody is a form that flatters the reader; in *Parody Party* it was even more colluding, in that the reader is informed at the inception of each contribution of the identity of the author who is being parodied; it is easy crossword-clue country. Only one parody stands out as being in any sense discomfiting, and that is Wyndham Lewis's modernist slight on Stanley Baldwin's vacuous appeals to English whimsy, the corrosive and directly on-target 'More on England'.[4] By contrast, and despite, or because of, its concentrated anti-intellectualism, *England, their England* was a comfortable and comforting book, one of many reflections on England and the English that proliferated in the 1930s, and involving authors as disparate and as subtly interconnected as Stanley Baldwin, H. M. Morton, George Orwell, and J. B. Priestley. The difference is that they wrote, variously, as insiders; Macdonell wrote, consciously, as an outsider—albeit by way of his education at Winchester—with something of an insider's knowledge. Macdonell had been acculturated into

3. Leonard Russell (ed.), *Parody Party* (London: Hutchinson, 1936), pp. vii–viii, 169–81, 123–36.
4. Russell (ed.), *Parody Party*, 97–103.

England, but always kept a self-conscious distance from it, as is very clear in the asperity of his deeply nationalist work, *My Scotland*, published in 1937, not quite a work of what Hugh Trevor-Roper would have described as 'Scotch' *mythistoire*, but very far from the North British unionism familiar from the work of Colin Kidd; Macdonell was a Highland Celt by ancestry, and his nationalism extended to a pan-Celtic championing of Irish nationalism. *My Scotland* is littered with racial theorizing and far from disinterested historical summaries, informed throughout by a perspective on Anglo-Scottish relations that might be summarized by his pervasive claim that the Scots have had 'too much England'.[5] He made this deliberately alarming statement within four years of completing *England, their England*.

There can be no surprise that books such as *England, their England* proliferated in what was a decidedly troubled decade. The English, in common with many other nations, were in need of self-validating myths, and light fiction and insular travelogues provided exactly such reassuring narratives. That many such accounts were provided by veterans of the First World War gives some poignancy to what can otherwise be a blandly discomfiting scenario. After the bestselling accounts of life in the trenches, provided by members of the officer class—Siegfried Sassoon, Robert Graves, Edmund Blunden, et al.—had begun to appear with some regularity in the 1920s, those same authors were in search of new territory.[6] And a new generation of men too young to fight in that war were beginning to express their distance from, even their distaste for, the generation of the First World War, nowhere more shockingly or more repeatedly than in the novels and memoirs of Evelyn Waugh. The Waugh of the 1930s could have had no inkling that in his *Men at Arms* trilogy he would himself write one of the greatest series of novels about war, and about the frustrations of would-be combatants keen to make up for their own callow disapprobation of an earlier generation of decidedly more militarily experienced men of letters.

The 1930s was also a decade in which Herbert Butterfield—who narrowly avoided conscription by virtue of having been born in 1900 and gaining a place to study Modern History at Peterhouse, Cambridge—sought to bury

5. Hugh Trevor-Roper, *The Invention of Scotland: Myth and History* (New Haven, CT, and London: Yale University Press, 2008); Colin Kidd, *Union and Unionisms: Political Thought in Scotland 1500–1800* (Cambridge: Cambridge University Press, 2008), and 'The Politics of the Scottish Enlightenment', in Blair Worden (ed.), *Hugh Trevor Roper: The Historian* (London: I. B. Tauris, 2016), 145–61; A. G. Macdonell, *My Scotland* (1937; repr. Stroud: Fonthill, 2012), 13.
6. The classic treatment remains Paul Fussell, *The Great War and Modern Memory* (Oxford: Oxford University Press, 1975).

the comforting delusions of what he influentially identified as *The Whig Interpretation of History*, consigning self-consciously progressive accounts of a more than mildly patriotic kind to the dustbin in preference for what he approvingly called 'technical history'.[7] But it was precisely such anti-Whig technical history that had only slightly earlier rejuvenated an account of English exceptionalism, and this in a study written by a historian early reared in continental traditions of historical thought. Lewis Namier's *Structure of English Politics at the Accession of George III* appeared in 1928, three years before Butterfield's premature burial of English historical exceptionalism.[8] A celebration of English politics as being securely founded in the experiences and activities enjoyed by an exclusive, civilized, and responsible elite, Namier's work was to become typical of an émigré theorization—one is tempted to say, rather, an anti-theorization—of English history, which later included such successful practitioners as G. R. Elton and Nicolas Pevsner, the author of a study of *The Englishness of English Art*. The 1930s proved a rich and varied decade intellectually, and for perfectly explicable reasons it was one in which émigrés and semi-outsiders often proved more charitable to the English than did the English themselves. In his own very particular way, A. G. Macdonell was one such charitably inclined semi-outsider, so far as a Wykehamist can ever be considered an outsider.[9]

In fact, his academically and athletically successful years at Winchester College are not the only reason to query aspects of Macdonell's 'outsider' status. Proudly Scottish though he undoubtedly was, Macdonell belonged to a class of North Britons intimately related to empire and traditions of public service, exactly the sort of cadre that gives currency to the notion of a more narrowly *Scottish*, rather than a more widely British, Empire.[10] Archibald Gordon Macdonell was born in Poona, India, in 1895, the son of a box wallah, who had served as chairman of the Bombay Chamber of Commerce; India and its various imperial absurdities and colonial tragedies

---

7. See Michael Bentley, *The Life and Thought of Herbert Butterfield: History, Science and God* (Cambridge: Cambridge University Press, 2011).

8. See, further, Isaiah Berlin, 'L. B. Namier', in *Personal Impressions* (London: Hogarth Press, 1980), 91–111; G. R. Elton, *The English* (Oxford: Wiley Blackwell, 1992), and Susie Harris, *Nikolaus Pevsner: The Life* (London: Pimlico, 2011). Both Namier and Pevsner became conforming Anglicans.

9. There is no biography; the *ODNB* entry by Bill Deedes, revised by Clare L. Taylor, is excellent, and it can be profitably supplemented by reference to the introductions to the Fonthill reprints of many of Macdonell's books.

10. For decidedly contrasting views of which, see Michael Fry, *The Scottish Empire* (East Linton: Tuckwell, 2001), and T. M. Devine, *Scotland's Empire: The Origins of the Global Diaspora* (London: Allen Lane, 2003).

was to recur at several times in his fiction, not least in *England, their England*. An implied critique of 'orientalism' is current throughout the novel, but rather more palpable is a sense of distance from what David Cannadine has subsequently called 'ornamentalism':[11] the unnamed 'Anglo-Indian Major-General' who first appears at Lady Ormerode's country-house party, and then returns in the roof-top fire at the Hôtel Joséphine, is quite literally neither use nor ornament, but a man whose somewhat paradoxically wide—yet, to a First World War veteran such as Macdonell, actually rather restricted—experience is all too predictably reflected in his conventionally narrow views:

> he had soldiered on veld and kopje, on Himalayan hillsides, on Chinese rivers, on burning plains and deserts, and had even, once or twice, visited front-line trenches, or at least got as far as battalion headquarters. He knew how to deal with Boers and Pathans and Waziris and Afridis and Chinks and Bolshies and hecklers...[12]

'Mrs Major-General', as Macdonell invariably denominated 'the portly wife of the warrior', holds, if anything, even more startling views, telling Donald Cameron, the hero of the novel:

> a good many times that no one could really understand the Indian problem unless they had actually lived there, and that the only solution of the difficulty, now that the initial blunder of not hanging Mr Montagu and Lord Chelmsford years ago had been irrevocably committed, was to let the natives try another Mutiny and then show them what was what.[13]

In *England, their England,* the familiar identification of representatives of the Raj with reaction was made again and again; the Liberal partisan Macdonell had the Major-General sit as a Conservative MP, although the Conservative Party was decidedly capacious in the novel, containing not only the major-general but also, as a 'Die-hard Conservative', the ideologically promiscuous Lady Ormerode, whose obscurely Canadian origins are held to explain much, both by her allies and her enemies.[14] (Lady Ormerode, is a caricature melding Ottoline Morrell and Nancy Astor, with perhaps a nod to being a feminized equivalent of that most masculine of men, Lord Beaverbrook).

More typical is another member of the house party at Ormerode Towers, Captain de Wilton-ffallow, a Conservative MP whose dubious qualities are

---

11. David Cannadine, *Ornamentalism: How the British saw their Empire* (London: Allen Lane, 2001).
12. A. G. Macdonell, *England, their England* (1933; repr. Cambridge: Oleander Press, 2011), 69.
13. Macdonell, *England, their England*, 70.   14. Macdonell, *England, their England*, 56–7.

resentfully intimated by Macdonell by remarking that the 'gallant captain' was one of those whose military rank 'had mysteriously survived into the days of peace; some have survived, others have not, and no one knows the reason', although dubious and probably sinister pomposity of some sort seems the most likely imputed explanation on Macdonell's part.[15] There is an amused quality to Macdonell's bitter veteran status, but it is a bitterness that is discernible at several moments in the novel. By remaining committed to the Liberal Party in its years of decline, Macdonell likewise retained his 'outsider' status. For in 1933 he expressed distaste not only for the Conservatives, but also for a Labour Party whose Scottish leader, Ramsay McDonald, was not exactly to Macdonell's taste, any more than is an exceptionally well-tailored old dandy attending the house party, who, it transpires, is an ex-Secretary of State, the Right Honourable Robert Bloomer, a former president of the TUC and 'for thirty-five years Secretary of the Amalgamated Union of West-end Journeymen Tailors, Hem-stitchers, and Cutters', a typical 'branch of English labour'.[16] (One wonders if Macdonell is slyly alluding to Tressell's *The Ragged Trousered Philanthropists* here.) Bloomer is identified as 'a Coalition Socialist', but is a Tory in all but name, unlike another Labour MP attending the house party, Miss Prudence Pott, who is described as being 'a woman of painstaking industry, of sterling worth, and of extreme dullness'. It is Bloomer who begins a tirade against Liberals as 'poisonous', and he is rapidly joined by the Tory chorus constituted by the unnamed and unnameable major-general, Captain de Wilton-ffalow, and Sir Ethelred Ormerode.[17] (Ethelred is a name lazily associated by novelists and film-makers with the most ultra-conservative of Anglo-Saxons; it is best instanced by the duke of Chalfont, whose murder is the last undertaken by the anti-hero of Robert Hamer's *Kind Hearts and Coronets*.) But Sir Ethelred is not so extreme as his interlocutors, concluding amicably: ' "I agree profoundly that Liberals are insane, but it will need more than that to persuade me that they are treacherous as well." '[18] The strange death of Liberal England saw Macdonell as a grieving Scottish pallbearer; but dignity was salted with humour in its obsequies.

Brought up conventionally in Scotland, Macdonell entered Winchester as a scholar, which he left in 1914; from 1916 to 1918 he served as a lieutenant in the 51st Highland Division; thereafter his life was to take a less prescribed,

15. Macdonell, *England, their England*, 69.   16. Macdonell, *England, their England*, 63.
17. Macdonell, *England, their England*, 71–5.   18. Macdonell, *England, their England*, 75–6.

and less circumscribed, route than might otherwise have been expected. In many ways, the First World War liberated him from the conventional career of an Edwardian Wykehamist: not for him the closed scholarship to New College, Oxford, followed either by the Bar and politics or a prominent place in the civil service, or, slightly more eccentrically, by a fellowship of an Oxford college.[19] Nor yet, as he put it in one a series of potboiler detective novels that he wrote under the not exactly impenetrable pen names of Neil Gordon and John Cameron (and more occasionally under his own name), did he choose to become 'the ordinary type which goes from public school to the army or the Indian or Colonial Civil Service'.[20] Unusually for a scholar of Winchester, there was for Macdonell no university study after the First World War; his life was, instead, to prove conventionally unconventional. One aspect of his Winchester schooling clearly marked Macdonell out, and that is a characteristically resentful sense of superiority, usually disguised as satire, directed against more socially, if arguably less academically, prestigious schools, as instanced in an observation about modern novelists:

> Donald had also learnt much about country-house life from the ... books of astonishingly brilliant young men, mostly about one-and-twenty years of age. These books, for some reason, were always on the same model. They began with life at Eton, or Harrow, in the proportion of about eighty of the former to twenty of the latter, and the first part invariably contained two descriptions. There was always a rather sardonic description of the Harrow match, or, in twenty per cent, the Eton match, and always a description of a small boy being whipped by a larger boy.

After these novelistic preliminaries, Macdonell continues, 'the scene automatically moves' to the weekend party:

> and there the hero, his contempt for cricket having been duly flaunted and his injured posterior healed, finds himself in surroundings that are worthy of him and his brilliance ... he ... exchanges dazzling epigrams until luncheon with others of his own age and brilliance, all about the Hollowness of Life, the Folly of the Old, the Comicality of the War, the Ideas of the Young, the Brilliance of the Young, the Novels of D. H. Lawrence, the Intelligence of the Young, the Superiority of Modern Photography over Velazquez, and the Futility of People of Forty.[21]

19. As apparently in the case of Brookes, a character in A. G. Macdonell, *The Seven Stabs* (London: Victor Gollancz, 1929), as described at pp. 47–8.
20. Macdonell, *The Shakespeare Murders*, 89.   21. Macdonell, *England, their England*, 54–5.

It is not hard to detect behind the humour an expression of anger and resentment by the thirty-eight-year-old veteran; and one such man, a product of Eton and Balliol, was Huxley, a year older than Macdonell, and an astringent student of the world of Ottoline Morrell's literary house parties, although the world he describes in such novels as *Crome Yellow*, published in 1921, is less indulgently characterized than Macdonell suggests when consigning his 'Etonian' and 'Harrovian' novelists to such ill-disguised outreaches of literary contempt. But the young Huxley knew that he was not necessarily considered to be a great novelist, and his admiration for those he considered truly great, such as D. H. Lawrence, went so far as to see him quoted at length in *Eyeless in Gaza*, his pacifist-aligned novel of 1936, and undoubtedly a masterpiece to invoke one of the most overused categories of our times. And two even younger Etonian novelists, Anthony Powell and Henry Green, both far too young to have served in the war, were beginning to publish, as *England, their England* conspired against them and the worlds they intimately described.

Eton and Harrow were portrayed by Macdonell as institutions that produced decorous, languid, and generally useless if pukka Englishmen; not only Conservative MPs, but a trio of absurdly English diplomats—Messrs Carshalton-Stanbury, Woldingham-Uffington, and Carteret-Pendragon—who elegantly ensure that nothing whatever untoward happens at the League of Nations, are inevitably identified as Etonians.[22] Towards Winchester there was, on Macdonell's part, a becomingly astringent loyalty, a devotion to a peculiar establishment whose self-conscious eccentricities and sense of apartness can be appreciated in the pages devoted to it by Kenneth Clark in the first volume of his memoirs, *Another Part of the Wood*. Clark, eight years younger than Macdonell, was a singular Wykehamist who wore his Scottish lineage with pride, recalling in his first volume of memoirs that, at a school play-reading society, he had read the part of the porter in *Macbeth* with 'a genuine Highland accent', but he went on to note: 'No one present had ever heard a Highland accent and expected it to be played in Harry Lauder Scots; they thought my accent was Welsh (which historically, it is) and I was severely reprimanded.'[23]

In common with the young Clark, a few years behind him at the school, Macdonell seems to have ingested Winchester's peculiarities into his own

22. Macdonell, *England, their England* , 128–32.
23. Kenneth Clark, *Another Part of the Wood: A Self-Portrait* (London: Harper Collins, 1974), 64.

sense of being an outsider; he had, as it were, his own 'Notions', which he took forward with him in a somewhat angular life. At the country-house party, the absurdly named Porson Wilamowitz Möllendorf Jebb (named by a father with an excessive enthusiasm for Classical philology) is revealed as an academic dud in a revealing sequence, first failing the Winchester entrance examination before being 'superannuated from Eton after four successive failures in "Trials"'. (And, like many a hack writer, Macdonell was not above recycling jokes; in his tale of scholars unexpectedly beating school hearties, 'Mind over Matter', a calculating swot is called Porson Wilamowitz Bates). But Jebb has quite other skills, scoring 160 in the Sheffield Test Match against Australia, 'a masterpiece of classic batsmanship'.[24] Cricket, as all readers of *England, their England* know, is the centre of all that is best about England for Macdonell, and, in the visionary closing chapter of the novel, a nostalgic visit to Winchester, an exchange between Cameron and a Winchester boy provides, in every sense of the word, 'closure' to all that has gone before.

Spotting an unusual-looking tree, Cameron asks the black-gowned boy what it is, and their desultory conversation provides the ideal of 'Manners Makyth Man' by which Macdonell had tried to live his own life, a public-spirited motto that he felt marked out Winchester from all other schools, from Eton (and he proudly noted that Winchester was fifty years older than Eton), to the purely imagined St Ethelburga's, Worksop, and St Francis Xavier's-in-partibus, Tel-el-Kebir:

The boy took off his straw hat and replied with equal politeness:

'That is Lord's tree, sir.'
'Lord's tree?' said Donald, also taking off his hat. 'What is that?'
'It is called that, sir, because only men in Lord's are allowed to sit
    on the seat at the foot of it,' explained the child.
'I am sorry to appear stupid,' Donald apologized, 'but when you say
    "Men in Lord's" do you refer to the Peers of the Realm?'
'By no means,' replied the infant. 'Men in Lord's are the men
    in the cricket eleven.'
'Oh, I see. The cricket eleven is called Lord's because they go
    to Lord's to play cricket.'
'No, sir. They don't go to Lord's.'
'Then why are they called Lords?' Donald was getting confused.
'Because we used until quite recently to play at Lord's against Eton.'

24. Macdonell, *England, their England*, 67–8.

'Ah! Now I begin to understand. Until a few years ago;
   how many years, by the way?'
'About seventy or eighty, sir.'

Donald kept a firm grip upon himself, and tried to speak naturally as he answered:

'Quite so. Just the other day. I see. And the boys in the cricket eleven—'
'Men,' interrupted the child firmly.
'I beg your pardon.'
'Men,' repeated the child. 'We are all men here. There are no boys.'
Donald by now quite dizzy, bowed and thanked the man for his trouble.
'It was a pleasure,' replied the man, bowing courteously
   and removing his hat again and going on his way.[25]

In that final cadence there is something almost biblical after this otherwise potentially bewildering *Alice in Wonderland* exchange; for Macdonell there is something sacred about Winchester as a city as well as a school, the city of King Alfred, the Round Table, and William of Wykeham. And the novel closes with something very like *The Vision of Piers Plowman*, as a sleeping Donald Cameron sees dimly in a misty field a group of fat men and a group of thin men, who begin to fight one another, but who are then revealed to be masquerading poets, chief among whom, absurdly, is Shakespeare. Pastoralism is of the essence: 'the muted voices of grazing sheep, and the merry click of bat upon ball, and the peaceful green fields of England, and the water-meads, and the bells of the Cathedral.'[26] Cameron/Macdonell, the shell-shocked figure at the opening of the novel, repairs himself after his tour of England as one of the 'men' of Winchester. Winchester represented a great deal for English patriots; it is pivotal to H. M. Morton's classic of travel literature, *In Search of England*, and Macdonell dedicated his collection of short stories, *The Spanish Pistol*, in which his Winchester/Silchester story appears, to Morton, a name he also gives to a sympathetic character in his first detective novel, *The Factory on the Cliff*, published in 1928.

Both Morton and Macdonell had much to repair after the First World War, but it took much to achieve, and the episodic plot of *England, their England* is a 1930s equivalent of the eighteenth-century picaresque novel, a fictional genre appropriately pioneered by another Scots observer of the English, Tobias Smollett. There are two components to this rehabilitation of

25. Macdonell, *England, their England*, 239–41.
26. Macdonell, *England, their England*, 244–8.

Cameron/Macdonell: the consolations of literature and the humour of games, particularly cricket; sometimes the two come together, and the cricket chapter of *England, their England* draws directly on Macdonell's experience of playing for the Invalids, an amateur squad that still exists and that regularly draws on the world of letters and the stage for its membership.[27] Its founder was a literary man, J. C. Squire, to whom *England, their England* is dedicated, and he was identified by Jeremy Paul, the chronicler of the Invalids (whose colours are supposedly based on the hospital pyjamas worn by recuperating First World War officers, completed by two walking sticks, crossed), as the inspiration behind the character of Hodge—a proverbial name for a rustic, of course, and Macdonell's Hodge is 'at heart an agrarian, for all his book-learning and his cadences'. That the early years of the Invalids were punningly known as The Squirearchy tells one a great deal about the club's ethos; early players included Alec Waugh—who once recruited his younger brother, Evelyn, to play—Macdonell's fellow humorist J. B. Morton, alias Beachcomber of the *Daily Express*, as well as Hilaire Belloc, G. K. Chesterton, and a brace of publishers. First World War veterans naturally played for the Invalids alongside Macdonell, notably J. B. Priestley and Edmund Blunden.[28] In common with Blunden, Macdonell drew on literature and cricket to reorientate his post-war life; *England, their England* is littered with literary allusions, but Macdonell knew his middlebrow audience, and usually drew attention to his literary play.

Cameron (the son of a Dante-fancying Abderdonian), describing his encounter with a group of vintage Hardyesque rustics, points out that one of them had unknowingly quoted Shakespeare: 'I am a true labourer: I earn that I get, eat that I wear, owe no man hate, envy no man's happiness, glad of other men's good, content with my own harm; and the greatest of my pride is to see my ewes graze and my lambs suck.' What is more, one of the rustics, two years short of his century, had met Dickens. (Never one to lose the chance of an obvious joke, Macdonell christened one of his elderly retinue Mr Young.) So conscious is Macdonell of invoking a Hardy fantasy that he has Cameron corrected by an Englishman as being likely to turn him into the Mayor of Casterbridge, just as he himself parallels the Scotsman Farfrae in that novel. Inevitably, bucolic Buckinghamshire contains its 'village Hampdens' (an allusion he was to repeat in his cricketing tribute to Dickens,

27. Macdonell, *England, their England*, 82–103.
28. Jeremy Paul, *Sing Willow: The True Story of the Invalids Cricket Club* (Lewes: The Book Guild, 2002); Macdonell, *England, their England*, 96.

'Dingley-Dell *v.* All Muggleton Cricket Match'); contemporaneously, a rail guard reminds Macdonell of the already 'immortal Jeeves'. [29] And Macdonell the literary journalist evokes lower forms of literature at several moments in the novel. The Conservative MP Sir Henry Wootton might well share the name of a great humanist diplomat, but his initially impressive library soon disappoints Cameron:

> the books were not the books of a reader, but more like the reference section of a public library or a dusty corridor in a West End Club. The *Dictionary of National Biography* stretched out its interminable array; above it was an old edition of the *Encyclopaedia Britannica.* The *Annual Register* occupied shelf after shelf. Bailey's *Guide to the Turf,* Hansard's *Parliamentary Debates,* the *Gentleman's Magazine,* huge bound volumes of the *Illustrated London News,* the *Field, Country Life, Horse and Hound,* and other periodicals of bygone ages stood massively, leathery, shoulder to shoulder, rather like the massive, prosperous years of Victorianism which they recorded in their pages.[30]

Macdonell was a modern, if not quite a Modernist, and he gleefully parodied his own detective novels, whose gloriously preposterous plots, replete with their routinely exotic racism, are paraded in Cameron's absorbed reading of *The Trail of the Poisoned Carpet*:

> He read the great scenes of Dick's fight with Ah Boo Wu and his gang in the Limehouse main drain, the reappearance of the secret submarine off Valparaiso, the forgery of Sir Dalhousie Canning's signature to the Bungiskhan Treaty, and the theft of the Poisoned Carpet itself from the nunnery in Hull, and he had just reached the point at which La Sapphirita has put cyanide upon the claws of a Siamese cat and, disguised in black satin trousers as a Government window cleaner, has inserted the animal into the Far Eastern Department of the Foreign Office where huge, ugly Dick Trelawney is at work with an atlas and a manual of geography trying to discover exactly where Bungiskhan is, with which he has negotiated the Treaty.[31]

Such routine silliness informed his own work in the genre, from *The Seven Stabs* in 1928 to the anti-appeasement thriller, *The Crew of the Anaconda,* his last published book, in 1940. A typical sentence in one of these reads: 'A fanfare of an electric horn made him look up just in time to see Streatfield

29. Macdonell, *England, their England,* 183–96, 199, 201, 205; A. G. Macdonell, 'Dingley-Dell *v.* All Muggleton Cricket Match', in Macdonell, *The Spanish Pistol, and Other Stories* (London: Macmillan, 1939), 179–94: Mr Dumkins is described as 'an authentic village, or rather town, Hampden.'

30. Macdonell, *England, their England,* 119.   31. Macdonell, *England, their England,* 209.

and the two girls, and the Columbian man-servant, tearing down the avenue in a large, pale-blue Bentley.'[32]

A younger Scotsman, Ian Fleming, would absorb reams of such stuff at Eton; Macdonell had a penchant for vast global conspiracies involving dubious Russians and Slavs, including a vast anarcho-socialist network, a tendency that was to have a lasting influence. The pedigrees and filiations of Scottish middlebrow fiction between and immediately after the wars await their historian. And sometimes the brow is pointing upwards, if occasionally gesturing downwards; Macdonell's first essay in this genre, *The Factory on the Cliff*, looks back to Conrad's *Secret Agent* and forward to James Bond (the subject of a late and brilliant Connolly parody, 'Bond strikes camp'.) But its literary quality is vitiated by casual racism, as when the hero, Templeton— typically for Macdonell an idealized self-portrait; he is a moneyed if prin- cipled loafer, a decorated First World War veteran who had served in an infantry regiment and who lives for golf and rugby football—observes of the occupant of a car that he was 'a man of exceptionally swarthy complex- ion. He was quite clearly not a native of the British Isles, and Templeton judged that he must be an Arab or something akin to an Arab.'[33] That phrase, 'something akin to', is characteristic of the author, a studied lack of preci- sion mocking a knowing accuracy at all times. In this forensic looseness, Macdonell had much in common with members of the Detection Club, sharing their fascination with Sherlock Holmes: the villain of *The Factory on the Cliff* is a variant of Professor Moriarty, a fantasy figure (and in a Dorothy Sayers-like essay on Conan Doyle's anti-hero, Macdonell would claim, from a close dating of 'The Valley of Fear', that Moriarty was a fantasy projection made by Sherlock Holmes).[34] The inevitable 'Professor'—whose organization of Balkan anarchists, Liberty (which reappears in subsequent novels), like- wise foreshadows, if in a slightly more benevolent form, SMERSH—claims to be behind most of the assassinations of the 1900s; one detects some sympathy on Macdonell's part for a man who claims to have shot the Turk who inspired the Armenian Massacre, if not exactly for his villainous methods: ' "I am getting old. Killing one tyrant here and there is slow work.

32. Macdonell, *The Shakespeare Murders*, 111.
33. A. G. Macdonell, *The Factory on the Cliff* (London: Longmans & Co., 1928), 7.
34. A. G. Macdonell, 'Mr Moriarty: A Study in the Sherlock Holmes Saga', in *The Spanish Pistol*, 208–20. Rather than being the 'Napoleon of crime', Macdonell's professor declares of himself: 'I am the new Rousseau' (*The Factory on the Cliff*, 212). For the wider (if agreeably narrow) context, see Martin Edwards, *The Golden Age of Murder: The Mystery of the Writers who Invented the Modern Detective Story* (London: Harper Collins, 2015).

I haven't time for it. That is why I have taken to germ-running. The germs
will kill in thousands. They begin in a fortnight's time. Give me another
fortnight and my work will be complete." '[35] Naturally, the elderly anarchist
does not get his fortnight, and his fiendish plot is foiled by Templeton and
his fellow veterans, the germs ending up safely in a canal (after some business in the Scottish heather reminiscent of Buchan's *The Thirty-Nine Steps*),
with some remaining to be examined in their laboratories by Aberdeen
professors (Macdonell was the nephew of a professor of Classics at Aberdeen).

Macdonell's detective novels, written at speed and with panache, betray
an ambivalent love of England and the English, but when the crimes are not
solved at their considerable leisure by gifted gentlemen-amateurs in search
of post-war camaraderie and adventure, they are scrupulously resolved by
omniscient Scottish detectives, such as the omnipresent Inspector Fleming
of Scotland Yard (intellectually far ahead, in the engagingly absurd *The Seven
Stabs,* of the 'flawless' if necessarily deeply flawed reasoning of a Berlin
detective, Von Hoffman, educated at Buchan's old Oxford college, Brasenose),
ably abetted by men with such dependable names as Maitland (and
Macdonell evidently enjoyed in his essay on Moriarty his references to
Doyle's Inspector Macdonald).[36] The archetype is characterized with jour-
nalistic aplomb in *The Silent Murders*. Such is the sociological deftness of
touch here that Macdonell merits quotation *in extenso*, beginning with the
superb redundancy of its opening sentence:

> Inspector Dewar was a Scotsman. Born on a farm in Dunbartonshire, the
> eldest of a family of seven sons and three daughters, he had from an early age
> helped his father to provide for the rest of his family. His official education
> had, therefore, been somewhat neglected as he had left school at the first
> instant permitted by the law. But his real education had continued in his spare
> moments during the day and every evening on his return home from work.
> His father taught him practically simultaneously how to drive a plough and to
> read Livy, so that at the age of nineteen he was able to take the usual plunge
> that young Scotsmen take. He borrowed sufficient money for the railway-fare
> and went to London. On arriving, he went straight to the home of a
> Dunbartonshire acquaintance who had taken the plunge successfully a few
> years earlier and lodged with him for six weeks. He employed the time in
> finding out the qualifications and conditions for entry into the Metropolitan
> Police Force, and then presented himself as a candidate. His fine physique, and
> his "book-learning" caught the fancy of the authorities and shortly afterwards
> he was accepted as a recruit.

35. Macdonell, *The Factory on the Cliff*, 214.   36. Macdonell, *The Seven Stabs*, 88, 264.

Immediately thereafter, everything is attributable to Dewar's distinctively and dependably Lowland nature:

> His rise was unspectacular but steady, and he owed his Inspectorship to his dogged courage, his attention to detail, his persistence and his capacity for studying the theory of detection, rather than to any particularly brilliant feats of daring or intellect. He had no trace of Highland dash or instability. He studied the facts and pursued a case to the bitter end. The result was that he was trusted by his superiors and affectionately chaffed by his juniors. He was a bachelor and had no recreations or hobbies outside his profession. When he was in charge of a case, he thought of the case and dreamt of the case. It practically took possession of him for twenty-four hours a day.[37]

(As can readily be observed, Macdonell loved his adverbs, particularly 'particularly'.) The detective novel allowed Macdonell to play with cliché, and he perpetrated that most knowing of plots, the detective-novelist caught up in a genuine mystery, in his 1930 excursion *The Big Ben Alibi*.

As a busy jobbing writer, Macdonell relished playing with different literary, and occasionally subliterary, genres; games, in all their infinite variety, intellectual and physical, appealed to him strongly (the most effective moments in his 1935 travelogue, *A Visit to America*, involve trips to American Football and Baseball matches). The literary miscellany that is constituted by *England, their England* was to be reconciled by cricket, as in the reference to the poetry Hodge (patently a portrait of J. C. Squire) published in his literary magazine, the *London Weekly*:

> What consistent policy was there in printing three Shakespearean sonnets by one of the major Victorian Survivals, then a weird affair in chopped-up lines and no capital letters, all about violet-rayed bats in a-minor belfries, and then a ballade on the severe French model but with the refrain, 'I made a century in Zanzibar'?[38]

Davies, the Welshman who commissions Cameron to write his book on the English, tells him that, along with Lord Nelson, the English hold only two things sacred, the other being 'the team spirit in cricket'.[39] And the celebrated cricket match episode at the centre of the novel might well be entitled 'This Is Team Spirit'. The English 'national game' is, along with its literature, what Macdonell most admired about England. However absurd

---

37. A. G. Macdonell, *The Silent Murders* (London: Longmans & Co., 1929), 52–3.
38. Macdonell, *England, their England*, 32–3.
39. Macdonell, *England, their England*, 1–13, 40.

the course of play, what Cameron witnesses in the match is 'the Team Spirit at play'; later in the novel, when confronted by the terrifying headlines 'ENGLAND OVERWHELMED WITH DISASTER', 'IS ENGLAND DOOMED?', and 'COLLAPSE OF ENGLAND', Cameron is relieved to discover it is a series of reports concerning England playing test matches against Australia at Melbourne, although an elegant elderly gentleman remarks fiercely to him that, ' "It all comes of treating it as a game. We don't take things seriously enough in this country, sir, damnation take it all." ' But this is to take things too seriously, and Macdonell enjoys the ragging of the American, Shakespeare Pollock, when he is told that baseball is akin to a game of rounders. Indeed, most other sports are routinely dispatched with contemptuous economy by Macdonell: association football is associated with financial self-interest, and the Varsity Rugby Match is satirized through its superannuated supporters.[40] Where Macdonell is most critical of the English, however, is in his depiction of fox hunting, the cruelty of which he accentuates even as he notes that the woman who nearly knocks Cameron over in pursuit of her quarry is recognized by him as a self-sacrificing nurse who had served dutifully in the First World War.[41] For Macdonell, the English can be both cruel and self-sacrificing. And Macdonell was a Bonapartist who published the year after *England, their England* a study in military history, *Napoleon and his Marshals;* but when he evokes the bravery of the English, it is often as the successful opponents of Napoleon, a very Scottish paradox, perhaps, as the 'auld alliance' gives way to a grudging admiration for Nelson, Wellington, and the men they led. The Napoleonic Wars inevitably looked rather different to a veteran of the First World War who had served in France.

Cameron/Macdonell is at his most self-consciously Scottish when he writes about a sortie to a Home Counties golf club; the professional at the club, Glennie, is no less knowing, admitting to Cameron that he exaggerates his Scottish accent because it goes down well with the English members. Even here, satire quietly turns savage as Macdonell delineates the origins of the club with the unrelenting irony of a veteran, and of an Asquithian, rather than a Lloyd George, Liberal:

> Cedar Park is one of the newest of the great golf clubs which are ringed round the north, west, and south of London in such profusion, and what is now the clubhouse had been in earlier centuries the mansion of a venerable line of marquesses. High taxation had completed the havoc in the venerable finances which had been begun in the Georgian and Victorian generations by high gambling,

---

40. Macdonell, *England, their England*, 155–9. 41. Macdonell, *England, their England*, 206–13.

and the entire estate was sold shortly after the War by the eleventh marquess to a man who had, during it, made an enormous fortune by a most ingenious dodge. For, alone with the late Lord Kitchener, he had realized in August and September of 1914 that the War was going to be a very long business, thus providing ample opportunities for very big business, and that before it was over it would require a British Army of millions and millions of soldiers. Having first of all taken the precaution of getting himself registered as a man who was indispensable to the civil life of the nation during the great Armageddon, for at the outbreak of hostilities he was only thirty-one years of age, and, in order to be on the safe side, having had himself certified by a medical man as suffering from short sight, varicose veins, a weak heart, and incipient lung trouble, he set himself upon his great task of cornering the world's supply of rum...He was, of course, knighted for his public services during the War. It was not until 1925 that the rum knight shot himself to avoid an absolutely certain fourteen years for fraudulent conversion, and Cedar Park was acquired by a syndicate of Armenian sportsmen for the purpose of converting it into a country club.[42]

That casual reference to the Armenian sportsmen can be paralleled throughout *England, their England* with conventionally nasty-minded allusions to Jews, Hampstead Zionists, 'a Kaffir', blacks, Rolls Royce-driving Maharajas, and a black jazz singer incongruously singing a First World War ballad in a Modernist German play. None of this casual racism would have surprised the likes of Waugh and Powell, the sort of young English novelists Macdonell otherwise so evidently disliked. But then, in 1940, Macdonell married, as his second wife, Rose Paul-Schiff, a member of a Jewish banking family; he was to be actively involved with wartime broadcasting for the BBC, but died early and unexpectedly at his Oxford home, in 1941.

Indeed, what is striking in much of his writing is a taste for what he would have called miscegenation; in *The Shakespeare Murders*, the hero, Paul Kerrigan, is the product of a union between an Irish adventurer and 'a beautiful Latvian girl'; born in Riga, Kerrigan does the right thing and fights for an Irish infantry regiment in the First World War before following his own avocation as an adventurer.[43] Similarly, the cunning hero of 'Mind over Matter', Diarmid di Colonna Ramsay, is the son of a Jewish Antwerp diamond merchant and a mother whose origins are lovingly evoked by Macdonell in his minute characterization of young Ramsay:

There is no doubt that his lavish endowment of personality and intellect was due to heredity. His mother was a hard, forceful, old-fashioned, learned, dogmatical Scotswoman from the north-west coast of Inverness-shire, near the

42. Macdonell, *England, their England*, 106–16.
43. Macdonell, *The Shakespeare Murders*, 10–11.

Kyle of Lochalsh . . . and Susanna MacIsaac was the descendant of a long line
of shrewd, pugnacious, and resourceful clansmen. In her youth she had been
sent, like all young ladies of the impoverished Highland gentry, to learn the
violin at Dresden and polish up the German irregular verbs in which she
had been so well grounded by the parish priest on the misty shores of Loch
Toridon.[44]

In a knowing parody of racial essentialism, 'Ali Baba and the Forty Thieves',
Macdonell allowed himself an in-joke about one Fergus O'Donell Barber,
an Accrington shopkeeper whose uncertainty as to whether he is of Irish or
Scottish Celtic origin leads to one son being named as if Irish, the other
(inevitably the hero of the story) as if Scottish, whose good fortune at the
end of the story is clearly a fantasy projection:

> As for Alastair Barber, he was now a man of such prodigious wealth that the
> University of Accrington, fully alive to the fact that the novels of so rich a man
> must be of exceptional merit, made him an Honorary LL.D., and in the
> following year he was awarded the Hawthornden Prize, and elected Vice-
> President of the P.E.N. Club.[45]

(*England, their England* won for Macdonell the James Tait Black Memorial
prize on its publication in 1933.)

As this award attests, Macdonell could write, and his prose indicates an
impressive, if sadly curtailed, classical education; what would in other hands
have led to lengthy and dense exposition, he concentrated and distilled to
immediate purpose. In this respect, his experience is akin to that of two of
his English contemporaries, P. G. Wodehouse and Raymond Chandler,
indebted as both men were to the same classics master at Dulwich College
for their own idiosyncratic, pitch-perfect styles. Macdonell often made
classical allusions; the difference between the hearties and the scholars of
Silchester in 'Mind over Matter' is made clear by their respective powers of
description: 'Then the scrum collapsed on the ground; bodies were super-
imposed upon one another in a sold mass, like "sardines in a damned tin",
as George Hogg put it, or, in young Porson Bates' words, "like the seven
layers of Ionian civilisation which Dr Schliemann discovered on the site of
Troy".'[46] The doubtlessly Scottish expatriate William Young Boyd apostro-
phizes Inspector Dewar and Superintendent Bone thus, in *The Silent*

44. A. G. Macdonell, 'Mind over Matter', in *The Spanish Pistol*, 164–78, at 169–70.
45. A. G. Macdonell, 'Ali Baba and the Forty Thieves', in *The Spanish Pistol*, 221–44.
46. Macdonell, 'Mind over Matter', 176.

Murders: 'Ah! My gallant defenders,' he said. 'Come in. You are welcome. I feel like Priam at the siege of Troy, seated in the safest part of the palace while the young men go out to fight his battles. Sit down.'[47] Bathos is the order of the day in most of his classical allusions; erudition is sometimes an indication that something is amiss, and above all that a literary man is not sufficiently addicted to sports, as with Oliver Maddock's retreat in retirement to St Andrews: 'He lived on the outskirts of the town, read Greek and Latin and Hebrew and Sanskrit till all hours of the morning, and never set foot on the golf links.'[48] One wonders if, for his creator, this is sufficient justification for Maddock's grisly murder.

What is most obviously lacking in *England, their England*, and elsewhere in Macdonell's writing, is serious engagement with religion; the only religion ever imputed to Cameron is a love of golf, 'a religion to him far more inspiring and appealing than the dry dogmatics of the various sections of the Presbyterian Church which wrangled in those days so enthusiastically in the North-East of Scotland'.[49] Nor is it only the Presbyterians of whom he proves critical; in those years of redevelopment and quick commercial killings, he invents a policy attributed to the Church of England for the selling-off and demolition of Wren's London churches in order to finance an evangelistic crusade. When he attempts to attend the New Year service at St Paul's Cathedral, allegedly a 'Mecca' for London-resident Scots, he is put off by a crowd, and 'by many voices saying, "Do you know the one about the Aberdonian and the Jew?"', an unfinished joke earlier begun at their different elections meetings by the Tory Sir Henry Wootton and his Labour opponent, Ernest Dodds (alas, one suspects, not named in honour of E. R. Dodds, the Classical scholar). The by-election ends in a dead heat, and the one thing that unites the two newly returned parliamentarians is a widely shared suspicion of Jews and Scotsmen.[50] It proves a turning point in the sentimental and political education of a Celtic Liberal.

Aside from an agreeable bit of 'slumming it' at greyhound racing, Cameron/Macdonell abhors the urban, be it in London or the sadly predictably excoriated Hull, about which he is brazenly rude (the professional Yorkshireman Priestley was, by contrast, deeply approving of that city in his own travelogue of 1934, *An English Journey*). In the Hull to Danzig episode in the novel, Cameron is confronted, in the figure of William Rhodes, by a

---

47. Macdonell, *The Silent Murders*, 263.   48. Macdonell, *The Silent Murders*, 12.
49. Macdonell, *England, their England*, 104.
50. Macdonell, *England, their England*, 153–4, 164–7, 181–2.

parody Yorkshireman, a solipsist who finds everywhere beyond Leeds and the East Riding of Yorkshire 'queer'; but it is Rhodes who saves the useless upper-class characters from the hotel fire towards the end of the novel.[51] The fire at the Hôtel Joséphine is a depiction of London as a form of Hell; it is the southern countryside that forms Heaven in *England, their England*, and Macdonell is most explicit about this: 'Donald was enchanted at his first sight of rural England. And rural England is the real England, unspoilt by factories and financiers and tourists and hustle.' It is, similarly, a Mr Fielding (whose name evokes the eighteenth-century novelist whose quintessentially English form of ribald gentility appealed to Macdonell) who delivers one of the moments of post-war repair in the novel, when he tells of how a Londoner had recently looked through the records of the village of Eynesbury St Clement, where 'he found a list of the bowmen that went from Eynesbury St Clement to Agincourt. There were the names of twenty-four bowmen, and eighteen of their names are on Eynesbury St Clement war memorial for the Great War.' The repetition of the name of this rural paradise is evidently deliberate. But the rehabilitation is destined to remain incomplete, for it is only a matter of pages afterwards that Cameron, attempting to defend the First World War, is confronted by the reasoning of one of the ancient rustics, the equally named 'impartial voter', Mr Stillaway:

> 'But can you tell me, sir, what national honour does for me? I've worked on the land all my life, and the least I've ever earned is four-and-six a week and the most is twenty-nine shillings. It isn't a fortune, either of them. In 1914 a man comes down to the green here, and he makes a speech about just that very national honour that you've been talking about. Mind you, sir, in 1914 the nation and all its honour was giving me twenty-two shillings a week and I was working seventy-four hours a week for it. But I had to give three sons and eight grandsons to fight for the national honour. Eleven of them. And three were killed and two lost legs. And what good did that do to them or to me or to Mr Davis here, or Mr Darley? Cost of living is higher. Beer is more expensive and so is tobacco. And my grandsons, the ones that weren't killed, can't get work. And all that for what you call national honour.'[52]

It is in the immediate wake of this speech that, after discussing the French, Nelson, and the Napoleonic wars, the chief rustic unknowingly cites Shakespeare. But is it enough to dissipate the speech of Mr Stillaway?

---

51. Macdonell, *England, their England*, 216, 168–80, 226–35.
52. Macdonell, *England, their England*, 84, 187, 195.

Poetry and cricket are at the heart of *England, their England*, but it is a Welshman, the man alongside whom Macdonell was wounded in the opening chapter of the novel, who makes so much of the English addiction to cricket and the 'team spirit', and he it is who, after chiding them for their occasionally militaristic appetite for dressing up in fancy dress, declares that '"I've got an idea that all their queernesses and oddities and incongruities arise from the fact that, at heart, fundamentally, they're a nation of poets'.[53] Years later, he once again declares to an increasingly sceptical Cameron that he isn't to forget what he had told him 'in that infernal pill-box':

> 'I've got a sort of instinctive notion that the English character—'
>   'There's no such thing,' interrupted Donald. 'They're all different.'
>   'That the English character', went on Davies firmly, 'is based fundamentally upon kindliness and poetry. Just keep that notion in mind, whether you agree with it or not.'[54]

England, their England is a book supposedly devised by a Welshman and executed by a Scot: can it be anything other than occasionally delusional, and occasionally acute, in its judgements? After Donald's Winchester vision, the novel concludes with studied matter-off-fact-ness: 'Donald got up and yawned and stretched himself and went off to find some tea.'[55] Is there an allusion here to the *Vision of Piers Plowman*, replete with its 'field full of folk'? If so, there is no religious consolation for this Scottish visionary, only nostalgia for a school whose motto he was to parody, rather too obviously, in 'Mind over Matter', complete with a self-lacerating joke about scholarly precision languishing dangerously close to mocking, pedagogic pedantry: 'That would have been Bad Form, and Bad Form had been specially banned at Silchester in the famous edict of the Founder himself in A.D. 1290, which begins *Ne malam formam in Collegium* (the corrupt, silver-age Latin use of the word *forma* will be noticed, and, of course, deplored).'[56]

But where does the curtly visionary, yet curiously matter-of-fact, close of *England, their England* leave the modern reader? It is a decidedly Anglo-Scottish moment, but younger Englishmen were altogether less nostalgically pluralistic than Macdonell in the 1930s. In 1935, Graham Greene produced his scathing portrayal of class-bound nastiness, *England Made Me*, in which the old school tie denotes fraudulence and depravity of a depth undreamed of

53. Macdonell, *England, their England*, 10.   54. Macdonell, *England, their England*, 40, 117.
55. Macdonell, *England, their England*, 248.   56. Macdonell, 'Mind over Matter', 166.

in *England, their England*; educated at Berkhamstead, the minor public school of which his father was headmaster, Greene unrelentingly chronicled a dispiriting decline of his native country in a politically combustive Europe. And already, in 1928, Evelyn Waugh had mocked the team spirit in the semi-murderous prep school sports' day at Llanabba Castle in *Decline and Fall*.

The last indirectly English word might be left to a figure from another novel published in 1933, *From A View to a Death*, by an Anglo-Welsh novelist, Anthony Powell. A dispassionate portrayal of precisely the types Macdonell excoriated in *England, their England*, it is a former First World War soldier, reduced to running a pub, who sees exactly what is wrong with that generation of dissipated English men and women. Captain McGurk has retained his wartime rank, and has been put in as landlord of the *Fox and Hounds* by a syndicate that has bought the pub. And there can be no doubt that McGurk has been placed by the syndicate because he is ornamental; although not a member of the upper middle classes from whom Macdonell securely came, 'he made up for this with the traditional virtues of his race. He always wore plus-fours and a school tie and had once appeared at a local fancy dress ball in a kilt.' McGurk's attitudes are akin to those of Macdonell, but Powell cannot resist commenting on the fact that, while McGurk considers the young Oxford man who holds a cocktail party in his pub 'a degenerate', he 'saw no reason why this should debar him from having a drink at Torquil's expense'.[57] McGurk is a participant-observer, and in this sense a more critical, less sentimental fictional counterpart to Macdonell's Donald Cameron. The England that Powell would go on to depict in his mature, post-Second World War novels was altogether less sentimentally described than that evoked by Macdonnell's account of England, *his* England. And Kenneth Widmerpool, the repellently recurrent presence in *A Dance to the Music of Time*, is, unhappily, a Scot.

But it would be grossly unfair to leave Macdonell beached in his Neverland portrayal of England and his dreams of an independent Scotland. At the end of his short life, something like a mature style was beginning to be discernible in Macdonell, otherwise a fairly representative type of the Squirearchy recently and indulgently studied by D. J. Taylor in *The Prose Factory*, but, because of Macdonell's early death, this late style remained sadly undeveloped.[58] His disillusion with much that he had chronicled earlier

---

57. Anthony Powell, *From A View to a Death* (London: Duckworth, 1933), 110–11.
58. D. J. Taylor, *The Prose Factory: Literary Life in England since 1918* (London: Chatto and Windus, 2016), 32–45.

becomes apparent in three places: in his 1936 conspiracy-thriller *Lords and Masters*, perched somewhere between Graham Greene's division between the serious novel and the entertainment, Macdonell wrote chillingly about an Anglo-German industrial matrix working selfishly against international peace, a theme that intrudes into his ostensibly light play *Where Next Baby?, or, shall I go to Tanganyika?*, the preface to which unconvincingly attempted to distance it from the tense international politics of the 'Munich Crisis' era during which it was produced. But it is in his disarmingly titled *Autobiography of a Cad*, published in 1938, that Macdonell distilled all that was most power-ful in his style and intelligence. It is a book that ought to be much better known, and is greatly superior to *England, their England*. There is no nostalgia in the later novel, and the humour is brittle. In reading it one should remember a rare joke against the public-school system, and one told by a woman: '"Another old Borstalian, eh?" Lady Caroline finished the sentence for him with a flutter of an ancient eyelid that was surprisingly like a wink.'[59] Criminality knew no social boundaries in Macdonell's fiction; it often united the working and upper classes, although only members of the former social stratum ever actually spent any time in a Borstal.

The artless narrator of *Autobiography of a Cad*, the archly named Edward Fox-Ingleby, and given a date of birth that makes him Macdonell's slightly older contemporary, is an unmitigated bad hat, a womanizer who thinks himself *gallant*, a snob (the conforming scion of a nonconformist northern industrial family) who considers himself a gentleman, a mendacious coward who piques himself on having been a good soldier; he is a dime-store Machiavellian, a much less intelligent progenitor of Francis Urquhart. Many of Macdonell's prejudices, from schools and games to political convictions, are turned to great account as the ghastly story unfolds. Suspicions begin early, as when Fox-Ingleby recalls:

> I greatly enjoyed Eton—I was a wet-bob, of course. Cricket never appealed to me very much and even in those Edwardian days, when the Harrow eleven was dimly perceptible on the field at Lord's—it has not been perceptible to the naked eye since 1910—I could never muster any enthusiasm for it, even as a spectator on a fashionable coach... every second year we were invaded by the Winchester boys, quiet, gentlemanly lads with their eyes fixed, even at that early age, upon the various branches of the Civil Service.[60]

59. Macdonell, *The Shakespeare Murders*, 103.
60. A. G. Macdonell, *Autobiography of a Cad* (London: Macmillan, 1938), 30.

As a 'non-competitive wet-bob', the young Fox-Ingleby gained 'complete scope for the two main activities of any rational Etonian, the cultivation of friends likely to be useful in after life and the avoidance of Collegers'.[61] (The former Winchester Scholar had some feeling for the travails of King's Scholars at Eton; a parallel comes to mind with the experience of George Orwell.) Social comedy rapidly turns sinister, as the indolent narrator asks, 'What is there to say about the war which has not been said already? Blunden, Remarque, Sassoon, Barbusse, Graves, Mottram, and the rest of them have escribed it *ad nauseam*.'[62] Fox-Ingleby is portrayed, with deadly precision, as recklessly imbibing the prejudices of the Waugh generation as he grows older only in terms of years.

A Tory of exactly the wrong kind to Macdonell, a Liberal internationalist (and a Celtic Nationalist who had explored the deepest reaches of Depression-era America), who had served at the League of Nations in the interwar years, Fox-Ingleby displayed an imperial isolationism that is unequivocally displayed:

> My first year in Parliament was dominated by the negotiations in Paris about the treaties. I must confess that they bored me. While our own flesh and blood was being assassinated by cowardly Irish-American blackguards (for there was not a single gentleman among the whole crew, and very few who did not hail from the Bowery or the lower quarters of Chicago), being shot at in ambulances and treacherously waylaid in traps, it was very difficult for me to take an interest in the fate of Syrians, Jews, Iraquists, Bessarabians, and all the rest of the dagoes who clutter up the map.

And he continues, relentlessly:

> So naturally the whereabouts of Teschen, the massacre of Armenians, the native land-laws of a place that was called, apparently Tanganyika, and the deaths of a million or so refugees from Russia left me cold... The only detail of those post-war international politics of the world which moved us with any emotion was the League of Nations, and the only emotion to which the League moved us was laughter.[63]

His is savage laughter; he plots with officers at the Curragh against Irish Nationalism, denouncing Irish Nationalists as 'traitors' and 'scoundrels'; and at the Carlton Club meeting that ended Lloyd George's coalition government, Fox-Ingleby voted 'in favour of live, vital, resilient, bounding Conservatism

---

61. Macdonell, *Autobiography of a Cad*, 31.   62. Macdonell, *Autobiography of a Cad*, 104.
63. Macdonell, *Autobiography of a Cad*, 159–60.

as personified by Mr Bonar Law.'[64] So lacking in self-knowledge is he that he interprets his time as Minister for the Fine Arts as having allowed him to lay down 'a broad basis for a new national culture, just as Pericles or Ruskin did in their days'. (Macdonell's fellow Wykehamist, Kenneth Clark, the author of *Ruskin Today*, would have relished the joke.) This is the bleakest variety of black comedy, in striking contrast with the light comedy of *England, their England*. It concludes with terse economy:

> And so I bring my memoirs to a close. There is nothing more to say.
>
> In May 1926 I had defeated all my enemies. I was a Minister of the Crown. I was rich and young and a bachelor again. I was untainted by public scandal. I was respected and honoured by all. And I was at peace with myself.[65]

With the defeat of Lloyd George's coalition, there was no possibility, even remotely, of England (and Britain) becoming a country fit for heroes; with the advent of Fox-Ingleby and his ilk it had become, in Macdonell's view, the public stage for cads. And the narrator's self-congratulatory prose leaves him on the cusp of the General Strike.

Unfortunately, Macdonell is remembered for the wrong novel: *England, their England* is essentially an entertainment; *Autobiography of a Cad* is a novel of consummate distinction, the Scottish insider/outsider skewering all that was wrong in the England of the 1920s and 1930s as brilliantly and effectively as had the younger generation of Greene, Green, Powell, Waugh, *and* Huxley.

---

64. Macdonell, *Autobiography of a Cad*, 94, 190, 193.
65. Macdonell, *Autobiography of a Cad*, 310, 311.

15

England's Scotland

Robert Crawford

Modern scholarship has demonstrated many Scots' eagerness to articulate literary discourses of Britishness between the Renaissance and the early twentieth century.[1] Conservative scholars use this to make a case for British Unionism, or at least argue for a sense of an 'Anglo-Celtic archipelago' (to invoke Les Murray's phrase), which gives rise in literature to what John Kerrigan has called 'Archipelagic English'.[2] However, broad-brush versions of such thinking can suppress political issues even as they claim to reveal them, particularly if commentators assume the early twenty-first century arrangements of the British and Irish governments represent a terminus rather than simply a stage in an often volatile process. Identity is dynamic, not static. While T. M. Devine's statement that 'the referendum campaign of 2014 was the most extraordinary political episode in the modern history of Scotland' may be true, few imagined the 'panic' Devine discerned at 'the very highest levels of the British state' would return with even greater intensity in 2016, bringing with it the fall of a prime minister and crises in the Conservative and Labour parties.[3] In a Scotland whose pro-independence

1. Such work includes Robert Crawford, *Devolving English Literature* (1992; 2nd edn, Edinburgh: Edinburgh University Press, 2000); Leith Davis, *Acts of Union: Scotland and the Literary Negotiation of the British Nation 1707–1830* (Stanford: Stanford University Press, 1998); and work by the contributors to the present volume.
2. John Kerrigan, *Archipelagic English: Literature, History, and Politics 1603–1707* (Oxford: Oxford University Press, 2008).
3. T. M. Devine, *Independence or Union: Scotland's Past and Scotland's Present* (London: Allen Lane, 2016), 232, 233.

political leadership was dramatically regendered after the 2014 independence referendum and re-energized after the 2016 European Union referendum, we appear to be in a period of excited waiting; at Holyrood the dominant pro-independence government, and across the country many supporters of independence and of 'Scotland in Europe' (not all of whom define themselves as 'nationalists' or belong to the SNP) anticipate a second independence referendum when circumstances seem right. Supporters of Scottish independence have everything to play for. Just a 6 per cent swing to 'Yes' in September 2014's referendum would have produced a very different result, while in the June 2016 referendum 62 per cent of Scots voted to remain in the European Union.

In England, though sometimes cloaked in the Union flag, a resurgent English nationalism very different from the Scottish civic nationalism of recent decades has led not just to 'Brexit' but to heightened xenophobia and even, in the 2016 stabbing of Labour MP Jo Cox, to political assassination. While the neo-Thatcherite Conservative Theresa May has articulated a determination to oppose 'divisive nationalists in Scotland' and to 'reunite Britain' outside the European Union, it seems to many people in Scotland that the United Kingdom is heading in several wrong directions.[4] Seldom has the topic of the way Scotland, England, and Britain regard one another assumed greater importance.

At such times it is useful to turn to literature, rather than simply to headlines. Any search for explanations behind a modern weakening of unifying 'Britishness' and a resurgent sense of 'Englishness' as well as 'Scottishness' gains from taking a long view. In literature, though far from the only one, the political is a persistent element. To consider 'English literature' or 'Australian literature' or 'Chinese literature' or 'European literature' makes good sense. Yet so does thinking about 'literature' as a whole, and pondering other, more aesthetically nuanced ways of categorizing literary works, such as 'Romantic-era writing' or 'poems in iambic pentameter'. What matters when we categorize literary productions is that we are aware of what we are doing. My first poetry collection, *A Scottish Assembly* (1990), was followed by my prose book *Devolving English Literature* (1992);[5] though I would not like all my work to be seen in purely political terms, I have tried to enhance a sense of Scottish culture appropriate to an independent country, without seeking to deny

---

4. Theresa May, 'We can Make Britain Work for Everyone', *The Times*, 30 June 2016, p. 7; Francis Elliott and Sam Coates, 'May: I Will Reunite Britain', *The Times*, 30 June 2016, p. 1.
5. Robert Crawford, *A Scottish Assembly* (London: Chatto & Windus, 1990).

that Scotland still lacks independence and remains deeply involved in debates about Britishness.

Often, in thinking about English literature, commentators blur the distinction between 'English' meaning 'written in the English language' and 'English' meaning 'emanating from England'. For some—particularly people in dominant cultures—such issues may seem trivial, confined to what Deleuze and Gauttari call 'minor literatures' and relating to the narcissism of small differences.[6] Even Hugh MacDiarmid mocked the sort of 'members o' | St Andrew's Societies' who wrote to the papers complaining about the 'use o' England whar the UK's meent'.[7] Yet differences between the use of the words 'England' and 'Britain', and a slipperiness in the use of the term 'English' (not least when it comes to 'English Literature') hint at a deep-running aspect of the literature and culture of England that everyone interested in English literature and the politics of the British Union must address.

The championing of Britishness by post-1707 Scottish writers including Tobias Smollett, James Thomson, Walter Scott, and (as the last of this line) John Buchan is a familiar, if dated, trope. More striking but less remarked on is the fact that the literary articulation of Britishness has interested almost no major English-born imaginative writer. Though Rivka Swenson in her recent study of 'the idea of Unionism' shrewdly reminds us that Francis Bacon and Daniel Defoe pondered issues of union, for these English authors the British Union was but a passing literary concern.[8] To understand the full and lasting failure to develop a literary identity of Britishness in England is to comprehend why today's British identity is so problematic, and why it seems so likely that sooner or later Scotland will leave the Union. After William Camden's *Britannia* (a Latin work of 1586 that was Englished in 1610 and is now read only by specialist scholars), no major creative writers from England have engaged in sustained imaginative projects to articulate Britishness, and very few have engaged in a detailed way with Scotland.

This chapter concentrates on the three most lasting and widely read English literary representations of Scotland during the period of 'Britishness'; that *Macbeth*, Samuel Johnson's *A Journey to the Western Islands of Scotland*, and Virginia Woolf's *To the Lighthouse* are the *only* three really widely read and

---

6. Gilles Deleuze and Félix Guattari, *Kafka: Towards a Minor Literature*, trans. Dana Polan (Minneapolis: University of Minnesota Press, 1986).

7. Hugh MacDiarmid, *Collected Poems* (New York: Macmillan, 1962), 76.

8. Rivka Swenson, *Essential Scots and the Idea of Unionism in Anglo-Scottish Literature, 1603–1832* (Lewisburg, PA: Bucknell University Press, 2016), 25–66.

canonical literary works from England that deal with Scotland is both remarkable and revealing. *Macbeth* (a drama that can be read in the context of the Union of the Crowns) and Johnson's *Journey* (a work illuminated by the historical contexts of the Union of the Parliaments and the Jacobite Rebellions) present Scotland as broken, ruined, even dangerous. For Shakespeare and Johnson, the Scots are often disturbingly alien; Scotland can advance only if it adopts English models. In part, such representations are countered by the topographical prose of Defoe's now little-read 1724–6 *Tour through the Whole Island of Great Britain*, but Defoe too favours a model of English domination. In the wake of *Macbeth* and Johnson's *Journey*, no major nineteenth-century novels by English writers are set in Scotland, but the Scotophilia of poets from Wordsworth to Clough and Hopkins presents a northern nation whose otherness and wildness can have a radical political edge. Ultimately, this plays into the hands of Scottish nationalist-inclined writers. Woolf's *To the Lighthouse* avoids the propagandistic elements present in *Macbeth* and Johnson's *Journey*, but presents in a different way what is very much England's Scotland.

The world's best-known extended literary work about Scotland was written by England's most celebrated author. Deservedly, *Macbeth* is widely termed (with a certain superstitious wariness) 'the Scottish play'. *Macbeth* is not solely about Scotland, but the condition of Scotland is essential to it, and it has conditioned how Scotland is perceived. There has been some considerable examination of Shakespeare's Scotland, but the scrutiny has been carried out sporadically. Contributors to Willy Maley and Andrew Murphy's 2004 co-edited collection of essays *Shakespeare and Scotland* (the modern standard work) seem unaware of Sir James Fergusson's 1957 *Shakespeare's Scotland*, while insightful comments by Terry Hawkes about Shakespeare in the light of the rise of Scottish nationalism, and about Shakespeare's perceived ' "Englishing" ' of Scotland, Ireland, and Wales, have had too little impact on Scottish literary studies.[9] Critics and commentators on Scottish literature can focus too narrowly on their topic, rather than surveying it within wider international contexts—contexts including literature from England.

9. Willy Maley and Andrew Murphy (eds), *Shakespeare and Scotland* (Manchester: Manchester University Press, 2004); Sir James Fergusson, *Shakespeare's Scotland* (Edinburgh: T. Nelson, 1957); Terence Hawkes, *That Shakespherian Rag: Essays on a Critical Process* (London: Methuen, 1986), 121; Terence Hawkes, *Shakespeare in the Present* (London: Routledge, 2002), 143.

While there should not be *one* distinctively nuanced Scottish view of English literature (there need to be several), it is surely a difficulty if there sometimes seem to be *none*. Part of this problem is explained by the 'Scottish invention of English literature' as a university subject. Its pioneers, including Adam Smith and Hugh Blair, liked to champion Anglocentric values; but, alert to Classical and modern European literatures, they did not only do that, and, in any case, their Anglocentric emphases waned in Scotland some time ago. In England, however, such Anglocentric emphases complemented all too easily the rise of 'Eng. Lit.' in universities, and so, even today, Scottish literature courses in England are revealingly few.[10] Just as there is a need for a deeper understanding of Scottish literature in England, so it is time for Scottish literary studies to pay more attention to English literature, and not least to what I call here England's Scotland.

Famously, some years after the composition of *Macbeth*, Shakespeare's contemporary Ben Jonson walked to Scotland to converse with William Drummond of Hawthornden; Jonson praised the Union of the Crowns in a masque but also went on to co-author the play *Eastward Ho*, which evidently ridiculed the Scots. For every reader who knows something about Jonson's attitudes to Scotland, there are a thousand familiar with *Macbeth*; yet scholars of Scottish literature have paid surprisingly little attention to the Scottish play in terms of its relationship with Scottish, English, and British politics. Perhaps as a result, its assumptions about Scotland have been all the more influential, shaping discourse about Scotland not just in later English and Scottish writing, but around the world.

Though there is no hard evidence that he visited Scotland, Shakespeare read about it in Raphael Holinshed's *Chronicles* and, probably, in George Buchanan's *Historia*. The 'Mac' alone in the title of his play would have been enough to identify *Macbeth* as Scottish in a London whose royal court had so recently been modified by an influx of Scots following James VI of Scotland's accession to the throne of England in 1603, after the death of Queen Elizabeth. The word 'Scotland' is not uttered by *Macbeth*'s very first speakers, but the opening scenes articulate Scottishness: the first people's names uttered are 'Macbeth' (1.1.7) and 'Macdonwald...from the western isles' (1.2.9, 12); a little later Duncan is hailed as 'King of Scotland' (1.2.28).[11]

---

10. Crawford, *Devolving English Literature*, ch. 1; Robert Crawford (ed.), *The Scottish Invention of English Literature* (Cambridge: Cambridge University Press, 1998).
11. William Shakespeare, *Macbeth*, ed. Kenneth Muir (London: Methuen, 1979), is the text to which act, scene, and line numbers in my chapter refer.

Through early mention of 'Kernes and Gallowglasses' (1.2.13) and 'Norweyan' (1.2.50), this Scotland is linked to Ireland and Norway, exoticizing it before there is any talk of 'England'. The words 'Thane' (1.2.46), 'Cawdor' (1.2.54) and 'Fife' (1.2.49) heighten notes of cultural difference that would have struck seventeenth-century English audiences at least as much as they do modern ones. Most emphatically, Scotland is made strange by the play's famous opening scene, whose only characters are witches. From the outset this is a drama of 'thunder' and 'lightning', 'rain' and 'battle', all associated with the distinctively Scottish word 'Macbeth', and with a destabilizing 'hurlyburly' that upends expectations and values:

> ALL. Fair is foul, and foul is fair:
> Hover through the fog and filthy air.[12]

So, immediately, Scotland is linked to perverse inversions, wildness, and disorder. A study in both individual and group psychology, but also seemingly written to psychologize a nation, *Macbeth* may have been angled in part to fascinate a king preoccupied with witches and witch trials; it was, too, authored in a way likely to unsettle a monarch whose love of divine order matched his keen sense of the divine right of kings. An accomplished poet, James VI sets his sonnet 'The Argument' at the head of his treatise on kingship, *Basilicon Doron*. First published in an elite, limited edition in Edinburgh in 1599, this was soon reprinted in a new, widely read edition in London in 1603. Thanks to marked interest in this Scottish king who was taking over the English throne, it was rapidly translated into French, German, Dutch, and Danish:

> God giues not Kings the style of *Gods* in vaine,
> For on his throne his Scepter do they swey:
> And as their subjects ought them to obey,
> So Kings should feare and serue their God againe.
> If then ye would enjoy a happie raigne,
> Obserue the Statutes of your Heauenly King...[13]

Macbeth violates all such statutes. Scotland in *Macbeth* is a land of mayhem whose divine-right monarch is murdered. A topic of considerable interest among Renaissance Europe's political theorists including Buchanan, regicide was much discussed in Britain. During Shakespeare's early 20s, it was not

12. *Macbeth*, 1.1.11–12.
13. King James VI, *Basilicon Doron*, ed. James Craigie, 2 vols (Edinburgh: Blackwood for the Scottish Text Society, 1944–50), i. 4.

Scotland but England that had executed a divine-right monarch: the killing of James's mother, Mary, Queen of Scots, by order of Queen Elizabeth at the English castle of Fotheringay, was the most shocking violation of all that her son James's *Basilicon Doron* sought to uphold. More recently, since James's accession to the English throne, the 1605 Gunpowder Plot had been an attempt by English Catholics to assassinate King James at the Houses of Parliament. Making much of Shakespeare's probable detailed knowledge of this attempted murder of a king, James Shapiro has pointed out in passing how *Macbeth* contains (in its protagonist's vision in a magic mirror) 'a clear nod to the anticipated Union'.[14] Yet a crucial point ignored by commentators is that, in a brilliant piece of political propaganda, Shakespeare transfers all ideas of regicide from England to Scotland, where, during Shakespeare's infancy, James's father, Henry Darnley, King of Scots, had been murdered in 1567. Though England, not Scotland, was the country most involved with regicide in Shakespeare's lifetime, the dramatist turns to older Scottish history and presents in his medieval Scottish play a vision of a country that is ruinously riven, unnaturally governed, supernaturally disordered, and can be saved only by English orderliness and intervention.

The daring of this is striking: the play has no suggestion that England might be a regicidal place. Sometimes across his oeuvre Shakespeare presents England as a land of internecine and king-killing violence, sometimes as a haven of delight; in his sole 'Scottish play', however, Scotland is wholly a zone of chaos, the topographical incarnation of regicide. The witches' heath, Macbeth's castle, Birnam Wood, and Dunsinane are all locations of horrific disorder. There may be disagreement over whether the word in the line 'We have scotch'd the snake, not killed it' (3.2.13) should be 'scorch'd' or 'scotch'd', but appropiately in *Macbeth* the very word 'scotch' may pun on violent wounding as well as on Scottish nationality. *Macbeth*'s Scotland is a wounded place whose balm can come only in the form of English aid. As an anonymous lord tells Lennox,

> The son of Duncan,
> From whom this tyrant holds the due of birth,
> Lives in the English court; and is receiv'd
> Of the most pious Edward with such grace,
> That the malevolence of fortune nothing
> Takes from his high respect. Thither Macduff

14. James Shapiro, *1606: William Shakespeare and the Year of 'Lear'* (London: Faber and Faber, 2015), 243.

> Is gone to pray the holy King, upon his aid
> To wake Northumberland, and warlike Siward;
> That, by the help of these (with Him above
> To ratify the work), we may again
> Give to our tables meat, sleep to our nights,
> Free from our feasts and banquets bloody knives,
> Do faithful homage, and receive free honours,
> All which we pine for now.[15]

The English King is Edward the Confessor, a monarch of holiness, piety, and grace: a quasi-divine, divine-right ruler who is everything that Macbeth is not—and everything that King James I of England aspired to be. Only through this English monarch, Edward, can Scotland be redeemed from ruin and, to use Macduff's word 'dolour' (4.3.8). Malcolm's saving grace must come from 'gracious England' (4.3.43). Malcolm in that same scene thinks of himself as lacking 'the king-becoming graces' (4.3.91), and lists them; while at the English court, he discovers in himself both his own flaws and, eventually, what may make him 'fit to govern' (4.3.101). During his 'here-remain in England' (4.3.148) he has seen the 'healing benediction' (4.3.156) that the English monarch, 'full of grace' (4.3.159), can bestow upon his people.

All this contrasts absolutely with the situation in Scotland, its awfulness summed up in the famous exchange between Macduff and Rosse:

> MACDUFF. Stands Scotland where it did?
> ROSSE.   Alas, poor country!
> Almost afraid to know itself. It cannot
> Be call'd our mother, but our grave; where nothing,
> But who knows nothing, is once seen to smile;
> Where sighs, and groans, and shrieks that rent the air
> Are made, not mark'd; where violent sorrow seems
> A modern ecstacy: the dead man's knell
> Is there scarce ask'd for who; and good men's lives
> Expire before the flowers in their caps,
> Dying or ere they sicken.[16]

In this hell-scape, the tyrannous usurper Macbeth's later dismissal of the English as 'epicures' (5.3.8), or his wish to 'scour these English hence' (5.3.56) can appear only as dreadful and perverse. Salvation comes with a rightful king who has learned how to be a king in England. After the defeat of

---

15. *Macbeth*, 3.6.24–37.   16. *Macbeth*, 4.3.164–73.

Macbeth, in the play's final speech Malcolm's first royal act is one of clear Anglicization: he gets rid of one of the Scottish play's most distinctive Scottish-sounding words (ironically it is an Anglo-Saxon word, but it would have sounded exotic to seventeenth-century English theatregoers), substituting instead an English diction far more familiar to the original audience:

> My Thanes and kinsmen,
> Henceforth be Earls; the first that ever Scotland
> In such an honour nam'd.[17]

The play's last line ends with Malcolm inviting his followers 'to see us crown'd at Scone', which sounds very Scottish; yet, as early—and later—audiences would have known, the Stone of Scone or Stone of Destiny had been pillaged from Scotland by another Edward, the 'Hammer of the Scots', in 1296, and had long resided at Westminster Abbey as the Coronation Stone. Indeed, it was the very stone on which King James VI of Scotland had recently been crowned as King James I of England, beginning the process of his Anglicization. So, though the mention of 'Scone' might sound like a reassertion of Scottish power at the very end of the play, it can be heard also as a final reminder of Scotland's assimilation to English values—a symbol of England's Scotland. In *Macbeth*, as in different ways in *King Lear* and *Henry V*, Shakespeare produces a masterpiece one of whose aspects is propagandistic: it presents the evidence for English assimilation, guidance, and dominance. The 'Scottish play' shows the need for England's Scotland.

One and three-quarter centuries later, after the Union of Parliaments in 1707 and after the 1746 defeat at Culloden of those 'rebellious Scots' mentioned in a verse for a time attached to Britain's national anthem, Britishness may have seemed much more fully developed; yet to England's greatest eighteenth-century man of letters Scotland still required English assimilation if it were to develop from ruin to civilized prosperity. Though Samuel Johnson's *A Journey to the Western Islands of Scotland* (1775) is substantially a volume detailing his travels in the Hebrides, it also chronicles his progress across the Scottish mainland, and was read as a book about Scotland. Published at the height of the Scottish Enlightenment (it appeared the year before Adam Smith published *The Wealth of Nations* and recounts a tour

---

17. *Macbeth*, 5.9.28–30.

made while David Hume—whom Johnson detested and omits from his *Journey*—was still alive in the Scottish capital), Johnson's volume gives a view of Scotland that continually emphasizes the country as broken and primitive. Johnson skirts over the greatest intellectual and cultural centres of what is now known as the Scottish Enlightenment.

In his book's second paragraph Johnson dismisses Edinburgh as 'a city too well known to admit description'; yet, unless one excepts Daniel Defoe, none of the great English men of letters had so far described it.[18] Towards his conclusion, Johnson revisits Edinburgh, only to gloss over most of its intellectual and other achievements: 'We now returned to *Edinburgh*, where I passed some days with men of learning, whose names want no advancement from my commemoration, or with women of elegance, which perhaps disclaims a pedant's praise'.[19] The only Edinburgh institution of which he gives an account is 'a college of the deaf and dumb'. Johnson writes humanely about this 'subject of philosophical curiosity', but his discussion of this place where the physically impaired must learn articulation follows after (and is in the context of) a paragraph where he broods on the general need for the Scots to learn correct Anglicized articulation, ridding themselves of markers of '*Scotch*' linguistic and cultural difference, and assimilating to the assumed superiority of English standards:

> The conversation of the *Scots* grows every day less unpleasing to the *English*; their peculiarities wear fast away; their dialect is likely to become in half a century provincial and rustic, even to themselves. The great, the learned, the ambitious, and the vain, all cultivate the *English* phrase, and the *English* pronunciation, and in splendid companies *Scotch* is not much heard, except now and then from an old Lady.[20]

With these words Johnson aligns himself with the Anglocentric emphases of such teachers of rhetoric and belles lettres as Smith, Blair, and Robert Watson, all of whom stressed the importance of Anglocentric linguistic propriety. Robert Burns would counter that attitude with his 1787 *Poems, Chiefly in the Scottish Dialect*, following on from Burns's admired poetic predecessor, Robert Fergusson, who satirized Johnson in both Scots and English. However, in Johnson's *Journey* the English man of letters remarks on the Scots tongue not with a nod to Smith, Blair, or Hume, but in the

18. Samuel Johnson, *A Journey to the Western Islands of Scotland*, ed. R. W. Chapman (Oxford: Oxford University Press, 1974), 3.
19. Johnson, *A Journey to the Western Islands of Scotland*, 147.
20. Johnson, *A Journey to the Western Islands of Scotland*, 147.

context of the disabled people of Thomas Braidwood's school for the deaf and dumb. By association, the Scottish dialect is presented as a disability. Likewise, having described how Braidwood's school educates the disabled in such matters as writing and arithmetic, Johnson continues, 'after having seen the deaf taught arithmetic, who would be afraid to cultivate the *Hebrides*?'[21] Gaelic and Hebridean culture, too, are linked to disability which must be cured through Anglocentric cultivation.

If Johnson gives Enlightenment Edinburgh short shrift, then Adam Smith's Glasgow fares little better. Johnson mentions it in passing just twice, noting in half a sentence near the beginning of his *Journey* that '*Glasgow*, though it no longer has an archbishop, has risen beyond its original state by the opulence of its traders',[22] and then spending just over a page on the city towards the end of his book. Here again his tactic is to maintain that 'to describe a city so much frequented as *Glasgow*, is unnecessary',[23] though one wonders just how many of the citizens of Johnson's literary London had ever set eyes on or read much about Glasgow in Defoe or elsewhere. The Glaswegian institutions that interest Johnson fleetingly are the cathedral ('*Gothick*' and a rare survivor of 'the rage of Reformation') and Glasgow University. Johnson opines that Glasgow University's session dates make more sense than the term dates of Oxford and Cambridge; however, he leaves his reader in no doubt about the inferiority of the Scottish universities when it comes to intellectual content and style:

> Yet when I have allowed to the universities of *Scotland* a more rational distribution of time, I have given them, so far as my inquiries have informed me, all that they may claim. The students, for the most part, go thither boys, and depart before they are men; they carry with them little fundamental knowledge, and therefore the superstructure cannot be lofty. The grammar schools are not generally well supplied; for the character of a school-master being the less honourable than in *England*, is seldom accepted by men who are capable to adorn it, and where the school has been deficient, the college can effect little.
>
> Men bred in the universities of *Scotland* cannot be expected to be often decorated with the splendours of ornamental erudition, but they obtain a mediocrity of knowledge, between learning and ignorance, not adequate to the purposes of common life, which is, I believe, very widely diffused among them, and which countenanced in general by a national combination so invidious,

21. Johnson, *A Journey to the Western Islands of Scotland*, 148.
22. Johnson, *A Journey to the Western Islands of Scotland*, 21.
23. Johnson, *A Journey to the Western Islands of Scotland*, 145.

that their friends cannot defend it, and actuated in particulars by a spirit of
enterprise, so vigorous, that their enemies are constrained to praise it, enables
them to find, or to make their way to employment, riches, and distinction.[24]

This last sentence pays Scottish university graduates at best a very back-
handed compliment. Johnson perceives Scotland has a markedly different
educational tradition from that of England's private schools, grammar schools,
and Oxbridge; like many researchers today, he is shocked by how young
eighteenth-century Scottish university students were. Yet, rather than giving
any deeper consideration to a system that had educated men such as David
Hume and the Common Sense philosophers, he denigrates it in language
sometimes linked to his dislike of Presbyterian plainness (no 'splendours of
ornamental erudition' there) and throughout bonded to an assumption that
English mores are and should be the benchmark. Johnson simply does not
understand the Scottish Enlightenment, and has no wish to showcase it to his
readers when he can snipe at the poetry of Ossian instead. His version of
England's Scotland presents the latter country as crude, primitive, and poet-
ically spurious even when Scotland was at its most intellectually splendid.

So, passing over Edinburgh and Glasgow, Johnson devotes far more
attention to eighteenth-century St Andrews. Hardly celebrated as a hotbed
of Enlightenment genius, St Andrews eminently fits Johnson's presentation of
Caledonia. St Andrews University merely 'subsists'. Johnson pays lip service
to past glories: St Andrews was where 'philosophy was formerly taught by
Buchanan', that great Renaissance Latin poet, dramatist, historian, and thinker
whom Johnson admired. However, instead of suggesting how Reformation
iconoclastic energy such as that in Buchanan's elegy for Calvin might fuel artistic work, Johnson sees the Scottish Reformation only as ruination. St Andrews
offers 'ruins of ancient magnificence' that 'have been till very lately so much
neglected'. To blame is 'the tumult and violence of Knox's reformation' with its
'ruffians'.[25] Johnson sees the Scottish Reformation solely in terms of 'epidemical
enthusiasm', which 'by trade and intercourse with England, is now visibly abat-
ing'. St Andrews for Johnson epitomizes both Scottish culture and persistent rot:

> It is surely not without just reproach, that a nation, of which the commerce is
> hourly extending, and the wealth increasing, denies any participation of
> its prosperity to its literary societies; and while its merchants or its nobles are
> building palaces, suffers its universities to moulder into dust.[26]

24. Johnson, *A Journey to the Western Islands of Scotland*, 145–6.
25. Johnson, *A Journey to the Western Islands of Scotland*, 5–6.
26. Johnson, *A Journey to the Western Islands of Scotland*, 6–7.

While 'Saint Andrews' is 'a place eminently adapted to study and education', Johnson sees in it 'an university declining, a college alienated, and a church profaned and hastening to the ground'. St Andrews makes manifest 'atrocious ravages'; Johnson associates 'Knox and his followers' with 'the irruptions of Alaric and the Goths'. This is a site struck by barbarity: 'to see it pining in decay and struggling for life, fills the mind with mournful images and ineffectual wishes'.[27] St Andrews is the most significant topographical set piece, which establishes Johnson's attitude towards Scottish history, culture, and prospects right at the start of his *Journey*. Ruined, in dire need of renovation, its only hope lies in benefiting from 'the Union'.[28] This is England's Scotland with a vengeance. Johnson's portrayal of Scotland continues on the same trajectory.

So, for instance, his famous comments on Scotland's perceived treelessness develop just after he leaves St Andrews: 'From the bank of the Tweed to St Andrews I had never seen a single tree, which I did not believe to have grown up far within the present century.' This implies that the Union of 1707 has brought Scotland even its forestation. Johnson contends that 'it may be doubted whether before the Union any man between Edinburgh and England had ever seen a tree'.[29] Though he goes on to write with real interest and sometimes sympathy about supposedly primitive Highland culture, Johnson's sidelining of the Scottish Enlightenment and his presentation of Scotland as a place in dire need of English influence and support in every area from ecclesiastical affairs and universities to arboriculture establishes his Scotland as attuned to that presented to English and other audiences by Shakespeare's *Macbeth*.

Revealingly, *Macbeth* is the first English literary work Johnson mentions in his *Journey*; he remarks on travelling along the road near Forres 'on which *Macbeth* heard the fatal prediction', which related to that Scottish king 'promises of kingdoms'.[30] This allusion is to Shakespeare's revealing to Macbeth a lineage of monarchs stretching towards the eventual Union of the Crowns in 1603. Macbeth, however, is linked by Johnson less to eventual monarchical Britishness than to the perennial theme of Scottish ruin: at Inverness, Johnson records, 'is a castle, called the castle of Macbeth, the walls of which are yet standing'; the implication again is that this is a ruin, and

27. Johnson, *A Journey to the Western Islands of Scotland*, 8.
28. Johnson, *A Journey to the Western Islands of Scotland*, 9.
29. Johnson, *A Journey to the Western Islands of Scotland*, 9.
30. Johnson, *A Journey to the Western Islands of Scotland*, 22.

both *Macbeth* and Macbeth's castle can be taken as synecdoches for the ruinous state of Scotland. Stands Scotland where it did? For readers of Johnson's *Journey*, the answer is manifestly Yes.

Though Johnson's Caledonian travels have been presented perceptively by Pat Rogers as a British alternative to the continental Grand Tour, and attempts have been made to defend Johnson's attitudes to Scotland and the Scots, my impression is that students who read the *Journey* today—be they Scottish, English, or from other countries—are increasingly conscious of it as a work of pointed prejudice and resist Johnson's attitudes towards Scottish culture.[31] In *Devolving English Literature* I presented Boswell's life of Johnson as a biography of Britishness, part of that Scottish effort to articulate through a deliberately 'British literature' a unionist identity that remained strong from Boswell's day until the era of John Buchan; but Johnson's is not a work that articulates such Britishness. Tellingly, the words 'Scotch', 'Scots', and 'English' occur frequently in Johnson's *Journey*, but 'Briton' and British' are not used at all, while the noun 'Britain' features on just four occasions. Johnson does not share Boswell's investment in Britishness; instead, what he presents through a haze of prejudice is vehemently England's Scotland.

Astonishingly, no major English novel of the eighteenth or nineteenth centuries is set north of the Anglo-Scottish border. This again reveals something about England's lack of imaginative investment in British identity. Whereas Scottish novelists including Smollett and Scott joined Boswell in articulating Britishness as distinct from Englishness, Britishness just was not something that excited England's novelists in their creative work. A relatively minor exception to this rule might appear to be the English writer Jane Porter's bestselling *The Scottish Chiefs*, a historical novel about William Wallace that culminates with the battle of Bannockburn and whose publication pre-dates Scott's prose fictions; as I have argued in *Bannockburns: Scottish Independence and Literary Imagination, 1314–2014*, this English-authored novel is an important link between the popular writings of William Hamilton (who recast Blind Hary's Wallace epic in a way that fired up Robert Burns) and Hollywood's *Braveheart*.[32] Porter, however, is hardly a major English novelist, and her book is not an articulation of British identity.

31. Pat Rogers, *Johnson and Boswell: The Transit of Caledonia* (Oxford: Oxford University Press, 1995).
32. Robert Crawford, *Bannockburns: Scottish Independence and Literary Imagination, 1314–2014* (Edinburgh: Edinburgh University Press, 2014), 106–26.

One can look in vain through the fictions of Austen, the Brontës, Dickens, George Eliot, Gaskell, Gissing, Hardy, Thackeray, Trollope, and all the canonical novelists of nineteenth-century England for a single novel set north of the border. It is almost as if, with the exception of the occasional curiosity such as Ann Radcliffe's *The Castles of Athlin and Dunbayne*, for the canonical nineteenth-century English novel Scotland does not exist, and Britishness (as distinct from Englishness) has scarcely any meaning. On the relatively rare occasions when Scottish characters do feature in well-known English fiction during the era of the zenith of the British Empire—for instance, Hardy's Donald Farfrae in *The Mayor of Casterbridge*—they serve principally as foils for the major players. In poetry from England, post-Ossianic Romanticism and the success of Burns and Byron spurred a marked scotophilia in Wordsworth, Coleridge, Keats, and other Romantics, but the only Victorian poems from England that are set in Scotland and approach greatness are Clough's celebration of radical freedom in *The Bothie of Toperna-Fuosich* (1848) and Hopkins's marvellously energetic 'Inversnaid'.[33]

In the twentieth century, English creative writers pay less and less attention to Scotland. The sole major English novel set there is *To the Lighthouse*, but Woolf's Scotland scarcely masks her preoccupation with English behaviours. David Bradshaw builds on Hermione Lee's point that Woolf spent childhood holidays in Talland House overlooking a lighthouse near St Ives in Cornwall, while Woolf's mother wrote for her children a story featuring boats, fishermen, and 'a long pier which ran out to sea and far off, rising straight out of the sea was a white lighthouse on whose windows the sun was burning fiercely'; some years later, Woolf 'read with great relish the little leatherbound set of Lockhart's *Life of Scott* Leslie [her father] gave her (where she found "his diary of a voyage to the lighthouses on the Scotch coast" '—a voyage that included Skye).[34] Given these associations, it may not be so surprising that when Woolf authored *To the Lighthouse*, a novel that draws heavily on memories of Cornwall and her parents, she chose—perhaps to avoid over-biographical readings—to set it somewhere quite different, and selected Skye. At this time (1925–7) Woolf had hardly visited Scotland, and

---

33. On Clough's poem and Scotland, see Robert Crawford, *The Modern Poet* (Oxford: Oxford University Press, 2001), 113–41.
34. Hermione Lee, *Virginia Woolf* (London: Vintage, 1997), 28, 142 (quoting Woolf); see also David Bradshaw's edition of *To the Lighthouse* (World's Classics; Oxford: Oxford University Press, 2006).

had never been near Skye. That most topographically stunning of Scottish islands had attracted Turner and generations of tourists; striking paintings of its mountainous landscape by Wycliffe Egginton were exhibited at London's Fine Art Society in late 1925.[35] *To the Lighthouse*, however, has no set-piece landscape descriptions. Its Skye is largely tokenistic; its novelist eschews the words 'loch' or 'Cuillins' or 'Gaelic' or 'ferry', and refers only in generalized terms to 'the Lighthouse', 'the town', or 'the fishing village'.[36] The specific place names of *To the Lighthouse* are predominantly English.

In Woolf's day, Scotland viewed from London could still seem an other-world best known from a few familiar books. During the summer of the year when she began her novel, an advertisement in the London *Times* headed 'Skye to Schiehallion' maintained:

> The map of Scotland is a trumpet call. Ordnance survey? Not even a Government office can prevent it from being a song. The contours are like music. Your feet beat time to the printed word.
>
> The names linger like notes. You heard them in childhood, the mighty names of Scotland. They flamed in the page of history; they gave poetry its thunder. "Glamis thou art and Cawdor." They vibrate in the memory.
>
> Follow up the name. Turn old sounds to new sights. Realise romance. Get on the heels of doomed Macbeth. From the haunted heath of Forres to the keep of Inverness. From Inverness to fatal Dunsinane.[37]

Woolf's Scotland is neither that of advertising copywriters, nor that of Macbeth, but nor is her Skye very substantial. Jane Goldman's *'With You in the Hebrides'* makes a sustained case for Woolf's engagement with aspects of Scottish culture, and it is clear she had read (or had read to her) a good number of Scotland-related works, including the entire Waverley Novels and Johnson's *Journey*.[38] Some recent critics argue Woolf's Scotland is more thoroughly presented than her early audiences—and many readers today— assume. David Bradshaw mentions Woolf's noting that on Skye 'the fishing is bad, unemployment is a fact of life and the islanders are emigrating', but such an awareness (even in a novel that mocks a guide-book approach) is a very general, guide-book awareness.[39] Richard Zumkhawala-Cook too

35. 'Art Exhibitions', *The Times*, 16 November 1925, p. 12.
36. Virginia Woolf, *To the Lighthouse* (1927; repr. Harmondsworth: Penguin Books, 1964), 12, 13.
37. 'Skye to Schiehallion' (LMS advertisement), *The Times*, 5 June 1925, p. 18.
38. Jane Goldman, *'With You in the Hebrides': Virginia Woolf and Scotland* (London: Cecil Woolf, 2013).
39. David Bradshaw, 'The Socio-Political Vision of the Novels', in Sue Roe and Susan Sellers (eds), *The Cambridge Companion to Virginia Woolf* (Cambridge: Cambridge University Press, 2000), 200.

sees social concern manifested in this novel where on Skye 'the English enjoy leisure time and the Scots serve them'; Zumkhawala-Cook has an interesting argument that, because it lingers on Skye while Mrs Ramsay dies elsewhere, the novel is one whose principal characters 'in the end are shown to be tourists; the novel, however, is not'. Yet, surely, and even if Goldman and Bradshaw modify it, there is much truth in Zumkhawala-Cook's contention that 'the narrative reproduces what even in this time period would have been a well-worn cliché of Scotland as both the literal and psychic escape from English modern life and the exotic backdrop for the main characters' personal, philosophical and aesthetic contemplations'.[40] Such clichés may have been promoted not just by non-Scottish writers but also at times by Scottish ones from Alexander Smith in *A Summer in Skye* to Fiona Macleod and Mrs Kennedy-Fraser, several of whose Skye songs featured in BBC broadcast concerts when Woolf was at work on her novel. That Woolf was conditioned by exoticizing clichés of Skye is reinforced, Zumkhawala-Cook points out, by Mrs Ramsay's feeling that on that island she and her friends and family are ' "three thousand miles" away from their English lives'; just such a sensation was felt by Woolf when in 1938 she eventually visited Skye and wrote vividly to her Scottish-born friend Duncan Grant that it was 'remote as Samoa; deserted; prehistoric'.[41]

Rather than lambasting Woolf for failing to match the Scottish cultural fidelity of work by such contemporaries as Nancy Brysson Morrison or Lewis Grassic Gibbon, or exaggerating her Scottish filiations, it is better to admit that her Scotland in *To the Lighthouse* is largely a fictional device, a distancing technique. Woolf's incorporation into her book of references to Scott's *The Antiquary* indicates not only that Scott (on whose work she had written the year before she began *To the Lighthouse*) was a lifelong presence to her but also that his Scottish fiction of thick description, however impressive and moving, is exactly what she is attempting to avoid. Her allusions to Scott signal, perhaps, that she is attempting to match him; but at least as much they hint that her project is far removed from his. For Woolf's generation, Scott remained the emblematic, pre-eminent, Scottish novelist— a favourite of their parents if not of their own generation. Whatever else

40. Richard Zumkhawala-Cook, 'Tae the Lichthoose: Scotland and the Problem of the Local', in Diana Roger and Madelyn Detloff (eds), *Virginia Woolf: Art, Education and Internationalism* (Clemson, SC: Clemson University Press, 2008), 62, 57.
41. Zumkhawala-Cook, 'Tae the Lichthoose', 57 (quoting Woolf).

it is, *To the Lighthouse* marks a break with Scott's fictional techniques. Woolf's Skye, her Scotland, is an English modernist novelist's fictional device in a novel whose principal interests lie elsewhere.

And so it is that the sole great English novel to be set in Scotland has strikingly little to say about the place. Goldman quotes Woolf from *Three Guineas*: 'As a woman I have no country. As a woman I want no country. As a woman, my country is the whole world.'[42] This is, as Goldman says, a 'ringing' declaration; but it is also one much easier to make because it comes not from a refugee or a colonized subject but from someone who has a powerful country and financial security. Rather than seeing Woolf as defined solely by gender, it is worth seeing her as the author of many meditations on England and Englishness produced at the same time as Joyce was interrogating Ireland and Irishnesss and MacDiarmid and writers of the Scottish Renaissance movement were interrogating Scotland and Scottishness. If *Mrs Dalloway* and *Orlando* may be among Woolf's most searching examinations of England and Englishness, then *To the Lighthouse* too has its attention directed principally to the English. In that sense, at least, its Scotland is England's Scotland.

Again, for W. H. Auden and George Orwell, both of whom (unlike Woolf) lived in twentieth-century Scotland for extended periods, the country is at best a backdrop for English concerns. In Scotland Auden writes *The Orators*, his *English Study*, and Orwell authors *Nineteen Eighty-Four*. In their treatment of Scotland as 'other' and, even more, in their frequently ignoring it all together, a succession of England's greatest writers expose how much the literary articulation of Britishness is a Scottish-driven phenomenon, one that has never gained much traction in the literature of England. England, not Britain, is England's focus. If one of England's greatest eighteenth-century immigrant writers, James Thomson, penned 'Rule, Britannia' and celebrated Britishness, then for its greatest twentieth-century immigrant poet, T. S. Eliot, as for so many native-born English writers, when it came to what might have been regarded as the matter of Britain, it was very clear, as Eliot puts it in 'Little Gidding', that 'History is now and England'.[43]

---

42. Goldman, '*With You in the Hebrides*', 59.
43. T. S. Eliot, 'Little Gidding', in *The Poems of T. S. Eliot*, ed. Christopher Ricks and Jim McCue, 2 vols (London: Faber and Faber, 2015), i. 208.

16

Postscript
The Strange Death of Literary Unionism

Gerard Carruthers

There is a curious tale to be told about the solipsism of twentieth-century
Scottish literary criticism. Stranger still is the dominance of nationalist
criticism, which is not simply a reaction to British cultural and intellectual 'conditions', but is even—irony of ironies—decidedly English, if not
Anglocentric, in provenance. As I have argued at some length elsewhere, the
ultimate foundational figure in Scotland's distinctive, navel-gazing tradition
of nationalist criticism is—somewhat bizarrely—England's Matthew Arnold
(1822–88).[1] Owing to various pressures in Victorian culture and society, not
least the crisis of faith, most generally a crisis in Christian faith, Arnold
attempted to substitute English Literature for the vacuum left by the redundancy of the Christian scriptures.[2] Central to his project was Arnold's essay
'On the Study of Celtic Literature' (1866), in which he advances his notion
of English poetry comprising 'Celtic' and 'Saxon' characteristics, with a dash
of something 'Roman' thrown in.[3] This last characteristic, one can infer, is a
venerable classical element, a crucial part of Arnold's attempt to cement the

---

1. Gerard Carruthers, *Scottish Literature: A Critical Guide* (Edinburgh: Edinburgh University Press,
   2009), 4–28.
2. See Chris Baldick, *The Social Mission of English Criticism, 1848–1932* (Oxford: Clarendon Press,
   1983), 18–58 and *passim*.
3. Matthew Arnold, *Lectures and Essays in Criticism*, ed. R. H. Super (Ann Arbor, MI: University of
   Michigan Press, 1962), 339–44.

intellectual and cultural respectability of vernacular English Literature as a subject of study. He calculated that plans to promote the study of vernacular English would potentially attract hostility from the well-entrenched university discipline of Classics, where down to the twentieth century the study of great literature (and the ethical issues it embodied) was most naturally housed. These qualities together, implicitly, also offset a 'Germanic' element (presumably to be held at arm's length owing to the growing power and rivalry of Prussia at the time when Arnold was writing). Arnold's mid-Victorian encouragement of Celticism lent permission for a whole raft of Scottish critics to advance a strong Celtic component in their accounts of Scottish literature; and this happens through the latter part of the century and into the next.[4] Race played a crucial part in Arnold's project,[5] and in the gradual transition in Scotland's critical circles from a loosely defined British literature[6] to an emergent study of Scotland's distinctive national literature. Arnold's project of inculcating the teaching 'English Literature', in both schools and universities, was increasingly successful, and witnessed the rise of the English Association, of whose Scottish Branch, James Cruickshanks Smith (1867–1946) was the President when he published 'Some Characteristics of Scots Literature' (a lecture printed in pamphlet form) in 1912. On the topic of Scottish 'humour', Smith opines:

> If humour implies, as it seems to do, some perceived incongruity between points of view, then Scottish humour lies above all in the perception of incongruity between the romantic and the vulgar, the general and the personal, the sacred and the profane. Some of these differences, it is not to be denied, correspond to differences between the Celtic and Saxon temperaments, and in the clash of these temperaments Scottish humour finds one of its choicest fields.[7]

This passage is the crucial missing link between the Arnoldian racial grammar accepted in unproblematic fashion by J. C. Smith, and the most influential text of Scottish literary criticism in the twentieth century: *Scottish Literature:*

4. For instance, a new emphasis upon 'Celticism' can be found in John Ross, *Scottish History and Literature to the Period of Reformation* (Glasgow: J. Maclehose and Sons, 1884), 2 and *passim*; in John Veitch, *The Feeling for Nature in Scottish Poetry* (Edinburgh: Blackwood, 1887); in Patrick Geddes, 'The Scots Renascence', *Evergreen: A Northern Seasonal*, 1 (Spring 1895), 136–7; in George Douglas, *Scottish Poetry: Drummond of Hawthornden to Fergusson* (Glasgow: J. Maclehose, 1911), 66, 151, and *passim*.
5. F. E. Faverty, *Matthew Arnold the Ethnologist* (Evanston, IL: Northwestern University Press, 1951).
6. Colin Kidd, 'British Literature: The Career of a Concept', *Scottish Literary Review*, 8 (2016), 1–16.
7. J. C. Smith, *Some Characteristics of Scots Literature* (London: English Association, 1912), 5.

Character and Influence (1919) by G. Gregory Smith (1865–1932). Here Gregory Smith coins the notion of the 'Caledonian Antisyzygy', the essential condition of the Scottish literary tradition, effectively a creative tension between the 'polar twins' of 'realism' and 'fantasy'—often in operation together—apparent in Scottish literary texts from at least the medieval period until the nineteenth century.[8] We might, of course, ask the obvious question: do we not in fact find just such a creative dialectic, especially given such generalized qualities as 'realism' and 'fantasy', in literature and other creative art forms everywhere and anywhere? If we examine the underlying motivation for Gregory Smith's 'diagnosis' (precisely what it is, of course, stemming as it does from mass psychology), we discover that it arises from his perception that Scottish literary history, indeed Scottish history generally, is so hopelessly fractured. There is no obvious and continuous one-to-one correspondence between nationhood and a Scottish language. Language use in Scotland, and in its literature, is plural, disjointed, and far from straightforwardly congruent with the nation. Again, this is not particularly uncommon in multinational states, whether sprawling multi-ethnic empires, union states, or even small polyglot states. However, the particular problem that Gregory Smith confronts, we can infer, is that the increasing dominance of English as the language of Britain and its Empire curtails options for untrammelled Scottish self-expression; instead, distinctiveness of expression and the power of the Scots language—cultural as well as political—recede. The hyphenated 'Saxon-Celtic' British identity patented by Arnold provides the template for Smith's Caledonian Antisyzygy; realism is a manifestation of Saxon practicality, fantasy of a Celtic mentality, the twin racial genealogies of a disrupted and divided Scottish identity.[9] Gregory Smith's attempt to couch his division in positive terms (to the extent of providing a catch-all label) really does not cohere, since it is done against the baseline assumption that culture, literary and national, is something ideally that is cogent, and indeed a unitary phenomenon. What he ends up projecting is a rather manic sensibility in Scottish literature that never settles, one that constantly bounces between two 'extremes' of expression: 'realism' and 'fantasy'.

8. G. Gregory Smith, *Scottish Literature: Character and Influence* (London: Macmillan, 1919), 4–27.
9. For the underacknowledged presence of race in modern Scottish culture, see Colin Kidd, 'Teutonist Ethnology and Scottish Nationalist Inhibition, 1780–1880', *Scottish Historical Review*, 74 (1995), 45–68; Kidd, 'Race, Empire and the Limits of Scottish Nationhood', *Historical Journal*, 46 (2003), 873–92.

Nevertheless, Gregory Smith's influential formulation was eagerly appropriated by the magpie-poet and critic Hugh MacDiarmid, who famously
proclaimed himself to 'aye be whaur extremes meet'.[10] The Caledonian
Antisyzygy became MacDiarmid's personal and creative manifesto in his
campaign to revive the Scots language—not without some success—as a
literary medium fit for modernity. The interwar period marked a major
turning point in the history of Scottish literature. The story of Scots-
language literature before MacDiarmid's recasting of it as synthetic Lallans
was happily enmeshed in the experience of Britishness and of Britain's
imperial expansion overseas. As far back as the eighteenth century, Scots and
English had been championed by antiquary-philologists as Saxon–British
cognates. The emergence of an antithetical relationship of Scots and English
was largely a twentieth-century phenomenon. Indeed, MacDiarmid entirely
reconceptualized the relationship of Scottish literature to the post-1707
British state. Scotland, a partner nation composed of enthusiastic imperial-
ists, was reimagined as an oppressed colony. The practitioners and critics of
Scottish literature embarked on a process of forgetting Scotland's complicity
in Britishness and Empire.

However, there were problems immediately ahead. As MacDiarmid's
erstwhile ally in the Scottish cultural 'renaissance' from the 1920s, Edwin
Muir (1887–1959), comes to realize, the Antisyzygy is ultimately delusional:
an attempt to make a virtue out of a weakness. Following the publication of
his *Scott and Scotland: The Predicament of the Scottish Writer* (1936), Muir found
himself in bitter conflict with MacDiarmid. This was because Muir's book
argued that writing in Scots was no longer viable, that Scots lacked the
capacity to be the language of a modern, national literature, for it had dwin-
dled in utility and versatility during the eras of Reformation and Union and
was now little more than the displaced, withered ghost of what *once*—in the
bygone medieval period—had been a national language. An arch-disciple of
T. S. Eliot (1888–1965), Muir apprehended the hole at the heart of Gregory
Smith's 'theory', that it was actually a way of comprehending broken, or at
least discontinuous, 'tradition'. Indeed, in his quest for the integration, or

---

10. Hugh MacDiarmid, explicitly embraces Gregory Smith's concept, writing:

> I'll ha'e nae hauf-way hoose, but aye be whaur
> Extremes meet—it's the only way I ken
> To dodge the curst conceit o' bein' richt
> That damns the vast majority o' men.

(*A Drunk Man Looks at the Thistle* (1926), ii. 141–4, ed. Kenneth Buthlay (Edinburgh: Scottish
Aacademic Press, 1987).)

reintegration, of literature and nation, the Anglo-American Eliot was himself the heir to Matthew Arnold. Thus, yet again, in the interwar era as in the
late Victorian period, Scottish literary criticism evolved in the shadow of
England, co-opting the insights of Arnold and Eliot. Indeed, Eliot reviewed
Smith's *Scottish Literature: Character and Influence*, and—rather reductively—
saw like Smith the essential issue to be the question of a national literary
language; and logically deduced, as Muir was later to do, that the historic
annihilation of Scottish literature had happened at some point.[11] When, after
the medieval era, the Scots language had lost its national cultural authority,
it found itself undernourished and ghettoized into regional dialects. The
assumptions here—a matter, worthy of note, where English and Scottish
critics were in accord—are interesting. They rest on the idea of a national
(literary) language, essentially licensed by the state, whether that be crown,
parliament, or people (or preferably all of these things at the same time
within Eliot's much sought-after organic culture). Notwithstanding his own
diagnosis of periods of 'dissociation of sensibility' in English Literature (especially in the seventeenth century after the deposition of King Charles I),
Eliot is the critic who more than anyone establishes the idea of a strongly
continuous vernacular English literary tradition, a concept that takes increasing
hold in British universities through the twentieth century.[12] A by-product
of this was the displacement of Classics departments at the centre of the
humanities in British universities, in a way Matthew Arnold could not have
foreseen, and, at the same time, the foregrounding of English culture. Muir's
response to this elevation of Elizabethan drama, the metaphysical poets, and
the English Romantics was the central lament in *Scott and Scotland*, that
Scotland lacked the necessary components that made English Literature
such a compelling success.[13]

Muir's assumption that English Literature existed in a state of creative
development around what he called a 'homogenous' language is, of course,
open to all kinds of interrogation.[14] English Literature, like Scottish Literature,
shows—obviously enough—language in flux through time (how could it
be otherwise?); yet somehow tradition is felt by Eliot and Muir to cohere in
England in a way that does not happen in Scotland. After all, during the

11. T. S. Eliot, 'Was there a Scottish Literature?', *Athenæum,* 1 August 1919, pp. 680–1.
12. For his coinage of 'dissociation of sensibility', see T. S. Eliot, 'The Metaphysical Poets' (1921), in
    Eliot, *Selected Prose,* ed. John Hayward (Harmondsworth: Penguin, 1953), 288.
13. Edwin Muir, *Scott and Scotland: The Predicament of the Scottish Writer* (Edinburgh: Polygon, 1982),
    47–51.
14. Muir, *Scott and Scotland,* 72.

nation-building centuries of the Middle Ages in both England and Scotland, Latin and French remained powerful presences in the spheres of court, government, and law, as well as in broader literary practice. In Scotland, of course, Gaelic adds a further complicating dimension, as do numerous dialects and the phenomenon of mass illiteracy across the British Isles. The notion of a centralizing literary language in either England or Scotland is flawed both in the conception of any such unchallenged entity and in the reach that any language had throughout 'the state' or 'nation' (however defined). For Muir, we might see there is an overanxiety about the development of 'British' culture, and for Eliot too little consideration of 'English' as a subset of 'British' culture. For Muir, the Scottish cultural situation was to be explained historically by a series of wrong-headed trajectories. He saw this primarily in the Reformation, particularly its rigidly puritanical version in Scotland, which inhibited the emergence of the kind of exemplary 'humanist' drama that England developed in the later sixteenth and early seventeenth centuries. This glorious achievement was off limits in his own bigoted and benighted country. The Reformation also introduced English as the language of authority by way of the King James Bible and generally brought about a psychological cleavage within the community between 'thought' (in English) and 'feeling' (in Scots).[15] Here, then, we find another loosely turned iteration of Gregory Smith's Antisyzygy, in this instance also informed by Eliot's 'dissociation of sensibility', a phrase that Muir appropriates from Eliot to describe Scotland's predicament. If only Scotland had appreciated its secular culture (beyond the narrow permitted bounds of sacred literature policed by philistine Presbyterians) and maintained its national language, then it would have remained a full, versatile, and omnicompetent culture, instead of shrivelling in range and experiencing relegation to minority status within the dominant British state; not that the Union was the primary cause of Scotland's cultural difficulties.

Muir, a believer in an ideal but now impossible national culture, came to the sad conclusion that the only thing for a Scottish writer to do in 1936 was to write in English, even though this option could never be completely 'natural' for him or her. Throughout Muir's grand narrative of Reformation, Union of the Crowns in 1603, Union of Parliaments in 1707, and ensuing British imperial enterprise, Scottish 'culture' is viewed as a receding, rather than a transforming, entity. All of these things helped to bring about the

---

15. Muir, *Scott and Scotland*, 36.

triumph of a somewhat hollow 'Britishness': essentially nothing positive was left within Scottish culture, nothing in a strange and artificial 'Britishness' itself, and nothing that might be resuscitated from the residue of Scotland's former national literature in reaction to English dominance. Outraged, Hugh MacDiarmid rounded on his former friend. For MacDiarmid believed that resuscitation was a viable option for Scottish culture and its literature. He castigated Muir as the 'leader of the white mouse faction of the Anglo-Scottish literati', a man oblivious of what MacDiarmid believed had really been going on since the 1920s, the rebirth of a properly indigenous Scottish culture.[16] The rise of Scottish Nationalism in this period seemed to be of a piece with this literary revival. Certainly, a more intense engagement with Scottish themes, contemporary and historical, was characteristic of the period, and often fuelled by a sense of grievance about the trajectory of Scots–British history, and especially the fate of the Highlands. For example, Neil Gunn (1891–1973) had written a powerful novel about the Highland Clearances only two years before *Scott and Scotland* had appeared, *Butcher's Broom* (1934), and this was to be followed up by *Silver Darlings* (1941) about the rise of the herring industry in the nineteenth century; a hard life, but also a new culture emerging in the lives of those very often who had been cleared. Why, it has been asked, did it take so long for the Clearances to be addressed so explicitly in fiction? Did not the time lag prove that tranquillized Kailyard Scotland had been living anachronistically, failing to imagine its own reality? A possible response to this charge is that Modernism, generally, in the early twentieth century began to question received narratives, especially proud imperial ones, as well as the structures of hierarchy. After all, the Peace of Versailles of 1919 had begun to encourage the self-confidence of small nations. Invocations of 'the people' (from both political Left and Right) during the era of European Modernism opened up fresh perspectives on suppressed nations and ethnic minorities, as well as on class and gender. A focus on identity, on revisionist history, and indeed on revisionist historical fiction transformed cultures across Europe during the 1920s, and Scotland was no exception to the general trends of the era.

MacDiarmid's narrative—that Scots (in tandem with the claims of Gaelic) was the appropriate language for his nation's literature—gradually won out, though Edwin Muir's pessimistic assessment lurked in the background like Banquo's ghost. What was presented in works such as *The Scots Literary*

16. Hugh MacDiarmid, *Lucky Poet* (London: Methuen, 1943), 21.

Tradition (1940; revised 1962) by John Speirs (1906–79) was the case for
Scottish literature as literature in Scots. Speirs influentially set out the canon
of medieval Scots: *The Kingis Quair*, Robert Henryson, William Dunbar,
Gavin Douglas, David Lindsay; a trickle of Scots poetry in the sixteenth and
seventeenth centuries; Allan Ramsay, Robert Fergusson, Robert Burns; the
Scottish Ballads; '19th Century Scotland in Allegory'; and 'The Present and
C. M. Grieve'.[17] Here yet again, we see the centrality of England in Scottish
criticism, for Speirs was part of the grouping around *Scrutiny* magazine,
founded in 1932 by L. C. Knights (1906–97) and F. R. Leavis (1895–1978).
Scrutiny sought to praise what was good, within a rigidly defined English
literary tradition, and was forceful in its condemnation of anything else that
was perceived as an illegitimate, alien, or inappropriate presence in literature. Speirs interpreted Scottish literature in terms of the Leavisite agenda,
as well as MacDiarmid-inspired notions of Scots language-centredness and
some concession to Muir's pessimism. Speirs had little or nothing to say
about Gaelic, or about Latin (which exhibited vibrancy as a living literary
medium down to the eighteenth century), and also overlooked Scottish
literary achievement in English as by definition alien to the native tradition.
Where, for instance, did he properly account for the work of William
Drummond of Hawthornden (1585–1649), a virtuoso writer of pastoral,
elegy, and burlesque, who enjoyed a creative friendship with Ben Jonson,
and who is otherwise to be associated with 'mainstream' British poetic
culture from 1603 (although also with roots in James VI's late Renaissance
court culture from the 1580s)? Where was James Thomson (1700–48) author
of *The Seasons* (1726–30), which was, arguably, the most internationally
influential poem ever produced by a Scot? Thomson, of course, had sought
and made his fortune down south, and his panoramic *The Seasons* covers the
history and geography not only of Scotland but also of Britain more widely.
Moreover, it was also written in English, not Scots. In the zero-sum game of
the Scottish criticism practised by Speirs, the 'non-Scottish' dimensions
of a work are enough to condemn it to marginal, or indeed a sort of
quisling status.

Speirs paid particular attention to the ballads. Here he followed the line
advanced by Muir. The ballads are read as an underground phenomenon, as
less than full, sawn-off literary products. They are the result of Scots being
marginalized, rather than viewed as a form of song that pre-dated the medieval

17. John Speirs, *The Scots Literary Tradition* (London: Chatto and Windus, 1962), contents page.

period and all the 'calamities' that had occurred in Scottish history and culture, and was moreover in its borders version a transnational phenomenon, as much the product of Northumberland as of Selkirkshire. Instead, in the Muir–Speirs formulation, the ballads were to be read as part of a malfunctioning 'system', in which Scots literary culture was being disempowered and denuded. Speirs also singled out *The House with the Green Shutters* (1901) by George Douglas Brown (1869–1902) as the main text in his 'Nineteenth-Century Scotland in Allegory' section. This ferociously witty text, with its diagnosis that the Scottish 'imagination' had largely been hijacked, by way of Calvinism and British Empire, for thin materialist purposes, was a key source of inspiration of the MacDiarmidist movement. Brown's text mapped out the culture that MacDiarmid decried. Written in a Scot–English narrative voice, Douglas Brown's novel also featured vivid dialogue in Scots. Such dialogue had been a feature of Scottish fiction since at least the time of Walter Scott (though could be found even further back in the work of Tobias Smollett). Is this not counter-proof, we might ask, that a vibrant literary medium in Scots still pertained in Scotland? Yet Brown's novel is also an odd choice within Speirs's canon: it is to some extent an 'English-language' work, and it also speaks to a nineteenth-century Scottish fictional tradition that Speirs discounts.

Speirs provides yet another example of an essentialist and overly politicized Scottish critic, armed with a priori assumptions about the fate of Scotland's narrowly defined history, language, and culture and blind to the agency of Scots—as writers as well as careerists—within Union and Empire. Ironically, this was understandable enough when the Leavisite agenda predominated in British universities, as culture and society were then parsed in a largely symbiotic relationship. Energy was expended in Scotland on defining a literary tradition that was distinctively Scottish, or failed to be; and Britishness, whether cultural or political, was, to all intents and purposes, outlawed.

The Marxist critic David Craig (b. 1932), picked up Muir's theory of a deformed national culture in his *Scottish Literature and the Scottish People, 1680–1830* (1961).[18] Craig's work in turn paved the way for David Daiches (1912–2005), whose *The Paradox of Scottish Culture* (1964)[19] rounds out what might be termed the recessionist narrative of Scottish literature. For Craig and

18. David Craig, *Scottish Literature and the Scottish People, 1680–1830* (London: Chatto and Windus, 1961).
19. David Daiches, *The Paradox of Scottish Culture: The Eighteenth-Century Experience* (London: Oxford University Press, 1964).

Daiches, the eighteenth century is the crucial moment when Scottish culture finally splits asunder. The Union of Parliaments in 1707 contributes substantially to the strains of bifurcation, and a neoclassical Enlightenment represents 'an alienation from things native'.[20] The obverse of the Enlightenment is the vernacular Scots revival. Undernourished, though more organic than the false neoclassical veneer of the Enlightenment, the best the neo-vernacular can muster is 'the reductive idiom', a sneering, dissenting voice, which, while satirically effective, is somehow symptomatic of a culture less complete than it ought to be.[21] Daiches's 'paradox' builds on Craig's diagnosis of cultural deficiency, as he reads failure in what had previously been valued as the glories of the country's intellectual and cultural achievements. Daiches—following Craig—contends that it is in the period between the mid-eighteenth century and the 1830s—the period of Hume, Burns, and Scott, the very era when Scottish culture becomes world famous—that inauthenticity abounds. The canon between Hume and Scott is interpreted reductively by Daiches as a set of authors operating in an incomplete national culture. Here we reach the point that would have contented Muir: Scottish literature even when rather good—and internationally recognized—is never quite good enough.

The Scottish critical tradition from Gregory Smith to Daiches raises some fundamental questions. Does literature *need* a nation with a parliament, crown, and so forth—the ongoing British model, the erstwhile Scottish model—to thrive? Could Scots poetry have been healthier than it was in the eighteenth century, if, as Craig suggests, the network of country houses that provided a context for the circle of Alexander Pope had been available, say, to Robert Burns? According to Craig, had there been more aristocratic patronage for Scots writers, then this might have obviated their alleged trademark, the caustic, sardonic reductive idiom.[22] Yet again, we might note the curious Anglocentricity of our Scottish critics, an Anglo-fixation that flourished alongside rather naive notions about authenticity. Easy targets for Craig and Daiches in respect of 'authenticity' include the Ossian phenomenon, which today we know is much less easily dismissed for its supposed falsity,[23] and

20. Craig, *Scottish Literature and the Scottish People*, 63.
21. Craig, *Scottish Literature and the Scottish People*, 82 and *passim*.
22. Craig, *Scottish Literature and the Scottish People*, 81–3.
23. Derek S. Thomson, *The Gaelic Sources of Macpherson's Ossian* (Edinburgh: Oliver and Boyd, 1952); Fiona Stafford, *The Sublime Savage: James Macpherson and the Poems of Ossian* (Edinburgh: Edinburgh University Press, 1988).

Hume's cultivation of an accurate English style free of Scotticisms.[24] Of course, there was hardly a market for Scots prose in the eighteenth century, certainly not in England, where the majority of Hume's sales were tallied. Part of the supposed eighteenth-century cultural split rests on the somewhat asinine, a priori idea—found in both Craig and Daiches—that Scots poets wrote well in Scots and badly in English. As we know, Allan Ramsay, Robert Fergusson, and Robert Burns wrote not only excellent Scots–English and English poetry, but also vivid and compelling letters in English. We might also enquire about how we might evaluate the work of Tobias Smollett, in or near the first rank of the eighteenth-century 'English' novel. The overall effect of the Craig–Daiches line of criticism, though, was to add to the canon of large-scale Scottish cultural disaster. The belittling Craig–Daiches interpretation of the Scottish Enlightenment joined Muir's black account of the Scottish Reformation as milestones on a treacherous highway that ran downhill to eventual cultural perdition.

We might, of course, counter that twentieth-century Scottish critics, in thrall to their English counterparts and an idealized notion of English culture, had become—to use the language of colonial theory—inferiorized. Why should Scottish literary culture exhibit all of the same characteristics as its southern cousin? Can we, moreover, plausibly accept a narrative that sees Scotland so laggardly behind the pace of western culture? A repeated claim in the line of criticism we have just been considering is that Scotland misses out on Romanticism. What, then, about James Macpherson, Robert Burns, and Walter Scott (assuming that Byron is ceded completely to the English canon), all of whom would need to be taken account of in any serious version of European, let alone British, literary Romanticism? Of course, this also brings us to the realization that it is not only Scottish criticism that is at fault. The English critical engine too is sluggish and ungenerous. Even after the de-canonizing, revisionist instincts of the last few decades of literary theory, the 'big six' in 'English Romanticism', for instance, remain largely intact in their dominance of publications, teaching, and conferences. Blake, Coleridge, Wordsworth, Keats, Shelley, and the problematic Byron are still the staple fare of 'British' Romanticists. Burns remains out in the cold. Furthermore, the study of English Literature, although highly aware of particular forms of identity politics (especially, class, gender, and sexuality),

---

24. Cf. J. G. Basker, 'Scotticisms and the Problem of Cultural Identity in Eighteenth-Century Britain', in John Dwyer and Richard Sher (eds), *Sociability and Society in Eighteenth-Century Scotland* (Edinburgh: Mercat Press, 1993), 81–95.

remains somewhat immature in its appreciation of 'Englishness'. For it, clearly, 'Britishness' has worked rather differently, so that 'English' is a supposedly 'transparent' label referring simply to the medium of texts (as though this was anywhere as straightforward as supposed). The 'English'/British nation is elided and is regarded as a largely unproblematic arena of literary development (except in class, gender, or sexual terms). Notwithstanding decades of intense self-analysis by literary theorists, these remain the underlying assumptions of mainstream English literary study. It is in good part this purblindness—an ingrained cluster of Anglo-Saxon attitudes, if you will—in the field of English Literature that, alongside a growing cultural nationalism, accounts for the rise of courses in Scottish Literature from the 1960s.

Inevitably, the canon narrowed, and some later critics have been alert to the hobbling effects of older strains of Modernist criticism. Robert Crawford has called in his *Devolving English Literature* (1992) for a non-political 'British Literature' that among other things means English Literature, not simply appropriating Scottish (or Irish, or Welsh, or New Zealand Texts), and facing up to the interesting contradictions and difficulties of being British (which, even in its unique history, might be no more difficult than being French or Hungarian, or Chinese for that matter). We are more comfortable with ragged, hyphenated identities in 'nationality' in these postcolonial, postmodern days. In recent decades practitioners of Scottish historical and literary studies have learnt to interpret the Reformation or the Enlightenment in more nuanced and less decidedly judgemental terms; no moment in Scottish cultural history is seen as either altogether bad or all good. Our history has acquired greyish tints, and this costive, undogmatic balance is to be welcomed. Over the centuries Scotland has produced interesting, original, internationally important writers, but who in the twentieth century found themselves marginal to an overly determined Scottish tradition and unable to find a canonical home. James Boswell (1740–95), the inventor of modern biography, was for a long time adjudged a denizen exclusively of the London literary scene. Thomas Carlyle (1795–1881), the great Victorian sage, is likewise pigeonholed in British categories; after all, he writes not only about the French Revolution, but also about English monastic history. What have these concerns to do with us here in Scotland, ran twentieth-century critical assumptions? But does this British significance need to be pitched *against* his Scottish significance? In more modern times, Muriel Spark (1918–2006), like Carlyle of huge importance in Europe and North America too, is the most successful Scottish writer of the twentieth century. Writing as often as not of other places—France, Italy, Africa, America, London—as of Scotland, and with more interest in issues of religion than in nationhood, is Spark un-Scottish? Is she not a Scottish, British, and, indeed, a world writer? Arguably, moreover, Spark's obsessions with religion—in lieu of nation—align her more decisively than, say, MacDiarmid, with the dominant traditions of Scottish literature since the sixteenth century.

Unified national canons of literary texts have been overdetermined in Scotland, and underconceptualized at the heart of the British literary establishment. Of course, a crude unionism has been at work, or more properly a complacent metropolitan Anglocentricity. Nevertheless, a crude separatism north of the border has wrought almost as much damage as English indifference to our understanding of Scottish literature. Postmodernity holds out an uncertain prospect for Scottish literature. Postmodern perspectives have led to an overdue interrogation of the nationalist assumptions embodied within the Modernist-inspired tradition of criticism inaugurated by MacDiarmid. Yet unionism has also been evaporating in recent decades since the advent of Thatcherism, a process accelerated by the rise of English nationalism and the grim prospect of a Brexit largely unwanted by Scots. The literary intelligentsia is almost exclusively committed to independence— though its own postmodern critical compass warns of the dangers of uncritical nationalist perspectives. On the other hand, in the wider Scotland—Middle Scotland, as it were—a reluctant, and increasingly conditional, adherence to the Union has outlived enthusiastic Britishness and certainly overt Unionism, except in a few sectarian pockets. Where do we go from here, and how do we pick up the pieces?

Acknowledgements

The editors wish to thank the Carnegie Trust for the Universities of Scotland for their generous financial support of the various workshops in Glasgow and St Andrews between 2013 and 2016 that helped to shape this project. They are also keen to thank the various speakers at the workshops, as well as contributors from the floor, who helped to make the workshops so stimulating and enjoyable. Indeed, at a time when Scotland was divided so vociferously between Yes and No camps over the merits of independence, the workshops—which comprised a mixed cast of nationalists, unionists, and occasional outsiders from Canada, England and Northern Ireland—were, without fail, friendly, convivial and civilized. The success of the workshops owed much to Ralph McLean's talents for organization, and to the assistance of Lorna Harris and Andy Eccles. Valerie Wallace would also like to thank the Royal Society of Edinburgh for a research Visitor's grant in 2015.

Quotations from the poetry of Hugh MacDiarmid and the translations of Donald Davie are reproduced by kind permission of Carcanet.

We are also grateful to Dr Carol Baraniuk for compiling the index as well as providing other support and to Hilary Walford for compiling the Bibliography.

This book is dedicated to the memory of Tom Kennedy (1950–2016), one of the cleverest and best-read figures in Scottish life, who died suddenly as it was going to press, and in honour of Professor Andrew Hook, who has done so much in his career to bring Scottish literature into alignment with history and with literature outside Scotland.

Bibliography

A Complete Key to the Three Parts of Law is a Bottomless-Pit, and The Story of the St Alban's Ghost ([London: ?S. Bolton,] 1712).

A Continuation of the History of the Crown-Inn (London: J. Moor, [1714]).

A Dialogue between the Staff, the Mitre, and the Purse. With a Conclusion by Lord John Bull (London: J. Roberts, 1715).

A Farther Continuation of the History of the Crown-Inn (London: J. Moor, [1714]).

A Guide to the Electors of Britain (London: S. Popping, 1722).

A Memorial and Remonstrance Concerning the Proceedings of the Synod of Glasgow and Ayr and of the General Assembly in the Case of Dr William McGill (Edinburgh: n.p., 1792).

A Postscript to John Bull, Containing the History of the Crown-Inn (London: J. Moor, [1714]).

A Review of the State of John Bull's Family, ever since the Probat of his Last Will and Testament (London: J. Moor, 1713).

A Satyr upon Allan Ramsay Occasion'd by a Report of his Translating Horace (Edinburgh, 1720).

Adams, James, *Rule Britannia or the Flattery of Free Subjects, Paraphrased and Expounded* (London: n.p., 179ch. 48).

Addison, Joseph, *The Miscellaneous Works of Joseph Addison*, ed. A. C. Guthkelch, 2 vols (London: G. Bell & Sons Ltd, 1914).

Aird, Andrew, *Reminiscences of Editors, Reporters, and Printers during the Last 60 Years* (Glasgow: Aird and Coghill, 1890).

Aitken, George A., *The Life and Works of John Arbuthnot* (Oxford: Clarendon Press, 1892).

Alker, Sharon, 'John Arbuthnot's Family Ties: Anglo-Scottish Relations in the John Bull Pamphlets', *Scottish Studies Review*, 9/2 (Autumn 2008), 1–20.

Allan, David, *Making British Culture: English Readers and the Scottish Enlightenment, 1740–1830* (New York and London: Routledge, 2008).

Altholz, Josef, *The Religious Press in Britain, 1760–1900* (Westport, CT: Greenwood, 1989).

Altick, Richard, *The English Common Reader: A Social History of the Mass Reading Public 1800–1900* (Chicago and London: University of Chicago Press, 1957).

An Appendix to the History of the Crown-Inn (London: J. Moor, [1714]).

Anderson, Benedict, *Imagined Communities: Reflections on the Origin and Spread of Nationalism* (London: Verso, 1983).

Anderson, Benedict, *Imagined Communities: Reflections on the Origin and Spread of Nationalism*, rev. edn (London: Verso, 2002).

Anderson, James, *Sir Walter Scott and History* (Edinburgh: Edina, 1981).

Anderson, R., 'University Teaching, National Identity and Unionism in Scotland, 1862–1914', *Scottish Historical Review* 91 (2012), 1–41.

Anderson, R., 'The Development of History Teaching in the Scottish Universities, 1894–1939', *Journal of Scottish Historical Studies* 32 (2012), 50–73.

Anderson, R., 'University History Teaching and the Humboldtian Model in Scotland, 1858–1914', *History of Universities*, 25 (2010), 138–84.

Arbuckle, James, *James Arbuckle: Selected Works*, ed. Richard Holmes (Lewisburg, PA: Bucknell University Press, 2014).

[Arbuthnot, John], *Of the Laws of Chance, or, a Method of Calculation of the Hazards of Game* (London: Randall Taylor, 1692).

[Arbuthnot, John], *A Sermon Preach'd to the People, at the Mercat Cross of Edinburgh; on the Subject of the Union* ([Edinburgh?,] 1706).

Arbuthnot, John, *The History of John Bull*, ed. Alan W. Bower and Robert A. Erickson (Oxford: Clarendon Press, 1976).

Armitage, David, 'The Scottish Vision of Empire: Intellectual Origins of the Darien Venture', in John Robertson (ed.), *A Union for Empire: Political Thought and the British Union of 1707* (Cambridge: Cambridge University Press, 1995), 97–118.

Armitage, David, *The Ideological Origins of the British Empire* (Cambridge: Cambridge University Press, 2000).

Arnold, Matthew, *Lectures and Essays in Criticism*, ed. R. H. Super (Ann Arbor, MI: University of Michigan Press, 1962).

Ash, Marinell, *The Strange Death of Scottish History* (Edinburgh: Ramsay Head Press, 1980).

Atherton, Herbert M., *Political Prints in the Age of Hogarth* (Oxford: Clarendon Press, 1974).

Aytoun, Robert, *The Poems of Sir Robert Aytoun*, ed. C. Rogers (Edinburgh: Adam and Charles Black, 1843).

Aytoun, William Edmondstoune, *Poems of William Edmondstoune Aytoun* (London: H. Milford and Oxford University Press, 1921).

Backscheider, Paula R., 'No Defense: Defoe in 1703', *PMLA* 103/3 (1988), 274–84.

Bainbridge, Cyril, and Stockdill, Roy, *The News of the World Story: 150 Years of the World's Bestselling Newspaper* (London: HarperCollins, 1993).

Bakhtin, Mikhail, *Dostoevsky's Poetics*, ed. and trans. Caryl Emerson (Minneapolis, University of Minnesota Press, 1984).

Baldick, Chris, *The Social Mission of English Criticism, 1848–1932* (Oxford: Clarendon Press, 1983).

Ballantyne, James, *Chronicle of the Hundredth Birthday of Robert Burns* (Edinburgh and London: Fullarton & Co, 1859).

Bank of England Archive, 'Britannia and the Bank 1694–1961', ADM 30/59.

Baranuik, Carol, *James Orr, Poet and Irish Radical* (London: Pickering and Chatto, 2014).

Barringer, Terry, 'What Mrs Jellyby Might Have Read: Missionary Periodicals: A Neglected Source', *Victorian Periodicals Review*, 37/4 (2004), 46–74.

Barrell, John, *Imagining the King's Death: Figurative Treason, Fantasies of Regicide, 1793–1796* (Oxford: Oxford University Press, 2000).

Barrow, Tim, *Union* (Portsmouth: Playdead Press, 2014).

Basker, J. G., 'Scotticisms and the Problem of Cultural Identity in Eighteenth-Century Britain', in John Dwyer and Richard Sher (eds), *Sociability and Society in Eighteenth-Century Scotland* (Edinburgh: Mercat Press, 1993), 81–95.

Beattie, Lester M., *John Arbuthnot: Mathematician and Satirist* (Cambridge, MA: Harvard University Press, 1935), 36–57.

Beckett, J. C., *The Anglo-Irish Tradition* (London: Faber and Faber, 1976).

Beetham, Margaret, 'The Agony Aunt, the Romancing Uncle and the Family of Empire: Defining the Sixpenny Reading Public in the 1890s', in Laurel Brake, Bill Bell, and David Finkelstein (eds), *Nineteenth-Century Media and the Construction of Identities* (Houndmills: Palgrave, 2000), 253–70.

Bell, Barbara, 'The Age of the Periodical', in B. Bell (ed.), *The Edinburgh History of the Book in Scotland*, iii. *Ambition and Industry 1800–1880* (Edinburgh: Edinburgh University Press, 2007).

Bell, Bill, (ed.), *The Edinburgh History of the Book in Scotland*, iii. *Ambition and Industry 1800–1880* (Edinburgh: Edinburgh University Press, 2007).

Benedict, Barbara M., 'Encounters with the Object: Advertisements, Time, and Literary Discourse in the Early Eighteenth-Century Thing-Poem', *Eighteenth Century Studies*, 40/2 (Winter 2007), 193–207.

'Bennet, William', *The History of Parliament: The House of Commons 1690–1715*, ed. Eveline Cruickshanks, Stuart Handley, and D. W. Hayton, 5 vols (Cambridge: Cambridge University Press, 2002).

Bentley, Michael, *The Life and Thought of Herbert Butterfield: History, Science and God* (Cambridge: Cambridge University Press, 2011).

Berg, Maxine, and Eger, Elizabeth (eds), *Luxury in the Eighteenth Century: Debates, Desires and Delectable Goods* (Basingstoke: Palgrave Macmillan, 2003).

Berger, S., and Niven, B., 'Writing the History of National Memory', In S. Berger and B. Niven (eds), *Writing the History of Memory* (London and New York: Bloomsbury Academic, 2014), 140–6.

Berger. S., and B. Niven, B. (eds), *Writing the History of Memory* (London and New York: Bloomsbury Academic, 2014).

Berlin, Isaiah, *Personal Impressions* (London: Hogarth Press, 1980).

Beveridge, Craig, and Turnbull, Ronald, *The Eclipse of Scottish Culture* (Edinburgh: Polygon, 1989).

Bew, John, *The Glory of Being Britons: Civic Unionism in Nineteenth-Century Belfast* (Dublin: Irish Academic Press, 2009).

Billington, Louise, 'The Religious Periodical and Newspaper Press, 1770–1870', in M. Harris and A. Lee (eds), *The Press in English Society from the Seventeenth to Nineteenth Centuries* (London and Toronto: Associated University Presses, 1986), 113–32.

Black, A., *Gilfillan of Dundee, 1813–1878: Interpreting Religion and Culture in Mid-Victorian Scotland* (Dundee: Dundee University Press, 2006).

Black, Jeremy, *Politics and Foreign Policy in the Age of George I, 1714–1727* (Farnham: Ashgate, 2014).

Blacklock, Thomas, 'A Parody on the Ode, "Britannia rule the waves", written by Dr Blacklock on the Capture of the West & East India Fleet', National Library of Scotland MS.24593.

Blair, Kirstie (ed.), *The Poets of the People's Journal: Newspaper Poetry in Victorian Scotland* (Glasgow: Association for Scottish Literary Studies, 2016).

Blake, George, *Barrie and Kailyard School* (London: A. Barker, 1951).

Blaney, Roger, *Presbyterians and the Irish language* (Belfast: Ulster Historical Foundation, 1996).

Bloom, Edward A., and Bloom, Lilian D., *Joseph Addison's Sociable Animal* (Providence, RI: Brown University Press, 1971).

Bolton, H. Philip, *Novels on Stage*, ii. *Scott Dramatized* (London: Mansell Publishing, 1992).

Boswell, James, *Life of Johnson* (1791; World's Classics; Oxford: Oxford University Press, 1980).

Bottingheimer, Karl S., 'The Glorious Revolution and Ireland', in Lois G. Schwoerer (ed.), *The Revolution of 1688–89: Changing Perspectives* (Cambridge: Cambridge University Press, 2004), 234–43.

Bowie, K., *Scottish Public Opinion and the Anglo-Scottish Union, 1699–1707* (Woodbridge: Boydell Press, 2007).

Boyse, Samuel, 'To the Honourable Sir John Clerk, Baronet', *Translations and Poems* (London, 1738), 180–2.

Brabrook, Henry R., 'If it's Scotch it's Scotch; if it's English it's–British', *Publishers' Circular*, 29 July 1916, p. 89.

Bradshaw, Brendan, and Morrill, John (eds), *The British Problem: State Formation in the Atlantic Archipelago 1534–1707* (Houndmills: Palgrave, 1996).

Bradshaw, Brendan, and Roberts, Peter (eds), *British Consciousness and Identity: The Making of Britain 1533–1707* (Cambridge: Cambridge University Press, 1998).

Bradshaw, David, 'The Socio-Political Vision of the Novels', in Sue Roe and Susan Sellers (eds), *The Cambridge Companion to Virginia Woolf* (Cambridge: Cambridge University Press, 2000), 124–41.

Bremner, G. A., and Conlin, Jonathan (eds), *Making History: Edward Augustus Freeman and Victorian Cultural Politics* (Oxford: Oxford University Press, 2015).

Brewer, John, 'The Misfortunes of Lord Bute: A Case Study in Eighteenth-Century Political Argument and Public Opinion', *Historical Journal*, 16 (1973), 3–43.

Britannia in Mourning: Or, a Review of the Politicks and Conduct of the Court of Great Britain (London: J. Huggonson, 1742).

Brockliss, L., and Eastwood, D. (eds), *A Union of Multiple Identities: The British Isles c.1750–c.1850* (Manchester: Manchester University Press, 1997).

Brooke, Peter, 'Controversies in Ulster Presbyterianism, 1790–1836', Ph.D. thesis, University of Cambridge, 1980.

Brooke, Peter, *Ulster Presbyterianism: The Historical Perspective, 1610–1970* (2nd edn; Belfast: Athol Books, 1994).

Brotherstone, T. (ed.), *Covenant, Charter and Party: Traditions of Revolt and Protest in Modern Scottish History* (Aberdeen: Aberdeen University Press, 1989).

Brown, Candy G., *The Word in the World: Evangelical Writing, Publishing, and Reading in America, 1789–1880* (Chapel Hill, NC, and London: University of North Carolina Press, 2004).

Brown, George Mackay, *Beside the Ocean of Time* (1994; Edinburgh: Polygon, 2011).

Brown, Iain Gordon, *The Clerks of Penicuik, Portraits of Taste and Talent* (Edinburgh: Penicuik House Preservation Trust, 1987).

Brown, K., *Kingdom or Province? Scotland and the Regal Union, 1603–1715* (Basingstoke: Palgrave, 1992).

Brown, Keith M., 'The Vanishing Emperor: British Kingship and its Decline 1603–1707', in Roger A. Mason (ed.), *Scots and Britons: Scottish Political Thought and the Union of 1603* (Cambridge: Cambridge University Press, 1994), 58–88.

Brown, K., and Mann, A. J. (eds), *The History of the Scottish Parliament II: Parliament and Politics in Scotland, 1567–1707* (Edinburgh: Edinburgh University Press, 2004).

Brown, S. J., 'Outside the Covenant: The Scottish Presbyterian Churches and Irish Immigration, 1922–38', *Innes Review*, 42 (1991), 19–45.

Brown, S. J., *Providence and Empire: Religion, Politics and Society in the United Kingdom, 1815–1914* (Harlow: Pearson Longman, 2008).

Bruce, Steve, *No Pope of Rome: Militant Protestantism in Modern Scotland* (Edinburgh: Mainstream, 1985).

Bruckmüller, E., et al., 'Striving for Visibility: Nationalists in Multinational Empires and States', in I. Porciani and J. Tollebeek (eds), *Setting the Standards: Institutions, Networks and Communities of National Historiography* (Basingstoke: Palgrave, 2012), 372–93.

Buchan, John, *Midwinter* (2nd edn, London: Thomas Nelson and Sons, Ltd., 1925).

Buchan, John, *The Blanket of the Dark* (2nd edn, London: Thomas Nelson and Sons Ltd, 1933).

Burgess, G. (ed.), *The New British History: Founding a Modern State 1603–1715* (London: I. B. Tauris, 1999).

Burke, Edmund, *Reflections on the Revolution in France*, ed. J. G. A. Pocock (Indianapolis: Hackett Publishing Company, 1987).

Burns, Robert, *The Poems and Songs of Robert Burns*, ed. James Kinsley (Oxford: Clarendon Press, 1968).

Burns, Robert, *The Letters of Robert Burns: Volume II, 1790–1796*, ed. J. De Lancey Ferguson; 2nd edn, ed. G. Ross Roy (Oxford: Clarendon Press, 1985).

Burns, Robert, *Burns Poems and Songs*, ed. J. Kinsley (1969; paperback edn, Oxford: Oxford University Press, 1990).

Burns' Centenary: Are Such Honours due to the Ayrshire Bard? (Glasgow: printed privately, 1959).

Burns Day in Detroit, Being a History of the Movement for a Burns Statue in Detroit (Detroit: Detroit Burns Club, 1921).

Burrow, John, *A Liberal Descent* (Cambridge: Cambridge University Press, 1981).

Burrow, J. W., 'Victorian Historians and the Royal Historical Society', *Transactions of the Royal Historical Society*, 39 (1989), 125–40.

Butler, Marilyn, *Maria Edgeworth* (Oxford: Clarendon Press, 1972).

Butler, Samuel, *Hudibras Parts I and II and Selected Other Writings*, ed. John Wilders and Hugh de Quehen (Oxford: Clarendon Press, 1973).

Butterfield, Herbert, *The Englishman and his History* (Cambridge: Cambridge University Press, 1944).

Byron, Lord, *Lord Byron: The Complete Poetical Works*, ed. Jerome McGann (Oxford: Clarendon Press 1980–93).

Campbell, T. D., 'Hutcheson: "Father of the Scottish Enlightenment"', in R. H. Campbell, and A. S. Skinner (eds), *The Origins and Nature of the Scottish Enlightenment* (Edinburgh: John Donald, 1982), 167–85.

Cannadine, David, 'British History: Past, Present—and Future?', *Past and Present*, 116 (1987), 169–91.

Cardwell, M. John, *Arts and Arms: Literature, Politics and Patriotism during the Seven Years War* (Manchester: Manchester University Press, 2004).

Carey, John, *The Intellectuals and the Masses: Pride and Prejudice among the Literary Intelligentsia, 1880–1939* (London: Faber and Faber, 1992).

Carey, John, *The Unexpected Professor: An Oxford life in Books* (London: Faber and Faber, 2013).

Carretta, Vincent, *George III and the Satirists from Hogarth to Byron* (Athens, GA: University of Georgia Press, 1990).

Carruthers, Gerard, 'James Thomson and Eighteenth-Century Scottish Literary Identity', in Richard Terry (ed.), *James Thomson: Essays for the Tercentenary* (Liverpool: Liverpool University Press, 2000), 165–90.

Carruthers, Gerard (ed.), *The Edinburgh Companion to Robert Burns* (Edinburgh: Edinburgh University Press, 2009).

Carruthers, Gerard, *Scottish Literature: A Critical Guide* (Edinburgh: Edinburgh University Press, 2009).

Carruthers, Gerard, 'Presbyterianism and the Legacy of Thomas Muir', unpublished paper presented at 'Presbyterianism and Scottish Literature' colloquium, University of St Andrews, 7 October 2016.

Carswell, Donald, *Brother Scots* (London: Constable & Co., 1927).

Cartwright, John, *The Trident: Or, the National Policy of Naval Celebration* (London: J. Johnson, J. White & T. Payne, 1802).

Cash, Arthur H., *John Wilkes: The Scandalous Father of Civil Liberty* (New Haven: Yale University Press, 2006).

Chibnall, Marjorie, *The Debate on the Norman Conquest* (Manchester: Manchester University Press, 1999), 53–68.

Churchill, Charles, *The Prophecy of Famine* (London, 1763),

Clark, Kenneth, *Another Part of the Wood: A Self-Portrait* (London: Harper Collins, 1974).

Clarke, Tristram, '"Nurseries of Sedition"?: The Episcopal Congregations after the Revolution of 1689', in James Porter (ed.), *After Columba—After Calvin: Community and Identity in the Religious Traditions of North East Scotland* (Aberdeen: Elphinstone Institute, 1999), 1–9.

Clerk, Sir John, *Memoirs of Sir John Clerk of Penicuik*, ed. John M. Gray (Edinburgh: T. and A. Constable, 1892).

Coleman, James, 'The Double Life of the Scottish Past: Discourses of Commemoration in Nineteenth-Century Scotland', Ph.D. thesis, University of Glasgow, 2005.

Coleman, James, 'Unionist–Nationalism in Stone? The National Wallace Monument and the Hazards of Commemoration in Victorian Scotland', in E. J. Cowan (ed.), *The Wallace Book* (Edinburgh: John Donald, 2007), 137–50.

Coleman, James J., *Remembering the Past in Nineteenth-Century Scotland: Commemoration, Nationality and Memory* (Edinburgh: Edinburgh University Press, 2014).

Coleman, James J., 'The Scottish Covenanters', in Gareth Atkins (ed.), *Making and Remaking Saints in Nineteenth-Century Britain* (Manchester: Manchester University Press, 2016), 177–92.

Colley, Linda, *Britons: Forging the Nation 1707–1837* (New Haven and London: Yale University Press Vintage, 1992).

Connell, Philip, 'British Identities and the Politics of Ancient Poetry in Later Eighteenth-Century England', *Historical Journal*, 49/1 (2006), 161–92.

Connolly, Claire, 'The National Tale', in Peter Garside and Karen O'Brien (eds), *The Oxford History of the Novel in English*, ii. *English and British Fiction 1750–1820* (Oxford: Oxford University Press, 2015), 216–33.

Conrad, Joseph, *The Collected Letters of Joseph Conrad*, ed. Frederick R. Karl, Laurence Davies, et al., 9 vols (Cambridge: Cambridge University Press, 1988–2007).

Cooper, J. Nicoll, 'Dissenters & National Journalism: "The Patriot" in the 1830s', *Victorian Periodicals Review*, 14/2 (1981), 58–66.

Courthope, W. J., *A History of English Poetry*, 6 vols (London: Macmillan, 1910).

Cox, Philip, *Reading Adaptation: Novels and Verse Narratives on the Stage, 1790–1840* (Manchester: Manchester University Press, 2000).

Craig, Cairns, *Out of History: Narrative Paradigms in Scottish and British Culture* (Edinburgh: Polygon, 1996).

Craig, Cairns, *The Modern Scottish Novel: Narrative and the National Imagination* (Edinburgh: Edinburgh University Press, 1999).

Craig, Cairns, *Intending Scotland: Explorations in Scottish Culture since the Enlightenment* (Edinburgh: Edinburgh University Press, 2009).

Craig, David, *Scottish Literature and the Scottish People, 1680–1830* (London: Chatto and Windus, 1961).

Crawford, Robert, *A Scottish Assembly* (London: Chatto and Windus, 1990).

Crawford, Robert, *Devolving English Literature* (Oxford: Oxford University Press, 1992).

Crawford, Robert (ed.), *The Scottish Invention of English Literature* (Cambridge: Cambridge University Press, 1998).

Crawford, Robert, *Devolving English Literature* (1992; 2nd edn, Edinburgh: Edinburgh University Press, 2000).

Crawford, Robert, Presbyterianism and Imagination in Modern Scotland', in Devine (ed.), *Scotland's Shame? Bigotry and Sectarianism in Modern Scotland* (Edinburgh: Mainstream, 2000), 187–96.

Crawford, Robert, *The Modern Poet* (Oxford: Oxford University Press, 2001).

Crawford, Robert, *Bannockburns: Scottish Independence and Literary Imagination, 1314–2014* (Edinburgh: Edinburgh University Press, 2014).

[Croker, John Wilson], *Two Letters on Scottish Affairs from Edward Bradwardine Waverley, Esq, to Malachi Malagrowther, Esq* (2nd edn; London: John Murray and Oliver and Boyd, 1826).

Crosland, T. W. H., *The Unspeakable Scot* (London: Grant Richards, 1902).

Crownshaw, R., 'History and Memorialization', in S. Berger and B. Niven (eds), *Writing the History of Memory* (London and New York: Bloomsbury Academic, 2014), 222–6.

Cummings, W. H., *Dr Arne and Rule, Britannia* (London: Novello and Co., 1912).

Curran, Kevin, *Marriage, Performance, and Politics at the Jacobean Court* (Farnham: Ashgate, 2009).

Daiches, David, *The Paradox of Scottish Culture: The Eighteenth-Century Experience* (London: Oxford University Press, 1964).

D'Arcy, Julian Meldon, *Subversive Scott: The Waverley Novels and Scottish Nationalism* (Reykjavic: University of Iceland Press, 2005).

Darlow, T. H., *William Robertson Nicoll: Life and Letters* (London: Hodder and Stoughton, 1925).

Davie, Donald, *Slavic Excursions* (Manchester: Carcanet, 1990).

Davies, Norman, *God's Playground: A History of Poland*, 2 vols (Oxford: Clarendon Press, 1981).

Davies, Norman, 'Polish National Mythologies', in Geoffrey Hosking and George Schöpflen (eds), *Myths and Nationhood* (London: Hurst & Company, 1997), 141–57.

Daviot, Gordon, *Leith Sands and Other Plays* (London, 1946).

Davis, Evan R., 'The Injured Lady, the Deluded Man, and the Injured Creature: Swift and the 1707 Act of Union', in David A. Valone and Jill Marie Bradbury (eds), *Anglo-Irish Identities, 1571–1745* (Lewisburg, PA: Bucknell University Press, 2008), 126–42.

Davis, Leith, *Acts of Union: Scotland and the Literary Negotiation of the British Nation 1707–1830* (Stanford: Stanford University Press, 1998).

Dee, John, *General and Rare Memorials Pertaining to the Perfect Art of Navigation* (London: John Daye, 1577).

Defoe, Daniel, *The Shortest-Way with the Dissenters* (London, 1702).

Defoe, Daniel, *An Essay on the Regulation of the Press* (London, 1704).

Defoe, Daniel, *A Tour thro' the Whole Island of Great Britain* (London, 1724–6).

Deleuze, Gilles, and Guattari, Félix, *Kafka: Towards a Minor Literature*, trans. Dana Polan (Minneapolis: University of Minnesota Press, 1986).

Devine, T. (ed.), *Irish Immigrants and Scottish Society in the Nineteenth and Twentieth Centuries* (Edinburgh: John Donald, 1991).

Devine, T. (ed.), *Scotland's Shame? Bigotry and Sectarianism in Modern Scotland* (Edinburgh: Mainstream, 2000).

Devine, T. M., *Scotland's Empire: The Origins of the Global Diaspora* (London: Allen Lane, 2003).

Devine, T. M., *Independence or Union: Scotland's Past and Scotland's Present* (London: Allen Lane, 2016).

Dibdin, Charles, *The Songs of Charles Dibdin*, i (London: E. Lloyd, 1847).

Donaldson, William, *Popular Literature in Victorian Scotland: Language, Fiction and the Press* (Aberdeen: Aberdeen University Press, 1986).

Donaldson, William, *The Jacobite Song: Political Myth and National Identity* (Aberdeen: Aberdeen University Press, 1988).

Douglas, George, *Scottish Poetry: Drummond of Hawthornden to Fergusson* (Glasgow: J. Maclehose, 1911).

Downie, J. A., *Robert Harley and the Press: Propaganda and Public Opinion in the Age of Swift and Defoe* (Cambridge: Cambridge University Press, 1979).

Drake, George A., '"The ordinary rules of the pave": Urban Spaces in Scott's *The Fortunes of Nigel*', *Studies in the Novel*, 33/4 (Winter 2001), 416–29.

Dresser, Madge, 'Britannia', in Harry Goldbourne (ed.), *Race and Ethnicity: Solidarities and Communities* (London: Routledge, 2001), 26–49.

Drummond, A. L., and Bulloch, J., *The Scottish Church 1688–1843* (Edinburgh: St Andrew Press, 1973).

Drummond, A. L., and Bulloch, J., *The Church in Victorian Scotland 1843–1874* (Edinburgh: St Andrew Press, 1975).

Drummond, A. L., and Bulloch, J., *The Church in Late Victorian Scotland 1874–1900* (Edinburgh: St Andrew Press, 1978).

Duffy, C. G., *Young Ireland: A Fragment of Irish History, 1840–45. Final Revision* (London: T. Fisher Unwin, 1896).

Duncan, Douglas, *Thomas Ruddiman: A Study in Scottish Scholarship of the Early Eighteenth Century* (Edinburgh: Oliver and Boyd, 1965).

Duncan, Ian, *Modern Romance and the Transformations of the Novel: The Gothic, Scott, Dickens* (Cambridge: Cambridge University Press, 1992).

Duncan, Ian, 'Walter Scott, James Hogg and Scottish Gothic', in David Punter (ed.), *A Companion to the Gothic* (Oxford: Blackwell, 2000), 70–80.

Duncan, Ian, *Scott's Shadow: The Novel in Romantic Edinburgh* (Princeton: Princeton University Press, 2007).

Eaude, M., *Catalonia: A Cultural History* (Oxford: Signal Books, 2007).

Edinburgh Miscellany (Edinburgh: M'Euen, 1720).

Edwards, Martin, *The Golden Age of Murder: The Mystery of the Writers who Invented the Modern Detective Story* (London: Harper Collins, 2015).

Edwards, Michael, *Poetry and Possibility* (London: Macmillan, 1988).

Edwards, Michael, *Of Making Many Books* (London: Macmillan, 1990).

Edwards, Owen Dudley (ed.), *A Claim of Right for Scotland* (Edinburgh: Polygon, 1989).

Eliot, T. S., 'Was there a Scottish Literature?', *Athenæum,* 1 August 1919, pp. 680–1.

Eliot, T. S., 'The Metaphysical Poets' (1921), in Eliot, *Selected Prose,* ed. John Hayward (Harmondsworth: Penguin, 1953), 105–14.

Eliot, T. S., *The Poems of T. S. Eliot,* ed. Christopher Ricks and Jim McCue, 2 vols (London: Faber and Faber, 2015).

Elliott, Francis, and Coates, Sam, 'May: I Will Reunite Britain', *The Times,* 30 June 2016, p. 1.

Elliott, J. H., 'A Europe of Composite Monarchies', *Past and Present,* 137 (1992), 48–71.

Ellis, S., and Barber, S. (eds), *Conquest and Union: Fashioning a British State 1485–1725* (London: Longman, 1995).

Elton, G. R., *The English* (Oxford: Wiley Blackwell, 1992).

Emerson, Roger L., *Academic Patronage in the Scottish Enlightenment: Glasgow, Edinburgh and St Andrews Universities* (Edinburgh: Edinburgh University Press, 2008).

Erim, Kenan T., 'A New Relief Showing Claudius and Britannia from Aphrodisias', *Britannia,* 13 (1982), 279–81.

Ewing, A. McL., *A History of the Glasgow Herald 1783–1948* (Glasgow: Printed for Private Circulation, [c. 1948]).

Fabricant, Carole, *Swift's Landscape* (Baltimore: Johns Hopkins University Press, 1982).

Faverty, F. E., *Matthew Arnold the Ethnologist* (Evanston, IL: Northwestern University Press, 1951).

Fenyo, K., *Contempt, Sympathy and Romance: Lowland Perceptions of the Highlands and the Clearances during the Famine Years, 1845–1855* (East Linton: Tuckwell Press, 2000).

Ferguson, F., *Should Christians Commemorate the Birthday of Robert Burns?* (Edinburgh: A. Elliot, 1869).

Ferguson, Frank (ed.), *Ulster-Scots Writing: An Anthology* (Dublin: Four Courts Press, 2008).

Ferguson, Frank, Erskine, John, and Dixon, Roger, 'Commemorating and Collecting Burns in the North of Ireland, 1844 to 1902', in Frank Ferguson and A. R. Holmes, *Revising Robert Burns and Ulster: Literature, Religion and Politics, c. 1770–1920* (Dublin: Four Courts Press, 2009), 127–47.

Ferguson, Frank, and Holmes, A. R. (eds), *Revising Robert Burns and Ulster: Literature, Religion and Politics, c. 1770–1920* (Dublin: Four Courts Press, 2009).

Ferguson, William, *Scotland's Relations with England: A Survey to 1707* (Edinburgh: John Donald, 1977).

Fergusson, Sir James, *Shakespeare's Scotland* (Edinburgh: T. Nelson, 1957).

Fergusson, Robert, *Robert Fergusson Selected Poems,* ed. James Robertson (Edinburgh: Polygon, 2000).

Ferris, Ina, *The Romantic National Tale and the Question of Ireland* (Cambridge: Cambridge University Press, 2002).

Fielding, Penny, *Writing and Orality: Nationality, Culture, and Nineteenth-Century Scottish Fiction* (Oxford: Clarendon Press, 1996).

Finlay, R., 'Nationalism, Race, Religion and the Irish Question in Inter-War Scotland', *Innes Review*, 42 (1991), 46–67.

Finlay, R., 'For or Against? Scottish Nationalists and the British Empire, 1919–1939', *Scottish Historical Review*, 71 (1992), 184–206.

Finlay, R. J., 'The Burns Cult and Scottish Identity', in K. Simpson (ed.), *Love & Liberty: Robert Burns, A Bicentenary Celebration* (East Linton: Tuckwell Press, 1997), 74–5.

Finlay, Richard J., 'Heroes, Myths and Anniversaries in Modern Scotland', *Scottish Affairs*, 18 (Winter 1997), 108–25.

Finlay, R., *A Partnership for Good? Scottish Politics and the Union since 1880* (Edinburgh: John Donald, 1997).

Finlay, Richard, 'The Burns Cult and Scottish Identity in the Nineteenth and Twentieth Centuries', in Kenneth Simpson (ed.), *Robert Burns a Bicentenary Celebration* (East Linton: Tuckwell Press, 1997).

Finn, Thomas, 'The Painter Cut, A Vision', in *The Irish Magazine, or Monthly Asylum for Neglected Biography* (July 1810), 293–5.

Flaningam, John, 'The Occasional Conformity Controversy: Ideology and Party Politics, 1697–1711', *Journal of British Studies*, 17/1 (Autumn 1977), 38–62.

Fletcher, Andrew, *Political Works*, ed. John Robertson (Cambridge: Cambridge University Press, 1997).

Fletcher, C. R. L., and Kipling, Rudyard, *A School History of England* (Oxford: Clarendon Press, 1911).

Folkenflik, Robert, 'Self and Society: Comic Union in Humphry Clinker', *Philological Quarterly*, 53 (1974), 195–204.

The Fourth and Last Part of the History of the Crown-Inn (London: J. Moor, [1714]). *An Appendix to the History of the Crown-Inn* (London: J. Moor, [1714]).

Fox, Christopher, 'Swift's Scotophobia', *Bullan: An Irish Studies Journal*, 6/2 (2002), 43–66.

Francis, Philip, *The Odes, Epodes, and Carmen Secularae of Horace in Latin and English*, 2 vols (Dublin: S. Powell, 1742).

Franke, W., 'Smollett's *Humphry Clinker* as a Party-Novel', *Studies in Scottish Literature*, 9 (1971–2), 97–106.

Frédéricq, Paul, 'The Study of History in England and Scotland', *Johns Hopkins University Studies in Historical and Political Science* (October 1887).

Freeman, F. W., 'The Intellectual Background of the Vernacular Revival before Burns', *Studies in Scottish Literature*, 16/1 (1981), 160–87.

Freeman, F. W., and Law, Alexander, 'Allan Ramsay's First Published Poem: The Poem to the Memory of Dr Archibald Pitcairne', *Bibliotheck*, 9 (1979), 153–60.

Frost, Robert I., *The Oxford History of Poland–Lithuania*, i. *The Making of the Polish–Lithuanian Union 1385–1569* (Oxford: Oxford University Press, 2015).

Fry, Michael, 'The Disruption and the Union', in S. J. Brown and M. Fry (eds), *Scotland in the Age of the Disruption* (Edinburgh: Edinburgh University Press, 1993), 31–43.

Fry, Michael, *The Scottish Empire* (East Linton: Tuckwell, 2001).

Fulford, Tim, 'Britannia's Heart of Oak: Thomson, Garrick and the Language of Eighteenth-Century Patriotism', in Richard Terry (ed.), *James Thomson: Essays for the Tercentenary* (Liverpool: Liverpool University Press, 2000), 191–216.

Fussell, Paul, *The Great War and Modern Memory* (Oxford: Oxford University Press, 1975).

Galbraith, Douglas, *The Rising Sun* (2000; New York: Grove Press, 2001).

Gallagher, Tom, *Glasgow the Uneasy Peace: Religious Tension in Modern Scotland* (Manchester: Manchester University Press, 1987).

Galt, John, *Annals of the Parish* (1821; Oxford: Oxford University Press, 1986).

Galt, John, *Ringan Gilhaize* (1823; Edinburgh: Canongate, 1995).

Gardiner, Michael, *The Cultural Roots of British Devolution* (Edinburgh: Edinburgh University Press, 2004).

Gardiner, Michael, *The Constitution of English Literature: The State, the Nation and the Canon* (London: Bloomsbury, 2013).

Gardiner, Michael, Macdonald, Graeme, and O'Gallagher, Niall (eds), *Scottish Literature and Postcolonial Literature: Comparative Texts and Critical Perspectives* (Edinburgh: Edinburgh University Press, 2011).

Garside, P. D., 'Union and the Bride of Lammermoor', *Studies in Scottish Literature*, 19 (1984), 72–93.

Geddes, Alexander, 'Three Scottish Poems, with a Previous Dissertation on the Scoto-Saxon Dialect', *Archaeologia Scotica*, 1 (1792), 402–68.

Geddes, Patrick, 'The Scots Renascence', *Evergreen: A Northern Seasonal*, 1 (Spring 1895), 131–40.

Geoghegan, Patrick, *Liberator: The Life and Death of Daniel O'Connell, 1830–1847* (Dublin: Gill Books, 2010).

Gibb, Andrew Dewar, *Scotland in Eclipse* (London: H. Toulmin, 1930).

Gifford, Douglas, 'Myth, Parody and Dissociation: Scottish Fiction 1814–1914', in Gifford (ed.), *History of Scottish Literature Vol. III* (Aberdeen: Aberdeen University Press, 1987), 217–60.

Gillies, Mary Ann, *The Professional Literary Agent in Britain, 1880–1920* (Toronto: University of Toronto Press).

Gisbal, an Hyperborean Tale: Translated from the Fragments of Ossian the Son of Fingal (London: printed for the author, 1762).

The Glorious Privilege: The History of 'The Scotsman' (London: Nelson, 1967).

Goldman, Jane, *'With You in the Hebrides': Virginia Woolf and Scotland* (London: Cecil Woolf, 2013).

Goldstein, Doris S., 'The Organizational Development of the British Historical Profession, 1884–1921', *Bulletin of the Institute of Historical Research*, 55 (1982), 180–93.

Goldstein, Doris S., 'The Professionalization of History in Britain in the Late Nineteenth and Early Twentieth Centuries', *Storia della Storiografia*, 3 (1983), 3–27.

Goodwillie, Edward, *The World's Memorials of Robert Burns* (Detroit: Waverley Publishing, 1911).
Gordon, R. C., *Under which King? A Study of the Scottish Waverley Novels* (Edinburgh and London: Oliver and Boyd, 1969).
Grainger, J. H., *Patriotisms: Britain 1900–1939* (London: Routledge & Kegan Paul, 1986).
Grant, A., and K. Stringer, K. (eds), *Uniting the Kingdom? The Making of British History* (London: Routledge, 1995).
Green, Roger Lancelyn, *Andrew Lang: A Critical Biography* (Leicester: Edmund Ward, 1946).
Gribben, C., 'James Hogg, Scottish Calvinism and Literary Theory', *Scottish Studies Review*, 5 (2004), 9–26.
Giuseppi, John, *The Bank of England* (London: Evan Brothers, 1966).
Guest, Harriet, *Unbounded Attachment: Sentiment and Politics in the Age of the French Revolution* (Oxford: Oxford University Press, 2013).
Gunn, S., *The Public Culture of the Victorian Middle Classes: Ritual and Authority in the English Industrial City 1840–1914* (Manchester: Manchester University Press, 2000).
Haddington, Earls of, *The Memorials of the Earls of Haddington*, ed. W. Frazer, 2 vols (Edinburgh: privately printed, 1889).
Harris, Bob, 'Scotland's Herring Fisheries and the Prosperity of the Nation, *c.*1660–1760', *Scottish Historical Review*, 79/207, pt 1 (April 2000), 39–60.
Hames, Scott (ed.), *Unstated: Writers on Scottish independence* (Edinburgh: Word Power Books: 2012).
Hamilton, John, Lord Belhaven, *The Lord Beilhaven's Speech in Parliament Saturday the Second of November, on the Subject-matter of an Union betwixt the Two Kingdoms of Scotland and England* ([Edinburgh: n.p.,] 1706).
Hamilton, Valerie, and Parker, Martin, *Daniel Defoe and the Bank of England: The Dark Arts of Projectors* (Alresford: Zero Books, 2016).
Harris, Bob, 'The Press, Newspaper Fiction and Literary Journalism, 1707–1918', in Susan Manning (ed.), *The Edinburgh History of Scottish Literature*, ii. *Enlightenment, Britain and Empire (1707–1918)* (Edinburgh: Edinburgh University Press, 2007), 308–16.
Harris, Bob, and McKean, Charles, *The Scottish Town in the Age of Enlightenment 1740–1820* (Edinburgh: Edinburgh University Press, 2014).
Harris, Susie, *Nikolaus Pevsner: The Life* (London: Pimlico, 2011).
Harvie, Christopher, 'Nineteenth-Century Scotland: Political Unionism and Cultural Nationalism, 1843–1906', in R. G. Asch (ed.), *Three Nations—a Common History? England, Scotland, Ireland and British History* c.*1600–1920* (Bochum: Universitatsverlag Dr N. Brockmeyer), 191–228.
Hawkes, Terence, *That Shakespherian Rag: Essays on a Critical Process* (London: Methuen, 1986).
Hawkes, Terence, *Shakespeare in the Present* (London: Routledge, 2002).
Hay, Ian, *The Oppressed English* (London: J. M. Dent & Sons, 1917).

Hayden, John O. (ed.), *Walter Scott: The Critical Heritage* (London: Routledge, 1970).

Hayton, D. W., *The Anglo-Irish Experience, 1680–1730: Religion, Identity, and Patriotism* (Woodbridge: Boydell, 2012).

Hearn, J., *Claiming Scotland: National Identity and Liberal Culture* (Edinburgh: Polygon, 2000).

Hechter, Michael, *Internal Colonialism: The Celtic Fringe in British National Development, 1536–1966* (London: Routledge and Kegan Paul, 1975).

Hegel, Georg Wilhelm Friedrich, *The Science of Logic*, trans. and ed. George Di Giovanni (Cambridge: Cambridge University Press, 2010).

The Heimskringla or, Chronicle of the Kings of Norway, Translated from the Icelandic of Snorro Sturleson, 3 vols (London: Longman, Brown, Green, and Longmans, 1844).

Hempton, David, *Religion and Political Culture in Great Britain and Ireland from the Glorious Revolution to the Decline of Empire* (Cambridge: Cambridge University Press, 1996).

Henderson, Jennifer M., *Josephine Tey: A Life* (Dingwall: Sandstone Press, 2015).

Herron, A., *Kirk by Divine Right: Church and State: Peaceful Coexistence* (Edinburgh: St Andrew Press, 1985).

Hervey, Lord, *Memoirs*, ed. Romney Sedgwick, 3 vols (London: Eyre Methuen, 1931).

Hewitt, John, 'Ulster Poets', MA thesis, Queen's University Belfast, 1951.

Hewitt, John, *Rhyming Weavers and Others Poets of Antrim and Down*, new edn. (Belfast: Blackstaff Press, 2004).

Hibernicus's Letters (Dublin and London: Smith and Bruce, Grierson and others, 1729).

Higgins, Ian, 'Censorship, Libel, and Self-Censorship', in Paddy Bullard and James McLaverty (eds), *Jonathan Swift and the Eighteenth-Century Book* (Cambridge: Cambridge University Press, 2013), 179–98.

Hill, Christopher, *Puritanism and Revolution* (London: Penguin Books, 1986).

Hilton, B., *Corn, Cash and Commerce: The Economic Policies of the Tory Governments 1815–1830* (Oxford: Clarendon Press, 1977).

Hilton, Boyd, '"Sardonic Grins" and "Paranoid Politics": Religion, Economics, and Public Policy in the *Quarterly Review*', in Jonathan Cutmore (ed.), *Conservatism and the Quarterly Review: A Critical Analysis* (London: Pickering and Chatto, 2007), 41–60.

Hinsley, F. H., *Sovereignty* (2nd edn; Cambridge: Cambridge University Press, 1986).

Historical Sketch of the Ulster Institution for the Deaf and Dumb, and Blind (Belfast: Belfast News-Letter, 1933).

The History of John Bull. Part III (London: M. Cooper, 1744).

Hobsbawm, Eric, *Nations and Nationalism* (Cambridge: Cambridge University Press, 1990).

Hobsbawm, Eric, 'Introduction: The Invention of Tradition', in E. Hobsbawm and Terence Ranger (eds), *The Invention of Tradition* (Cambridge: Cambridge University Press, 2010), 1–14.

Hogg, James, *The Brownie of Bodsbeck* (1818; Edinburgh: Scottish Academic Press, 1976).

Hogg, James, *The Private Memoirs and Confessions of a Justified Sinner* (1824; Harmondsworth: Penguin, 1983).

Hogg, James, *The Jacobite Relics of Scotland*, ed. Murray G. H. Pittock, 2 vols (Edinburgh: Edinburgh University Press, 2002, 2003).

Holmes, A. R., *The Shaping of Ulster Presbyterian Belief and Practice, 1770–1840* (Oxford: Oxford University Press, 2006).

Holmes, A. R., 'The Uses and Interpretation of Prophecy in Irish Presbyterianism, 1850–1930', in Crawford Gribben and A. R. Holmes (eds), *Protestant Millennialism, Evangelicalism, and Irish Society, 1790–2005* (Basingstoke: Palgrave Macmillan, 2006), 144–73.

Holmes, A. R., 'Irish Presbyterian Commemorations of their Scottish Past, c.1830 to 1914', in James McConnel and Frank Ferguson (eds), *Across the Water: Ireland and Scotland in the Nineteenth Century* (Dublin: Four Court Press, 2009), 48–61.

Holmes, A. R., 'Presbyterian Religion, Historiography and Ulster Scots Identity, c.1800 to 1914', *Historical Journal*, 52 (2009), 615–40.

Holmes, A. R., 'Covenanter Politics: Evangelicalism, Political Liberalism, and Ulster Presbyterians, 1798–1914', *English Historical Review*, 125 (2010), 340–69.

Holmes, A. R., 'From Francis Hutcheson to James McCosh: Irish Presbyterians and the Scottish Philosophy in the Nineteenth Century', *History of European Ideas*, 40 (2014), 622–43.

Holmes, A. R., 'The Scottish Reformations and the Origin of Religious and Civil Liberty in Britain and Ireland: Presbyterian Interpretations, c.1800–1860', *Bulletin of the John Rylands University Library*, 90 (2014), 135–54.

Holmes, Geoffrey, *British Politics in the Age of Anne* (London: Macmillan, 1967).

Holmes, R. F. G., *Henry Cooke* (Belfast: Christian Journals, 1981).

Holmes, Richard 'James Arbuckle's Glotta (1721) and the Poetry of Allusion', *Journal for Eighteenth-Century Studies*, 35/1 (March 2012), 85–100.

Hoppen, K. T., *Elections, Politics, and Society in Ireland 1832–1885* (Oxford: Oxford University Press, 1984).

Housman, A. E., *A Shropshire Lad* (Ludlow: Palmers, 1987).

How a Newspaper Is Printed: Being a Complete Description of the Offices and Equipments of the Dundee Advertiser, People's Journal, Evening Telegraph, and People's Friend (Dundee: John Leng & Co, n.d. [1891]).

Howsam, Lewlie, *Past into Print: The Publishing of History in Britain, 1850–1950* (London: British Library, 2009).

Hutchison, Matthew, *The Reformed Presbyterian Church in Scotland: Its Origin and History 1680–1876* (Paisley: J and R. Parlane, 1893).

Hume, David, *The History of England, from the Invasion of Julius Caesar to the Revolution in 1688*, intr. William B. Todd, 6 vols (Indianapolis: Liberty Fund, 1983).

Humphreys, R. A., *The Royal Historical Society* (London: Royal Historical Society, 1969).

Hunt, Tamara L., *Defining John Bull: Political Caricature and National Identity in Late Georgian England* (Aldershot: Ashgate, 2003).

Ives, Keith A., *Voice of Nonconformity: William Robertson Nicoll and the British Weekly* (Cambridge: Lutterworth Press, 2011).

Jackson, Clare, *Restoration Scotland, 1660–1690: Royalist Politics, Religion and Ideas* (Woodbridge and Rochester: Boydell Press, 2003).

Jacobite Minstrelsy (Glasgow: R. Griffin & Co., 1828).

James VI, *Basilicon Doron*, ed. James Craigie, 2 vols (Edinburgh: Blackwood for the Scottish Text Society, 1944–50).

Jenkins, Robin, *The Awakening of George Darroch* (1985; Edinburgh: B&W Publishing, 1995).

J. G., *The Charmer: A Choice Collection of Songs, Scots and English* (Edinburgh: J. Yair, 1752).

John Bull's Last Will and Testament, as it was Drawn by a Welch Attorney (London: S. Popping, 1713).

John Knox and the Rev. Thomas Drew; Or, the Book of Common Order No Liturgy (Belfast: William McComb, 1840).

John Knox's Book of Common Order No Liturgy. To the Rev. John Cuming, Minister of the Scottish Church, London, from James M'Neight, Editor of the Belfast News-Letter (Belfast: n.p., 1840).

Johnson, Samuel, *A Journey to the Western Islands of Scotland*, ed. R. W. Chapman (Oxford: Oxford University Press, 1974).

Kearney, Hugh, *The British Isles: A History of Four Nations* (Cambridge: Cambridge University Press, 1989).

Keating, Peter, *The Haunted Study: A Social History of the English Novel 1875–1914* (London: Secker & Warburg, 1989).

Keith, Thomas, 'Burns Statues of North America, a Survey', in G. Ross Roy (ed.), *Robert Burns & America* (Columbia, SC: Thomas Cooper Library and Akros Publications, 2001), 23–33.

Kelly, James, 'Regulating Print: The State and the Control of Print in Eighteenth-Century Ireland', *Eighteenth-Century Ireland*, 23 (2008), 142–74.

Kelly, Lionel (ed.), *Tobias Smollett: The Critical Heritage* (London: Routledge & Kegan Paul, 1987).

Kelly, Stuart, *Scott-land: The Man who Invented a Nation* (Edinburgh: Polygon, 2010).

Kenyon, John, *The History Men: The Historical Profession in England since the Renaissance* (London: Weidenfeld and Nicolson, 1983).

Kerrigan, John, *Archipelagic English: Literature, History, and Politics 1603–1707* (Oxford: Oxford University Press, 2008).

Keymer, Thomas, 'Smollett's Scotlands: Culture, Politics and Nationhood in *Humphry Clinker* and Defoe's *Tour*, *History Workshop Journal*, 40/1 (1995), 118–32.

Keymer, Thomas, 'Paper Wars: Literature and/as Conflict during the Seven Years' War', in Frans De Bruyn and Shaun Regan (eds), *The Culture of the Seven Years' War: Empire, Identity, and the Arts in the Eighteenth-Century Atlantic World* (Toronto: University of Toronto Press, 2014), 119–46.

Kidd, Colin, 'The Ideological Significance of Scottish Jacobite Latinity', in Jeremy Black and Jeremy Gregory (eds), *Culture, Politics and Society in Britain 1660–1800* (Manchester: Manchester University Press, 1991), 110–30.

Kidd, Colin, *Subverting Scotland's Past: Scottish Whig Historians and the Creation of an Anglo-British Identity* (Cambridge: Cambridge University Press, 1993).

Kidd, Colin, 'Religious Realignment between Restoration and Union', in John Robertson (ed.), *A Union for Empire: Political Thought and the British Union of 1707* (Cambridge: Cambridge University Press, 1995), 153–7.

Kidd, Colin, 'Teutonist Ethnology and Scottish Nationalist Inhibition, 1780–1880', *Scottish Historical Review*, 74 (1995), 45–68.

Kidd, Colin, 'Conditional Britons: The Scots Covenanting Tradition and the Eighteenth-Century British State', *English Historical Review*, 117 (2002), 1147–76.

Kidd, Colin, 'Race, Theology and Revival: Scots Philology and its Contexts in the Age of Pinkerton and Jamieson', *Scottish Studies Review*, 3 (2002), 20–33.

Kidd, Colin, 'Race, Empire and the Limits of Scottish Nationhood', *Historical Journal*, 46 (2003), 873–92.

Kidd, Colin, 'Eighteenth-Century Scotland and the Three Unions', in T. C. Smout (ed.), *Anglo-Scottish Relations from 1603 to 1900: Proceedings of the British Academy*, 127 (2005), 171–87.

Kidd, Colin, *The Forging of Races: Race and Scripture in the Protestant Atlantic World, 1600–2000* (Cambridge: Cambridge University Press, 2006).

Kidd, Colin, *Union and Unionisms: Political Thought in Scotland 1500–2000* (Cambridge: Cambridge University Press, 2008).

Kidd, Colin, 'Assassination Principles in Scottish Political Culture from Buchanan to Hogg', in R. Mason and C. Erskine (eds), *George Buchanan* (Farnham: Ashgate, 2012), 269–88.

Kidd, Colin, 'Scottish Independence: Literature and Nationalism', *Guardian*, 19 July 2014 <http://www.theguardian.com/books/2014/jul/19/scottish-independence-literature-nationalism> (accessed 21 May 2015).

Kidd, Colin, 'British Literature: The Career of a Concept', *Scottish Literary Review*, 8 (2016), 1–16.

Kidd, Colin, 'The Politics of the Scottish Enlightenment', in Blair Worden (ed.), *Hugh Trevor Roper: The Historian* (London: I. B. Tauris, 2016), 145–61.

The Kilmarnock Burns Monument and Statue (1882).

King, Kathryn R., *A Political Biography of Eliza Haywood* (London: Pickering & Chatto, 2012).

Kingsley, Charles, *Hereward the Wake: The Last of The English* (London: Collins, 1954).

Kipling, Rudyard, *Puck of Pook's Hill and Rewards and Fairies*, ed. D. Mackenzie (World's Classics; Oxford: Oxford University Press, 1993).

Kipling, Rudyard, *The Letters of Rudyard Kipling*, ed. Thomas Pinney, 6 vols (London: Macmillan, 1990–2004).

Klein, L., 'Joseph Addison's Whiggism', in David Womersley (ed.), *Cultures of Whiggism* (Newark: University of Delaware Press, 2005), 108–26.

Klein, L., 'Addisonian Afterlives: Joseph Addison in Eighteenth-Century Culture', *Journal for Eighteenth-Century Studies*, 35/1 (2012), 101–18.

Knapp, Lewis M., 'Rex versus Smollett: More Data on the Smollett-Knowles Libel Case', *Modern Philology*, 41/4 (1944), 221–7.

Koenigsberger, H. G., 'Dominum regale or dominium politicum et regale: Monarchies and Parliaments in Early Modern Europe', in Koenigsberger, *Politicians and Virtuosi: Essays in Early Modern History* (London: Hambledon, 1985), 1–25.

Kompeckyj, Ramon, 'Adam Mickiewicz and Polish Romanticism', in Michael Ferber (ed.), *The Companion to European Romanticism* (London: Blackwell, 2005).

Koropeckyj, Roman, *Adam Mickiewicz: The Life of a Romantic* (Ithaca, NY: Cornell University Press, 2008).

Koss, Stephen, *Nonconformity in Modern British Politics* (London: Batsford, 1975).

Koss, Stephen, *The Rise and Fall of the Political Press in Britain* (Chapel Hill, NC, and London: University of North Carolina Press, 1984).

Leask, Nigel, *Robert Burns and Pastoral: Poetry and Improvement in Late Eighteenth-Century Scotland* (Oxford: Oxford University Press, 2010).

Leavis, F. R., *The Great Tradition* (London: Chatto & Windus, 1948).

Ledger-Lomas, Michael, 'Mass Markets: Religion', in D. McKitterick (ed.), *The Cambridge History of the Book in Britain*, vi. *1830–1914* (Cambridge: Cambridge University Press, 2016).

Lednicki, Wacław, *Pushkin's Bronze Horseman: The Story of a Masterpiece* (Westport, CT: Greenwood Press, 1978).

Lee, Hermione, *Virginia Woolf* (London: Vintage, 1997).

Lenihan, Maurice, 'Portrait of Turlough O'Callaghan', *Notes and Queries*, 4th ser., 6 (15 October 1870).

Lenman, Bruce, *The Jacobite Risings in Britain, 1689–1746* (London: Eyre Metheun, 1980).

Lenman, Bruce, 'The Scottish Episcopalian Clergy and the Ideology of Jacobitism', in Eveline Cruickshanks (ed.), *Ideology and Conspiracy: Aspects of Jacobitism, 1689–1759* (Edinburgh: John Donald, 1982), 36–48.

L'Estrange, Roger, *Fables, of Aesop and Other Eminent Mythologists* (London: for R. Sare, 1692).

Levack, Brian P., *The Formation of the British State: England, Scotland and the Union 1603–1707* (Oxford: Clarendon Press, 1987).

Levine, Philippa, *The Amateur and the Professional: Antiquarians, Historians and Archaeologists in Victorian England, 1838–1886* (Cambridge: Cambridge University Press, 1986).

Levy, Buddy, *River of Darkness: Francisco Orellana's Legendary Voyage of Death and Discovery down the Amazon* (New York: Random House, 2011).

Lewis, C. S., *Surprised by Joy* (London: Geoffrey Bles, 1955).

Lieuallan, R., 'A Sculptor for Scotland: The Life and Work of Sir John Robert Steell, RSA (1804–1891)', unpublished Ph.D. thesis, 2 vols, University of Edinburgh, 2003.

Lincoln, Andrew, *Walter Scott and Modernity* (Edinburgh: Edinburgh University Press, 2007).

Lindley, David, *The Trials of Frances Howard: Fact and Fiction at the Court of King James* (London: Routledge, 1993).

Lockhart, J. G., *Memoirs of the Life of Sir Walter Scott, Bart.*, 7 vols (Edinburgh: Robert Cadell, 1837–8).

Lomas, Robert, *Freemasonry and the Birth of Modern Science* (Gloucester, MA: Fair Winds Press, 2003).

Low, Donald (ed.), *Robert Burns: The Critical Heritage* (London and Boston: Routledge and Kegan Paul, 1974).

Low, Donald (ed.), *The Scots Musical Museum, 1787–1803* (Aldershot: Scolar Press, 1991).

Lugubres Cantus (Edinburgh: M'Euen, 1720).

Lukács, Georg, *The Historical Novel*, trans. H. and S. Mitchell (London: Merlin Press, 1962).

Lukács, Georg, *The Historical Novel*, trans. H. and S. Mitchell (Boston: Beacon Press, 1963).

Lukács, Georg, *The Historical Novel*, trans. H. and S. Mitchell (Lincoln, NE, and London: University of Nebraska Press, 1983).

Lumsden, Alison, 'Walter Scott', in Adrian Poole (ed.), *The Cambridge Companion to English Novelists* (Cambridge: Cambridge University Press, 2009), 116–31.

Lumsden, Alison, *Walter Scott and the Limits of Language* (Edinburgh: Edinburgh University Press, 2010).

Lynch, Michael, *Scotland: A New History* (London: Century, 1991).

Lytton, Bulwer, *Harold: The Last of the Saxon Kings* (London: George Routledge and Sons, 1887).

McBride, I. R., *Scripture Politics: Ulster Presbyterians and Irish Radicalism in the Late Eighteenth Century* (Oxford: Oxford University Press, 1998).

McCleery, A. (ed.), *Nation and Nationalism* (Dunbeath: Whittles Publishing, 2013).

McClelland, Aiken, 'The Early History of Brown Street Primary School', *Ulster Folklife*, 17 (1971), 55.

McComb, William, *The School of the Sabbath: A Poem* (Belfast: T. Mairs, 1822).

McComb, William, *McComb's Guide to Belfast, the Giant's Causeway, and the Adjoining Districts of the Counties of Antrim and Down* (Belfast: William McComb, 1861).

McComb, William, *Poetical Works of William McComb* (London: Hamilton, Adams & Co., 1864).

McConnel, James, and Ferguson, Frank (eds), *Across the Water: Ireland and Scotland in the Nineteenth Century* (Dublin: Four Court Press, 2009).

McCormack, W. J., *Ascendancy and Tradition in Anglo-Irish Literary History* (Oxford: Clarendon Press, 1985).

McCracken-Flesher, Caroline, *Possible Scotlands: Walter Scott and the Story of Tomorrow* (Oxford: Oxford University Press, 2005).

McCrie, Thomas, *Miscellaneous Writings, Chiefly Historical of the Late Thomas McCrie, DD*, ed. Thomas McCrie Jr (Edinburgh: Johnstone, 1841).

McCrie, Thomas, *The Works of Thomas McCrie, DD: A New Edition*, ed. Thomas McCrie Jr (Edinburgh: William Blackwood, 1857).

McCrie, Thomas, Jr, *Life of Thomas McCrie, DD* (Edinburgh, 1840).

McCulloch, Katie Louise, 'Building the Highland Empire: The Highland Society of London and the Formation of Charitable Networks in Great Britain and Canada, 1778–1857', unpublished Ph.D. thesis, University of Guelph, 2014.

MacDiarmid, Hugh, *Lucky Poet* (London: Methuen, 1943).

MacDiarmid, Hugh, *Collected Poems* (New York: Macmillan, 1962).

MacDiarmid, Hugh, *Selected Essays of Hugh MacDiarmid*, ed. Duncan Glen (London: Jonathan Cape, 1969).

MacDiarmid, Hugh, *A Drunk Man Looks at the Thistle* (1926), ed. Kenneth Buthlay (Edinburgh: Scottish Aacademic Press, 1987).

MacDiarmid, Hugh, *Complete Poems, Volume I*, ed. Michael Grieve and W. R. Aitken (Manchester: Carcanet, 1993).

MacDiarmid, Hugh, *Lucky Poet*, ed. A. Riach (Manchester: Carcanet, 1994).

MacDiarmid, Hugh, *Hugh MacDiarmid: Selected Poems*, ed. Alan Riach and Michael Grieve (Harmondsworth: Penguin, 1999).

Macdonald, C. (ed.), *Unionist Scotland 1800–1997* (Edinburgh: John Donald, 1998).

Macdonald, Catriona M. M., 'Montrose and Modern Memory: The Literary Afterlife of the Frist Marquis of Montrose', *Scottish Literary Review*, 6/1 (2014), 1–18.

Macdonald, Catriona M. M., 'Andrew Dewar Gibb', in James Mitchell and Gerry Hassan (eds), *Scottish National Party Leaders* (London: Biteback, 2016), 105–25.

Macdonell, A. G. *The Factory on the Cliff* (London: Longmans & Co., 1928).

Macdonell, A. G., *The Seven Stabs* (London: Victor Gollancz, 1929).

Macdonell, A. G., *The Silent Murders* (London: Longmans & Co., 1929).

Macdonell, A. G., *England, their England* (1933; repr. Cambridge: Oleander Press, 2011).

Macdonell, A. G., *The Shakespeare Murders* (London: Arthur Baker, 1933).

Macdonell, A. G., *My Scotland* (1937; repr. Stroud: Fonthill, 2012).

Macdonell, A. G., *My Scotland* (1937; repr. Stroud: Fonthill, 2012), 13.

Macdonell, A. G., *Autobiography of a Cad* (London: Macmillan, 1938).

Macdonell, A. G. 'Ali Baba and the Forty Thieves', in *The Spanish Pistol, and Other Stories* (London: Macmillan, 1939), 221–44.

Macdonell, A. G., 'Dingley-Dell *v.* All Muggleton Cricket Match', in Macdonell, *The Spanish Pistol, and Other Stories* (London: Macmillan, 1939), 179–94.

Macdonell, A. G., 'Mind over Matter', in *The Spanish Pistol, and Other Stories* (London: Macmillan, 1939), 164–78.

Macdonell, A. G., 'Mr Moriarty: A Study in the Sherlock Holmes Sage', in *The Spanish Pistol, and Other Stories* (London: Macmillan, 1939), 208–20.

Macdonell, *The Spanish Pistol, and Other Stories* (London: Macmillan, 1939).

McDowall, W., *History of Dumfries* (Edinburgh: Adam & Charles Black, 1867).

McEwan, P. J. M., *The Dictionary of Scottish Art and Architecture* (Ballater: Glengarden Press, 1988).

McFarland, Elaine, *Protestants First: Orangeism in Nineteenth-Century Scotland* (Edinburgh: Edinburgh University Press, 1990).

McGinn, Clark, '"Every Honour Except Canonisation":The Global Development of the Burns Supper, 1801 to 2009', unpublished Ph.D. thesis, University of Glasgow, 2013.

McGuirk, Carol, 'Jacobite History to National Song: Robert Burns and Carolina Oliphant', *Eighteenth Century*, 47/2–3, 'Ballads and Songs in the Eighteenth Century' (Summer/Fall 2006), 253–87.

Machin, G. I. T., 'Voluntaryism and Reunion 1874–1929', in N. Macdougall (ed.), *Church, Politics and Society: Scotland 1408–1929* (Edinburgh: John Donald, 1983), 221–38.

Machin, G. I. T., *Politics and the Churches in Great Britain 1869 to 1921* (Oxford: Clarendon Press, 1987).

McIlvanney, Liam, *Burns the Radical: Poetry and Politics in Late Eighteenth-Century Scotland* (East Linton:Tuckwell Press, 2002).

Mcilwham, Thomas, *The McIlwham Papers: In Two Letters from Thomas Mcilwham, Weaver, to his Friend, James Mcneight, Editor of the Belfast Newsletter. Edited, and Illustrated with Notes and a Glossary, by John Morrison, a Student, Glasgow* (Belfast: William McComb, 1838).

Mack, Douglas, 'The Rage of Fanaticism in Former Days: James Hogg's *Confessions* and the Controversy over *Old Mortality*', in Ian Campbell (ed.), *Nineteenth-Century Scottish Fiction* (Manchester: Carcanet, 1979), 37–50.

Mackay, James A., *Burnsiana* (Alloway: Alloway Publishing, 1988).

Mackay, Pauline A., 'Objects of Desire: Robert Burns the "Man's Man" and Material Culture', *Anglistik*, 23/2 (2012), 27–39.

Mackenzie, Donald, 'Edwardian Idyll, Edwardian Mapping', in Laura Colombino and Max Saunders (eds), *The Edwardian Ford Madox Ford* (Amsterdam: Rodolpi, 2013), 105–24.

McKenzie, Raymond, *Public Sculpture of Glasgow* (Liverpool: Liverpool University Press, 2002).

McKeon, Michael, 'Aestheticising the Critique of Luxury: Smollett's *Humphry Clinker*', in Maxine Berg and Elizabeth Eger (eds), *Luxury in the Eighteenth Century: Debates, Desires and Delectable Goods* (Basingstoke: Palgrave Macmillan, 2003), 57–70.

McKerrow, John, *History of the Secession Church* (Glasgow:A. Fullarton, 1841).

Mackillop, A., and Siochru, M. O. (eds), *Forging the State: European State Formation and the Anglo-Scottish Union of 1707* (Dundee: Dundee University Press, 2009).

McKnight, James, *Extracts from Original Letters of James McKnight, LL.D. Ninth Annual Report of the Presbyterian Historical Society of Ireland, 1915–16* (Belfast: Presbyterian Historical Society of Ireland, 1916).

McLaverty, Jim, 'An Introduction to *The Story of an Injured Lady*', *Jonathan Swift Archive* <jonathanswiftarchive.org.uk/browse/year/intro_jsa_9_1_1.html> (accessed July 2017).

MacLeod, C., *Heroes of Invention: Technology, Liberalism and British Identity 1750–1914* (Cambridge: Cambridge University Press, 2007).

Macleod, D. S., *Art and the Victorian Middle Classes: Money and the Making of Cultural Identity* (Cambridge: Cambridge University Press, 1996).

Macleod, J. L., *The Second Disruption: The Free Church in Victorian Scotland and the Origins of the Free Presbyterian Church* (East Linton: Tuckwell Press, 2000).

McMahon, Marie, *The Radical Whigs, John Trenchard and Thomas Gordon* (Lanham, MD: University Press of America, 1990).

McMaster, Graham, *Scott and Society* (Cambridge: Cambridge University Press, 1981).

Macpherson, James, *Original Papers; Containing the Secret History of Great Britain, from the Restoration, to the Accession of the House of Hannover*, 2 vols (London: W. Strahan and T. Cadell, 1775).

McVie, J., *The Burns Federation: A Bicentenary Review* (Kilmarnock: Kilmarnock Standard, 1959).

Madden, Richard R., *The United Irishmen, Their Lives and Times*, 2nd edn, 4 vols (Dublin: J. Duffy, 1858).

Maidment, James (ed.), *A Third Book of Scotish Pasquils, & c.* (Edinburgh, 1828).

Mair, John, *A History of Greater Britain*, trans. A. Constable (Edinburgh: Scottish History Society, 1892).

Majerus, B., '*Lieux de memoire*—A European Transfer Story', in S. Berger and B. Niven (eds), *Writing the History of Memory* (London and New York: Bloomsbury Academic, 2014), 157–71.

Maley, Willy, and Murphy, Andrew (eds), *Shakespeare and Scotland* (Manchester: Manchester University Press, 2004).

Mallet, David, *The Works of David Mallet*, 3 vols (London: A. Millar, 1759).

Mallett, David, *The Plays of David Mallet*, ed. Felicity Nussbaum (New York: Garland, 1980).

Maloney, Paul, *Scotland and the Music Hall, 1850–1914* (Manchester and New York: Manchester University Press, 2003).

Maloney, Paul, *The Britannia Panopticon Music Hall and Cosmopolitan Entertainment Culture*, Palgrave Studies in Theatre and Performance History (London: Palgrave Macmillan, 2016).

Maltzahn, Nicholas von, 'Marvell's Ghost', in Warren Chernaik and Martin Dzelzainis (eds), *Marvell and Liberty* (Basingstoke: Macmillan, 1999), 50–74.

Manning, Susan, *The Puritan–Provincial Vision: Scottish and American Literature in the Nineteenth Century* (Cambridge: Cambridge University Press, 1990).

Manning, Susan, *Fragments of Union: Making Connections in Scottish and American Writing* (Basingstoke: Palgrave, 2002).

Marcus, Leah S., 'Literature and the Court', in David Loewenstein and Janel Mueller (eds), *The Cambridge History of Early Modern Literature* (Cambridge: Cambridge University Press, 2002), 487–511.

Marsden, George, *Jonathan Edwards: A Life* (New Haven: Yale University Press, 2003).

Marshall, Ashley, *The Practice of Satire in England, 1658–1770* (Baltimore: Johns Hopkins University Press, 2013).

Marshall, Ashley, *Swift and History: Politics and the English Past* (Cambridge: Cambridge University Press, 2015).

Mason, Roger, 'Kingship, Nobility and Anglo-Scottish Union: John Mair's *History of Greater Britain*', *Innes Review*, 41 (1990), 182–222.

Mason, Roger, 'The Scottish Reformation and the Origins of Anglo-British Imperialism', in Mason (ed.), *Scots and Britons: Scottish Political Thought and the Union of 1603* (Cambridge: Cambridge University Press, 1994).

Mason, Roger, (ed.), *Scots and Britons: Scottish Political Thought and the Union of 1603* (Cambridge: Cambridge University Press, 1994).

Mason, Roger, 'Posing the East Lothian Question', *History Scotland*, 8 (January–February 2008), 40–8.

Mason, Roger, 'Debating Sovereignty in Seventeenth-Century Scotland: Multiple Monarchy and Scottish Sovereignty', *Journal of Scottish Historical Studies*, 35 (2015), 1–24.

Mason, Roger, 'Divided by a Common Faith? Protestantism and Union in Post-Reformation Britain', in J. McCallum (ed.), *Scotland's Long Reformation* (Leiden: Brill, 2016), 202–25.

Masson, David, *British Novelists and their Styles: Being a Critical Sketch of the History of British Prose Fiction* (Cambridge: Macmillan, 1859).

Maume, Patrick (ed.), *The Repealer Repulsed by William McComb* (Dublin: UCD Press, 2003).

Maume, Patrick, 'Repealing the Repealer: William McComb's Caricatures of Daniel O'Connell', *History Ireland*, 13/2 (March–April 2005), 43–7.

Maume, Patrick, 'From Scotland's Storied Land: William McComb and Scots–Irish Presbyterian Identity', in James McConnel and Frank Ferguson (eds), *Across the Water: Ireland and Scotland in the Nineteenth Century* (Dublin: Four Court Press, 2009), 76–92.

May, Theresa, 'We can Make Britain Work for Everyone', *The Times*, 30 June 2016, p. 7.

Mayo, Thomas F., 'The Authorship of *The History of John Bull*', *Proceedings of the Modern Language Association*, 45 (1930), 274–82.

Meikle, James, *Our Scottish Forefathers, a Tale of Ulster Presbyterians* (Belfast: H. Clark and Co., 1837).

Mickiewicz, Adam, *Konrad Wallenrod and Other Writings of Adam Mickieiwcz*, trans. G. R. Noyes et al. (Berkeley and Los Angeles: University of California Press, 1925).

Mickiewicz, Adam, *Konrad Wallenrod*, in *Konrad Wallenrod and Other Writings of Adam Mickieiwcz*, trans. G. R. Noyes et al. (Berkeley and Los Angeles: University of California Press, 1925), i. 136–62.

Mickiewicz, Adam, *Pan Tadeusz*, trans. G. R. Noyes (London: J. M. Dent, 1930).

Mickiewicz, Adam, *Pan Tadeusz*, trans. K. R. Mackenzie (New York: Hippocrene Books, 1992).

Mickiewicz, Adam, *Polish Romantic Drama*, ed. Harold B. Segal (Amsterdam: Harwood Academic Publishers, 1997).

Mickiewicz, Adam, *Forefather's Eve, Part III*, in *Polish Romantic Drama*, ed. Harold B. Segal (Amsterdam: Harwood Academic Publishers, 1997).

Millar, J. H., *A Literary History of Scotland* (London: T. F. Unwin, 1903).

Miller, D. W., *Queen's Rebels; Ulster Loyalism in Historical Perspective* (Dublin: Gill and Macmillan, 1978).

Miller, Karl, *Doubles* (1985; London: Faber and Faber, 2008).

Miller, William L., *The End of British Politics? Scots and English Political Behaviour in the Seventies* (Oxford: Clarendon Press, 1981),

Miller, W. L. (ed.), *Anglo-Scottish Relations from 1900 to Devolution*, Proceedings of the British Academy, 128 (Oxford: Oxford University Press, 2005).

Millgate, J., 'Text and Context: Dating the Events of *The Bride of Lammermoor*', *Bibliotheck*, 9 (1979), 200–13.

Milne, A. T., 'History in the Universities: Then and Now', *History*, 59 (1974), 33–46.

Milton, John, *A Manifesto of the Lord Protector* (London: A. Millar, 1738).

Miłosz, Czesław, *The History of Polish Literature* (Berkeley and Los Angeles: University of California Press, 1983).

Mineka, Francis, *The Dissidence of Dissent:* The Monthly Repository *1806–1838* (Chapel Hill, NC: University of North Carolina Press, 1944).

The Mirror of Literature, Amusement and Instruction (London: J. Limbird, 1832).

Mitchell, James, *Governing Scotland: The Invention of Administrative Devolution* (Houndmills: Palgrave Macmillan, 2003).

Mitchell, James, *Devolution in the UK* (Manchester: Manchester University Press, 2009).

Mitchell, Jerome, *The Walter Scott Operas: An Analysis of Operas Based on the Works of Sir Walter Scott* (Alabama: University of Alabama Press, 1977).

Mitchell, Jerome, *More Scott Operas: Further Analyses of Operas Based on the Works of Sir Walter Scott* (Lanham, MD, New York: University Press of America, 1996).

Mitchell, M. J., *The Irish in the West of Scotland* (Edinburgh: John Donald, 1998).

Modrzewska, Miroslawa, 'Pilgrimage or Revolt?: The Dilemmas of Polish Byronism', in Richard A. Cardwell (ed.), *The Reception of Byron in Europe*, 2 vols (London: Thoemmes Continuum, 2004), ii. 310–14.

Mooney, Thomas, *The History of Ireland, from its First Settlement to the Present Time* (Boston, 1845).

Moores, John Richard, *Representations of France in English Satirical Prints* (Basingstoke: Palgrave Macmillan, 2015).

Morton, Graeme, *Unionist Nationalism: Governing Urban Scotland, 1830–1860* (East Linton: Tuckwell Press, 1999).

Morton, Graeme, *William Wallace: A National Tale* (Edinburgh: Edinburgh University Press, 2014).

Murdoch, Alexander J., 'The Importance of Being Edinburgh: Management and Opposition in Edinburgh Politics, 1746–1784', *Scottish Historical Review*, 62 (1983), 1–16.

Muir, Edwin, *Scottish Journey* (Edinburgh: Mainstream Publishing, 1979).

Muir, Edwin, *Scott and Scotland* (London: Routledge, 1936).

Muir, Edwin, *Scott and Scotland: The Predicament of the Scottish Writer* (Edinburgh: Polygon, 1982).

Muir, Edwin, *Edwin Muir: The Complete Poems*, ed. P. Butter (Aberdeen: Association for Scottish Literary Studies, 1991).

Murphy, Michael, 'Marriage as Metaphor for the Anglo-Scottish Parliamentary Union of 1707: The Case of *Humphry Clinker*', *Etudes Ecossaises*, 3 (1996), 61–5.

Murphy, P., *Nineteenth-Century Irish Sculpture: Native Genius Reaffirmed* (New Haven and London: Yale University Press, 2010).

Murray, Douglas, 'Martyrs or Madmen? The Covenanters, Sir Walter Scott and Dr Thomas McCrie', *Innes Review*, 43 (1992), 166–75.

Murray, Douglas, *Rebuilding the Kirk: Presbyterian Reunion in Scotland 1909–1929* (Edinburgh: T & T Clark, 2000).

Myers, Mitzi, ' "Completing the Union": Critical *Ennui*, the Politics of Narrative, and the Reformation of Irish Cultural Identity', *Prose Studies*, 18/3 (1995), 41–77.

Nash, Andrew, 'William Robertson Nicoll, the Kailyard Novel and the Question of Popular Culture', *Scottish Studies Review*, 5 (2004), 57–73.

Nash, Andrew, 'Authors in the Literary Marketplace', in David Finkelstein and Alistair McCleery (eds), *The Edinburgh History of the Book in Scotland*, iv. *Professionalism and Diversity, 1880–2000* (Edinburgh: Edinburgh University Press, 2007), 388–408.

Nash, Andrew, *Kailyard and Scottish Literature* (Amsterdam: Rodopi, 2007).

National Association for the Vindication of Scottish Rights, *Address to the People of Scotland, and Statement of Grievances* (Edinburgh: Johnstone & Hunter, 1853).

The Naval Chronicle, i. *1793–1798*, ed. Nicholas Tracy (London: Chatham, 1998).

Nesstor, Mary Catherine, 'Adapting the Great Unknown: The Evolving Perception of Walter Scott', unpublished Ph.D. thesis, University of Aberdeen, 2016.

Newman, Steve, 'The Scots Songs of Allan Ramsay: "Lyrick" Transformation, Popular Culture, and the Boundaries of the Scottish Enlightenment', *Modern Language Quarterly*, 63 (2002), 277–314.

Nicoll, Mildred Robertson (ed.), *The Letters of Annie S. Swan* (London: Hodder & Stoughton, 1945).

Nicoll, William Robertson, *'Ian Maclaren': Life of the Rev. John Watson, DD* (London: Hodder and Stoughton, 1908).

Noble, A., 'Burns and Scottish Nationalism', in K. Simpson (ed.), *Burns Now* (Edinburgh: Canongate, 1994), 176–7.

O'Flaherty, P., 'John Pinkerton (1758–1826): Champion of the Makars', *Studies in Scottish Literature*, 13 (1978), 159–95.

Osborne, John W., *John Cartwright* (Cambridge: Cambridge University Press, 1972).

Pae, David, *Lucy, the Factory Girl: Or the Secrets of the Tontine Close* (Edinburgh, Thomas Grant, 1860).

Parker, Alice, 'Tobias Smollett and the Law', *Studies in Philology*, 39 (1942), 545–58,

Paterson, Lindsay, *The Autonomy of Modern Scotland* (Edinburgh: Edinburgh University Press, 1994).

Parting Words to the Members of the Royal Historical Society in a Letter to the President, Rt Hon. Lord Aberdare (London, 1881).

Paton, David, *The Cergy and the Clearances: The Church and the Highland Crisis 1790–1850* (Edinburgh: John Donald, 2006).

Patrick, D. J., and Whatley, C. A., 'Persistence, Principle and Patriotism in the Making of the Union of 1707: The Revolution, Scottish Parliament and the *Squadrone volante*', *History*, 92/306 (April 2007), 162–86.

Patterson, Annabel, *Censorship and Interpretation: The Conditions of Writing and Reading in Early Modern England* (Madison: University of Wisconsin Press, 1984).

Paul, Jeremy, *Sing Willow: The True Story of the Invalids Cricket Club* (Lewes: The Book Guild, 2002).

Peacham, Henry, *Minerva Britanna* (London: Wa: Dight, 1612).

Peebles, William, *Burnomania: The Celebration of Robert Burns Considered: In a Discourse Addressed to All Real Christians of Every Denomination* (Edinburgh: J. Ogle, 1811).

Penman, M. A., 'Robert Bruce's Bones: Reputations, Politics and Identities in Nineteenth-Century Scotland', *International Review of Scottish Studies*, 34 (2009), 7–73.

Pentland, Gordon, ' "We speak for the ready": Images of Scots in Political Prints, 1707–1832', *Scottish Historical Review*, 90 (2011), 64–95.

Pepys, Samuel, *The Diary of Samuel Pepys*, ed. Robert Latham and William Matthews, 11 vols (London: Harper Collins, 2000).

Platt, Jane, *Subscribing to Faith? The Anglican Parish Magazine 1859–1929* (Houndmills: Palgrave Macmillan, 2015).

Phillips, Alastair, *Glasgow's Herald: 1783–1983* (Glasgow: Richard Drew, 1983).

Phillipson, N., 'Politics, Politeness and the Anglicization of Early Eighteenth Century Scottish Culture', in R. A. Mason (ed.), *Scotland and England 1286–1815* (Edinburgh: John Donald, 1987), 226–47.

Phillipson, Nicholas, *Adam Smith: An Enlightened Life* (London: Allen Lane, 2010).

Pinkerton, John, 'An Essay on the Origin of Scotish [*sic*] Poetry', in Pinkerton, *Ancient Scotish Poems* (2 vols; London: C. Dilly, 1786).

Pitcairne, Archibald, *The Assembly, A Comedy* (London, 1722).

Pittock, Murray, 'Were the Easy Club Jacobites?', *Scottish Literary Journal*, 17/1 (1990), 91–4.

Pittock, Murray, *The Invention of Scotland: The Stuart Myth and the Scottish Identity 1638 to the Present* (London: Routledge, 1991).

Pittock, Murray, *Poetry and Jacobite Politics in Eighteenth-Century Britain and Ireland* (Cambridge: Cambridge University Press, 1994).

Pittock, Murray, 'Allan Ramsay and the Decolonization of Genre', *Review of English Studies*, NS 58 (2007), 316–37.

Pittock, Murray (ed.), *The Reception of Walter Scott in Europe* (London: Continuum, 2007).

Pittock, Murray, ' "A Long Farewell to All My Greatness": The History of the Reputation of Robert Burns', in Murray Pittock (ed.), *Robert Burns in Global Culture* (Lewisburg, PA: Bucknell University Press, 2011).

Pittock, Murray, *The Road to Independence? Scotland in the Balance* (London: Reaktion Books, 2013).

Pittock, Murray, and Whatley, Christopher, 'Poems and Festivals, Art and Artefact and the Commemoration of Robert Burns, *c.*1844–*c.*1896', *Scottish Historical Review*, 93/1 (April 2014), 56–79.

Pocock, J. G. A., 'Burke and the Ancient Constitution', in *Politics, Language and Time* (London: Methuen & Co, 1971), 202–32.

Pocock, J. G. A., 'British History: A Plea for a New Subject', *New Zealand Journal of History*, 8 (1974), 3–21, repr. in *Journal of Modern History*, 47 (1975), 601–24.

Pocock, J. G. A., 'The Limits and Divisions of British History: In Search of the Unknown Subject', *American Historical Review*, 87 (1982), 311–36.

Pocock, J. G. A., *The Ancient Constitution and the Feudal Law*, rev. edn (Cambridge: Cambridge University Press, 1987).

Pocock, J. G. A., *The Discovery of Islands* (Cambridge: Cambridge University Press, 2005).

Poems on Several Occasions, with a Dissertation upon the Roman Poets (London: [E.Curll], 1718).

Poems on Several Occasions (London: L. Gilliver, 1729).

Powell, Anthony, *From A View to a Death* (London: Duckworth, 1933).

The Present State of the Crown-Inn, for the First Three Years under the New Landlord (London: S. Baker, 1717).

Price, R., *British Society, 1680–1880* (Cambridge: Cambridge University Press, 1999).

Prothero, G. W., 'Historical Societies in Great Britain', *Annual Report of the American Historical Association for the Year 1909* (Washington, 1911), 229–42.

Quinault, R., 'The Cult of the Centenary, *c.*1784–1914', *Historical Research*, 71 (1998), 303–23.

Raffe, Alasdair, 'Episcopalian Polemic, the London Printing Press and Anglo-Scottish Divergence in the 1690s', *Journal of Scottish Historical Studies*, 26 (2006), 23–41.

Raffe, A., '1707, 2007 and the Unionist Turn in Scottish History', *Historical Journal*, 53 (2010), 1071–83.

Ragaz, Sharon, 'Walter Scott and the *Quarterly Review*', in Jonathan Cutmore (ed.), *Conservatism and the Quarterly Review: A Critical Analysis* (London: Pickering and Chatto, 2007), 107–32.

Ramsay, Allan, *The Works of Allan Ramsay I*, ed. Burns Martin and John W. Oliver (Edinburgh: Scottish Text Society, 1944).

Ramsay, Allan, *The Works of Allan Ramsay*, ed. Burns Martin, A. M. Kinghorn, and A. Law, 6 vols (Edinburgh: Scottish Text Society, 1951–74).

Ramsay, John, *Scotland and Scotsmen in the Eighteenth Century from the MSS of John Ramsay of Ochtertyre*, ed. Alexander Allardyce (Edinburgh and London: W. Blackwood and Sons, 1888).

Rawson, Claude Rawson, *Swift's Angers* (Cambridge: Cambridge University Press, 2014).

Records of the Parliaments of Scotland to 1707, ed. Keith M. Brown et al. (St Andrews, 2007–15) <http://www.rps.ac.uk/> (accessed July 2017).

The Register of the Privy Council of Scotland, 3rd ser., ed. P. Hume Brown, Henry Paton, and E. Balfour-Melville, 16 vols (Edinburgh: HM General Register House, 1908–70).

Reid, David (ed.), *The Party-Coloured Mind: Selected Prose Relating to the Conflict between Church and State in Seventeenth-Century Scotland* (Edinburgh: Scottish Academic Press, 1982).

Renfrew, Alastair, 'Brief Encounters, Long Farewells: Bakhtin and Scottish Literature', *International Journal of Scottish Literature*, 1 (Autumn 2006).

The repealer repulsed! A correct narrative of the rise and progress of the repeal invasion of Ulster: Dr Cooke's challenge and Mr O'Connell's declinature, tactics, and flight. With appropriate poetical and pictorial illustrations. Also, an authentic report of the great Conservative demonstrations, in Belfast, on the 21 and 23 of January 1841 (Belfast: William McComb, 1841).

Rigney, Ann, *The Afterlives of Walter Scott: Memory on the Move* (Oxford: Oxford University Press, 2012).

Ritson, Joseph (ed.), *Scotish Songs Volume II* (London: J. Johnson, 1794).

Ritson, Joseph, *Robin Hood: A Collection of all the Ancient Poems, Songs and Ballads, now Extant, Relative to that Celebrated English Outlaw*, 2 vols (London: Routledge/Thoemmes Press, 1997; repr. of 1887 edn).

Robertson, James, *And the Land Lay Still* (London: Hamish Hamilton, 2010).

Robertson, John, *The Scottish Enlightenment and the Militia Issue* (Edinburgh: John Donald, 1985).

Robertson, J., 'Andrew Fletcher's Vision of Union', in R. A. Mason (ed.), *Scotland and England 1286–1815* (Edinburgh: John Donald, 1987), 203–25.

Robertson, John, 'An Elusive Sovereignty: The Course of the Union Debate in Scotland, 1698–1707', in John Robertson (ed.), *A Union for Empire: Political Thought and the British Union of 1707* (Cambridge: Cambridge University Press, 1995), 198–227.

Robertson, J. (ed.), *A Union for Empire: Political Thought and the British Union of 1707* (Cambridge: Cambridge University Press, 1995).

Robbins, K., *Nineteenth-Century Britain: Integration and Diversity* (Oxford: Oxford University Press, 1988).

Rodger, Johnny, 'The Burnsian Constructs', in J. Rodger and Gerard Carruthers (eds), *Fickle Man: Robert Burns in the 21st Century* (Dingwall: Sandstone Press, 2009), 50–79.

Rogers, C., *A Few Testimonials in Favour of the Rev. Charles Rogers, LL.D.* (Edinburgh: Grant Bros., 1857).

Rogers, C., *The Issues of Religious Rivalry: A Narrative of Five Year's Persecution* (London: Alfred Boot, 1866).

Rogers, C., 'Preface', *Transactions of the Historical Society*, 1 (1872), 3–5.

Rogers, C., *Leaves from my Autobiography* (London: Longmans, Green & Co., 1876).

Rogers, C., 'Notes on the Study of History', *Transactions of the Royal Historical Society*, 8 (1880), 1–11.

Rogers, C., *The Serpent's Track: A Narrative of Twenty-Two Years Persecution* (London, 1880).

Rogers, C., *Memorials of the Scottish Family of Glen* (Edinburgh: privately printed, 1888).

Rogers, C., *Memorials of the Scottish House of Gourlay* (Edinburgh: privately printed, 1888).

Rogers, Pat, *Johnson and Boswell: The Transit of Caledonia* (Oxford: Oxford University Press, 1995).

Rogers, Pat, 'Dr Arbuthnot and his Family', *Notes and Queries*, 51 (2004), 387–9.

Rose, R., *Understanding the United Kingdom: The Territorial Dimension in Government* (Harlow: Longman, 1982).

Ross, John, *Scottish History and Literature to the Period of Reformation* (Glasgow: J. Maclehose and Sons, 1884).

Ross, J. D. (ed.), *Burnsiana: A Collection of Literary Odds and Ends* (2 vols; Paisley and London: A. Gradner, 1892).

Ross, J. D., 'Statues of Burns', *Burns Chronicle and Club Directory*, 4 (January 1895), 121–9.

Rostvig, Maren Sophie, *The Happy Man: Studies in the Metamorphosis of a Classical Ideal* (Trondheim: Norwegian Universities Press, 1971).

Rothstein, E., 'Scotophilia and *Humphry Clinker*: The Politics of Beggary, Bugs and Buttocks', *University of Toronto Quarterly*, 52 (1982), 63–78.

Rounce, Adam, 'Stuarts without End: Wilkes, Churchill and Anti-Scottishness', *Eighteenth-Century Life*, 29 (2005), 20–43.

Roxburghe, Duke of, *The Manuscripts of the Duke of Roxburghe*, Historical Manuscripts Commission 14th Report (London: HMSO, 1894).

Russell, Conrad, *The Causes of the English Civil War* (Oxford: Oxford University Press, 1990).

Russell, Conrad, *The Fall of the British Monarchies 1637–1642* (Oxford: Clarendon Press, 1991).

Russell, Leonard (ed.), *Parody Party* (London: Hutchinson, 1936).

Russell, M., 'A Writer in a Time of Change: Gunn, Walsh and the Process of Independence', in Alistair McCleery (ed.), *Nation and Nationalism* (Dunbeath: Whittles Publishing, 2013).

Rymes of Robin Hood, ed. R. B. Dobson and J. Taylor (London: Heinemann, 1976).

Sahlins, Peter, *Boundaries: The Making of France and Spain in the Pyrenees* (Berkeley and Los Angeles: University of California Press, 1989).

Sambrook, James, *James Thomson: 1700–1748, A Life* (Oxford: Clarendon Press, 1991).

Schama, Simon, *Landscape and Memory* (London: Harper Collins, 1995).

Schmeichen, J., 'Glasgow of the Imagination: Architecture, Townscape and Society', in W. H. Fraser and I. Mavor (eds), *Glasgow*, ii. *1830 to 1912* (Manchester: Manchester University Press, 1996), 490–9.

Scott, Alexander, 'Arne's Alfred', *Music and Letters*, 55 (1974), 385–97.

Scott, Dixon, *Men of Letters* (1916; London: Hodder & Stoughton, 1923).

Scott, Hew, *Fasti Ecclesiae Scoticanae: The Succession of Ministers in the Church of Scotland from the Reformation*, rev. edn, 8 vols (Edinburgh: W. Paterson, 1915–50).

Scott, Mary Jane W., *James Thomson, Anglo-Scot* (Athens, GA: University of Georgia Press, 1988).

Scott, Patrick, 'The Business of Belief: The Emergence of "Religious" Publishing', in D. Baker (ed.), *Sanctity and Secularity: The Church and the World* (Oxford: Blackwell, 1973), 213–23.

Scott, Patrick, 'The First Publication of "Holy Willie's Prayer"', *Scottish Literary Review*, 7/1 (2015), 1–18.

Scott, Paul Henderson, *Walter Scott and Scotland* (Edinburgh: William Blackwood, 1981).

[Scott, Walter], *Ivanhoe; or, the Knight Templar, and the Jew's Daughter: An Ancient Tale of English Chivalry* (London, [1821]).

[Scott, Walter], *Letters of Malachi Malagrowther on the Currency* (1826; Edinburgh: R. Cadell, 1844).

Scott, Walter, *Minstrelsy of the Scottish Border*, ed. T. F. Henderson, 4 vols (Edinburgh: William Blackwood and Sons, 1902).

Scott, Walter, *The Letters of Sir Walter Scott*, ed. H. G. C. Grierson et al., 12 vols (London: Constable, 1932–7).

Scott, Walter, *Ivanhoe* (Classic Comics 2; New York, Gilberton Company, 1946).

Scott, Walter, *The Heart of Midlothian* (1818; New York: Holt, Rinehart and Winston, 1963).

Scott, Walter, *The Journal of Sir Walter Scott*, ed. W. E. K. Anderson (Oxford: Clarendon Press, 1972).

Scott, Walter, '*The Fortunes of Nigel* (1822; St Albans: Panther, 1973).

Scott, Walter, 'General Preface to the Waverley Novels', repr. in D. Hewitt (ed.), *Scott on Himself: A Selection of the Autobiographical Writings of Sir Walter Scott* (Edinburgh: Scottish Academic Press, 1981).

Scott, Walter, 'General Preface' (1829), in *Waverley; or, 'Tis Sixty Years Since*, ed. Claire Lamont (Oxford: Oxford University Press, 1981).

Scott, Walter, *Rob Roy* (1817; London: Penguin, 1962 edn; repr. 1986).

Scott, Walter, *The Black Dwarf*, ed. P. D. Garside (1816; Edinburgh: Edinburgh University Press, 1993).

Scott, Walter, *Ivanhoe*, ed. Graham Tulloch (EEWN 8; Edinburgh: Edinburgh University Press, 1998).

Scott, Walter, *Ivanhoe*, ed. Graham Tulloch (Penguin Classics; Harmondsworth, Penguin, 2000).

Scott, Walter, *Redgauntlet*, ed. G. A. M. Wood with David Hewitt (Penguin Classics; Harmondsworth, Penguin, 2000).

Scott, Walter, *The Fortunes of Nigel*, ed. Frank Jordan (EEWN 13; Edinburgh: Edinburgh University Press, 2004).

Scott, Walter, *Waverley*, ed. P. D. Garside (EEWN; Edinburgh University Press, 2007).

Scott, Walter, 'Introduction to *Ivanhoe*', in *Introduction and Notes from the Magnum Opus*, ed. J. H. Alexander with P. D. Garside and Claire Lamont (EEWN 25B; Edinburgh; Edinburgh University Press, 2012).

Scott-Moncrieff, George, 'Balmorality', in David Cleghorn Thomson (ed.), *Scotland in Quest of her Youth* (Edinburgh: Oliver and Boyd, 1932), 69–86.

Scottish Government, *Scotland's Future* (Scottish Government, 2013).

Sekora, John, *Luxury: The Concept in Western Thought, Eden to Smollett* (Baltimore: Johns Hopkins University Press, 1977).

Shaftesbury, Earl of, *Characteristics of Men, Manners, Opinions, Times*, ed. Lawrence Klein (Cambridge: Cambridge University Press, 1999).

Shakespeare, William, *Macbeth*, ed. Kenneth Muir (London: Methuen, 1979).

Shapiro, James, *1606: William Shakespeare and the Year of 'Lear'* (London: Faber and Faber, 2015).

Shattock, Joanne, 'Problems of Parentage: The *North British Review* and the Free Church of Scotland', in J. Shattock and M. Wolff (eds), *The Victorian Periodical Press: Samplings and Soundings* (Leicester and Toronto: Leicester University Press, 1982), 145–66.

Shebbeare, John, *A Sixth Letter to the People of England, on the Progress of National Ruin* (London: J. Morgan, 1757).

Sher, Richard, '"Those Scotch Imposters and their Cabal": Ossian and the Scottish Enlightenment', *Man and Nature/L'Homme et la nature*, 1 (1982), 55–63.

Sher, Richard, *Church and University in the Scottish Enlightenment: The Moderate Literati of Edinburgh* (Princeton: Princeton University Press; Edinburgh: Edinburgh University Press, 1985).

Shuttleton, David E., '"A modest examination": John Arbuthnot and the Scottish Newtonians', *British Journal for Eighteenth-Century Studies*, 18 (1995), 47–62.

Simpson, K., *The Protean Scot: The Crisis of Identity in Eighteenth-Century Scottish Literature* (Aberdeen: Aberdeen University Press, 1988).

Simpson, Kenneth G., *The Protean Scot: The Crisis of Identity in Eighteenth Century Scottish Literature* (Aberdeen: Aberdeen University Press, 1988).

Simpson, Kenneth (ed.), *Robert Burns a Bicentenary Celebration* (East Linton: Tuckwell Press, 1997).

Sinclair, John, *Observations on the Scottish Dialect* (London: n.p., 1782).

Sister Peg: A Pamphlet Hitherto Unknown by David Hume, ed. David R. Raynor (Cambridge: Cambridge University Press, 1982).

Sister Peg's Memorial to one of her Clerks, on the Subject of Some Late and Present Grievances (Edinburgh: n.p., 1763).

Sivasundaram, Sujit, 'The Periodical as Barometer: Spiritual Measurement and the *Evangelical Magazine*', in L. Henson, G. Cantor, G. Dawson, R. Noakes, S Shuttleworth, and J. R. Topham (eds), *Culture and Science in the Nineteenth-Century Media* (Aldershot: Ashgate, 2004), 43–55.

Skinner, John, *John Skinner: Collected Poems*, ed. David M. Bertie (Peterhead: Buchan Field Club, 2005).

Slack, Paul, *The Invention of Improvement: Information and Material Progress in the Seventeenth Century* (Oxford: Oxford University Press, 2015).

Smith, Erin, 'Religion and Popular Print Culture', in Christine Bolt (ed.), *The Oxford History of Popular Print Culture 1860–1920* (Oxford: Oxford University Press, 2012).

Smith, G. Gregory, *Scottish Literature: Character and Influence* (London: Macmillan, 1919).

Smith, J. C., *Some Characteristics of Scots Literature* (London: English Association, 1912).

Smith, John, *A Short Account of the Late Treatment of the Students of the University of G—w* (Dublin, 1722).

Smollett, Tobias, *The History of England, from the Revolution to the Death of George the Second*, new edn, 5 vols (London: T. Cadell; R. Baldwin, 1790).

Smollett, Tobias, *Travels through France and Italy*, ed. Frank Felsenstein (Oxford: Oxford University Press, 1981).

Smollett, Tobias, *The Expedition of Humphry Clinker* (1771; Harmondsworth: Penguin, 1967; repr. 1982).

Smollett, Tobias, *Humphry Clinker*, ed. Lewis M. Knapp, rev. Paul-Gabriel Boucé (World's Classics; Oxford: Oxford University Press, 1984).

Smout, T. C., 'Problems of Nationalism, Identity and Improvement in Later Eighteenth-Century Scotland', in T. M. Devine (ed.), *Improvement and Enlightenment* (Edinburgh: John Donald, 1989).

Smout, T. C., 'Perspectives on the Scottish Identity', *Scottish Affairs*, 6 (Winter 1994), 101–13.

Snelling, Thomas, *A View of the Silver Coin and Coinage of England* (London: T. Snelling, 1762).

Songs, Odes, and Other Poems, on National Subjects, ed. William McCarthy (Philadelphia: Wm McCarthy, 1842).

Southey, Robert, *The Life and Correspondence of Robert Southey*, ed. Charles Cuthbert Southey, 6 vols (London: Longman's, 1849–50).

Speedily will be Published, the History of Rachel, commonly called Auld Reikie, eldest Daughter of Sister Peg ([Edinburgh: n.p.,] [1761]).

Speck, W. A., *Stability and Strife: England, 1714–1760* (Cambridge, MA: Harvard University Press, 1977).

Speirs, John, *The Scots Literary Tradition* (London: Chatto and Windus, 1962).

Stafford, Fiona, *The Sublime Savage: James Macpherson and the Poems of Ossian* (Edinburgh: Edinburgh University Press, 1988).

Stafford, Fiona, *The Last of the Race: The Growth of a Myth from Milton to Darwin* (Oxford: Clarendon Press, 1994).

The Statutes at Large, from Magna Charta, to the End of the last Parliament, 1761, ed. Owen Ruffhead, 8 vols (London: Mark Baskett, Henry Woodfall and William Strahan, 1763–4).

Steensma, Robert C., *Dr John Arbuthnot* (Boston: Twayne, 1979).

Stephen, Jeffrey, *Scottish Presbyterians and the Act of Union 1707* (Edinburgh: Edinburgh University Press, 2007).

Stephens, Frederic George, and George, M. Dorothy (eds), *Catalogue of Prints and Drawings in the British Museum*, 11 vols (London: British Museum, 1870–1954).

Stewart, M. A., 'John Smith and the Molesworth Circle', *Eighteenth-Century Ireland*, 2 (1987), 89–102.

Struthers, Gavin, *The History of the Rise, Progress, and Principles of the Relief Church* (Glasgow: A. Fullarton, 1843).

Sutherland, John, *Life of Walter Scott* (Oxford: Blackwell, 1995).

Swan, Annie S., *My Life: An Autobiography* (London: Ivor Nicholson and Watson, 1934).

Swenson, Rivka, *Essential Scots and the Idea of Unionism in Anglo-Scottish Literature, 1603–1832* (Lewisburg, PA: Bucknell University Press, 2016).

Swift, Jonathan, 'The Story of the Injured Lady', in *The Works of Jonathan Swift, D.D.*, ed. Walter Scott, 19 vols (Edinburgh: Archibald Constable and Company, 1814).

Swift, Jonathan, *The Works of Jonathan Swift, D.D.*, ed. Walter Scott, 19 vols (Edinburgh: Archibald Constable and Company, 1814).

Swift, Jonathan, *The Conduct of the Allies*, ed. C. B. Wheeler (Oxford: Clarendon Press, 1916).

Swift, Jonathan, *Irish Tracts, 1720–1723, and Sermons*, ed. Louis Landa (Oxford: Basil Blackwell, 1948).

Swift, Jonathan, *A Tale of a Tub, to which is added The Battle of the Books and the Mechanical Operation of the Spirit*, ed. A. C. Guthkelch and D. Nichol Smith (2nd edn; Oxford: Oxford University Press, 1958).

Swift, Jonathan, *The Correspondence of Jonathan Swift*, ed. Harold Williams, 5 vols (Oxford: Clarendon Press, 1963–5).

Swift, Jonathan, 'The Story of the Injured Lady', in *The Basic Writings of Jonathan Swift*, ed. with introduction by Claude Rawson and notes by Ian Higgins (New York: Modern Library, 2002).

Swift, Jonathan, *The Basic Writings of Jonathan Swift*, ed. with introduction by Claude Rawson and notes by Ian Higgins (New York: Modern Library, 2002).

Szechi, D., 'The Politics of "Persecution": Scots Episcopalian Toleration and the Harley Ministry, 1710–12', in W. J. Sheils (ed.), *Persecution and Toleration*, Studies in Church History, 21 (Ecclesiastical History Society; Oxford: Blackwell, 1984), 275–87.

Szechi, Daniel, *Britain's Lost Revolution? Jacobite Scotland and French Grand Strategy, 1701–1708* (Manchester: Manchester University Press, 2015).

Taylor, D. J., *The Prose Factory: Literary Life in England since 1918* (London: Chatto and Windus, 2016).

Taylor, Miles, 'John Bull and the Iconography of Public Opinion in England, c. 1712–1929', *Past and Present*, 134 (February 1992), 93–128.

Tey, Josephine, *The Singing Sands* (1952; London: Arrow Books, 2011).

Thackeray, William Makepeace, *Rebecca and Rowena, Or, Romance upon Romance*, first published *Fraser's Magazine* (August–September 1846); repr. in *Christmas Books: Rebecca and Rowena and Later Minor Papers, 1849–1861*, ed. George Saintsbury (The Oxford Thackeray; Oxford: Oxford University Press, 1908).

Thompson, Alex M., 'Was Shakespeare a Scotsman?', in Thompson, *The Haunts of Old Cockaigne* (London: Clarion, 1898), 87–115.

Thomson, Derek S., *The Gaelic Sources of Macpherson's Ossian* (Edinburgh: Oliver and Boyd, 1952).

Thomson, James, *The Tragedy of Sophonisba* (London: A. Millar, 1730).

Thomson, James, *Alfred: A Masque* (London: A. Millar, 1740).

Thomson, James, *Britannia, A Poem*, in James Thomason, *Liberty, The Castle of Indolence and Other Poems*, ed. James Sambrook (Oxford: Clarendon Press, 1986), 21–30.

Thomson, James, *Liberty, The Castle of Indolence and Other Poems*, ed. James Sambrook (Oxford: Clarendon Press, 1986).

Thomson, James, *Liberty, The Castle of Indolence and Other Poems*, ed. James Sambrook (Oxford: Clarendon Press, 1986).

Thomson, James, and Mallet, David, *Alfred: An Opera. Altered from the Play Written by Mr Thomson and Mr Mallett* (London: A. Millar, 1745).

Topham, Jonathan, '*The Wesleyan–Methodist Magazine* and Religious Monthlies in Early Nineteenth-Century Britain', in G. Cantor, G. Dawson, G. Gooday, R. Noakes, S. Shuttleworth, and J. R. Topham (eds), *Science in the Nineteenth-Century Periodical: Reading the Magazine of Nature* (Cambridge: Cambridge University Press, 2004), 67–90.

Torrance, David, *The Battle for Britain: Scotland and the Independence Referendum* (London: Biteback Publishing, 2013).

Townend, G. M., 'Religious Radicalism and Conservatism in the Whig party under George I: The Repeal of the Occasional Conformity and Schism Acts', Parliamentary History, 7 (1988), 24–43.

Tranter, Nigel, *The Patriot* (1982; London: Coronet Books, 1984).

Trevor-Roper, Hugh, *Religion, the Reformation and Social Change* (London: Macmillan, 1972).

Trevor-Roper, Hugh, *The Invention of Scotland: Myth and History* (New Haven, CT, and London: Yale University Press, 2008).

Trumpener, Katie, *Bardic Nationalism: The Romantic Novel and the British Empire* (Princeton: Princeton University Press, 1997).

Tuan, Yi-Fu Tuan, *Space and Place: The Perspective of Experience* (University of Minnesota Press: Minneapolis and London, 1977).

Tulloch, Graham, 'Introduction', in Walter Scott, *Ivanhoe* (London: Penguin, 2000).

Tulloch, Graham, 'Essay on the Text', in Walter Scott, *Ivanhoe*, ed. Graham Tulloch (Edinburgh Edition of the Waverley Novels (EEWN), 8; Edinburgh: Edinburgh University Press, 1998).

Tyrell, A., 'Paternalism, Public Memory and National Identity in Early Victorian Scotland: The Robert Burns Festival at Ayr in 1844', *History*, 90/1 (2005), 42–61.

Tytler, Alexander, 'Remarks on the Genius and Writings of Allan Ramsay', in *The Poems of Allan Ramsay*, ed. George Chalmers (London: T. Cadell and W. Davies, 1800).

Tytler, William, *The Poetical Remains of James I, King of Scotland* (Edinburgh: J. and E. Balfour, 1783).

Uglow, Jenny, *A Gambling Man: Charles II and the Restoration* (London: Faber and Faber, *Ulster Biographies, Relating Chiefly to the Rebellion of 1798* (Belfast: J. Cleeland, 1897).

Vance, M. E., 'Burns in the Park: A Tale of Three Monuments', in Sharon Alker, Leith Davis, and Holly F. Nelson (eds), *Robert Burns and Transatlantic Culture* (Farnham and Burlington: Ashgate, 2012), 209–32.

Vance, Norman, *Irish Literature: A Social History. Tradition, Identity, and Difference* (Oxford: Basil Blackwell, 1990).

Veitch, John, *The Feeling for Nature in Scottish Poetry* (Edinburgh: Blackwood, 1887).

Verne, Jules, *Twenty Thousand Leagues under the* Sea, trans. William Butcher (World's Classics; Oxford: Oxford University Press, 1998).

Viner, Brian, 'Why Murray is a Brit when he wins and a Scot when he loses', *Independent*, 1 July 2010 <http://www.independent.co.uk/voices/columnists/brian-viner/brian-viner-why-murray-is-a-brit-when-he-wins-and-a-scot-when-he-loses-2016381.html> (accessed 12 August 2016).

Volo, James M., *Blue Water Patriots: The American Revolution Afloat* (London: Praeger Publishers, 2007).

[Wagstaffe, William], *The Story of the St Alb[a]ns Ghost, or the Apparition of Mother Haggy* (London: n.p., 1712).

Wagstaffe, William, *Miscellaneous Works of Dr William Wagstaffe* (2nd edn; London: Jonah Bowyer, 1726).

Waller, Phillip, *Writers, Readers and Reputations: Literary Life in Britain 1870–1918* (Oxford: Oxford University Press, 2006).

Walpole, Horace, *Memoirs of the Reign of King George III*, ed. G. F. Russell Barker, 4 vols (London: Lawrence and Bullen, 1894).

Wasserman, E. R., *The Subtler Language: Critical Readings of Neoclassic and Romantic Poems* (Baltimore: Johns Hopkins University Press, 1959).

Watson, James, *James Watson's Collection of Comic and Serious Scots Poems* (Glasgow: M. Ogle, 1869).

Watson, Nicola J., *The Literary Tourist: Readers and Places in Romantic & Victorian Britain* (Houndmills: Palgrave Macmillan, 2006).

Wawn, Andrew, *The Vikings and the Victorians* (Cambridge: D. S. Brewer, 2000).

Weber, Eugen, *Peasants into Frenchmen: The Modernization of Rural France 1870–1914* (Stanford: Stanford University Press, 1976).

Weinbrot, Howard, *Britannia's Issue: The Rise of British Literature from Dryden to Ossian* (Cambridge: Cambridge University Press, 1995).

Weintraub, Wiktor, *The Poetry of Adam Mickiewicz* ('S-Gravenhage: Mouton & Co, 1954).

Wells, J. E., 'Thomson's *Britannia*; Issues, Attribution, Date, Variants', *Modern Philology*, 40 (1942), 46–9.

Welsh, Alexander, *The Hero of the Waverley Novels with New Essays on Scott* (Princeton: Princeton University Press, 1992).

Whatley, Christopher, 'Burns and the Union of 1707', in Kenneth Simpson (ed.), *Robert Burns a Bicentenary Celebration* (East Linton: Tuckwell Press, 1997).

Whatley, Christopher, 'Contesting Memory and Public Spaces: Albert Square and Dundee's Pantheon of Heroes', in C. A. Whatley, B. Harris, and L. Miskell (eds), *Victorian Dundee: Image and Realities* (Dundee: Dundee University Press, 2000), 173–96.

Whatley, Christopher, *The Scots and the Union* (Edinburgh: Edinburgh University Press, 2007).

Whatley, Christopher, 'Robert Burns, Memorialisation, and the "Heart-Beatings" of Victorian Scotland', in Murray Pittock (ed.), *Robert Burns in Global Culture* (Lewisburg, PA: Bucknell University Press, 2011), 204–28.

Whatley, Christopher, *Immortal Memory: Burns and the Scottish People* (Edinburgh: Birlinn, 2016).

Whatley, Christopher A., '"It is said that Burns was a Radical: Contest, Concession, and the Political Legacy of Robert Burns, *c.*1796–1859', *Journal of British Studies*, 50/3 (July 2011).

Whatley, Christopher A., with Patrick, Derek J., *The Scots and the Union* (Edinburgh: Edinburgh University Press, 2006).

Wilkinson, David, 'Smollett, Sir James (c.1648–1731), of Stainflett and Bonhill, Dumbarton', in David Hayton, Eveline Cruickshanks, and Stuart Handley (eds), *The House of Commons 1690–1715*, 5 vols (Cambridge: Cambridge University Press for the History of Parliament Trust), v. 515–17.

Williams, Abigail, *Poetry and the Creation of a Whig Literary Culture 1681–1714* (Oxford: Oxford University Press, 2005).

Williamson, A., 'Scotland, Antichrist and the Invention of Great Britain', in J. Dwyer, R. Mason, and A. Murdoch (eds), *New Perspectives on the Politics and Culture of Early Modern Scotland* (Edinburgh: John Donald, 1982).

Wilson, Kathleen, *The Island Race: Englishness, Empire and Gender in the Eighteenth Century* (London: Routledge, 2003).

Wilson, P., 'Ringan Gilhaize: A Neglected Masterpiece?' in Christopher Whatley (ed.), *John Galt 1779–1979* (Edinburgh: Ramsay Head Press, 1979), 120–50.

Wilt, Judith, *Secret Leaves: The Novels of Walter Scott* (Chicago: University of Chicago Press, 1981).

Wolf, Reva, 'John Bull, Liberty and Wit: How England Became Caricature', in Todd Porterfield (ed.), *The Efflorescence of Caricature, 1759–1838* (London: Ashgate, 2011), 49–60.

Wolffe, John, *The Protestant Crusade in Great Britain 1829–1860* (Oxford: Clarendon Press, 1991).

Womersley, David (ed.), *Augustan Critical Writing* (London: Penguin, 1997).

Woolf, Virginia, *To the Lighthouse* (1927; repr. Harmondsworth: Penguin Books, 1964).

Woolf, Virginia, *To the Lighthouse*, ed. David Bradshaw (World's Classica; Oxford: Oxford University Press, 2006).

Wright, Frank, *Two Lands on One Soil: Ulster Politics before Home Rule* (Dublin: Gill and Macmillan, 1996).

Zumkhawala-Cook, Richard, 'Tae the Lichthoose: Scotland and the Problem of the Local', in Diana Roger and Madelyn Detloff (eds), *Virginia Woolf: Art, Education and Internationalism* (Clemson, SC: Clemson University Press, 2008), 57–63.

Zwicker, Stephen N., *Lines of Authority: Politics and English Literary Culture, 1649–1689* (Ithaca, NY: Cornell University Press, 1993).

Index

Dibdin, Charles 138
'There never was a Scot who was true
to his clan' 138
'Tom Bowling' 138–9
Dick, Thomas 253
Dickens, Charles 315, 345
Disarming Act (1782) 137
Dissenters 47–9, 50, 206, 208, 210
occasional conformity 48–9
Dodds Mr 251, 251n36
Donald, Robert 267
Donaldson, William 272, 273
Donaldson, Williamson 137–8
Douglas, Gavin 126, 356
Eneados 126
Douglas-Home, Alexander Frederick 20
Dove, Patrick Edward 247
Doyle, Sir Arthur Conan 214, 267,
317, 318
'The Valley of Fear' 317
A Duet 214
Drake, George A. 157, 161
drama 90, 289, 334, 336, 354
dramatic adaptations 151n18, 152–3,
153n24
Elizabethan 353
Romantic 290
Scottish 30
Drummond, William, of
Hawthornden 263, 335, 356
Drury Lane Theatre 90
Dryden, John 63, 66, 74
Duff, Sir Mountstuart Grant 255
Dulwich College 322
Dumfries 122
Dunbar, William 356
Duncan, Ian 99, 148, 286
Dundee Advertiser 272, 275
Dundee Warder 184
Dunn, James Nicol 267

Easy Club 68, 70
Eaton, Daniel Isaac 108–9, 108n35, 110
Ecclesiastes 282
Edgar, John 171
Edgeworth, Maria 24–5, 113, 139
Edinburgh
city fathers 125
Enlightenment 340–1
Faculty of Advocates 124

intellectuals 126
literary life 248
and Union 26, 38
and Union Parliament 107
University of 84, 124, 254, 271
Edinburgh Christian Instructor 199, 200,
201, 207, 211, 213
Edinburgh Miscellany 66
Edinburgh Review 267
Edinburgh Theological Magazine 198, 199,
200, 207, 208, 210, 213
Edinburgh Voluntary Churchman 208
Edinburgh Weekly Journal 37
Edward the Confessor, King 338
Edward I, 'Hammer of the
Scots' 285, 339
Edwards, Michael 303
Egginton, Wycliffe 346
Elector of Hanover 138
elegiac, the 280, 281, 283, 284–5, 286–7,
291, 292, 303
as canonical mode 280, 281, 282
and memory sites 280, 281
political 282
elegy 280, 281, 292, 303, 356
conventions 281
Elgin, Earl of 250
Eliot, T. S. 352–3, 353n12
and English literary
tradition 353, 354
'Little Gidding' 348
Elizabeth I, Queen 80, 88, 89, 335, 337
Elton, G. R. 308
England:
focus of 348
and identity of Britishness 344
literature and culture of 333
Middle 27
over-mighty 22
relations with Scotland 276
scotophobic prejudices 9
Scots in 263, 265, 271, 276
in Scottish culture 271
the Unions with 14
see also John Bull; Arbuthnot, *History of
John Bull,* Britannia
English
slipperiness of the term 333
English Association 350
English critical tradition 215